The Oxford History of Literary Translation in English

GENERAL EDITORS
Peter France (University of Edinburgh)
Stuart Gillespie (University of Glasgow)

Volume 1 To 1550
edited by Roger Ellis

Volume 2 1550–1660
edited by Gordon Braden, Robert Cummings, and Theo Hermans

Volume 3 1660–1790
edited by Stuart Gillespie and David Hopkins

Volume 4 1790–1900
edited by Peter France and Kenneth Haynes

Volume 5 1900–2000
edited by Lawrence Venuti

The Oxford History of Literary Translation in English

Volume 4
1790–1900

Edited by
PETER FRANCE
and
KENNETH HAYNES

OXFORD
UNIVERSITY PRESS

Great Clarendon Street, Oxford OX2 6DP

Oxford University Press is a department of the University of Oxford.
It furthers the University's objective of excellence in research, scholarship,
and education by publishing worldwide in

Oxford New York

Auckland Cape Town Dar es Salaam Hong Kong Karachi
Kuala Lumpur Madrid Melbourne Mexico City Nairobi
New Delhi Shanghai Taipei Toronto

With offices in

Argentina Austria Brazil Chile Czech Republic France Greece
Guatemala Hungary Italy Japan Poland Portugal Singapore
South Korea Switzerland Thailand Turkey Ukraine Vietnam

Oxford is a registered trade mark of Oxford University Press
in the UK and in certain other countries

Published in the United States
by Oxford University Press Inc., New York

© The various contributors 2006
© In the editorial matter Peter France and Kenneth Haynes 2006

The moral rights of the authors have been asserted
Database right Oxford University Press (maker)

First published 2006

All rights reserved. No part of this publication may be reproduced,
stored in a retrieval system, or transmitted, in any form or by any means,
without the prior permission in writing of Oxford University Press,
or as expressly permitted by law, or under terms agreed with the appropriate
reprographics rights organization. Enquiries concerning reproduction
outside the scope of the above should be sent to the Rights Department,
Oxford University Press, at the address above

You must not circulate this book in any other binding or cover
and you must impose the same condition on any acquirer

British Library Cataloguing in Publication Data

Data available

Library of Congress Cataloging in Publication Data
The Oxford history of literary translation in English / edited by
Stuart Gillespie and David Hopkins.
v. cm.
Includes bibliographical references and index.
Contents : — v. 3. 1660–1790.
ISBN 0–19–924622–X (v. 3 : alk. paper)
1. Literature—Translations into English–History and criticism.
2. Translating and interpreting–English-speaking countries.
I. Gillispie, Sturart, 1958–   . II. Hopkins, David, 1948–
PR131.0944 2005 820.9—dc22 2005020693

Typeset by Newgen Imaging Systems (P) Ltd., Chennai, India
Printed in Great Britain
on acid-free paper by
Biddles Ltd., King's Lynn, Norfolk

ISBN 0–19–924623–8 978–0–19–924623–6

1 3 5 7 9 10 8 6 4 2

Contents

General Editors' Foreword	viii
List of Contributors	ix
List of Abbreviations	xi
Transliteration	xii
Preface	xiii

1. Translation in Britain and the United States

   1.1 Translation and British Literary Culture   3
       Kenneth Haynes

   1.2 Translation in the United States   20
       Colleen Boggs

   1.3 Readers and Publishers of Translations in Britain   34
       Terry Hale

   1.4 Translation, Politics, and the Law   48
       Susan Bassnett and Peter France

2. Principles and Norms of Translation   59
       Matthew Reynolds

3. The Translator

   3.1 Professionals   85
       Margaret Lesser

   3.2 Amateurs and Enthusiasts   98
       Peter France

   3.3 Writers   105
       Stephen Prickett and Peter France

   3.4 Academics   117
       Adrian Poole

   3.5 Women   125
       Susanne Stark

4. The Publication of Literary Translation: An Overview   133
       Peter France and Kenneth Haynes

5. Greek and Latin Literature

   5.1 Introduction   155
       Kenneth Haynes

5.2	Homer *David Ricks*	168
5.3	Greek Drama *Adrian Poole*	178
5.4	Latin Poetry *John Talbot*	188
5.5	Greek and Latin Prose *Stuart Gillespie*	200

6. Literatures of Medieval and Modern Europe

6.1	German *David Constantine*	211
6.2	French *Peter France*	230
6.3	Italian *Ralph Pite*	246
6.4	Spanish and Portuguese *Anthony Pym and John Style*	261
6.5	Early Literature of the North *Andrew Wawn*	274
6.6	Modern Scandinavian *Robert Bjork*	286
6.7	Celtic *Mary-Ann Constantine*	294
6.8	Literatures of Central and Eastern Europe *Peter France*	308

7. Eastern Literatures

7.1	Arabic *Wen-chin Ouyang*	323
7.2	Persian *Dick Davis*	332
7.3	Literatures of the Indian Subcontinent *Harish Trivedi*	340
7.4	Chinese *Lauren Pfister*	355
7.5	Japanese *Anne Commons*	363

8. **Popular Culture**

    8.1 Popular Fiction   371
          Terry Hale

    8.2 Popular Theatre   382
          Terry Hale

    8.3 Children's Literature   394
          David Blamires

9. **Texts for Music and Oral Literature**

    9.1 Hymns   411
          J. R. Watson

    9.2 Opera, Oratorio, Song   420
          Denise Gallo

    9.3 Oral Literature   430
          Kenneth Haynes

10. **Sacred and Religious Texts**

    10.1 Christian Texts   443
          Kenneth Haynes

    10.2 The Revised Version of the Bible   451
          David Norton

    10.3 Sacred Books of the East   458
          Richard Fynes

11. **Philosophy, History, and Travel Writing**

    11.1 Greek and Roman Philosophy   473
          Alexandra Lianeri

    11.2 Modern Philosophy, Theology, Criticism   481
          Susanne Stark

    11.3 Modern History and Socio-political Theory   489
          Ian Patterson

    11.4 Exploring the World   498
          Laura Dassow Walls

12. **The Translators: Biographical Sketches**   505

Index   561

General Editors' Foreword

Peter France and Stuart Gillespie

Since the time of Cicero, translation has been at the heart of literary culture in Europe. In the English-speaking world, now that English has become a lingua franca around the globe, this is perhaps less obvious than it once was; by many measurements, translation today contributes less to literature in English than to any other major European literature. Even so, it is hard to overstate the importance of translations in the history of anglophone culture. Its sacred books are translations for most readers, as are many of the works that are central to our literary experience, from Homer to Dostoevsky, from Plato to Nietzsche.

In the five volumes of the *Oxford History of Literary Translation in English* we aim to present for the first time a critical and historical overview of the development of this art or craft in the English-speaking world. The story of English-language translation begins in England but eventually expands to include Scotland, Ireland, and Wales, and from the late eighteenth century America, India, and all the other parts of the world where English became one of the languages of culture. Over this wide geographical area, these volumes show how literary translation has challenged, enriched, and transformed the native traditions. While we emphasize the value of such high artistic achievements as Pope's Homer or FitzGerald's *Rubáiyát*, we use the word 'literary' in the broad old sense which it has still not completely lost, to encompass something like the full range of non-technical work which has made up the reading of the literate public. And since the history of translation is also the history of translators, we explore the activities of the sometimes famous, often obscure men and women who contributed to it, the conditions they worked in, the norms and principles which governed their practice.

This is an unprecedented undertaking and has been a correspondingly challenging task. The story of English literature has been told many times, but that of English literary translation has never been accorded full-scale treatment. While certain subjects—the making of the King James Bible, the extraordinary translation work of John Dryden or Ezra Pound—have been visited by many scholars and critics, other parts of our extensive field were virtually *terra incognita*. Inevitably, then, even after the work of our host of contributors, parts of our map are still less comprehensively filled in than others. Our hope is that we have provided a helpful outline, with enough detailed critical discussion to show how richly worthwhile is the study of a kind of writing whose importance both in itself and in its immediate effects has all too rarely been acknowledged.

Contributors

Susan Bassnett
University of Warwick

Robert Bjork
Arizona State University

David Blamires
University of Manchester

Colleen Boggs
Dartmouth College

Anne Commons
University of Alberta

David Constantine
The Queen's College, Oxford

Mary-Ann Constantine
University of Wales

Dick Davis
Ohio State University

Clara Drummond
Boston University

Peter France
University of Edinburgh

Richard Fynes
De Montfort University

Denise Gallo
Library of Congress

Stuart Gillespie
University of Glasgow

Terry Hale
University of Hull

Kenneth Haynes
Brown University

Margaret Lesser
University of Manchester

Alexandra Lianeri
Darwin College, Cambridge

David Norton
Victoria University of Wellington

Wen-chin Ouyang
School of Oriental and African Studies,
University of London

Ian Patterson
Queens' College, Cambridge

Lauren Pfister
Hong Kong Baptist University

Ralph Pite
University of Liverpool

Adrian Poole
Trinity College, Cambridge

Stephen Prickett
Baylor University

Anthony Pym
Universitat Rovira i Virgili

Matthew Reynolds
St Anne's College, Oxford

David Ricks
King's College London

C. N. Smith
University of East Anglia

Susanne Stark
Stuttgart

John Glenmore Style
Universitat Rovira i Virgili

John Talbot
Brigham Young University

Harish Trivedi
University of Delhi

Laura Dassow Walls
Lafayette College

Phil Walsh
Brown University

J. R. Watson
University of Durham

Andrew Wawn
University of Leeds

Jane Yeoman
University of Edinburgh

Abbreviations

Journals

MLR	*Modern Language Review*
N&Q	*Notes and Queries*
PMLA	*Publications of the Modern Language Association of America*
SEER	*Slavonic and East European Review*
T&L	*Translation and Literature*

Reference Works

CBEL3 Joanne Shattock *et al.*, eds., *The Cambridge Bibliography of English Literature*, 3rd edn., 5 vols. (Cambridge, 1999–)
DNB1 *The Dictionary of National Biography*, editions to 2003
ESTC *English Short-Title Catalogue* (online version)
NSTC *Nineteenth-Century Short-Title Catalogue* (online version and CD-ROM)
ODNB *The Oxford Dictionary of National Biography*, ed. H. C. G. Matthews and Brian Harrison, 60 vols. (Oxford, 2004)

Transliteration

Our policy has been to use the non-academic British convention for transliterating Russian names; to transliterate Sanskrit and Japanese in accordance with the standard academic conventions, and Arabic and Persian in accordance with the old system of the *International Journal of Middle East Studies* (with diacriticals); to give the Pinyin transliteration of Chinese with diacriticals added to indicate tone; and not to transliterate Greek terms with the exception of some common words (e.g. *polis*).

Preface

Peter France and Kenneth Haynes

In the late seventeenth and eighteenth centuries translated works, principally from the familiar literatures of Greece, Rome, and France, and often made by the most important writers of the age, occupied a central place within the mainstream of English literature. After 1790 fewer translations attained a classic status, and for the 110 years covered by this volume translation was concerned not only with revisiting widely known literatures but also with discovering new ones. By opening up Anglo-American culture to 'world literature', a phrase which was itself characteristic of the age, these contacts helped shape the course of British and American literature.

The number of published translations increased dramatically, they were made from an ever wider range of sources, and the potential readership for them grew rapidly. For this expanding public, translation was a necessity, not a luxury. While many of the great poetic translations of the eighteenth century were directed, at least in part, to those who had enough knowledge to compare source and translation, nineteenth-century translations were more often a replacement for an inaccessible original. For all but a few, most of the literature of the world—from the classical texts of Greece, Persia, or India to the Icelandic sagas, the folklore of Celtic or Slavic countries, and the newly discovered cultures of northern and eastern Europe—could be appreciated only through translation, and even the more widespread knowledge of French and Latin was mainly the prerogative of the upper class and the professional middle class; Latin was learned mostly by the men of those classes. The activity of publishers, who saw in this new demand for translations not only a mission to be accomplished but also an opportunity for profit, is an essential part of our story.

While translation in the period did not typically form part of the literary mainstream, it provoked much literary experimentation and public debate. More than in the previous century, translators adopted a variety of different styles, and many discussions about what the translator should be doing were published in the periodical press and elsewhere. The dispute between Matthew Arnold and Francis Newman on translating Homer remains one of the most illuminating discussions of translation. The old consensus favouring naturalization of the foreign was shaken by a new tendency to stress the foreignness of the foreign and to search for new ways of doing justice to it—where the 'new' in some cases takes the form of a deliberate recourse to archaism, as in Robert Browning's *Agamemnon* or William Morris's *Beowulf*.

The first four chapters of the volume deal with the contexts and circumstances of translation and offer a preliminary quantification of translated material. The first chapter looks at translation under the aspects of literary culture, commerce, and politics, as well as the special situation of translation in the United States. The subjects of copyright, censorship, publishing houses, literacy, etc. are covered here in their relation to translation. Readers should be aware that many such topics are discussed not only in Chapter 1 (sometimes in more than a single section) but also in subsequent chapters; the cross-references and the index will offer guidance here and throughout the volume. The first section of Chapter 1 discusses translation and British literature and is meant to serve as an introduction to the volume.

Chapter 2 deals with the norms and principles of nineteenth-century translation; it too draws on examples that in some cases receive fuller treatment or are examined from a different perspective elsewhere. Chapter 3 surveys the translators themselves, their different backgrounds, and the place occupied by translations within their lives and careers. Chapter 4 attempts to provide an overview of the body of translated material and of the place occupied by literary translation within the British and American book trade of the period; it also offers a selective account of the presence of translations in the periodicals which were so important a part of the literary landscape.

Chapters 5 to 7 cover literary translation by source language: Greek and Latin, modern European languages, and eastern languages, respectively. The treatment is unavoidably selective because the body of translated literature in the period is vast and unwieldy. A balance has to be struck between an overview of the material and critical discussion of particular cases; in practice, this balance varies in relation to the quantity of the material (much more French literature was translated than Latin verse), its literary value, and the particular interests of the contributors. In discussing literatures newly introduced in English translation (Russian, Chinese, etc.), the pioneering efforts of the first translators generally receive special attention.

Chapters 8 to 11 are devoted to specific types of literature. These types include works intended for performance (§ 8.2,[1] on popular theatre, and Chapter 9); works directed to specific audiences (Chapter 8, covering popular fiction and children's literature as well as popular theatre); works with a religious dimension (Chapter 10); and works which without being 'literary' in the narrow sense of the word (that is, fiction, drama, or poetry), constituted major reading areas of the literate public (Chapter 11). Of necessity, these four chapters sometimes take up again topics already broached in the preceding chapters. The final chapter consists of brief biographical sketches of translators. Its goal is to complement the discussions in the previous chapters by providing in one place basic information (sometimes not easily available in other publications) and also to draw attention

---

[1] Most chapters in the volume are divided into sections. Chapter 1, Section 1 is referred to in cross-references as § 1.1.

to individual translators as figures worthy of study for their intrinsic merit, historical influence, or other interest.

Except for Chapter 12, each section or chapter includes a 'List of Sources', which usually consists first of the principal translations mentioned or discussed in the main body and second of the other sources that are cited in the main text or are indispensable for further reading on the topic. These lists, in particular the lists of translations, are of course selective and do not aim to provide full bibliographies of the subject. Publishers are not indicated, with the exception of Bohn, whose various Libraries have a distinct importance for translation in this period.

The editors would like to thank all the contributors to this volume and also the many individuals and institutions who gave advice and support, in particular Richard Cronin and Christopher Ricks, who read the manuscript and suggested improvements; Stuart Gillespie who offered invaluable assistance at every stage of our work; our research assistants, Rebecca Bradburd and Jane Yeoman; the excellent editorial team at Oxford University Press; the Leverhulme Trust, which provided valuable financial assistance; the University of Edinburgh, Boston University, and Brown University.

1
Translation in Britain and the United States

1.1 Translation and British Literary Culture   3
     Kenneth Haynes
1.2 Translation in the United States   20
     Colleen Boggs
1.3 Readers and Publishers of Translations in Britain 34
     Terry Hale
1.4 Translation, Politics, and the Law   48
     Susan Bassnett and Peter France

1.1 Translation and British Literary Culture

Kenneth Haynes

English and Foreign Literatures

In an essay of 1821, Thomas De Quincey insisted that English literature needed the stimulus of foreign literatures: 'So it is with the literatures of whatsoever land: unless crossed by some other of different breed, they all tend to superannuation.' He was pleading for the study of 'some exotic, but congenial' foreign literature, namely German, to protect English from the dotage, nervelessness, and imbecility that had befallen French because of its refusal to admit influences from without or to form alliances with exotic literature (De Quincey 2000–3: III, 18). His view, needless to say, was exaggerated and prejudiced: not only were some Frenchmen eager to understand contemporary German culture, but it was a French study—Madame de Staël's *De l'Allemagne* (1810; translated into English in 1813)—that played an important role in making Britain more receptive to Germany after the Napoleonic wars. The discovery of German literature and philosophy took place not just in Britain and France but throughout Europe and beyond, from St Petersburg and Moscow to Concord and Cambridge, Massachusetts.

In the essay ('John Paul Frederick Richter'), De Quincey took as his subject his favourite German writer, Jean Paul; his first translation from him followed immediately in the same issue of the *London Magazine*. Over the next ten years he published further translations from Jean Paul as well as from Kant and other German writers, first in the *London Magazine* and later in *Blackwood's*; both magazines also carried his essays about them. His essay on Jean Paul imitated the style of his original (see Black 1985: 309), and his mature style—digressive, emphatically incongruous, grotesque, comic, and sentimental—continued to owe much to Jean Paul, an influence he always acknowledged (he named his fifth child Paul Frederick). The stimulus of German literature was a matter of both style and ideas, and translation served a dual purpose, bringing new works into English and suggesting new styles for writing English.

Jean Paul himself had been influenced by Sterne, who was widely read in Germany. In fact in the eighteenth century the whole Continent had discovered Britain, and British works of literature, philosophy, and science were extensively reprinted and translated, resulting in 'one of the most momentous literary and cultural impacts in the history of Europe' (Fabian 1992: 3). Other European-wide discoveries and revaluations followed. Not only were German literature and philosophy read throughout Europe for the first time, but in mid-century American literature was discovered by Britain and the Continent, and at the end of the century and into the twentieth, Russian literature became widely known.

Modern Scandinavian literature, too, was much read and translated by the end of the century. In addition, a new excitement over ancient Greek literature and Greek democracy was prominent throughout Europe at the end of the eighteenth and in the beginning of the nineteenth century; in Germany and Britain for the rest of the century, Greek assumed an importance it had never before possessed in Western Europe.

Translation played a large part in these literary discoveries and in many more besides. In the wake of the Peninsular War, popular translations by Southey and Lockhart introduced British readers to the chivalric Spain of ballad and epic, a shift away from a general indifference in which Spanish literature meant little more than *Don Quijote*. Among Italian writers, Dante was read widely for the first time, often in Cary's translation. Contemporary French literature was repeatedly able to *épater le bourgeois*, whether in the hands of Swinburne or later among the Decadent poets of the 1890s. French novels had an even greater appeal, and the shock value of Zola was considerable.

The discovery of the Middle Ages was yet another powerful literary refocusing in this period, influencing both Romantics and Victorians. For 'Isabella', Keats drew on a seventeenth-century English translation of Boccaccio, and Tennyson's 'Geraint and Enid' was founded on a story from the *Mabinogion* in Lady Charlotte Guest's translation. Swinburne and Rossetti translated Villon and the lyrics of other medieval poets, while Morris translated the sagas. Old ballads from a number of languages were collected, translated, and imitated throughout the century, an enthusiasm that received a strong impetus from translations of German literary ballads made in the 1790s and subsequently also from translations of folk ballads, especially Celtic. These were essential to the development of the literary ballad in English, from Wordsworth and Coleridge to Keats and Tennyson and to Morris and Swinburne.

New discoveries were not limited to the European literatures. From the last quarter of the eighteenth century, Persian, Arabic, and Sanskrit were studied in England. This direct knowledge of the languages is 'what distinguishes the Orientalism of the Romantic Age' from its 'earlier manifestations' (Yohannan 1952: 137). Towards the end of the eighteenth century, Sir William Jones inaugurated a new, more closely verbal attention to eastern literatures, an attention which would be further sponsored by the East India Company (after the India Act of 1784 gave joint oversight to Parliament), the Royal Asiatic Society (founded in 1823), and the universities. These bodies supported some of the large series of translations that made many eastern texts available in English, like the Oriental Translation Fund and Max Müller's Sacred Books of the East.

This new informed interest eventually bore fruit within British literary culture more generally, as in Shelley's imitation of the ghazal, 'From the Arabic', or Tennyson's 'Locksley Hall', influenced by one of the *Muʻallaqāt* in Jones's translation. Persian poetry yielded Edward FitzGerald's bestselling *Rubáiyát of Omar Khayyám*, and in America Emerson was translating via German a number of Persian poems, while Whitman espoused a sort of Sufism in 'A Persian Lesson'.

The literatures of China and Japan began to be translated, and in the early twentieth century they were to be a major component of British and American modernism. But dozens of other eastern literatures were not translated at all.

All these developments depended on accident as well as design, on minor figures as well as major ones, and on provincial cities as well as London. If, from one point of view, the British discovery of German literature formed part of a European-wide phenomenon, from another that discovery was the product of various accidents. It began in the 1780s and 1790s with the efforts of 'dispersed enthusiasts' (Renwick 1963: 6) such as William Taylor of Norwich and Henry Mackenzie of Edinburgh, whose translations, criticism, lectures, and example promoted knowledge of German. After the Napoleonic wars, figures like Henry Crabb Robinson and R. P. Gillies were also influential. From 1819 to 1827, Gillies contributed to *Blackwood's* a number of translations from German that were widely read; in 1824 he introduced E. T. A. Hoffmann to England with the publication of *The Devil's Elixir*.

Such minor figures as these laid necessary groundwork for the major appropriations of German poetry by Beddoes, Byron, and Scott; of German philosophy and criticism by Coleridge, De Quincey, and George Eliot; of German prose by Carlyle. A path toward these major engagements began to be cleared when fashionable trends like the late eighteenth-century cult of sentiment or taste for the Gothic led to an enthusiastic, if superficial, reading of German literature. Sometimes the influential minor characters riding these fashions lacked basic competence in German (Mackenzie lectured and wrote on German plays though he had read them only in French translations; he subsequently learned some German before undertaking his own translations). Often the early reception of German literature was a matter of personal contacts and local associations. Scott discovered German literature by attending a lecture by Mackenzie. Taylor's influence was felt not only through published articles and translations, but also through manuscripts, through the Norwich literary group, and through his friends and students. Crabb Robinson's influence was mediated almost entirely through his friendships, with Carlyle, Coleridge, Lamb, Southey, and Wordsworth. The new importance of periodicals for translation was also in evidence: *Blackwood's*, for example, gave prominence to translations of foreign literature in the first few decades of its run, and both Gillies and John Gibson Lockhart translated specimens for its series 'Horae Germanicae'.

Accident and individual proclivities combined unpredictably with political, economic, social, and cultural forces in making translations. The first chance encounter behind the *Rubáiyát* was that which brought Edward FitzGerald and Edward Byles Cowell together in 1844. The accidents of individual temperament which would soon lead to their friendship had first made them amateur linguists: FitzGerald was a gentleman of leisure, while Cowell, the son of a merchant, taught himself several eastern languages after encountering Sir William Jones's work in a public library. In 1852, Cowell urged FitzGerald to study Persian, and in 1856, shortly before leaving for India, he gave him a copy of some of the quatrains attributed to 'Umar Khayyām. This next encounter, FitzGerald's reading of Khayyām at a difficult time in his life, led him to sympathize and even identify himself with the Persian poet, and later to recreate in translation the Epicurean and sceptical spirit he found in or imparted to him. He translated first into Latin and subsequently into English. When *Fraser's Magazine* did not publish the translation (although the editor expressed interest in it), he printed it at his own expense in 1859 and arranged for the bookseller Bernard Quaritch to distribute it. In contrast to the more usual Victorian practice, he neither let his name as translator be known nor permitted the book to be advertised except very modestly; as a result, the translation went unnoticed. Its popular success was due to another chance encounter, two years later, when an acquaintance of Dante Gabriel Rossetti's bought him a copy of the *Rubáiyát*, which he had found in the penny box outside Quaritch's shop. With the discovery of the poem by the Pre-Raphaelites, the translation began to sell; it would go through three more editions in his lifetime, and innumerable ones after his death. (For more information, see FitzGerald 1997, from which this account derives, as well as pp. 335–7, below.)

The Literature of the World in Translation

Carlyle thought he could discern in the new British openness to German literature an incipient era of 'world literature'—an idea and a phrase he added to the English language in 1831, translating it from Goethe. The emphasis was on contemporary writers, and since Goethe developed the concept partly in letters to and reviews of Carlyle, the history of the phrase illustrates in miniature the process it was coined to describe. Goethe first used it in 1827. In the next year he wrote to Carlyle about an English translation of his drama *Tasso*, remarking that 'it is precisely the bearing of an original to a translation, which most clearly indicates the relations of nation to nation, and which one must especially know and estimate for the furtherance of the prevailing, predominant and universal world literature' (Goethe and Carlyle 1887: 42). This was to be a gradual process, rooted in individual readers and writers, starting with Europe and then spreading to encompass the world. Carlyle subscribed wholeheartedly to it at the time, asking in a review of William Taylor's *Historic Survey of German Poetry* whether the growing knowledge of German literature in England did not in fact 'betoken that a new era in the spiritual intercourse of Europe is approaching; that instead of isolated, mutually repulsive National Literatures, a World Literature may one day be looked for? The better minds of all countries begin to understand each other; and, which follows naturally, to love each other, and help each other' (Carlyle 1899: XXVII, 369). There is evidence that 'world literature' was a popular ideal, or at least a fashionable phrase, in the 1830s although it did not retain its appeal in Britain in later decades (Strich 1949: 281). In the United States Longfellow may be seen as attempting to realize the German ideal (More 1908: 140), both in his translations and in works like *Hiawatha* (on Longfellow, see further pp. 24, 29, and 433 below).

By the middle of the century, 'world literature' began to assume its modern meaning of the literary works written in the many different languages of the world, a descriptive rather than programmatic usage. This became the normal usage: FitzGerald in 1879 and Tennyson in 1880 refer descriptively to the 'literature of the world' (FitzGerald 1997: 113; Tennyson 1990: III, 183). From the second half of the nineteenth century, it is not anachronistic to speak of a 'canon' of world literature (or for that matter European literature), although the word 'canon' was not used in its current sense. Two factors combined to make this possible: programmes of reading directed toward the social classes who did not typically attend university and radical changes in the price and supply of books. The first might be dated from the appearance in Britain of Auguste Comte's 'religion of humanity'. At the end of the preface to his *Catéchisme positiviste* (1851), Comte had published a list of 150 items that would constitute a basic course of reading for all educated people; he revised and reprinted the list as an appendix to the fourth volume of the *Système de politique positive* (1854). It consisted of four categories: 'poésie' (including prose fiction), science, history, and 'synthèse' (i.e. philosophy and religion). With a few exceptions, the thirty items selected for the category 'poetry' could be found in modern lists of great books. Famous works of Greek, Latin, French, Italian, Spanish, and English literature are included; German is represented by selections from Goethe and non-European literature by the *Arabian Nights*. No mention is made of any particular translator or translation.

Comte's influence in Britain was large (see pp. 493–4, below), and his list soon appeared in English translation. Moreover, his disciples in England did much to promote his educational aims. For example, in 1886 Frederic Harrison published a translation of Comte's list, with a preface and commentary (revised and reprinted in Harrison 1912: 395–408), which included desultory remarks about translation. The year 1886 was one of 'Great Books'. Sir John Lubbock, Principal of the Working Men's College, gave an address at the college featuring his list of the best hundred books. Shortly afterwards other lists appeared in the *Pall Mall Gazette* and the *Contemporary Review*. A strenuous battle of the best books was fought subsequently, especially in the *Pall Mall Gazette*; a special supplement devoted to the debate sold 40,000 copies (Carnochan 1998: 56). The works on Lubbock's list (which was several times revised and never claimed to be authoritative) were almost all items that could be found on such lists today. Only about half the books were originally written in English, and a number of works in non-western languages were represented, including Arabic, Chinese, Persian, and Sanskrit. No living authors were included. The list had a great impact among those excluded from higher education, and in particular it had a formative influence on the culture of the working-class autodidact (see Rose 2001: 128–30). Lubbock, however, said very little about translations, even though they were implied by his programme of reading; the translators and even the fact of translation remained invisible.

The translations were supplied by publishers, notably those specializing in cheap reprints. Often these translations were included within series devoted to a particular topic, genre, or area. For example, Henry Colburn formed a British and Foreign Library, which he sold to Otley in 1824. He had more success after becoming a partner with Richard Bentley; together they launched the highly successful series of Standard Novels, which included some translations. In 1848 George Routledge inaugurated the Railway Library, thereby 'ushering in the era of mass marketing' of books (Anderson and Rose 1991: 106); it was followed by several other 'libraries', which often included translations. Such series continued throughout the century. Tauchnitz began his 'Collection of German Authors' in 1862; Henry Vizetelly in the 1880s was offering 'Popular French Novels', 'Boulevard Novels: Pictures of French Morals and Manners', and 'Russian Novels'; and in 1890, with his first list, William Heinemann offered an 'International Library' of designated modern European classics in translation.

However, it was Henry Bohn, more than any other publisher, whose series actively influenced the formation of a canon of world literature in translation. The son of a German bookbinder settled in England, Bohn had dealt in rare books before launching his famous 'Libraries'. His Standard Library and Classical Library were carefully aimed to make a profit not by entertaining readers but from their desire for self-improvement. The former series was launched in 1846, and came to consist of eighty-three volumes by the time of his retirement in 1864.[1] The smaller Classical Library (discussed on p. 165, below) was inaugurated in 1848. After Bohn's retirement, his various libraries passed into the ownership of Bell & Daldy (after 1872, George Bell & Sons), who augmented the series in addition to selling them. No new items were added after 1914.

From 1846 to 1864, under Bohn's supervision, just over half of the books in the Standard Library were translations. The ratio holds whether the items are counted by title or by number of volumes (the single title *Works* by Goethe ran to fourteen volumes). Counting by titles, we find that just over half of the translations were from German, while a little over a third were from French; Italian, Spanish, and Swedish made up the few remaining items. By genre, almost three-quarters were historical works; literary works in a narrow sense (poetry, drama, fiction) included only Bremer, Goethe, Heine, and Schiller.

The translations were mostly reprints; Bohn had been purchasing the copyrights of remainders since 1841 and reissuing them cheaply. However, commercial considerations were not the only factor determining the contents of his lists. When Bohn absorbed the stock of Bogue (whose European Library had inspired the Standard Library), he would have gained *Marguerite de Valois* (1846), an English translation of Alexandre Dumas's *La Reine Margot* (1845), but it never appeared in the 'Libraries'; Bohn actively excluded translations of French novels from his series, in contrast to other publishers' series. He himself translated some works by Schiller that were included in the Standard Library.

The key to the success of Bohn's series was the fact that he issued the volumes cheaply. 'One significant consequence of Bohn's Standard Library and his

---

[1] Since Bohn classified the individual titles in his series in different ways at different times, there is always some uncertainty about how to count them. The bibliography by Cordasco (1951) has been followed.

subsequent series was the reduction in the average cost of all titles published in England ... Bohn's prices became the standard for the market for twenty years' (Anderson and Rose 1991: 60). Bohn's books sold for five shillings a volume; in 1828 the average price of a book was sixteen shillings (Anderson and Rose 1991: 60). According to the *Gentleman's Magazine*, it was Bohn who with his Standard Library established 'the habit, in middle-class life, of purchasing books, instead of obtaining them from a library' ('Sylvanus Urban' 1884: 413).

Of the seventy-six titles which were added to the Standard Library between 1865 and 1900, thirty-four (45 per cent) were translations. Of the translations, eighteen were from German (53 per cent), nine from French (26 per cent), and the rest from Greek, Portuguese, Russian, Sanskrit, and Spanish. The most pronounced difference is that the majority of those volumes were literary in the narrow sense. Only three works of history were added. A few of these translations appear to have been commissioned and indicate on their title pages that they are new or have been 'newly translated' (Molière, Richter, Plutarch).

The success of the series—Anna Swanwick's verse translation of *Faust* sold around 1,000 copies each year for almost half a century (Cordasco 1951: 16)—ensured that the commercial category of 'standard' or 'classic' world literature would have a long life. Bohn's dominated this category until Israel Gollancz created the Temple Classics in the last decade of the nineteenth century, and in the twentieth century they would be followed by Everyman's Library, the Harvard Classics, the Oxford World's Classics, and Penguin Classics. Classic older translations were notably revived in the 1890s, when W. E. Henley and Charles Whibley oversaw the creation of the Tudor Translations series (1892–1903), including Florio's Montaigne and North's Plutarch; from this time on, series consisting not just of world literature but of classic translations of world literature competed for commercial success.

High Points of Nineteenth-Century Translation

Did the period from 1790 to 1900 produce translations that ought to be seen as classic? Ezra Pound, as tendentious as De Quincey, thought so:

British literature ... was kept alive during the last century by a series of exotic injections. Swinburne read Greek and took English metric in hand; Rossetti brought in the Italian primitives; FitzGerald made the only good poem of the time that has gone to the people.
(Pound 1968: 33–4)

Even with its polemical thrust, Pound's case for the vital dependence of nineteenth-century British literature on foreign sources is a valuable corrective to the common view that the literature of the period was inhospitable to translation. It is easy (and essential) to see translation as an integral part of literary history in the eighteenth or twentieth centuries. Dryden's *Works of Virgil*, Pope's *Iliad* and *Imitations of Horace*, and Johnson's imitations of Juvenal all deserve their fame, and Pound's influential re-launching of the imitation with the *Homage to Sextus*

Propertius, as well as his translations from Anglo-Saxon, Chinese, Italian, and Provençal, occupy a central place in literary modernism. It would be deceptive to reduce the history of literary translation to the handful of translations commonly recognized as great: poetry tends to be favoured over prose, free translations over literal, and entire decades within periods may be ignored. Nonetheless, if overvaluing great translations can distort literary history, so can undervaluing them. The translations of FitzGerald, Shelley, Swinburne, and Rossetti have not been rightly valued as part of nineteenth-century British literature. In addition, other translations merit sustained literary attention; some of these are among the best translations of a particular author. A handful of examples will be discussed here, Verlaine in versions by the writers of the 1890s, Charlotte Guest's *Mabinogion*, and Constance Garnett's Turgenev. Other examples are argued for in subsequent chapters.

Few of Shelley's translations were published in his lifetime. The collection *Alastor* (1816) has two sonnets in translation, one from Dante and the other from an epigram by Moschus, and 'Epipsychidion' (1821) opens with the translation of a stanza from one of Dante's *canzoni*. Only with the publication of *Posthumous Poems* (1824) was Shelley's range and skill as a translator revealed. The volume included versions of the 'Homeric Hymn to Mercury', Euripides' *Cyclops*, scenes from Calderón's *El mágico prodigioso*, and scenes from Goethe's *Faust*—perhaps his four finest translations. Other noteworthy translations, including further Homeric hymns, Greek epigrams, and fragmentary versions from Dante and Virgil, were published later in the century. The prose translations from Plato first appeared in 1840 in expurgated versions.

Shelley's translation of Plato's *Symposium* was made with extreme rapidity from Ficino's edition, without recourse to a dictionary. His mistranslations, Neo-Platonizing, and bowdlerization of the text have been closely documented. His version has nonetheless been called a 'masterpiece', in full awareness of the apparent paradox (Nelson 2007). Shelley's primary attention went to the larger prose rhythms of the text. To interrupt the flow of comprehension by consulting a dictionary would not have served his purpose of creating an English version that could be read rapidly and passionately.

Two reviews of the *Posthumous Poems* praised the translations particularly. Leigh Hunt called them 'masterly' and singled out the 'Hymn to Mercury' (on which see pp. 161–2, below) for praise. J. G. Lockhart wrote that Shelley's deficiencies as a poet—his lack of distinct conceptions, his lapses in taste—were overcome in the translations where he was 'chastened and inspired' by the originals. Although tendentiously expressed, this view (which Matthew Arnold also held) may help to clarify the nature of his achievement. The translations were praised for their 'classical gracefulness' by Lockhart, their 'animal spirits' by Hunt, and their strength and ease by Swinburne (quoted in Webb 1976: 123–4)—not qualities that come first to mind in describing Shelley's own poetry. Although we may learn to see such qualities in the original verse (see for example Davie 1952: 133–59), they are foregrounded and unmistakable in several translations.

The 'Prologue in Heaven' of Goethe's *Faust* opens with three archangels who praise the universal harmony which contains within itself, and resolves, all the violent discord of the world. As a sublime statement of cosmic affirmation, this 'astonishing chorus' appealed to Shelley immensely, and his translation was especially attentive to 'the volatile strength and delicacy of the ideas' (as he describes the chorus in a note to his translation, Shelley 1970: 749). Still, it is not free of some awkward poetical inversions (the ineffable regularly tempts Shelley to poeticisms); immediately after the chorus, however, Mephistopheles enters and changes the register by speaking like an experienced courtier. Shelley is able to map the shifts from sublime worship to courtly politesse to urbane irony, even as the scene echoes the Book of Job. In rendering the 'Walpurgisnacht' scene, Shelley likewise encountered a diversity of tones corresponding to a wide range of experiences. To some extent, he was able to bring them to bear on each other, and though he was unable to face fully the grotesque elements in the scene, he does permit May-Day's nocturnal mysteries of love and death to impinge and be impinged on by Mephistopheles' aristocratic irony (for a full discussion see pp. 223–4, below).

Swinburne's *Poems and Ballads* appeared in 1866. Original poems are found side by side with the translations, and in many cases the distinction between original and translated is blurred. In the collection Swinburne surveyed the literature of Europe with an eye especially to what had previously been neglected or not turned to account by poets. Fragments of Greek poetry, the Provençal alba, the traditional ballads of Europe, the rococo of the eighteenth century, the *formes fixes* of medieval French lyrics, English medieval miracle plays, and contemporary French poetry (Baudelaire, Gautier, Hugo) are among his sources. Sometimes these result in free translation: 'A Song Before Death' (subtitled 'From the French') is a version from a short lyric by Sade; 'Love at Sea' is an imitation, or free translation, of Théophile Gautier; and 'April' translates an amatory epistle of a thirteenth-century French poet. In other poems, translation is included in part: 'Phaedra' translates a four-line fragment from Aeschylus, 'Anactoria' incorporates several fragments of Sappho, and 'In the Orchard' takes its refrain from a Provençal alba. Many others are inspired by a literary source, either in its subject or in its stanza form or metre, and sometimes such inspiration should be seen as a form of translation (see, for example p. 161, below, on Swinburne's 'Sapphics').

Though *Poems and Ballads* contains much of his finest poetry, perhaps the best translations are found in subsequent volumes: ten translations from Villon in *Poems and Ballads, Second Series* (1878) and the 'Grand Chorus of Birds from Aristophanes' in *Studies in Song* (1880), the latter discussed on p. 185, below. Translating from Villon is demanding in several respects: the stanza forms are strict; the language is concentrated; and diverse emotional registers are combined, including pathos, mockery, piety, obscenity, and humour. Swinburne has obvious qualifications only for the first (formal) demand, which he met with great exuberance. Of the ten translations, eight follow the original rhyme scheme closely. A typical *ballade* may require fourteen rhyming words in twenty-eight lines, and Swinburne not only manages this in several poems, he also includes a double *ballade* with twenty-four rhyming words. A cost is incurred, mainly in the form of some poetical inversions and vague expressions, but nonetheless the rhymes are generally good, neither obvious nor outré (except when they were in Villon's French), usually belonging to different parts of speech, and only rarely relying on participles.

That Swinburne rose to the second and third demands is more surprising (see also p. 232, below). It surprised the *Athenaeum* reviewer, who had supposed that Swinburne's diffuse muse would have been 'ill-adapted to rendering Villon—the most concise of all French poets' (quoted in Hyder 1970: 179). Besides their concentration, he praises them for their vitality and closeness, and it was this closeness which obliged Swinburne to write in a more concentrated vein than elsewhere. Here is the penultimate stanza of the section from *Le Testament* which Swinburne translated as 'The Complaint of the Fair Armouress':

> 'Thus endeth all the beauty of us.
>   The arms made short, the hands made lean,
> The shoulders bowed and ruinous,
>   The breasts, alack!, all fallen in;
>   The flanks too, like the breasts, grown thin;
> As for the sweet place, out on it!
>   For the lank thighs no thighs but skin,
> They are speckled with spots like sausage-meat.'
>   (Swinburne 1904: III, 136)

Because of the additions 'ruinous' and 'alack!', the third and fourth lines do not quite capture the brute self-knowledge of 'Des espaulles? Toutes bossues; | Mamelles, quoy? toutes retraictes', but the stanza as a whole, especially its end, is nonetheless impressive for its directness and relative lack of fillers. Villon begins the stanza with a more abstract and literary reflection, and Swinburne skilfully reproduces the stylistic range involved in moving from 'Thus endeth all the beauty of us' to 'speckled with spots like sausage-meat'.[2]

Dante Gabriel Rossetti's *Poems* of 1870 includes both original and translated verse, including Sappho, Villon, and others. Rossetti's activities as a translator were far more extensive than Swinburne's and resulted in the several editions of *Dante and his Circle*. In its final form, the collection would consist of Dante's *La vita nuova* and some of his shorter poetry; sonnets, *ballate*, and *canzoni* by Cavalcanti; and a wide selection of Italian lyrics from the twelfth and thirteenth centuries. Rossetti had an idealizing vision of early medieval writers, and the *dolcestilnovisti* themselves had an 'idealizing' vision of courtly love. But the difference between them is great: for Dante and Cavalcanti, the vocabulary of love was technically precise and theologically informed. Rossetti's vocabulary is archaizing and very literary, and his versions of the great poets (Dante, Cavalcanti, Guinizelli)

---

[2] When the poem was first published, Swinburne omitted the last three lines because of their indecency; the last two lines he restored in 1904. The sixth line, restored here, was finally printed in T. J. Wise's *Bibliography* of 1919–20. (The most obscene of the Villon translations, 'The Ballad of Villon and Fat Madge', could not be published at all; see Swinburne 1964: 13–14, 183–6.)

tend to lose the tight semantic focus of the originals by depending so heavily on the medievalizing flavour of his diction. On the other hand, no other translator can match Rossetti for the gracefulness and the musical aspect of the verse, the melopoeia of the translation.

The cosmopolitanism of the 1890s was hospitable to translation. Poets of the Rhymers' Club—John Davidson, Ernest Dowson, John Gray, G. A. Greene, Arthur Symons, Oscar Wilde—translated much verse and prose, mostly from French, though D'Annunzio also enjoyed a brief vogue at the time. Poetic translation formed a central part of many of these writers' oeuvre (though not Davidson's, which includes little beyond an adaptation of Hugo's *Ruy Blas* in 1904). Dowson, Gray, and Symons all published collections which combine translated and original verse. Gray's *Silverpoints* (1893) contains versions of Verlaine, Mallarmé, and Baudelaire, and three-quarters of his *Spiritual Poems* (1896) are translations, mostly of medieval and early modern devotional poetry. Symons's versions of Baudelaire fall outside the chronological boundary of this volume, but three of his first five books include translations (twenty-nine altogether), and more follow in *Knave of Hearts: 1894–1908* (1913) and later. Dowson has four poems 'After Paul Verlaine' in his *Decorations* (1899).

The translations from Verlaine tended to be of higher quality than those of other French poets. It has been suggested that one reason for this lies in Verlaine's short verse lines, which avoid the '*ampleur* and the final climax of the traditional alexandrine' so notoriously difficult to render in English, and in his phrasing, which is so far 'from conventional French phrasing that they may frequently be scanned in the manner of English verse, as anapests or iambs' (Temple 1953: 148). In consequence, fairly close semantic translation can on occasion also be metrically close. That an affinity between Verlaine and English poetry was felt at the time is evident in the fact that 'Spleen' was decently translated by three contemporary poets, Dowson (1899), Gray (1893), and Symons (1913). Though Verlaine did not write the kind of concentrated poetry whose power is evident in shorter passages, all three translators were responsive to the atmosphere and the syntactical rhythms of the original. Moreover, they were much closer to Verlaine's own world than subsequent translators, sharing similar historical experiences and aesthetic assumptions, and for that reason they had a significant advantage over their successors. Translating from contemporary authors is not like translating from Greek and Latin, where new translations will always be called for because no subsequent age can claim to have a privileged access to the original. In contrast, 'when the translator is more or less coeval with his author and there is a real affinity of spirit ... a relation of privilege can exist' (Carne-Ross 1992: 39).

Some fine translations were made by figures not otherwise known to literary history. Francis Howes's versions of Horace's Satires and Epistles are among the most convincing ever made; though published in mid-century, he adopted an earlier, eighteenth-century style to render them with a natural, unforced ease (see p. 195, below). Charlotte Guest managed the considerable feat of translating the *Mabinogion* into a pseudo-archaic idiom that nonetheless relayed the action of the story movingly and without waste. Tennyson told her that he considered her English 'the finest he knew, ranking with Malory's *Morte d'Arthur*' (Schreiber 1952: 111).

Guest's version shows that some nineteenth-century translations in prose retain far more than the historical interest of having opened up a new field. Constance Garnett provides another example. Her earliest translations, of Goncharov and Tolstoy, were apprentice work, accomplished with much help from Russian friends exiled in England while she was still learning the language. Fifteen volumes of her translations of Turgenev appeared between 1894 and 1899 (Vols. 16 and 17 appeared in 1921). The choice of Turgenev had been suggested by Garnett's friend Stepniak (S. M. Kravchinsky), who before his death in 1895 worked closely with her on the first few volumes. With Turgenev, Garnett perfected her clear and fluent style of translating. Justifiably, this style has been criticized as too elegant for Dostoevsky, whom Garnett impoverished by smoothing over his heterogeneous styles and occasional weirdness. It is, however, well suited to Turgenev. As critics have pointed out (most dismissively Wilson 1958: 48), Garnett makes mistakes and omits things that are difficult; she is also at times insensitive to the rhythm and idiom of dialogue, removing spoken eccentricities and flattening vigorous speech, particularly among peasants (see Turton 1992: 190–4). Even so, she was generally able to catch the movement of Turgenev's narrative and the tone of the narrator, a success that is evident less in detail than in the pace and rhythm of longer passages. Joseph Conrad praised her in May 1917: 'Turgenev for me is Constance Garnett and Constance Garnett *is* Turgenev. She has done the marvellous thing of placing the man's work inside English literature and it is there that I see it—or rather that I feel it' (Jean-Aubry 1927: II, 192).

Translation, Imitation, Inspiration

As De Quincey had hoped, the presence of foreign literature would repeatedly serve as a stimulus to English literature. It is, however, often difficult to tell whether a foreign work exerted an influence on writers directly or through translation, or both. Some works were most often read in translation, above all the Bible in the King James version. No other translation, and perhaps no other text, had a greater literary impact in the nineteenth century. Allusions to it are continually found in authors of all sorts, and by no means only Christian writers. Byron and Swinburne, for example, draw heavily on it, Byron offering paraphrases in *Hebrew Melodies* (1815) and Swinburne writing lyrics that can be regarded as a 'profane and fighting parody of the Old Testament' (Chesterton 1913: 94). The rise of the critical reputation of the King James Bible in the second half of the eighteenth century continued in the nineteenth. All the major Romantic poets, 'from Wordsworth through to Byron (with the exception of Keats)', admired the Bible as literature (Norton 1993: II, 169), as did most writers throughout the century. The very phrase 'the Bible as literature' is a Victorian invention; it was first used by Matthew Arnold in 1872 (quoted and discussed by Norton 1993: II, 272–4). Prose writers like Charlotte Brontë, Dickens, and Ruskin show the influence of the King James Bible stylistically not only by allusion, but through prose rhythms, parallelism, and diction (see further Lewis 1950 and Norton 1993: II, 172–5, 302, and 312–13).

All but a few read the *Arabian Nights* in translation. Coleridge, De Quincey, Dickens, and Wordsworth each recorded the impact which those tales had on them when they were children (Irwin 1994: 266–70). One of Dickens's biographers has called the *Arabian Nights* 'the literary love of his life', a work 'which played a formative role in the texture of Dickens's imagination'; he further points to its influence on the 'violent aspect of Dickens's own imagination' in works like *Little Dorrit* and *Our Mutual Friend* (Smith 1996: 45). A passionate childhood reading of the *Arabian Nights* must have helped to shape the adult imagination, even if that shaping is not strictly demonstrable, and the same is true of the Grimms' *Tales*, the stories of Hans Christian Andersen, and other works in translation commonly read by children.

Translation, in addition, has always been a means to introduce stylistic innovations into English literature; grappling with a foreign text leads to discoveries about language. De Quincey not only translated from German but in doing so he was helped to form his own English style. Carlyle's distinctive style in *Sartor Resartus* (1833–4)—a style which the *North American Review* complained was 'very strongly tinged throughout with the peculiar idiom of the German language' (quoted in Haynes 2003: 85)—was first developed in certain of his experiments in translation which sought to preserve the foreign idiom of German (see p. 71, below).

How should a foreign metrical system be translated into English verse? The question was polemically argued over in mid-century with reference to the hexameter, which some believed to be intrinsically unsuited to English but which others thought not just desirable in English but essential (see Arnold 1960: 148–53; Haynes 2003: 131–3; Saintsbury 1939: 271–5; Whewell 1847). This close attention to the hexameter, however, did not result in successful translations. Despite being earnestly desired by Matthew Arnold, Homer translated into English hexameters (e.g., Lockhart, Clough) was never convincing, not even for short passages. On the other hand, in the nineteenth century, and for the first time since the Renaissance, a wide variety of prosodic experimentation was attempted. Swinburne's 'Sapphics' and Tennyson's 'Milton' are modelled on the sapphics and alcaics of Greek verse; Swinburne's 'Hendecasyllabics' and Tennyson's 'The Daisy' and 'To the Rev. F. D. Maurice' on the hendecasyllabics and alcaics of Latin verse (with accent replacing classical quantity). However, such translation, in a broad sense, of foreign metres only rarely coincided with translation in a narrow sense, as with some of the odes in Bulwer Lytton's *Odes and Epodes of Horace*, or Swinburne's translation from the *Birds*, mentioned above, or Bayard Taylor's *Faust* (see also pp. 193–4, below, on John Conington).

In addition to metres and rhythms, stanza forms were adopted, or readopted, from foreign poetry. Not only was Dante widely read and translated, but his stanza, the *terza rima*, was revived, most notably in Byron ('The Prophecy of Dante') and Shelley, who used it not only in his translation from Dante but also in his poems ('Ode to the West Wind' and 'The Triumph of Life'). Here too we see important continuities between a foreign work, its English translation, and original English works shaped by the encounter with it. 'The Triumph of Life' is one of Shelley's finest works, and its debts, both specific and general, to Dante have been noted by subsequent critics. 'Through his apprenticeship in Italian literature Shelley has here attained to certain qualities which are very rare in English', Timothy Webb writes, remarking not only on the skill with which he handles *terza rima* but also on a larger debt: 'he demonstrates an ability to handle abstractions ... together with an ability to reproduce the particularities of everyday life with great force and intensity ... Here we can observe Shelley coming close to the functional simplicity of Dante's visual imagination' (Webb 1976: 328–9).

Luigi Pulci, one of the great comic-epic poets of the Italian Renaissance, was first translated, in part, into English by John Herman Merivale in 1806–7 (Merivale 1978: II, 1–33). Pulci's stanza, like that of Boiardo and Ariosto, was the *ottava rima*, which had a greater impact on English poetry than the *terza rima*: it was not just the stanza but the whole genre of the romance epic that was reinvented. In 1812, William Tenant's *Anster Fair* appeared, the first original long poem in English since the Renaissance to use the *ottava rima*. In 1814, Merivale published his poem in octave stanzas, *Orlando in Roncesvalles*, incorporating stanzas from Pulci. A decisive development was precipitated when John Hookham Frere read some extracts from Pulci and became so animated by them that he translated them the same night. He soon decided that he would write an imitation of Pulci. *The Monks and the Giants* (1817–18) not only used the *ottava rima*, but also recreated other aspects of the Italian poem: comic rhymes, rapid movement from serious to humorous moods, and a friendly, conversational tone.

When Byron read the first volume of Frere's comic poem, he responded at once, imitating it in *Beppo* (1817). The imitation extended to the verse form and to some extent the style, though Byron's digressions, slang, and ferocious satire are his own, not Frere's. In 1819, Byron turned to the Italian sources directly, translating in *ottava rima* the first canto of the *Morgante Maggiore*. It is a close translation, and it is possible to see in Byron's choice to convey the 'low-keyed style' of the original (Byron 1980–93: IV, 509) a development away from impassioned satire to 'a more detached and unruffled ridicule, which, with its implication of command and easy superiority, was a more powerful weapon than angry vituperation' (Frere 1926: 56). *Don Juan* and *The Vision of Judgement* are an illustration, even as late as the nineteenth century, of the 'struggle between native and foreign elements as the result of which our greatest poetry was created' (Eliot 1964: 40).

Other genres developed in response to foreign sources. Sir Walter Scott's early immersion in Goethe's historical drama *Götz* (which he translated) was formative for the development of the historical novel in English. Goethe had shown how 'in the course of history one way of life, one society, one set of values gives way to another' (Lamport 1990: 44), and the Waverley novels explore that theme in a Scottish setting. Fantastic fairy tales and stories of the uncanny and the supernatural were stimulated by the fiction of E. T. A. Hoffmann in particular, whom

Gillies and Carlyle translated, and whom Scott influentially characterized as an extravagant visionary (see Bauer 1999: 24–136). Later in the century, the decisive change in the British novel toward greater realism and psychological depth was influenced not only by French novels but by translations of Turgenev (see further pp. 314–16, below). A good deal of popular fiction—Gothic novels, science fiction, detective stories, the *Mysteries of London*—was inspired by foreign literature (see further § 8.1 below) that was translated, adapted, and imitated in English.

Original prose works sometimes incorporated translation directly. Coleridge infamously interpolated entire passages from Schelling in the *Biographia Literaria* (see pp. 109 and 221 below). However, in between the extremes of translation as inspiration and as plagiarism, we might conclude with an emblematic instance of translation as imitation and re-creation, taking an example drawn from American literature, a famous paragraph from Thoreau's *Walden*:

I long ago lost a hound, a bay horse, and a turtle dove, and am still on their trail. Many are the travellers I have spoken concerning them, describing their tracks and what calls they answered to. I have met one or two who had heard the hound, and the tramp of the horse, and even seen the dove disappear behind a cloud, and they seemed as anxious to recover them as if they had lost them themselves. (Thoreau 1971: 17)

The paragraph has its origin in a passage in Mengzi (Mencius), which Thoreau read in French translation, and which he translated in *A Week on the Concord and Merrimack Rivers*:

Mencius says: 'If one loses a fowl or a dog, he knows well how to seek them again; if one loses the sentiments of the heart, he does not know how to seek them again ... The duties of practical philosophy consist only in seeking after those sentiments of the heart which we have lost; that is all.' (Thoreau 1980: 264)

Guy Davenport traced the steps by which the Chinese fowl and dog became an American hound, bay horse, and turtle dove, and he showed how Thoreau made their loss into the loss of the sentiments of the heart (1993: 77–86; see also Edel 1970: 34–5). Translation here is a primary means of literary invention, of finding one's own voice through another's, following the injunction of another Confucian source, which Pound would translate 'Make it new'.

LIST OF SOURCES

Translations
Byron, George Gordon (1980–93). *The Complete Poetical Works*, ed. Jerome J. McGann, 7 vols. Oxford.
Dowson, Ernest (1962). *Poems*, ed. Mark Longaker. Philadelphia, PA.
FitzGerald, Edward (1997). *Rubáiyát of Omar Khayyám: A Critical Edition*, ed. Christopher Decker. Charlottesville, VA.
Garnett, Constance (1894–9). *The Novels of Ivan Turgenev*, 15 vols. London (two supplementary volumes pub. 1921).
[Gillies, Robert Pearse] (1824). *The Devil's Elixir* [E. T. A. Hoffmann]. Edinburgh.
Gray, John (1988). *The Poems*, ed. Ian Fletcher. Greensboro, NC.

Guest, Charlotte (1849). *The Mabinogion: From the Llyfr Coch o Hergest, and Other Ancient Welsh Manuscripts*, 3 vols. London.
Howes, Francis (1845). *The Epodes, Satires, and Epistles of Horace*. London.
Merivale, John Herman (1978). *Poems Original and Translated*, 2 vols. in 1. New York (first pub. 1838).
Rossetti, Dante Gabriel (1892). *Dante and his Circle: With the Italian Poets Preceding Him*. London.
—— (2003). *Collected Poetry and Prose*, ed. Jerome McGann. New Haven, CT.
Shelley, Percy Bysshe (1970). *Poetical Works*, ed. Thomas Hutchinson and corrected by G. M. Matthews. Oxford (first pub. 1905).
—— (1989–). *Poems*, ed. Geoffrey Matthews and Kelvin Everest, 2 vols. to date. London.
Swinburne, Algernon Charles (1904). *Poems*, 6 vols. London.
—— (1964). *New Writings*, ed. Cecil Y. Lang. Syracuse, NY.
Symons, Arthur (1902). *Poems*, 2 vols. London.
—— (1913). *Knave of Hearts: 1894–1908*. London.
Thoreau, Henry David (1980). *A Week on the Concord and Merrimack Rivers*, ed. Carl F. Hovde. Princeton, NJ.
[Whewell, William], ed. (1847). *English Hexameter Translations from Schiller, Göthe, Homer, Callinus, and Meleager*. London.

Other Sources
Anderson, Patricia J., and Rose, Jonathan, eds. (1991). *British Literary Publishing Houses, 1820–1880*. Detroit, MI.
Arnold, Matthew (1960). *On the Classical Tradition*, ed. R. H. Super. Ann Arbor, MI.
Ashton, Rosemary (1980). *The German Idea: Four English Writers and the Reception of German Thought, 1800–1860*. Cambridge.
Bauer, Petra (1999). 'The Reception of E. T. A. Hoffmann in 19th Century Britain.' Ph.D diss. University of Keele.
Black, Joel D. (1985). 'Confession, Digression, Gravitation: Thomas De Quincey's German Connection', pp. 308–37 in Robert Lance Snyder, ed., *Thomas De Quincey: Bicentenary Studies*. Norman, OK.
Carlyle, Thomas (1899). *Works*, ed. H. D. Traill, 30 vols. London.
—— (2000). *Sartor Resartus*, ed. Rodger L. Tarr and Mark Engel. Berkeley, CA.
Carne-Ross, D. S. (1992). 'Pantagruelism for our Time? Rabelais Reconsidered.' *New Criterion* 10/9: 33–9.
Carnochan, W. B. (1998). 'Where Did Great Books Come From Anyway?' *Stanford Humanities Review* 6/1: 51–64.
Chesterton, G. K. (1913). *The Victorian Age in Literature*. New York.
Cordasco, Francesco (1951). *The Bohn Libraries: A History and a Checklist*. New York.
Davenport, Guy (1993). *A Table of Green Fields: Ten Stories*. New York.
Davie, Donald (1952). *Purity of Diction in English Verse*. London.
De Quincey, Thomas (2000–3). *Works*, ed. Grevel Lindop, 21 vols. London.
Edel, Leon (1970). *Henry D. Thoreau*. Minneapolis, MN.
Eliot, T. S. (1964). *The Use of Poetry and the Use of Criticism*. London (first pub. 1933).
Fabian, Bernhard (1992). *The English Book in Eighteenth-Century Germany*. London.
Frere, John Hookham (1926). *The Monks and the Giants*, ed. R. D. Waller. Manchester.
Goethe, Johann Wolfgang, and Carlyle, Thomas (1887). *Correspondence between Goethe and Carlyle*, ed. Charles Eliot Norton. London.

Harrison, Frederic (1912). *Among my Books*. London.
Haynes, Kenneth (2003). *English Literature and Ancient Languages*. Oxford.
Holmes, Richard (1974). *Shelley: The Pursuit*. London.
Hyder, Clyde K., ed. (1970). *Swinburne: The Critical Heritage*. New York.
Irwin, Robert (1994). *The Arabian Nights: A Companion*. London.
Jack, Ian (1963). *English Literature 1815–1832*. Oxford.
Jean-Aubry, G. (1927). *Joseph Conrad: Life and Letters*, 2 vols. London.
Lamport, F. J. (1990). *German Classical Drama: Theatre, Humanity and Nation, 1750–1870*. Cambridge.
Lewis, C. S. (1950). *The Literary Impact of the Authorised Version*. London.
More, Paul Elmor (1908). *Shelburne Essays*, 5th ser. New York.
Nelson, Stephanie (2007). 'Shelley and Plato: The Poet's Revenge.' *International Journal of the Classical Tradition* (forthcoming in Vol. 13)
Norton, David (1993). *A History of the Bible as Literature*, 2 vols. Cambridge.
Pound, Ezra (1968). *Literary Essays*, ed. T. S. Eliot. New York (*How to Read*, first pub. 1929, is reprinted on pp. 15–40).
Renwick, W. L. (1963). *English Literature: 1789–1815*. Oxford.
Rose, Jonathan (2001). *The Intellectual Life of the British Working Classes*. New Haven, CT.
Saintsbury, George (1939). 'The Prosody of the Nineteenth Century', pp. 250–82 in Vol. 13 of A. W. Ward and A. R. Waller, eds., *The Cambridge History of English Literature*. Cambridge (first pub. 1917).
Schreiber, Charlotte [Lady Charlotte Guest] (1952). *Lady Charlotte Schreiber: Extracts from her Journal 1853–1891*, ed. V. B. Ponsonby, Earl of Bessborough. London.
Smith, Grahame (1996). *Charles Dickens: A Literary Life*. Basingstoke.
Strich, Fritz (1949). *Goethe and World Literature*, tr. C. A. M. Syan. New York.
'Sylvanus Urban' [i.e. editors of *Gentleman's Magazine*] (1884). 'Table Talk: Bohn's Libraries and the Purchase of Books.' *Gentleman's Magazine* 257: 413–14.
Temple, Ruth Zabriskie (1953). *The Critic's Alchemy: A Study of the Introduction of French Symbolism into England*. New York.
Tennyson, Alfred (1990). *Letters*, ed. Cecil Y. Lang and Edgar F. Shannon, Jr., 3 vols. Cambridge, MA.
Thoreau, Henry David (1971). *Walden*, ed. J. Lyndon Shanley. Princeton, NJ.
Turton, Glyn (1992). *Turgenev and the Context of English Literature*. London.
Webb, Timothy (1976). *The Violet in the Crucible: Shelley and Translation*. Oxford.
Wilson, Edmund (1958). 'Turgenev and the Life-Giving Drop', pp. 3–64 in Ivan Turgenev, *Literary Reminiscences*, tr. David Magarshack. New York.
Yohannan, John D. (1952). *The Persian Fad in England 1770–1825*. New York.

1.2 Translation in the United States

Colleen Boggs

Introduction

American writers came late to the practice of publishing major translations. In eighteenth-century Britain, Dryden's and Pope's renditions of classical texts rivalled those of their Elizabethan predecessors and drew renewed attention to translation as a literary art. No similarly prestigious American translations were produced until after the Civil War. And yet the absence of major translations associated with renowned authors does not signify indifference; it reflects rather the different ways in which Americans and Britons valued authorship and print. British culture was increasingly driven by a celebration of authorship and of major works (see Woodmansee 1984; Rose 1993: 2). In the United States, on the other hand, the practice of unauthorized publication and anonymous translation remained appealing to publishers well into the nineteenth century.

The reasons for this were both political and economic. In the first place, the practice corresponded with the ideology of a democratically egalitarian society that thrived on its citizens' universal and easy access to print (see Warner 1990: 34, 61). By facilitating communication between the different language groups present in America and at the same time connecting the new republic to the larger literary world, translations played an important role in this print culture. But translation was also attractive to American publishers for economic reasons, because translated works were not protected by copyright. Copyright laws in Britain gave individual people control over their writings, but Americans by and large did not like the idea of private intellectual property; the free circulation of texts and ideas was a key democratic value in the early republic. Americans saw written texts as public property that copyright removed only temporarily from the public sphere to a realm of private ownership (McGill 2003: 93).

When the first Copyright Act of the United States was enacted in 1790, it initially protected only American authors. Publishers were not required to pay royalties to foreign authors, which made it advantageous for American publishers to republish British works or translations of other European works. Under these provisions arose a practice of reprinting: it was common practice to republish or translate texts, the publishing house of Harper's being especially notorious for reissuing previously published texts. Most publishers, however, respected the 'courtesy of the trade', by which they voluntarily refrained from publishing one another's titles. Because drawing up print plates was expensive, this courtesy was overall in everyone's best economic interest. But increasingly, even this protectionist habit became insufficient in a fiercely competitive market.

American and British authors tried to tighten American law and to achieve international (and especially Anglo-American) agreement on copyright. James Fenimore Cooper had been among the first to voice strong support for tighter copyright provisions that would pay Sir Walter Scott royalties for republications of his works in the United States, and Charles Dickens was a prominent voice among the supporters of copyright restrictions. A petition for copyright protection was signed by fifty-six 'Authors of Great Britain' and submitted to Congress. The debate grew particularly fierce in the 1840s, when publisher Evert Duyckinck took a leading role in 1843 and organized the American Copyright Club at the Athenaeum Hotel in New York (Greenspan 1992: 680). In Britain copyright had been extended by mid-century to foreign nationals under certain conditions (see pp. 55–6, below), but the United States proved resistant to such an extension of its copyright provisions. It was not until the amendment of the Copyright Act in 1891 that copyright was extended to foreign authors and to translations.

Most translations in the United States were initially published in the thriving American magazine and newspaper market of the early nineteenth century and became books later, if at all. For instance, in the preface to a collection of his translations, Charles Timothy Brooks expressed the hope that 'readers of the *Dial* and the *Diadem*, the *Child's Friend* and the *Christian Examiner*' would recognize the translations included in *Schiller's Homage of the Arts* (Brooks 1846: p. iv). Two publications proved particularly important for distributing translations and generating a readership: the *North American Review* and *The Dial*. These magazines popularized translations, but also set new standards for translators; looking at them allows us to understand what texts Americans were interested in translating, and how they thought about the practice of translation.

Romanticism and Orientalism

The *North American Review* was founded in 1815 and set itself the task of creating a literary culture in America that could compete with Britain's accomplishments while remaining true to the former colony's new national values. Although the magazine had been founded to rival British publications such as the *Edinburgh Review* and to provide a literary, critical, and historical review of important publications and intellectual developments, its focus had initially been somewhat parochially dedicated to the promotion of American letters. That changed when Edward Everett took over as editor in 1819. Everett received his Ph.D. from the University of Göttingen in 1817; he had been among a group of friends who had gone abroad together, and who 'became known as "the Göttingen Four"' (Harding 1979: 62); the other members were Harvard librarian Joseph G. Cogswell, historian George Bancroft, and George Ticknor, who became the first professor of modern languages and *belles-lettres* at Harvard.

These young men were the vanguard of a growing group of German-educated Americans: by one estimate, over 9,000 Americans studied at German universities in the nineteenth century (Fallon 1980: 51–2). Everett and his friends systematically set out to make America more cosmopolitan and to change the intellectual landscape, both by revising the university system at institutions such as Harvard and by publishing for a wider audience. Everett set out to pass on his learning to the general public through his editorial and written contributions to the *North American Review* (see Goodnight 1907: 33). His attempts met with success: in the two years of his editorship, the *North American Review* increased in circulation from 600 to 2,500 (Mott 2001: 110). Translation played an important role in Everett's endeavour to introduce his fellow Americans to European literature. In articles on writers such as Goethe, whom Everett first introduced to a wide American readership, he provided lengthy passages in translation (usually his own) to illustrate his literary interpretations.

Such translations from the German Romantic writers apparently caused or at least responded to shifting intellectual tastes, fuelled by the work of Thomas Carlyle and Germaine de Staël in Britain and France respectively (on this see § 6.1, below). France had long been the focus of American intellectual and political engagement with Europe. For instance, Benjamin Franklin thought that the universal language of the eighteenth century was French, and in a letter to Noah Webster of 1789 described English as holding at best second place to this lingua franca of educated men (Franklin 1987: 1175). But as Franklin's generation of founding fathers passed away, the Enlightenment values of the revolution were superseded by the Romanticism of the younger generations. What particularly interested them about German Romanticism was its dual attempt to create a national, German literature, and to make that German literature part of a broader world literature. That dual desire echoed their own wishes regarding American culture. The ground had been prepared by John Quincy Adams, who on various diplomatic assignments had acquired several European languages. He desired not only to perfect his ability to speak those languages, but also to refine his literary skills in them, and to that end, he developed the habit of translating texts. For instance, during the little spare time he had, he began to translate Wieland's *Oberon* in 1799. But he also translated less belletristic and more overtly political texts. His translation of an important essay by Friedrich von Gentz as *The Origin and Principles of the American Revolution Compared with the Origin and Principles of the French*, was serialized in the *Port Folio* in 1801 and also published anonymously as a book.

Yet his largest contribution to the growing field of American language training and literary translation was perhaps his support of the expansion of Harvard Library's holdings—which Everett's friend Cogswell reorganized along German lines when he was the college librarian from 1821 to 1823 (Harding 1979: 66). Aided by Goethe's gift of a copy of his collected works in 1818 to Harvard University and the acquisition of Hamburg merchant Christoph Daniel Ebeling's collection of Americana, George Ticknor and his successor Henry Wadsworth Longfellow began shopping extensively in Europe for important works of literature. As books became increasingly more accessible in the original languages, they also became increasingly available for translation.

The fascination with translation extended beyond European contexts. Explorers such as Alexander von Humboldt and Heinrich Schliemann also generated and participated in a fascination for all things exotic and Oriental. This interest was largely driven by two crucial discoveries: first, *The Arabian Nights*, which circulated widely in translation and created an Orientalist vogue in the late eighteenth and early nineteenth century, and second, the Rosetta Stone. Bayard Taylor published a whole volume of newly composed *Poems of the Orient* (1855), and Ralph Waldo Emerson was fascinated with the language, poetry, and philosophy of Persia. His volume of *Poems* (1847) included two works 'From the Persian of Hafiz', one by that title, and another, 'Ghaselle', with that subtitle. Despite these titles, the poems were not directly translated: in a note to the first poem, Emerson acknowledged the work of Ḥāfiẓ's German editor, Von Hammer, on whom he had relied for his translations (see Yohannan 1943). Emerson also popularized translations from Persian in magazines. In its 1851 edition, *The Liberty Bell*, an abolitionist annual, included one poem, 'Word and Deed', from Niẓami, and four poems—'The Phoenix', 'Faith', 'The Poet', 'To Himself'—that were from Ḥāfiẓ.

Champollion's deciphering of Egyptian hieroglyphics in the 1820s with the help of the Rosetta Stone sparked keen interest in the antiquities of Egypt and preoccupied the American literary imagination (as discussed in Irwin 1980). The *North American Review* published many articles on this subject, and specialized journals such as the *Journal of the American Oriental Society* (1843–99) came into circulation and proved to have staying power. But the broader cultural ramifications can also be seen in the references American authors make to hieroglyphics in their writings—for instance when Walt Whitman talks in *Leaves of Grass* (1855) about grass as a 'uniform hieroglyphic' (Whitman 1982: 193). The impact of deciphering on Edgar Allan Poe was especially significant for the development of American literature: Poe's creation of the detective genre in works such as 'Murders in the Rue Morgue' (1845) or his fantasies of translation in the *Narrative of Arthur Gordon Pym* (1838) partly stem from his fascination with Champollion (Irwin 1980: 43). Translation was a central practice and preoccupation even in original American literature that is not explicitly a translation of another text.

Even if there was much interest in translation, relatively little theoretical work on translation was produced in America, especially in contrast to Germany, where a veritable cottage industry of treatises on translation burgeoned in the early nineteenth century. But even if there was a relative dearth of treatises, Americans engaged extensively with theories of translation in their practice and their experiments with translation. Theories were discussed in articles on other languages and literatures and in the prefaces that accompanied book-length translations. Although the nineteenth century is often understood as a time of intense nationalism, a nationalist agenda did not exclude but on the contrary fostered an interest in translation. For instance, the New York-based editor and *littérateur* Evert Duyckinck actively promoted a national agenda, but nevertheless one of the books he helped to finance was Parke Godwin's translation of Goethe's autobiography *Dichtung und Wahrheit* (on this publication see Greenspan 1992: 679).

Academic Translation and Entertainment

The *North American Review* proved an important testing ground for translators who desired to develop a theory of their practice. In particular, it provided an outlet for the early writings of the nineteenth century's most prominent American poet and translator: Henry Wadsworth Longfellow. Among Longfellow's first publications are several magazine articles, such as the 'History of the Italian Language and Dialects' (1832), that tried to explain to an educated but general audience the linguistic and literary peculiarities of different languages and literatures. Longfellow's articles were meant to educate readers in what we would now think of as comparative linguistics: translations enabled readers to appreciate linguistic peculiarities and differences. These articles were meant to popularize foreign literature. But that did not mean that what was foreign had to be made familiar: Longfellow was adamant about appreciating foreign literature on its own terms and tried to translate in a way that showed his readers how the language worked in the original text.

Scholars of the classical languages in particular often saw translations from modern languages as frivolous. The centrality of translation to the American stage may very well have contributed to that perception, since translations of continental drama were popular on the American stage and in many cases the translators were also performers. Thus John Howard Payne appeared in 1811 at the Chestnut Street Theatre, Philadelphia, as Frederick in his own version of Kotzebue's *Das Kind der Liebe*, which, as *Lovers' Vows*, was already popular in English translations by Mrs Inchbald and Benjamin Thompson (see Hartnoll and Found 1996: 373). This performance was part of a much broader phenomenon: according to Zipes (1974: 273–4), Kotzebue 'dominated the entire Western stage during the first half of the nineteenth century', but in America, he owed his success to the translations of the 'father of the American stage', William Dunlap. Although Dunlap later disavowed the importance and influence of Kotzebue on the American theatre, his translations 'led to a vogue for melodrama which tended to eclipse more serious works and pandered to a craving for sensationalism' (Hartnoll and Found 1996: 261). The popularity of Dunlap's translations helped to launch the American stage, but French drama was also popular, especially in the many translations and adaptations of current French successes by John Howard Payne, who had visited Paris, winning the friendship of the actor Talma and the freedom of the Comédie-Française (see Hartnoll and Found 1996: 373). Among his translations are Ducange's *Thérèse, the Orphan of Geneva* (1821), Jouy's *Sylla* (1827), and Pixerécourt's *Adeline, the Victim of Seduction* (1822).

Given the success of translation as entertainment, Longfellow was in an odd position as a popularizer of European literature. Like his good friend and fellow translator James Russell Lowell, he was active in the academic field as professor of modern languages at Harvard. What made that position difficult at times was the reluctance on the part of the Greek and Latin faculty at Harvard to allow modern languages into the curriculum. A Harvard committee concluded that 'the simplistic grammatical structures and base literature of modern languages would irreparably harm a student's capacity for disciplined learning' (cited in Longfellow 2003: p. xii). Even after the modern languages secured their position in the American academy around mid-century, the academic study of languages was still largely dominated by scholars of antiquity: 'next to Christianity, the central intellectual project in America before the nineteenth century was classicism' (Winterer 2002: 1), so it is not surprising that many translation practices were developed in relation to the languages of antiquity. Because modern languages and national literatures were closely aligned at this time with political and often revolutionary goals, the emphasis on classicism points to a deep cultural conservatism that American translators of modern languages were beginning to challenge.

The Transcendentalists

That challenge was launched from within the heart of the New England educational élite. Although the importance of the *North American Review* was recognizable at the time of its publication, in retrospect at least, a relatively short-lived publication must also be seen as central to the development of translation practices in America. *The Dial* (1840–4) never reached wide circulation and was primarily a publication for the New England Transcendentalists, that is, for an important American branch of Romanticism. As such, it proved a testing ground for a school of authors we have come to see as central to American letters: Margaret Fuller, Ralph Waldo Emerson, and Henry David Thoreau are among the best-known contributors to *The Dial*.

Among this group of friends, attitudes towards translation were far from uniform. Fuller embraced translation as a means of expressing linguistic and cultural variety, whereas Emerson felt threatened by that plurality and wished for a uniform return to an Edenic language of nature (see Boggs 2004). In his training as a minister, Emerson had encountered translation theory in the model of 'higher criticism' for biblical scholarship, which viewed biblical texts as a cultural matrix 'that only the modern comparatist was in a position to comprehend' (Ellison 1984: 6). For Emerson, such comprehension meant transcending linguistic and intellectual differences. Yet he was sometimes troubled by the question whether such transcendence was ever truly possible, and he shared that concern with his younger friend Henry David Thoreau.

The question whether language was always derivative and could ever be original interested Thoreau, alongside the question of the extent to which language could be used for individual expression or was always a socially shared language (see Cavell 1972: 62–5). Thoreau adopted from the continental authors he was reading at the time the idea that national languages function as a 'quasi-organic embodiment of collective consciousness' that both inspires and limits 'all individual thought and expression' (West 1984: 768). Translation was a particularly interesting enterprise for him in that it allowed him to examine individual languages and to think about common elements and differences. He had studied Greek at Harvard with Longfellow's friend C. C. Felton, who had been trained in Germany. After graduating, he continued to read classically trained European writers such as Friedrich von Schlegel and Henry Nelson Coleridge, and was influenced by the theories of primitive and national poetry popularized by Johann Gottfried von Herder and Madame de Staël (Thoreau 1986: 187; West 1984: 753, 768).

Four of Thoreau's translations were published in *The Dial*: his translations of the Aeschylean *Prometheus Bound* (January 1843), of Anacreon (April 1843), of Pindar (January 1844), and again of Pindar (April 1844). The other translations survived in manuscript, and some have recently been published, including an episode from a later addition to the *Mahābhārata, The Transmigration of the Seven Brahmans*, Aeschylus' *Seven Against Thebes*, and others. In working on his translations, Thoreau turned not only to the ancient texts, but also to contemporary translations into languages other than English: although he was well versed in Greek and Latin, he relied for his Pindar translations on Friedrich Thiersch's German translation, and for the *Seven Brahmans* on S. A. Langlois's French translation of the *Harivaṃśa* (Thoreau 1986: 173).

Thoreau's notebooks reveal a careful consideration of alternatives when he was translating, and a concern for accuracy that is so pronounced that his translations can be traced back to the specific editions of the classical authors he used. He tried to maintain a sense of the original by finding English stylistic equivalents—his translations have been described as 'fairly faithful to the syntax, diction, and sounds of his originals', yet he 'avoids stilted literalism' (Anglen in Thoreau 1986: 203–4). He was particularly drawn in his translations to texts that had the literary qualities he hoped to achieve in his writings on nature. In an essay entitled 'Homer. Ossian. Chaucer', he remarks that 'Ossian reminds us of the most refined and rudest eras, of Homer, Pindar, Isaiah, and the American Indian' (Thoreau 1986: 177). Primitivism enabled such sweeping comparisons (see Carr 1996: 2–3), but it also points out that for Thoreau, translating was a way of reconnecting with a more natural form of linguistic expression. He wished to recover what he considered the 'heathenish integrity' that connected primitive poetry directly with the natural world.

Although women by and large did not have the same educational opportunities as men, some of them were very interested in acquiring language skills. For them, translation provided an entry into the public intellectual life from which they were largely excluded. Women writers such as Susan Warner and Harriet Beecher Stowe were hugely successful by mid-century, but their writing was largely confined to the popular genres of romance fiction. Translation functioned as a gateway to more scholarly literary pursuits, at least in their more accessible aspects. In this way Margaret Fuller and her fellow Transcendentalist Elizabeth Peabody, the American Sarah Helen Whitman, and the Canadian Anna Jameson all made their mark as translators.

Fuller saw translation as a means of connecting different national literatures (see Boggs 2004), but she also used translation to enact a feminist politics. For her, translations were a way of imagining an intimate connection between women worldwide—a form of friendship (see Berkson 1994: 13–14, 21–2). Specifically, she thought of them as a means of having a conversation with someone who was not present in person but present in print (Bean 1997: 31). She also recognized the political importance of translation—alongside contemporaries such as John Greenleaf Whittier, whose translation of Lamartine's poetry strengthened support for the provisional government that had been established in France in 1848 and that had immediately abolished slavery in the colonies (see Reynolds 1988: 19). Sarah Helen Whitman praised Fuller's translation of Johann Peter Eckermann's *Conversations with Goethe* as an 'admirably translated volume', speaking of the 'increasing interest with which the German is looked upon among us. We are in no way disturbed by the fear, that its subtleties, refinements and abstractions, should have an evil influence on our national character ... the individuality of which seems in no danger of being neutralized by such antagonistic principles, though it may perchance be favorably modified by them' (Whitman 1840: 22). In the mid-1840s, Fuller translated articles from the German-American *New Yorker Staatszeitung* for the *New York Tribune*. Among those translations was the earliest mention of Karl Marx and Friedrich Engels in an English-language context in the United States. Fuller's work became even more explicitly political when she became a foreign correspondent for Horace Greeley's *New York Tribune* and wrote dispatches from Italy, where she lived during the revolution of 1848. The circulation of translations in magazines and newspapers, far from being merely belletristic, was an important factor in political discussion.

Anthologies and Major Translations

The Dial at times read almost like an anthology of translated and original compositions, and the anthology format was central as well to the publications that grew out of this literary magazine. For example, Margaret Fuller had published an article in *The Dial* on 'Bettina Brentano and her friend Günderode' which was a condensed version of her book-length translation published that same year (Fuller 1842). Similarly, Charles Timothy Brooks contributed translations to *The Dial* that later became part of a book publication (1842). The popularity that translations enjoyed was also apparent in the frequency with which they appeared in the 'gift books', and their inclusion in these volumes gives us some indications of the role that gender played in this literary practice. Enormously popular in the nineteenth century, gift books were compilations of literary texts that were meant to entertain and morally elevate the reader. They functioned as tokens of friendship, and were used—as the name suggests—as gifts around the holidays and on other occasions throughout the year. To give just one example, *The Cabinet Annual—A Christmas and New Year's Gift for 1855* contained a poem entitled 'New Year's Eve. From the German of Jean Paul Richter. By Mrs. Charles Richardson.'

Many of the editors and the contributors of original and translated poetry were women, such as L.E.L, Mrs Hemans, and Lydia Sigourney (though Longfellow's works were also often reprinted in these volumes).

Another of *The Dial*'s legacies was its close connection with the first series of new literary translations of book length: the fourteen-volume collection called Specimens of Foreign Standard Literature that was published between 1838 and 1842. The series was edited by George Ripley, and volumes included Margaret Fuller's translation of Eckermann's *Conversations with Goethe* and Charles Timothy Brooks's translated *Songs and Ballads* (1842). Ripley's series was the first attempt to bring a sustained and high-quality series of literary translations to an educated American readership. Rather than simply translating individual authors these volumes attempted to facilitate a broader cultural understanding of literatures produced in other countries.

Contributors to the Specimens of Foreign Standard Literature tried to establish a qualitative standard for translation. They emphasized fidelity to the original, but also valued literary creativity. Charles Timothy Brooks's prefaces to his translations play out these competing desires. He explains of his translation of Ferdinand Freiligrath's poem 'The Lion's Ride' that he 'has seen two other versions of the following piece', but complains that neither maintains 'the exact measure of the original, which is here given' (Brooks 1846: 61). Such comments demonstrate that different theories of translation competed at the time, but that Brooks for one desired to replicate the formal qualities of the original. The desire for accuracy reflects an increasing emphasis on the role of authors and their stylistic choices, and a move away from the appreciation of text as a culturally mobile artefact that exists in relative independence from an author. But it also suggests an attempt to understand the differences between languages. For instance, Brooks set himself the task of retranslating Burns's 'Farewell to his Native Land' from Ferdinand Freiligrath's German translation, and published the results. He says that the 'only thing which makes it impossible for the Germans to give the characteristic beauties of Burns is, that they have no dialect which bears the same relation to a German ear that the Scottish does to an English ear' (Brooks 1846: 87). In the preface to his *Songs and Ballads*, he writes that his 'translations will be found faithful to the word of the original, so far as the difference of idiom between the two languages and the comparative deficiency of English in rhyme would permit' (Brooks 1842: p. x).

These collections set out to represent the linguistic diversity of any given culture and as such were used for ethnographic purposes. The cultures represented were not always the cultures of others, but also American culture. Walt Whitman's anthologies of literary specimens, *Leaves of Grass* (1855) and *Specimen Days* (1882), evoke the formulaic title of a particular type of early nineteenth-century anthology, the literary specimen collection that aimed at a broadly inclusive representation of poetry (see Boggs 2002: 35–40). The first collection of American literature edited and published in the United States, Samuel Kettell's *Specimens of American Poetry* (1829), included translations, for instance Revd John Adams's 'Translation of an Ode of Horace'(first pub. 1745), in a collection that aimed to call 'into notice what is valuable and characteristic in the writings of our native poets' (Kettell 1829: I, p. iii). The most extensive effort to create an anthology of translations was undertaken by Longfellow. In 1845, he published his *Poets and Poetry of Europe*. The initial publication had over 700 pages, and Longfellow added to that a supplement of over 340 pages in 1871. The poems in the volume ranged in time from the Nordic *Eddas* and *Beowulf* to the work of Lamartine and Heine, and Longfellow himself translated poetry from eight languages into English, his translations making up about one tenth of the whole. This was an unprecedented undertaking, and for all its inevitable shortcomings, it played 'a genuinely Arnoldian role ... for some decades, in helping to propagate among American readers "the best that is known and thought in the world" ' (Arvin 1962: 59).

Although we might now assume that people who were academically schooled were not interested in translation because they could read works in the original, that assumption does not hold true for the nineteenth century, when academics often compared translations, or read them with pleasure as texts that were important in their own right. Longfellow was at the forefront of the movement in favour of translations that were not only accurate but also valuable in themselves. Although British translations of Dante existed and Emerson had begun translating the *La vita nuova* by 1843, no American had published a full translation of the *Divine Comedy*, in part because the poem remained suspect to a predominantly anti-Catholic readership. Despite his own earlier dislike of the poem, Longfellow began translating the *Inferno* in March 1863. His full translation was published in 1867 (along with six sonnets that he composed on the process of translation) and went through four printings within a year. Longfellow translated Dante in blank verse and tried to represent his language and rhythm, but he also aimed to produce a literal version: 'while making it [the poem] rhythmic, I have endeavoured to make it also as literal as a prose translation. ... The business of the translator is to report what the author says, not to explain what he means. ... what an author says, and how he says it, that is the problem of the translator' (cited in Cunningham 1965: 67). The reception was mixed, but the translation sold very well; Longfellow has recently been praised by Lino Pertile for his 'punctilious adherence to the original text' and for having rendered Dante's language into English with 'extraordinary precision, richness, and variety' (preface to Longfellow 2003: p. xviii).

The years after the Civil War saw important contributions to translation from the languages of antiquity: William Cullen Bryant translated both the *Iliad* (1870) and the *Odyssey* (1871) in blank verse and a relatively plain style. And the interest in German literature continued: although a partial translation of *Faust* had been available since 1856 in Charles Timothy Brooks's translation, Bayard Taylor was the first to produce a full translation of the work. Taylor began translating *Faust* seriously in 1863 after having been recalled from Europe by news of his brother's death at Gettysburg (see Prahl 1945). His work was published in a large edition in December 1870 and sold well; in 1878, Taylor was sent to Germany as an ambassador.

Multilingualism

The role of translation in bridging the gaps between different communities in the United States has already been mentioned. It can be illustrated in the career of Charles Godfrey Leland, whose work also exemplifies the increasingly frequent intersections in the popular press between translation and dialect writing, and the way in which this entertainment culture branched into areas of what we would today consider anthropology. Although Mark Twain's reflections on the difficulties of German are probably the most famous example of the linguistic humour sparked by these interests, this genre grew from the widespread philological interests and translation practices pioneered by people such as Leland.

After graduating from Princeton in 1845, Leland studied in Heidelberg and Munich, and participated in the Paris uprising of 1848. Back in the United States, he worked as an editor on numerous magazines, including P. T. Barnum's *Illustrated News*. He collaborated with George Ripley and Charles Dana on *Appleton's Encyclopedia* and began publishing monographs in the 1850s. Like other writers of his era, he was fascinated by German Romanticism and its early radical politics, but he was also among the first Americans to publish Native American stories for their literary value. At a time when 'there were not many linguists on the American press', he wrote 'reviews in half-a-dozen languages' (Leland 1893: 197). He was the first American to translate Heine's *Reisebilder*, and his translation (Leland 1855) remained in print into the twentieth century. He also compiled dictionaries of demotic language, such as the *Dictionary of Slang, Jargon & Cant embracing English, American, and Anglo-Indian Slang, Pidgin English, Tinker's Jargon and other Irregular Phraseology* (1889–90).

Becoming interested in applying his linguistic knowledge and observations to the American scene, Leland wrote a series of humorous German-English dialect poems known collectively as *Hans Breitmann's Ballads* (1870). These poems create a blended language that often requires knowledge of both German and English, and acts of translation, to understand the punning and phonic humour of the poems. Leland's interest in dialect writing also caused him to write in Chinese-English (Leland 1876), and he began collecting speech patterns from around the world. His linguistic interests increasingly drew him towards the cross-cultural study of folk legends. He collected these tales in publications such as *The Algonquin Legends of New England* (1884). (The collection and translation of texts in Native American languages is considered more fully in § 9.3, below.)

One of the things that Leland's translation activities point to is the existence of many and diverse linguistic environments in the United States. It is important to remember that 'American multilingual literature is not only a literature of immigration and assimilation ... multilingual American literature is part of a transnational world—though authors who complicate the fit of authorship, citizenship and language have been marginalized by the pervasive national organization of literature' (Shell and Sollors 2000: 7–8). The American press was and remains to this day intensely multilingual. It was Benjamin Franklin who in 1732 issued the first German newspaper in the United States, *Die Philadelphia Zeitung*, and it was not uncommon for predominantly English-language presses to publish in other languages as well. From 1828, for instance, Carey and Lea, the publishers of Washington Irving and James Fenimore Cooper, published an annual magazine called *El Aguinaldo* in which many articles had been translated from the *Atlantic Souvenir* into Spanish (Kaser 1957: 46). Multilingual literature thrived on translations. These other linguistic environments cannot be examined at greater length here, but it is worth noting that literary translation in English is only a fraction of the translation activity that was taking place within the United States in the nineteenth century.

LIST OF SOURCES

Translations

Anon., ed. (1839). *Select Minor Poems, Translated from the German of Goethe and Schiller*. Boston, MA.

[Adams, John Quincy] (1800). *The Origin and Principles of the American Revolution Compared with the Origin and Principles of the French* [Gentz]. Philadelphia, PA.

Brooks, Charles Timothy (1842). *Songs and Ballads, Translated from Uhland, Körner, Bürger and other German Lyric Poets*. Boston, MA.

—— (1846). *Schiller's Homage of the Arts, with Miscellaneous Pieces from Rückert, Freiligrath, and other German Poets*. New York.

—— (1856). *Faust* [Goethe]. Boston, MA.

Bryant, William Culler (1870). *The Iliad* [Homer]. Boston, MA.

—— (1871). *The Odyssey* [Homer]. Boston, MA.

Emerson, Ralph Waldo (1994). *Collected Poems and Translations*. New York.

Fuller, Margaret (1839). *Conversations with Goethe in the Last Years of his Life* [Eckermann]. Boston, MA.

—— (1842). *Günderode* [von Arnim]. Boston, MA.

Godwin, Parke (1846). *The Auto-biography of Goethe. Truth and Poetry: From my Life*. New York.

Kettell, Samuel, ed. (1829). *Specimens of American Poetry*, 3 vols. Boston, MA.

Leland, Charles Godfrey (1855). *Pictures of Travel* [Heine]. Philadelphia, PA.

—— (1876). *Pidgin-English Sing-song, or, Songs and Stories in the China-English Dialect. With a Vocabulary*. London.

—— (1884). *The Algonquin Legends of New England, or, Myths and Folk Lore of the Micmac, Passamaquoddy, and Penobscot Tribes*. Boston, MA.

Longfellow, Henry Wadsworth, ed. (1845). *The Poets and Poetry of Europe*. Philadelphia, PA.

—— (2003). *Inferno* [Dante], ed. Matthew Pearl and with an introduction by Lino Pertile. New York (first pub. 1867).

Payne, John Howard (1821). *Thérèse, the Orphan of Geneva* [Ducange]. New York.

—— (1822). *Adeline, the Victim of Seduction* [Pixerécourt]. London.

—— (1827). *Sylla* [Jouy]. New York.

Shell, Marc, and Sollors, Werner, eds. (2000). *The Multilingual Anthology of American Literature: A Reader of Original Texts with English Translations*. New York.

Taylor, Bayard (1871). *Faust* [Goethe], 2 vols. Boston, MA.

Thoreau, Henry David (1986). *Translations*, ed. K. P. Van Anglen. Princeton, NJ.

Other Sources

Arvin, Newton (1963). *Longfellow: His Life and Work*. Boston, MA.

Bean, Judith (1997). 'Conversation as Rhetoric in Margaret Fuller's Woman in the Nineteenth Century', pp. 27–41 in Sherry Linkon, ed., *In her own Voice: Nineteenth-Century American Women Essayists*. New York.

Berkson, Dorothy (1994). ' "Born and Bred in Different Nations": Margaret Fuller and Ralph Waldo Emerson', pp. 3–30 in Shirley Marchalonis, ed., *Patrons and Protégées: Gender, Friendship, and Writing in Nineteenth-Century America*. New Brunswick, NJ.

Boggs, Colleen Glenney (2002). 'Specimens of Translation in Walt Whitman's Poetry.' *Arizona Quarterly* 58: 33–56.

—— (2004). 'Margaret Fuller's American Translation.' *American Literature* 76: 31–58.

Carr, Helen (1996). *Inventing the American Primitive: Polities, Gender, and the Representation of Native American Literary Traditions, 1789–1936*. New York.

Cavell, Stanley (1972). *The Senses of Walden*. New York.

Cunningham, Gilbert (1965). *The Divine Comedy in English: A Critical Bibliography 1782–1900*. Edinburgh.

Ellison, Julie (1984). *Emerson's Romantic Style*. Princeton, NJ.

Fallon, Daniel (1980). *The German University: A Heroic Ideal in Conflict with the Modern World*. Boulder, CO.

Franklin, Benjamin (1987). *Writings*, ed. J. A. Leo Lemay. New York.

Goodnight, Scott (1907). *German Literature in American Magazines Prior to 1846*. (Bulletin of the University of Wisconsin, no. 188). Madison, WI.

Greenspan, Ezra (1992). 'Evert Duyckinck and the History of Wiley and Putnam's Library of American Books, 1845–1847.' *American Literature* 64: 677–93.

Harding, Annelise (1979). *John Quincy Adams: Pioneer of German-American Literary Studies*. Boston, MA.

Hartnoll, Phyllis, and Found, Peter, eds. (1996). *The Concise Oxford Companion to the Theatre*, 2nd edn. Oxford.

Irwin, John (1980). *American Hieroglyphics: The Symbol of the Egyptian Hieroglyphics in the American Renaissance*. New Haven, CT.

Kaser, David (1957). *Messrs. Carey & Lea of Philadelphia: A Study in the History of the Booktrade*. Philadelphia, PA.

Leland, Charles Godfrey (1893). *Memoirs*. New York.

McGill, Meredith (2003). *American Literature and the Culture of Reprinting, 1834–1853*. Philadelphia, PA.

Mott, Wesley T., ed. (2001). *Dictionary of Literary Biography*, Vol. 235: *The American Renaissance in New England, Third Series*. Detroit, MI.

Parkhill, Thomas C. (1997). *Weaving Ourselves into the Land: Charles Godfrey Leland, "Indians," and the Study of Native American Religions*. Albany, NY.

Prahl, Augustus (1945). 'Bayard Taylor in Germany.' *German Quarterly* 18: 16–25.

Reynolds, Larry (1988). *European Revolutions and the American Literary Renaissance*. New Haven, CT.

Rose, Mark (1993). *Authors and Owners: The Invention of Copyright*. Cambridge, MA.

Warner, Michael (1990). The *Letters of the Republic: Publication and Public Sphere in Eighteenth-Century America*. Cambridge, MA.

West, Michael (1984). 'Thoreau and the Language Theories of the French Enlightenment.' *English Literary History* 51: 747–70.

Whitman, Sarah Helen (1840). Review of Margaret Fuller's *Conversations with Goethe*. *Boston Quarterly Review* 3: 20–57.
Whitman, Walt (1982). *Complete Poetry and Selected Prose*. New York.
Winterer, Caroline (2002). *The Culture of Classicism: Ancient Greece and Rome in American Public Life, 1780–1910*. Baltimore, MD.
Woodmansee, Martha (1984). 'The Genius and the Copyright: Economic and Legal Conditions of the Emergence of the "Author".' *Eighteenth-Century Studies* 17: 425–48.
Yohannan, J. D. (1943). 'Emerson's Translations of Persian Poetry from German Sources.' *American Literature* 14: 407–20.
Zipes, Jack (1974). 'Dunlap, Kotzebue, and the Shaping of American Theater: A Reevaluation from a Marxist Perspective.' *Early American Literature* 8: 272–85.

1.3 Readers and Publishers of Translations in Britain

Terry Hale

Introduction

During the nineteenth century the British publishing industry expanded enormously. It is hard to give precise figures for book publication, since much depends on what statisticians choose to count as a book, but the growth is clear: a recent literary historian writes that 'whereas between 1800 and 1825 only about 580 books appeared each year, by mid-century the figure has risen to over 2,600 titles, and by 1900 it was over 6,000' (Davis 2002: 201). Nor was it only books that were in demand. In 1800, British readers had some 264 periodicals of all kinds from which to choose; in 1859, some 115 new periodicals were started in London alone (Graham 1930: 16–17, 301). Newspapers also proliferated; by 1870, a large city such as Liverpool had five daily papers while even a small town such as Exeter could sustain three (Feather 1988: 164). One commentator estimates that more than 25,000 journals, including newspapers, saw the light of day during the Victorian era (Houghton 1982: 4). Though many of these new ventures quickly floundered—the competition was intense across all sectors of print media—there can be no doubt that fortunes were there to be made by enterprising publishers.

How did translation fare amidst all this feverish activity? The picture is contradictory. On the one hand, in certain genres such as children's fiction, translation flourished throughout the period. Likewise, one can point to an impressive sequence of major translations—ranging from Henry Cary's version of Dante (1814) or Edward FitzGerald's *Rubáiyát of Omar Khayyám* (1859) through to Richard Burton's *Book of the Thousand Nights and a Night* (1885)—which might tend to suggest that translation held a central position in Victorian publishing. With regard to the novel, often considered the pre-eminent literary form of the nineteenth century, the evidence is less clear. The mainstream publishing houses issued relatively little fiction in translation. More generally, the work of many of the major European and Russian novelists had to wait decades before English translations became available. Balzac, for example, did not become fully available in translation until the very eve of the twentieth century. Similarly, there was little translation in the majority of the (middle-class) literary periodicals of the mid-century and later (see Ch. 4, below).

By contrast, several of the more popular journals, notably the *Family Herald* and the *London Journal*, were largely dependent on translation at various moments round about the mid-century. At the same time, Eugène Sue's *Les Mystères de Paris* attracted the attention of six different British publishers simultaneously (see pp. 375–6, below). Later in the century, translation also appealed to some of the newer publishing houses, especially those producing 'railway literature' (i.e. books to be consumed on long railway journeys). Notable amongst the latter is the firm of Vizetelly and Co. in the 1880s. Towards the end of the century, several publishers of pornography likewise tended to specialize in translation. In general, then, the market for translations appears to have been quite uneven.

The market for printed matter, including translation, was much affected by the changing demography of nineteenth-century Britain. In 1801, the first national census put the British population at nearly eleven million, just over nine million of that population in England and Wales. By 1870, that figure had more than doubled to twenty-six million. By 1900, though growth had slowed, the figure was forty million, with the population of England and Wales standing at thirty million. But it is not just a question of population size, however great the impact of the economies of scale on book production might be, especially when coupled with technological developments which, by the mid-century, had made large print runs increasingly viable (Davis 2002: 202–3). By 1900, 80 per cent of the population lived in towns, and that new urban population was increasingly literate. By the end of the century, moreover, living conditions had visibly improved, and in the final decades of the century working hours fell quite sharply. A new middle class of professional or commercial white-collar workers was developing, ranging from clerks and teachers to civil servants. Numbering around 300,000 in the 1851 census, that class had swollen to 650,000 by 1881 (Davis 2002: 202). If reading was a principal leisure activity of the nineteenth century, by the mid-century it was no longer the sole preserve of a small élite (the minimum subscription to a circulating library such as Mudie's was a guinea) but the preferred pastime of the new middle classes (the main audience for the new shilling fiction-carrying monthlies).

Lower down the social scale, a new sector was also developing which catered for a still wider popular audience. Working-class readers could obtain access to standard literature (see below), but they also constituted the main audience for fiction in penny instalments and penny periodicals such as the *Family Herald*. The Victorian world was so socially stratified that the gulf between the shilling monthlies and the penny weeklies was almost unbridgeable. Middle-class commentators only ventured into this territory on an occasional basis, and even then purely for sociological purposes. James Payn, editor of the *Cornhill Magazine*, the archetypal shilling monthly, referred disparagingly to this new class of readers as 'the Unknown Public'. Though the penny press was already of 'considerable dimensions' in the early 1860s when it was first described by Wilkie Collins (from whom Payn borrows the expression 'the Unknown Public'), two decades later 'the luxuriance of its growth has become tropical' (Payn 1882: 149). This new popular audience was the chief beneficiary of the educational reforms of the second half of the century.

Historically, the main market for books had been a small educated élite, whose personal libraries were sometimes extensive. In the case of Britain, at the beginning of the nineteenth century, this élite consisted mainly of the families of the peerage and local gentry; as the century wore on, it was augmented by a rising class of large landowners, often industrialists, and high officials without any hereditary titles (Colley 1994: 164). Though numerically small, this group was not only well informed and wealthy (an important consideration given that books were expensive), it was also by no means narrowly British in outlook; indeed, it has been described as 'in some respects ostentatiously unBritish' (ibid. 177).

The market for translation was affected by the socially stratified nature of the reading public. It might seem that since the élite group had relatively little need for translation, particularly from French, there was little incentive for publishers to take on translation projects for this audience. To put it at its worst, translation was caught between an 'unBritish' élite with little use for translation and a patriotic general public unsure of the moral value of foreign literature. This resulted in a culture where 'concealed' translation (primarily adaptation) flourished, notably in popular fiction and the theatre (see §§ 8.1 and 8.2, below). On the other hand, there was a continuing demand for such things as non-fiction translation (especially history and religion), literal translations of the classics as student cribs, and, more generally, translation from languages other than French and Latin (see Ch. 4, below). As the century progressed, moreover, new market opportunities opened up for the publishers of translations of all kinds.

The Cultural Élite and their Circulating Libraries

In 1818, when Richard Rush, the newly appointed American ambassador, attended his first official dinner at the London town house of the British Prime Minister, Lord Castlereagh, he was astonished to discover not only that the general topics of conversation 'related to France, and French society' but that 'the conversation was nearly all in French': 'This was not only the case when the English addressed the foreigners, but in speaking to each other. Before dinner, I had observed in the drawing-room, books lying about. As many as I glanced at were French. I thought of the days of Charles II when the tastes of the English all ran upon the models of France. Here, at the house of an English minister of state, French literature, the French language, French topics were all about me; I add, French *entrées*, French wines!' (Rush 1987: 177).

French increasingly established itself as the second language of well-educated people everywhere in the eighteenth and nineteenth centuries. Not surprisingly, the extent to which the British cultural élite invested in foreign languages is most thoroughly documented in relation to writers. Horace Walpole and William Beckford, for example, both wrote French with ease. Walpole conducted a voluminous correspondence in French; Beckford wrote his most enduring contribution to British letters, *Vathek* (1786), in French. Among the Gothic novelists, M. G. Lewis, who like Walpole and Beckford had the benefit of a classical education, learned French at Westminster, where the boys were allowed to converse only in French during the school day. He spent the summer vacation of 1791, while still only 16, in

Paris (where he regularly attended the theatre); the following year, he had a six-month stint in Weimar learning German in preparation for the diplomatic service (see Peck 1961: 5–9). Women writers did not lag far behind. Ann Radcliffe certainly knew French well enough to read eighteenth-century trial reports; Harriet and Sophia Lee, Charlotte Smith, and Clara Reeve all had enough French (on the evidence of their own writing) to be able to cope with authors such as the Abbé Prévost in the original (see pp. 371–3, below).

Matters had not greatly changed by the mid-nineteenth century. Thackeray, who had earned a living there as a journalist, and Bulwer Lytton both knew Paris almost as well as London. Charlotte and Emily Brontë spent nine months at the Pensionnat Heger in Brussels in 1842, an experience modern critics see as having a major impact on their future literary careers. Wilkie Collins and M. E. Braddon, two of the most prolific authors of the 1860s and 1870s, were both saturated in French culture, as was Robert Louis Stevenson. Collins and Stevenson left behind substantial libraries on their deaths: approximately half the books they owned were in French. Braddon's French was so accomplished that she was able to write a novel in the language for serial publication in a French newspaper (Woolf 1979: 492–3). The spell cast by French was possibly even stronger towards the end of the century. The key authors associated with *fin-de-siècle* decadence were all thoroughly imbued with French culture: Oscar Wilde wrote his verse drama *Salomé* in French, Ernest Dowson published translations of Balzac and Zola, while much of the writing of Arthur Symons served to introduce French writers and ideas to a British audience.

But such linguistic proficiency was by no means limited to authors. Lord Castlereagh, Richard Rush's host in 1818, was an accomplished linguist. A Cambridge-educated classicist whose knowledge of modern languages had further benefited from the Grand Tour, Castlereagh in his accomplishments was typical of the patrician order to which he belonged and to which most of the writers mentioned above aspired in some measure to belong. Nor was it only in Britain that a knowledge of French was essential for advancement. When Edgar Allan Poe began his cadetship at West Point in March 1830 he was no doubt surprised to discover that the commanding officer, Colonel Thayer, who had studied at the École Polytechnique in Paris, insisted on recruits undertaking French conversation classes. Not only that, but most of the books in the library, especially those used to provide the mathematical rudiments necessary for training in such areas as artillery bombardments and the building of fortifications, were also in French (Messac 1929: 11).

Other languages, it is true, fared considerable less well than French, though Italian became more fashionable, whether through travel or the appeal of the opera. German, which began to attract British intellectuals around the turn of the century, usually involved a conscious decision to learn the language. Coleridge was able to visit Germany and devote himself to the study of German (see pp. 107–9, below), because of the offer of an annuity from Josiah and Thomas Wedgwood. Others, including Sir John Bowring, John Stuart Mill, and George Eliot, were largely self-taught. But generally speaking, as one might expect given the emphasis on classical languages at school and university, modern European languages did not represent a particular problem for the educated classes of the nineteenth century. Sir Thomas Phillipps, the leading bibliophile of the age, ransacked the bookshops and auction houses of continental Europe to put together a library which took more than half a century to disperse. When, in 1825, he advertised for a successor to his principal assistant, he demanded a knowledge of 'Saxon, Greek, Latin, French, German, Persian, Arabic and Domesday characters' (cited in Munby: 1967, 52).

Some confirmation of the hypothesis being developed here—namely that the wealthiest and most literate segment of society could read much foreign literature without the help of translation—is provided by the catalogues of the circulating libraries. One such institution was Booth's Library in Regent Street, which was broadly typical of the well-to-do end of the market. Around the year 1855, Booth's stocked some 10,000 titles. The subscription terms were much the same as elsewhere, the lowest annual rate of two guineas entitling the reader to borrow four volumes at a time. The catalogue (Anon. *c.*1855) is divided into five sections: 'History, Antiquities, Voyages, Travels, Poetry, Drama, Miscellaneous' (representing approximately 50 per cent of stock); 'Novels, Romances and Tales' (approximately 26 per cent); 'French, Italian, and Spanish' (16 per cent); 'German' (7 per cent); and 'Divinity and Ecclesiastical History' (1 per cent).

The high proportion of books in languages other than English is particularly emphasized in the title of the catalogue, which draws attentions to holdings in 'English, French, German, Italian and Spanish Books'. Readers were clearly expected to read many foreign texts without the aid of translations, which barely account for 3 per cent of the overall stock. This figure is at the lower end of the estimated proportion of translation in books published (see Ch. 4, below). Nevertheless the catalogue does contain a fair number of translated volumes in both the non-fiction and fiction sections.

The translations of non-fiction works in Booth's Library largely fall into two predictable categories, already well represented in the previous century. First, as befitted a trading nation, there are accounts of voyages by French travellers and explorers, especially those whose journeys took them to places of strategic importance to British interests. These include Bougainville's *History of a Voyage to the Malouine (or Falkland) Islands, made in 1763 and 1764*, first published in French in 1771 and translated into English the following year; René Caillé's *Travels through Central Africa to Timbuctoo, and across the Great Desert to Morocco* (1830; tr. 1830), which includes an account of the crossing of the Sahara; and the Marquis de Custine's *The Empire of the Czar* (1843; tr. 1843). Second, we find a number of memoirs dealing with recent historical events, especially those connected with the French Revolution and the Empire such as: Clausewitz's *Account of the Campaign of 1812 in Russia* (1843), first published in German in 1835 and translated anonymously by Francis Egerton, a friend of Wellington; Las Cases's *Mémorial de Sainte-Hélène* (1822–3; tr. 1823), a primary source, if not always an reliable one, of Napoleon's last years;

the *Memoirs* of Joseph Fouché, Napoleon's chief of police (1824; tr. 1825); and, to bring subscribers closer to the present day, Louis Blanc's *History of Ten Years, 1830–1840* (1843; tr. 1844–5), an account of the reign of Louis-Philippe by one of the leading socialists of the period.

Libraries are, of course, accumulative enterprises, and it is not surprising to find that a considerable body of Booth's stock is quite old. This is also true of the 'Novels, Romances, and Tales' section with its generous stock of Gothic novels. Once again, the most remarkable aspect of the library's acquisition policy is the absence of translations of contemporary works. Alexandre Dumas *père*, for example, is represented by just two titles: *The Count of Monte-Cristo* and a one-volume edition (or possibly an odd volume) of his *Celebrated Crimes* series; Eugène Sue is represented by four titles (including, of course, *The Mysteries of London* and *The Wandering Jew*); Balzac is entirely absent, for the very good reason that translations of his work would not commence for another four years (and even then would take the form of cheap one-shilling editions issued by Routledge); likewise absent are most of the major *feuilletonistes*, including Frédéric Soulié, Paul Féval, and the more versatile George Sand. On the basis of Booth's catalogue, the most popular author in translation with subscribers was the Swedish novelist and travel writer Fredrika Bremer (see pp. 288–9, below).

As with non-fiction, though to an even greater degree, one reason why Booth's stocked so little translated fiction is that the proprietors expected their readers to read such material in the language in which it was written. In fact, more than a fifth of the books held by the library were in languages other than English, mainly French and German. Catalogued separately, with fiction and non-fiction titles indiscriminately listed together, the books in the foreign languages section tend to be more recent acquisitions than those listed under the 'Novels, Romances, and Tales' rubric. Of the French novelists, those most in evidence are Dumas *père* (74 titles); Balzac (57 titles); Paul de Kock, a writer famed for his coarse humour (43 titles); George Sand (38 titles); Eugène Sue (25 titles); Frédéric Soulié (19 titles); and Madame la Comtesse Dash (i.e. Cisterne de Courtiras, vicomtesse de Poilloüe de Saint-Mars), a prolific minor writer and occasional collaborator of Dumas *père* (15 titles).

Booth's library was clearly somewhat exclusive, but similar acquisition policies can be seen elsewhere, whether in public institutions (the Leeds Library, a subscription library, for example, has considerable French holdings acquired during the course of the nineteenth century) or in private settings (of the country house libraries still intact there are few indeed which do not possess a couple of shelves of choice French fiction). The very fact that Booth's enjoyed a relatively long existence (it had been in operation since 1830 and may have been much older) indicates that the selection policy met with the approval of its subscribers.

It seems therefore that translations of modern prose works, particularly from French, were not needed by many educated readers. In order to appeal to this group, translation, especially in the first half of the century, had generally to offer more than merely a straightforward account of a new work. By and large, the projects that aroused the greatest interest involved poetry rather than prose, less familiar languages than French, or works from historically remote periods. The sort of ambitious translation projects noted at the beginning of this section—Cary's Dante, FitzGerald's *Rubáiyát* (see §§ 6.3 and 7.2, below)—generally met these criteria. More broadly, a considerable retranslation market developed with regard to certain key texts, notably Greek and Latin works, but also those of such figures as Dante, Tasso, Cervantes, and Camões, as poets and scholars competed with each other to create ever more compelling readings of the originals. Significantly, there were relatively few such retranslations of French literature.

The New Middle Classes and their Periodicals

By 1861, Mudie's Circulating Library, which had long since overtaken all its rivals, was claiming that it purchased 180,000 volumes a year on behalf of some 25,000 subscribers (Griest 1971: 21). From its premises in New Oxford Street, it not only lent books to its London subscribers but also sent them out in boxes to clients in the provinces and even overseas. Given the commercial clout wielded by a firm such as Mudie's, it is hardly surprising that the three-decker novel and the circulating library had become mutually interdependent by this stage. With the exception of Dickens (and the partial exception of Thackeray), the bulk of mainstream British fiction was published in three-decker format until the 1890s. Even American authors whose work had been published in one-volume editions in their own country succumbed to the three-decker treatment in Britain, a process that did not spare Fenimore Cooper, Herman Melville, Nathaniel Hawthorne, Mark Twain, or even Henry James (Griest 1971: 55–6).

Foreign authors (i.e. those who wrote in languages other than English) were largely ignored both by the circulating libraries and by the main producers of multi-volume fiction, including such established publishing houses as Smith, Elder and Co. and Richard Bentley and Son. Foreign writing, especially French fiction, suffered from a specific disadvantage with regard to the world of the circulating libraries: it was perceived as morally dangerous. This was a view that had been growing for some time. In the mid-1830s, the conservative *Quarterly Review* had published two influential articles by John Wilson Croker on the subject of contemporary French literature. Though one dealt with drama and only the second dealt with fiction, both pieces came to the same conclusion: the novel was even more reprehensible than the drama, and both exhibited 'the same extravagance, absurdity and immorality' (see also, p. 230, below). In fact, so great was the moral threat posed by such works (the authors passed under review included Victor Hugo and Alexandre Dumas *père*) that Croker saw them as preparing the way for a new French Revolution.

From the outset, Mudie had exercised some form of control over the books that he welcomed into his library, as did other circulating libraries such as W. H. Smith's. His subscribers, he claimed in a letter to the *Athenaeum* in 1860, 'are evidently willing to have a barrier of some kind between themselves and the lower floods of literature' (Griest 1971: 145). The same reluctance to offend middle-class taste can also be seen in the fiction-carrying magazines in the second half of the century. Of these, the *Cornhill Magazine* (1860–1975), owned by Smith, Elder and Co., is generally considered the most important. The *Cornhill* sought, in the context of a shilling magazine, to combine serialized fiction for family reading with essays and articles; it remained the market leader among British periodicals for over two decades, publishing major works by authors as diverse as Wilkie Collins, George Eliot, Anthony Trollope, and Thomas Hardy. But only one foreign novel ever found its way into print between its covers, a translation of *L'Histoire du plébiscite*, a novel based on recent history by the very popular Émile Erckmann and Alexandre Chatrian; in this case serialization was rapidly followed by book publication in 1872 by Smith, Elder and Co. In addition, the *Cornhill* printed a number of shorter texts in translation.

The position was much the same with the *Cornhill*'s principal rivals, including *Belgravia* (1866–99), which was largely a vehicle for the fiction of its editor, M. E. Braddon; *Temple Bar* (1860–1906), which, after a slightly chequered career, passed into the control of Richard Bentley and Son in 1866; the short-lived *Saint Paul's Magazine* (1867–74), initially edited by Anthony Trollope; and the slightly later *Longman's Magazine* (1882–91), which was likewise a monthly miscellany specializing in fiction. The *Strand Magazine*, appearing in the 1890s, was unusual in making extensive use of foreign short stories in translation (see p. 145, below).

The other main exception to the general tendency to ignore foreign fiction concerns novels that were entirely rewritten for an English audience. A number of M. E. Braddon's serializations, notably *The Doctor's Wife* (*Temple Bar*, January to December 1864) and *Circe* (*Belgravia*, April to September 1867), fall into this category. *The Doctor's Wife* follows the main plot outline of Flaubert's *Madame Bovary*, while *Circe*, a minor work which the author initially published under the pseudonym Babington White, is a version of Octave Feuillet's *Dahlia*, a Parisian boxoffice hit of ten years earlier. In both cases, though she may have appropriated French originals, Braddon covers her tracks convincingly: to all intents and purposes these works belong to the tradition of British sensation fiction (see Hale 2000).

In the light of the considerable demand for new fiction which all these periodicals occasioned, the absence of translated works is all the more remarkable. But not only were these periodicals, and the publishers who owned them, like Mudie's, jealous of their wholesome reputation, there was also a small army of struggling writers ready to produce supposedly original work on demand, especially in the early stages of their career. Such work was better paid than translation, but often drew heavily on foreign sources. This is particularly true of the nonfiction market. Most periodicals, in addition to serialized fiction, also included around half-a-dozen self-contained articles. For these, the authors were paid varying rates. The *Cornhill*, one of the more generous in this respect, typically paid around four guineas a page (and sometimes as much as twelve); *All the Year Round* (1859–93), edited by Charles Dickens, was considered as one of the more stingy at a guinea a page, perhaps because it was a twopenny weekly (Drew 1999: 10–11).

A contributor could not lose too much sleep over ephemeral productions of this kind, and the vast majority of these articles essentially constitute a clever reworking of other sources, often foreign.

This is particularly apparent with regard to some of the articles in *All the Year Round* concerning French subjects. In some case, the articles are little more than paraphrases of French sources. Vidocq, the famous French detective, is the subject of articles in issues 64 (14 July 1860), 65 (21 July 1860), and 73 (8 September 1860), for example, while Pierre-François Lacenaire, whose posthumous *Mémoires* confirmed his reputation as a criminal dandy, is the subject of a lengthy article in issue 118 (27 July 1861). In fact, all four articles merely recycle material that would be extremely familiar to a French reader. One should not be too surprised at this: news gathering (and these articles, after all, are but journalism) has always been largely a matter of selective quotation and the juxtaposition of sources; in any event, the working conditions of the periodical contributor, even one on the lower rungs of the ladder, were much to be preferred to those of the jobbing translator.

By the 1880s, however, the world of the illustrated monthlies, the three-decker novels, and the circulating libraries was already under severe attack, and new initiatives greatly increased the sales of translations to the middle classes. In the 1840s Henry Bohn had established his Standard Library and Classical Library (see respectively pp. 8–9, above and p. 165, below); the latter consisted entirely of translations, and in the former they made up a sizeable minority of the titles. At about the same time, Routledge had launched its Railway Library, a collection of one-shilling reprints aimed at travellers. Various translations made their way into this series, notably Balzac's *Balthazar* and *Eugénie Grandet* in 1859. This effectively marked the beginning of the piecemeal translation of Balzac into English, with Ward and Lock bringing out an undated *Daddy Goriot* the following year.

The main favourites of the new yellowback fiction (so called after the colour of their glossy, board covers) tended, however, to be the old favourites of the circulating libraries, and considerable sums were paid for the right to produce cheap editions of authors such as Bulwer Lytton. After Bohn, the publisher who really broke the mould of Victorian publishing as far as translation was concerned was Henry Vizetelly (on whom see Anderson and Rose 1991: 314–20). By the time Vizetelly returned to his former calling as publisher in 1880, he was 60 years old and had served a long apprenticeship in virtually every aspect of print media: wood engraver, printer, newspaper proprietor, journalist, and author. In the early 1850s, his elder brother James, possibly with some assistance from Henry, had already tried his hand at a comprehensive series entitled Contemporary French Literature, including history, travel, and fiction, but the experiment does not seem to have been a success and was discontinued in 1855 (see Korey *et al.* 2003: 27).

Although Vizetelly and Co. in its final incarnation existed for barely ten years (1880–90), it published an astonishing catalogue of fiction in translation. Indeed, of the 250 or so titles published by the firm, about 140 were translations from French (see Portebois in Korey *et al.* 2003: 56). Of these, more than half were by just four authors. Interest has tended to focus on Vizetelly's relationship with

Émile Zola, eighteen of whose novels were issued under his imprint, and on the two obscenity trials that were to cost the publisher both his livelihood and his life (see Speirs and Landon in Korey *et al.* 2003; also p. 54, below). But Vizetelly also published a number of works by George Moore, one of Zola's warmest admirers and the leading British naturalist novelist of the day. Significantly, Moore was one of Mudie's most outspoken opponents (Griest 1971: 83–5).

Linked to Vizetelly's championing of Zola is his keen interest in the French and Russian realists. Flaubert's *Madame Bovary* (1857), for example, remained untranslated in Britain until 1886, when Vizetelly published Eleanor Marx-Aveling's version under the title *Madame Bovary: Provincial Manners*. Texts such as *Madame Bovary* or Dostoevsky's *Crime and Punishment* were published with the subtitle 'a realistic novel'. Lower down the literary scale was Georges Ohnet, the best-selling author of sentimental fiction aimed at a female readership; seven of his works were published by Vizetelly, who also made a considerable contribution to the development of the detective story. Émile Gaboriau and Fortuné du Boisgobey, generally considered the main exponents of the genre prior to the creation of Sherlock Holmes in 1887, were the main beneficiaries of this trend with twelve and thirty-nine titles respectively.

Zola, who was issued in a variety of formats (7*s.* 6*d.* illustrated, 6*s.* illustrated, 5*s.* unillustrated, 3*s.* 6*d.*, and 2*s.* 6*d.*), generated considerable revenues for the firm, which quickly expanded its list. Gaboriau and Fortuné du Boisgobey, who were issued in shilling editions (the longer works occupying two such volumes) in striking maroon covers, also sold respectably. Later overprints of some titles note 'Fifteenth thousand' or even 'Twentieth thousand', though this is a far cry from the 272,000 copies that Hugh Conway's *Called Back*, a 'shilling shocker' produced by the Bristol firm of J. W. Arrowsmith in 1883, is reputed to have sold. But such was the competition on the market between some of the newer entrants that Vizetelly's rights to these authors did not go altogether unchallenged. Ward, Lock & Co., Routledge, and J. & R. Maxwell (whose fortune was based on its founder's long association with M. E. Braddon) also issued cheap editions of these authors in the mid-1880s, the latter claiming to be the 'sole and authorized copyright translation'.

Whatever the truth of this last claim, it made sense for new entrants to the publishing business, lacking the benefit of the considerable backlists of their more established rivals, to turn their attention to foreign, including American, works. Prior to the Berne Convention of 1887 and the 1891 American Copyright Act, and even for some time afterwards, the various legislation in force in different countries was complex, contradictory, and difficult to enforce (see pp. 55–6, below). In 1852, for example, Routledge made a fortune by issuing cheap pirated reprints of *Uncle Tom's Cabin*; the following year, an American court even found that an unauthorized German translation of Harriet Beecher Stowe's novel did not infringe the author's interests (Venuti 1995: 57).

Vizetelly was an exception to the common run of British publishers in that he looked to France rather than the USA for his titles. Even before his editions of

Zola, though, cheap unauthorized American translations of the French naturalist's work 'enjoyed brisk sales from under the counters in London's infamous Holywell Street' (Speirs in Korey *et al.* 2003: 85). Likewise, publishers at the cheap end of the market such as Routledge, who issued half a dozen works by Balzac between 1886 and 1891, also occasionally sourced material from America. In the case of Routledge's Balzac translations, these had been initially published by the prominent Boston firm of Roberts Brothers (who also published translations of the controversial George Sand in the early 1870s). More generally, the advent of cheap books in Britain was clearly heralded by the American publishing industry. In the first half of the nineteenth century, North American publishing had been very much overshadowed by the British book trade. But by the closing decades of the century, price, which had long been a major factor in the US market, also proved to be the principal catalyst for change in British publishing practice.

The 'Unknown Public': The Penny Press and the 'Self-Made Reader'

The same constraints which defined Vizetelly's publishing strategy—the unfettered availability of French texts, the lack of a history of dealings with local authors—also defined the penny press in the mid-century. As Louis James notes, though American fiction was popular with British readers, the main influence after about 1844 came from France: 'French fiction formed the backbone of *The London Journal*, *The London Pioneer*, and *The Family Herald* between 1845 and 1849, and appeared liberally elsewhere: not a single issue of *The London Journal* between these years was without some French literature in translation' (James 1974: 159). James is quite correct as far as the dates are concerned. Take the *Family Herald*, for example, which was founded in December 1842. From 20 July 1844 to 18 October 1845, the main serial was a translation of Eugène Sue's *The Wandering Jew* while the periodical published other translations too. But it is quite clear that British writers were quickly taking to the trade of writing a French-style serial so that translations first coexisted with original fiction (another lengthy Sue serialization occurred in 1848) before being entirely supplanted. Worse still, French serializations were not guaranteed to draw an audience. *The Black Cabinet* (obviously a French work though the original remains untraced), which began promisingly enough on 5 August 1848, disappeared abruptly six weeks later. By the 1850s, translations had become exceedingly rare in the *Family Herald*.

It was the same with the *London Journal*, initially edited by the prolific G. W. M. Reynolds. At one moment in the early life of this paper (from August 1846 to May 1847), three French serials were running concurrently: Dumas's *The Count of Monte-Cristo*, Sue's *Martin the Foundling, or, Memoirs of a Valet de Chambre*, and Thiers's *History of the Consulate and the Empire of France under Napoleon*. But Reynolds, who quickly fell out with the *London Journal*, understood that there was more money to be derived from authorship, however derivative, than from translation. Throughout the rest of his life he penned an astonishing sequence of popular serials, essentially calqued equally on earlier Gothic fiction and contemporary French *feuilletons*. Mrs Braddon, writing for a slightly more sophisticated audience, refers to this sort of work as the 'combination novel': 'Why, you see, when you're doing four great stories a week for a public that must have a continuous flow of incident,' one or her characters remarks, 'you can't be quite as original as a strict sense of honour might prompt you to be... I'm doing a combination novel now—*The Heart of Midlothian* [Scott] and *The Wandering Jew* [Sue]. You've no idea how admirably the two stories blend' (cited in Hale 2000: 229–30).

The stratification of the Victorian publishing industry is further exemplified by the publication history of the translations of an author such as Dumas (on which see Munro 1978). The *London Journal* version of *The Count of Monte-Cristo*, like the abridged edition published by George Peirce in 1846, was no doubt intended primarily for James Payn's 'Unknown Public'. But texts could percolate up the social ladder as well as down. Chapman and Hall quickly brought out a sumptuous illustrated two-volume edition, presumably intended for the circulating libraries and carriage trade, costing 24 shillings the set (1846). Somewhere between the two extremes was a three-volume edition published by W. S. Orr, Simms and M'Intyre as part of their Parlour Novelist collection, also in 1846. Finally, in 1888, Routledge produced a five-volume edition containing nearly 500 plates (Munro 1978: 91–9). The same held true for other popular novelists such as Eugène Sue. Chapman and Hall produced illustrated editions of *The Wandering Jew* (1844) and *The Mysteries of Paris* (1845); Appleyard in Farringdon Road more modestly priced editions of the same texts in the same years; and W. Dugdale, a veteran of Hollywell Street, cheaper still one-volume editions (both 1844).

While poorer readers were the principal market for such sensational fiction, both in the penny press and in the cheap editions that became more and more numerous as the century progressed, it should not be forgotten that what Richard Altick called the 'self-made reader', the working-class autodidact with a thirst for a more demanding literary culture, was 'particularly a product of the age' (Altick 1957: 240). Some, like Hardy's Jude, embarked on the study of foreign languages, but for many translation was essential. For rural and industrial workers anxious to educate themselves, serious literature was available through a variety of channels: libraries, journals, and 'mutual improvement' organizations of all kinds (well described in Rose 2001). In addition, after 1870, the new Board Schools introduced children of all classes to the great texts of English and world literature.

Religious and political groups both had their reasons for seeking to limit the amount of modern fiction or drama made available to libraries and reading circles, but the classics of world literature were generally more acceptable. This included the sort of great books included in the reading lists discussed on p. 7, above, many of these being translations of the kind published by Bohn's Libraries. At the very end of the century, the firm of J. M. Dent (who were shortly to launch the revolutionary Everyman's Library), aimed for a popular audience with the demanding international repertoire of their small-format Temple Classics, while in a less elevated sphere George Newman's Penny Library of Famous Books included novels by Mérimée and Dumas alongside the works of Goldsmith, Scott, and Dickens. That there was nothing narrowly national about this 'self-made' culture is suggested by the radical politician J. Bruce Glasier, who had herded sheep in Ayrshire and served as an apprentice in Glasgow in the 1870s; writing of his youth, he declares that Bunyan, Burns, Shelley, Byron, Aeschylus, Dante, Schiller, and *Les Misérables* 'all helped to rouse and nourish in me a passionate hatred of oppression and an exalting hope of the coming of a new era' (cited in Rose 2001: 48). In this perspective, the publishers of translations were auxiliaries of the 'men of culture' who in the idealistic words of Matthew Arnold's *Culture and Anarchy* were seeking 'to do away with classes; to make the best that has been known and thought in the world current everywhere' (Arnold 1965: 113).

Conclusion

The class stratification of the reading public outlined at the beginning of this section was vulnerable to the commercial logic that made all kinds of books, including translation, increasingly available to all kinds of reader. If the penny press was the first to exploit the new technology that was becoming available to produce cheaper books, it was soon joined by more entrepreneurial mainstream publishers. Collectively, their innovations destroyed the long-standing partnership between the circulating libraries and the publishers of multi-volume novels: in 1897, only four novels were published in the old format (Griest 1971: 208). 'We have become a novel-reading people', declared Anthony Trollope as early as 1870; 'Novels are in the hands of us all; from the Prime Minister down to the last appointed scullery maid' (Trollope 1938: 109). Only ten years later, Henry Vizetelly would puff Émile Gaboriau, whose detective stories he published in shilling editions, as 'the favourite reading of Prince Bismarck'. Now the scullery maid could even afford to read the same author as a German Chancellor.

By the same token, by the second half of the century such 'élite' authors as Goethe or Sophocles were more readily available to a popular audience. Translations such as those published by Bohn and Vizetelly played a role in this democratic transformation, even if the market for such works, and in particular translations from French, suffered from the disadvantage that some of their most likely readers could read those works in the original language.

LIST OF SOURCES

Anon. (*c.*1855). *A Catalogue of English, French, German, Italian and Spanish Books, Contained in L. Booth's Library*. London.

Altick, Richard D. (1957). *The English Common Reader: A Social History of the Mass Reading Public*. Chicago, IL.

Anderson, Patricia J., and Rose, Jonathan (1991). *British Literary Publishing Houses, 1820–1880*. Detroit, MI.

Arnold, Matthew (1965). *Culture and Anarchy*, ed. R. H. Super. Ann Arbor, MI.

Colley, Linda (1994). *Britons: Forging the Nation, 1707–1837*. London.

Davis, Philip (2002). *The Victorians*, Oxford.
Drew, John (1999). '*All the Year Round* ', pp. 8–12 in Paul Schlicke, ed., *The Oxford Reader's Companion to Dickens*. Oxford.
Feather, John (1988). *A History of British Publishing*. London.
Graham, Walter James (1930). *English Literary Periodicals*. New York.
Griest, Guinevere Lindley (1971). *Mudie's Circulating Library and the Victorian Novel*. Newton Abbot (first pub. 1970).
Hale, Terry (2000). 'The Imaginary Quay from Waterloo Bridge to London Bridge: Translation, Adaptation and Genre', pp. 199–238 in Miriam Salama-Carr, ed., *On Translating French Literature and Film II*. Amsterdam.
Houghton, Walter E. (1982). 'Periodical Literature and the Articulate Classes', pp. 3–27 in Joanne Shattock and Michael Wolff, eds., *The Victorian Periodical Press: Samplings and Soundings*. Leicester.
James, Louis (1974). *Fiction for the Working Man, 1830–50*. Harmondsworth.
Korey, Marie Elena, *et al.* (2003). *Vizetelly & Compan(ies): A Complex Tale of Victorian Printing and Publishing*. Toronto.
Messac, Régis (1929). *Influences françaises dans l'œuvre d'Edgar Poe*. Paris.
Munby, A. N. L. (1967). *Portrait of an Obsession: The Life of Sir Thomas Phillipps, the World's Greatest Book Collector*, ed. Nicolas Barker. London.
Munro, Douglas (1978). *Alexandre Dumas père: A Bibliography of Works Translated into English to 1910*. New York.
Payn, James (1882). *Some Private Views*. Leipzig.
Peck, Louis F. (1961). *A Life of Matthew G. Lewis*. Cambridge, MA.
Rose, Jonathan (2001). *The Intellectual Life of the British Working Classes*. New Haven, CT.
Rush, Richard (1987). *A Residence at the Court of London*, ed. Philip Ziegler. London (first pub. 1833).
Trollope, Anthony (1938). 'On English Literature as a Rational Amusement', pp. 94–139 in his *Four Lectures*, ed. Morris L. Parrish. London.
Venuti, Lawrence (1995). *The Translator's Invisibility: A History of Translation*. London.
Woolf, Robert Lee (1979). *Sensational Victorian: The Life and Fiction of Mary Elizabeth Braddon*. New York.

1.4 Translation, Politics, and the Law

Susan Bassnett and Peter France

Introduction: Power in Translation

Translation always takes place within a context of power; there is always a history out of which a text emerges and into which that text is transposed (for a fuller discussion see Bassnett and Lefevere 1990). The study of translation involves an exploration of power relationships within textual practice, since the activity of translation reflects and responds to the power structures of the world in which it takes place. For instance, translators working in languages and literatures that occupy a more prominent position on the world stage (for example, German, French, or English) may exercise very different criteria in the choice of texts to be translated from those adopted by translators working in less well-known languages and literatures, where translation is particularly important as a source of innovation or renewal. For these reasons, the history of the translation into English of classical Greek and Latin works in our period is very different from the history of translation of works written in non-European languages or in some of the less familiar languages of Europe, which took on a new importance in the nineteenth century. The status of the classical texts as sources of European culture meant that translators had to engage directly with issues of ownership and fidelity, but when the source text was in a language that few if any readers knew and from a culture that was perceived as distant both geographically and psychologically, translators sometimes felt able to take greater liberties, with the result that the original tended to disappear, having been fully assimilated within a text wholly directed to the target audience.

Goethe saw the dangers inherent in a translation practice of this kind when he complained about Horace H. Wilson's translation of Kālidāsa's *Meghadūta* as *The Cloud Messenger* in 1813 (on this see p. 346, below). Wilson, he suggested, should be praised for having introduced readers to the Sanskrit work, but condemned for taking too many liberties and creating a text intended to flatter 'the Northern ear and senses' (cited in Schulte and Biguenet 1992: 62). Certainly, some translations that did seek to flatter northern ears and senses were well received. One of the most successful translations ever made in English is Edward FitzGerald's *The Rubáiyát of Omar Khayyám*, which radically altered the Persian original, following the translator's declaration that he perceived both the poem and its author to be lacking in sophistication and aesthetic value before his intervention. Writing about Persian poetry in a letter to E. B. Cowell in 1857, FitzGerald remarked that 'these Persians', with the exception of Ḥāfiẓ, 'really *do* want a little *Art* to shape them' (FitzGerald 1980: II, 261).

FitzGerald's position was by no means shared by the many scholarly translators who endeavoured to translate from eastern languages in the nineteenth century, but it raises the important questions of assimilation and misrepresentation through translation, questions which postcolonial research has begun to explore more fully. Translation has played a key role in the production of our knowledge about other cultures and their artistic heritage, and at times it has been used to uphold notions of the cultural inferiority of one group vis-à-vis another. Referring to the Indian context (on which see further § 7.3, below), Tejaswini Niranjana has argued that translation participated 'in the fixing of colonized cultures, making them seem static and unchanging rather than historically constructed' (Niranjana 1992: 3). From another perspective, however, translation challenges rather than reinforces, enacts, or mirrors assumptions of cultural superiority. The existence of works in translation, after all, is an implicit claim that such works deserve the attention of the target audience. An imperialist assumption of cultural superiority may well lead to the absence of translation. In this polemical area, scholarly translations, translations that seek to acculturate the source text, and the absence of translations have all been found imperialist.

For the nineteenth century was also an age when a very different idea of translation prevailed, when translation was used by peoples all over Europe as part of their struggle for political independence and cultural autonomy. Political liberation could be fought for in the streets, whereas cultural autonomy could be achieved through translation, which expanded the horizons of literatures such as Czech, Finnish, Serbian, or Hungarian and led to the introduction of new literary models. By the same token, in Britain and America, translations of the ballads of Serbia, of the works of the exiled Polish poet Mickiewicz, or indeed of Irish songs, could be seen, as their prefaces sometimes made clear, as acts of sympathy and solidarity with the political struggles of oppressed peoples (see §§ 6.7 and 6.8, below). And more generally, political developments in Europe and beyond, from the Revolutionary and Napoleonic wars to the upheavals of 1848, the Crimean War, the struggle for Empire, and the Boer War, were all reflected, often in contradictory ways, in the production and consumption of literary translation.

The history of power relationships and translation in the nineteenth century is therefore a complex one. Both dominant societies and less powerful ones used translations for political purposes, selecting the texts most helpful for their purposes and adjusting them in translation. But whether the translators belonged to a dominant or a dominated culture, it was possible for the translation strategies employed to differ hardly at all.

Translation and Imperialism

Interest in works written by non-European writers had been growing steadily throughout the eighteenth century at the same time as Chinese porcelain, Persian carpets, Indian shawls, tea, spices, and other valued goods from the East flooded into Europe. In English, *The Thousand and One Nights* had proved popular with readers of all ages. In 1789, Sir William Jones published his translation of the Sanskrit drama *Śakuntalā*, which was received with great enthusiasm. Interest in Sanskrit, which Jones demonstrated was related to European languages through a common Indo-European linguistic ancestor, grew steadily, and a number of important Indian works subsequently appeared in English versions (see §§ 7.3 and 10.3, below).

Many of the early Orientalist translators set high standards of scholarship and believed in the genuine importance of the works they were translating, but in assessing their achievements today, it is important not to lose sight of the context in which they worked. For translation was very much a one-way process, with Indian and later Chinese texts being imported into English, while the few texts exported were religious tracts used by missionaries, and works which were perceived to have some moral purpose, such as Lamb's *Tales from Shakespeare* or Bunyan's *Pilgrim's Progress*. This imbalance in literary traffic has been underlined by some scholars, who see in the importation of Oriental texts through translation a parallel phenomenon to the commercial exploitation of the colonies.

Certainly, literary power relationships reflected broader cultural ones; the colonizing powers genuinely believed in their cultural superiority. Lord Macaulay asserted famously in his 'Minute on Indian Education' (1835) that all Orientalists agreed that 'a single shelf of a good European library was worth more than the whole native literature of India and Arabia' (Macaulay 1972: 241). Postcolonial scholars such as Niranjana who argue that the act of translation in such a context should be viewed as an aggressive act of cultural appropriation have prima facie a strong case. But it is also important to remember that translation will always, by its very nature, be an activity that lends itself to different political uses. Tymoczko and Gentzler describe the translator as having divided allegiances, as 'a kind of double agent in the process of cultural negotiation' (Tymoczko and Gentzler 2002: xix). Moreover, a view of power relations in translation that is premissed on polarities (e.g. a 'strong' culture and a 'weaker' one) is simplistic. Harish Trivedi has pointed out that Charles Wilkins, an early translator from Sanskrit, also designed and cast the first font of Bengali characters and set up a printing press in Calcutta in 1778, thereby enabling the publication of works in that language. Trivedi has also argued that while the history of translation into English has received a great deal of attention, the history of translation between Indian languages has received only scant attention, yet this was a parallel phenomenon to the British importation of classical Indian texts (Bassnett and Trivedi 1999: 9). The traffic in texts through translation was never simply one dominated by the colonial power.

The translation of writings in Sanskrit and other ancient eastern languages is the outcome of two distinct nineteenth-century phenomena: scholarly interest in the history of languages and civilizations and more widespread popular interest in travel accounts. Indeed, the success of much travel writing was reinforced by the work of Orientalist translators. The preface to Richard Burton's *The Book of the Thousand Nights and a Night* (on which see § 7.1, below) combines scholarly detail with criticism of previous translators who, he argues, have failed to grasp all the nuances of the Arabic work, and with a lyrical description of the Arabian desert. Burton's travels in the region coloured his translation. Yet faced with translations such as his, with their extensive footnotes and detailed cultural information, the present-day reader feels a sense of unease, for here too the implicit colonial power structures are apparent. Burton's notes are anthropological in tone and content, transforming the very people he claimed to admire into specimens, into the objects of the gaze of curious European readers. The very scholarship that perceived itself as objective can be seen, with hindsight, as reflecting the ideology of the imperial age.

National Identity and Archaism

There was a strong political element to the study of philology in the nineteenth century. The codification of languages into families located Indo-European in a superior position globally, and the tracing of languages back to their roots ensured that direct links could be made between the great civilizations of Greece and Rome, the heroic Germanic civilizations, and contemporary England. While the Sanskritists introduced English readers to many of the great works of classical Indian antiquity, other translators working with European languages sought to introduce readers to their own authentic past. The identification of historic relationships between Germanic and Nordic languages became linked for some scholars to the development of nationalistic myths of Englishness. There had been much antiquarian interest in Old English in the eighteenth century and before, but from the 1830s onwards that interest grew considerably, manifesting itself not only in translations, but also in the publication of adventure stories for boys and adults that glorified the world of the Anglo-Saxons and Vikings (see § 6.5, below).

The translation of old Germanic epics was mirrored, though to a lesser extent, by the translation of works written in the Celtic languages (on which see § 6.7, below). Though largely dismissed in England as literary forgeries, the impact of James Macpherson's Ossian rewritings in the age of revolutions is undeniable; the collection and translation of Celtic folklore prompted by the success of Ossian served to consolidate cultural identities on the periphery of the British Isles. Lady Charlotte Guest's translation of the *Mabinogion* (1849) was closely associated at its inception with the movement for the propagation of Welsh culture, and the translation of Irish songs sometimes, though not always, carried with it a strong nationalist and anti-English charge; later in the period, the Irish Literary Revival was premised on the recovery of early texts, both written and oral, through translation and transcription.

What is striking about the translations of the sagas, of the *Nibelungenlied*, of *Beowulf* and other Anglo-Saxon poems, is the conscious archaizing employed by translators. Implicit in the desire to translate these texts was the forging of a link between contemporary England and those ancient societies, whose heroes were viewed as models of manliness and physical courage; the employment of an archaic form of English was intended to remind readers of that past continuity. Archaizing (as also in Robert Browning's version of Aeschylus' *Agamemnon*) reflected the respect in which the medieval and ancient world was held, in contrast with the corruption of the modern world.

The nostalgic yearning for an idealized past which found its expression in archaic English is particularly apparent in the translations of two of the leading figures of the age, William Morris and Dante Gabriel Rossetti. Both translated a great deal, but, like many of their contemporaries, they said little about the actual process of translating. However, Rossetti's preface to his translations in *Early Italian Poets*, published in 1861, contains what may be considered a representative statement on the role and powers of the translator. The purpose of translation, he maintains, is primarily an aesthetic one: to turn a good poem in one language into an equally good poem in another. However, he acknowledges that the task of the translator is 'one of some self-denial' (Rossetti 2003: 240). A translator would, he argues, use particularities of idiom belonging to his own time, 'if only his will belonged to him'. The translator is compared to Aladdin in the enchanted cave, bent on searching for the lamp and compelled to ignore many of the beautiful things around him. He is a servant of the original, a feudal lordling bound through an oath of fealty to a much greater lord. The task of the translator is to serve, and hence to remain invisible. Rossetti's view of the subservient translator contrasts with FitzGerald's opinion of the inadequacy of Persian poets, and reflects the different status attributed to the source cultures.

A further example of the reflection of power relations in the debate over archaism and modernity is the Arnold–Newman debate about the translation of Homer, sparked in 1861 by Matthew Arnold's hostile reaction to Francis Newman's archaizing translation of the *Iliad*, which was meant to remind readers of the great gap between their own time and Homer's. This debate (more fully discussed in Ch. 2 and § 5.2, below) reveals a great deal not only about translation but about the politics of language in nineteenth-century England. Arnold's is perhaps an élitist view, privileging scholarship and insisting on the desirability of a knowledge of ancient Greek, but at the same time he advocates the use of modern English, rather than the faux-archaic English preferred by Newman. In this respect, although his own sample translation in hexameters rather belies his theoretical position, Arnold is the more modern of the two, for he argues that contemporary language can be a fitting vehicle for Homer. Arnold's challenge to the archaizing convention is an important landmark in thinking about the politics of language in nineteenth-century Britain.

Acculturation and the Policing of Translation

Translation theorists have at different times engaged in different ways with debates about the desirability or otherwise of acculturating their foreign texts by erasing signs of foreignness in them. While many nineteenth-century critics and theorists of translation favoured literalism above the traditional virtue of fluency (see Ch. 2, below), it was also the case that acculturation was widespread in the nineteenth century, partly because of the proliferation of translations for mass consumption. In such popular novels, plays, and scientific and religious tracts, what was most important was accessibility, and this objective could lead to considerable textual manipulation. In the translation of a work from one literary system to another, the needs of the target audience can often take precedence over a more abstract notion of fidelity to the source. The more powerful an audience is, in economic and social terms, the more likely it is that translators will reshape texts according to the expectations of those for whom the work is destined.

An important dimension to acculturation is the refusal of whatever is offensive to the receiving culture. In France and Britain in the eighteenth century, prevailing norms had prevented the representation on stage of material that violated norms of taste and decency. Under the influence of such norms, the nineteenth-century translator often acted as a censor by bowdlerizing the source text; many nineteenth-century translations of Sappho, for example, removed all references to lesbian sexuality. In addition, bookshops such as W. H. Smith's, circulating libraries such as Mudie's (see pp. 38–41, above), or publishers, editors, or printers might refuse to accept compromising material. The case of Richard Burton is illuminating here. In 1886 Stanley Lane Poole, discussing translations of *The Thousand and One Nights*, categorized them as follows: 'Galland for the nursery, Lane for the library, Payne for the study, and Burton for the sewers' (Poole 1886: 184). In 1875 the English printers had refused to complete work on Burton's and Arbuthnot's translation of the *Kāma Sūtra* (Thomas 1969: 251), and after Burton's death his widow Isabel is said to have destroyed the manuscript of his erotic translation *The Scented Garden*. In the face of such resistance it is not surprising that many translators of dangerous material had recourse to private publication; in the later years of the nineteenth century a variety of societies and private presses issued translations of potentially scandalous texts by classic authors from Rabelais to Zola, Petronius to Boccaccio.

On the other hand, were a translator to disregard those norms in a published work, the consequences could in theory be severe. The nineteenth century was not only the century of Thomas Bowdler, the great age of expurgation; it also saw the establishment of bodies dedicated to suppressing indecent or blasphemous publications. The Society for the Suppression of Vice and the Encouragement of Religion and Virtue was set up in 1802 and was active for more than half a century, bringing law cases against books which included a certain number of translations, notably from France, the great source of corruption. In 1822, for example, the Society brought an unsuccessful case against a new translation of Louvet's *Les Amours du chevalier de Faublas* and in 1829–30 against a version of the notorious pornographic work the *Histoire de Dom B... portier des Chartreux*.

In the last third of the century, attitudes to supposedly obscene writings hardened. This may be explained, as many contemporaries saw it, by a greater availability of such material at all levels of the market. At all events, when Henry Bohn was testifying in a court case in 1877, he admitted that when Bell and Co. took over his business they had been 'obliged to withdraw from circulation such works as the *Memoirs of the Chevalier de Grammont* and editions of Rabelais' (Thomas 1969: 266). In 1886, the torch of decency was taken up by the newly formed National Vigilance Association, which, after a failed prosecution of the *Decameron*, was more successful against Henry Vizetelly.

Vizetelly (on whom see also pp. 42–4, above) was a reputable publisher who in the 1880s specialized in foreign literature. Among the authors he promoted in English were Dostoevsky, Tolstoy, and Flaubert, but it was above all his promotion of the novels of Émile Zola that caused the crisis. Between 1884 and 1888, Vizetelly had issued eighteen Zola translations, for the most part lightly expurgated to respect the sensibilities of Victorian taste. However, in May 1888 a somewhat sparsely attended House of Commons unanimously approved a motion that 'this House deplores the rapid spread of demoralizing literature in this country and is of the opinion that the Law against obscene publications and indecent pictures and prints should be vigorously enforced and, if necessary, strengthened'. Samuel Smith, who proposed the motion, named Vizetelly as the 'chief culprit' and told the House that 'nothing more diabolical had ever been written by the pen of man' and that Zola's work was 'only fit for swine' (*Hansard's Parliamentary Debates* 325: 1707–25). It is not surprising then that in October of the same year the National Vigilance Association took Vizetelly to the Central Criminal Court on charges of publishing obscene matter, the titles named being translations of *La Terre*, *Nana*, and *Pot-Bouille*. He was found guilty, fined £100, and had to withdraw the volumes from circulation. *The Times* (1 November 1888) noted approvingly: 'In future anyone who publishes translations of ZOLA's novels and works of a similar character will do so at his peril.' Six months later, Vizetelly was again on trial for publishing eight further French novels; this time he was sent to prison for three months. He died five years later, a broken and ruined man. The Vizetelly case (described in a somewhat partisan way in Vizetelly 1904: 242–99) is an example of the risk run by translators and publishers in a hostile climate.

The theatre was more directly affected by censorship. Since the Licensing Act of 1737, drama in Britain had been regulated and censored by the Lord Chamberlain and his Examiner of Plays. The Act required that all new plays be submitted to the Lord Chamberlain two weeks before the performance, or else the theatre managers would risk being fined and losing their theatre licence. It also gave a monopoly on the staging of plays to three theatres (see further p. 383, below). The Theatres Act of 1843 ended the monopoly, but also further strengthened the censorship powers of the Lord Chamberlain. In fact, few plays were actually denied licences, and the majority of these were in foreign languages (Johnston 1990: 35). English translations were sometimes proscribed. *La Perouse*, a play adapted from Anne Plumptre's translation of Kotzebue, was denied a licence in 1801 because it featured bigamy; the objection in this case was less moral than political, since many people considered the Prince of Wales to have committed bigamy with his second marriage (Conolly 1976: 128). Half a century later, *La Dame aux camélias* by Dumas *fils* (published as a novel in 1848 and as a play in 1852) was far too sexually explicit for English audiences, and in 1853 the Lord Chamberlain forbade the Drury Lane Theatre from performing the English translation *Camille* (Stephens 1980: 82). Dumas's play was given a licence only in 1881 (Johnston 1990: 38). However, Verdi's opera *La Traviata*, based on Dumas's work, was not only given a licence to be performed at Her Majesty's Theatre in 1856 but received reviews so favourable that the Lord Chamberlain permitted an English translation (*La Traviata, or, The Blighted One*) to be staged at the Surrey Theatre a few months later (Stephens 1980: 83).

French plays generally raised suspicions as to their morality, especially after the 1850s when they were increasingly imported (Stephens 1980: 81); by the 1880s, however, attitudes toward them were more relaxed, and this tolerance extended even to some English adaptations (Stephens 1980: 138). At this time, a deliberate challenge to the authority of the Lord Chamberlain was launched with the productions of Shelley's *Cenci* in 1886 and Ibsen's *Ghosts* in 1891: both plays were refused licences but staged nonetheless by the subterfuge of a 'private performance'. The fact that Sophocles' *Oedipus the King* was also banned (even though Aristophanes' *Lysistrata* was not) gave further ammunition to the campaign to end theatre censorship (Macintosh 1995: 60).

The power of the government was evident not only in its threat to ban certain plays but also in its consequent ability to require them to be altered before being performed. For example, Victor Hugo's *Ruy Blas* had its licence rapidly withdrawn in 1852 because Queen Victoria was displeased by the representation of a queen forming a romantic attachment with a footman in livery. A translation (*The Secret Passion*) was finally approved in 1858 under the condition that the term 'footman' be expunged and that Ruy Blas be dressed as a retainer and not as a valet (Stephens 1980: 51). Depending on the particular character of the Examiner, the changes required could be extensive, especially if any religious reference were made.

Copyright

Translators and publishers had to negotiate with the law in one other important respect: copyright. The legal definition of copyright in the period from 1790 to 1900 evolved piecemeal, in response to more than a dozen statutes and to legal decisions which were sometimes in conflict with each other or overturned on appeal. The most important statutes include the first English copyright statute (passed in 1710), which assigned a copyright period of fourteen years, renewable once if the author was alive at the end of the period; the Copyright Act of 1814, which extended the period to twenty-eight years or the author's lifetime, whichever was longer; the International Copyright Act of 1838, which allowed reciprocal copyright agreements with other nations to be reached; and the 1842 Copyright Act, which attempted to repair the poorly drafted international provisions of the 1838 Act and also extended the copyright term to the author's lifetime or forty-two years, whichever was longer. In the 1840s and 1850s copyright agreements were reached with France, Belgium, Spain, and many German states; in 1887 the Berne Convention instituted a uniform system of international copyright among signatories. In 1891 a copyright agreement was reached at last with the United States. For much of the period the rights within Britain of foreign authors remained obscure.

Translation was frequently a grey area within copyright. 'Translations into English from other languages generated little discussion, because often there was no English copyright holder to protest' (Seville 1999: 245). The translations themselves, however, were protected, at least in theory. In 1814 the defendant in the case *Wyatt* v. *Barnard* insisted that the 'usual practice among publishers of magazines and monthly publications was to take from each other articles translated from foreign languages' (quoted in Seville 1999: 245). The defence was not successful, and Lord Eldon ruled that translations could not be distinguished from original works. This view that translations were original works meant that translations of copyrighted works could not be considered piracy; however, the position was sometimes rejected (Seville 1999: 246). In 1843, the publisher Bogue was cleared of the charge of copyright infringement after he published an English translation of a German version of a book published by his rival Murray, but this was because the German translation was found to be substantially original (Seville 1999: 246).

In its early formulation, the Copyright Act of 1842 would have resolved the question of copyright of translations: 'the Copyright in every translation shall be deemed to be the property of the Translator thereof and his assignees as though it were an original work' (quoted in Seville 1999: 247). However, the clause was deleted by the House of Lords, and the matter remained unclarified. It was only with the Anglo-French convention, brought into effect in 1852, that the issue of copyright for translated works was faced squarely. The French negotiators were unhappy with the wide-scale adaptation of French drama for the English stage without permission; the agreement, however, did little to relieve the situation (see further § 8.2, below and Nowell-Smith 1968: 32). Effective copyright for translations had to await the Berne Convention and the reform of copyright in the United States.

Conclusion

We have seen that power relations, both within a society and in the international arena, had an impact not only on the choice of texts to be translated and the ways in which they were received, but also on the nature of the translations. The Arnold–Newman debate represents two polarized views about what constitutes good translation. Ultimately Arnold's views won the day in the sense that his call for translation practice to be rooted in good, contemporary English consolidated the domesticating tendency that has since become established across different translation genres. This led English-speaking readers to ignore the differences between their own universe of discourse and other such universes—and this in turn led to translation being perceived as a second-class activity. In many other

European countries, on the other hand, where translation served to enrich the emergent national literature, acculturation served the opposite purpose and produced an opposite result. That Byron was an inspiration for many central, eastern, and southern European poets is undeniable, and that translation played a vital role in this process is equally clear.

The issue is not whether acculturating translation is desirable or undesirable in itself, but rather what the context is in which that translation takes place. The early attempt at defining a cultural theory of translation in terms of power relations sketched by Itamar Even-Zohar (Even-Zohar 1978) still retains its validity. Even-Zohar argued that in cultures which are 'young', 'weak', or in a state of crisis, translation occupies a crucial position in the literary system. In more established literary cultures, on the other hand, translation is likely to be seen as making a less important contribution to the development of the literature. There are times when translation is central to a literature, other times when it is more peripheral. In the nineteenth century translation played a vital role in the establishment of new national cultures in many countries; in English-speaking culture, by contrast, despite the vast number of works translated from all over the world and the interesting debates about how to translate, the role of translation was relatively marginal.

LIST OF SOURCES

Alvarez, Roman, and Vidal, M. Carmen-Africa, eds. (1996). *Translation, Power, Subversion*. Clevedon.
Bassnett, Susan, and Lefevere, André, eds. (1990). *Translation, History, and Culture*. London.
—— and Trivedi, Harish, eds. (1999). *Post-Colonial Translation: Theory and Practice*. London.
Conolly, L. W. (1976). *The Censorship of English Drama 1737–1824*. San Marino, CA.
Even-Zohar, Itamar (1978). 'The Position of Translated Literature within the Literary Polysystem', pp. 117–27 in James S. Holmes, José Lambert, and Raymond van den Broeck, eds., *Literature and Translation: New Perspectives in Literary Studies*. Leuwen.
FitzGerald, Edward (1980). *The Letters of Edward FitzGerald*, ed. Alfred McKinley Terhune and Annabelle Burdett Terhune, 4 vols. Princeton, NJ.
Johnston, John (1990). *The Lord Chamberlain's Blue Pencil*. London.
Macaulay, Thomas Babington (1972). *Selected Writings*, ed. John Clive and Thomas Pinney. Chicago. IL.
Macintosh, Fiona (1995). 'Under the Blue Pencil: Greek Tragedy and the British Censor.' *Dialogos* 2: 54–70.
Niranjana, Tejaswini (1992). *Siting Translation: History, Post-Structuralism and the Colonial Context*. Berkeley, CA.
Nowell-Smith, Simon (1968). *International Copyright Law and the Publisher in the Reign of Queen Victoria*. Oxford.
Poole, Stanley Lane (1886). 'The Arabian Nights.' *Edinburgh Review* 164: 166–99.
Rossetti, Dante Gabriel (2003). *Collected Poetry and Prose*, ed. Jerome McGann. New Haven, CT.
Schulte, Rainer, and Biguenet, John, eds. (1992). *Theories of Translation: An Anthology of Essays from Dryden to Derrida*. Chicago, IL.

Seville, Catherine (1999). *Literary Copyright Reform in Early Victorian England*. Cambridge.
Sova, Dawn B. (2004). *Banned Plays: Censorship Histories of 125 Stage Dramas*. New York.
Stephens, John Russell (1980). *The Censorship of English Drama 1824–1901*. Cambridge.
Thomas, Donald (1969). *A Long Time Burning: The History of Literary Censorship in England*. London.
Tymoczko, Maria, and Gentzler, Edwin, eds. (2002). *Translation and Power*. Boston, MA.
Vizetelly, Ernest (1904). *Émile Zola: Novelist and Reformer*. London.

2
Principles and Norms of Translation
Matthew Reynolds

Principles and Norms of Translation

Matthew Reynolds

Introduction: Varying Norms and Complex Principles

How should we distinguish between a 'norm' and a 'principle'? One view might be that norms tend to inhere in and define societies while principles belong to individuals. From this angle, Edward FitzGerald can be described as sensing a disparity between his principle and the norm when, thinking of publishing a version of Calderón in 1853, he worried that 'my Translation would be so free as to be rather a dangerous Experiment' (FitzGerald 1980: II, 53; on FitzGerald's Calderón see further p. 270, below). The norm he both feared and hoped to threaten ('dangerous' cuts both ways) was widely evident around him. Prominent journals such as *Fraser's Magazine* and the *Edinburgh Review* habitually prized 'fidelity' and 'accuracy' in the many translations they discussed. The popular 'Standard' and 'Classical' libraries recently launched by the publisher Henry Bohn included many literal versions, suggesting that the market had the same taste as the reviewers. Early responses to the finished *Six Dramas of Calderon* were indeed chilly (see FitzGerald 1997: xxiv), but there was a happy surprise when *Fraser's* welcomed the book in terms that had seemed to be out of fashion: 'the freedom, vigour and liveliness of Mr Fitzgerald's translation it is almost impossible to commend too highly ... his version reads like an original composition' (Donne 1857: 457). Shall we say that a principle shared becomes a norm, albeit a minor one? A binary of societal norms vs individual principles is too stark: there are many intermediate categories such as groups, trends, and influences that need to be taken into account. The play of assumption and innovation which this chapter aims to map is at once complex and hazy; in consequence, our descriptive terms will inevitably multiply and blur.

Norms change over time: principles can expand into norms, and norms can shrink to principles. A couple of centuries earlier, when Cowley's very free *Pindarique Odes* (1656) enjoyed a vogue, FitzGerald's *Calderon* would have seemed dangerous to nobody. And only three decades later he might have felt rather less experimental. When Michael Field (the pen name of Katharine Bradley and Edith Cooper) published some 'extensions' of Sappho in 1889, he (or she, or they) warningly introduced them as 'audacious'—but audacity is different from danger: it expects to be welcomed. Gideon Toury suggests that we track such shifts of mood by distinguishing between 'mainstream', 'previous', and 'new' norms (1995: 62–3). This is a necessary step, but three such enormous categories are never going to be enough. What of the 'quite new', the 'semi-mainstream', or the 'very previous indeed'? Even then the question of which label to apply may still be vexed. Should we think of FitzGerald as inaugurating a new norm with his 'dangerous' assertion of principle, or resurrecting an old one?

Norms vary in rigour, spawning new terms as they do so. Toury thinks they occupy a continuum between 'whims' and 'rules' (1995: 54); Hermans distinguishes them from 'conventions' on the one hand and 'decrees' on the other (1996: 29, 32). But, again, more words are needed if we are to describe the weave of expectation and surprise with any subtlety: 'trend', 'tradition', 'habit', 'provocation'. 'Principle' is itself a word of this sort: though vital to Alexander Tytler's *Essay on the Principles of Translation* (1791) it is absent from the recent literature on norms. And then norms shift according to the genre of the translated text and the use to which it is put. Had FitzGerald been aiming at stage performance rather than a closet reading his freedoms would have been uncontroversial (see 'The Importance of Genre' below).

Trickiest of all is the fact that norms can seem uncertain even to the translators most affected by them. In 1877, Robert Browning englished Aeschylus' *Agamemnon* according to principles directly opposed to FitzGerald's. It was, he said, a 'transcript', designed 'to be literal at every cost save that of absolute violence to our language' (Browning 2000–: XIV, 7). Which norms bear on this endeavour? Browning's preface sends out mixed signals. It announces a commitment to rendering the play's 'ideas' in contrast to the 'abundant musicality' available 'elsewhere' (8). This looks like a gibe at Swinburne's melodious imitations of Greek drama *Atalanta in Calydon* (1865) and *Erechtheus* (1876), and suggests a Browning idiosyncratically objecting to a resurgent norm of freedom—shall we call it 'decadent'?—that had been initiated by FitzGerald and was to be consolidated by Field. But then Browning dedicates his transcript to one grand old theorist of translation, Thomas Carlyle, and alludes to another, Matthew Arnold. This looks more as if he thought of himself as defending a status quo. But both notions are likely to have occurred to him, and he may not have distinguished between them.

Even if we were to discover a clear attitude in Browning's preface, it does not follow that his readers would have characterized his translation in the same way. Toury is right to contend that discussion of translation must invoke norms; the assertion he quotes from Wexler is irrefutable: 'without a norm all deviations are meaningless' (Paul N. Wexler, cited in Toury 1995: 55). But we must keep in mind that the meaning of any deviation—and indeed whether it counts as a deviation at all—will vary according to whom you ask. Hermans claims with reason that norms 'help to bring about the coordination required for continued existence with other people' (1996: 26); but we must also recognize that *lack* of coordination—disagreement, misunderstanding—is no less constitutive of social interaction. What strikes some people as the expression of an exciting new principle may look to others like just another instance of the tired old norm.

With these caveats in place, let us venture a few approximate truths regarding norms and principles of translation between 1790 and 1900. The period is remarkable for the variety of its translation styles (in this it differs from the preceding century) and also for their air of being in competition (in this it differs from the century after). In his *Defence of Poetry* (1821), Shelley directed a memorable surge of rhetoric against close translation: 'it were as wise to cast a violet into a crucible that you might discover the formal principle of its colour and odour, as seek to transfuse from one language into another the creations of a poet. The plant must spring again from its seed, or it will bear no flower' (Shelley 1988: 280). This needed to be said because the opposite view was gathering strength: translation increasingly connoted fidelity, even literalism, in prose as well as poetry. The trend continued during the succeeding decades, when the desire for closeness to the source also fostered the dictional archaism common in versions from older texts. But, as the example of FitzGerald indicates, this norm was by no means all-pervasive (though its distant presence can be discerned even in him: his Calderon is lightly archaic).

Meanwhile, much popular fiction was being translated, notably during the 1840s in penny weeklies such as the *London Journal* and the *Family Chronicle*, both of which sometimes adopted lightly foreignizing styles (see under 'National Difference', below). Beneath the notice of reviewers and untrammelled by international copyright, these publications were free to steal and cut as they wished, but in practice they typically altered their sources rather little; certainly nothing like so much as the English playwrights who rifled contemporary French drama throughout the century.

Towards the end of the period it was again tempting and permissible for highbrow poets to work more freely, blending translation and imitation often in response to contemporary French verse. But again this was only one feature of the landscape: the prose cribs of the Bohn imprint and faithful versions of the classics, of Dante, and of major novelists such as Balzac continued to appear.

Tytler's Literal-Mindedness

In his *Essay on the Principles of Translation*, Alexander Tytler, professor of history and judge-advocate at Edinburgh, adduces many precedents (for further discussion of Tytler in an eighteenth-century context see Vol. 3 of this *History*). He finds that some translators, especially in the sixteenth and seventeenth centuries, have been too much in thrall to the 'style' of the source text. Their ringleader is Ben Jonson, whose version of Horace is no more than a 'literal and servile transcript'. On the other hand, a translator confident in his ability to find new words for his source's 'ideas' is in danger of 'licentiousness'. Dryden is found guilty of incitement to this crime (Tytler 1791: 50, 52, 57).

Judge that he is, Tytler grounds his opinions in 'laws':

I. THAT the Translation should give a complete transcript of the ideas of the original work.
II. THAT the style and manner of writing should be of the same character with that of the original.
III. THAT the Translation should have all the ease of original composition. (13)

Tytler's Jonsonian and Drydenian extremes anticipate the poles set up by later theorists: Schleiermacher's alternatives of moving the reader towards the writer or vice versa (1992: 42); Nida's 'static' vs 'dynamic' equivalence (2000: 129); Venuti's 'domesticating' vs. 'foreignizing' strategies (1995: 20). But his laws I and II are worded to make it seem that the reasonable demands of both parties can be met. A translator *can* re-embody his source's 'ideas', so long as he does so with the tightness of a 'transcript'; and he *can* reproduce the 'style and manner' of the source, so long as he allows himself the latitude implied by 'of the same character'. Law III then unsettles this compromise by giving the treaty a decisive bias against the Jonson tendency.

When Tytler gets down to discussing examples (the detailed case studies are his book's main novelty and virtue), a fourth principle appears: 'taste'. Translators should imitate the character of their originals only so long as that character is good. When it is not, it must be reformed: 'ambiguity' and 'obscurity', for instance, are faults which the translator should correct (24). Lord Roscommon was mistaken when he assured translators: 'Your author always will the best advise; | Fall when he falls, and when he rises, rise'; 'far from adopting the former part of this maxim', Tytler protests, 'I conceive it to be the duty of a poetical translator, never to suffer his original to fall' (59). The translator must ensure that his author appears to best effect in the best company, speaking nothing but standard English in elegant style. It was wrong of Dryden and his collaborators to make Tacitus 'express himself in the low cant of the streets'; wrong of Thomas Brown to give Lucian 'the ease of Billingsgate and of Wapping' (79, 141).

For all his criticism of Dryden's practice, Tytler draws deeply, though silently, on his theorizing: 'a translator ought always to figure to himself, in what manner the original author would have expressed himself, if he had written in the language of the translation' (123; compare Dryden 1987: 330–1). For him, as for Dryden, what should be translated is not the text but the author, i.e. a construction of authorial intention. Translation is thought of as continuing the process of composition, adjusting the source text to suit its changed circumstances. But what is distinctive in Tytler is his wish to clarify the terms of the translator's power of authorial representation (again this is a lawyerly emphasis). It is affected by genre, 'the liberty of adding or retrenching' being less allowable in prose than in verse, and by the relationship between the 'genius' (i.e. grammar, idiom, and nuance) of source and target languages (48, 111). Any 'idea' omitted by a translator 'must be only such as is an accessory, and not a principal in the clause or sentence' (such as honorific epithets in Homer) while any 'superadded idea shall have the most necessary connection with the original thought, and actually increase its force' (32–3).

With all this detail, even doggedness, of illustration, Tytler's *Principles* is an encyclopedia of the tradition of domestication. At last we can find out what might really be meant by the 'transfusion' of 'spirit' from a text in one language to a text in another. But Tytler's literal-mindedness, his determination to lay down the letter of the law, also puts that tradition under pressure. Tellingly, he avoids Dryden's and Pope's word 'spirit', preferring to talk of the transfusion of something that sounds solider and more measurable: 'merit' (3). If it is possible to list the procedures available to a translator and the conditions under which he should apply them, how can translation continue to be thought of as metempsychosis? In this respect, Tytler opens the way for an enquiry that gathered force over the ensuing decades. Could a recognizably English style really be said to be 'of the same character' as a style in a foreign language? And might not the foreignness of a foreign text be something to be valued and therefore preserved in its English representative?

The Definition of a Copy

Later critics of translations echo many of Tytler's assumptions and use many of the same words. Often, a translation will be described as a compromise between two opposites—say 'fidelity' and 'elegance'. But frequently the meaning of the words and the purchase of the assumptions turns out to have changed. Take for instance the following, printed in the *Edinburgh Review* in 1835: 'in translation ... we have of late been acquiring some new ideas; and it seems now to be pretty generally felt that the main object of a translator should be to exhibit his author and not himself. If a work is worth translating at all it is worth translating *literally*' (Moir 1835: 355). Tytler would have agreed that a translator's main object should be to present an author (though he might well have protested at the word 'exhibit', with its clinical and fairground connotations). But he did not think that the way to do so was by 'translating *literally*'. For this *Edinburgh* reviewer, the word 'author' has shifted function. It no longer licenses the translator to correct what he takes to be errors of judgement in the source text, to improve its manners and clarify its ideas. Rather, you exhibit an author by mirroring his words.

One should always distrust a claim that anything is 'generally felt': the anonymous writer of this essay in the *Edinburgh*, George Moir, was himself a translator and likely to be biased. Nevertheless, by mid-century, 'literalness' was a quality often manifested and welcomed in translation. For example, the volumes in the Bohn Classical Library almost all advertised themselves as being 'literally translated' (see Cordasco 1951: 56–66). In Bohn's Standard Library too, versions from the modern languages kept to what was presented as a new stringency. When William Julius Mickle's 1777 translation of *The Lusiad* was reissued a century later, its editor, E. Richmond Hodges, marked Mickle's interpolations and corrected him in footnotes (Mickle 1877: vii, xiv, and throughout). This visible editing differs from silent revision: it not only gives readers greater literalness but points it out to them and asks for their approval.

A contrasting reissue in the Classical Library bears the marks of the same norm. When Christopher Smart's *Works of Horace Translated Literally into English Prose* had first been published in 1756 it had included the Latin in parallel text and opened with repeated apologies: on the title page: 'For the Use of those who are desirous of acquiring or recovering a competent Knowledge of the LATIN LANGUAGE'; and on p. ii: 'The learned reader need not be informed that this version was not intended for him.' The lightly revised Bohn reissue of 1850 cut both the Latin and the prefatory excuses. Literal translation could now stand alone and without embarrassment.

Parallel text volumes did appear during this period, but more typical are the translations issued with *implied* parallel text. An obvious instance is *The Prometheus Bound of Aeschylus Literally Translated into English Verse* by Augusta Webster (1866) whose line numbers were keyed to a separate edition of the Greek. But the gesture did not need to be so explicit. *Specimens of the Russian Poets* and similar collections translated by John Bowring in the 1820s kept the absence of the source text present in the reader's mind by allowing shards of it onto the page in titles and notes. This style of presentation tallies with the metaphors of translation as 'mirror' and as 'copy' which frequently appear in reviews and prefaces at this time. If, like Dryden or Tytler, you think of translation as metempsychosis or transfusion, it follows that, after each act of translation, the source text can be buried or cast away, a dead body or a dry skin. But a copy always refers back to an original, while a mirror only contains an image so long as there is something to reflect.

All this advocacy of 'literalness' concealed—and indeed relied on—differences as to what the word precisely meant. One possibility was that the 'literal' meaning excluded meanings contributed by verse form: in this case a 'literal' translation would always (as with Smart's Horace) be in prose. Tytler had ridiculed this idea with an argument from generic identity. Poetry, with its 'boldness of figures, luxuriancy of imagery, a frequent use of metaphors, a quickness of transition, a liberty of digressing' had an irreducibly different character from prose and so could not be translated into it (Tytler 1791: 125). Many later writers shared his hostility, but for a different reason. Typically their concern was expressed through the metaphors of mirror or copy. It focused on structure, not character; and the key term was in consequence not 'poetry' but 'verse'.

A copy can, and a reflection must, be in a different medium (in this case a different language) from its original. But verse form looked temptingly as though it might be carried across without alteration from source to target. Obviously Petrarch's words would mutate in translation, but surely his metre and rhyme scheme need not? Far from being excluded from literal translation, poetic form might be the only linguistic element amenable to it.

But there were difficulties. The Petrarchan sonnet was unusual in having long been assimilated into the repertoire of English verse. Stranger forms such as Dante's *terza rima* and Homer's hexameters were harder to accommodate to our habitual rhythms and rhymes. And then how much definition should one expect the formal copy to have? Was a pattern of metrical stress an acceptable substitute for the pattern of quantity with which Homer had worked? Matthew Arnold thought so; the scholar James Spedding disagreed (Arnold 1960: 192–3). Like all verse forms, Dante's *terza rima* is more than a metre plus a rhyme scheme: its other characteristics include a very high incidence of paroxytone line-endings (those with stress on the penultimate syllable, common in Italian) and a marked tendency to align rhymes with syntactic pauses. Should a translator attempt to copy these? Charles Lancelot Shadwell thought them essential: 'nothing could be more unlike the *Commedia* than the movement of Byron's *Prophecy of Dante*, professing to be written in terza rima, but allowing the break between the sentences to occur at random, at any part of the verse' (Shadwell 1892: viii). But he also thought them impossible to recreate without fatal damage to the sense, and so chose for his *Purgatory of Dante Alighieri . . . An Experiment in Literal Verse Translation* an easier though frankly English form, the stanza of Marvell's Horatian Ode. Even were it magically possible to mirror a verse form in all its detail while maintaining an acceptable degree of semantic closeness there would still be the problem that the feel, the 'character', of a form differs in different languages. There was no way out of this dilemma. Successive versions of Dante are a chronicle of dissatisfaction: Cary's Miltonic blank verse (1814; see pp. 250–1, below) prompting attempts in *terza rima* by Dayman (1843), Cayley (1851), and Haselfoot (1887), which in turn produced a reaction in favour of English forms: Shadwell, and George Musgrave who in 1893 draped Dante in Spenserian stanzas.

Then as now, no one meant the word 'literal' literally: a letter-for-letter translation would not be in a language but in code. Even when 'literal' was allowed the latitude of meaning 'word-for-word', and even when the question of verse form had been fudged one way or another, further qualifications were required. John Fletcher Davies, 'First Classical Master in Kingstown School, Ireland', presented his *Agamemnon of Aeschylus* (1868) as 'a "literal" translation', i.e. 'one which follows the construction of the Greek'. But: 'the ordinary and well-known deviations from the Greek to the English idiom are systematically made', for example: 'the participle and finite verb usually become two finite verbs. The aorist participle is most frequently rendered by the English present'—and so on (Davies 1868: vi). He attempts to map the difference in 'genius' between Greek and English so as better to overcome it. But is English idiom, and particularly the idiom of English verse, so readily defined? Can rules for what counts as a copy ever hold? Following what he took to be the ordinary deviations, Davies produced an unexceptionable first line: 'I have been asking of the gods relief'. It obeys the conventions of syntax and verse, but as the heralding of a great tragedy it is not impressive. Robert Browning had less respect for the 'well known' and so could be more literally literal. His version begins as follows: 'The Gods I ask deliverance from these labours' (Browning 2000–: XIV, 13). With its inverted word order and omission of a preposition, this clings closer to the Greek and departs further from Fletcher's notion of 'the English idiom'. But such departures have long been welcomed in poetry, especially when they are embedded in a pentameter and accompanied by a flicker of metaphorical suggestion ('deliverance' is almost 'delivery', and 'labours' almost 'labour'). Browning's less ordinary English creates a more compelling line of English poetry.

Arnold and Archaism

In the preface to his *Iliad of Homer Faithfully Translated into Unrhymed English Metre* (1856), F. W. Newman pitched himself against a different norm from the one that had troubled FitzGerald only three years before. 'Some reviewers of my translation of Horace's Odes'—he wrote—'laid down as axioms . . . principles which I regard to be utterly false and ruinous to translation. One of these is, that the reader ought, if possible, to forget that it is a translation at all, and be lulled into the illusion that he is reading an original work.' There would be none of this Circean seductiveness about Newman's Homer: 'I aim at precisely the opposite;— to retain every peculiarity of the original, so far as I am able, *with the greater care, the more foreign it may happen to be*' (1856: xv–xvi).

One might think that Newman is about to launch into Browningesque Graecification of syntax and word forms; but in fact he is more like Tytler than he sounds. His idea of what it is to 'adhere closely' to Homer's 'manner and habit of thought' is basically what Tytler would recommend—though he has more sympathy with Billingsgate and Wapping. He aims to create a style that will be equivalent to Homer's in the sense of having the same position on a putative scale of English styles as Homer's on a putative scale of Greek ones. This line of argument is at odds with the widespread interest in literalism chronicled above, and comes close to contradicting Newman's own flag-waving for the foreign on adjacent pages. Homer's language is 'direct, popular, forcible, quaint, flowing, garrulous' and Newman hopes his English will attract the same adjectives. It will be 'foreign' not because of any residual Greekness (though Newman does produce some lexical compounds on the Greek model) but in the metaphorical sense of being 'foreign' to received ideas. These, Newman thinks, have not sufficiently recognized Homer's variety: he is 'alternately Poet, Orator, Historian, Theologian, Geographer, Traveller, jocose as well as serious, dramatic as well as descriptive'; his poem is like 'a good novel' or a 'book of travels'; and his way with verse (this was by no means a new suggestion) bears comparison with 'the old English ballad' (iii–iv).

As a sample, let us take the description of Calchas in Book I:

> Who knew the present and the past, and all hereafter coming,
> And had as far as Ilium the Achaian galleys guided,
> Because of that sage art of his, which bright Apollo gave him:
> Who thus with kindly soul harangu'd, and spake his word among them.
> (1886: 3)

The only hint of foreignness in this verse comes from the persistent paroxytone endings. Home-grown ballads echo in the very regular iambic beat, while the marked caesura and tendency to alliteration recall Old English poetry. The verbosity is not a Homeric characteristic either: it is Newman who has opted to write 'as far as' (not 'to'), '*bright* Apollo' (the epithet is not in the source), 'spake *his word*' and 'hereafter *coming*'. Calchas, 'sage' and of 'kindly soul', is not only englished but made Anglican. Lawrence Venuti has celebrated Newman as a radically 'foreignizing' translator (1995: 119–41): Calchas the clergyman shows that this *Iliad* also includes marked domesticating elements.

When Matthew Arnold attacked Newman in his lectures as Oxford Professor of Poetry (1860–1) his focus was not a principle of translation *per se*. Like Newman (and again fundamentally like Tytler) he held that a translator should aim for what we now call 'dynamic equivalence' or 'equivalence of affect'. And both he and Newman assumed that the affect to be equalled was that provoked by Homer in an Athenian of the fifth century BCE (Victorians being latter-day Pericleans). Arnold introduces the caveat that since 'we cannot really know ... how Homer seemed to Sophocles' we should rely on the judgement of 'intelligent scholars' such as 'the Provost of Eton'. But this proviso is soon dropped. The trouble with Newman is that his words 'do not correspond in their effect upon us with Homer's words in their effect upon Sophocles' (Arnold 1960: 120, 182). Homer's style is not 'garrulous' but 'rapid'; it *is* 'direct', but in a 'plain' sort of way. It is not 'popular' but rather 'noble'. And there is certainly nothing 'quaint' about it. Above all, Newman was wrong to think it 'essentially archaic': it was to Sophocles, and mysteriously is to us, 'never antiquated' (120–2).

Arnold's cultural politics are evident here and they have been thoroughly documented (Venuti 1995: 129–46). But just perceptible through the suave embattled eloquence is a sharp point about translation and history. Judging Homer to be 'essentially archaic', Newman wants to give his version 'a plausible aspect of moderate antiquity' so as 'to break off mental association with the poetry later than Dryden' (1856: x). Arnold's objection is, not that this holds on to Homer's foreignness, but on the contrary that it saddles him with an identifiable English character which is, because identifiably English, necessarily un-Homeric. For Arnold, Homer's English translators have always done this: Chapman gave him 'the fancifulness of the Elizabethan age' and Cowper an 'elaborate Miltonic manner' (1960: 103). But Homer is different from all these characterizations. Here, it is Arnold who insists on Homer's foreignness.

At times Arnold places Homer not only outside English culture but outside culture altogether. Homer 'sees his object and conveys it to us immediately' (116). The argument creates a circle whereby the absolutely foreign becomes 'natural' and therefore absolutely familiar, closer to us even than Englishness. This allows Arnold to be confident that he knows Homer, and knows him to be 'simple'; had he been as learned a classicist as Newman he might well have been less sure of the transparency of Homer's words. Still, when it comes to producing his own sample translations, Arnold is closely attentive to the detail of the *Iliad*'s language. And, finding encouragement in experiments with hexameters by Longfellow, Clough, Hawtrey, and Spedding, he takes the crucial copyist's step of mirroring Homer's metre, albeit with the substitution of metrical stress for quantity:

> Then, perhaps, thou shalt work at the loom of another, in Argos,
> Or bear pails to the well of Messeïs, or Hypereia,
> Sorely against thy will, by strong Necessity's order.
> And some man may say, as he looks and sees thy tears falling:
> *See, the wife of Hector, that great pre-eminent captain*
> *Of the horsemen of Troy, in the day they fought for their city.*
>
> (1960: 164)

Though Arnold claims that all his words are current English, at least for poetry, the idiom ('bear pails', 'in the day they'), the concatenation of clauses, and the rhythm are more peculiarly foreign than anything in Newman.

Arnold's strictures did not prevent later translators from putting on an 'aspect of moderate antiquity'. Swinburne's 'translations from the French of Villon' in *Poems and Ballads: Second Series* (1878) exploit the mode with some subtlety (see pp. 11–12, above, and p. 232, below), but the mass production of archaized diction in William Morris's *Aeneids of Virgil* (1876) and *Odyssey of Homer* (1887) justifies the label of 'Wardour-Street early English' stuck on it by one reviewer (Wardour Street shops sold antique and reproduction furniture). A peculiarity of Morris's translations, as of his style in general, was a preference for words of Anglo-Saxon origin even though, as Arnold had pointed out, 'we owe to the Latin element in our language most of that very rapidity and clear decisiveness by which it is contradistinguished from the German, and in sympathy with the languages of Greece and Rome' (1960: 100–1). Arnold's assimilation of Greek and Latin is dubious, but his main thrust is nonetheless strong. Latinate words that feel modern (say, 'idealism') may have roots at least as old as those of the Anglo-Saxonisms deployed by Newman and Morris; and what is more, they go back to the language in which Virgil wrote. A translator who neglects this linguistic resource exaggerates the otherness of the classical and Romance languages. He secludes himself within a contentiously insular English.

The preface to Dante Gabriel Rossetti's *Early Italian Poets . . . in the Original Metres Together with Dante's Vita Nuova* does not mention this danger, but his translations quietly avoid it by cultivating overlaps between English and Italian (see also pp. 254–6, below). 'Pleasant' for 'piacente', 'creature' for 'creatura', 'courteous' for 'cortese', 'spirits' for 'spiriti': none of these choices feels archaic or foreignizing in itself (2003: 268, 266, 258, 266). But their collaboration awakens slumbering medieval nuances; and readers who catch these will find themselves following etymologies back across the channel towards an origin that English and Italian have in common.

Browning's *Agamemnon* (discussed further on pp. 179–80, below) likewise blurs the boundaries of English, using latinate vocabulary as a bridge towards Greek in just the way Arnold had recommended: 'cognate', 'vociferate', 'symphonious'. On the other hand, it makes frequent visits to Wardour Street: its preface bluntly defends 'the use of certain allowable constructions which, happening to be out of daily favour, are all the more appropriate to archaic workmanship' (Browning 2000–: XIV, 7). Phrases such as 'the spear-captured Troic habitations' (27) are as novel as they are antiquated: according to the *OED*, 'spear-captured' is a coinage, while 'Troic' had appeared in the language only recently in works of Homeric scholarship. The point is to argue that Aeschylus can neither (in the manner of Newman) be placed on an English time-line nor (in the manner of Arnold) be thought ageless. 'Early' is the word that best catches the ambivalent temporality of Browning's Aeschylus. The most ancient writing was also the newest, for history was yet to come.

National Difference

Modern originals, like the classical texts that interested Newman, had 'peculiarities' which translators endeavoured to 'retain'. In 1830, Thomas Carlyle translated 'Jean Paul Friedrich Richter's Review of Madame de Stael's "Allemagne"' for the first number of *Fraser's Magazine*, announcing in a preface his ambition 'to preserve the quaint grotesque style so characteristic of Jean Paul; rendering with literal fidelity whatever stood before us' (Carlyle 1899: XXVI, 476–7). As so often in the period, terms dear to Tytler are deployed with another purpose, the imitation of a writer's 'characteristic style' being taken to require 'literal fidelity'. Carlyle's aim is not (as Newman's would be) to find an English analogue for the foreign manner, but to give his English readers a sense of what Richter's style is like *in German*. For instance: 'We Germans are in the habit of limning Paris and London from the distance, which capitals do sit to us, truly,—but only on the book-stall of their works' (477). Fraser's editor was unusually adventurous (he later serialized *Sartor Resartus*), but still it is striking that such un-English English should be allowed to appear in the vital first number of a new magazine. Foreignized English—translationese—was not only tolerated: it was thought likely to sell.

The principles animating this mode of translation were a new respect for national difference, and a new interest in its embodiment in language. Richter matters, not only as an individual, but because he is an exemplary German: 'students of German literature will be curious to see ... in what fashion the best of the Germans write reviews'—and since his Germanness is interesting it should be preserved in translation. The focus on nationhood will have seemed the more attractive to Carlyle because it is asserted by Richter himself: he condemns Mme de Staël's domesticating translations and praises the German foreignizers Voss and A. W. Schlegel. Carlyle does unto Richter as Richter would be done unto. From this point of view, Dryden's ambition 'to make Virgil speak such *English* as he wou'd himself have spoken, if he had been born in *England*, and in this present Age' looks nonsensical (Dryden 1987: 330–1). If he had been born in England and in this present age he would not have been Virgil.

Carlyle's stance was extreme, but other translators in the second and third decades of the century also responded to the German emphasis on national difference. John Bowring, an editor of the *Westminster Review*, produced anthologies from several European literatures (on which see also § 6.8, below). He was convinced of their public utility: in *Specimens of the Russian Poets*, he urged 'the statesman ... to study the tendency and the character of that fountainhead of popular feeling whose waters will spread over ... the widest empire of the world' (1821–3: II, vii). 'Character', of course, is a word Tytler had used; but here the character that matters is not an author's but a nation's. Hence Bowring's commitment to anthologies in which poets appear as 'specimens' of their nationality.

Once national difference has been asserted, international understanding must be advanced to bridge it. As Bowring assures us in his *Poetry of the Magyars*, 'my mission ... is one of benevolence' (1830: viii). The translations that embody this dual intent are necessarily a hybrid of copy and transfusion. On the one hand, Bowring 'generally' reproduces 'the measure of the original ... a practice which has been made of late quite a point of conscience in Germany' (1821–3: I, xxi–xxii). On the other, his diction consists largely of the most quiescent inherited poeticisms, all cool grots, laved welkins, and effluences of lights divine. No doubt one cause of this familiar air is Bowring's lack of inventiveness as a writer. But there is a rationale for it too. Prosody stands for the letter that separates nations; diction for the literary spirit they all share.

Bowring does occasionally break this pattern, especially for 'Popular Poems' since, as he came to think, 'the language of art and civilization differs little among different nations; nationality must be sought among popular masses' (1832: 85). Folk songs and similar verses did not have to be shown to be literary. Bowring allowed them to remain strange:

> THE BUGACZIAN* CSARDA†
> Csikós 's gulyás nép clubbja rossz vityilló
>
> Now, *Csikos*,¶ *Gulyas*,§ now — come hither — hither,
> And make your way through fly-swarms numberless,
> And armies of loud croaking frogs ...

> * Bugacz, A Hungarian village
> † A sort of inn or public house ...
> ¶ A keeper of wild horses
> § A keeper of wild oxen
> (Bowring 1830: 32)

An additional nudge towards foreignization comes from a trend often discernible in this period but rarely if ever formulated: thematic continuity. Since the stanza is all about Hungarian noises, Bowring fills his English page with the static of Hungarian words.

Carlyle and Bowring wrote for a highbrow market. But translations designed for mass circulation could also register the 'peculiarity' of other languages. The publishing sensation of the 1840s was Eugène Sue's *Les Mystères de Paris*, in Britain no less than in France: according to Chevasco (2003: 119) six rival translations were printed in 1844. This book offered a particular challenge to translators because it engages in translation itself. The inner-city dwellers whose doings were its main attraction are shown, not only to obey different codes of behaviour from its implied readers, but to speak a different language. Footnotes and parentheses provide running Standard French translations: '*tapis-franc*' = 'cabaret du plus bas étage'; '*bougeron*' = 'sorte de blouse'; '*ogre*' = 'repris de justice'; and so on (Sue *c*.1844: 1). Spoken by thieves and prostitutes, the *argot* is offered up to be disapproved of: it is, the narrator says, a 'vocabulaire infâme' (10). But the possibility that it might nonetheless have a sort of autochthonous authority, so as to be more French than French itself, is opened when the first speaker of 'très bon français' turns out to be English (44).

In translation—at least, in the anonymous version published by Chapman and Hall in 1845—the linguistic affiliations are even harder to plot. Sometimes the *argot* is imported unchanged onto the English page while the Standard French translation is translated, as when the nickname 'la *Goualeuse*' is explained as 'sweet-throated' (Anon. 1845: I, 2). This aligns the English and French implied readers as being equally foreign to the language and environment represented. But more often the *argot* is rendered as London slang: this has the effect which always attaches to dialects (and not to standard languages) of relocation: its speakers belong in London not Paris. But then part of the attraction of the *Mystères de Paris* was the feeling that Paris might as well be any city—witness the many imitations it spawned: *The Mysteries of London, Les Mystères de Marseille*, and so on. Occasionally *argot* and slang appear side by side, both requiring explanation: 'The Schoolmaster saw at the Pré (the galleys) the man who brought you to my *crib* when you were a brat, and he has proofs that the people who had you first were *"gentry coves"* (rich people)' (I, 41–2). This makes the slang look like a foreign language. And sometimes slang is given what looks like an explanation in *argot*, as though readers were more at home in Paris than in London: 'you must pay me the glass of "tape" (*eau d'aff*)' (I, 3). Native novels such as *Oliver Twist* (1837–8) had explored the different Englishes spoken within England, and especially in London; but this anonymous translation of Sue gives a more vertiginous impression of the dislocations of urban identity. The principles it embodies are nowhere explicitly formulated; but they can be inferred. This style of translation follows a principle of scepticism about the consistency of national identity, and therefore about the solidity of national difference. In its pages, the inner city can suddenly look international, and English seem stranger than French.

The Mysteries of Paris shared much of its readership with penny weeklies of the time, such as the *London Journal* (circulation *c.*500,000) and the *Family Chronicle*. These were miscellanies that included topical information but gave most space to short stories and serial novels of romantic and moralistic tenor, often (especially before the international extension of copyright in 1851) translated from European languages, usually French (see King 2004: 70–1 and pp. 44–5, above). The styles of writing in these magazines were as various as their content, and translationese flourished, doubtless fostered by the speed at which the translations must have had to be done. Take for instance the following, from *It was Time* by Frédéric Soulié serialized in the *London Journal*:

Oh! lady, lady! what a great fault it was thus to carry off that flower, and to caress it thus! Melchior did not witness it; but you, when you went to sleep with smiling lips, and that flower hidden in your bosom, you knew full well that there now remained no bar between him and you, except the one defence of honour. Oh! yes, it was a great fault.

(Anon. 1846: 45)

The underlying French syntax and idiom show through clearly. But the question of how foreign this English would have seemed to an 1840s reader is difficult, for its repetitions and exclamations were common to romance and Gothic styles which had long been in the English repertoire.

Nevertheless, readers of such passages must have felt exposed to foreignness—of origin, scene, behaviour, and possibly of language. But this opening up of identity is impeded by obvious barriers. Readers were after all generally in Britain, and stuck there (it was only in later decades that the penny weeklies developed worldwide circulations); and the text had been on a double journey to reach them: translocation and translation. This complex situation produces a mingling of the principles evident in Carlyle's and Bowring's translations on the one hand, and *The Mysteries of Paris* on the other. The possibility of dissolving national difference is simultaneously advanced and resisted. A characteristic of romance in general is that the opportunity for transformation it holds out to its readers is balanced, and therefore intensified, by its manifest distance from them. Translation increases both the sense of possibility and the sense of distance. Romance translated is romance squared.

The Importance of Genre

Names of translators did not figure in the pages of the *London Journal* and *Family Chronicle*: sometimes it is even unclear whether a text has been translated or not. Of course, anonymity was the norm in periodicals of all heights of brow, for nonfiction contributors as much as for translators (though fiction and poetry were often signed): the magazine stood as 'author' of the views it expressed, and likewise as 'translator' of foreign material. Nonetheless, the absence of translators' names is significant: it implies that the translator has not made an individual contribution to the text; that the translation should count as impersonal, if not invisible.

In general, the treatment of a translator's signature is a marker of genre. This is revealing because different genres of text were translated according to different principles and judged by different norms. Prose in free-standing volumes, both fictional and non-fictional, could be translated anonymously just like texts in periodicals. Sometimes—as with the anonymous translator(s) of the Vizetelly Zolas prosecuted for obscenity in 1888—anonymity may have been prompted by circumspection; sometimes—as with the equally anonymous translator of Sismondi's unexceptionable *History of the Italian Republics* (1832)—no specific reason can now be recovered (see also p. 86, below). Even when, as was much more common, translators of prose were named, they might as well not have been for all the attention reviewers paid to their labours. Routine praise of 'fidelity with elegance' was the most they could hope for (see for instance Anon. 1825: 174).

In scholarly versions, however, the translator's signature mattered because it functioned as a certificate of competence and authority. Title pages often list relevant qualifications: when a translation of Lucian's *Dialogues* is said to be by 'Howard Williams, M. A. Late Scholar of St John's College, Cambridge' the translator is flagged, not in himself, but in his capacity as someone who knows Greek. Augusta Webster's *Prometheus Bound* presents itself as being 'edited by Thomas Webster, M. A., Late Fellow of Trinity College, Cambridge'—and a preface explains why: 'my wife wished for some better guarantee of accuracy than a lady's name could give' (Webster 1866: 5). For modern fiction also, a translator's credentials could be more important than his personality: *German Romance* (1827) is announced as being englished, not by Thomas Carlyle, but 'by the translator of Wilhelm Meister and Author of the Life of Schiller'.

The names of poetical translators of poetry were presented differently. In the Bohn *Greek Anthology* (Burges 1852), the literal prose versions were credited only on the title page to 'George Burges, M. A. Trinity College Cambridge'. But 'metrical versions' by different translators were also included in the volume, sometimes two or more to each source poem—and these were individually signed. Some were reprinted from elsewhere; some were written specially by 'the author's friends' (Burges 1852: iv). The different status of these verse translations is obvious: they are offered as Merivale's refashioning of the Greek, or Bland's, or someone else's, not as *the* impersonal translation. Translations of this sort are felt to involve more of a translator's individuality. They offer themselves to be read in relation to a different criterion: not 'accuracy' but something less measurable such as 'spirit' or 'tone'.

Since translations of poetry—especially into verse—were allowed to be more personal than translations of prose they were also understood to be more partial, in both senses of that word. In consequence, it sometimes seemed that for verse originals one translation was not enough. This idea is evident in the Bohn *Greek Anthology* with its large-scale gathering of multiple versions, but single-translator books sometimes created similar kaleidoscopes of translation styles. For example, Coleridge remarks at one point in his version of Schiller's *Piccolomini*: 'I found it not in my power to translate this song with *literal* fidelity, preserving at the same time the Alcaic Movement'; he therefore supplements his verse translation by quoting the original with a prose crib. But once the illusion of equivalence has been broken any number of alternatives can crowd in. Coleridge opts to balance the extreme of fidelity with its opposite: 'an imitation of this song'—by Charles Lamb—'which appears to me to have caught the happiest manner of our old ballads' (Coleridge 2001: 379–80). A comic variant of this strategy appears in F. A. Paley's otherwise solemn prose *Agamemnon*. Dissatisfied with his rendering of Cassandra's wild first noises as 'woe, woe, woe! alas!', he was moved to explain at the foot of the page: 'Greek exclamations, the same in sound as our *tut tut* and *pooh pooh*' (1864: 160).

Being more personal and partial than prose translation, verse translation was also felt to be more creative. This meant that it could stimulate other kinds of textual transformation. Both prose and verse translators could anthologize—witness on the one hand Thomas Roscoe's *Italian Novelists, Selected from the Most Approved Authors in that Language* (4 vols., 1825), and on the other Bowring's ethno-poetical collections—but (as at other periods) translators of poetry were freer to refashion their sources as extracts. Dante's *Commedia* was especially susceptible to this treatment because of its episodic structure: orphaned speeches and divorced cantos were brought into English throughout the period—by Byron, Shelley, Montgomery, Barrett Browning, to name but a few (see Griffiths and Reynolds 2005). Conversely, the disjoined elements of a source text could be combined in surprising ways: J. H. A. Tremenheere (1897) arranged Catullus' lyrics to form a narrative, while FitzGerald in his *Rubáiyát* gave emotional sequence to what had been an alphabetical collection of aphorisms.

Versions as transformative as these challenged the boundary between translation and composition. The norms that bounded them were loose and their animating principles included something deserving the name of creativity. The printing of verse translations recognized their uncertain identity, for they were permitted to mingle in collections of original poems. Sometimes they were corralled into a special section at the end, but even then they could be arranged so as to participate in the expressive arc of a volume. The last original poem in Byron's *Hours of Idleness: A Series of Poems, Original and Translated* is 'Oscar of Alva', which ends with a death. The next page announces the new section of 'Translations and Imitations', the first of which is 'Adrian's Address to his Soul, when Dying', given in Latin and then English: 'Ah! gentle, fleeting, wav'ring sprite . . . | To what unknown region borne, | Wilt thou, now, wing thy distant flight?' (Byron 1807: 67–72). No doubt it would be glib to respond: 'England, as it turns out'—nonetheless, the layout clearly suggests comparisons between translation and other kinds of passing across and away: of the soul in death and of originality in imitation. The version has been creatively placed so as to take on new, distinctively Byronic connotations.

It was even possible for passages of verse translation to be incorporated into an otherwise original continuous work. When this happened, the identity of the translation was obviously weakened, but it did not disappear completely. Browning's *The Ring and the Book* (1868–9) is for the most part a prodigious imaginative expansion of its prose Italian and Latin source text, but at times it settles down to close translation: at one point the narrator says 'nay, | Better translate' and proceeds to do so (I, 120–1). The ensuing passage takes its place alongside response, increase, disagreement, invention, and others as one of a gamut of ways in which Browning gets to grips imaginatively with his source (see Reynolds 2003: 114–25). Translation is recognized as belonging to a continuum of imaginative activity.

Do such embedded texts have to be explicitly marked if they are to count as translations rather than echoes or allusions? If not, how long do they have to be? And how close? In Tennyson's 'Ulysses', which derives from Dante's *Inferno* 26, the word 'little' appears twice in successive lines (25–6). Is this a translation of the Italian 'picciola', an emphatically repeated word in the Dante (ll. 102, 114, 122)? Or is it rather that the whole poem is a translation, if a very free one? Criticism in the period touches on such questions only rarely and lightly, but the practice of poets explores them deeply and often. Byron had wanted to publish his *Hints from Horace* in parallel text, not so that readers could measure his fidelity, but so that his departures from the source could be mapped. As we noted above, literal translations were often published with implied parallel text. The same was true of much freer versions, even of poems that counted as original works—but with a Byronesque expectation that the point of the comparison was to notice change more than sameness. The distant parallel may be signalled (as in Tennyson's 'Ulysses') by title and scene, or else (and very frequently) by verse form: the *terza rima* of Shelley's 'The Triumph of Life' points to Dante; the hexameters of

Clough's *The Bothie of Tober-na-Vuolich* to Homer and Virgil (a work can have two distant parallels and more).

Poems that were this far from and creative with their sources did not call themselves translations or even imitations. But then a trait of poetry in general was its readiness to draw expressively on texts in other languages: translation loosely conceived was a constituent of the genre. In this period as in others, the boundaries of the norms, trends, and principles that bear on and define poetry translation were uncertain. Poetry opened the category of translation to question.

Prose did not have the same ability to work with distant parallels (though it soon developed it: witness Joyce's *Ulysses*). And even in close translation its adjustments of its sources—such as the frequent bowdlerization of French novels—were designed to go unnoticed. Zola's Denise, in *Au Bonheur des dames* spends the night with her lover, whereas in English she goes to stay with an aunt (Anon. 1888: 167–8) but this metamorphosis has no thematic significance: it is simply an index of public taste. Translation for the theatre could transform its source texts as freely as poetry; but the conditions were different, and so were the implications. On the one hand, there were openly advertised adaptations of novels, both English and foreign (usually French). On the other, there was silent appropriation of plays from abroad, again usually French (see § 8.2, below). Sometimes the same English play could incur both kinds of debt, for instance *The Corsican Brothers*, first produced by Charles Kean in 1852. The programme for Henry Irving's 1881 revival announces the work as being *Founded upon Dumas' Novel, 'Les Frères Corses,' and altered for the English Stage by Dion Boucicault*. The source in Dumas is a selling point; but nothing is said of Boucicault's reliance on the French dramatization of *Les Frères corses* by E. Grangé and Xavier de Montépin. Such plagiarism was frequent, unashamed, and barely criticized: it scorned anything that might be called a 'norm' of 'translation'. This textual libertinism was fostered by commercial forces, the prestige of French drama, the laxity of copyright arrangements—and also by the presentism and ephemerality of acting. If each performance is in a sense a new version, why worry if the script is a version too?

The Translator Translated

A text need not be all that is translated in an act of translation. It is possible to think that translators, and indeed readers, are translated too. This thought was not much formulated in our period but, as with the assumptions underlying *The Mysteries of Paris by Eugène Sue*, it can be extrapolated from the practice of translators. When translation is viewed from this angle, distinctive principles emerge.

One kind of personal translation is trans-gendering. This was mainly done by women: there were many fewer female translators than male and, as might be expected from the gender balance of literary production, the works they translated were usually by men (it was, and is, much rarer for men to translate women). One of Augusta Webster's aims in her *Prometheus Bound* was—as the preface shows— to prove herself in the masculine domain of the classics, and the same had been true of Elizabeth Barrett Browning's successive versions of the same work (1833 and 1850). But the imaginative gender reassignment was not all one way. Prometheus' complaints of injustice could sound like expressions of feminist aspiration. Having found feelings of sisterhood in this masculine, classical work, Barrett Browning was able to launch herself into trans-gendering a masculine, classical genre by writing the feminized epic *Aurora Leigh*. Webster likewise makes free with the tradition she had at first mouthed. In her poem 'Circe' she transforms the classical story of entrapment by feminine wiles into a new-womanly parable of male shortcoming.

Katharine Bradley and Edith Cooper combined and trans-gendered themselves into the pseudonym 'Michael Field'. When Michael Field then translated Sappho, the doubling of gender was compounded—the more so because the source texts of the translations (or 'extensions') were for the most part lost. At the head of each page is a fragmentary line or two of Sappho's Greek which is translated as the opening of the English verses. But whom should we think of as being the origin of the lines that follow? Sappho—if they are a reconstruction of her writing? Michael Field—if they represent a masculine imagining of her? Bradley and Cooper—if the imagining is really feminine, and the merging of identities in translation (or is it pseudo-translation?) echoes the merging of their identities in authorship? When we read 'Cyprus' daughter smiles on me at night | Through Hades' mournful myrtles in a dream', 'me' might be any of the above, and Cyprus's Daughter (i.e. Venus) a figure of any of the others (Field 1889: 50). The doubling—no, dissolution—of identity in translation reflects the doubling—no, dissolution—of identity in desire. Bradley and Cooper and Field and Sappho are all one, thanks to the lack of resistance offered by the source. Sappho projects her shadow through Bradley and Cooper and Field; but then she is herself a shadow projected by them.

This exploration of the mutability of the translating self is decadent in tone and time. Similar interests are evident in the ecstasies, first sensuous then religious, that are staged via translation in John Gray's *Silverpoints* (1893) and *Spiritual Poems, Chiefly Done out of Several Languages* (1896). If these works ask to be judged by a norm of fidelity at all, it is only a very loose one. The principle they embody is rather that of personal transformation. The translator is shown to have expanded and dissolved himself through translation; and readers are invited to follow.

Since they represent themselves as being transformed in translation, Field and Gray assimilate translation to romance. They exaggerate and make explicit the possibilities we found to be latent in the *London Journal*. But translation could also be governed by a norm of realism. This was when the source text was taken to be clearly knowable, and when the identities of translator and readers were taken to be reinforced by contact with it. The literal translations in the Bohn library are like this: they offer up the source text as an object of study. And so is Goethe's *Wilhelm Meister's Apprenticeship* translated by Carlyle in 1824.

In the preface, Carlyle warns his readers that there will be no 'romance interest' in the succeeding pages. What he admires in Goethe are the realist qualities of 'keen glances into life and art' and 'minute ... delineation of men', all performed with the coolest narratorial 'indifference' (Carlyle 1899: XXIII, 6–7). Carlyle has aimed to embody the same virtues in his translation: 'to alter any thing was not in my commission'—though, like many others in this period, he takes for granted that some passages should nonetheless be 'dropped as evidently unfit for the English taste' (XXIII, 10). His version is to be a realistic representation of a realist representation of life. It reads like this: 'If the first love is indeed, as I hear it everywhere maintained to be, the most delicious feeling which the heart of man, before it or after, can experience ...' (XXIII, 40). There is none of the Gothic self-abandonment of the version of Richter in this style, but it is not fluently domesticating either. Slight awkwardnesses of idiom ('*the* first love') and the stiff succession of clauses imply a translator who is not deliciously communing with his source but observing it keenly and delineating it minutely. In the opening chapters, Wilhelm is in love with an actress and since she is good at impersonation he cannot be sure that she corresponds with his view of her. When he sees the romance figure of a 'phantom' issuing from her door he is puzzled; but soon a 'letter' makes clear to him that he has been deceived. With its air of hard-won accuracy, Carlyle's style of translation implies that by attending to the letter, one will form a 'correct impression' of Goethe, of one's difference from him, and therefore of one's self (5). Here translation adopts the principle of empirical observation.

In translation as romance, the familiar is transformed by contact with the foreign; in translation as realism, it is all the more clearly defined. Both these modes can work through foreignizing styles; in translation as romance, foreignization indicates an imaginative transformation that has been undergone by the translator and is open to his readers; in translation as realism, it establishes a distance between 'us' and 'them'. Coexisting with these two modes is a third which snakes around them, suggesting deconstructively that their opposition is ill founded because the familiar has been foreign all along. This implication appears sporadically in all sorts of translations (e.g. *The Mysteries of Paris*, Rossetti's *Early Italian Poets*, Browning's *Agamemnon*) and it assumes the consistency of a principle in FitzGerald's *Rubáiyát of Omar Khayyám* (on which see also pp. 101 and 335–7, below). As a model for translating Persian, FitzGerald took the King James Bible, not as being a specially English text (for all that it was at the heart of Anglicanism) but because it preserved 'the Oriental Idiom' while using 'the most idiomatic Saxon *words* to convey the Eastern Metaphor', as he wrote to Mrs Cowell in 1854 (FitzGerald 1980: II, 119). In consequence, the *Rubáiyát* is inseparably foreignizing and domesticating.

In the first edition (reproduced in FitzGerald 1997: 3–23), the poem and day begin with a wake-up call to the presence of Eastern Metaphor: 'Awake! for Morning in the Bowl of Night | Has flung the Stone that puts the Stars to Flight' (in later editions this shock was attenuated by a less conspicuous metaphor: 'who scatter'd into flight | The Stars before him from the Field of Night'). The exotics continue: there are unglossed strange names 'Jamshýd', 'Kaikobád' (stanza 8), and even references that seem familiar turn out to have a foreign aspect. 'The WHITE HAND OF MOSES on the bough' is glossed: 'Exodus iv. 6; where Moses draws forth his Hand—not, according to the Persians, "*leprous as Snow*,"—but *white* as our May-Blossom in Spring perhaps!'—though notice the twist whereby the surprising Persian interpretation is illustrated with an English image (stanza 4). Equally, there are domesticating tactics: stark colloquialisms ('take the Cash in hand') and allusions to Shakespeare: 'Sans Wine, sans Song, sans Singer, and—sans End!'—though again the gesture is complex as the line selected from our national poet is half in French (stanzas 12, 23; compare *As You Like It* II.vii.166). But it is metaphor that, in FitzGerald's hands, most creates disunities within English:

> And this delightful Herb whose tender Green
> Fledges the River's Lip on which we lean—
> Ah, lean upon it lightly! for who knows
> From what once lovely Lip it springs unseen!
> (stanza 19)

Some aspects of this are firmly grounded in English poetry. 'Fledges' is a thoroughly rural word, with its connections to fledglings and sedges and hedges; while the whole stanza has a root in Gray's 'Elegy' ('Full many a flower is born to blush unseen'). But then the extraordinary violence of the image—the river's lip might have a human lip beneath it ('lovely' implies a girl's or a boy's) from which the grass grows like a moustache—upends the English idyll, not only because of what is imagined, but because of how the imagining emerges through the writing. Usually, a metaphor compresses two meanings into one appearance of a word, but FitzGerald deploys the same word twice. This exploits and emphasizes the fact that the same combination of letters can take on different senses in different circumstances. There are boundaries within one language as well as between it and others: 'lip' differs from 'lip' just as 'pain' in English differs from 'pain' in French. Metaphor is etymologically related to translation and in FitzGerald's writing the two become incestuously one. 'Lip' is translated into 'lip'. For once, a translation is literally literal, indeed more than literal: the target is a perfect mirror of its source. But the result is a vertiginous grotesque.

The broadest norm of all regarding translation in this period (and indeed always) is that it should accomplish a transfer out of one language and into another. But, in the *Rubáiyát*, FitzGerald disrupts that assumption. He revels in revealing that languages are not entirely separate and that none of them is whole. English is not all English. It can be translated into itself.

LIST OF SOURCES

Translations
Anon. (1845). *The Mysteries of Paris by Eugène Sue*, 3 vols. London.
Anon. (1846). *It was Time* [Frédéric Soulié]. *London Journal* 3: passim.
Anon. (1888). *The Ladies' Paradise* [Zola]. *London Journal* 77: passim.
Bowring, John (1821–3). *Specimens of the Russian Poets*, 2 vols. London.
—— (1830). *Poetry of the Magyars*. London.
—— (1832). *Cheskian Anthology: Being a History of the Poetical Literature of Bohemia, with Translated Specimens*. London.
Browning, Robert (2000–). *The Complete Works*, 16 vols. to date. Athens, OH.

Burges, George (1852). *The Greek Anthology, as Selected for the Use of Westminster, Eton, and other Public Schools*. London.
Byron, George Gordon, Lord (1807). *Hours of Idleness: A Series of Poems Original and Translated*. Newark.
Carlyle, Thomas (1899). *Works*, 30 vols. London.
Cary, Henry Francis (1814). *The Vision, or, Hell, Purgatory, and Paradise of Dante Alighieri*. London.
Cayley, C. B. (1851). *Dante's Divine Comedy: The Vision of Hell Translated Line for Line in the Original Ternary Rhyme*. London.
Coleridge, Samuel Taylor. (2001). *Plays*, Part 1 (includes *The Piccolomini* and *Wallenstein's Death* [Schiller]). Princeton, NJ (Vol. 16, III, Part 1 of the Princeton *Collected Works* of Coleridge).
Davies, John Fletcher (1868). *The Agamemnon of Aeschylus*. London.
Dayman, John (1843). *The Inferno Translated in the Terza Rima of the Original*. London.
Field, Michael [pseud. Katharine Bradley and Edith Cooper] (1889). *Long Ago* [Sappho]. London.
FitzGerald, Edward (1853). *Six Dramas of Calderon, Freely Translated*. London.
—— (1997). *Rubáiyát of Omar Khayyám: A Critical Edition*, ed. Christopher Decker. Charlottesville, VA.
Griffiths, Eric, and Reynolds, Matthew, eds. (2005). *Dante in English*. London.
Haselfoot, F. K. H. (1887). *The Divina Commedia of Dante Alighieri Translated Line for Line in the Terza Rima of the Original*. London.
Mickle, William Julius (1877). *The Lusiad, or, The Discovery of India*. [Camões] 5th edn., rev. E. Richmond Hodges. London.
Musgrave, George (1893). *Dante's Divine Comedy*. London.
Newman, F. W. (1856). *The Iliad of Homer Faithfully Translated into Unrhymed English Metre*. London.
Paley, F. A. (1864). *Aeschylus Translated into English Prose*. Cambridge.
Rossetti, Dante Gabriel (2003). *Collected Poetry and Prose*, ed. Jerome McGann. New Haven, CT.
Shadwell, Charles Lancelot (1892). *The Purgatory of Dante ... An Experiment in Literal Verse Translation*. London.
Smart, Christopher (1756). *The Works of Horace. Translated Literally into English Prose*, 2 vols. London.
—— (1850). *The Works of Horace. Translated Literally into English Prose*, new edn., rev. Theodore Alois Buckley. London (Bohn).
Tremenheere, J. H. A. (1897). *The Lesbia of Catullus Arranged and Translated*. London.
Webster, Augusta (1866). *The Prometheus Bound of Aeschylus Literally Translated into English Verse*. London.
Williams, Howard (1888). *Lucian's Dialogues*. London (Bohn).

Other Sources
Anon. (1825). 'Roscoe's *Italian Novels.*' *Edinburgh Review* 42: 174–206.
Arnold, Matthew (1960). *On the Classical Tradition*, ed. R. H. Super. Ann Arbor, MI.
Chevasco, Berry Palmer (2003). *Mysterymania: The Reception of Eugène Sue in Britain 1838–1860*. Berne.
Coleridge, Samuel Taylor (1983). *Biographia Literaria*, ed. James Engell and W. Jackson Bate. Princeton, NJ (Vol. 7 of the Princeton *Collected Works* of Coleridge).

Cordasco, Francesco (1951). *The Bohn Libraries: A History and a Checklist.* New York.
[Donne, W. B.] (1857) 'Calderon.' *Fraser's Magazine* 55: 455–70.
Dryden, John (1987). *The Works*, Vol. 5: *The Works of Virgil in English 1697*, ed. William Frost and Vinton A. Dearing. Berkeley, CA.
FitzGerald, Edward (1980). *The Letters of Edward FitzGerald*, ed. A. McK. Terhune and A. B. Terhune, 4 vols. Princeton, NJ.
Hermans, Theo (1996). 'Norms and the Determination of Translation. A Theoretical Framework', pp. 25–51 in Román Álvarez and M. Carmen-África Vidal, eds., *Translation, Power, Subversion*. Clevedon.
King, Andrew (2004). *The London Journal 1845–83: Periodicals, Production and Gender*. Aldershot.
[Moir, George] (1835) 'Glassford's *Lyrical Translations*.' *Edinburgh Review* 60: 353–63.
Nida, Eugene (2000). 'Principles of Correspondence', pp. 126–40 in Lawrence Venuti, ed., *The Translation Studies Reader*. London.
Reynolds, Matthew (2003). 'Browning and Translationese.' *Essays in Criticism* 53: 97–128.
Schleiermacher, Friedrich (1992). 'On the Different Methods of Translating', tr. Waltraud Bartscht, pp. 36–54 in Rainer Schulte and John Biguenet, eds., *Theories of Translation: An Anthology of Essays from Dryden to Derrida*. Chicago.
Shelley, Percy Bysshe (1988). *Shelley's Prose, or, The Trumpet of a Prophecy*, ed. David Lee Clark. London.
Sue, Eugène (*c.*1844). *Les Mystères de Paris*. Paris.
Toury, Gideon (1995). *Descriptive Translation Studies and Beyond*. Amsterdam.
[Tytler, Alexander Fraser] (1791). *Essay on the Principles of Translation*. London (rev. edn., Edinburgh, 1831).
Venuti, Lawrence (1995). *The Translator's Invisibility: A History of Translation*. London.

3
The Translator

3.1	**Professionals** *Margaret Lesser*	85
3.2	**Amateurs and Enthusiasts** *Peter France*	98
3.3	**Writers** *Stephen Prickett and Peter France*	105
3.4	**Academics** *Adrian Poole*	117
3.5	**Women** *Susanne Stark*	125

3.1 Professionals

Margaret Lesser

This chapter is concerned with the careers of the men and women who made the translations, their social situation and motivation, the part translation played in their lives. They are presented in five groups: the professionals, for whom translation offered a way of earning at least a partial living; the amateurs and enthusiasts, for whom it was above all a pastime or a passion; the major literary figures, for whom it was only a part of their writing activity; the academics, whose translations were an extension and an application of their scholarly work; and finally the women, for whom translation might present particular possibilities. These categories overlap considerably—members of all five groups might receive payment for translation, some of the 'amateurs and enthusiasts' had ambitions as writers, and women might be professionals, amateurs, or writers, though hardly ever academics. Nevertheless, each category represents a distinctive approach to the work of translation. We begin with the professionals.

Definitions and Status

With the expansion of popular reading and theatregoing (see §§ 8.1, 8.2, below), publishers and theatre managements increasingly needed translators who could be called on when required in return for payment—professionals, in short, although in the field of translation 'professional' is never an easy term to define. Even the jobbing translators of the earlier years were not necessarily uncommitted to the texts they handled, while some late nineteenth-century translators (professionals in the modern sense) were as eager to introduce Russian literature, for example, as Carlyle had been to introduce German. Conversely, even the most committed of the 'non-professionals' might well be interested in material rewards.

Few professionals translated full-time before the latter part of the century. Fewer still placed their major ambitions in translation: they often saw themselves as novelists, poets, or dramatists who translated to supplement their incomes. Alternatively, translation might be the more creative leaven in lives otherwise occupied by teaching or the law. Some, like Hazlitt's son William,[1] began their careers with translation and largely abandoned it when they could get more regular work; others, like the schoolmaster William Robson (1785–1863), only adopted the translating life when they had fallen on hard times. They were always a heterogeneous group: even when inadequate translations often passed muster, as in the

---

[1] For biographical notices on the more important translators discussed in this and the following sections of this chapter, see Ch. 12, below.

earlier years of the period, there were always some professionals who did better work, while the new craftsmen of the 1890s coexisted with others who were considerably less skilled.

The texts they worked on were equally varied. The best-selling novels of each period naturally gave much employment, but they were far from being the only material for the professionals, who also handled memoirs of contemporary notables, travel books, histories, and much else. In the theatre they translated not only plays but libretti. Many ranged over various genres and worked with several languages. The numerous, and often prolific, translators of classical literature, whether aiming at the schoolboy or the general reader, were often clerics, schoolmasters, or academics who confined themselves to that area, but classical texts were also handled by 'mixed' translators such as Theodore Martin (Catullus and Horace, as well as Goethe, Dante, and others) or Walter Keating Kelly (Catullus and Petronius, as well as Michelet, Cervantes, Ranke), and by all-purpose writers, like the largely self-taught Theodore Buckley, who not only translated Aeschylus, Homer, and Euripides, but edited both classical and English texts and wrote, among other things, *The Boy's First Help to Reading* (1854) and *The Natural History of Tuft-Hunters and Toadies* (1848). Broadly speaking, it was not until the end of the century that specialists began to adopt translation as a serious profession of choice, concentrating on single authors, genres, or languages.

For much of the period jobbing translators attracted little respect or even notice; in the earlier years they were frequently anonymous. This was not entirely a consequence of their low status. Anonymity and pseudonymity—for authors (sometimes even publishers) as well as translators—were more common generally than they are today, particularly for novels and other prose genres, and were often seen as protection, rather than neglect. As the century progressed, anonymity became largely confined to potboilers, although right up to the 1900s it sometimes reflected a translator's reluctance to be identified with possibly immoral works, such as Daudet's *Sapho*, published in two anonymous translations in 1886. Indeed for the 'bolder' books in the London publisher J. M. Dent's complete edition of Balzac's *Comédie humaine* (1895–8), Ellen Marriage, its chief translator, adopted the male pseudonym of 'James Waring', according to one of Dent's employees (Swinnerton 1956: 67–8).

In the theatre the low status of the translator manifested itself differently: much stress was laid on the fact that works had been not merely translated but 'adapted' or 'altered' for English tastes, so as to produce something new (see § 8.2, below). There were some translators in the classic sense of the term, such as the German drama specialist Benjamin Thompson (1776?–1816), even in the first half of the century, but many who 'translated' were essentially men of the theatre quarrying in German or French plays for exploitable plots and 'pathetic or humorous situations', as Macready advised Bulwer Lytton to do in 1838 (Shattuck 1958: 82).

There was a general awareness throughout the period that translation, particularly from French, was a buyers' market. Though the profession might confer little prestige, it attracted several overlapping groups, including would-be writers, linguists of various sorts, and women—or rather ladies, whose education normally included a modern language and whose options for non-dependent work were notoriously limited (translation had many obvious advantages over governessing). Many, both male and female, could see themselves as qualified for the work, since most language teaching relied heavily on translation exercises, as it had since Roger Ascham and before. Consequently publishers were beset by applicants throughout the period, ranging from future celebrities like J. G. Lockhart, who in 1816 asked Blackwood for translations to pay his travelling expenses in Germany, to an unknown Annie Garstin, who in 1897 offered Richard Bentley translations of 'many Swedish novels superior to Miss Bremer'.[2]

In the early years of our period it was rare for reviews or publishers' advertisements to comment on the quality of professional translations, but by the 1850s Bohn, among others, was regularly mentioning translators' names in his advertising, while by 1887 T. Y. Crowell and Co. of New York were positively promoting their *Les Misérables* with a quotation from the *National Republican*: 'The name of the translator is sufficient guaranty... Miss Hapgood becomes one with her author.' In 1896 the publicity for Dent's *Comédie humaine* stressed, as a selling point, that 'the translations of Miss Ellen Marriage and her co-labourers... have received the highest praises for the admirable manner in which the flavour and piquancy of the language are preserved'. In some areas at least, professional translators were beginning to be noticed.

Pay, Conditions, and Recruitment

As a profession, translation was always uncertain. For the better known the remuneration could be reasonable. In 1833, for instance, the highly regarded Frederic Shoberl received £50 from Richard Bentley (not known for his generosity) for his translation of Hugo's *Notre-Dame de Paris* (1833). The novel is 466 pages long in this English edition; it might have taken Shoberl anything from 50 to 150 or more working days, depending on his speed and assiduity. At seventy-two days he would have been receiving some £4 3s. a week, at a time when 'a family was thought to be "respectable" if it had a weekly income of £2. 8s' (Altick 1957: 276). But the supply of work was often fitful; in 1835 Isabel Hill, who had translated Mme de Staël's *Corinne* for Bentley a few years earlier with considerable commercial success, earned less than £14 by translation. Moreover, translations of books with uncertain sales were often accepted on the 'half-profits' system (half each to publisher and translator after all expenses had been paid), which meant that payment was always delayed and often small or non-existent.

Fees varied according to the publisher, the probable popularity of the book, and the reputation of the translator. By 1847 Bentley was offering Mary Howitt, already a successful translator, £250 for a three-volume novel by Sophie von Knorring, but the unknown Charles Cocks was offered only £53 12s. for Scribe's 400-page *Piquillo Alliaga* in the same year. In 1858 J. R. Planché, very well known

---

[2] Here and in what follows unreferenced quotations are from the relevant publishers' archives.

in the theatre, received £240 for his translation of *Four-and-Twenty Fairy Tales* from Routledge (Mumby 1934: 75), whereas six years later Bentley paid one A. Baillot only £120 for J. H. Michon's three-volume *The Nun*.

In the last third of the century fees rose overall, but translations of works not certain to be profitable were often still poorly paid. Ernest Dowson and Havelock Ellis received only £50 each for Zola's *La Terre* and *Germinal* (both 1894) in the Lutetian Society's unexpurgated 'private' edition. Constance Garnett too received only £40 from Heinemann for Goncharov's *A Common Story* (283 pages) in 1893—but this was at the beginning of both her career and the Russian boom. For *War and Peace* (1904) she was paid £300 but until the last minute had been left in doubt whether the project would go ahead or whether Heinemann would simply buy in sheets of a recent American translation. In 1901 she 'had no further translations in prospect' (Garnett 1991: 192), despite having already established a considerable reputation with her Turgenev and Tolstoy translations, and was anxious for work of any kind, whether revision or translation proper.

There was obviously a strong incentive to work as fast as possible while work was available. Ernest Vizetelly (son of the popular publisher Henry Vizetelly), who knew this world from both the translator's and the publisher's standpoint, observed that 'the prices paid for translations are usually so low that few men of real ability are willing to undertake them'. The work often had to be 'done hastily, in a rough and ready manner' (Vizetelly 1904: 386–7), not only to earn a living but also for copyright reasons, and the effects of haste can be seen throughout the period.

In the early years particularly, and for cheap editions throughout the period, many publishers took little care in their recruitment of translators, using whoever was to hand—Cassell, for example, casually committed Blanc's *Histoire des peintres de toutes les écoles* to 'the gentlemen composing his editorial staff' (Nowell-Smith 1958: 37) in 1852—or acting on self-proposals or recommendations. 'Please if you have any work in the way of Russian translation ever in your hands think of Tchaikovsky. Mrs Wilson would be very glad to get any translation from the French to do', is a typical request, in this case from Olive Schreiner to Havelock Ellis in 1888 (Draznin 1992: 443). Recommendations from the originator of the text obviously carried more weight, although those described as 'authorized translators' were not necessarily vetted by publisher or author. Some authors exercised their power of veto; 'a person who started off with *alterations*', wrote George Sand in 1848, 'did not seem best placed to ask me to guarantee the fidelity of her translation' (Sand 1964–95: VIII, 258)—but many, then as now, were either unable or unwilling to check.

Gradually publishers became more aware of the importance of finding good translators. By the end of the century some, such as Vizetelly or Routledge, who handled many foreign best-sellers, had lists of regular translators (who often worked anonymously). Others, on both sides of the Atlantic, were finding that serious translation projects brought prestige and so recruited for them with more care. In the 1880s, for example, after T. Y. Crowell's surprise successes with *Anna*

Karenina and *War and Peace*, he 'was the first publisher anywhere to understand how profitable it would be to publish a uniform edition of Tolstoy' and recruited accordingly (Tebbel 1975: 368). In the 1890s, even more painstakingly, J. M. Dent recruited Professor George Saintsbury to gather a team of crack professional translators for a complete *Comédie humaine*. (In 1903 Methuen even produced a collected edition, all translated by Alfred Allinson, of Dumas's works—which, as best-sellers, had often been rushed out with very little care in earlier years.) Editorial values became more important: Saintsbury even focused on details of house style, writing to one of his team: 'A word on titles. I have not allowed your "Comte" etc. in the Sceaux Ball ... The more excellent way is to translate when the title alone is used.' Less superficially, the unexpurgated Lutetian Society edition of Zola required translators to conform in other ways: Teixeira de Mattos was engaged to 'hold [the translators] up rigorously round the editorial boat', though 'like hooked fish we struggled desperately to escape the ultra-literal in places' (Plarr 1914: 96).

The Early Years

After this overview of the conditions under which translators worked, we shall now consider the way in which the profession developed over the century, using particular case histories by way of example. At the beginning of the century, there was a clearly defined demand for journeyman translators to satisfy the popular demand for romance, exciting theatre, memoirs, or history, but the definition of the translator's task was less clear. As has been mentioned, adaptation was usually the aim for drama translators, but book translators too might take considerable liberties with the source text, to suit supposed 'English tastes' or simply their own or their publishers' convenience. Thus the Revd Charles Swan removes about a third of Manzoni's *Promessi sposi* in his 1828 translation, and Elizabeth Gunning frankly describes *The Foresters* (1796) as 'A Novel. Altered from the French'. It was usually taken for granted that translators would bowdlerize indecencies. They might also incorporate previous versions, a practice that lasted well into the century, as cheerfully acknowledged by John Oxenford, referring to an unidentified translation: 'The Translator ... found many successful renderings in the work of his predecessor, and these he has engrafted without hesitation' (Oxenford 1848: iii). At the start of the century this labour-saving device was too common to be worth mentioning.

Latin, French, and sometimes Italian were taught in the schoolrooms of the educated classes, but there was a shortage of British translators who knew German, so that the German vogue (see § 6.1, below) presented something of a problem. This was alleviated partly by translating from French versions and partly by using émigrés whose mother tongue was not English. These—they included translators of French, German, and both languages—were sometimes aware that the target language might present difficulties. In 1809 Daniel Boileau, for example, touchingly hopes that 'the severity of criticism will be tempered by the consideration that the omnipotence of parliament, which admits a foreigner to the invaluable benefits of the British constitution, does not initiate him into the knowledge of the... countless beauties of the English language' (Boileau 1809: I, viii). Some émigrés, including Boileau himself, succeeded reasonably well, if with a certain stiffness. (He translated nine books and, like various other émigrés, also produced a number of 'courses of instruction' in French and German to supplement the limited dictionaries and grammars then available to translators.) Others needed extensive revision, but did not always get it.

The translators included many casual workers, each of whom might translate only a few Cottin romances here, a *Corinne* there. Many clearly had literary or (above all) theatrical ambitions, to judge from their original published works, but are otherwise obscure. However, there is a record of one—Isabel Hill—who is perhaps not unrepresentative of the least fortunate. An obituary memoir by her brother indicates the pattern. In 1823 'a prose Tale and a poem... received most favourable mention, and visions of fame and fortune often arose in both our minds, but as though to check the ardour of her Genius... the Publisher failed'. Plays, novels, and anthologies were rarely more productive; the only substantial rewards came from her translations, including de Staël's *Corinne*, although the translator's station was made very plain:

L. E. L. [a fashionable London poet, Letitia Landon] had already converted the Improvisings of the heroine into blank verse; of this fact my sister was not aware till after she had closely imitated the *rhymes* of Corinne and rendered them as like the French versions as the difference between the two languages would allow. She learnt at the same time that L. E. L.'s version, having been paid for, *must* be introduced. (Hill 1842: 85, 91)

Perhaps as a feeble gesture of personal rebellion—or influenced by the literary taste of the 1830s, now that the early enthusiasm for *Corinne* had cooled—Hill peppers the text with carping 'translator's footnotes' such as:

A religious moral English gentlewoman propose a romantic falsehood! This anti-national inconsistency neutralises all the rest of Mme de Staël's satire!
If this was Corinne's first English dinner, how did she know the *usual* time for retiring!
(Hill 1833: II, 300, 235)

Fortunately this habit was not common among translators, unlike the small inaccuracies which sprinkle Hill's text. (It nevertheless went into at least three further editions and was still being reprinted in New York in 1882.)

Hill did relatively few translations and died in distress; others were more successful, artistically or personally. There were respectable craftsmen on a small scale, like the solicitor Edgar Taylor, a pioneer of early German literature who translated the Grimms' stories in 1823 (see p. 396, below), *Lays of the Minnesingers* in 1825, and *Master Wace* in 1837, or the miscellaneous writer Anne Plumptre, who dealt competently with books on literature, travel, and history, as well as several Kotzebue plays. Others, like Shoberl, were full-time translators and all-purpose writers. But the professionals who made the most impact were those who insured against powerlessness by acting as editors as well as translators. The most notable of these were perhaps Thomas Roscoe and William Hazlitt the younger, both of whom were well placed to commission translations as well as making them. Both had been precipitated into the translating life by their fathers' financial failures and were sustained in it, at least at first, by their fathers' literary contacts. The distinguished writer William Roscoe had 'failed' in 1816, from which time Thomas entered on a busy career, translating Silvio Pellico, Benvenuto Cellini, and others, while at the same time editing many works, including series of Spanish, Italian, and German novels. Hazlitt the essayist had already separated from his wife eight years before he died in 1830, leaving his son at 19 untrained and penniless. The son's great aim was a permanent post, which he did not achieve until in 1854 he became a registrar in the London Bankruptcy Court. While waiting, he worked as a journalist and made many translations, including the historians Guizot and Thierry as well as the 'naughty' Paul de Kock and a *Notre-Dame* (1833) which had three more chapters than any other translation, as he asked Leigh Hunt to stress in his review. His main editorial work was his Romancist and Novelist's Library, an inexpensive periodical in which translations were 'a very important feature' (letter to Leigh Hunt, cited in Gates 1998: 344). For twenty-four years he personified the professional translator-*littérateur*, although he was always (according to his son) looking for safer employment.

Artistically, his success was vitiated above all by the period's besetting weakness, literalism (on which see further Ch. 2, above). To some extent this was deliberate, though the need for speed no doubt made polishing difficult. Professional translators of the classics were of course often aiming to produce teaching tools (or cribs) and advertised their 'literal translations' as such, but others too clung to the letter of the source text for safety. 'The doubt whether the traditional story of the origin of Rome is history is not a doubt of yesterday' (Hazlitt 1847: iii) is fairly characteristic of Hazlitt's at times owlish translating style. It is easy to see why the highest praise for the Constance Garnetts of later years usually took the form: 'It does not read like a translation.'

Mid-Century: Expansion

From the point of view of the professional translator, the middle years of the century were marked by two developments in particular: the arrival of popular successes in an increasing number of languages and the demand for multiple translations of best-sellers in the cheaper editions which were now technically possible and marketable to an ever-widening public (see Ch. 4, below). The new languages were still often tackled by relay translation (thus Hans Christian Andersen and Turgenev, for instance, provided work for translators from German and French), but it was now widely accepted that the practice was not ideal. In 1846 Joseph C. James, editor of the ambitious (but ultimately unsuccessful) new Library of Foreign Romance, published in sixpenny weekly parts for a wide readership, made a special point of direct translation: 'We shall not venture to incur a double risk of misconception and enervation by *translating translations*. Our Swedish novels will not be taken from the German, nor our German from the French; but writers familiarly versed in these several topics will be engaged' (preface to Barrow 1846: 6). In many cases this remained a pious hope, but gradually translators emerged who were prepared (if not always well equipped) to tackle a variety of 'rare' languages.

The day-to-day working life of one of these, Mary Howitt, is conveniently documented in the correspondence of Fredrika Bremer, the popular Swedish novelist, even if her working experience was somewhat exceptional. Unlike many in the profession, Mary and her husband William came of non-literary, non-metropolitan stock. In the 1830s they decided on literary careers, but soon found that their original work would need to be supplemented by translation. For this purpose they taught themselves German, which gave access to various popular domestic novelists as well as the increasingly popular Hans Andersen. In the 1840s Mary spotted the potential of Bremer and 'embarked a considerable capital' on translating her, at a time when 'not a person could be found who dared undertake the risk of publication' (Howitt 1843: v). She had taught herself Swedish, which she claimed to find delightfully easy after German. Bremer was polite—'No matter if some words are mistaken when the life and heart are there!' (Bremer 1996: 36)—though confiding to third parties that Howitt's knowledge was 'very imperfect'. The inaccuracies in Howitt's version of the non-fiction *Homes of the New World* (1853) actually produced complaints. Bremer published a disclaimer, which in its turn provoked a resentful letter to *The Times* from Howitt. Nevertheless the author stuck to her translator, excusing her mistakes and periodically supplying her with useful vocabulary and explanations. By the end Howitt, together with her husband, had translated over twenty of her works (see pp. 288–9, below) and was never really challenged as the authorized translator, despite the fact that from the 1840s onwards various others tried to climb on the bandwagon, to Howitt's considerable indignation.

As understood by Bremer, the translator's task was not straightforward. Speed was often essential. Usually the translator worked from proofs, but in time of need she might be faced with manuscript—'a little difficult to read, as the paper was too thin'. There were many late emendations. Moreover she was expected, on occasion, to eliminate word repetitions on her own initiative, make suggestions about the plot, and remove redundancies (Bremer 1996: 62, 101, 124, 156). Some of these features were peculiar to the Howitt–Bremer relationship; others, such as the need for speed and the late emendations, remained standard throughout the century.

Inaccuracies too were not uncommon; dictionaries and grammars were available for most of the languages facing journeyman translators, but they were often misleading or inconvenient; Brisman's Swedish *Handlexicon* of 1801, for example, has 670 pages on the English–Swedish side, but only 170 in the opposite direction. Libraries, for more extensive research, were only just becoming accessible to the general public: the London Library in 1841, the Reading Room of the British Museum in 1857, American and English public libraries in the second half of the century. The more conscientious used these facilities; over the years several applied for readers' tickets to the British Museum. Some, too, consulted native speakers—even, occasionally, translating 'with the assistance of the author' (Hardman 1854). But most translation could, it was felt, be done at home—that was one of its attractions to women—either alone or, if the translator was lucky, in circumstances like those described much later by Havelock Ellis: '[In our Cornish cottage] I dictated the translation while [my wife] wrote the whole ... in her swift, clear handwriting, without weariness or complaint, now and then bettering my translation of dialogue with some more idiomatic phrase' (Ellis 1940: 274).

Swedish was not the only new adventure. More translators began to engage, directly or indirectly, with the languages of Eastern Europe: J. M. D. Meiklejohn, primarily an educationalist, ventured into Turgenev (via French) in 1855 (*Russian Life in the Interior*) and the American diplomat Eugene Schuyler followed him with a direct translation of *Fathers and Sons* in 1867. German was increasingly popular—not only the domestic novels handled by Mary Howitt, but (for smaller audiences) Goethe, Schiller, and Heine, who provided work for Edgar Bowring, R. D. Boylan, and John Oxenford among others. As for genre, there was a strong demand for travel and history, particularly Michelet and Guizot, supplied by such translators as Frederick Hardman, G. H. Smith, and the prolific Sir Andrew Scoble, who dealt with seven Guizots and a Mignet, as well as three Mérimées (see § 11.3, below). But undoubtedly it was the big best-sellers which engaged the majority of the journeymen. Many were anonymous, but Dumas's named translators in mid-century alone included William Robson, William Barrow, Henry Llewellyn Williams, Franz Demmler, and Emma Hardy. Both Sue and Sand occupied many translators; *Notre-Dame* attracted Hazlitt, Shoberl, and Henry Llewellyn Williams, while the authorized translator of *Les Misérables*, Lascelles Wraxall, also englished many other popular texts by Edmond About, Gustave Aimard, and others.

Many of the best-seller translations were poor or at least patchy (and particularly in their lowest 'Penny Popular' versions often presented in execrable type on the cheapest paper). Literalism was still rife. One version of *Les Trois Mousquetaires* faced entertainment-seeking readers with: 'His mother ... was waiting for him with the famous recipe of which the counsels we have just repeated would necessitate the so frequent employment' (Robson 1853: 3)—and it would not be difficult to cite many comparable passages.

Late Century: Mass-Producers and the 'New Breed'

It was in the 1870s that full-time translators began to appear in some numbers, although the majority of professionals still combined their translating activities with original writing or some quite different occupation. Thus Henry Llewellyn Williams, translator or adaptor of at least fifty-six works, following popular taste from Dumas to Émile Gaboriau, also wrote some thirty-seven of his own, on topics ranging from *Gay Life in New York* (1866) to *The Elephant Tamer* (1890). The same pattern was usually followed, if less energetically, by the many translators of

Jules Verne, Victor Cherbuliez, Georges Ohnet, and other best-sellers. Translators of less popular works were still often members of the professions or, now that modern languages were beginning to be taken seriously at boys' schools, language masters. (One of the more distinguished of these was Henri van Laun, whose achievements included Taine's *History of English Literature* in 1871, a six-volume *Dramatic Works of Molière*, 1875–6, and *Gil Blas*, 1886—all produced while he was successively a master at three prestigious schools and an examiner for the Civil Service Commission.)

But full-timers were beginning to be seen. Clara Bell, for instance, wrote nothing of her own but translated at least fifty-six full-length books (some in two or more volumes) between 1876 and 1906. Many of these were solid, 'researched' historical romances by the German Egyptologist Georg Ebers and others (very popular for a period, particularly in America, where Bell's counterpart was Mary Safford). But she was also called on to translate Maupassant, Loti, and Huysmans, as well as Galdós, Couperus, and Firenzuola, from Spanish, Dutch, and Italian. A professional in the modern sense, she could be relied on to complete Moltke's *Franco-German War* in the year of his death (1891) when it was topical, and would, when required, turn her hand to short monographs on painters, or even an illustrated *Cats and Kittens* (1894). She must have seemed an ideal choice when Saintsbury was recruiting his team for the *Comédie humaine* of 1895, but the habit of haste proved difficult to throw off; there are still disquieting inaccuracies, and the old woodenness has not been completely banished.

Bell's contributions to the *Comédie* contrast with those of Ellen Marriage, who belonged to the next generation. By the 1890s there was a new serious-mindedness regarding modern languages in schools and universities, which would bear fruit in the following century. Women, moreover, who were increasingly prominent in translation, were beginning to receive university educations. Constance Garnett, one of the new breed, was a graduate (in classics) of Cambridge, and fully conscious of the need for systematic study and knowledgeable native contacts (on Garnett's Turgenev see p. 14, above, and pp. 314–16, below).

For much of the century languages outside the juvenile curriculum had been 'mastered' (or not) by turning to grammars and dictionaries—or indeed translation itself; as late as 1887 Havelock Ellis was 'not ashamed' of his (published) translation of *Florentine Nights*, 'done for my own instruction when I was learning German out of Heine' (Ellis 1940: 164). Garnett herself began to study Russian in this fashion, but after two years of practice, consultation with Russian exiles, and even publishing versions of Goncharov and Turgenev, she still felt that her translations needed checking. 'Now that I have a prospect of permanent work as a translator', she wrote to her collaborator Sergey Stepniak in 1893, 'I absolutely must have help I can rely upon in correcting my work. I should like to make a definite *business* arrangement (paying a certain percentage of what I receive to my coadjutor). Could you do this for me?' Twenty per cent was agreed on; she was still regularly consulting native Russians in 1900 and probably (to a lesser extent) throughout her career (Garnett 1991: 76, 109).

Garnett was a particularly conscientious craftsman, but for others too, seriousness was in the air, aided by an enormous improvement in dictionaries, both general and specialized. Ernest Vizetelly, the translator of Zola, prided himself on his research: 'The English version of *Travail* necessitated the perusal of several textbooks on metallurgy and a visit to some large English steel works. An American version of the same book was made by a person who did not take that precaution, with the result that it literally bristled with technical errors' (Vizetelly 1904: 387). The expertise of the American Nathan Haskell Dole, best known for translating (in the 1880s) the newly discovered Tolstoy (see pp. 316–17, below), now seems doubtful; when pressed for time he was still, though apologetically, using 'an anonymous French paraphrase of *Anna Karenina* ... in a few passages, but always with the Russian original at hand' and, like the easygoing cutters of earlier years, 'more or less modifying' certain scenes whose 'realism is too intense for our Puritan tastes' (Dole 1886b: iii). Nevertheless he devotes many pages of his introductions to debating translation principles: 'No attempt has been made to make smooth, easy reading: the effort has been rather to reproduce the crisp, sharp staccato of the Russian. When Count Tolstoi says *On shol, shol*, the rendering is: *He went, went* ... Of course the [resultant] style is crabbed and will very likely invite criticism' (Dole 1887: ii).

By the end of the century overall expectations had risen; among others, Garnett, Isabel Hapgood, and Louise and Aylmer Maude were applying more rigorous standards to Russian, William Archer to the Norwegian of Ibsen, Teixeira de Mattos to Dutch, Ellen Marriage and Katharine Prescott Wormeley to French. However, it would be a mistake to think that the old ways were changed at a stroke. 'Heinemann has a most unfortunate system', writes Garnett in 1900, 'of giving translation work to quite incompetent persons who don't know English—and then giving their unintelligible translations to be revised to Edward [her husband], who does not know the original languages. I feel for the poor authors almost as much as for the reviser' (Garnett 1991: 192).

As might be expected, the nineteenth-century professionals left little lasting mark on the Anglo-Saxon literary consciousness. Many of the best-sellers which occupied them have rarely been read in more recent times except by historians. The authors who have stayed in the canon are now usually better read in more recent versions, although a few of the 'new breed', notably Constance Garnett, are still satisfying. On the other hand, the professionals, along with the other categories of translator discussed in the rest of this chapter, were immensely influential in bringing the non-anglophone world to a readership which expanded throughout the century in both Britain and America as literacy became widespread and eventually universal. From the 1830s, when Chartist newspapers were introducing their proletarian readers to George Sand, Eugène Sue, and Victor Hugo, to the turn of the century, when autodidacts such as the music critic Neville Cardus, for example, were steeping themselves in the Goncourts, Huysmans, and Dostoevsky, professional translators played a vital role in bringing continental writing to the English-speaking countries.

LIST OF SOURCES

Translations

Archer, William (1906–12). *The Collected Works of Henrik Ibsen*, 12 vols. London.
Barrow, William (1846). *The Three Musketeers* [Dumas]. London.
Bell, Clara (1885). *Serapis* [Ebers]. New York.
—— et al. (1895–8). *Comédie humaine* [Balzac], 40 vols. London (includes many volumes translated by Ellen Marriage).
Boileau, Daniel (1809). *Letters and Reflections of the Austrian Field-Marshal Prince de Ligne*, 2 vols. London.
Dole, Nathan Haskell (1886a). *The Great Masters of Russian Literature in the Nineteenth Century*. New York.
—— (1886b). *Anna Karénina* [Tolstoy]. New York.
—— (1887). *Ivan Ilyitch and Other Stories* [Tolstoy]. New York.
Dowson, Ernest (1894). *La Terre* [Zola]. London.
Ellis, Havelock (1887). *The Prose Writings of Heinrich Heine*. London.
—— (1894). *Germinal* [Zola]. London.
Garnett, Constance (1894). *A Common Story* [Goncharov]. London.
—— (1901–4). *The Novels of Leo Tolstoy*, 6 vols. London.
Hapgood, Isabel (1887). *Les Misérables* [Hugo]. New York.
—— (1903–4). *The Novels and Stories of Iván Turgénieff*, 16 vols. New York.
Hardman, Frederick (1854). *History of the French Protestant Refugees* [Weiss]. Edinburgh.
Hazlitt, William (1833). *Notre-Dame* [Hugo]. London.
—— (1847). *History of the Roman Republic* [Michelet]. London.
Hill, Isabel (1833). *Corinne* [de Staël]. London.
Howitt, Mary (1843). *The President's Daughters* [Bremer]. London.
—— (1852–3). *Fredrika Bremer's Works*, 4 vols. London.
Kelly, Walter Keating (1842). *The History of the Popes* [Ranke]. London.
—— (1855). *The Heptameron of Margaret, Queen of Navarre*. London.
Meiklejohn, J. M. D. (1855). *Russian Life in the Interior, or, The Experiences of a Sportsman* [Turgenev]. London.
Oxenford, John (1848). *The Auto-biography of Goethe: Truth and Poetry: From my own Life*. London.
Plumptre, Anne (1798). *The Natural Son* [Kotzebue]. London.
—— (1805). *A Historical Relation of the Plague at Marseilles* [Bertrand]. London.
Robson, William (1853). *The Three Musketeers* [Dumas]. London.
Roscoe, Thomas (1832). *The Spanish Novelists*. London.
—— (1833). *My Imprisonments* [Pellico]. London.
Shoberl, Frederic (1833). *The Hunchback of Notre-Dame* [Hugo]. London.
—— (1838). *The History of the French Revolution* [Thiers]. London.
Swan, Charles (1828). *The Betrothed Lovers* [Manzoni]. Pisa.
Taylor, Edgar (1823). *German Popular Stories* [Grimm]. London.
Teixeira de Mattos, Alexander, and Dowson, Ernest (1894). *Majesty* [Couperus]. London.
Thompson, Benjamin (1801). *The German Theatre*. London.
Vizetelly, Ernest (1901). *Work* [Zola]. London.
Williams, Henry Llewellyn (1869). *Mysteries of Paris* [Sue]. London.
—— (1884). *Warrant No. 113* [Gaboriau]. London.

Wormeley, Katharine Prescott (1885–93). *The Comedy of Human Life* [Balzac], 7 vols. Boston, MA.
—— (1899). *Memoirs of the Duc de Saint-Simon*. Boston, MA.
Wraxall, Lascelles (1862). *Les Misérables* [Hugo]. London.
—— (1864). *The Smuggler Chief* [Aimard]. London.

Other Sources
Altick, Richard D. (1957). *The English Common Reader: A Social History of the Mass Reading Public, 1800–1900*. Chicago, IL.
Archer, Charles (1931). *William Archer: Life, Work and Friendships*. London.
Bates, E. Stuart (1936). *Modern Translation*. London.
Black, Alistair (1996). *A New History of the English Public Library*. London.
Bremer, Fredrika (1996). *Brev*, ed. Carina Burman. Stockholm.
Collison, Robert (1982). *A History of Foreign-Language Dictionaries*. London.
Cross, Nigel (1985). *The Common Writer: Life in Nineteenth-Century Grub Street*. London.
Draznin, Yaffa Claire, ed. (1992). *'My Other Self': Letters of Olive Schreiner and Havelock Ellis, 1884–1920*. New York.
Ellis, Havelock (1940). *My Life*. London.
Garnett, Richard (1991). *Constance Garnett: A Heroic Life*. London.
Gates, Eleanor M., ed. (1998). *Leigh Hunt: A Life in Letters*. Essex, CT.
Hazlitt, W. C. (1897). *Four Generations of a Literary Family*. London.
Hill, Benson (1842). 'Memoir of the Authoress', in Isabel Hill, *Brian, the Probationer*. London.
Howitt, Mary (1889). *Mary Howitt: An Autobiography*, ed. Margaret Howitt. London.
Lee, Amice (1955). *Laurels and Rosemary: The Life of William and Mary Howitt*. London.
Mumby, Frank Arthur (1934). *The House of Routledge, 1834–1934. With a History of Kegan Paul, Trench, Trübner and Other Associated Firms*. London.
Nowell-Smith, Simon (1958). *The House of Cassell, 1848–1958*. London.
Plarr, Victor (1914). *Ernest Dowson, 1888–1897: Reminiscences, Unpublished Letters and Marginalia*. London.
Sand, George (1964–95). *Correspondance*, ed. Georges Lubin, 26 vols. Paris.
Shattuck, Charles H. (1958). *Bulwer and Macready: A Chronicle of the Early Victorian Theatre*. Urbana, IL.
Sutherland, J. A. (1976). *Victorian Novelists and Publishers*. London.
Swinnerton, Frank (1937). *Swinnerton: An Autobiography*. London.
—— (1956). *Background with Chorus*. London.
Tebbel, John (1975). *A History of Book Publishing in the United States*, Vol. 2: *The Expansion of an Industry, 1865–1919*. New York.
Vizetelly, Ernest (1899). *With Zola in England*. London.
—— (1904). *Émile Zola, Novelist and Reformer*. London.

3.2 Amateurs and Enthusiasts

Peter France

Amateurs and Professionals

As is clear from the previous section, even those who translated for a living rarely worked at it full-time. In addition, many translations were done by people from a variety of backgrounds for whom translation was less a source of income than a pastime or a private passion; indeed, many of the most celebrated literary translations of the nineteenth century were the work of men and women who can best be described as amateurs or enthusiasts. This was notably the case with the translation of poetry, not generally a serious source of income. To take just one example, the nineteenth-century translators of Luís de Camões included a diplomat, an engineer, two explorers, an agent for a shipping company, and a paper manufacturer (see p. 269, below).

The distinction between 'amateur' and 'professional' translators is not a clearcut one. Some who could not be regarded as professional translators were nevertheless paid for their work, while others were not. Richard Burton, whose main professional activity was as a soldier and diplomat, wrote at the end of his life, after his successful translation of *The Thousand and One Nights*: 'I have struggled for forty-seven years ... I never had a compliment, nor a "thank you", nor a single farthing', but then in old age 'I translate a doubtful book ... and I immediately make sixteen thousand guineas' (quoted in Lovell 1998: 689). For many, translation was part of a varied literary career, involving original writing, editorship, and journalism, but in addition to these, there was a host of clerics, missionaries, lawyers, librarians, physicians, merchants, tradesmen, soldiers, politicians, government officials, colonial servants, or people of private means who translated, often quite copiously, from most of the principal languages of the world. Sometimes they had learned these languages (notably the classical languages, French, and Italian) at school or with governesses, but in many cases they learned languages by residence abroad or through private study. Some translated out of love, some out of boredom, some in search of fame, some from a sense of duty or the desire to open people's eyes to an unfamiliar masterpiece.

The clergy included many educated men whose pastoral duties left them time for literary work. Naturally enough, they often translated religious writings, including hymns (see § 9.1, below). Newman and Pusey translated the Church Fathers and some devotional literature as part of their campaign to combat 'national apostasy' and to revitalize the Anglican Church. Others preferred secular literature, often returning to the classics they had studied at school and university. Francis Howes, for instance, who became a minor canon of Norwich Cathedral, translated the Satires of Persius (1809), some Anacreon and Homer (1806), and the Satires and Epistles of Horace (1845). More ambitious was his contemporary Henry Cary, who enjoyed two ecclesiastical livings and eventually became Assistant Keeper of Printed Books at the British Museum (for a biography see King 1925); a respected member of London literary circles, he combined his other duties with the first important translation of Dante's *Commedia* (1814) and a trailblazing study (with translations) of *The Early French Poets* (1846).

Alongside these figures one can set many clergymen whose names survive only on their title pages. A curious case is provided by the translations of Archbishop Fénelon's *Télémaque*. This prose continuation of Homer's *Odyssey*, originally written for the edification of Fénelon's royal charge, the duc de Bourgogne, became a bestseller in France and abroad in the two centuries following its publication in 1699. In nineteenth-century Britain it was used as a language-teaching text and generated many translations.[1] Improbably, several of these were in verse, and this timeconsuming exercise tempted a number of otherwise unknown clergymen, including Gibbons Bagnell, vicar of Home-Lacy, Hertfordshire (1790), the Revd W. E. Hume (1849, also the author of *The Pilgrim's Progress Versified* and *Don Quixote Versified*), and the Revd John Lockhart Ross, vicar of Averbury-cum-Winterbourne (1860).

Then there were the missionaries, who, as well as translating the Bible or *The Pilgrim's Progress* into foreign languages, might also become interested in indigenous culture and seek to record it in English. The first translations from traditional Swahili oral literature were the work of Bishop Edward Steere of the Universities Mission to Central Africa and the Revd W. E. Taylor of the Church Missionary Society in Mombasa (Steere 1870; Taylor 1891). More controversially, the Revd James Long was fined and sent to prison for publishing the translation of a Bengali play about the oppression of Indian peasants (Anon. 1860, see pp. 351–2, below).

The missionaries were one of many groups whose work took them overseas for long periods of time: colonial servants, diplomats, military men, or businessmen such as John Bowring (for whom see pp. 308–10, below). Such people sometimes learned the local languages, explored the unfamiliar culture of the people among whom they lived, and tried to convey it to the public back home. Their translations were often undertaken in a spirit of generosity and openness, as a service to both the source and target culture. Herbert Giles, himself the son of a translator, served in the Chinese consular service between 1867 and 1892, and this enabled him, in his *Gems of Chinese Literature* (1884), to overcome preconceived western ideas about the oddity of China and to lay the foundations for the modern reception of Chinese writing in the English-speaking world (he later became the first professor of Chinese at Cambridge). James Legge, a missionary, had opened the way for Giles by making the first substantial translation of Chinese poetry (Legge 1861–72), and the pioneer in the Japanese field was a naval physician, F. V. Dickins with his 1866 translation of Japanese verse (see pp. 358–60 and 365–6, below).

[1] Thomas De Quincey, having noted how young ladies customarily translated the opening pages of *Télémaque*, remarked in 1854: 'It is amongst the standing hypocrisies of the world, that most people affect a reverence for this book, which nobody reads' (De Quincey 1970: 408).

Less far from home (culturally speaking), it was periods spent on military leave in Goa and as a consul in Brazil that enabled Richard Burton to engage with the works of Camões. The posting to Brazil also resulted in Burton's translation of the eighteenth-century epic *O Uraguay* (Burton 1982) and led his wife Isabel to make the first translation into English of a Brazilian work (Burton 1886). Russian literature benefited similarly from the efforts of soldiers and diplomats; the first translation of Pushkin's *Eugene Onegin* was the work of the otherwise unknown Lieutenant-Colonel Spalding, while Jeremiah Curtin, for several years an American diplomat in St Petersburg, went on to produce translations of Russian and East European folklore as well as of the Polish novels of Henryk Sienkiewicz.

The collection and translation of unknown texts went on in Britain and America too, and here again government officials might well be involved. Curtin, on his return from Russia, worked for the American Bureau of Ethnology, studying Native American languages and folklore, and across the Atlantic John Francis Campbell of Islay used his leisure as Secretary to the Lighthouse Commission in Scotland to complete his four volumes of *Popular Tales of the West Highlands*, translated from Gaelic (1860–2; see p. 302, below). One of his collaborators was Alexander Carmichael, a Customs and Excise official whose duties took him to the Hebrides; here he collected the Gaelic hymns, charms, and incantations which he translated in *Carmina Gadelica* (1900).

It was more common, however, for government officials and politicians in Britain to use their free time translating the literature of continental Europe. While Chancellor of the Exchequer, Gladstone published skilful verse translations from ancient and modern languages (Gladstone 1861), but this is small beer compared to the quantity of translations produced by the young Francis Leveson-Gower (later Francis Egerton, then the first Earl of Ellesmere), while he was a Member of Parliament, a Secretary of State, and a Privy Counsellor. It was no doubt literary ambition which led Leveson-Gower to translate plays by Goethe, Schiller, Hugo, and Dumas. His Dumas (*Catherine of Cleves*, 1832) was performed with some success at Covent Garden, and his Hugo (*Hernani*, 1832) before a royal audience at Bridgewater Castle.

Other translators came from the men of law, judges, solicitors, or barristers. One such was Charles Stuart Calverley, an accomplished translator of Latin and Greek verse, though he was more a man of leisure than a practising barrister, since a skating accident forced him to give up legal work only eighteen months after being called to the bar. Others, such as the Irish judge John O'Hagan, who translated the Old French *Song of Roland* (1880), or the Scottish-born parliamentary solicitor Theodore Martin, a translator of poetry from many languages, combined literary production (e.g. translations of Horace and Goethe) with an active public and professional life. The same might be said of John Bowring; most of his translating was done in his early years, between 1820 and 1830, while he was successively a merchant and a journalist, but even much later on, when he had been a Member of Parliament, an industrialist, and a consular official in China, he produced a volume of *Translations from Alexander Petőfi* (1866) from the Hungarian.

Two Enthusiasts: FitzGerald and Guest

While some occasional translators such as Calverley might be properly described as 'amateurs', for others translation was less a pastime than a compelling passion. Examples of such enthusiasts abound. Richard Burton has already been mentioned; in a well-filled life as soldier, explorer, and diplomat, he threw himself into learning the languages of the East and producing a series of important translations. Apart from *The Thousand and One Nights*, these brought him little or no financial reward, but they satisfied deeper needs, from the erotic verse of *The Perfumed Garden*, into which he poured 'my whole life and all my life blood' (quoted in Lovell 1998: 729), to the six-volume limited edition of Camões, with whose adventurous spirit he felt a close kinship. A less eye-catching, but equally devoted, enthusiast was William Ralston, a modest scholar whose work in the British Museum enabled him to develop a taste for Russian literature and folklore and to champion and translate Turgenev (see Waddington 1995: 17–56). To see this kind of passionate engagement in more detail, let us consider two remarkable enthusiasts, Edward FitzGerald and Lady Charlotte Guest, authors of some of the most durable translations of the period.

FitzGerald did not need to translate for money. Enjoying a private income, he lived a life of leisure in the Suffolk countryside (for an account of his life see Martin 1985). He was on good terms with many literary people, devoting much of his time to reading and art, but also writing in a somewhat desultory way. Many of his books, including the translations, were privately printed—or in some cases, not printed at all during his lifetime—and he seems to have made little money from his *Rubáiyát of Omar Khayyám* (1859; for the translation, see pp. 335–7, below), which was to become one of the most successful translations ever published. In 1872 he wrote about the second edition to his publisher Bernard Quaritch: 'you will owe me something for it—of so little consequence to me, or to you, that I shall desire you to give it some Charity . . . as I daresay old Omar would have done—had he translated the works of your truly E. FG.' (FitzGerald 1980: III, 371).

Translation was only one of FitzGerald's occupations, coming to the fore from time to time, but then giving way to other passions, notably his venture into boat owning and herring fishing. Nor did he always accord much importance to this work. He preferred not to be named on the title pages of his translations, and the dominant note in his correspondence is one of gentlemanly self-deprecation. Aware of the weakness of his own poetic efforts, he described himself in a letter as 'little more than a Versifier' (IV, 325). And writing about his 'small Escapades in print' he declared: 'I am always a little ashamed of having made my leisure and idleness the means of putting myself forward in print, when really so many much better people keep silent, having other work to do' (III, 119).

This stance was prompted partly by the modesty of one whose friends included Tennyson, Thackeray, and Carlyle; compared with the creators, the translator is a humble figure. Another factor was no doubt a well-bred distaste for tedious self-promotion; in a letter of 1857 FitzGerald notes: 'I think I shall become a bore, of the Bowring order, by all this translation' (III, 273). But one should not take such statements at face value; the modesty topos is belied by other remarks which show FitzGerald well aware of the value of what he is doing. In the letter just quoted, addressed to his young friend E. B. Cowell, whose prompting largely decided him to translate Calderón and Khayyām, FitzGerald goes on: 'I really think I have the faculty of making some things readable which others have hitherto left unreadable'—he is referring to his translation of Aeschylus' *Agamemnon*.

And certainly, when the mood was on him, he threw himself into translation with an enthusiasm that belies the 'gentleman amateur' attitude—the corollary being that when what he called his 'Go' deserted him, and translation became work, he tended to abandon it. In 1850, with the help and encouragement of Cowell, he embarked on Calderón, learning to read more accurately as he went along, and producing free translations of eight plays 'at odd times' over the two following years. The seriousness of this commitment is only partly concealed by his casual tone in writing to Cowell: 'His Drama may not be the finest in the world: one sees how often too he wrote in the fashion of his time and Country— but he is a wonderful fellow; one of the Great Men of the world' (II, 63).

The same familiar tone of voice appears in his comments to Cowell on 'old Omar', whose work he did not hesitate to treat with great freedom, 'tesselating' the original quatrains into 'a sort of Epicurean Eclogue in a Persian Garden' (II, 323). He knew French from boyhood and Latin and Greek from school and university, but he was over 40 when he began to study Persian, again under the influence of Cowell, and his letters make it clear that this pastime became for some years a serious passion to which he sacrificed not only time, but health. As with Burton, translation grew naturally out of language learning; the letters bear witness to FitzGerald's fascination with the culture he was discovering. He was in no way in awe of Persian poets such as Jāmī and 'Aṭṭār, who 'really *do* want a little Art to shape them' (II, 261), but his letters make it clear that in Khayyām he found a consolation and a kindred spirit who helped to give meaning to his life.

As has been suggested above, the majority of 'amateur' translators were members of the professions, and therefore probably men; women were rather more likely to see translation as a profession in its own right (see § 3.5, below). A remarkable exception to this generalization is provided by Lady Charlotte Guest. Like FitzGerald, the translator of the *Mabinogion* had more than one string to her bow— her biographers describe her as 'a translator, a businesswoman, a collector, an educator' (Guest and John 1989: xv). In a sad and lonely aristocratic childhood, she had found comfort in reading and self-education, learning languages (Latin, Italian, Arabic, Persian) and developing a taste for medieval history and legend. Then, at the age of 21, she married John Guest of Dowlais in South Wales, the master of the largest ironworks in the world. She noted in her diary: 'since I married I have taken up such pursuits as in this country of business and iron-making would render me conversant with what occupied the male part of the population' (Guest and John 1989: 31). She became a considerable businesswoman and was active in public life, working to set up schools in the area. She had ten children in the space of thirteen years, but still found time to edit and translate medieval Welsh tales.

The young Englishwoman who arrived in Wales in 1833 knew no Welsh. But she soon began to learn it, influenced by the powerful Welsh cultural renaissance (she attended the newly created National Eisteddfod in Cardiff in 1834). Her romantic view of old Welsh culture and her desire for some sort of literary fame led her to begin translating the old stories before she had the necessary command of Welsh, but like FitzGerald with Cowell, she was able to rely on expert advisers, in her case the Revd John Jones (bardic name Tegid) and the Revd Thomas Price (bardic name Carnhuanawc). These two ministers had a large hand in the *Mabinogion*, but the controlling force was Lady Charlotte, who for a matter of ten years made translation the centre of her life. A diary entry for 28 March 1839 reads: 'today I worked hard at the translation of *Peredur*. I had the pleasure of giving birth to my fifth child and third boy today' (Phillips 1921: 24). She took the work with her on European holidays, worked in the British Museum, corresponded with scholars, and was responsible for getting together long and learned introductions, appendices, and fine illustrations for the noble three-volume edition produced by Longmans in 1849. The introduction reveals the diffidence of the neophyte, but also pride in her achievement.

As she worked on the tales, she tested them out on her children, to some of whom she gave appropriate Welsh names. But once the work was done, she announced (in her diary) that 'it is quite right that I should have done with authorship' so as to do her duty as a wife and mother (Phillips 1921: 36). And so, suddenly, translation disappeared from her life. After her husband's death in 1852, she ran the ironworks, then remarried and as Lady Charlotte Schreiber found new activities—and a new celebrity—as a philanthropist and a collector of ceramics and fans. Her involvement with translation had been limited to just over ten years, but it was intense and in no way amateurish. Her enthusiasm, like FitzGerald's, gave nineteenth-century English-language culture one of its great acquisitions.

LIST OF SOURCES

Translations
Anon. (1860). *Nil Darpan, or, The Indigo Planting Mirror* [Mitra], ed. James Long. Calcutta.
Burton, Isabel (1886). *Iraçéma, the Honey-lips: A Legend of Brazil* [Alencar]. London.
Burton, Richard Francis (1880). *Os lusiadas* [Camões], 2 vols. London.
—— (1884). *Camoens. The Lyricks: Sonnets, Canzons, Odes and Sextines*. London.
—— (1982). *The Uruguay: A Historical Romance of South America* [Da Gama], ed. F. C. H. Garcia and Edward F. Stanton. Berkeley, CA.
Calverley, C. S. (1866). *Translations into English and Latin*. Cambridge.
—— (1869). *Theocritus, Translated into English Verse*. Cambridge.
Cary, Henry Francis (1814). *The Vision, or, Hell, Purgatory, and Paradise of Dante Alighieri*, 3 vols. London.
—— (1846). *The Early French Poets: A Series of Notices and Translations*. London.
[FitzGerald, Edward] (1859). *The Rubáiyát of Omar Khayyám*. London.
—— (1906). *Eight Dramas of Calderon*. London ('Six Dramas' published 1853).

Giles, Herbert A. (1884). *Gems of Chinese Literature*. London/Shanghai.
Gladstone, William Ewart (1861). *Translations by Lord Lyttelton and the Right Hon. William Ewart Gladstone*. London.
Guest, Lady Charlotte (1849). *The Mabinogion: From the Llyfr Coch o Hergest, and Other Ancient Welsh Manuscripts, with an English Translation and Notes*, 3 vols. London.
Howes, Francis (1806). *Miscellaneous Poetical Translations*. London.
—— (1809). *The Satires of A. Persius Flaccus*. London.
—— (1845). *The Epodes, Satires, and Epistles of Horace*. London.
Legge, James (1861–72). *The Chinese Classics*, 5 vols. Hong Kong.
Newman, John Henry (1842). *Select Treatises of S. Athanasius*. Oxford.
—— (1842–4). *The Ecclesiastical History of M. l'Abbé Fleury*, 3 vols. London.
O'Hagan, John (1880). *The Song of Roland*. London.
Steere, Edward (1870). *Swahili Tales, as Told by the Natives of Zanzibar*. London.
Taylor, W. E. (1891). *African Aphorisms, or, Saws from Swahili-land*. London.

Other Sources
Calverley, C. S. (1885). *The Literary Remains of Charles Stuart Calverley. With a Memoir by Walter J. Sendall*. London.
De Quincey, Thomas (1970). *Recollections of the Lakes and the Lake Poets*, ed. David Wright. Harmondsworth.
FitzGerald, Edward (1980). *The Letters of Edward FitzGerald*, ed. Alfred McKinley Terhune and Annabelle Burdick Terhune, 4 vols. Princeton, NJ.
Guest, Revel, and John, Angela V. (1989). *Lady Charlotte: A Biography of the Nineteenth Century*. London.
King, Robert W. (1925). *The Translator of Dante: The Life, Work and Friendships of H. F. Cary, 1772–1844*. London.
Lovell, Mary S. (1998). *A Rage to Live: A Biography of Richard and Isabel Burton*. London.
Martin, Robert Bernard (1985). *With Friends Possessed: A Life of Edward FitzGerald*. London.
Phillips, D. Rhys (1921). *Lady Charlotte Guest and the Mabinogion: Some Notes on the Work and its Translator, with Extracts from her Journals*. Carmarthen.
Waddington, Patrick, ed. (1995). *Ivan Turgenev and Britain*. Oxford.

3.3 Writers

Stephen Prickett and Peter France

Introduction

As Volume 3 of this *History* makes clear, the period from 1680 to 1730 was a high point in the involvement of major British writers in translation. Much of Dryden's greatest work was translation, particularly in the last twenty years of his career, and his *Aeneid*, together with Pope's *Iliad*, is one of the outstanding poetic creations of the period; although both these texts came under attack during the Romantic period, their commercial appeal continued into the nineteenth century and beyond. One cannot point to an exactly equivalent phenomenon in the period covered by this volume (though see pp. 9–14, above), but many major writers did engage sporadically in translation, particularly at the beginning of their career, and for some it was an activity of central importance.

Some writers, notably those whose formal education was limited, did little or no translation. Such were Jane Austen and Dickens, whose own work, though it owes something to the Bible, draws very little on any other translations (though we may remember that the young people in *Mansfield Park* act *Lovers' Vows*, Elizabeth Inchbald's version of a play by the very popular Kotzebue). There were others for whom foreign literature was more important, though they did not themselves translate, for example the Brontë sisters (Charlotte did however translate one canto of Voltaire's *Henriade* as a school exercise).

For many writers, and especially poets, translation served as an apprenticeship, since they had learnt (the men at least) to translate Greek and Latin poetry as part of their schooling. Byron's first published work, for instance, was *Hours of Idleness: A Series of Poems Original and Translated* (1807); he was 18 at the time. A few years later he returned to the classics in his polemic against the Lake poets, using Horace as a model in his Popean imitation *Hints from Horace* (1811). This early training in the classics might bear rich fruit later on; such was notably the case with Tennyson, even if he did little actual translation. Wordsworth too was much influenced by classical poetry (on which see Clancey 2000); Hawkshead Grammar School had developed in him a passion for Ovid, Virgil, and Homer, and some of his earliest poems are translations or imitations of Anacreon, Catullus, Virgil, Horace, and others. Translation thus helped him to find his own voice, and he would come back to it from time to time in later years, imitating Juvenal, modernizing some Chaucer, extending his range to Italian (Metastasio, Michelangelo, Chiabrera), and in 1823 beginning a new verse translation of the *Aeneid* in opposition to that of Dryden (for a comprehensive modern edition of the Virgil, of which only three books were completed, and the Chaucer, see Wordsworth 1998).

A different kind of apprenticeship was served by women writers like George Eliot or Harriet Martineau, who did not have the advantage of a classical education and who began their writing career with important translations from modern languages (for a discussion see pp. 127–8, below). While Eliot ceased translating once she became a novelist, her later work is marked by her early work as a translator (on this see Ashton 1980: 147–77). German, as we shall see later on in this section, provided a particularly stimulating challenge for male and female translators alike; the language was little known at the beginning of the nineteenth century, but the literature was increasingly seen as the most fertile source of new ideas and models. It was German which attracted the young and classically educated Walter Scott at the outset of his writing career (see p. 219, below).

Scott's translation of German ballads preceded and influenced his work on the 'minstrelsy' of the Scottish borders. In this he belongs (if only in a small way) to another category of writer/translators, those who translated in order to bring something new to English literature. For the translation of ballads and old popular literature one could also cite Robert Southey and John Gibson Lockhart; Southey's *Chronicles of the Cid* (1808) and Lockhart's *Ancient Spanish Ballads* (1823) both helped to open British eyes to the richness of old Spanish literature. A more unusual figure is George Borrow, who in the middle years of the century, even after he had achieved fame with *The Bible in Spain*, continued to labour—with almost no success in terms of public recognition—on his versions of ballads from many nations; here translation was an activity conducted in parallel with what we now see as his essential work (on Borrow as translator see pp. 287, 301, 310, 313, and 436, below; also Hyde 1999).

Towards the end of the century, in particular, many writers felt the urge to bring the new literature of the Continent to Britain. The poets of the 1890s translated a good deal, incorporating translated verse into their own poetry, and also translating much prose: John Davidson translated the *Lettres persanes* of Montesquieu (1892); Ernest Dowson translated Zola's *La Terre* (1895), Balzac's *La Fille aux yeux d'or* (1896), and others; Arthur Symons translated Zola's *L'Assommoir* (1894). The motivation for these prose translations was primarily financial, but the challenge of doing an unexpurgated Zola for the Lutetian Society (see p. 242, below) also played a part.

Some of the greatest poetic translators of our period attempted to use translation to enlarge the scope of English literature, and many of them are discussed at various other points in this volume. They include Shelley, who not only translated Dante, but in 'The Triumph of Life' wrote a Dantesque English (for the full range of Shelley's translations see pp. 10–11, above and 161–2, and 221–4, below); Robert Browning, attempting in his *Agamemnon* to use his Greek model in such a way as to make the English language do things it had never done (see pp. 179–80, below); Swinburne, who played an important part in recovering the forgotten figure of Villon and so in shaping Victorian medievalism (see pp. 11–12, above, and 232, below); and Dante Gabriel Rossetti, whose translation of the early Italian poets was a challenge to the literary canon comparable to that of the Pre-Raphaelites in the world of art (see pp. 254–6, below). The remainder of this section, however, is devoted to case studies of four other writers for whom translation and the confrontation with foreign texts were in interestingly different ways essential elements in their creative work: Samuel Taylor Coleridge, Thomas Carlyle, Elizabeth Barrett Browning, and William Morris.

Coleridge and German Literature

Coleridge offers the fascinating case of a writer and thinker who largely reinvents himself by intensive immersion in a foreign culture, that of Germany. Even if the yield of major translations was limited, the reading and translation of German writings made up an integral part of Coleridge's intellectual and poetic development. His translations of Schiller earned him neither the fame nor the money he had hoped for, but they helped to bring the nascent revival of letters in Germany to a wider public. Certainly among the second-generation Romantics, it was axiomatic that in German studies Coleridge was the pioneer in whose steps all others followed. It is ironic therefore that just when Coleridge's real scholarship was being appreciated by Julius Hare, George Henry Lewes, John Stuart Mill, Henry Crabb Robinson, and others, his other 'translations' (i.e. the unacknowledged reuse in his later lectures and writings of material he had translated from German philosophers) were coming to light, and he was being vilified for them by rivals like De Quincey.

Coleridge's direct experience of Germany and German literature stands in almost direct contrast to Wordsworth's. When Coleridge was 25, he had sailed with William and Dorothy Wordsworth to Hamburg. The Wordsworths were immediately seasick, and fled to their cabin, but Coleridge remained on deck, engaging the less afflicted foreign passengers in animated if fragmented multilingual conversation (see Coleridge 1956–71: I, 420–5; Holmes 1989: 204–7). It was symbolic of a more profound difference between the authors of the *Lyrical Ballads*, published the same month in Bristol, than either could have recognized at the time. During their stay in Germany, and to a great extent for the rest of their lives, William and Dorothy were to remain isolated within their own domestic bubble, more concerned with the construction of their own interiorized narrative than with external affairs, while for Coleridge it was the beginning of what was to prove a lifelong fascination with German manners, customs, and thought. Literary translation was merely one aspect—though an important one—of this passionate contact with the foreign. Coleridge's translations of Schiller are discussed elsewhere in this volume; here we shall be considering the context which enabled them to be made.

Once in Germany Coleridge separated from the Wordsworths and settled in Göttingen, learning the language and integrating rapidly into the life of the university, which had already gained a formidable academic reputation. It was what was happening in philosophy and theology that made the greatest long-term impact on the young poet. From notebook evidence (Coleridge 1957–90: I, no. 249 n.), he seems to have heard of Kant as early as 1796, but it was only on his arrival in Göttingen, and under the intellectual stimulation of university circles there, that he began serious study of Kantian and idealist philosophy. The result was to reorientate his mental landscape: passing from Hartley to Kant was, for Coleridge, an intellectual turning point, and his later writings and lectures made ample use of terminology translated from the German.

In retrospect the ground had been well prepared. As early as 1795 he had read Herbert Marsh's multi-volume English translation of J. D. Michaelis's *Introduction to the New Testament*. During his stay in Göttingen, Coleridge was to attend the lectures of Michaelis's successor, J. G. Eichhorn, who was using the material which was later to appear in his own *Introduction to the New Testament* (on Michaelis and Eichhorn see Shaffer 1975: 22–30). Though Coleridge was to reject some of his more sceptical conclusions, the encounter with Eichhorn was to transform his way of thinking about the Bible quite as radically as his reading of Kant was to reshape his philosophy. When, in the 1820s, Coleridge started on his own investigation of the New Testament, it was with the tools given him during his stay in Germany (see Prickett 1976: 38–69).

One other German writer at this time brought together Coleridge's philosophical, theological, and literary interests to provide a lasting influence on his thought: Lessing. Coleridge had begun reading him while in Ratzeburg, and despite his crowded programme at Göttingen, he made full notes (in English and in German) on a recent brief life of Lessing (Coleridge 1957–90: I, no. 377). To Thomas Wedgwood he wrote, somewhat mysteriously, that he had chosen to study Lessing 'because it would give me an opportunity of conveying under a better name, than my own ever will be, opinions, which I deem of the highest importance' (Coleridge 1956–71: I, 519). Some of these opinions appear to relate to a projected critical history of German literature, but in a later letter to Wedgwood, of January 1800, he describes his 'greater work' as a 'Life of Lessing' (which was never written) (1956–71: I, 559).

There was one aspect of Lessing's career that was important in offering a role model for the young English poet. This was the way in which Lessing had managed to combine poetic, philosophical, and theological concerns in a single career, producing a body of writing that was at once popular, controversial, and of lasting importance. Coleridge's interest in poetry and the theatre at the time of his stay in Germany was almost as strong as his interest in philosophy, and Lessing was no doubt a source of inspiration for the poet and aspiring playwright. At this time he translated a number of short poems or extracts by Friedrich Leopold Stolberg, Lessing, Schiller, Goethe, and others; some of these are close translations, often seeking to transpose into English the adventurous prosody of the originals, while others are free adaptations and expansions, notably the poem inspired by a short lyric of the Swiss poet Friederike Brun that became 'Hymn before Sun-Rise, in the Vale of Chamouni' (Coleridge 1912: I, 376–80; the original is printed in an appendix). One in particular, his version of the famous song of Mignon from Goethe's *Wilhelm Meister* ('Know'st thou the land where the pale citrons grow . . .', 1912: I, 311) is one of his most haunting lyrics.

Far more important than these short pieces, however, were his translations of plays by Schiller. As early as 1794 he had been overwhelmed by *Die Raüber* in Tytler's translation; now, when approached by Longman after his return from Germany, he set to work vigorously on the second and third parts of the very recent *Wallenstein* trilogy. These creative yet faithful versions (discussed on pp. 219–21, below) are Coleridge's most important dramatic writings. He found the work of translation wearisome, but later in life referred to these plays as 'a specimen of my happiest attempt, during the prime manhood of my intellect' (*Table Talk*, cited in Holmes 1989: 268). It is not surprising that some years after his *Wallenstein*, he was seen by some as the only possible translator for Goethe's *Faust*, even though this idea came to nothing.

Although Coleridge was not responsible for a great volume of translation, it was thus an integral part of his own mental and literary development. This no doubt accounts for his more controversial use of material that he had translated from German sources throughout his later writings, an unusual form of 'translation' that has been much discussed (see for instance McFarland 1969: 1–52; McFarland 1974). His use of whole pages of Schelling in *Biographia Literaria* (1817) soon became notorious, but there is considerable unacknowledged use of German material in *The Friend*, *Aids to Reflection*, and the *Philosophical Lectures*, and his wholesale reliance on Lessing, even in the second posthumous edition of his *Confessions of an Inquiring Spirit* (1849), was enough to provoke a nervous and defensive preface by his daughter Sara. As Richard Holmes puts it (1989: 232 n.), 'it is worth noticing that for Coleridge, plagiarism begins in translation—and specifically the attempt to carry over and interpret German literature and philosophy into an insular, English culture'.

Carlyle versus Coleridge

Coleridge's greatest successor as a mediator of German literature was another major writer, Thomas Carlyle. As a student at Christ's Hospital, Coleridge had done a great deal of translation from the classics by the time he reached Cambridge in the early 1790s; in such a context, 'translation' would automatically imply: 'from Latin and Greek'. The excitement with which he discovered contemporary German thought at the end of the century, therefore, can hardly be exaggerated. For him, translation became part of the search for a philosophical identity. Carlyle, by contrast, a generation later, coming from a totally different Scottish context, and educated at Edinburgh University, was able to found for himself a career as 'man of letters' on the translation and presentation of German literature and thought in the English-speaking world.

For some twenty-five years after the French Revolution, continental ideas—whether French or German—were popularly seen as atheistic, politically suspect, and (if understood) probably sexually immoral as well. Meanwhile, literacy had increased dramatically in Britain between 1790 and 1820, and, supported by a variety of technical innovations, a new and rapidly growing reading public had at its disposal a remarkable variety of critical journals—second only in numbers to those of Germany. Given this combination of a flourishing literary culture with a considerable ignorance of developments in neighbouring countries, it was hardly surprising that Carlyle, twenty years younger than Coleridge, should appropriate the role of interpreter of contemporary German culture as his entry point into the world of letters—and as such find himself in competition with the older poet.

As has often been pointed out, despite the obvious differences in nationality, education, and religious conviction, many of Carlyle's own ideas and his intellectual development were too close to Coleridge's for comfort. Crabb Robinson noted that the 'philosophy' of Carlyle's only novel, *Sartor Resartus*, was essentially that of Coleridge (see Ashton 1980: 98) and while Carlyle shared something of what he claimed in his *Life of Sterling* was the popular contempt for Coleridge, at the same time he remained uneasily aware, despite himself, of the real scope of the older writer's achievements. The unwilling admiration for Coleridge is clearly visible in an 1829 article on Novalis in the *Foreign Review* (Carlyle 1899: XXVII, 3).

What is interesting about Carlyle's continuing jealousy was that by 1829 his own reputation as a translator was already higher than Coleridge's was ever to be. His monumental translation of the two parts of Goethe's *Wilhelm Meister* had been published in 1824 and 1827, and even if it had not been the resounding success he might have hoped for, it had been recognized, at least by the discerning few, as a major literary achievement in its own right. This was followed by translations of stories by Hoffmann, Tieck, and others, and such critical essays as 'The State of German Literature' in the *Edinburgh Review*, both in 1827. Carlyle's position as the principal mediator of German culture was later strengthened by his *Sartor Resartus*, which (after some delays) was finally serialized in *Fraser's Magazine* in 1833 (on the 'Germanic' nature of this text see p. 71, above), and by his monumental *Life of Frederick the Great* (1858–63).

Unlike Coleridge, Carlyle learnt German at home, beginning in Edinburgh in 1818. For all his eminence as a commentator on German culture, he did not actually visit Germany until 1852. Nor was his translation and exposition of German literature and culture necessarily more scholarly than Coleridge's. To take just one example, for many 'Kantians' the virtual identity of poetry and philosophy was an article of faith. In 1796, however, Kant had criticized those who introduced an undue aesthetic emphasis on intuition and feeling into philosophy. The fact is, declared Kant, 'philosophy is fundamentally prosaic; and to attempt to philosophize poetically is very much as if a merchant should undertake to make up his account-books not in prose but in verse' (quoted in Lovejoy 1961: 11; on the first translator of this essay, John Richardson, see p. 482, below). Carlyle, however, had no qualms in tacitly assuming the more mystical interpretation of Kant, nor, indeed, in giving it qualities that sound more like Carlyle than anything else:

Not by logic or argument does [the Kantian Reason] work; yet surely and clearly may it be taught to work; and its domain lies in that higher region whither logic and argument cannot reach; in that holier region where Poetry and Virtue and Divinity abide, in whose presence Understanding wavers and recoils, dazzled into utter darkness by that 'sea of light', at once the fountain and termination of all true knowledge.

(Carlyle 1899: XXVI, 27)

But if the phraseology is Carlyle's, the enthusiasm for the ineffable certainties of Reason is virtually identical to Coleridge's in *Aids to Reflection*.

Given this unanimity on the poetic nature of Reason from both the major expounders of German thought in the period, it is perhaps not surprising that one important long-term influence of Carlyle's translations was on the later development of Victorian fantasy, which often sought to use poetic fiction as a means of directly apprehending spiritual truths. The interest aroused, especially by the second volume of Carlyle's translation of *Wilhelm Meister*, quickly extended to include Novalis's *Heinrich von Ofterdingen* and E. T. A. Hoffmann's *The Golden Pot* (also translated by Carlyle) and had a profound influence on the writings of Edgar Allan Poe, Lewis Carroll, Charles Kingsley, and, above all, George MacDonald, all of whom drew heavily on this strain in German Romanticism, even while not themselves publishing direct translations. Ironically, however, it was not Carlyle's German scholarship in any form, but his French scholarship, resulting in the *French Revolution* (1837), that was to bring him real literary and financial success for the first time.

Elizabeth Barrett Browning

While Carlyle was struggling to make his way on the back of German translation, two brilliant young women were attempting the much more difficult task of creating literary careers through translation without the help of universities in either England or Scotland. Marian Evans—George Eliot—is discussed elsewhere (see pp. 127–8, below). As for Elizabeth Barrett, later Elizabeth Barrett Browning, she might well be seen as one of Eliot's creations—say a successful version of Maggie Tulliver, the heroine of *The Mill on the Floss*, who was prevented from receiving the 'boy's education' in classics to which she was eminently suited, and to which her less academic brother was most eminently not. However, while Barrett's father may have been the tyrannical paterfamilias portrayed by *The Barretts of Wimpole Street*, he was also proud of his daughter's intelligence (her first published work, *The Battle of Marathon*, appeared in 1819, when she was only 13), and he gave her every assistance in developing her academic talents at home. Elizabeth, unlike Maggie, was able to follow closely her brothers' classical education at Charterhouse and enjoyed the friendship and tutelage of two classical scholars, Uvedale Price and Hugh Stuart Boyd.

Her early translation of the Aeschylean *Prometheus Bound* (1833) reflected not only her passionate admiration of the ancient Greeks, but also the relative isolation of her upbringing and education, since she laboured under the assumption, as the prefatory essay makes clear, that knowledge of, and translation from, the classics were the necessary prerequisites for a literary career. This primary love of the classics was not superseded by her later mastery of both Italian and German (her *Sonnets from the Portuguese*, contrary to what the title suggests, is not a translation). Though her last translation (and virtually her last work) consisted of paraphrases of her near-contemporary Heine, she continued her early habit of translating from Greek, not only revising her *Prometheus* (see the edition of Clara Drummond, Browning 2004), but also translating passages from Theocritus, Bion, Apuleius, Nonnus, Hesiod, Homer, and Anacreon. She also, in 1845, made a *terza rima* translation of the first canto of Dante's *Commedia*; this was echoed in her political poem 'Casa Guidi Windows' (1851), but remained unpublished in her lifetime (it is reproduced in Griffiths and Reynolds 2005: 197–203).

Barrett's regular recurrence to translation, however, seems to have stemmed neither from the process of philosophical self-discovery that drove Coleridge, nor from the more programmatic desire of Carlyle to bring foreign literature to the notice of the British public, but rather from a conviction that poetry was a single, organically unified, art form, and that any practitioner must understand the roots from which his or her art had grown. In a long review of a poetry anthology (*The Book of the Poets*) written for the *Athenaeum* in 1842, the 36-year-old Elizabeth Barrett sketches out her own professional map:

> Our poetry has an heroic genealogy. It arose, where the sun rises, in the far East. It came out from Arabia, and was tilted on the lance-heads of the Saracens into the heart of Europe, Armorica catching it in rebound from Spain, and England from Armorica. It issued in its first breath from Georgia, wrapt in the gathering cry of Persian Odin: and passing from the orient of the sun to the antagonistic snows of Iceland, and oversweeping the black pines of Germany and the jutting shores of Scandinavia, and embodying in itself all wayward sounds, even to the rude shouts of the brazen-throated Cimbri—so modified, multiplied, resonant in a thousand runic echoes, it rushed abroad like a blast into Britain. In Britain, the Arabic Saracenic Armorican and the Georgian Gothic Scandinavian mixed sound at last; and the dying suspirations of the Grecian and Latin literatures, the last low stir of the 'Gesta Romanorum', with the apocryphal personations of lost authentic voices, breathed up together through the fissures of the rent universe, to help the new intonation and accomplish the cadence. Genius was thrust onward to a new slope of the world.
>
> (Browning 1904: 628)

The sometimes over-flowery language, the looseness of syntax, and the geographical hyperbole are all (perhaps unfortunately) reminiscent of Carlyle; still, in the broad sweep of its internationalism, in its belief both in a historic tradition and in the unpredictable flowering of individual genius, this is Romantic criticism in the best tradition of Coleridge and Shelley. Like her essay on 'The Greek Christian Poets', published in January of the same year, this is a thorough and detailed essay in criticism by someone who has read her sources carefully—and, more often than not, in the original languages. What is impressive in all this is perhaps the last thing the age might have expected from a woman: a note of academic authority.

Before she could attain this note, she had first to repudiate a false ambition of academic exactitude. She came to see her first translation of *Prometheus* as marred by its unswerving literalism. Anxious that her command of Greek might be called into question, she produced a translation that is little more than a crib. She had her doubts about it as soon as it was published, enquiring in a letter to a friend whether it was stiff and so much like translated poetry that it was no poetry at all (Browning and Browning 1984–: VIII, 259). She began to revise it in 1844 in order to right the wrong she believed she had committed against Aeschylus. By this time, however, her *Poems* had appeared, and she undertook the work of revision with the confidence in her own powers that was necessary for her to write with genuine authority (see further p. 178, below).

Barrett's literary apprenticeship came to an end with the first translation of *Prometheus Unbound*. Her deep involvement with European literature would continue throughout her career, taking the several forms of essays, translations, and original poetry.

William Morris: Translation and Retelling

Important though translation was to Elizabeth Barrett Browning, her actual publications in this field were relatively slight. The case of William Morris is very different; of the major writers of the period he is the one in whose work translation bulks largest. His numerous and varied translations make up about a quarter of his published writings, they are an essential part of his work, and are spread throughout the whole length of his career, rather than being concentrated in his apprentice years.

Some of his early works, notably *The Life and Death of Jason* (1867) and *The Earthly Paradise* (1869), had involved the reworking of foreign material, but literary translation proper began for him in 1869, when he discovered and fell in love with the literature of medieval Iceland. Reading the sagas and the verse of the *Edda* with the Icelandic scholar Eiríkr Magnússon, Morris immediately began to translate them—or rather to work up Magnússon's literal versions into texts that satisfied his own literary standards (for Magnússon's description of the process see Morris 1910–15: VII, xv–xix). In the first instance, then, translation was part of the process of language learning, but it quickly became much more, as Morris took on the task of bringing the sagas into contemporary English culture. With Magnússon, he published some twenty-seven saga translations as well as innumerable verse fragments. What is more, this activity continued until the end of his life; the 1890s saw a new burst of life with the publication of the six volumes of the Saga Library.

Why this enormous expenditure of energy? For Morris, as he explains in the introduction to the Saga Library, old Icelandic literature had a special significance for English society of the nineteenth century—these views had been strengthened by his two visits to Iceland in the 1870s. The largely forgotten roots of English culture were Nordic, and Morris declared in the preface to *The Story of the Volsungs and Niblungs*: 'this is the Great Story of the North, which should be for all our race what the Tale of Troy was to the Greeks' (Morris 1910–15: VII, 286). The sagas, as he read them, offered a vision of democratic equality and of moral virtues (independence, fortitude, individuality) that had been lost in modern commercial civilization. This old world had become strange to modern readers, and Morris's translating style seems designed to enhance this feeling of estrangement. Starting from Magnussón's plain literals, he created highly wrought texts, plain and vigorous in their way, but also marked by self-conscious archaism, with a predominance of Germanic words (for an example see p. 281, below).

Introducing Morris's adaptations of three Old French romances in 1896, Joseph Jacobs wrote that the style used first by Morris for the sagas had since 'been adopted by all who desire to give an appropriate English dress to their versions of classic or medieval masterpieces' (Jacobs 1896: x). In his verse translations of the *Aeneid* (1875) and the *Odyssey* (1887), while sticking closely to his original texts, Morris remained true to his archaizing impulse, which reaches its peak in one of his last works, the translation of *Beowulf* (1895), done from a literal version by A. J. Wyatt. These translations, with their strange phraseology and (in the *Aeneid* and *Odyssey*) their cumbersome long lines, have won little favour with later readers, and in their time opinion was strongly divided on them (see Faulkner 1973). Even a sympathetic critic like Andrew Lang regretted that Morris's translations from Latin and Greek, with their 'almost literal closeness', were marred by the 'strain of the philologist' who insisted on such a peculiar language in which to render them (Lang 1912: 116–17). What is important, however, is to see that they form part of a coherent strategy of artistic production, based on a thoroughgoing critique of contemporary culture, and finding expression equally in the physical presentation of the translations. Between 1869 and 1875, Morris was deeply involved in calligraphy, producing illuminated manuscripts of Latin poems (Virgil and Horace), but also of some 2,000 pages of saga translation. Such labours of love, like the translations themselves, can be seen as a refuge from, and a challenge to, the values of the machine age and commercial publishing (for a full discussion see Whitla 2001). Similarly with printed books: the translation of *Beowulf* first appeared in the splendid livery of the Kelmscott Press.

In Morris, as in Coleridge, there is a continuity between translation proper and the creative reworking of foreign sources. His early romances, from *The Defence of Guinevere* (1858) to *The Earthly Paradise* (1869), are almost all retellings of stories from classical or medieval literature (on the romances see Hodgson 1987). Sometimes they can be regarded as very free translations; in *The Earthly Paradise*, for instance, 'The Lovers of Gudrun' translates and expands a central episode in the *Laxdæla Saga*. But the most remarkable instance is that offered by his long poem *The Story of Sigurd the Volsung and the Fall of the Niblungs* (1876), a retelling of 'the Great Story of the North'. This story was the subject not only of Wagner's *Ring* cycle, but of one of Morris and Magnússon's first saga translations, *The Story of the Volsungs and the Niblungs* (1870). The poem of 1876 is an epic for the nineteenth century, but written in the same long lines, and with the same archaic terminology, as the *Aeneid* translation of the previous year; it is Morris's own poem, yet it carries with it the aura of a translation from an ancient and prestigious work.

Sigurd was not Morris's most popular work—nothing like as popular as *The Earthly Paradise*—but it won much critical praise and for Morris himself represented a high point in his writing. If we regard it as paraphrasing an existing text, we might observe that this system of paraphrase is typical of his artistic life. Just as the Pre-Raphaelite Brotherhood recreated a medieval past which was partly of their own invention, using history, gothic architecture, and legend as pegs on which to hang their own visions—in effect 'paraphrasing' rather than translating the medieval world for contemporary Victorian reality—so even the furniture design, wallpapers, tapestries, etc. of Morris & Co. were, like his writings, 'paraphrases' through which he could find his own distinctive artistic voice. It is, perhaps, hardly surprising that of all the later nineteenth-century poets, it was W. B. Yeats, with his theory of poetic 'masks', who was most to admire Morris.

LIST OF SOURCES

Translations
Browning, Elizabeth Barrett (1904). *The Poetical Works*. London.
—— (2004). 'Two Translations of Aeschylus', ed. Clara Drummond. Ph.D. diss. Boston University.
Carlyle, Thomas (1899). *Works*, 30 vols. London.
Coleridge, Samuel Taylor (1912). *The Complete Poetical Works*, ed. Ernest Hartley Coleridge, 2 vols. Oxford.
—— (2001). *Plays*, Part 1 (includes *The Piccolimini* and *Wallenstein's Death* [Schiller]). Princeton, NJ (Vol. 16, III, Part 1 of the Princeton *Collected Works* of Coleridge).
Griffiths, Eric, and Reynolds, Matthew (2005). *Dante in English*. London.
Morris, William (1910–15). *The Collected Works*, ed. May Morris, 24 vols. London.
Wordsworth, William (1998). *Translations of Chaucer and Virgil*, ed. Bruce E. Graver. Ithaca, NY (The Cornell Wordsworth).

Other Sources
Ashton, Rosemary (1980). *The German Idea: Four English Writers and the Reception of German Thought, 1800–1860*. Cambridge.
Browning, Elizabeth, and Browning, Robert (1984–). *The Brownings' Correspondence*, ed. Phillip Kelley and Ronald Hudson, 14 vols. to date. Winfield, KS.
Clancey, Richard W. (2000). *Wordsworth's Classical Undersong: Education, Rhetoric and Poetic Truth*. London.
Coleridge, Samuel Taylor (1956–71). *Collected Letters of Samuel Taylor Coleridge*, ed. Earl Leslie Griggs, 6 vols. Oxford.
—— (1957–90). *The Notebooks of Samuel Taylor Coleridge*, ed. Kathleen Coburn, 4 double vols. London.
Faulkner, Peter, ed. (1973). *William Morris: The Critical Heritage*. London.
Hodgson, Amanda (1987). *The Romances of William Morris*. Cambridge.
Holmes, Richard (1989). *Coleridge: Early Visions*. London.
Hyde, George (1999). ' "Language is First of All a Borrowed One": George Borrow as a Translator from Polish.' *MLR* 77: 74–92.
Jacobs, Joseph (1896). 'Introduction' to William Morris, *Old French Romances*. London.
Lang, Andrew (1912). *Adventures among Books*. London.
Lovejoy, A. O. (1961). *The Reason, the Understanding, and Time*. Baltimore, MD.
McFarland, Thomas (1969). *Coleridge and the Pantheist Tradition*. Oxford.
—— (1974). 'Coleridge's Plagiarisms Once More.' *Yale Review* 63: 252–84.

Prickett, Stephen (1976). *Romanticism and Religion: The Tradition of Coleridge and Wordsworth in the Victorian Church.* Cambridge.
Shaffer, Elinor (1975). '*Kubla Khan*' *and* '*The Fall of Jerusalem*'*: The Mythological School in Biblical Criticism and Secular Literature 1770–1880.* Cambridge.
Taplin, Gardner B. (1957). *The Life of Elizabeth Barrett Browning.* London.
Webb, Timothy (1976). *The Violet in the Crucible: Shelley and Translation.* Oxford.
Whitla, William (2001). ' "Sympathetic Translation" and the "Scribe's Capacity": Morris's Calligraphy and the Icelandic Sagas.' *Journal of Pre-Raphaelite Studies* 10 (NS): 27–108.

3.4 Academics

Adrian Poole

Universities

The emergence of the 'academic translator' is inseparable from the transformation of the universities and the development of university teaching as a profession. By the end of the nineteenth century the ancient universities had been largely released from their old theological ties, the celibate clergyman had turned into a married don, college tutors were moulding a new civic élite, and students were plagued with examinations. In Britain and America new colleges and universities were founded and new fields of scholarship opened up to which translation was essential, in historiography, philosophy, theology, and comparative philology. German thought migrated into English culture through 'a tightly knit network of intellectuals' (Stark 1999: 176), many of whom had positions in or close links to the academic world. (The first chair of German was established at University College London in 1828.) Niebuhr's *History of Rome* was particularly influential through the English version (3 vols., 1828–42) by two Fellows of Trinity College, Cambridge, Julius Hare and Connop Thirlwall. Kant was translated by William Hastie in Glasgow and John Henry Bernard in Dublin, and Hegel by William Wallace in Oxford (see § 11.2, below). Though Latin and Greek retained their central status in the curriculum, other languages gained recognition within the academy (and beyond). Chinese was enthusiastically promoted by James Legge in Oxford and Herbert Allen Giles in Cambridge (see § 7.4, below), and the Slavonic languages by William Richard Morfill in London. One should note that not all 'academic translators' spent their whole careers within 'the academy'. Bernard was Archbishop of Dublin before becoming Provost of Trinity College Dublin, for example, while Legge and Giles served in the Far East as, respectively, a missionary and a consular diplomat.

For most students, however, translation was a matter of 'the classics' and its function was pedagogical. Translation into and out of Latin and Greek was central to the developing system of examinations at Oxford and Cambridge and to the schooling that prepared pupils for university admission. At its most severe it was a form of punishment for naughty schoolboys. It was also an ordeal facing applicants to the Indian Civil Service—Oxford graduates were unsurprisingly successful. From this perspective translation was a way of instilling in civil servants and others the virtues of accuracy, speed, and precision in the discharging of strictly defined tasks, and deprecating independent, creative, or sceptical thought.

The task of coaching students for exams was not an elevated one, and model versions designed to help them, of Aeschylus' *Agamemnon* by 'a Balliol Man' (1880) or of Euripides' *Hercules Furens* by Augustus C. Maybury in the candidly entitled series 'How to Pass' (1886), did not strive for immortality. A loftier concept of translation and teaching was based on a belief in the ancient languages as living literature and a desire to read the classics alongside literature in English and other modern languages. To translate Aeschylus or Plato or Thucydides might be a means to redemption, of yourself, of others, or even of the degenerate modern world itself. Thus Benjamin Jowett and his modern followers, among many others. The rewards were not merely spiritual. One group of liberal academics that included Jowett and Mark Pattison saw in the study of Greek culture the means to an imperial end: 'Britain as a world civilization, with Oxford as its intellectual center' (Dowling 1994: xiv).

Though opposed in principle, these two ideas were not always at loggerheads: if you were to bring Sophocles to life in modern English, you had to know your Greek particles. The century boasts many virtuoso translators who commanded the admiration of pupils and peers. This was often a matter of live performance. W. H. Thompson, for example, professor of Greek at Cambridge from 1853 to 1867, was renowned for the apparently impromptu translations that illuminated his lectures; R. Y. Tyrrell, professor of Latin (1871), then Greek (1880), at Trinity College Dublin, was another such figure, whose graceful English renderings 'filled the note-books of his admiring pupils' (Clarke 1959: 124, 166). Thompson was succeeded by the elderly Benjamin Hall Kennedy, 'the greatest classical teacher of the nineteenth century' (*ODNB*); most of his career had been spent turning out a long line of distinguished pupils from Shrewsbury School. Kennedy's translations included Aristophanes' *Birds* (1874), Aeschylus' *Agamemnon* (1878), and Sophocles' *Oedipus Tyrannus* (1882). The Cambridge tradition was continued by Kennedy's successor in the chair of Greek, Richard Claverhouse Jebb, whose crowning achievement was the complete edition of Sophocles (1883–96), of which a prose translation and commentary were an integral part. Like other academics Jebb saw translation as one element in a nexus of activities bringing together scholarship, analysis, and imaginative engagement.

Reflecting in 1861 on the market for new translations, John Conington noted that teachers had become more tolerant of the weakness to which translation 'cribs' ministered and more interested in providing their pupils with models of good practice. The hunger for self-improvement could lead readers to learn Greek and Latin from books without teachers, and many who would never learn the languages still wanted to know what the ancients thought and did (Conington 1872: I, 181). Passing exams was important but so too was self-development, or *Bildung* as the Germans called it. Through the second half of the century Oxford and Cambridge saw a new breed of college tutors zealously promoting it in their young charges. But for those outside the hallowed walls, one vital means of access to the wisdom of the ancients was provided by translation. In a relaxed sense of the term this included the paraphrases of W. Lucas Collins's popular 'Ancient Classics for English Readers' in twenty-five volumes (Edinburgh, 1870–9).

Scotland, Ireland, and America had their own hallowed walls to which enthusiastic liberals brought back ideas and sometimes first-hand experience of German universities, such as George Ticknor in America (Vanderbilt 1959: 27) and John Stuart Blackie in Scotland. On taking up a chair at Aberdeen in 1841, Blackie sounded a representative note when he vowed 'through Latin to awaken wide human sympathies, and to enlarge the field of vision' (*DNB1*). He had already translated Goethe's *Faust* (1834) and would go on to Aeschylus (1850), before moving to the chair of Greek at Edinburgh. He translated the *Iliad* (1866), published a good deal of mediocre original verse, and helped to found a new chair of Celtic. Meanwhile Oxford made its influence felt in Scotland through Lewis Campbell's association of more than thirty years with St Andrews. Campbell was one of Jowett's prize protégés at Balliol, and his biographer. He wrote with enthusiasm about the Greek tragedians and Shakespeare, and produced verse translations of Sophocles (1883) and Aeschylus (1890), some of which were performed in the private theatricals run by Edinburgh's remarkable professor of engineering, Fleeming Jenkin. In the last decades of the century Greek drama spilled out of the study on to the stage, both in English and the original. This was a movement to which academics eagerly contributed, including Jowett in Oxford and Jebb in Cambridge.

Conington's Latin, Max Müller's Sanskrit

Ancient Europe, ancient India. Brief comparison of the work of John Conington and Friedrich Max Müller can serve to indicate the range of academic translation in the second half of the nineteenth century.

A product of Thomas Arnold's Rugby, Conington was elected in 1854 to the new chair of Latin at Oxford and held it until his early death. Though drawn to the Greek tragedians, especially Aeschylus—he edited *Agamemnon* (1848) and *Choephori* (1857), the former with a verse translation—he became best known for his edition and translation of Virgil. The 1860s were his heyday, with versions of Horace's *Odes* (1863), the *Satires, Epistles*, and *Ars Poetica* (1869), Virgil's *Aeneid* (1866), and the last twelve books of Homer's *Iliad* (1868), a task he took over from his dying friend Philip Stanhope Worsley. Conington experimented boldly with different verse forms, translating the *Aeneid* into the octosyllabics of Scott's 'Marmion'. This roused the scorn of some scholars, but it proved popular in the world at large (for a discussion of this and his Horace see pp. 192–4, below).

In his critical writings he reflected intelligently on the resources of verse forms in different languages, as for example the absence in English of any equivalent for Homer's and Virgil's hexameters and for Greek choral lyric metres. He mistrusted blank verse and was attracted to the possibilities of good English prose, producing a prose version of Virgil that now reads more impressively than his metrical one. He was attractively unpretentious about the different aims of the academic translator and the 'genuine poet'. As 'a piece of embodied criticism' a translation could have a value it might not otherwise have in itself (1866: ix). He looked up with intelligent but critical awe towards the heights of Dryden's Virgil (his 'clear unaffected musical English' and 'easy strength') and to Pope's Homer ('the delight of every intelligent schoolboy'). He saw his own work as part of an ongoing tradition. In 'The English Translators of Virgil' he remarked on the sea-change that had overtaken translations of Virgil since 1830: 'the old notion of translation—that which aims at substituting a pleasing English poem for an admired original—has been well-nigh abandoned, and experiments as multiform as those practised by Elizabethan scholars and poets have become the order of the day' (1872: I, 166). This suggests something of the excitement and belief in 'experiment' that characterizes the Victorians' attitude to translation, not only of Virgil, of course.

Conington believed that as the great works of antiquity had to be regularly translated afresh to preserve their value, so too did Shakespeare need reinterpretation for an expanding modern readership. This conviction prompted his lectures on *King Lear* and *Hamlet*, delivered both in Oxford, at the Working Men's Association and Woodstock Night Schools, and his home town of Boston in Lincolnshire. Through the efforts of classical scholars and translators like Conington modern literature was becoming a possible object of study, analysis, and appreciation. It is no surprise that the first King Edward VII Professor of English Literature at Cambridge (1911) was Arthur Woollgar Verrall, editor, translator, and interpreter of the Greek tragedians.

Max Müller also believed in the value of the great works of antiquity, but for him they lay in the East and their value was less literary than anthropological: they were vital evidence for understanding the evolution of language, religious belief, and philosophical thought. Born and educated in Germany, Max Müller settled in Oxford in 1848. Though appointed Taylorian Professor of Modern European Languages in 1854, his real passion was for the Sanskrit he had begun studying as a young man in Leipzig, where as a mere 20-year-old he translated into German the collection of tales known as the *Hitopadeśa*. Two decades later he turned it into English. His prolific publications included a ground-breaking edition of the *Ṛg Veda* (1849–74), *A History of Ancient Sanskrit Literature* (1859), *A Sanskrit Grammar for Beginners* (1866), and the *Lectures on the Science of Language* (2 vols., 1861, 1864) that won him the new Oxford chair of comparative philology in 1868. He also did pioneering, often controversial work on the study of comparative mythology and religion. Translation was a key element in all of his activities, but it took specific form in the translations of the *Ṛg Veda* (1869–74) and of the *Upaniṣads* (1879). A major undertaking of his last twenty-five years was his editorship of the fifty volumes of Sacred Books of the East, by various hands including his own (see § 10.3, below). These were translations not only from Sanskrit, Pali, and Prakrit, but also from Chinese, Arabic, Zend, and Pahlavi.

Max Müller's idea of the ancient world was very different from Conington's, and so was the kind of continuity he sought with it. He emphasized that his interest in all religions was chiefly historical: 'I want to see what has been, in order to understand what is' (cited by Chaudhuri 1974: 89). His own work had an immediate impact on 'what is', far greater than Conington's. In 1881 he published a translation of Kant's *Critique of Pure Reason*, in the preface to which he avowed his belief in 'the bridge of thoughts and sighs that spans the whole history of the

Aryan world'. Its first arch was the *Ṛg Veda* and its last Kant's *Critique*; in the former we could perceive the 'childhood', and in the latter 'the perfect manhood of the Aryan mind' (1881: lx–lxi). Such a myth was not without its uses to the then current rulers of India.

Jowett's Plato, Norton's Dante

Benjamin Jowett and Charles Eliot Norton are comparable figures in their intellectual eminence, their commitment to liberal education, their involvement with a powerful academic institution (Oxford and Harvard respectively), and their influence on the wider culture of their nations. Jowett wrote on theology and translated Thucydides and Aristotle, and late in life Norton edited the poetry of John Donne, but both owed their renown to association with a single great figure from the past. In Plato and Dante respectively they located an ethical, philosophical, and literary authority needed by a modern world increasingly liberated from the grip of dogmatic theology. Both travelled a long way from their fathers' fierce religious beliefs. Jowett's father, a failed furrier, had strong and narrow Evangelical views; Norton's, at one time a Harvard professor, was a biblical scholar who engaged in fierce controversy with the Transcendentalists.

For both Jowett and Norton, translation played a central role in promoting the study and appreciation of their chosen figures. Jowett's translation of the *Dialogues of Plato* came out in 1871, a few months after he became Master of Balliol; it was revised and expanded in 1875, and again, conclusively, in 1892. He had been teaching Plato from at least 1847 when he announced to his students: 'Aristotle is dead, Plato is alive' (Turner 1981: 374). But he turned decisively from St Paul to Plato after the bitter controversy surrounding the publication of *Essays and Reviews* (1860), to which he and other theological liberals had contributed. The ancient Greeks were safer.

Yet they were still exciting, so Jowett declared: 'under the marble exterior of Greek literature was concealed a soul thrilling with spiritual emotion' (1892: I, 423). Lewis Campbell applies this image to Jowett's own personality (Abbott and Campbell 1897: I, 388), but it also bears on the act of translation, which may be thought to release the 'soul' of meaning from the forbidding marble of an alien language. The idea of releasing the soul was for Jowett at the heart of Plato's thought, and it was also his mission as a teacher. But it is revealing that in Jowett's formulation, the flesh and the body have been displaced by 'marble'. The physical aspects of Greek culture presented him with some difficulties, especially when it came to dealing with certain passages in the *Phaedrus* and the *Symposium*, where 'love' had to be forcibly translated into heterosexual (and married) terms.

Never slow to find fault, A. E. Housman is said to have been 'disgusted by his disregard for the niceties of scholarship' (Clarke 1959: 210). But Jowett's Plato was readable and hence very popular. He was sensitive to the difficulties of writing good English prose and he could command a pithy turn of phrase. When his Socrates says that 'the unexamined life is not worth living' (1892: II, 131), he lives again, unforgettably, in English. Jowett wrestled with the lifeless pronouns that are hard to avoid in an uninflected language like English, and he envied the delicacy of particles, 'these gleaming imps of Greek speech', as one of his biographers strikingly calls them (Faber 1957: 327). He himself ascribed Plato's durability to his melodious voice, and despite the comparative poverty of sound in English (all those monosyllables), he sought to match it, not least by the discreet use of archaic, quasi-scriptural language—'fain', 'abide', 'righteous', 'clothed in bright raiment', 'this earthly tabernacle'. His introductions suggest that readers think of the dying Socrates as Christ and compare his sayings to St Matthew.

Discreet connections are also made with English literary tradition. A footnote illustrates the imprisonment of the soul in the body with lines from Milton's *Comus*, where 'The soul grows clotted by contagion, | Imbodies, and imbrutes'. When the philosopher Edward Caird, Jowett's successor as Master of Balliol, introduced a little volume of the latter's *Four Socratic Dialogues* (first published 1903 and frequently reprinted), he illustrated the dying soul's release from the body with phrases from *The Merchant of Venice*, 'that muddy vesture of decay', and from George Eliot's famous poem 'Oh may I join the choir invisible'. Through such moves was Plato translated into—or 'imbodied' in—the mainstream of English literary culture (see further the discussion on pp. 475–7, below).

Charles Eliot Norton's Dante was similarly translated into some powerful currents in American culture. In his mid-twenties Norton was fired with enthusiasm for the art, architecture, and poetry of the European Middle Ages, and he began his published work on Dante with a translation of the *Vita nuova* in 1859 (revised in 1867). His prose translation of the *Commedia* first appeared in 1891–2 and was painstakingly revised in 1902. Like Jowett, Norton favoured quasi-biblical or pseudo-Elizabethan diction: 'thee', 'thou', 'mayest', 'behoves', 'girt', 'And lo!', 'miscreant', 'dames of eld'. In Dante he found an elevating contrast to modern Italy and, in the years after the Civil War, to his degenerate native land. When he returned to Harvard in 1874 he taught the history of the fine arts up to 1600, but no further. He undertook readings of the *Divine Comedy* with a select group of students, out of which there grew the Dante Society of America. Among the many Harvard students who came under his influence were Irving Babbitt and Paul Elmer More, who would in turn leave their mark on the young T. S. Eliot.

In the late 1840s, shortly after graduating from Harvard, Norton had started evening classes for men and boys unable to complete their school education, and in his later years he helped to found the Loeb Classical Library. In the interim he had been, in the words of his biographer, 'a businessman, humanitarian, magazine editor, teacher, scholar, and citizen' (Vanderbilt 1959: 1). He was no ivory tower academic, but nor were Jowett, Jebb, and Max Müller across the Atlantic. All were figures for whom the activity of translation drew on a sense of the academy's involvement in the world at large, a belief that would be enthusiastically embraced in the early years of the twentieth century by another key figure in the history of translation, Gilbert Murray.

3.4 Academics

LIST OF SOURCES

Translations

Blackie, John Stuart (1834). *Faust: A Tragedy by J. W. Goethe; Translated into English Verse, with Notes, and Preliminary Remarks*. Edinburgh.

—— (1850). *The Lyrical Dramas of Aeschylus Translated into English Verse*, 2 vols. London.

—— (1866). *Homer and the Iliad*, 4 vols. Edinburgh (Vols. 2 and 3, *The Iliad in English Verse*).

Campbell, Lewis (1883). *Sophocles: The Seven Plays in English Verse*. London.

—— (1890). *Aeschylus: The Seven Plays in English Verse*. London.

Conington, John (1848). *The Agamemnon of Aeschylus: The Greek Text, with a Translation into English Verse and Notes Critical and Explanatory*. London.

—— (1866). *The Aeneid of Virgil Translated into English Verse*. London.

—— (1868). *The Iliad of Homer*, Vol. 2 (Vol. 1 by Philip Stanhope Worsley, 1865). Edinburgh.

—— (1882). *The Poems of Virgil Translated into English Prose*. London.

Jebb, Sir R. C. (1862). *Translations*. [Cambridge.]

—— (1904). *The Tragedies of Sophocles. Translated into English Prose*. Cambridge.

Jowett, Benjamin (1892). *The Dialogues of Plato, Translated into English, with Analyses and Introductions*, 3rd edn., 5 vols. Oxford (first pub. 1871).

Kennedy, Benjamin Hall (1874). *The Birds of Aristophanes Translated into English Verse, with Introduction, Notes and Appendices*. London.

—— (1882). *The Agamemnon of Aeschylus with a Metrical Translation and Notes Critical and Illustrative*, 2nd edn. Cambridge (first pub. 1878).

Müller, Friedrich Max (1864–5). *Hitopadesa: Containing the Sanskrit Text, with Interlinear Translation*, 2 vols. London.

—— (1869). *Rig-Veda-Sanhita: The Sacred Hymns of the Brahmans, Translated and Explained*. London.

—— (1879–84). *The Upanishads*, 2 vols. Oxford (Sacred Books of the East, Vols. 1 and 15).

—— (1881). *Immanuel Kant's Critique of Pure Reason*. London.

Norton, Charles Eliot (1859). *The New Life of Dante: An Essay with Translations*. Cambridge, MA.

—— (1902). *The Divine Comedy of Dante Alighieri*, 3 vols. Boston, MA (first pub. 1891–2).

Other Sources

Abbott, Evelyn, and Campbell, Lewis (1897). *The Life and Letters of Benjamin Jowett*, 2 vols. London.

Chaudhuri, Nirad C. (1974). *Scholar Extraordinary: The Life of Professor the Rt. Hon. Friedrich Max Müller, P.C.* London.

Clarke, M. L. (1959). *Classical Education in Britain, 1500–1900*. Cambridge.

Conington, John (1872). *Miscellaneous Writings*, ed. J. A. Symonds, with a memoir by H. J. S. Smith, 2 vols. London.

Dowling, Linda (1994). *Hellenism and Homosexuality in Victorian Oxford*. Ithaca, NY.

Engel, A. J. (1983). *From Clergyman to Don: The Rise of the Academic Profession in Nineteenth-Century Oxford*. Oxford.

Faber, Geoffrey (1957). *Jowett: A Portrait with Background*. London.

Rothblatt, Sheldon (1968). *The Revolution of the Dons: Cambridge and Society in Victorian England*. London.

Stark, Susanne (1999). *'Behind Inverted Commas': Translation and Anglo-German Cultural Relations in the Nineteenth Century*. Clevedon.

Stray, Christopher (1998). *Classics Transformed: Schools, Universities, and Society in England, 1830–1960*. Oxford.

Turner, Frank M. (1981). *The Greek Heritage in Victorian Britain*. New Haven, CT.

Vanderbilt, Kermit (1959). *Charles Eliot Norton: Apostle of Culture in a Democracy*. Cambridge, MA.

3.5 Women

Susanne Stark

Introduction

Historical research on women translators has tended to concentrate mainly on case studies of individuals and specific translations or, at a more general and theoretical level, on female attitudes and approaches to translation. It would be valuable to possess systematic statistical information about such topics as the proportion of women translators in the totality of translators, but such an undertaking poses considerable problems. In the fullest records available, those of the *Nineteenth-Century Short Title Catalogue* (*NSTC*), many translations are not attributed, and of those that are, many translators are identified in a form (initial plus surname) that makes it difficult to know whether it is a man or a woman. Nevertheless, a sampling of runs of literary translations in the *NSTC* produces the following figures: in 1830, about 70 per cent of translations are attributed to male translators, 4 per cent to female translators, 16 per cent to translators of uncertain sex, and 10 per cent are anonymous. For 1890, the figures are respectively 75, 16, 2, and 7 (the reduction of the number of translators of uncertain sex is due to the fuller information given on the *NSTC* records after 1871). Male translators are clearly in a large majority, but the proportion of identified female translators has grown markedly over the century. Unsurprisingly, women were more likely to be employed on the translation of fiction, history, biography, or religious writing from French and German than on classical or Oriental texts.

A number of important or prolific female translators such as Elizabeth Barrett Browning, Mary Howitt, Anna Swanwick, Katherine Wormeley, Mary Margaret Busk, Ellen Marriage, Clara Bell, Constance Garnett, and Lady Charlotte Guest are treated elsewhere in this chapter or in Chapter 12, below (for women's translation of poetry see also the discussion of 'Michael Field' on p. 78, above and George 2002: 274–7). The women selected for discussion here, though undoubtedly varied in background and situation, form a reasonably typical group; together, they shed some light on the situation of the female translator in the nineteenth century. They belonged to the middle or upper classes (like most women translators), enjoyed a high standard of education, moved in cultivated circles, and chose to translate intellectually challenging texts. On the other hand, a number of them, including Sarah Austin and Susanna and Catherine Winkworth, depended on the income they received from their translations; for them this occupation was more than a literary pastime. They had to face the economic necessities encountered by many male translators and to develop entrepreneurial talents by dealing with publishers and settling on the right texts.

This professional approach also encouraged many of them to reflect on their work as translators.

Many of the problems facing the woman translator were connected with the values underlying female education. Even women who grew up in a liberal and intellectually stimulating environment, which enabled them to study a wide range of subjects including the languages they needed in order to translate, were likely to have experienced a bias against expressing their opinions in public or engaging in literary creation. Translation, as opposed to independent authorship, might thus be a sign of conformity with traditional values. Its ancillary nature allowed those who so desired to shy away from public recognition. At the same time, however, it could be seen as highly skilled and at times creative work. The ambivalence inherent in the process of translation, its simultaneous derivativeness and originality, was particularly significant for female translators; the double-sidedness of the task encouraged many women who might otherwise not have become writers to develop their talents in this field.

Translation as Self-Effacement

Sarah Austin was considered to be the foremost translator of her time by contemporaries such as Thomas Carlyle, the philosopher William Whewell, and C. K. J. von Bunsen, the Prussian ambassador to London. She was best known for her translations from German, including works by Pückler-Muskau, Ranke, Raumer, and Niebuhr, in a variety of genres such as travel writing, history, and fiction. She also translated French writers such as Guizot and Cousin. Although she received encouragement from J. S. Mill, Southey, and Carlyle to write her own books, she insisted that she had to follow her 'calling of translator'. This allowed her to secure herself 'behind the welcome defence of inverted commas' (Austin 1854: vi–vii) for fear of exposing herself to criticism and provoking 'a possible polemic', which she considered to be improper in a woman (see Ross 1888: I, viii–ix). She also maintained that it was 'the peculiar and invaluable privilege of a translator' to be able to abstain from having opinions (Austin 1836: I, xiv). In contrast, far from receiving encouragement, Susanna Winkworth had been urged as a child to stifle her imagination and was deterred by her aunt from becoming a novelist (Winkworth 1883–6: I, 108–9). As an adult, when she considered undertaking a biography of Niebuhr, she came to the conclusion that she lacked the powers of judgement for original written work, which her sister considered to be unsuitable for a woman (Shaen 1908: 41; Stark 1999: 37). Under the guidance of her mentor Bunsen, Susanna decided to translate mainly theological, historical, and biographical works from the German. Her sister Catherine felt she could serve her religion best by translating a wide range of German protestant hymns; these were published under the title *Lyra Germanica* and went into over twenty editions (see pp. 412–14, below). While this is the work for which she is best known, she also made available to English readers the lives of Amalia Sieveking and Theodor Fliedner, whom she admired for their philanthropic and educational work.

If these women explicitly rejected going beyond translation in their literary endeavours, for others who were brought up with similar attitudes to the literary profession, notably Harriet Martineau and George Eliot, translation was a form of training leading to independent authorship. Martineau was Sarah Austin's cousin and grew up in the same educated and open-minded circles in Norwich as her more conservative relative. She acknowledged that in her youth young ladies were discouraged from studying conspicuously, 'especially with pen in hand' (Martineau 1983: I, 100), but she opposed Austin's views on women, since she did not believe that she did justice to her own 'natural powers', and criticized her for discrediting the pursuits of other women (I, 352). At the same time, she defended the activity of translation and, in contrast to George Eliot, did not abandon it after she had become established as an author active in a wide range of genres including journalism, history, fiction, and travel writing. Unlike some of her friends, she did not think that translating, which for her was 'like going back to school again while doing the useful work of mature age' (II, 391–2), was a task below her intellectual abilities. Moreover, in her rendering of Comte's *Philosophie positive*, she condensed the six volumes of the French original into two volumes of English text with a view to making Comte's ideas accessible to a wide audience in Britain. Comte welcomed Martineau's efforts and was in favour of getting her version of the text translated back into French.

Like Susanna Winkworth, George Eliot in her youth considered the novel to be a potentially pernicious genre and initially shrank from writing fiction (Eliot 1954: I, 21–4). She started her career by translating controversial German theological works which reflected her own questioning of orthodox religion at that time (see pp. 486–7, below). It was when she was turning herself from a translator into a creative writer that she published her most comprehensive statement on translation, a review of two pages in *The Leader* (1855), devoted to a Kant translation by J. M. D. Meiklejohn and a translation of German poetry by Mary Anne Burt. This article summarizes her ambivalent feelings about translation; on the one hand she emphasizes the professional training it requires, on the other hand she dismisses it as inferior to original work. An earlier letter, written shortly after the anonymous publication in 1846 of her first major translation, D. F. Strauss's *Life of Jesus*, had in many ways anticipated the conclusions of her later review. In this amusing document she invented an eccentric German professor of considerable learning who came to Britain to 'secure a wife and translator in one' (Blind 1883: 46). Even though she, like many readers, thought that it required male intellect and learning to translate Strauss, translation in this letter became a female occupation, which was carried out in a marital bond between a male author and his educated, though intellectually inferior, subservient wife. Despite the fact that Eliot showed more assertiveness in her rendering of Feuerbach's *Essence of Christianity* (1854), both in her translation style and through the fact that she attached her real name, Marian Evans, to the work, it is significant that, unlike Martineau, she stopped translating when she started to write novels, no longer finding translation an adequate way to express her ideas.

The women who shared Sarah Austin's concerns and undertook translation because it was a literary occupation to which their society objected less than to independent authorship did not therefore remain mute, transparent, and devoid of opinions. The example of Harriet Martineau's rendering of Comte makes it particularly clear that translation, like every other form of rewriting, cannot be divorced from creative processes. Even Sarah Austin contradicted herself in that she not only translated, but also wrote reviews in the periodicals and lengthy prefaces to her translations. Moreover, her *Germany from 1760 to 1814* (1854), which includes some of her lucid statements on translation, goes well beyond the mere reproduction of German original texts. Likewise Susanna Winkworth spent time in Bonn in 1850–1 and did a substantial amount of original research for her *Life of Niebuhr* (1852). She was also determined not to translate every text Bunsen suggested, refusing on religious grounds to undertake Kuno Fischer's history of philosophy. The texts her sister Catherine chose to translate reflected the major concerns of her life, the promotion of religion, philanthropic work, and education for women, and her history of German hymnody entitled *Christian Singers of Germany* (1869), which contains many translations, was a natural outcome of her translation work. George Eliot, too, did not translate Strauss, Feuerbach, and Spinoza arbitrarily; her own spiritual development is related to the theological texts she chose to render into English (see Ashton 1980: 147, 155–6, 159). The ideal of self-effacement was not absolute; all the translators mentioned so far either deliberately or inadvertently slipped into a role involving creativity and the expression of their values and convictions.

Translation as Professional Self-Assertion

Sarah Austin, an ardent defender of self-effacement in women translators, also repeatedly offered well-informed discussions of translation and the role of the translator in her prefaces. The most elaborate of these can be found in her preface to the *Characteristics of Goethe* (1833), in which she shows her familiarity with a wide range of ideas on the topic. Speaking of her own translation style, she made a point of defending a faithful literalness, even though she was aware that she might be criticized for advocating Germanisms (Austin 1833: xxxvii). But while close adherence to the original text was consonant with her view of the woman translator as a faithful, uncreative servant, this was not always the translation style she practised herself. Especially in her rendering of Pückler-Muskau's travel experiences in the British Isles, she bowdlerized the author, a flamboyant dandy figure, and cut his text, whenever she considered it necessary.

In many ways the level of training required to cope successfully with the role of translator might seem *less* compatible with female domestic duties than the abilities required for writing fiction, since a high level of linguistic competence could best be achieved by spending time abroad. This is what many women translators did, for extended periods. Against her family's advice, Anna Swanwick, translator of Goethe, Schiller, and Aeschylus, spent the years from 1839 to 1843 in Berlin, where she studied German as well as Greek and Hebrew (Bruce 1903: 27). Elizabeth Eastlake, who studied German during her stay in Heidelberg from 1827 to 1829 and subsequently translated German books on art history, is of particular interest. She not only went abroad, but also reflected on the role of women travellers in the *Quarterly Review*, became known for her travel writing, and commented on German life, art, and architecture in various periodicals. For other women, too, travel writing emerged naturally from their sojourns abroad even when, unlike men, they were brought up with values which made it less likely for them to undertake original writing. One example of this phenomenon is Sarah Austin's daughter, Lucie Duff Gordon, who, before leaving Europe, travelled and lived in Britain, Germany, France, and Malta. Having been shaped by her mother's ideas about suitable feminine literary occupations, she followed in her footsteps and concentrated on translating French and German literature, historiography as well as texts on legal history, but eventually her time in South Africa and Egypt led her into independent authorship and the publication of her *Letters from the Cape* and her *Letters from Egypt*.

One of the most productive connections between translating and travel writing is seen in the career of the American Isabel Hapgood, who actively promoted internationalism in literature. Hapgood became best known for her translations from Russian, but she also translated influential works such as Victor Hugo's *Les Misérables* (1887) and *Notre-Dame de Paris* (1888) and Ernest Renan's *Recollections and Letters* (1892) and had a knowledge of Spanish, Portuguese, Dutch, and Polish. In her 1928 obituary in the *New York Times* she was lauded as 'one of the few members of an honorable profession who succeed in rising above the obscurity which is the common fate of the translator' and who raised 'the middleman's craft in world literature to the level of an art' (Anon. 1928: 24). Her translation activity interacted fruitfully with her travel writing, journalism, and lecturing, as well as her interest in the Orthodox Church and its music. She considered it her main task to introduce Americans, who knew very little about Russia, to this distant country. Her translations from Russian covered a wide range of authors including Tolstoy, Gorky, Gogol, and Turgenev. In many cases these translations had no prefaces, but the volumes of Turgenev's *Novels and Stories* were preceded by introductions to the texts and at times by a broader examination of Russian literary history. Moreover, Hapgood's translation of Orthodox hymns contributed much to encourage the dialogue between the Russian Orthodox and her own Episcopalian tradition.

Similar traces of a 'mission' can be found in the work of Karl Marx's daughter Eleanor Marx-Aveling. Her translations were closely linked to the political and social values she wished to promote and to her own personal experiences. The internationalism of the socialist movement facilitated exchange across national and linguistic borders and made it easy for its supporters to establish contacts abroad. Marx-Aveling's published translations were closely linked to her political convictions, and she undertook a considerable number of translations for the socialist presses of Germany, France, Italy, Latin America, and Russia. Her translation of political writings, such as Lissagaray's *History of the Paris Commune of 1871* from the French and Plekhanov's *Anarchism and Socialism* from the German, are closely related to her own writings that promote the cause of socialism.

In her literary translations, too, she engaged with movements she wished to support and, together with George Bernard Shaw and Edward Aveling, she organized readings of Ibsen's plays in her house at a time when the dramatist's work was still little known in Britain. She was particularly fascinated by *A Doll's House* and learned Norwegian for the specific purpose of translating Ibsen. Her translations include *An Enemy of Society* and *The Lady from the Sea*, as well as short stories by Alexander Kielland. Like other intellectuals of her time, she felt attracted by the themes of Ibsen's plays, their critique of bourgeois morality and progressive depiction of the role of women in society. Flaubert, whose *Madame Bovary* she translated for Vizetelly, appealed to her because of the stylistic and moral 'revolution in the literary world' he had created in that work (Marx-Aveling 1886: xv). The parallel between Emma Bovary's and her own suicide has frequently been noted. In her introduction to *Madame Bovary*, she also discussed her own translation strategy, distinguishing three types of translator, the ingenious recreator of a work, the hack, and the faithful interpreter, who does his or her best without the brilliance of the first type and the flawed superficiality of the second (Marx-Aveling 1886: xvi–xvii). Marx-Aveling considered herself to be one of these honest, steady workers. But even though her comments defend her attempts at literal faithfulness in a way reminiscent of Sarah Austin's earlier theoretical support for this method, the motives which were responsible for each woman's stylistic choices reflect entirely different world views and highlight some of the changes in the self-perception of female translators during the nineteenth century.

LIST OF SOURCES

Translations
Austin, Sarah (1832). *Tour in England, Ireland, and France, in the Years 1828 & 1829* [Pückler-Muskau], 4 vols. London.
—— (1833). *Characteristics of Goethe. From the German of Falk, Von Müller, & c. With Notes, Original and Translated, Illustrative of German Literature*, 3 vols. London.
—— (1836). *England in 1835* [Raumer], Vols. 1 and 2. London.
—— (1845–7). *History of the Reformation in Germany* [Ranke], 3 vols. London.
Duff Gordon, Lucie (1844). *Mary Schweidler, the Amber Witch* [Meinhold]. London.
—— and Duff Gordon, Sir Alexander (1849). *Memoirs of the House of Brandenburg and History of Prussia During the Seventeenth and Eighteenth Centuries* [Ranke], 3 vols. London.
Eastlake, Elizabeth (1854). *Treasures of Art in Great Britain* [Waagen], 3 vols. London.
—— (1874). *Handbook of Painting. 4th Edition, Revised and Remodelled from the Latest Researches by Lady Eastlake* [Kugler]. London.
Eliot, George (1981). *Ethics* [Spinoza], ed. Thomas Deegan. Salzburg (translation completed 1856, unpublished at the time).
[Evans, Marian] (1846). *The Life of Jesus, Critically Examined* [Strauss], 3 vols. London.
—— (1854). *The Essence of Christianity* [Feuerbach]. London.

Hapgood, Isabel Florence (1903–4). *The Novels and Stories of Iván Turgénieff*, 16 vols. New York.
Martineau, Harriet (1896). *The Positive Philosophy of Auguste Comte*, 3 vols. London (first pub. in 2 vols. 1853).
Marx-Aveling, Eleanor (1886). *Madame Bovary: Provincial Manners* [Flaubert]. London.
—— (1888). *An Enemy of Society* [Ibsen], in Havelock Ellis, ed., *The Pillars of Society and Other Plays*. London (subsequently *An Enemy of the People*).
—— (1890). *The Lady from the Sea* [Ibsen]. London.
Swanwick, Anna (1846). *Dramatic Works of Goethe*. London.
—— (1888). *Schiller's Dramas*. London.
Winkworth, Catherine (1855). *Lyra Germanica. Hymns for the Sundays and Chief Festivals of the Christian Year*. London.
—— (1858). *Lyra Germanica: Second Series*. London.
Winkworth, Susanna (1852). *The Life and Letters of Barthold George Niebuhr with Essays on his Character and Influence by the Chevalier Bunsen and Professors Brandis and Loebell*, 3 vols. London.
—— (1858). *German Love: From the Papers of an Alien* [Max Müller]. London.

Other Sources
Anon. (1928). 'Translators.' *New York Times* (28 June), 24.
Ashton, Rosemary (1980). *The German Idea: Four English Writers and the Reception of German Thought, 1800–1860*. Cambridge.
Austin, Sarah (1854). *Germany, from 1760–1814*. London.
Blind, Mathilde (1883). *George Eliot*. London.
Bruce, Mary L. (1903). *Anna Swanwick: A Memoir and Recollections, 1813–1899*. London.
Chamberlain, Lori (1988). 'Gender and the Metaphorics of Translation.' *Signs* 13: 454–72.
Eastlake, Elizabeth (1845). 'Lady Travellers.' *Quarterly Review* 76: 98–137.
Eliot, George (1954). *Letters*, Vol. 1: *1836–1851*, ed. Gordon S. Haight. London.
—— (1963). 'Translations and Translators', pp. 207–11 in Thomas Pinney, ed., *Essays of George Eliot*. London (first pub. 1855).
George, J.-A. (2002). 'Poetry in Translation', pp. 262–78 in Richard Cronin, Alison Chapman, and Antony H. Harrison, eds., *A Companion to Victorian Poetry*. Oxford.
Martineau, Harriet (1983). *Harriet Martineau's Autobiography*, 2 vols. London (first pub. 1877).
Ross, Janet (1888). *Three Generations of Englishwomen: Memoirs and Correspondence of Mrs. John Taylor, Mrs. Sarah Austin and Lady Duff Gordon*, 2 vols. London.
Shaen, Margaret J., ed. (1908). *Memorials of Two Sisters: Susanna and Catherine Winkworth*. London.
Simon, Sherry (1996). *Gender in Translation: Cultural Identity and the Politics of Transmission*. London.
Stark, Susanne (1999). *'Behind Inverted Commas': Translation and Anglo-German Cultural Relations in the Nineteenth Century*. Clevedon.
Winkworth, Susanna, ed. (1883–6). *Letters and Memorials of Catherine Winkworth*, 2 vols. Clifton.

4
The Publication of Literary Translation: An Overview

Peter France and Kenneth Haynes

The Publication of Literary Translation: An Overview

Peter France and Kenneth Haynes

Some significant new directions in literary translation in nineteenth-century Britain and America have already been traced in Chapter 1. The aim of the present chapter is to provide a more quantitative account of the total body of translations, particular aspects of which will be highlighted in the following chapters. There are two main areas to be investigated, book publication and periodicals.

Book Publication

Our picture of the corpus of translations published between 1790 and 1900 is necessarily approximate and incomplete. There are studies of particular parts of the corpus (many of them will be found in the bibliographies of the chapters that follow), but for the complete body of translations the fullest source of information is the *Nineteenth-Century Short Title Catalogue* (*NSTC*); this covers the period 1801–1919, and can be supplemented for 1790–1800 by the *English Short Title Catalogue* (*ESTC*). The *NSTC* is based on the holdings of eight major libraries in the UK, Ireland, and the USA,[1] while the vastly more complete *ESTC* is based on the collections of over 1,600 institutions worldwide. At the time of writing the *NSTC* is not complete even for the holdings of the eight libraries in the period after 1870. Moreover, of the holdings of the two American libraries included in the *NSTC*, only books published from 1816 on are included. Altogether, the *NSTC* includes 1.2 million records for a 120-year period.

Neither the *NSTC* nor the *ESTC* lists all the titles that were actually published. Various types of books—including ephemera, pornography, and some privately published items—were not acquired by the libraries in question, nor did they necessarily buy subsequent editions of texts they already possessed. Conversely, some of the items listed are 'ghosts', books that do not exist. Duplicate entries are frequent. And the records rarely give any indication of the size of the edition. Scholars (for instance Amory 2001) have issued salutary warnings against over-reliance on such sources. Nevertheless, Simon Eliot (1997–8), comparing the result of bibliographical searches in the *NSTC* for the period 1800–70 with previous findings made by book historians, concludes that it is a valuable, if not perfect, tool for quantitative book history, and our checks against such databases as COPAC and WorldCat show that the *NSTC* is without question the most

---

[1] The *NSTC* is based on the catalogues of the Bodleian Library, British Library, Cambridge University Library, Trinity College Dublin, National Library of Scotland, Newcastle University Library, Library of Congress, and Harvard University Library.

complete source of data currently available. However, it must be emphasized that reliance on it will result in systematic undercounts. In particular, we will expect to see undercounts of those books not regularly collected by major libraries in the nineteenth century (including popular fiction, drama, libretti, song texts, and others); books printed in the United States before 1816; books published outside the UK, Ireland, and the United States; and reprints and subsequent editions of a book.

In order to obtain useful information, moreover, it is necessary to go beyond bare statistics and inspect the records one by one. By doing this one can eliminate duplicate records, find out more about the different imprints of a given title, and see more clearly the nature of each item, which may vary from a single song to a multi-volume edition of the works of Balzac.

Let us begin by considering the literary translations into English identified in an inspection of all the *NSTC* records for two sample years, 1830 and 1890. The word 'literary' is taken in a broad sense, to include for instance devotional writing,[2] political pamphlets, or popular science, but excluding technical or strictly utilitarian translations such as manuals, medical textbooks, grammars, or catechisms. The tables on p. 137 give figures by source language and by genre.

The figures for both 1830 and 1890 must be taken as a lower limit for the actual numbers of translations published in those years. Moreover, given the incompleteness of the *NSTC* for 1871 on, the figure for 1890 must be considerably lower than was the case in reality.[3] As a consequence, it is necessary to look at the percentages rather than the absolute numbers if the two years are to be compared. Finally, while it is not possible to estimate confidently how the *NSTC* numbers correlate with the total numbers (both absolute and percentage) of books published,[4] it seems likely that compared with continental countries the British were translating relatively little—as they continued to do in the following century (for the comparison in the nineteenth century, see the tentative evidence in Moretti 1998: 151–8; for the twentieth century see Pym 2000: 80).

As far as source language is concerned, the most striking change is the increase in the number of titles from Germany and northern Europe—and the emergence of Eastern Europe (where fourteen of the seventeen titles are Russian). Figures for Greek are noticeably higher (the great majority being ancient Greek), but Latin too shows a slightly above-average increase. French, on the other hand, which easily dominates the 1830 figures, shows a relative decline. Translations from

---

[2] In view of the extreme and confusing proliferation of editions of the Bible and Psalms, of which only a few are new translations rather than reissues or revisions of the King James Bible, it has been decided to omit these from the count.

[3] The total number of *NSTC* records for 1830 is 12,614; that for 1890 is barely higher at 12,977 (whereas the figure for 1870 was 21,169).

[4] We would nonetheless speculate that on average translations into English might make up between 3% and 5% of the total 'literary' production for a given year. This highly speculative figure is based on the assumption (corroborated by sample checks) that at least half the total book production for 1830 and a somewhat smaller percentage for 1890 is made up either of duplicate records or of such non-literary material as official reports or rules and regulations.

Table 1. Translations in the *NSTC* by source language

	1830	% of total	1890	% of total
Latin	31	12.3	54	13.4
Greek	22	8.8	47	11.7
French	103	41.0	106	26.4
German	33	13.1	81	20.1
Italian	16	6.4	16	4.0
Spanish and Portuguese	10	4.0	8	2.0
Celtic	4	1.6	8	2.0
Scandinavian and Dutch	1	0.4	24	6.0
Russian and E. European	5	2.0	17	4.2
Eastern	20	8.0	35	8.7
Miscellaneous	6	2.4	7	1.7
Total	251		402	

Note: Figures are rounded to the nearest tenth of a percentage and may therefore not add up to 100%.

Table 2. Translations in the *NSTC* by genre

	1830	% of total	1890	% of total
Fiction	39	15.5	107	26.6
Drama and opera	39	15.5	46	11.4
Poetry	33	13.1	49	12.2
History/geography	40	15.9	50	12.4
Biography	21	8.4	31	7.7
Philosophy/essay/criticism	23	9.2	47	11.7
Religious texts	38	15.1	53	13.2
Science/social science	18	7.2	19	4.7
Total	251		402	

Note: Categorization by genre has of course an arbitrary element and is necessarily imprecise. Children's stories and fables are classified under fiction; travel literature comes under history/geography; 'social science' includes writings on politics, law, and education.

eastern languages are already well launched in 1830 and increase proportionately in 1890, with a greater number of Chinese titles.

As noted, there is an element of arbitrariness in the categorization of titles by genres, but the figures suggest a fairly even growth in all categories with the exception of fiction, where there is a large increase. The year 1830 comes at the end of a period which, according to an exceptionally thorough recent study (Garside, Raven, and Schöwerling 2000), saw a major decline in the proportion of newly published novels that were translated. Of the thirty-nine fiction titles noted in 1830, only ten were translated from languages other than French. Over a third, moreover, were intended for children (including nine short and edifying works by the Genevan minister César Henri Abraham Malan); among the remainder one finds one or two classics of the eighteenth century such as Smollett's *Gil Blas*, a few popular modern classics such as Bernardin de Saint-Pierre's *Paul et Virginie* or Fouqué's *Undine* (both of them also appealing to children), but almost nothing of the more demanding foreign literature of the period. By 1890 French (with 39 titles) has declined noticeably in relation to German (30), Scandinavian (7, including four by Hans Andersen), and Russian and East European (7). What is more, while there is still plenty of children's reading here, there is also a fair proportion of novels by modern writers who have subsequently become classics (Balzac, Sand, Maupassant, Gautier, Goethe, Meyer, Bjørnsen, Tolstoy, etc.).

The importance of drama in 1830 is largely attributable to the place occupied by theatrical adaptations from French or German, many of them very free (see § 8.2, below); in 1890 we see more in the way of experimental drama from Scandinavia or Russia. Poetry, by contrast, is dominated in both years by Latin and Greek, many of the translations being no more than prose cribs for students. Separate volumes of poetic translation from the modern languages are fairly uncommon, but of course many translated poems appeared in journals, and others (not necessarily reflected in the tables above) were included alongside original works in editions of a given author's poems (see for instance Byron's first collection, *Hours of Idleness: A Series of Poems Original and Translated*, 1807). Apart from the more obviously literary genres, it is worth stressing the important place occupied by translations of history, biography, religious texts, and other discursive writing. In some years (notably 1870, when the Edinburgh firm of T. and T. Clark published a great number of translated Bible commentaries) religious translations could be over 20 per cent of the total, and at times the number of translations from a given language or in a given genre reflects current political events such as the French Revolution, the Crimean War, or the Boer War.

Figures for the two years 1830 and 1890 are bound to be unrepresentative in various ways; in what follows we shall attempt to characterize the development of the corpus of translation for specific languages over the whole period. In order to do this, we can draw on a number of specialized bibliographies, even if many of these define the literary by more exclusive criteria than those used here. In addition, we have made keyword searches in the *NSTC*, using the words 'translated', 'translation(s)', and 'translator(s)' for a number of years spread across the period (1790, 1810, 1850, 1870, and 1900) and examining all the records hit by this method. The results of these keyword searches are given in Appendix 4.1 at the end of this chapter. They confirm that the figures for 1830 and 1890 are broadly representative.

For the classical languages, as already noted, there are a great many translations described as 'literal' and designed primarily for student use; these become markedly more numerous for Greek in the second half of the period. One notices also the continuing presence of older translations, Pope's Homer and Dryden's Virgil, of course, but also older versions of Plutarch, Aesop, Ovid, and many others. As for new literary translations, these are spread across the whole range, with a new emphasis on Greek drama. Horace and Virgil both appear frequently. Interestingly, at the end of the period, there is a surge of interest in the previously somewhat neglected philosophy of Marcus Aurelius—four different publications in 1900.

Translations from Latin are as much concerned with post-classical texts as with classical ones. In some years, notably 1850, classical authors are in a minority. A large majority of post-classical translations are Christian texts, including many editions of the Church Fathers, with Augustine very prominent. The year 1850 sees the publication of four different Calvin commentaries, and of two works by Swedenborg, who is a major presence from the beginning to the end of the period. One notes also the regular appearance of such neo-Latin classics as the works of More and Erasmus, and the perennial popularity of *The Imitation of Christ*, thought to be by Thomas à Kempis.

Fiction is the dominant genre for French and German, but not as overwhelmingly so as one might expect. To be sure, the French popular novelists, above all Alexandre Dumas *père* and Eugène Sue, but also Balzac, Hugo, and many others, figure repeatedly on the lists, whereas some of those who were to become classics (notably Flaubert and Stendhal) are conspicuous by their infrequent appearances. For both languages, however, religious writings and a variety of discursive prose texts (notably biographical and historical works) tend to be almost as numerous as stories, novels, and plays. The works of such historians as Ranke and Guizot are translated more than once, and frequently reissued (on the vogue for translated history see § 11.3, below). Many plays are translated or adapted from French and German, the early vogue of Kotzebue giving way to the appeal of the French melodrama and the 'well-made play'. There are relatively few volumes devoted to poetry, markedly fewer than for the classical languages; this is particularly true of French, where there are no poets of the acknowledged stature of Goethe and Schiller, both of whom are repeatedly translated throughout the period.

Of the other Romance languages, Italy is by far the richest source of translations, providing material in many genres, from saints' lives to opera. Very little modern literature from Spain or Portugal is translated (see § 6.4, below). But for all three languages, one striking feature is the continuing attraction of certain classic translations, such as Hoole's Tasso and Ariosto, and the *Don Quixote* of Motteux and above all Jarvis. To this we should add the rediscovery of medieval Spanish epic and ballad literature, a renewed interest in Calderón, the many new translations of Camões, and the extraordinary vogue of Dante (see pp. 141–2, below, for Cary's translation).

The figures for the other European languages are very low until the middle of the century, though Ossian and similar Celtic material is translated throughout the period. Old northern literature, notably the Icelandic sagas, begins to make an appearance by mid-century. More important in quantitative terms are modern Scandinavian plays and novels (see Bjork 2005); there are six publications of Fredrika Bremer in 1850, seven of Bjørnstjerne Bjørnson and nine of Hans Andersen in 1870, and four of Ibsen in 1890. The literatures of Central and Eastern

Europe barely register before the last third of the century, but then certain authors achieve great popularity, notably Tolstoy (for details, see Line 1972). The last year of the century also sees the vogue of the Polish novelist Henryk Sienkiewicz (5) and the Hungarian Jókai Mór (4). It is an indication of the interest in previously little-known European literatures in this decade that in 1895 there are advertisements for Heinemann's International Library, a collection of seventeen novels in cheap editions, translated from nine European languages, including Norwegian, Dutch, Polish, and Bulgarian.

Translations from eastern languages are varied in nature. There are some new translations from the Old Testament, as well as Hebrew hymns and prayers. From the Middle East, India, and the Far East, while there are a certain number of literary translations for the general public, from the *Thousand and One Nights* to classical Persian poetry or the Japanese novel of *Genji*, the majority of translations are designed for specialists and students. Many educational translations from Sanskrit are published in India, while in Britain the Oriental Translation Fund, inaugurated in 1828, makes available to scholars a variety of philosophical, historical, religious, or legal works, chosen to introduce the reader to the cultures of the 'Orient'. The Indian languages dominate, but Chinese and eventually Japanese make their appearance in the last third of the century. From 1879 Max Müller's great collection Sacred Books of the East (see § 10.3, below) brings into English many important writings, particularly from the Indian subcontinent.

It is important to bear in mind that the most influential and popular translations at any particular time are not necessarily the latest ones. Many of our records concern reissues, many of relatively recent translations, but some of standard classics or even of texts whose appeal lies partly in their antiquity (as with W. E. Henley's collection Tudor Translations, issued in the 1890s). It is not always easy to tell whether a given imprint is a new translation or a reissue, but there is certainly a progressively greater percentage of new translations as the century wears on. If old and new are fairly evenly balanced in 1810, by 1870 it seems that more than two-thirds of the translations published are new ones—but it is the reprints in popular collections such as the Bohn Libraries (on which see pp. 8–9, above) which enjoy the large print runs.

For any given translation, it is not generally possible to know the total number of copies printed, but it may be illuminating to consider the reprints of certain texts. Take for instance one of the French history books which found such a good market in the English-speaking world. For Guizot's *General History of Civilization in Europe*, published in translation in 1837, the *NSTC* lists twenty-two imprints by 1870; until 1846 these are mostly British, but thereafter there are some fifteen American impressions; towards the end of the century this was a work that found favour with popular publishers, appearing in more than one reprint series. In a more esoteric vein, we might take James Legge's *Chinese Classics*; this was published in five volumes in Hong Kong and London in 1861–72, with at least four further editions by Trübner before 1900 and a new edition by the Clarendon Press in 1893–5.

These were new translations, but some of the classics continued to thrive, often in revised or abridged form. Pope's *Iliad* was reissued (unrevised) almost every year from 1790 to 1825 and thereafter some thirty times before the end of the century, and Dryden's *Aeneid* was published at least thirty times during the nineteenth century. There were a dozen or more printings of Urquhart's Rabelais, Hawkesworth's *Télémaque*, and Johnes's Froissart, and twice as many of Smollett's *Gil Blas*. But the most popular translation was Jarvis's *Don Quixote*, with almost as many imprints as there were years in the century—and this in spite of the popularity of the rival translations of Motteux and Smollett, each of which was issued some twenty times. Of more recent translations, Helen Maria Williams's version of Bernardin de Saint-Pierre's *Paul et Virginie* was published some thirty times (probably more, since it was sometimes issued anonymously), while towards the end of the century Victor Hugo's and Alexandre Dumas's novels figured repeatedly in a variety of cheap collections, and Edward FitzGerald's *Rubáiyát of Omar Khayyám* was beginning its triumphal career as one of the most popular poetry books ever published in English.

The importance of reprints in enlarging the readership for translation may be illustrated by the case of Henry Cary's *The Vision, or, Hell, Purgatory and Paradise of Dante Alighieri*, the most commercially successful verse translation of the century. Its success is all the more remarkable in that it was competing with many other translations, including that of Longfellow and the prose version by John Aitken Carlyle, Thomas Okey, and Philip H. Wicksteed, which was eventually adopted by Gollancz's bilingual Temple Classics.

The first edition of Cary's translation, in three volumes, was privately printed in 1814, some years before the general introduction of the manufacturing techniques (notably stereotyping and machine presses) which revolutionized the publishing industry, making possible large, cheap editions (on book production and readership in Britain between 1790 and 1830 see St Clair 2004). At this time print runs were generally small (usually between 500 and 2,000 copies) and prices were correspondingly high. However, Cary's work was sufficiently well received to warrant four subsequent British and American editions by 1844, the date of the last revised edition. Soon thereafter, the *Vision* began to figure in the reprint series that a number of publishers were establishing, and that might achieve print runs of 20,000 or more. The pioneer here was Henry Bohn, and Cary's text was in Bohn's Standard Library by 1847; it was also included in such collections as Warne's Chandos Classics, Routledge's Popular Library, Methuen's Little Library, and even, despite the name of the series, in Gibbing's Standard British Classics, as well as being repeatedly reissued by a number of publishers, notably Cassell's, in both de luxe and popular editions, often with engravings by Gustave Doré. These were sold in both Britain and America, but there were specifically American reprints as well. The editions came in different formats and prices, with correspondingly different print runs—in 1888 for instance the *Inferno* figures in Bohn's Shilling Library, while the following year the *Purgatorio* is included in Bohn's Select Library, at a correspondingly higher price. In all there were upwards of fifty different editions by 1900; one can only guess at the total number of copies printed and at the number of readers reached by Cary's work in the eighty-six years following its first publication.

Periodical Publication

It is not currently possible to estimate reliably, let alone document, the presence of translation in nineteenth-century periodicals. *The Wellesley Index to Victorian Periodicals* is a basic reference, but it covers only the forty-three British serials it takes to be major, lacks a subject index, and worst of all omits most of the verse. As a result, it severely misrepresents the monthlies which carried much verse, both original and translated; some translations ran for dozens of pages.[5] For most purposes, *Poole's Index to Periodical Literature*, covering 479 'substantial' British and American periodicals from 1802 to 1906, remains the basic resource. In its print form, *Poole's Index* does not include 'translation' as a subject; however, in its electronic version, a keyword search gives 695 citations between 1802 and 1900 of 'translated', 'translator(s)', 'translating', and 'translation(s)'. Dropping translations into languages other than English, and a few technical translations, we arrive at approximately 630 citations.[6] (For comparison's sake, Poole's lists 152 articles with 'Afghanistan' in the title, and 2,383 titles with 'Shakespeare'.) These citations include translations and reviews of translations, as well as more general discussions.

The languages that dominate these citations are Greek (22 per cent), Latin (18 per cent), and German (11 per cent); next come Italian (5 per cent), French (4 per cent), and Spanish (2 per cent); the languages of a few citations (1 per cent) could not be determined. Translations of biblical, theological, and devotional texts account for about 14 per cent of the entries; eastern texts, 8 per cent; and general discussions of translation, 6 per cent. Italian translations are heavily dominated by Dante, and appear most often in the last quarter of the century; in contrast, a wide variety of French authors are discussed throughout the period that is indexed. To a lesser degree, eastern texts are dominated by the *Arabian Nights* and translations from Max Müller's Sacred Books of the East. Homer is the most common Greek author discussed, Horace the most frequent Latin author.

By using the electronic index to search all the articles in which the names of popular foreign authors appear in the title, we find the pattern confirmed by which the literature of a country is represented in a high degree by a single author: Homer for Greece (272 citations, while Plato, apparently the nearest competitor, has 171); Goethe for Germany (428, while Kant has 172); Hugo for France (273, while Balzac and Guizot have 127 and 122, respectively); and Dante for Italy

---

[5] Additions and corrections are printed in *Victorian Periodicals Review* and elsewhere; see the Curran Index to Wellesley Index Revisions, **http://victorianresearch.org/curranindex.html**. The 'illogic' of the indexing was criticized by Eileen Curran (1996: 103).

[6] The electronic index does not distinguish between original articles and subsequent reprints (if any); both are included here in the number of citations.

(302, while Petrarch has 60). Slightly under a third of the articles concerned with Homer and Dante announce their interest in translation; for other authors, and especially for French authors, translation is noted in titles much less often.

Translations were a regular feature of many British literary periodicals. They appeared both independently and as parts of reviews and essays. The reviews covered both foreign literature, sometimes offering extracts newly translated by the reviewer, and English translations, often quoting from them, sometimes at length. The line between review and essay was not a sharp one; for example John Wilson (writing under his pseudonym 'Christopher North') took Sotheby's translation of Homer's *Iliad* as a point of departure for a wide-ranging study of the poem in its many English guises; his seven essays in *Blackwood's* on the topic (April 1831–February 1834) run to almost 400 pages. In addition, translation itself was sometimes a topic for discussion. These reviews and discussions of translations in periodicals should be considered alongside the periodical publication of translations.

Tables 3, 4, and 5 indicate the number of translations published in two magazines in three decades: the 1830s, the 1850s, and the 1870s. The journals, *Blackwood's Edinburgh Magazine* (1817–1980) and *Fraser's Magazine* (1830–82), span much of the period, circulated widely, and consistently included translation. Counting translations in periodicals, however, is not a simple task. They are sometimes not marked as translations; not all pseudo-translations can be readily identified; it is not always easy to distinguish between translations that stand on their own and those that are part of a larger article; and the question of what constitutes a literary translation may be particularly difficult to answer because the contemporary interest in politics and current affairs was strongly mixed with literary interests. The same liberal definition of 'literary' has been adopted here as with translated books, but a fairly strict criterion has been applied in distinguishing independent translations from extracts of translations. Only free-standing translations are included, except for those cases in which a review or essay includes a substantial amount of new translation: either two or more poems complete or a page and half or more of continuous writing.[7] (This excludes all but lengthy translated extracts in reviews, and all excerpts in reviews of existing translations; the exception was made because it would be misleading and merely purist not to count, for example, a new translation of an entire scene from an Italian drama.) The category 'other' includes all languages for which only a single translation was made in the period. It must be emphasized that the pattern of numbers is more reliable, or even intelligible, than any single entry; different and equally defensible definitions of 'literary' and 'substantial' would alter the numbers significantly.

---

[7] We have counted as 'new' those translations which did not indicate they had been previously published; this will result in an overcount because reprinted translations were not always identified as such. A few more details: translations of poems in dialects of foreign languages are included in the category of the related major language; translations from two or more languages in a single article may be counted for each language, provided that each meets the criteria for inclusion; précis of foreign works (most commonly, novels) have not been included; some, but not all, imitations and adaptations are included, depending on how closely they follow the original; and finally, the few items translated via an intermediate language have been classed according to the intermediate language.

Table 3. Translations in *Blackwood's* and *Fraser's*, 1830–1839

	Blackwood's	*Fraser's*
Latin	4	15
Greek	47	37
German	20	30
French	7	18
Italian	1	8
Spanish	1	6
Irish Gaelic	0	4
Persian	1	4
Arabic	0	2
Chinese	0	2
Danish	2	0
Other	0	8

Table 4. Translations in *Blackwood's* and *Fraser's*, 1850–1859

	Blackwood's	*Fraser's*
Latin	2	3
Greek	2	2
German	8	10
Dutch	0	4
Italian	0	3
French	1	2
Persian	0	3
Sanskrit	0	2
Other	2	5

Table 5. Translations in *Blackwood's* and *Fraser's*, 1870–1879

	Blackwood's	*Fraser's*
Latin	6	0
Greek	2	1
German	11	3
Dutch	0	9
French	4	3
Irish	0	5
Italian	2	1
Persian	0	2
Other	0	3

A very large majority of these translations consists of short verse, mainly lyric; the remaining minority consists both of prose and longer verse. Because the space occupied by short verse did not require a large investment of money, time, or labour, a wide range of languages and authors could be included at relatively small cost; thus, a spike in the number of translations for a given period should not necessarily be interpreted as a response to or a perception of increased demand. In addition, the choice of decades skews the representation. For example, in no other period than the 1830s was Greek the most popular source language for *Blackwood's*; in the 1840s *Blackwood's* carried eight translations from Russian, as opposed to only two others for the rest of its run in the nineteenth century; the nine translations from Dutch that appeared in *Fraser's* in the 1870s represent a single novel published serially. The decline in translations after the 1830s is sharply evident in both magazines.

A consideration of two other journals will help to round out this statistical picture: *Bentley's Miscellany* (1837–68) and the *Dublin University Magazine* (1833–80). As mentioned above, the *Wellesley Index* gives only a partial picture of the translations carried by them; however, assuming that the translations indexed in it are representative of all the translations published in the magazines, just over half of the translations in *Bentley's* in the 1850s came from French, and just over a quarter from German; the remainder included translations from Italian, Spanish, Danish, and Breton. No translations from classical languages were included, and the large proportion of French was partly due to the serial publication of a single work of fiction and of history. The proportions for the *Dublin University Magazine* in the 1850s were German 25 per cent, Latin 17 per cent, Portuguese 14 per cent, and Sanskrit 11 per cent; other languages include Italian, Irish, Norse, Russian, and Spanish. In the 1870s, the total number of translations has increased from those of the 1850s by about a quarter; the breakdown by language is French 35 per cent, Greek 20 per cent, German and Russian equal at just over 10 per cent, and the remainder included Icelandic, Italian, Latin, and Spanish. This increase sharply contrasts with the fate of translations in journals for a more general audience, like *Fraser's* and *Bentley's*.

The *London Journal*, particularly in its first series (1845–83), and the *Strand Magazine* (1891–1950) were among the widely read magazines for fiction; both included much translation (on the *London Journal*, see James 1974: 136–45; also Ch. 2, above). The first British translation of Zola appeared in the former (for a discussion, see King 2004: 223–42). The *Strand Magazine*, beginning only in the last decade of the nineteenth century, made translation a critical part of its enterprise, carrying in its first year thirty-five translated stories, including children's stories. These came mainly from French (51 per cent), Russian (14 per cent), and German (11 per cent); for much of the remaining decade, it was carrying only about half as many translations, dominated by French, though German was consistently represented, and Russian did not disappear (for more information on the translation of popular fiction, see § 8.1, below).

Of three famous short-lived magazines of the nineteenth century, *The Germ* (1850), *The Dial* (1840–4), and the *Yellow Book* (1894–7), only the latter two featured translation. *The Dial* is discussed in § 1.2, above; it included not only much translated work but also many short reviews of translations. The *Yellow Book* eschewed reviews; the translations it carried appeared on their own, sometimes accompanied by the original, or in a discursive essay. It favoured short lyric poems: Horace's Ode I.5, a sonnet by Heredia and by Petrarch, poems by Verhaeren. Richard Garnett published translations of two sonnet sequences, one Italian (Luigi Tansillo) and one Portuguese (Antero de Quental).

More than two-thirds of the periodicals in the *Wellesley Index* have at least some interest in translation or foreign literature, and many others not recorded there specialized in it. This interest most often took the form of reviews. In an appendix to *British Literary Magazines*, Vol. 3, Eileen M. Curran writes:

Particularly in the 1820s, 1830s, and 1840s, a number of reviews were founded that concerned themselves principally or exclusively with foreign literatures. Most were short-lived; many are difficult to find today. In addition to these, some general reviews published more or less regular features on foreign literature or foreign life and thought; others showed as great an interest without establishing separate departments for the articles. If less attention was given to foreign literature in the latter part of the century, the reason may be that the proselytizing of the earlier years was no longer necessary.   (Sullivan 1983–6: III, 493)

She lists sixteen periodicals devoted to foreign literature, life, and thought; another fourteen journals whose titles indicate a probable interest in foreign literature; eight general periodicals with special features devoted to foreign literature; four more that gave considerable attention to it; and finally twenty-two periodicals concerned with foreign languages from a pedagogical perspective. The most successful and influential of these were *Blackwood's Edinburgh Magazine*, the *Westminster Review*, and *The Athenaeum*. But the *Westminster Review* covered foreign literature only for about a decade after its merger with the *Foreign Quarterly Review* in 1846, and only in its early years did *The Athenaeum* review foreign works of literature with some regularity (Marchand 1941: 215–21).

This leaves *Blackwood's* as perhaps the single most important British source for reviews of translations. Tables 8 and 9 in Appendix 4.2 list, by decade, the languages and genres of the translated works it reviewed (only those reviews which include more than very brief extracts have been included). Greek, Latin, French, and German dominate the citations, though in the second half of the century reviews of translations, with the exception of reviews of translated fiction, generally declined. The high proportion of reviews of French works contrasts with the smaller number of translations from French published in the journal.

In the United States, the only periodical comparable to *Blackwood's* in its longevity, influence, and coverage of translation was the *North American Review* (1815–present). Unlike *Blackwood's*, however, it quickly dropped the practice of printing translations, publishing more in the first half-decade of its run than in the remaining eighty years of the century. Translation was subsequently included mostly in the form of reviews. Tables 10 and 11 in Appendix 4.2 list, by decade, the languages and genres of the translated works under review (as with *Blackwood's*, only those reviews which include more than very brief extracts have been included). In comparison with *Blackwood's*, the *North American Review* includes proportionately less Greek and Latin; overall, a greater diversity of languages is evident in the *North American Review*.

Among the periodicals which featured reviews, the *Foreign Quarterly Review* (1827–46) should be mentioned. Its main focus was contemporary literature, and the large majority of its reviews contain translated excerpts. Many other topics were discussed in its pages, however, from classical literature to political and religious controversies. In the 1830s, when the issues on average contained ten reviews, literature in a narrow sense (poetry, fiction, drama, and literary criticism) was the subject of 20 per cent of the reviews. History and current affairs (including recent travel writing) each received about the same amount of attention as literature, while science, religion, economics, and the arts largely made up the rest. French and German were the most common languages of the foreign books under review, though often serving as intermediate languages. Much of European literature, history, and current affairs was discussed in the *Foreign Quarterly*, which also covered, albeit less consistently, Asia and North and South America.

The success of the review, Curran writes, was due in part to its timing: it ran during a period of great interest in foreign literature and attitudes:

> About ten years after the end of the Napoleonic Wars the English developed considerable interest in foreign thinking and writing. If the importation of books into Great Britain is any indication, this interest crested in the 1830's, began to subside with the growing political agitation of the 1840's, and reached its lowest point in the 1850's.
>
> (Curran 1973: 1)

This general pattern is seen also in the number of translated works in *Blackwood's* and *Fraser's*, which declines steeply by mid-century. Translation will never regain its former prominence in their pages, and new journals aiming at a wide audience only partially picked up the slack in the second half of the century. For example, the *Cornhill Magazine* (1860–1975) consistently paid some attention to translation (in the form of reviews, excerpts, and free-standing pieces), but only at about the same level of coverage as *Blackwood's* in the same period. The translation of popular fiction follows a somewhat different pattern. The cheap, mass-circulated magazines which emerged for the first time in the 1840s (*Family Herald*, *London Journal*, *Reynolds' Miscellany*) owed their success to the public's demand for melodramatic fiction which at that time could be cheaply met by translation from French (see § 8.1, below). Likewise, at the end of the century, the *Strand* was again able to enjoy mass sales of translation, having found a new lucrative market for short stories from the Continent.

LIST OF SOURCES

Amory, Hugh (2001). 'Pseudodoxia Bibliographica: or, When is a Book not a Book? When it's a Record', pp. 1–14 in Lotte Hellinga, ed., *The Scholar and the Data Base*. London.

Balay, Robert (2000). *Early Periodical Indexes: Bibliographies and Indexes of Literature Published in Periodicals before 1900*. Lanham, MD.

Bjork, Robert (2005). 'A Bibliography of Modern Scandinavian Literature (Excluding H. C. Andersen) in English Translation, 1533–1900, and Listed by Translator.' *Scandinavian Studies* 7: 105–42.
Curran, Eileen M. (1958). 'The "Foreign Quarterly Review" (1827–1846): A British Interpretation of Modern European Literature'. Ph.D. diss. Cornell University.
—— (1961). 'The *Foreign Quarterly Review* on Russian and Polish Literature.' *SEER* 40: 206–19.
—— (1973). 'Reviews of Foreign Literature: Some Special Problems.' *Victorian Periodicals Newsletter* 20/2: 1–7.
—— (1996). 'Verse in *Bentley's Miscellany* vols. 1–36.' *Victorian Periodicals Review* 32: 103–59 (omits verse translation).
Eliot, Simon (1994). *Some Patterns and Trends in British Publishing, 1800–1919*. London.
—— (1997–8). '*Patterns and Trends* and the *NSTC*: Some Initial Observations.' *Publishing History* 42: 79–104; 43: 71–112.
Garside, Peter, Raven, James, and Schöwerling, Rainer (2000) *The English Novel, 1770–1829: A Bibliographical Survey of Prose Fiction Published in the British Isles*, 2 vols. Oxford.
Hathaway, Lillie V. (1935). *German Literature of the Mid-Nineteenth Century in England and America, as Reflected in the Journals, 1840–1914*. Boston, MA.
Houghton, Walter E., ed. (1966–89). *The Wellesley Index to Victorian Periodicals, 1824–1900*, 5 vols. Toronto.
James, Louis (1974). *Fiction for the Working Man, 1830–1850*. Harmondsworth (first pub. 1963).
Joyaux, George (1965). 'French Fiction in American Magazines: 1800–1848.' *Arizona Quarterly* 21: 28–40.
King, Andrew (2004). *The London Journal 1845–83: Periodicals, Production, and Gender*. Aldershot.
Line, M. B. (1972). 'A Bibliography of Russian Literature in English Translation to 1900 (Excluding Periodicals)', pp. 7–75 in M. B. Line, A. Ettinger, and J. M. Gladstone, eds., *Bibliography of Russian Literature in English Translation to 1945*. Totowa, NJ.
Marchand, Leslie A. (1941). *The Athenaeum: A Mirror of Victorian Culture*. Chapel Hill, NC.
Moretti, Franco (1998). *Atlas of the European Novel, 1800–1900*. London.
Morgan, Bayard Quincy (1938). *A Critical Bibliography of German Literature in English Translation, 1481–1927*. Stanford, CA (first pub. 1922).
—— and Hohlfeld, A. R., eds. (1949). *German Literature in British Magazines, 1750–1860*. Madison, WI.
Mott, Frank Luther (1938–68). *A History of American Magazines*, 5 vols. Cambridge, MA.
Poole, William Frederick (1891). *Poole's Index to Periodical Literature, 1802–1881*. Boston, MA (rev. edn.; five supplements follow between 1888 and 1908 which cover the years 1882 to 1907).
Pym, Anthony (2000). 'Late Victorian to the Present', pp. 73–81 in Peter France, ed., *The Oxford Guide to Literature in English Translation*. Oxford.
St Clair, William (2004). *The Reading Nation in the Romantic Period*. Cambridge.
Sullivan, Alvin, ed. (1983–6). *British Literary Magazines*, 4 vols. Westport, CT.
Vann, J. Don, and VanArsdel, Rosemary T., eds. (1978–89). *Victorian Periodicals: A Guide to Research*, 2 vols. New York.
—— —— eds. (1994). *Victorian Periodicals and Victorian Society*. Toronto.
Wilson, John (1855–8). *The Works of Professor Wilson*, 12 vols. Edinburgh (Vol. 8 reprints his *Blackwood's* essays on 'Homer and his Translators').

APPENDIX 4.1: TRANSLATIONS IN THE *NSTC* FOR SELECT YEARS (KEYWORD SEARCH)

In the following tables, the translations were counted not in their entirety but by searching keywords ('translated', 'translation(s)', and 'translator(s)'). In 1830, this method picked up about 80 per cent of the total number of translations recorded by the *NSTC*, and in 1890 it picked up about 90 per cent. The results of the search will be given in percentages rather than the total numbers, because the percentages are more reliable and less misleading.[8]

Table 6. Translations in the *NSTC* by source language: keyword search (%)

	1790	1810	1850	1870	1900
Latin	13.9	22.6	13.2	12.4	10.7
Greek	7.3	16.8	7.3	6.5	9.0
French	46.7	22.6	33.9	30.2	20.2
German	12.4	11.0	19.7	24.7	19.1
Italian	0.7	9.0	8.8	4.1	5.2
Spanish and Portuguese	1.4	4.5	3.1	3.6	3.2
Celtic	2.9	0.6	1.0	1.4	1.2
Scandinavian and Dutch	2.2	0	3.6	4.1	6.3
Russian and E. European	0	0	0.6	0.4	6.1
Eastern	8.6	11.6	7	9.9	16.8
Miscellaneous	3.6	1.3	1.8	2.8	2.3
Total numbers	137	155	386	507	346

Note: It should be emphasized again that the total numbers can be directly compared only for the years 1810, 1850, and 1870. The totals for 1790 and 1900 were assembled by methods (the *ESTC* and the incomplete *NSTC*, respectively) that differed from the other years

Table 7. Translations in the *NSTC* by genre: keyword search (%)

	1790	1810	1850	1870	1900
Fiction	12.4	9.7	14.5	17.8	15.9
Drama and opera	1.5	4.5	12.4	6.9	8.7
Poetry	15.3	34.2	9.6	13.6	11.0
History/geography	19.0	8.4	21.0	13.6	11.3
Biography	6.6	9.7	6.0	4.1	7.2
Philosophy/essay/criticism	7.3	5.8	7.8	8.3	12.7
Religious texts	19.0	18.7	21.5	24.3	15.3
Science/social science	16.8	6.4	4.1	7.5	14.5
Unclassified	2.2	2.6	3.1	3.9	3.5
Total numbers	137	155	386	507	346

[8] How reliable are the percentages? We have compared the results of the keyword search and the full search for 1830 and 1890. In the earlier year, the languages and genres are reliable on average plus or minus 2.5% (the worst cases, French and religious texts, are undercounted by 5.2% and 6.6%, respectively). In 1890, the error is approximately half the error in 1830.

APPENDIX 4.2: REVIEWS OF TRANSLATED BOOKS IN *BLACKWOOD'S* AND THE *NORTH AMERICAN REVIEW* [9]

Table 8. Reviews of translated works, by language: *Blackwood's*

	1817–20	1821–30	1831–40	1841–50	1851–60	1861–70	1871–80	1881–90	1891–1900
Latin	1	2	2	8	0	4	6	2	1
Greek	5	2	16	12	5	6	9	3	0
French	4	7	24	15	19	11	14	8	15
German	1	8	12	6	7	1	5	4	8
Italian	2	5	0	4	1	3	0	6	4
Spanish	0	2	2	1	0	0	3	2	2
Russian	0	0	0	2	0	0	2	0	0
Other	0	5	2	1	5	4	0	1	0

Table 9. Reviews of translated works, by genre: *Blackwood's*

	1817–20	1821–30	1831–40	1841–50	1851–60	1861–70	1871–80	1881–90	1891–1900
Fiction	0	4	2	5	5	4	7	10	15
Drama	5	8	4	3	4	2	10	4	2
Poetry	1	9	15	8	5	10	6	7	5
History/geography	0	0	6	7	11	2	0	0	1
Biography	3	3	16	6	2	2	2	4	3
Phil./essay/crit.	4	5	10	11	6	8	8	0	4
Religious texts	0	1	0	0	0	1	0	0	0
Social science	0	0	3	3	3	0	0	0	0
Miscellaneous	0	1	0	0	0	0	2	1	0

Table 10. Reviews of translated works, by language: *North American Review*

	1815–20	1821–30	1831–40	1841–50	1851–60	1861–70	1871–80	1881–90	1891–1900
Latin	0	4	2	0	0	0	0	1	0
Greek	0	2	2	3	4	3	1	2	0
French	2	11	8	10	22	11	6	2	3
German	1	7	2	4	2	1	10	2	0
Italian	1	3	7	3	2	8	6	1	1
Spanish	0	0	2	2	1	0	0	0	0
Russian	0	1	0	0	0	0	2	1	0
Other	1	6	7	4	0	3	6	2	1

[9] The tables were prepared by Rebecca Bradburd.

Table 11. Reviews of translated works, by genre: *North American Review*

	1815–20	1821–30	1831–40	1841–50	1851–60	1861–70	1871–80	1881–90	1891–1900
Fiction	0	3	2	5	3	0	4	1	1
Drama	0	1	2	3	0	3	1	2	1
Poetry	1	9	7	7	5	10	9	3	0
History/geography	2	4	2	4	4	4	2	0	1
Biography	1	2	4	1	2	3	3	2	0
Phil./essay/crit.	0	12	6	5	14	3	10	0	2
Religious texts	0	3	0	0	1	1	1	0	0
Social science	0	0	2	1	1	2	1	0	0
Miscellaneous	1	0	0	0	1	0	0	0	0

5

Greek and Latin Literature

5.1	Introduction *Kenneth Haynes*	155
5.2	Homer *David Ricks*	168
5.3	Greek Drama *Adrian Poole*	178
5.4	Latin Poetry *John Talbot*	188
5.5	Greek and Latin Prose *Stuart Gillespie*	200

5.1 Introduction

Kenneth Haynes

Background

From the second half of the eighteenth century, there were signs that the dominant position which classics had maintained in British culture since the Renaissance was declining. Protests about the uselessness of teaching Latin in secondary schools became vigorous (Stray 1998: 21; Waquet 2001: 26). But the opposite happened, and in the nineteenth century classics experienced a large revival. This is peculiar, and the process by which Latin regained its status and Greek gained a new prominence, in the midst of large social and economic changes, is complex. Industry and commerce, not land, were now the major source of wealth, the nature of the social élite was changing, and the university changed its mission from forming gentlemen-amateurs and clergymen to training academics, civil servants, and other professionals. The classics were likewise transformed in this period, in order to continue to play a defining role in a changed society (the fullest account is Stray 1998).

In Britain, ancient Greece was revalued in the second half of the eighteenth century. The new interest in ancient Greece had its roots in a variety of phenomena, including descriptions of travel to the Levant, lavish publications documenting archaeological expeditions in Greece, the Greek statuary and vases recovered by British collectors, and a new enthusiasm for Greek architecture; in addition, the aesthetic sensibility formulated by Winckelmann in mid-century helped to change attitudes toward ancient Greece. The German art historian had polemically celebrated Greece over Rome and found in its art the exemplary virtues of 'noble simplicity and sedate grandeur', as Henry Fuseli translated the slogan in 1765 (see Webb 1982: 121). Both Fuseli and John Flaxman helped to spread this aesthetic in Britain, where the 'Grecian Taste', in some respects a new and stricter kind of neo-classicism, supplemented Roman classicism (discussed in Buxton 1978: 1–25).

By the end of the century, changes in attitudes toward democracy and mythology began to alter attitudes toward ancient Athens, and for the Romantic writers ancient Greece often had radical implications. The place of Greek literature in their own writings, however, varied. Byron's Hellenic and revolutionary enthusiasms are well known, but Greek literature did not directly inspire the poems, in contrast to Latin (his adaptation of Horace's *Ars Poetica* stands at the end of a long line of such eighteenth-century adaptations). Wordsworth, who in his youth translated the song of the ancient Greek revolutionary Harmodius in addition to the Latin classics, had to move away from the classics before finding his own voice (which, nonetheless, they helped to shape). Keats loved the Greek myths but remained Greekless. Shelley is unique in having found in this new vision of Greek antiquity a central inspiration for his own poetry. His most important work bears the direct impress of his Greek reading. Greek tragedy informed both his *Prometheus Unbound* and *Hellas*; Greek elegy, his *Adonais*; and his passion for Plato's Greek never dimmed.

For all the Romantic enthusiasm for Greek, it is difficult to assess how widely the language was known, even among the university-educated (for conflicting accounts, see Clarke 1945 and Ogilvie 1964). Many students at Oxford and Cambridge studied Greek; this was a practical course of study, as the Anglican Church offering livings to graduates of Oxford and Cambridge, for whom the knowledge of Greek was understood to be necessary. The existence of the 'Greek play' bishops—those bishops who were preferred because of their classical scholarship (see Trollope 1996: 327)—shows that at least some graduates learned the language very well. Yet it was often not taught well (see Ogilvie 1964: 83–5), and knowledge of it was often superficial and sometimes a mere pretence (see Haynes 2003: 14–17).

After Shelley's death, the study of Greek became more fully integrated within the education of the upper classes. From 1830, the universities slowly changed in order to serve new purposes. The religious restrictions were eased, examinations were introduced, and a new merit-based system would in time provide students of classics with career possibilities in the civil service and the academy. As a result, Greek was taught more rigorously. Moreover, the secondary schools themselves began to teach the classics with increasing emphasis; the quantity of classics in the curriculum and the presence of Greece were direct markers of the status of the school. The hierarchy in schools of Greek, Latin, and English would eventually be used to mark the boundaries of the Victorian social classes (Stray 1998: 31, 74, 79, and elsewhere).

The Romantic and radical implications of Hellenism were mostly lost as Athens began to be made over in a Victorian image. An influential figure in this change of attitudes was George Grote, whose *History of Greece* (1846–56) was designed to undo attitudes that resulted from more than a century of indicting Athens as a dangerous and failed democratic experiment. It sought to replace that polemic with the suggestion that Athens should be the model for the modern liberal state and democratic empire, that is, modern Britain. After Grote, ancient Greece and especially Athens became the crucial political example for the Victorians, and arguments about Homer or about the Sophists, for instance, would provide ways of talking about British politics (see Turner 1981: 135–86, 264–321). The study of Plato, who had been a revolutionary figure for Shelley, became at Oxford one of the ways to encourage the 'conscious creation of Platonic guardians for Britain and its empire' (Stray 1998: 122). Some of the things, it is true, which the Victorians knew about the ancient Athenians—their homosexuality, paganism, slaves—resisted being assimilated to nineteenth-century liberal humanism. Those aspects were usually ignored; it was only toward the end of the century that the 'great gulf' between the Victorians and the Greeks was acknowledged (Turner 1981: 425). 'Hellenism' was generally able to serve as an effective slogan and to set the terms of many political, social, and cultural debates.

In literature specifically, it was no longer uncommon for writers to know Greek well: Arnold, the Brownings, Eliot, Hardy, Hopkins, Housman, and Swinburne all read the language with fluency. It was no longer unusual for works of Greek literature to be taken as direct models for English. Tennyson's 'English Idyls' find inspiration in Theocritus' idylls, Arnold's *Sohrab and Rustum* draws on Homer, Swinburne's *Atalanta in Calydon* on Aeschylus. For evidence that the cultural authority of Greek poetry was sometimes overbearing, unsuccessful works by major English poets are revealing: Arnold's *Merope*, Browning's *Balaustion's Adventure*, Swinburne's *Erechtheus*. In prose, for example in the novels of Eliot, Gissing, and Hardy, Greek allusions, even quotations, are not uncommon.

Latin, needless to say, did not disappear. Greek was 'superimposed on a continuing preoccupation with the rote learning of Latin grammar and syntax in the lower forms. The disciplined framework provided by Latin was followed and completed by a Hellenism which added a sublime yet stable transcendence' (Stray 1998: 21). The discipline that derived from the rote study of grammar became moralized and celebrated as a general source of precision, firmness, and character (Waquet 2001: 190–1). Such an apologia for Latin was common across Europe. In Catholic France, Latin was sometimes defended as the language of sacred mystery, but in England as in Germany Greek had the higher prestige. (This elevated status is one of the reasons why outsiders, for example Victorian women and working-class men with intellectual ambitions, would often prefer it to Latin.) This makes it easy to forget that in England knowledge of Latin and Rome was always more extensive than knowledge of Greek and Athens. Nor was Rome defended only as part of the grammar grind. Lucretius, for example, was taken by some Victorians as emblematic of modern trends in science and philosophy. Roman history provided revolutionary Romantics with examples of republican liberty as well as with suggestive ruins of empire; it was also of service to the Victorians, by focusing anew questions about the empire and by providing examples of duty and sacrifice, though also of decadence and decline (see further Vance 1997). In *Lays of Ancient Rome* (1842) Macaulay turned stories honouring the martial spirit of the ancient Romans into vigorous ballads, and for most Victorians it is likely that this work, more than any other, formed their attitudes toward antiquity. Another reason why readers in the nineteenth century were more at home with Latin is that, unlike Greek, the Latin literature most commonly read did not condone or praise homosexual behaviour (Byron wittily drew attention to a flagrant exception, Virgil's second eclogue, in his run-through of the classics at the beginning of *Don Juan*).

Overview of Classical Translation

What does all this have to do with translation? Sometimes the connection is direct and obvious. The new importance of Greek resulted in a great increase in the amount of Greek translated.

The nineteenth century, quantitatively at least, is the most important period in the history of Greek translation, for more than half of the total number of translations printed between 1484 and 1916 were published during these years ... The great numerical advance came after 1860, although the preceding sixty years had been far ahead of the previous centuries in the work produced. (Foster 1918: xv–xvi)

Foster's survey is long out of date, and uncritical besides, but the trends he indicates were real. The number of new translations from Greek had begun to rise sharply in the decade after 1820; there were also large increases in the 1860s and 1880s (see also Ch. 4, above).

In addition to the quantity, the nature of the Greek that was translated changed: before the nineteenth century, philosophical works were most often translated; afterwards, drama. The broad presence of Greek tragedy in translation is new. Aeschylus is an extreme case: the first translation into English seems to be Thomas Morell's *Prometheus in Chains* of 1773;[1] the next was Robert Potter's translation of the complete tragedies in 1777, often reprinted in the nineteenth century; and scores of new translations followed. Thomas Francklin's translation in 1758–9 of Sophocles' tragedies was also repeatedly reprinted in the nineteenth century alongside the many new ones, and with better justification given its greater claim to literary merit than Potter's. Despite the appearance of translations by Potter and Francklin, and despite the fact that indispensable textual work on the Greek tragedians had been accomplished by the later eighteenth century, it would still take several generations before the tragedies would be read sympathetically and widely. Johnson dismissed Potter's translation as verbiage, though he was willing, at the urging of a friend, to read one play, but not two, in Potter (*Life*, 9 April 1778). Johnson's antipathy to Greek drama is explicit in his depreciation of *Samson Agonistes*: 'It could only be by long prejudice, and the bigotry of learning, that Milton could prefer the ancient tragedies, with their encumbrance of a chorus, to the exhibitions of the French and English stages'(Johnson 1905: I, 188–9). Greek tragedy was a late addition to the European recovery of ancient literature.

Nineteenth-century readers also had a new feeling for Homer, a response which began to emerge in the second part of the eighteenth century. Pope's had been by far the most enduring translation of Homer. However, after the middle of the eighteenth century tastes began to change. The success of Macpherson's Ossianic poems in the 1760s gave prominence to oral traditions, to the primitive and the folk, and Homer began to be described in such terms (see pp. 431–2, below). Romantic poets, most famously Keats, would reject Pope's translation as learned and artificial. Even so, it was widely read until about 1830, when the steady number of reprints began to decline. (Between 1791 and 1836, the reprints of Pope's *Iliad* outnumber its nearest competitor, Cowper's *Iliad*, first published in 1791, by about four to one.)

---

[1] The attribution of the play to Aeschylus was first denied in 1911, though doubts had been raised in the mid-nineteenth century. Morell's blank verse translation appears (with its own title page) in *Aischylou Prometheus Desmotes* (London 1773).

5.1 Introduction

For Victorians, the view of Homer as a folk balladeer was inadequate. In 'On Translating Homer', Matthew Arnold insisted that Homer was far more than a writer of ballads. 'The ballad-manner requires that an expression shall be plain and natural, and then it asks no more. Homer's manner requires that an expression shall be plain and natural, but it also requires that it shall be noble' (Arnold 1960: 129–30). The emphasis was now on Homeric nobility and sublimity:

The Victorians were dissatisfied with the 'primitive' Homer and found different reasons for admiration. Homer was natural, grand, a refuge from the spiritual ills of the time, a moral, sometimes even religious teacher. (Gillespie 1988: 97)

As Homer was increasingly esteemed, so Virgil was more often praised in somewhat muted ways; he was admired, for example, for his melancholy, for 'a sweet, a touching sadness', as Arnold put it in 'On the Modern Element in Literature' (Arnold 1960: 35). Sometimes readers found very little to praise. Coleridge criticized him: 'If you take from Virgil his diction and metre, what do you leave him?' (*Table Talk*, 8 May 1824). The criticism stands in exact contrast to Johnson's view of Homer as expressed in his 'Life of Pope': 'among the readers of Homer the number is very small of those who find much in the Greek more than in the Latin, except the musick of the numbers' (Johnson 1905: III, 114).

In some respects (the sense of decorum, the neo-classical diction), Pope's translation had been made in the image of Virgil. Conversely, some nineteenth-century translations of Virgil were now made in the image of Homer. For his translation of the *Aeneid* (1866), John Conington chose the ballad-like metre of Sir Walter Scott's *Marmion* (iambic tetrameter lines interspersed with iambic trimeters), a few years after Arnold had attacked Maginn for using that very metre in his *Homeric Ballads*. In 1867, following Philip Stanhope Worsley's translation into Spenserian stanzas of the *Odyssey* (1861) and the first half of the *Iliad* (1865), E. Fairfax Taylor published a translation of the first two books of the *Aeneid* into Spenserian stanzas (the complete *Aeneid* in this stanza appeared in 1903). William Morris adopted fourteeners, the metre of Chapman's Homer, for his *Aeneids of Virgil* (1876).

Translators in this period also had their own elective affinities to Greek and Latin poets not otherwise popular. Perhaps the most inadvertently famous translated lyric in the nineteenth century was William Cory's 'They told me, Heraclitus, they told me you were dead', a translation of Callimachus' second epigram (*Ionica*, 1858). Nonnus had an irresistible appeal to Thomas Love Peacock, who quoted and translated short passages from him three times in *Crotchet Castle* (1831). Elizabeth Barrett Browning, attracted to the Bacchus and Ariadne story, translated Nonnus at somewhat greater length; her intimacy with later Greek is further evident in her essay 'Some Account of the Greek Christian Poets' (1842), in which she translated poems from more than a dozen writers from the third to the sixteenth centuries. Writers were also drawn to later Latin verse: Charles Lamb translated the eighteenth-century Latin poetry of Vincent Bourne; Leigh Hunt gave English versions of Latin poems by Thomas Randolph, John

Milton, and others; and John Addington Symonds first introduced medieval Latin student songs to a broad public with *Wine, Women, and Song* (1884). In general, books written in post-classical Latin, especially those of the Church Fathers, were a major source of translations, outnumbering in some years translations of books by classical Latin authors (see further p. 139, above, and p. 443, below).

Three Classics in Translation: Sappho, the Homeric Hymns, Theocritus

The new appeal of Homer and of Greek tragedy yielded a large number of new translations, and these are surveyed and studied in §§ 5.2 and 5.3. The translation of Latin poetry is the subject of § 5.4; for translations of Greek and Latin philosophy, including Lucretius, see § 11.1, below. Other poets, too, though usually on a smaller scale, now enjoyed a new popularity in fresh translations. The large-scale exception was the *Anacreontea* in Thomas Moore's translation (1800); the combination of elegance and eroticism was irresistible to fashionable readers of the time, though to later readers the translation has seemed turgidly rhetorical.

In English, Sappho was introduced to a broad public (in a version by 'Namby-Pamby' Philips) in a discussion by Addison (*The Spectator*, 15 and 22 November 1711, Nos. 223 and 229); for most of the eighteenth century, she was not clearly distinguished from other ancient lyric poets. In the next century, however, her reputation grew to the wildest heights: she aroused the enthusiasm of Romantic poets, particularly Byron, and later won the rapturous praise of Swinburne and Symonds. Swinburne loved her as 'the greatest poet who ever was at all' (quoted in Swinburne 2000: 332), and Symonds attributed to her alone, 'of all the poets of the world, of all the illustrious artists of all literatures', an absolute perfection in every word (quoted in Gillespie 1988: 200). Her reputation for sublimity, established in antiquity, was the main reason for her attractiveness; the Victorians turned to Greek literature generally for this sublimity, and in particular to Homer, Greek tragedy, and Sappho.

Translations of Sappho sometimes took the form of paraphrases and adaptations embedded in other literary works. Byron combines a one-line fragment of Sappho with a three-line one to form stanza 107 of Canto III of *Don Juan* (1821): 'Oh Hesperus, thou bringest all good things'. The last stanza of Tennyson's early poem 'Eleänore' (1832) rewrites a substantial fragment. In 'Anactoria' (1866), Swinburne creates a dramatic monologue, elaborating on Sappho's theme of erotic jealousy, in which the character Sappho speaks many of the poet Sappho's own words and phrases. Echoes from Sappho occur in several other lyrics by both Swinburne and Tennyson. George Eliot translated Sappho's fragment about the apple on the topmost bough in *Middlemarch* (1871; Book I, Chapter 6): Sir James 'was not one of those gentlemen who languish after the unattainable Sappho's apple that laughs from the topmost bough'; she alludes to the same fragment in *Romola*.

Individual poems and fragments were translated or adapted by Walter Savage Landor, F. T. Palgrave, Dante Gabriel Rossetti, Thomas Wentworth Higginson, and C. D. Yonge; translations of several poems or the entire oeuvre were made by Edwin Arnold, 'Michael Field' (pseudonym of Katherine Bradley and Edith Cooper; see p. 78, above), John Addington Symonds, Frederick Tennyson, and Henry Thornton Wharton. The last-named translator published a volume that includes Sappho's Greek, his own prose translation, and a full selection of verse translations and imitations by others (four editions between 1885 and 1907).

The sapphic metre itself was translated in Swinburne's 'Sapphics' (1866). For the first time in English prosody, Sappho's metre is reproduced in English; previously it was the Latin version of sapphics that had determined the English pattern (Cowper's 'Hatred and vengeance, my eternal portion'). In Swinburne English words move in a Greek way:

> Saw the white implacable Aphrodite,
> Saw the hair unbound and the feet unsandalled
> Shine as fire of sunset on western waters;
>   Saw the reluctant
>
> Feet, the straining plumes of the doves that drew her,
> Looking always, looking with necks reverted,
> Back to Lesbos, back to the hills whereunder
>   Shone Mitylene.

More generally, Greek prosody played a critical role in the development of both Romantic and Victorian prosody (see pp. 15–16, above, and Haynes 2003: 130–7).

Shelley's translations of seven Homeric hymns have been called 'the classic version, elegant and lucid' (Felicity Rosslyn in France 2000: 355). Henry Crabb Robinson wrote that he could hardly think that the Homeric hymn to Mercury is a translation ('it is very like Goethe', Robinson 1938: I, 409). This is despite the fact that the translations—all published posthumously—are unfinished and contain numerous errors, whether careless, creative, or neutral (see further Webb 1976: 90–8). The most ambitious of these is his version of the 'Hymn to Mercury' into *ottava rima*. Finding it 'infinitely comical', Shelley responded with an urbane version emphasizing its ironic humour, the wayward irresponsibility of the child-god Mercury, and its evocation of the power of music. The newborn Mercury, the product of a 'love not quite legitimate' (l. 73), started to play on a lyre at noon. In telling the story of how Mercury makes the lyre from a tortoise shell, Shelley forces distinct levels of diction, poetical and savage, to collide. While the tortoise at his leisure 'the flowery herbage was depasturing' (l. 29), 'Jove's profitable son' (l. 31) grabbed it:

> Then scooping with a chisel of gray steel,
>   He bored the life and soul out of the beast. —
> Not swifter a swift thought of woe or weal
>   Darts through the tumult of a human breast
> Which thronging cares annoy — nor swifter wheel
>   The flashes of its torture and unrest
> Out of its dizzy eyes — than Maia's son
> All that he did devise hath featly done.
>
>   (ll. 49–56)

The poeticism 'featly' emphasizes the divorce between moral approval and the approbation which a technical accomplishment deserves. Shelley stresses the contradiction between song and immoral singer in a passage he expanded from the original:

> But such a strain of wondrous, strange, untired,
>   And soul-awakening music, sweet and strong,
> Yet did I never hear from thee,
> Offspring of May, impostor Mercury!
>
> (ll. 591–4)

The tension is to be resolved when Hermes (Shelley did not settle on a consistent name) gives the lyre to Apollo, 'who art as wise as thou art strong' (l. 657). However, the ending is not entirely convincing, or even motivated, in Shelley's version, because in the rest of the hymn Mercury's irresponsibility had been depicted with urbane charm. After killing and sacrificing Apollo's cows, 'his mind became aware | Of all the joys which in religion are' (ll. 164–5). Yet song is too important, too redemptive, in Shelley's view, for him to continue in this ironic vein. The artist may be irresponsible, but finally only within an acceptable limit. It is a tension that is also present in his translation of Plato's *Symposium*, where he responds to Plato's irony with great skill, but drops it when he becomes enthusiastic about particular positions.

For the 'Hymn to the Earth', Shelley adopts a different style and metre. The poem begins:

> O universal Mother, who dost keep
> From everlasting thy foundations deep,
> Eldest of things, Great Earth, I sing of thee!
> All shapes that have their dwelling in the sea,
> All things that fly, or on the ground divine
> Live, move, and there are nourished—these are thine;
> These from thy wealth thou dost sustain; from thee
> Fair babes are born, and fruits on every tree
> Hang ripe and large, revered Divinity!
>
> (ll. 1–9)

Medwin, in his life of Shelley, writes that 'another of the canons of Shelley, was, that translations are intended for those who do not understand the originals, and that they should be purely English' (Medwin 1913: 212). This is a translation that is intended to be 'purely English'; it employs rhyming couplets, Miltonic and biblical diction. That is, he expresses the Greek religious feeling in traditional Christian language and by traditional poetic means; far from straining to recover a Greece remote from us, the style suggests an easy familiarity with earth's divinity. The syntax of the translation is mostly unperplexed. In the twenty-eight lines of the translation, there are twice as many verbs as epithets, very few inversions of subject and verb, and only about half as many compound epithets as in the original. The movement of the writing, with the emphasis on direct statement, on verbs over adjectives, and on reducing the density of compound adjectives, is graceful and easy; it is meant to reproduce the graceful harmony of the Greeks.

Shelley's translation was the best verse translation of the Homeric hymns of the period. Several prose translations were also made: Theodore Alois Buckley's translation for Bohn in 1853, John Edgar's version in 1891, and Andrew Lang's *Homeric Hymns* of 1899. Lang's translation, accompanied by literary and mythological essays, provided parallels to the folklore elements in the original and was influential in favouring an anthropological approach to Greek antiquity.

Theocritus had been known and respected since the Renaissance, but only among the Victorians could it be said that he was loved. Tennyson told his son that he would be 'content to die' if he had written anything the equal of the Hylas idyll (Idyll 13); his poems 'Audley Court' and 'Edwin Morris' are among the most Theocritean works in English. Several reasons were behind the new appreciation of Theocritus: Victorians and ancient Alexandrians both found pleasure in imagining rural retreats, felt that they had come after the major period of poetry and needed to work instead in smaller forms, and wrote occasionally in wistful and nostalgic veins. Most Victorians focused too single-mindedly on the wistful element in Theocritus. Leigh Hunt had insisted that Theocritus had a 'hearty, out-of-door nature' (Hunt 1844: 63) while Elizabeth Barrett Browning's Theocritus, who sang of 'the sweet years, the dear and wished-for years', reminded her of her own 'sweet, sad years, the melancholy years', in the first of the *Sonnets from the Portuguese* (1850). Hunt's translation of the Cyclops idyll (Idyll 11) was published in 1818, and Browning's in 1862 (she made it in 1845; see the letter of 19 August 1845 in Browning and Barrett 1969: II, 162):

> and never want for cheese
> In summer, nor in autumn, nor dead winter,
> My dairies are so full. I too know how
> To play the pipe, so as no Cyclops can,
> Singing, sweet apple mine, of you and me,
> Often till midnight.
> (Hunt 1923: 399)
> I lack no cheese, while summer keeps the sun;
> And after, in the cold, it's ready prest!
> And then, I know to sing, as there is none
> Of all the Cyclops can, ... a song of thee,
> Sweet apple of my soul, on love's fair tree,
> And of myself who love thee ... till the West
> Forgets the light, and all but I have rest.
> (Browning 1920: 584)

The ironies of the idyll are both comic and tragic in Theocritus. The speaker is a country bumpkin whose own words betray his ignorance and inexperience, but at the same time he is the innocent who will be blinded by Odysseus. Neither translation captures that dual sense: Hunt's robustness is faux-naïf, and Browning's sentimentality is unrelieved. Hunt's ends blithely (' 'Twas thus the

Cyclops quieted his love | With pipe and song'), while Browning's ending ('Ease came with song, he could not buy with gold') is freighted with the melancholy associations which 'song' acquires in the course of her translation.

The combination of Theocritus' humour and forceful energy with nostalgia and wistfulness hardly exists in English translation. But one Victorian did justice to the latter: Charles Stuart Calverley, whose complete translation of the Idylls appeared in 1869. Hylas has been abducted by the water-nymphs because his beauty made their soft senses reel:

> So drops a red star suddenly from sky
>   To sea—and quoth some sailor to his mate:
> 'Up with the tackle, boy! The breeze is high.'
>   Him the nymphs pillowed, all disconsolate,
> On their sweet laps, and with soft words beguiled;
> But Heracles was troubled for the child.
>
> Forth went he; Scythian-wise his bow he bore
>   And the great club that never quits his side;
> And thrice called 'Hylas'—ne'er came lustier roar
>   From that deep chest. Thrice Hylas heard and tried
> To answer, but in tones you scarce might hear;
> The water made them distant though so near.
>   (Calverley 1883: 75)

Theocritus turns epic into idyll, the heroic into the fairy tale. Hercules appears as lover, rather than hero or fighter, and Calverley tells the story with delicacy and poignancy. By choosing the stanza of Shakespeare's 'Venus and Adonis', Calverley places himself within a literary tradition as firmly as Theocritus had done, though by eschewing epic associations and metre Calverley is not able to reproduce the rich Theocritean interplay of epic and idyll. As translator, he does best when love or erotic infatuation is the theme, as here or in the second idyll. He is hardly able to convey the bright liveliness of the harvest-home (Idyll 7), and he does not reproduce the mundane conversation of the two ladies en route to the Festival of Adonis in Idyll 15 as well as Matthew Arnold had done, in the prose translation he included in the essay 'Pagan and Mediæval Religious Sentiment' (Arnold 1962: 216–21). Within his relatively narrow range, however, the verbal surface of Calverley's translations attains a high polish. Theocritus appealed to many nineteenth-century translators: in addition to Arnold, Browning, Calverley, and Hunt, his translators include Edwin Arnold, J. H. Hallard, Andrew Lang, and John Addington Symonds.

New Vehicles for Translation

Two new kinds of translation series were consistently used in the nineteenth century. The first consisted of volumes of interlinear translations. Toward the end of his life, John Locke had proposed an interlinear Aesop as a pedagogical model, and in 1722 Dumarsais had popularized that model in France. In England, interlinear translations first attained considerable popularity in the 1820s, roughly the time when the modern textbook emerged. Different interlinear systems competed for sales. The first is associated with James Hamilton's system for teaching languages; in the ensuing controversy over the system, Sidney Smith endorsed it strongly in the face of its detractors. Hamilton began with an English interlinear translation of the Latin Gospel of John in 1824, and versions in German, Italian, and Greek followed. Classic texts were soon after introduced, including Aesop, Caesar, Nepos, Phaedrus, Sallust, Virgil, and Xenophon. A rival series, Locke's Classical System, was published by John Taylor. It began with Homer and Virgil in 1827. Taylor's venture was a commercial success, and Hebrew and German authors were later added to the Greek and Latin ones (see Stray 1996).

The second translation series was the 'classical library', multi-volume sets of classical authors in translation. The Works of the Greek and Roman Poets (eighteen volumes, 1809–12) and Valpy's Family Classical Library (1830–4) reprinted existing translations. The most famous and influential was Bohn's Classical Library, which included both reprints and new versions. Most of the volumes were published between 1848 and 1862, though titles continued to be added later. In 1887 the Classical Library consisted of ninety-eight volumes at five shillings apiece, with a few exceptions. The majority indicated that they had been translated 'literally'; verse was regularly translated into prose (the dramas of Aeschylus were translated into prose in one volume and verse in another).

Bohn's Classical Library was widely read, though not universally approved. Matthew Arnold objected to them, comparing them invidiously with their French equivalent: 'think of the difference between the translations of the classics turned out for Mr. Bohn's library and those turned out for M. Nisard's collection!' ('The Literary Influence of Academies' in Arnold 1962: 242). Ralph Waldo Emerson was more sanguine. After identifying those works of Greek literature to be considered indispensable, he added: 'The respectable and sometimes excellent translations of Bohn's Library have done for literature what railroads have done for internal intercourse. I do not hesitate to read all the books I have named, and all good books, in translations' ('Books', *Society and Solitude* (1870) in Emerson 1903–4: VII, 203–4).The modern scholar H. MacL. Currie evaluates Bohn's library in this way:

> Classically, the Bohn translations are usually sound. Some are offered specifically as literal renderings, but even here there is a certain quality which generally makes for smooth readings; they are not crude, and in fact they easily bear comparison with the Loeb series, I think, and can even be superior to it, showing a consistently workmanlike approach. The Bohn Petronius (1854) leaves in a surprising amount for its time of the more racy material, but some sections are retained in what Gibbon called the decent obscurity of a learned tongue ... No significant author is missing from the Bohn Library.
>
> (Currie 1996: 52)

It is difficult to determine how extensively the interlinears were used by students in the early part of the century; they were not at first intended for the college-going class, though they survive in great numbers from the latter part of the century. Both the Bohn series and the interlinears had the same goals: to find new markets for classics and to break the upper-class monopoly on classical learning.

LIST OF SOURCES

Translations

For translations of Homer, Greek tragedy, and Virgil, consult the bibliographies to §§ 5.2, 5.3, and 5.4 respectively.

Browning, Elizabeth Barrett (1862). *Last Poems* [Theocritus and Nonnus]. London.
—— (1920). *Poetical Works*. London (first pub. 1904).
Calverley, C. S. (1883). *Theocritus Translated into English Verse*, 2nd. edn. Cambridge (first pub. 1869).
Hunt, Leigh (1818). *Foliage, or, Poems Original and Translated* [Theocritus]. London.
—— (1923). *Poetical Works*, ed. H. S. Milford. London.
Jay, Peter, and Lewis, Caroline (1996). *Sappho through English Poetry*. London.
Lang, Andrew (1899). *The Homeric Hymns*. London.
Moore, Thomas (1800). *The Odes of Anacreon*. London.
Shelley, Percy Bysshe (1970). *Poetical Works*, ed. Thomas Hutchinson and corrected by G. M. Matthews. London (first pub. 1905).
—— (1986–). *The Bodleian Shelley Manuscripts*, 23 vols. New York (Vol. 14 for the Homeric hymn to Mercury; Vol. 18 for other Homeric hymns).
Stoneman, Richard, ed. (1982). *Daphne into Laurel: Translations of Classical Poetry from Chaucer to the Present*. London.
Swinburne, Algernon Charles (2000). *Poems and Ballads & Atalanta in Calydon*, ed. Kenneth Haynes. London (contains 'Anactoria' and 'Sapphics').
Symonds, John Addington (1873–6). *Studies of the Greek Poets*, 2 vols. London.
—— (1884). *Wine, Women, and Song: Medieval Latin Students' Songs*. London.
Tomlinson, Charles, ed. (1980). *The Oxford Book of Verse in English Translation*. Oxford.
Wharton, Henry Thornton (1885). *Sappho: Memoir, Text, Selected Readings, and Literal Translation*. London.

Other Sources

Anon. (1887). *Complete Catalogue . . . of Bohn's Libraries*. London.
Arnold, Matthew (1960). *On the Classical Tradition*, ed. R. H. Super. Ann Arbor, MI.
—— (1962). *Lectures and Essays in Criticism*, ed. R. H. Super. Ann Arbor, MI.
Browning, Robert, and Barrett, Elizabeth Barrett (1969). *The Letters of Robert Browning and Elizabeth Barrett Barrett, 1845–1846*, ed. Elvan Kintner. Cambridge, MA.
Buxton, John (1978). *The Grecian Taste: Literature in the Age of Neo-Classicism*. London.
Clarke, G. W., ed. (1989) *Rediscovering Hellenism: The Hellenic Inheritance and the English Imagination*. Cambridge.
Clarke, M. L. (1945). *Greek Studies in England, 1700–1830*. Cambridge.
Cordasco, Francesco (1951). *The Bohn Libraries: A History and a Checklist*. New York.
Crook, J. Mordaunt (1995). *The Greek Revival: Neo-Classical Attitudes in British Architecture, 1760–1870*, rev. edn. London (first pub. 1972).
Currie, H. MacL. (1996). 'English Translations of the Classics in the 19th. Century', pp. 51–8 in H. D. Jocelyn, ed., *Aspects of Nineteenth-Century British Classical Scholarship*. Liverpool.
Emerson, Ralph Waldo (1903–4). *The Complete Works*, 12 vols. Boston, MA.
Feldman, Burton, and Richardson, Robert D., eds. (1972). *The Rise of Modern Mythology, 1680–1860*. Bloomington, IN.
Foster, Finley Melville Kendall (1918). *English Translations from the Greek: A Bibliographical Survey*. New York.

France, Peter, ed. (2000). *The Oxford Guide to Literature in English Translation*. Oxford.
Gillespie, Stuart, ed. (1988). *The Poets on the Classics: An Anthology of English Poets' Writings on the Classical Poets and Dramatists from Chaucer to the Present*. London.
Greene, Ellen (1996). *Re-reading Sappho: Reception and Transmission*. Berkeley, CA.
Haynes, Kenneth (2003). *English Literature and Ancient Languages*. Oxford.
Hunt, Leigh (1844). *Imagination and Fancy*. London.
Jenkyns, Richard (1980). *The Victorians and Ancient Greece*. Cambridge, MA.
Johnson, Samuel (1905). *Lives of the English Poets*, ed. G. B. Hill. Oxford.
Medwin, Thomas (1913). *The Life of Percy Bysshe Shelley*. London.
Ogilvie, R. M. (1964). *Latin and Greek: A History of the Influence of the Classics on English Life from 1600 to 1918*. London.
Prins, Yopie (1999). *Victorian Sappho*. Princeton, NJ.
Reynolds, Margaret, ed. (2000). *The Sappho Companion*. London.
Robinson, Henry Crabb (1938). *On Books and their Writers*, ed. Edith J. Morley, 3 vols. London.
Smith, F. Seymour (1930). *The Classics in Translation: An Annotated Guide to the Best Translations of the Greek and Latin Classics into English*. London.
Spencer, Terence (1954). *Fair Greece, Sad Relic: Literary Philhellenism from Shakespeare to Byron*. London.
Stray, Christopher (1996). 'John Taylor and Locke's Classical System.' *Paradigm* 20: 26–38.
—— (1998). *Classics Transformed: Schools, Universities, and Society in England, 1830–1960*. Oxford.
Trollope, Anthony (1996). *Barchester Towers*, ed. Michael Sadleir and Frederick Page. Oxford.
Turner, Frank M. (1981). *The Greek Heritage in Victorian Britain*. New Haven, CT.
Vance, Norman (1997). *The Victorians and Ancient Rome*. Oxford.
Waquet, Françoise (2001). *Latin, or, The Empire of a Sign*, tr. John Howe. London.
Webb, Timothy (1976). *The Violet in the Crucible: Shelley and Translation*. Oxford.
—— ed. (1982). *English Romantic Hellenism 1700–1824*. New York.

5.2 Homer

David Ricks

Introduction

There has been no period in which the Homeric poems have been so widely (if often enforcedly) read as the nineteenth century, and no period in which a greater number of complete or partial versions have been produced in English—yet also no period whose translations have proved less durable a part of the tradition. Our anthologies of verse translation tell their own story (though we shall see that verse translation of Homer is not the whole story): four pages of Cowper, and Tennyson's classic fragments from the *Iliad*, are all that Charles Tomlinson (1980) has to show from this period, while Adrian Poole and Jeremy Maule (1995), with more space available, augment their coverage with portions from the undeservedly neglected hands of the Earl of Derby and George Meredith and little else. George Steiner's *Homer in English* provides a highly various hundred pages of nineteenth-century versions, many of them mere curiosities with no chance of the afterlife which an undiscovered Victorian poet can still earn. For a living *Iliad* or *Odyssey* Pope and Chapman respectively are still without serious rivals.

Why this should be so is both a delicate and a sweeping question. Poole and Maule (1995: xlv) face it unflinchingly, with the assessment that 'Far too many nineteenth-century translations are written on their knees.' A parallel case is provided by the nineteenth century's failure to add to the stock of classic versions of the Psalms (robustly interrogated by Donald Davie 1996: xxxii–xxxiii). The history of Homeric translation from Cowper to Butler, with its successful skirmishings and strategic failings, is a large subject to survey in a small compass, but an illuminating one.

Particularly illuminating because it is in the middle of this period that one of the acutest discussions of translation ever, and one of the few indispensable works of criticism on Homer, was produced, in the form of Matthew Arnold's classic lectures 'On Translating Homer' (1861) and the subsequent reply to F. W. Newman, translator of the *Iliad*. The complete debate (discussed on pp. 67–70, above) is to be found in the Everyman edition (Arnold 1907): simple justice and historical interest dictate that Newman's own wounded response be read with care; though it is a sign of scholarly perversity that we have recently been asked to take his enterprise seriously (Venuti 1995: 118–45). Newman's assailant was, it is true, conscious of the difficulty of applying his prescriptions to the translator's enterprise:

When I say, the translator of Homer should above all be penetrated by a sense of four qualities of his author;—that he is eminently rapid; that he is eminently plain and direct, both in the evolution of his thought and in the expression of it, that is, both in his syntax and in his words; that he is eminently plain and direct in the substance of his thought, that is, in his matter and ideas; and, finally that he is eminently noble;—I probably seem to be saying what is too general to be of much service to anybody. (Arnold 1907: 215)

While there is a strong case for saying that Arnold's insights into the qualities of Homer were without peer (for modern assessments of Arnold, see Macleod 1982: 39–40 and Silk 2004: 47–8), they were nonetheless inhibiting to or unhelpful for translators (see Mason 1972: 7–18 and Ricks 1997), for all his protestations that 'it is for the future translator that one must work'. Indeed, they were doomed to provoke a spate of new versions which are now numbered, in Homeric phrase, among 'the strengthless heads of the dead'. An intelligent contemporary translator of Homer, P. S. Worsley, made the point plaintively but prophetically (1861–2: II, xvi): 'I am of course not asserting that Mr Arnold's tribunal is a bad one in the abstract ... but that it is a bad one for the translator to keep in mind during the process of composition.' Since the 1860s are the critical decade for Homeric translation, it is worth beginning there, though with an occasional glance back to the inadequacy of Cowper to supplant Pope (the main discussion of Cowper appears in Vol. 3 of this *History*) and a glance forward to various new possibilities that the last third of the nineteenth century opened up but was in no position to exploit.

Homer in the Industrial Age: New Possibilities

Each age will gain some new possibilities for Homeric translation and lose others: the trick is knowing which are which. (Milman Parry's insights into the oral-formulaic tradition behind the Homeric poems have been relatively fruitless for the modern translator's enterprise.) The world's first industrialized war, the American Civil War, began in the year of Arnold's lecture, and the world it created was both inhibiting of a truly ambitious enterprise in Homeric translation and oddly propitious. Fittingly, it is two American poets who draw attention to ways in which Arnold's noble touchstones might not address all the ways in which a modern world might both occlude and illuminate Homer—and especially the *Iliad*, much the more likely of the two poems to falter in translation. 'All went on by crank, | Pivot, and screw, | And calculations of caloric', Melville (1995: 61–2) wrote in his poem 'A Utilitarian View of the Monitor's Fight' (1866). The poem finds a grandeur in the battle of the ironclads, a grandeur perhaps more elemental than a traditional sea-fight because founded on the very elements, yet inimical to a traditional poetics of war: 'War shall yet be, and to the end; | But war-paint shows the streaks of weather.' And if war-paint, then a fortiori, it would seem, 'well-greaved warriors', patronymics, and the whole Homeric order.

But the antidote often grows next to the poison, and Whitman's *Drum–Taps* (1865) provides hints (characteristically, in fragmentary form) of what a modern touchstone for Homeric translation might be. Take the last three lines of 'Bivouac on a Mountain Side':

The numerous camp-fires scatter'd near and far, some away up on the mountain,
The shadowy forms of men and horses, looming, large-sized, flickering,
And over all the sky—the sky! far, far out of reach, studded, breaking out, the eternal stars.
(Whitman 1975: 325–6)

This is very much in the spirit of the famous night piece at the end of *Iliad* VIII, with Pope's version of which Arnold (1907: 222–3) and Cowper (see Mason 1972: 62) had such difficulty. In a curious way, Arnold might have warmed more to a passage such as this, with its evocation, not only of the *Iliad* passage (with the difference that the shepherd's joy in the night scene is now the speaker's), but also of Homeric epithets (σκιόεις: 'shadowy', δολιχόσκιος: 'long-shadowed') and verbs (ὑπερράγη: 'break out') and even the metrical movement of the hexameter Arnold deemed more fitting than Pope's heroic couplets. Whitman did not possess Tennyson's immersion in Homeric expression, but he could see through to it, even through cribs. Yet such modern possibilities largely escaped translators of the period; and the combination of a renewed sense of wonder in Homer's cosmic sweep with attention to those ways in which the modern world would reshape our experience of Homer would need to await the erratic boldness of Christopher Logue in the mid-twentieth century.

Tennyson and the Homeric Fragment

One major Victorian poet, however, devoted attention to the matter. Tennyson's versions of passages from the *Iliad*, though the published ones total only fifty-five lines, and though their author disclaimed any value for them other than experimental ('No, I shan't read it. It's only a little thing. Must be judged by comparison with the Greek. Can only be appreciated by the difficulties overcome.') are the finest the century has to offer (Tennyson 1987: II, 653–6). They too date in their writing from the early 1860s, and were clearly produced as a riposte to Arnold's claims for (and dignified samples of) the English hexameter, as opposed to Milton's blank verse—or indeed the blank verse of 'Ulysses'. 'These lame hexameters the strong-winged music of Homer!', Tennyson had exclaimed in indignation (Tennyson 1987: II, 651); and his own development of a blank verse un-Miltonic in its contours and with a fire and invention beyond Cowper bears fruit in a simile such as this from the very passage evoked by Whitman:

> As when in heaven the stars about the moon
> Look beautiful, when all the winds are laid,
> And every height comes out, and jutting peak
> And valley, and the immeasurable heavens
> Break open to their highest, and all the stars
> Shine, and the Shepherd gladdens in his heart.

The 'freedom of movement' here (Tennyson's phrase, 1987: II, 654) is impressive, and not just in relation to the *Iliad*'s cumulative style that has recently attracted more systematic attention (Kirk 1985: 34–7). The plainness, for example, of 'Look beautiful' for φαίνετ'ἀριπρεπέα (*Iliad* VIII, 556) meets Arnold's challenge to Pope's gorgeous version head-on. Nor does this idiom have the taste of the schoolroom evident, though not obtrusive, in the hexameter experiments praised by Arnold.

No one could doubt the adequacy of such an idiom to the *Iliad*'s grand style; but the question remains how far one could bridge the gap between the, so to say, opera highlights we have here and the totality of the narrative. Even if one ignores the Catalogue of Ships, there is much in Homeric narrative that does not lend itself to the blank verse that is inherited from Milton even where it does not directly invoke him. Faced with twenty-four books to render, and the presence of Pope within the tradition, it was those with the most adamantine digestion, such as William Morris, who saw their way to completing English versions of whole Homeric poems. Indeed, it is symptomatic that when poets of some standing turned to the task, they usually did so in the experimental and provisional mode of Tennyson, translating as little as one book alone. In the case of one of the ablest, Charles Stuart Calverley, we have the chance to compare parallel renderings, again in response to Arnold, of *Iliad* I, 1–129 in both blank verse and hexameters (1897: 1–30, 70–9). In a further development in this direction, we find small tableaux specifically conceived as such: Meredith's 'Fragments of the *Iliad* in hexameter verse' from 1891, including—again, following Arnold—'The Horses of Achilles', but imparting to the material more fire, even if of a flickering kind. H. A. Mason (1972: 182) is willing—too willing—to acknowledge that we of the iron age might have to face up to the possibility that, where the *Iliad* is concerned, we can only hope to render the 'glowing centres where life is abundant and most abundantly apparent' and in effect accept Cowper's engaging admission that 'It is difficult to kill a sheep with dignity in a modern language' (in Derby 1910: vii). But the lack of mettlesomeness that makes so much of Homeric translation in this period a retirement occupation (as in the staid but sometimes weighty blank verse of William Cullen Bryant 1870, 1871–3), a stay against mental turmoil (see Cowper 1989: 128–9), or a piece of Victorian social service on behalf of 'backward students' (Barnard 1876: vii), is pervasive.

Homer and Statecraft

There is one honourable exception, among *Iliad* versions, to this tale of those who set out to translate the poem simply because they had Greek enough; the case tells us something about the sort of culture likely to produce an adequate version. Edward Stanley, fourteenth Earl of Derby, produced a privately printed blank verse version of Book I in 1862 and received sufficient encouragement for his 'attempt to infuse into an almost literal English version something of the spirit, as well as the simplicity of the original' (Derby 1910: xvii) to have the will to complete it by 1864. Like Gladstone, but to better effect, Derby worked on his version 'in the intervals of more urgent business' (notably as Prime Minister), reflecting a culture of aristocratic service ('to be a sayer of words and a doer of deeds') which Arnold acknowledged to be deeply rooted (1907: 220), especially in Derby's alma mater, Christ Church, Oxford. The dying Earl Granville could quote *Iliad* XII, 322 ff.; the former Dean could write to an old pupil, Sir Robert Peel, on his parliamentary maiden speech, and admonish him that Homer should continue to be his daily reading (Hassall 1911: 35–6). Derby, aiming at a literal rendering (though with romanized deities and keeping only epithets which have 'in the particular passage, anything of a special and distinctive character'), is markedly successful at conveying the politics of the *Iliad*, a preoccupation of modern scholarship, but not often at the forefront of translators' interest; he does so in a somewhat stiff blank verse (compare Cary's Dante) which is yet free of Cowper's sub-Miltonic inversions and syntactical tangles. With close attention to the core story of the Quarrel, Derby presents the siege of Troy as the work of those 'Charg'd with the public weal, and cares of state' (II, 28); he shows a proper preoccupation with the 'ancestral'; he can lead his protagonists to speak in a language both recognizably in the tradition of the political Milton and capable of evoking current political forms (II, 125 ff.): 'Friends, Grecian Heroes, Ministers of Mars.' The proem gives a good idea of Derby's strengths as well as his limitations, though he often rises above this:

> Of Peleus' son, Achilles, sing, O Muse,
> The vengeance, deep and deadly; whence to Greece
> Unnumber'd ills arose; which many a soul
> Of mighty warriors to the viewless shades
> Untimely sent; they on the battle plain
> Unburied lay, a prey to rav'ning dogs
> And carrion birds; but so had Jove decreed,
> From that sad day when first in wordy war,
> The mighty Agamemnon, King of men,
> Confronted stood by Peleus' godlike son.

Though stiff ('confronted stood') or poeticizing in passages of description—and the evident Shakespearian echoes in 'viewless' (*Measure for Measure* III.i.122; but see also Pope, *Odyssey* XVI, 173) and 'Untimely' (*Macbeth* V.vii.45) in initial position are features which could be said to add unwanted associations—Derby's version is in many ways closer to a tradition of public discourse than, say, Lang, Leaf, and Myers (see below). This is an idiom which can handle the tough argumentation of the Embassy of Book IX of the *Iliad* in ways which owe much to Milton (and also to Pope: 'wordy war' occurs e.g. in his *Iliad* XX, 301) but are not necessarily sub-Miltonic.

The Homeric Translator vs. Pope

It is notable that, in their prefaces, the authors of versions of such sober blank verse renderings do not, characteristically, take up nearly so adversarial an attitude to Pope as does Arnold—who in this follows in the line of Bentley ('A pretty poem, but you must not call it Homer') or Coleridge ('The main source of our *pseudo*-poetic diction')—but tend to approach the question with a degree of circumspection. This is not just mock-modesty: it is a sober assessment that a post-Pope version will not pass muster simply by avoiding his manner. Robert Wood had spoken for such when he wrote (1765: 77), 'I believe that it will be acknowledged that, of all the languages we know, in which Homer has hitherto appeared, it is in English alone that he continues to be a Poet.' The problem is that only four mainstream methods presented themselves as alternatives to Pope.

The most extreme reaction, perhaps, is represented by F. W. Newman's now unread *Iliad* of 1856, which provoked Arnold's critical assault. Newman's version, to cite his own apologia for it, rested on several assumptions which, if correct, would consign Pope to oblivion, but to which Arnold, though unsympathetic to Augustan poetry, was rightly resistant. For Newman, Homer '*not only was* antiquated, relatively to Pericles, but *is also* absolutely antique, being the poet of a barbarian age'; furthermore, 'the entire dialect of Homer being essentially archaic, that of a translation ought to be as much Saxo-Norman as possible, and owe as little as possible to the elements thrown into our language by classical learning' (Arnold 1907: 303, 213). These are exceedingly sweeping assumptions, about Greek culture and the English language alike, which cannot stand up to the fact that, whatever the origins of the Homeric *Kunstsprache*, the poems were at once the foundation and a living part of a whole literary culture. And Arnold was right to judge Newman's undiscriminating philological forays by their fruits: Newman is capable of beginning one of the *Iliad*'s most powerful and centrally important speeches (VI, 344) with Helen addressing Hector as follows: 'O brother thou of me, who am a mischief-working vixen, | A numbing horror' (Arnold 1907: 233).

A second mode was the biblically indebted prose of Butcher and Lang for the *Odyssey* and Lang, Leaf, and Myers for the *Iliad* (to cite the most widely read of such versions). The great Hellenist Richard Porson, who adored Pope, did not see a prose *Iliad* as a soft option: he estimated it would take ten years to produce a literal version (Rogers 1903: 172). For the English reader saturated in the cadences of the Authorized Version (it was then the boast of the Church of England that it read more of the Scriptures in the liturgy than any other denomination), biblical English had the merit of 'high seriousness'; it could also cut through childhood memories of Pope's Homer, memorably testified to by Browning (in his poem 'Development') and Ruskin (in the early pages of *Praeterita*), to what C. S. Lewis in his *Preface to Paradise Lost* would term 'primary epic'. The disadvantage was that almost any preconceived idea of Homer as such-and-such a kind of epic founders on the subtleties of the poems themselves—subtleties which require the full resources of the target language, forswearing nothing (see Worsley 1861–2: II, vi). It is no coincidence, for that matter, that the first appearance of Butcher and Lang and of Lang, Leaf, and Myers falls at the time of the Revised Version of the English Bible (1881–5; see § 10.2, below). Although neither the Bible revisers nor the Homeric translators allowed themselves to wield a Higher Critical/Analytical scalpel (as did, for example, the Liverpool-based Greek translator of the *Iliad*, Alexandros Pallis, from 1892), the 'defamiliarizing' effect of seeing Aias for Ajax and so on is notable. The connections between Hebraic and Hellenic expression, pointed out by the scholar Zachary Bogan in the seventeenth century (see West 1997), felt by Milton, and developed in modern scholarship, are also pertinent—yet Lang, Leaf, and Myers all too often sink from the 'timeless Biblical to the clumsy mock-Tudor' (Silk 2004: 46). Here is Agamemnon speaking at the beginning of Book IX:

My friends, leaders and captains of the Argives, Zeus son of Kronos hath bound me with might in grievous blindness of soul; hard of heart is he, for that erewhile he promised and gave his pledge that not till I had laid waste well-walled Ilios should I depart, but now hath planned a cruel wile, and biddeth me return in dishonour to Argos with the loss of many of my folk. Such meseemeth is the good pleasure of most mighty Zeus that hath laid low the heart of many cities, yea and shall lay low; for his is highest power.   (1891: IX, 17–25)

The biblical echoes and monotheist emphasis both add weight to and detract from such a passage. As one commentator notes of Butcher and Lang, 'They were less at home in classical English than they thought' (Shewring 1980: 312); and this is only one of the types of Victorian Homer that could not speak in a contemporary voice.

The third form of escape from Pope, as we have seen with Derby, is blank verse in the tradition of Milton; but Arnold's general criticisms of its appropriateness were weighty, and modern attacks on Milton by Eliot or Leavis have their greatest force when one reflects on an inheritance which was almost wholly unproductive for Homeric translation. The contrast is striking with Pope, who could freely acknowledge the influence of Eve's seduction of Adam on his rewriting of the Deception of Zeus in *Iliad* XIV, which had inspired Milton himself (see Pope 1996: 694–6).

A fourth way, without the latter disadvantage, and generously acknowledged by Arnold in his 'Last Words' on the subject (1907: 367 n. 1), was that of Worsley, who rendered the *Odyssey* in Spenserian stanzas. This work, with its prefaces to the two successive volumes, the first completed before reading Arnold, the latter an answer to him, still repays attention today. 'For the power of preserving the charms, while veiling the blemishes of rhyme, no metre existing in the English language is to be compared with the Spenserian' is Worsley's claim (1861–2: I, xii). One of his merits is his intelligent assimilation of the full resources of English poetry since Spenser, in order to get to Homer, so to speak, *round the back of Pope*. This embraces Keats—Worsley, it could be said extrapolates 'The Eve of St Agnes' from epyllion to epic length—and Tennyson; Odysseus, in Worsley's proem, hopes of his homeland's smoke 'to see it curling, and to die', and 'experience' is one of the first words of his version, echoing Tennyson's 'Ulysses':

> Sing me, O Muse, that hero wandering,
> Who of men's minds did much experience reap,
> And knew the citied realms of many a king,
> Even from the hour he smote the Trojan keep.
> Also a weight of sorrows in the deep
> Brooding he bore, in earnest hope to save,
> 'Mid hard emprise and labour all too steep,
> Himself and comrades from a watery grave –
> Whom yet he rescued not with zeal nor yearnings brave.

If the price is too many feres and lemans, or the off-key medievalizing of 'keep' above, it is, at least much of the time, worth paying—by comparison, William Morris's Anglo-Saxonizing *Odyssey* ('Tell me, o Muse, of the Shifty, the man who wandered afar, | After the Holy Burg, Troy-town, he had wasted with war', Morris 1910–15: XIII, 1) is puerile. Above all, the narrative in Spenserians, despite 'the regular recurrence of such mechanical breaks as every stanzaic system demands' (Worsley 1861–2: I, viii), is actually easier to follow than in most contorted blank verse versions. The main failing is, unsurprisingly in one who follows a poet who 'writ no language' (as Ben Jonson had gibed of Spenser), in dialogue.

The English dactylic hexameter enters the field of Homeric translation via the example of Voss's German version; and through Scott's biographer J. G. Lockhart in 1846 (see Scott 1996 and Steiner 1996: 143–8; it could be argued that the cult of the hexameter in Homeric translation over a long period was just another Germanic episode in Victorian life). Arnold astutely used the hexameter as a control to existing versions, but there is no doubt that the poetic life of the hexameter survives in the form of parody, such as Arthur Hugh Clough's 'Long Vacation pastoral', *The Bothie of Tober-na-Vuolich* (1848), with its tissue of playful Homeric echoes. Such an idiom, even as parody, points us to possibilities in the novelistic delineation of character which Samuel Butler would take up.

The Odyssey as Novel: Samuel Butler

If we are to judge an age of translation in part by its fruits in the original literature of the target language, then Butler's *Odyssey* (1900) must take a significant place, formative influence as it was on Joyce's *Ulysses*, the richest of modern Homerizing works (for this influence, see Kenner 1975: 46–50). Butler sets the tone from the start, Telemachus addressing Mentes/Athena in I, 158 ff. as follows:

'I hope, sir', said he, 'that you will not be offended with what I am going to say. Singing comes cheap to those who do not pay for it, and all this is done at the cost of one whose bones lie rotting in some wilderness or grinding to powder in the surf. If these men were to see my father come back to Ithaca they would pray for longer legs rather than a longer purse, for money would not save them.' (Butler 1900: 5)

Cowper had found in Homer 'the minuteness of a Flemish painter' (in Derby 1910: vii). Butler was to prove equal to the domestic comedy of the latter part of the *Odyssey* (see Butler 1913: 59–98), albeit not without cost. Part of the cost is the disappearance of most of the stock epithets; though in taking the step of excluding them, Butler showed astuteness, as he did in the resource of paragraphing. With its echoes of English prose from the Prayer Book to Fielding and Jane Austen, Butler's version is sometimes perilously close to 'domesticating' in the most loaded sense (as E. V. Rieu's best-selling Penguin versions certainly were to be), but its consistent intelligence in getting at the real meaning of spoken expressions commands respect and affection. ('With your hand raised against every man' for III, 72: μαψιδίως ('recklessly') is but one example.) With a flash of recognition, the reader gets deeper into the comedy of the poem than ever before, and Butler's eccentricities about the Authoress of the *Odyssey* (1897) leave his translation immune. (He had limbered up for the task by rendering a famous speech of Mrs Gamp in Homeric hexameters: Butler 1930: 380–1, 393.) This is a version which can allude neatly and appositely to Milton when the phrase 'in shadiest covert hid' (XIX, 514) can be appropriated back from *Paradise Lost* III, 39 to the simile that inspired it. Butler's preface to his translation displays due circumspection in acknowledging that 'there can be no final English translation of Homer' (viii); and if the nineteenth century came further than some others from finality in that area, it did not end inauspiciously.

LIST OF SOURCES

Translations

Bryant, William Cullen (1870). *The Iliad of Homer, Translated into English Blank Verse*. Boston, MA.

—— (1871–3). *The Odyssey of Homer, Translated into English Blank Verse*. Boston, MA.

Butcher, S. H., and Lang, Andrew (1879). *The Odyssey of Homer, Done into English Prose*. London.

Butler, Samuel (1900). *The Odyssey of Homer, Rendered into English Prose for the Use of Those who Cannot Read the Original*. London.

Calverley, C. S. (1897). *Translations into English and Latin*. Cambridge (first pub. 1866).

Derby, Edward, Earl of (1910). *The Iliad of Homer*. London (first pub. 1864).

Lang, Andrew, Leaf, Walter, and Myers, Ernest (1891). *The Iliad of Homer, Done into English Prose*, rev. edn. London (first pub. 1882).

Meredith, George (1912). 'Fragments of the *Iliad* in English Hexameter Verse' (composed 1891), pp. 553–9 in his *Poetical Works*. London.

Morris, William (1887). *The Odyssey of Homer, Done into English Verse*. London.

—— (1910–15). *Collected Works*, ed. May Morris, 24 vols. London (Vol. 13 contains the *Odyssey*).

Poole, Adrian, and Maule, Jeremy, eds. (1995). *The Oxford Book of Classical Verse in Translation*. Oxford.

Pope, Alexander (1996). *The Iliad of Homer*, ed. Steven Shankman. London.

Steiner, George, ed. (1996). *Homer in English*. London.

Tennyson, Alfred (1987). *Poems*, ed. Christopher Ricks, 2nd edn., 3 vols. London.

Tomlinson, Charles, ed. (1980). *The Oxford Book of Verse in English Translation*. Oxford.

Worsley, Philip Stanhope (1861–2). *The Odyssey of Homer, Translated into English Verse in the Spenserian Stanza*, 2 vols. London.

Other Sources

Arnold, Matthew (1907). *Essays Literary and Critical*. London.

—— (1960) *On the Classical Tradition*, ed. R. H. Super. Ann Arbor, MI.

Barnard, Mordaunt (1876). Preface to *The Odyssey of Homer Rendered into English Blank Verse*. London.

Butler, Samuel (1897). *The Authoress of The Odyssey*. London.

—— (1913). *The Humour of Homer and Other Essays*, ed. R. A. Streatfield. London.

—— (1930). *Selections from the Notebooks of Samuel Butler*, ed. Henry Festing Jones. London.

Cowper, William (1989). *Selected Letters*, ed. James King and Charles Ryskamp. Oxford.
Davie, Donald, ed. (1996). *The Psalms in English*. London.
Foster, Finley Melville Kendall (1918). *English Translations from Greek: A Bibliographical Survey*. New York.
Hassall, Arthur, ed. (1911). *Christ Church, Oxford: An Anthology in Prose and Verse*. London.
Jenkyns, Richard (1980). *The Victorians and Ancient Greece*. Cambridge, MA.
Kenner, Hugh (1975). *The Pound Era*. London.
Kirk, G. S. (1985). *The Iliad: A Commentary*, Vol. 1: *Books 1–4*. Cambridge.
Macleod, C. W., ed. (1982). *Homer: Iliad Book XXIV*. Cambridge.
Mason, H. A. (1972). *To Homer through Pope: An Introduction to Homer's Iliad and Pope's Translation*. London.
Melville, Herman (1995). *Battle Pieces and Aspects of the War*. New York (first pub. 1866).
Ricks, David (1997). 'On Looking into the First Paperback of Pope's Homer.' *Classics Ireland* 4: 97–120.
Rogers, Samuel (1903). *Reminiscences and Table Talk of Samuel Rogers*, ed. G. H. Powell. London.
Rosslyn, Felicity (2000). 'Homer and Other Epics', pp. 350–5 in Peter France, ed., *The Oxford Guide to Literature in English Translation*. Oxford.
Scott, Robert L. (1996). 'The English Hexameter: A Short History of a Long Line.' *Classical and Modern Literature* 16: 149–74.
Shewring, Walter (1980). 'Epilogue on Translation', pp. 299–330 in his *Homer: The Odyssey*. Oxford.
Silk, Michael (2004). *Homer: The Iliad*, 2nd edn. Cambridge (first pub. 1987).
Turner, Frank M. (1981). *The Greek Heritage in Victorian Britain*. New Haven, CT.
Venuti, Lawrence (1995). *The Translator's Invisibility*. London.
West, M. L. (1997). *The East Face of Helicon: West Asiatic Elements in Greek Poetry and Myth*. Oxford.
Whitman, Walt (1975). *The Complete Poems*, ed. Francis Murphy. Harmondsworth.
Wood, Robert (1765). *An Essay on the Original Genius and Writings of Homer*. London.
Young, Philip H. (2003). *The Printed Homer: A 3,000 Year Publishing and Translation History of the Iliad and the Odyssey*. Jefferson, NC.

5.3 Greek Drama

Adrian Poole

Aeschylus

The full range of extant Greek tragedy became accessible for the first time in English in the second half of the eighteenth century, with complete translations of Sophocles by Thomas Francklin (1758–9), Aeschylus by Robert Potter (1777), and Euripides by Michael Wodhull (1782). (Aristophanes would have to wait another fifty years until C. A. Wheelwright in 1837.) These three pioneers held the field unchallenged through the first decades of the nineteenth century, and their collective status was marked in 1809 when they were published together in five volumes as *The Greek Tragic Theatre*. Though they would in due course be superseded, they endured for a remarkably long time, Potter's Aeschylus being still reprinted in the early 1900s.

Fortunately the fate of Aeschylus in English did not rest with Potter and his successors alone. For the Romantic poets Aeschylus was above all the creator of Prometheus, the icon of defiance, philanthropy, and hope, the inspiration for Byron's 'Prometheus' (1816) and Shelley's *Prometheus Unbound* (1820). Shelley and Byron did relatively little by way of extended translation (the former's version of Euripides' *Cyclops* is discussed below), but they whetted the appetite of succeeding writers and readers for new versions of Prometheus in English (see p. 26, above).

The Aeschylean play attracted some notable women translators, beginning with the young Elizabeth Barrett Browning, who produced her first translation of *Prometheus Bound* in 1833. It was greeted with such scorn that she withdrew it from circulation, but she returned to the fray with a new version, more happily received, in 1850. Her important preface rejects the conventional definition of the 'classical' as 'regular, polished, and unimpassioned'. Properly understood, the classical *was* romantic, and Aeschylus was its epitome, 'a fearless and impetuous, not a cautious and accomplished poet'. Images of tyranny and bondage from the play infiltrate the correspondence with Robert Browning during their courtship; the lovers evidently saw it 'as a script for the unfolding drama of their own lives' (Prins 1991: 435).

Aeschylus was also an inspiration to the redoubtable Anna Swanwick. She studied German, Greek, and Hebrew in Berlin, and went on to publish well-received versions first of the *Oresteia* (1865), then of all seven extant plays (1873). Her substantial introductions draw on a wide range of modern scholarship, including Hegel and Max Müller. Though she concurred with the spirit of the age in holding that 'Poets of the highest order belong ... not to one age or country, but to humanity', she stressed the foreignness of ancient religious belief, 'only a dim but most wonderful foreshadowing' (Swanwick 1881: xiv, xlvii). She also took the side of Matthew Arnold's antagonist, F. W. Newman, in their arguments over naturalizing

Homer in English. Swanwick's Aeschylus brought her power and influence, and it created new respect for women's scholarship (see Hardwick 2000: 32–6).

Another leading figure was Augusta Webster, who issued her *Prometheus Bound* in 1866 and went on to Euripides' *Medea* (1868). Like Swanwick, she was active in the campaign for women's education and political rights, but she also had high ambitions for herself as a poet, dramatist, and novelist. She wrote two significant essays on translation (reprinted in *A Housewife's Opinions*, 1879), one of them a trenchant review of two recent translations of the *Agamemnon*, by E. D. A. Morshead and by Robert Browning (Webster 1879: 66–79). The former was too readable: Morshead turns a brute 'bull' in the Greek into 'The monarch of the herd, the pasture's pride'. The latter, magnificent in its perverse cacophonous way, was not readable enough: you needed the Greek to understand the Browning.

Along with *Prometheus Bound*, *Agamemnon* was the play of Aeschylus that attracted most attention through the century. Webster could have extended her critique to two other prominent versions by Edward FitzGerald and Benjamin Hall Kennedy. The former's *Agamemnon* was privately printed in 1865, and revised for publication in 1876; the latter's was issued in 1878. FitzGerald took an extreme line on the readability of translations, famously declaring 'the live Dog better than the dead Lion' (FitzGerald 1889: I, 434). Though he deprecated his Choruses as 'mostly "rot" quoad Poetry' (I, 360), his free version is distinguished by its metrical variety and invention, ranging from these terse four-beat iambics:

> For soon or late sardonic Fate
> With Man against himself conspires;
> Puts on the mask of his desires: . . .
>
> (III, 286)

to the violent dactyls into which Cassandra explodes, as if she were inspired by the very rhythm of the name 'Phoebus Apollo!':

> . . . —love-grinning Woman above,
> Dragon-tail'd under—honey-tongued, Harpy-claw'd
> Into the glittering meshes of slaughter
> She wheedles, entices, him . . .
>
> (III, 315–16)

Kennedy's translation is the polar opposite of FitzGerald's insofar as it accompanies the Greek text, learned commentary, and notes that one would expect from the Regius Professor of Greek at Cambridge. (His successor, Richard Jebb, gave Sophocles the same treatment.) His was 'not an attempt to poetise Aeschylus in English', Kennedy insisted (1882: xix). But his choice of alexandrines for the dialogue makes a striking change from the norm of blank verse that translators often too limply adopted.

Robert Browning also eschewed 'poetizing' Aeschylus, arguing in his preface the desirability of a translator being 'literal at every cost save that of absolute violence to our language'. Webster was not alone in finding the violence excessive.

'He has trampled upon his mother-tongue as with the hoofs of a buffalo', snorted *The Spectator* (cited in Litzinger and Smalley 1970: 441). Or, as Browning makes his Watchman say: 'on tongue a big ox | Has trodden'. Most translators of the play have recourse to ingenious compounds, such as FitzGerald's 'meteor-bearded', 'torch-handed', and 'manslaughter-madden'd', or Kennedy's 'barrel-emptying stress of weather' and 'luck-reversing brunt of life'. But Browning outdoes them all for outlandishness, making his Klutaimnestra declare that 'in my late-to-bed eyes I have damage', and as she contemplates the corpse of Cassandra, that 'me she brought to— | My bed's by-nicety—the whet of dalliance'. Yet there is a good case for taking what Browning audaciously called a 'transcript' as a serious experiment in the (im)possibilities of translation. The words he finds for Iphigeneia's thwarted utterance can be understood as the motto for his own endeavour: 'violence bridling speech'. Recent readers have admired the way Browning defies the allure of fluency to explore the disjunctions between speech and writing that are a deep concern of his poetry as a whole (Prins 1989; Reynolds 2003).

In 1880 Browning was in the audience for the historic staging of the *Agamemnon* in Greek at Balliol College, Oxford. The occasion marked a new interest in the performance of Greek drama, both in translation and the original (see Macintosh 1997). Earlier the same year a select audience in Edinburgh had witnessed the first full-length production of the play in English by Professor Fleeming Jenkin, in a fluent but undistinguished version by the Balliol-educated Lewis Campbell, professor of Greek at St Andrews. Another academic to advocate the performability of the Greeks was George Warr, professor of classical literature at King's College London. In 1886 his abridged version in English of the *Oresteia*, 'The Story of Orestes', was performed in the Prince's Hall, Piccadilly, and he went on to publish a complete translation of the trilogy in 1900, in which the needs of readers both with Greek and without are generously met by thorough annotation along with an informative introduction and illustrations. The range of work gathered in Warr's volume suggests how close, by the turn of the century, were the connections between translation, performance, and several fields of scholarship including archaeology and anthropology (see Hall and Macintosh 2005).

Sophocles

It is no accident that the Brownings translated Aeschylus and Euripides but not Sophocles. He played a quite different role in nineteenth-century culture, one that was steadying rather than stirring, disturbing, or dissolving. In Matthew Arnold's famous formulation Sophocles 'saw life steadily, and saw it whole' ('To a Friend', 1849); he also heard in the sound of the sea 'the turbid ebb and flow | Of human misery' ('Dover Beach', 1867). This made him a good patron for the moralized, humanized view of Greek tragedy to which Arnold gave authoritative formulation (in his preface to *Merope* for example). As E. M. Forster was to put it unkindly in *The Longest Journey*, Sophocles became for the Victorians 'a kind of enlightened bishop'.

This may explain why for readers now the nineteenth-century Sophocles seems relatively mild, even harmless. FitzGerald produced a disappointing adaptation of the two Oedipus plays entitled *The Downfall and Death of King Oedipus* (1880) 'taken from' the Greek (the same careful formula he had used for his *Agamemnon*, though he takes more liberties with Sophocles). He admitted that for him, 'Sophocles does not strike Fire out of the Flint, as old Aeschylus does'; he had no qualms about omitting 'much rhetorical fuss about the poor man's Fatality', and closing both parts of the drama promptly after the climax; for the choral lyrics he simply reprinted the uninspired renderings of 'old Potter' (FitzGerald 1889: I, 432, 448). After his Aeschylus old Potter had inexorably marched all Euripides and Sophocles into English as well (1781–3 and 1788, respectively). FitzGerald's drama is mainly interesting for the candour of his discomfort with certain aspects of Sophocles recalcitrant to domestication, including what he tetchily calls 'rhetoric'.

The dominant tradition was more dutiful towards Sophocles, though not towards predecessors needing ritual disparagement. In 1824 Thomas Dale deplored the 'rude and insipid familiarity' into which Francklin's still current version degraded the 'pathetic simplicity of the original' (1824). Near the end of the century Sir George Young agreed that Potter was more faithful but 'prosaic and clumsy'; Dale had a better ear for verse but his style was pompous. Young's own complete version (1888) displays an exceptionally sensitive ear for the subtleties of Sophoclean style both dramatic and lyric. His choral lyrics are intricately wrought, cleverly varied in metre and rhyme. His preface includes intelligent discussion of the translator's problems, and an incisive comparison of seven preceding versions of 'the small but very Sophoclean part of Eurydice' (*Antigone* 1183–91). Sophocles' other most impressive appearance in Victorian English was in the sonorous prose of Young's friend Sir Richard Jebb. Young and Jebb both held fellowships at Trinity College, Cambridge. Jebb ended his days there as professor of Greek while Young went on to become a high-ranking administrator, an example of the man of affairs who found time, in his own words, 'to lighten the numerous griefs of life by excursions on the lower slopes of Parnassus' (*DNB1*).

It is an index of the flexible role of translation in these late Victorian years that Jebb's translations should have been associated not only with his magisterial work as a scholar and editor but also with performance. The first Cambridge Greek Play was staged in 1882; the choice of Sophocles' *Ajax* reflects the high standing of Homeric subjects. Jebb's translation was printed alongside the acting text, as was Kennedy's the following year for *The Birds*, establishing a tradition that continued up to 1965 (Easterling 1999). The association of another eminent academic figure with performance has already been mentioned. Though his own edition of Sophocles was overshadowed by Jebb's, Lewis Campbell's verse translation (1883) draws on his involvement with staging the plays in Edinburgh and St Andrews. His introduction stresses the 'acting qualities' of Sophocles, and he recalls the inspiring production of *Antigone* in London and elsewhere in the mid-1840s with Helen Faucit in the title role, in a staging better known for its music by Mendelssohn than its words by William Bartholomew.

From the sixteenth century onwards Sophocles and Euripides have also enjoyed an English life in extracts. Good nineteenth-century examples include a rendering by Charles Stuart Calverley of Ajax's great 'deception speech' which effectively turns it into a Victorian dramatic monologue (1862). Alfred Pollard's anthology *Odes from the Greek Dramatists* (1890) prints versions of choral lyrics from *Ajax* and the three Theban plays, by Campbell, Young, A. W. Verrall, and others, that succinctly demonstrate the virtues and limitations of Victorian attempts to 'poetize' Sophocles. The lyric in which the old men of Colonus recognize the 'evil days' that have fallen on Oedipus, for example, concludes with this fine flourish:

> Blown from the fall of even,
> Blown from the dayspring forth,
> Blown from the noon in heaven,
> Blown from night and the North.

This is A. E. Housman, but it could be mistaken for Swinburne—skilful use of a contemporary poetic idiom.

Euripides

Like Potter's Aeschylus and Francklin's Sophocles, Wodhull's complete Euripides (1782) proved durable enough to see (partial) reprinting over a century later. He was eventually superseded by Arthur S. Way, whose three volumes (1894–8) were adopted in the early twentieth century by the newly founded Loeb Classical Library. The interim saw other complete versions including a reissue of the tenacious Potter's in Valpy's Classical Library (1832), and Theodore. A. Buckley's for Bohn's Classical Library (1850). Far more plays by Euripides have survived than those by his rivals, and in English they tend to appear in groups of two or three, as for example *Hippolytus and Alcestis* by 'A Member of the University of Oxford' (1822) or *Hecuba, Medea, and Phoenissae* by Roscoe Mongan (1865). If one takes the duos and trios into account alongside the versions of single plays, the popularity poll is easily topped by *Alcestis*, followed by *Medea, Hippolytus*, and *Hecuba*, with the *Bacchae* a little way behind them (but attracting increased interest towards the century's close).

Ever since Euripides first began to pass into modern European culture through Erasmus and the Tudor humanists, it had been his passionate women on whom the focus had fallen—'good' women like Alcestis, 'bad' women like Medea, and women like Phaedra who try to be good but come to a bad end. The nineteenth century was no different save that women themselves became more prominent as translators. From Elizabeth Barrett Browning onwards more women sought admission to the hitherto well-fortified domain of classical learning, especially in the later decades as educational opportunities began to open up. Augusta Webster has already been mentioned for her versions of *Prometheus Bound* and *Medea* (1868). Her 'literal' version of the latter encompasses with skill and feeling the vengeful fury of the wronged wife and the tenderness of the distracted mother.

Some sense of the passions that Medea could stimulate can be gleaned from the free adaptation made by the gifted, troubled Amy Levy, the first Jewish student to be admitted to Newnham College, Cambridge. In her dramatized version 'after Euripides' (1884), the Chorus disappears and a new character called Nikias is introduced to act as social commentator. Levy's Medea ends not in triumph but in destitute abandonment (see further Hardwick 2000: 40–1).

Another woman writer drawn to Euripides was Agnes Mary Francis Robinson. Like Levy she was a 'new woman' insofar as she studied English and classical literature at University College London, but she enjoyed a more extensive career than Levy, especially after moving to France in 1888, where she became well known as a literary and cultural historian. The role played near the start of this career by translation from the Greek was a vital one. Still only 24, in 1881 she gave pride of place in her second book of poems to her translation *The Crowned Hippolytus*. In the revealing prefatory 'Sonnet', Robinson distances herself from 'the first songs I said | With tremulous girlish voice'. She describes herself now, awaiting the verdict on this her true bid for creative maturity, 'as a heart-racked mother' who awaits the return of 'the lost son'. This is to transform and chasten the image at the heart of the play she has translated, in which a guilty woman and son await the judgement of a returning husband-father. In her sonnet's argument, the translation of *Hippolytus* becomes a key element in her rite of passage into 'truth' (her word).

The sense of context implicit in Robinson's translation—her motives, her readers, the values by which she asks to be judged—is a long way from that informing versions of the same play, 'literally translated into English prose, with notes, by a Graduate in Honours of the University of Oxford' (1846), or the parallel-text edition by John Thompson and B. J. Hayes in the University Tutorial Series (1898). A more radical approach to the question of 'context' is taken by Robert Browning in his two remarkable versions of *Alcestis* and *Heracles*. Both translations—or 'transcripts', as Browning insisted—are enfolded within encompassing narratives entitled, respectively, *Balaustion's Adventure* (1871) and *Aristophanes' Apology* (1875); in the former, it is also interspersed with commentary. In both cases Euripides' words are mediated through an enthusiastic admirer of the playwright, a young woman from Rhodes called Balaustion. She stands outside the original play but inside new dramatic contexts that involve antagonistic listeners, in the earlier work primarily hostile Sicilians and in the later the comic poet Aristophanes. The nature of the experiment is very different from the one conducted with the *Agamemnon* (1877). Indeed in terms of the debate with which all three 'transcripts' are concerned about the possibility of crossing from one language, time, situation, and person to any other, they express differing degrees of optimism and despair. *Balaustion's Adventure* takes a comparatively breezy liberty with the Greek it purports to translate, turning the *Alcestis* into a recognizably Victorian story of marital crisis resolved by a Christlike Heracles. In *Aristophanes' Apology*, by contrast, the debate between comedy and tragedy suggests that 'liberty' belongs more properly to the former than to the latter. As for his *Agamemnon*, it can seem like 'translation as tragedy' (Reynolds 2003: 112). Browning's three extraordinary engagements with Greek drama embody the nineteenth century's most intelligently agonized thinking about literary translation in English.

The other great English nineteenth-century poet to translate an entire Greek play was Shelley, to whom Browning's poetry owes a complex debt. Shelley made an unusual choice. Euripides' *Cyclops* is the sole surviving example of the satyr play that followed the performance of three tragedies at the Festival of Dionysus. Shelley was impatient with the prudishly domesticating view of the Greeks that would dominate the century till near its end. 'There is no book which shows the Greeks precisely as they were', he wrote in his 'Discourse on the Manners of the Ancient Athenians'; 'they seem all written for children, with the caution that no practice or sentiment highly inconsistent with our present manners should be mentioned, lest those manners should receive outrage and violation' (cited in Shelley 1989–: II, 372). Through the ribald, lascivious, god-defying Cyclops, he could explore 'the possibility, and the real difficulty, of producing a translation for adults' (Everest in Shelley 1989–: II, 373). Shelley did hesitate over some sexually explicit and suggestive passages and seems not to have told his wife Mary what he was up to. But though perhaps inevitably idealized, Shelley's *Cyclops* (published posthumously in 1824, and probably written in the summer of 1818) anticipates a ruder and more carnal aspect to Greek drama, more fully embodied in Aristophanic comedy, with which the nineteenth century negotiated nervously, when it did not simply ignore or deplore it.

Aristophanes

Given how much there is in Aristophanes to outrage and violate nineteenth-century manners and sensibilities, it may seem surprising how popular he was. The popularity came at the price of bowdlerizing much of the 'grossness', but there was admiration and even a certain yearning for his unbuttoned earthiness as well as for his aerial levity. In 1820 the *Edinburgh Review* complained that Richard Cumberland's translation of *The Clouds* (1797) represented 'Aristophanes imprisoned in brocade and mounted upon stilts into the bargain' (cited by Williams 1918: 255). The version of three plays issued by Thomas Mitchell that same year did little to release him or help him dismount, or so thought John Hookham Frere, friend and patron of Coleridge (Frere 1872: I, 167–200).

Four years later Henry Francis Cary, translator of Dante, turned out the first metrical version of *The Birds* in mainly iambic heptameters ('fourteeners'). This was one of many attempts to match the rollicking rhythm of the Greek. In 1839 Frere himself, now elderly and retired in Malta, privately printed his own metrical versions of four of the plays; these gradually became more widely known and rightly admired for their fluency and inventiveness. Reviewing (and publicizing) Frere's versions in 1847, his younger friend George Cornewall Lewis opined that 'Comedy is harder of translation than tragedy; it is easier to copy the lofty and serious than the ridiculous and familiar' (Frere 1872: I, cclvii). But Aristophanes could be lofty, ridiculous, serious, and familiar all at once or in rapid alternation, a bit like Shakespeare, and to a century obsessed with prosody, the endless variety of his style and metres made an attractive challenge.

Of the several fine musical versions of the great central chorus from *The Birds* one of the most notable is by Swinburne, who hailed its author as 'the half-divine humourist in whose incomparable genius the highest qualities of Rabelais were fused and harmonized with the supremest gifts of Shelley'. He thought the English language well suited to Aristophanes' anapaests and sought 'to renew as far as possible for English ears the music of this resonant and triumphant metre' (Swinburne 1904: V, 42). Here are his Birds celebrating the kingdom of Eros, and the things that wings can accomplish:

> We have wings, and with us have the Loves habitation;
> And manifold fair young folk that forswore love once, ere the bloom of them ended,
> Have the men that pursued and desired them subdued, by the help of us only befriended,
> With such baits as a quail, a flamingo, a goose, or a cock's comb staring and splendid.

Just a hint of Rabelais perhaps.

After Frere, the writer who dominated Victorian translations of Aristophanes through the latter part of the nineteenth century and far into the following was Benjamin Bickley Rogers. He was still an Oxford undergraduate when he completed his first Aristophanic venture, an edition of *The Clouds* 'with a translation into corresponding metres, and original notes', published in 1852. When his career as a barrister was cut short by deafness, he redevoted himself to Aristophanes, issuing editions with accompanying translations of all eleven extant plays, and being posthumously rewarded by their wholesale adoption into the Loeb Classical Library.

Of the plays that translators (and performers) tended to avoid, the most outrageous was *Lysistrata*. So it was just the play to suit the dying decadent years of the century. In 1896 Leonard Smithers published a limited edition 'now first wholly translated into English', and famously illustrated by Aubrey Beardsley. Taken together the drawings compose a grotesquely lyrical hymn to the phallus: 'this plague of erections is frightful', complain the Chorus of Old Men. The translator, Samuel Smith, sums up a century of helpless admiration for 'Aristophanes' marvellous literary swordplay, his bewildering wealth of pun and parody, his gradations of style, sometimes abrupt, sometimes sly, between the mock-heroic, the colloquial, the lyrical and the burlesque' (Smith 1896: v). Mention of the 'burlesque' is much to the point, for there is a sense in which it had been exactly the burlesques of the Victorian theatre, such as Frederick Robson's brilliant travesty of Adelaide Ristori's *Medea* (1856), that had kept the spirit of Aristophanic comedy alive (see Macintosh 2000).

The Victorians were not always adept at negotiating between the lyrical and the burlesque, and where Aristophanes was concerned they did more justice to the Shelley in him than to the Rabelais. Yet Shelley would have approved of Smith's belief that it was possible through translation to catch glimpses of 'the ribald melancholy, the significant buffoonery, and the grotesque animality' (Smith 1896: vi).

LIST OF SOURCES

Translations

Browning, Elizabeth Barrett (1850). *Poems*, 2 vols. London.

—— (2004). 'Two Translations of Aeschylus' *Prometheus Bound*', ed. Clara Drummond. Ph.D. diss. Boston University.

Browning, Robert (1871). *Balaustion's Adventure; including a Transcript from Euripides*. London.

—— (1875). *Aristophanes' Apology; including a Transcript from Euripides: Being the Last Adventure of Balaustion*. London.

—— (1877). *The Agamemnon of Aeschylus*. London.

C[alverley], C. S. (1862). *Verses and Translations*. London.

Campbell, Lewis (1883). *Sophocles: The Seven Plays in English Verse*. London.

—— (1890). *Aeschylus: The Seven Plays in English Verse*. London.

Cary, Henry Francis (1824). *The Birds of Aristophanes*. London.

Dale, Thomas (1824). *The Tragedies of Sophocles*, 2 vols. London.

FitzGerald, Edward (1889). *Letters and Literary Remains of Edward FitzGerald*, ed. William Aldis Wright, 3 vols. London (Vol. 3 contains *Agamemnon* and *The Downfall and Death of King Oedipus*).

Frere, John Hookham (1872). *The Works of John Hookham Frere in Verse and Prose*, 2 vols. London.

Jebb, Sir R. C. (1904). *The Tragedies of Sophocles, Translated into English Prose*. Cambridge.

Kennedy, Benjamin Hall (1882). *The Agamemnon of Aeschylus with a Metrical Translation and Notes Critical and Illustrative*, 2nd edn. Cambridge.

Levy, Amy (1884). *A Minor Poet and Other Verses*. London.

Pollard, Alfred W., ed. (1890). *Odes from the Greek Dramatists Translated into Lyric Metres by English Poets and Scholars*. London.

Robinson, A. Mary F. (1881). *The Crowned Hippolytus Translated from Euripides, with New Poems*. London.

Rogers, Benjamin Bickley (1924). *Aristophanes*, 3 vols. London (Loeb).

Shelley, Percy Bysshe (1824). *Posthumous Poems*. London.

—— (1989–). *Poems*, ed. Kelvin Everest and Geoffrey Matthews, 2 vols. to date (Vol. 2, pp. 371–412, contains 'The Cyclops').

[Smith, Samuel] (1896). *The Lysistrata of Aristophanes. Now First Wholly Translated into English and Illustrated . . . by Aubrey Beardsley*. London.

Swanwick, Anna (1881). *The Dramas of Aeschylus*, 3rd edn. London (Bohn).

Swinburne, Algernon Charles (1904). *Poems*, 6 vols. London (the translation from Aristophanes was first published in *Studies in Song*, 1880).

Warr, George C. W. (1900). *The Oresteia of Aeschylus*. London.

Webster, Augusta (1866). *The Prometheus Bound of Aeschylus Literally Translated into English Verse*, ed. T. Webster. London.

—— (1868). *The Medea of Euripides Literally Translated into English Verse*. London.

Wheelwright, C. A. (1837). *The Comedies of Aristophanes*, 2 vols. Oxford.

Young, Sir George (1888). *The Dramas of Sophocles Rendered in English Verse Dramatic and Lyric*. Cambridge.

Other Sources

Drummond, Clara (2006). ' "Dost Thou See How I Suffer This Wrong?": The Prometheus Bounds of Elizabeth Barrett Browning.' *International Journal of the Classical Tradition*, forthcoming in Vol. 12.

Easterling, P. E. (1999). 'The Early Years of the Cambridge Greek Play', pp. 27–48 in Christopher Stray, ed., *Classics in 19th and 20th Century Cambridge: Curriculum, Culture and Community* (*Cambridge Philological Society*, Supplement 24). Cambridge.
Foster, Finley Melville Kendall (1918). *English Translations from the Greek: A Bibliographical Survey*. New York.
Hall, Edith, and Macintosh, Fiona (2005). *Greek Tragedy and the British Theatre 1660–1914*. Oxford.
Hardwick, Lorna (2000). *Translating Words, Translating Cultures*. London.
Litzinger, Boyd, and Smalley, Donald (1970). *Browning: The Critical Heritage*. London.
Macintosh, Fiona (1997). 'Tragedy in Performance: Nineteenth- and Twentieth-Century Productions', pp. 284–323 in P. E. Easterling, ed., *The Cambridge Companion to Greek Tragedy*. Cambridge.
—— (2000). 'Medea Transposed: Burlesque and Gender on the Mid-Victorian Stage', pp. 75–99 in Edith Hall, Fiona Macintosh, and Oliver Taplin, eds., *Medea in Performance*. Oxford.
Prins, Yopie (1989). '"Violence bridling speech": Browning's Translation of Aeschylus' *Agamemnon.*' *Victorian Poetry* 27: 151–70.
—— (1991). 'Elizabeth Barrett, Robert Browning, and the *Différance* of Translation.' *Victorian Poetry* 29: 435–51.
Reynolds, Matthew (2003). 'Browning and Translationese.' *Essays in Criticism* 53: 97–128.
Webster, Augusta (1879). *A Housewife's Opinions*. London.
Williams, Stanley Thomas (1917). *Richard Cumberland: His Life and Dramatic Works*. New Haven, CT.

5.4 Latin Poetry

John Talbot

Translation from Latin verse in the nineteenth century, for the first time since the Renaissance, was not central to the work of major English poets. The Romantics looked more often to Greece, and by Victoria's reign many of the most influential translators were not the age's most renowned poets, a fact acknowledged—not entirely ruefully—by a leading scholar-translator, John Conington: 'The time appears to have gone by when men of great original gifts could find satisfaction in reproducing the thoughts and words of others; and the work, if done at all, must now be done by writers of inferior pretension' (Conington 1863: vii). Translations by the leading poets tend to survive as schoolboy exercises, occasional excursions from the real work of composing original verse, or—often most memorably—as reminiscences or imitations of Latin passages incorporated into original poems. Amateurs, scholars, and minor poets took up the slack and became an important presence in the translation of Latin verse.

Catullus

The first complete English Catullus, published in 1795 by the physician John Nott, is a scholarly affair, with facing Latin and copious learned notes. Nott was no poet: his prosy elaboration of Catullus' compressed epigram *odi et amo* is a case in point:

> Tho' I hate, yet I love—you'll perhaps ask me, how?
> I can't tell; but I'm vext, and feel that I do.
> (Nott 1795: 137)

But his renderings are usually readable and accurate, and he leaves promising leads for better writers to pick up and improve: the flower, for instance, at the end of poem 11, 'Which, springing on the meadow's sides, | Felt the share's iron touch, and dies' (Nott 1795: 39), Thomas Moore would later transform into 'Like a fair flower, the meadow's last | Which feels the ploughshare's edge, and dies!' (Moore 1867: 516). Nott's edition breaks ground not only for being the first unexpurgated Catullus, but in anticipating a trend: respectable work by scholar-translators rather than poets.

Poets, though, did not ignore Catullus. Wordsworth translated poem 3 freely, and published an elegant version—once attributed to Coleridge—of poem 7 (Wordsworth 1997: 371–7). Walter Savage Landor praised Catullus above all other classical poets, and translated him throughout his life. Urbane romps like poem 10 offered scope for Landor's own lapidary wit:

> Varrus would take me t'other day
> To see a little girl he knew,
> Pretty and witty in her way,
> With impudence enough for two.
> (Landor 1969: XV, 250)

Landor toned down racier passages, and paraphrase of the poet's less genteel patches is a marked feature of many translations. In George Lamb's 1821 translation, the tendency to paraphrase Catullus' violent invective means, in a later critic's view, that 'it was not Catullus which was presented, but the graceful sarcasms of a well-bred gentleman of the days of the Regency' (Martin 1861).

The metrical dexterity typical of many nineteenth-century poets sometimes found an outlet in Catullan translations. Thomas Moore introduced into his translations elements of classical prosody, most notably the choriamb, whose distinctive cadence is heard in most of Catullus' lyric metres: 'Gazing upon the world of shade | Witness some secret youth and maid' (Moore 1867: 70, translating poem 7). Metrical challenges also enticed Moore's contemporary Leigh Hunt, who produced, among other more conventional translations, a daring version of poem 63, composed in Catullus' most complex metre, the galliambic, which can include such tortuously staccato rhythms as ᴗᴗ–ᴗ ᴗᴗᴗ–– ᴗᴗᴗᴗ –ᴗ– (l. 91). Hunt's version suggests the violence by veering from trochaic lines of varying feet, to frantic anapests, on to iambic lines ranging from two to eight feet, finally resolving into pentameter.

It is typical of the period that the only Catullan translations by Byron—who might have been expected to find a soulmate in the passionate Roman—are juvenilia, entombed in his first volume of verse, privately printed at the age of 18. Translation could, however, remain the leisure activity of privileged amateurs like Gladstone, who found time to render poem 51 into competent octosyllabics, or of Theodore Martin, who balanced an active public life with a career as a writer, including translations of Catullus rearranged to link poems of similar themes and suggest the outlines of narrative (so poem 11 in his edition is followed by 70). And other notable amateurs, including Sir Richard Burton and Aubrey Beardsley, tried their hand at selected poems.

Lucretius

English Romantics were drawn to Lucretius' 'violent energies', his feel for nature, and his supposed atheism, but usually expressed their admiration by emulating those features in their own original poems rather than through translations (see Vance 1997: 89–96). Scholars and amateurs, on the other hand, produced several versions of Lucretius. John Nott brought out a translation of the first book of

De Rerum Natura in 1799, a competent rendering in heroic couplets; but the public's cool response led him to abandon further translation. Six years later, another physician, John Mason Good, produced a sumptuous complete edition with facing Latin and copious scholarly notes, including parallel passages from Hebrew, Greek, Latin, the modern languages, and even Arabic. Unlike most of his predecessors, Good translates in blank verse as better suited than the couplet to 'mixed subjects of description and scientific precept' (Good 1805: xiii). His translation has the virtues of clarity and precision, but it fails to make the English respond to Lucretius' style. It is a solid, serviceable translation; and its reappearance alongside a prose translation in Bohn's Classical Library (1851) kept it in public view for several decades. The partial translation of the Ulster clergyman W. H. Drummond (1808) was criticized in the *Monthly Review* as too accurate, allowing the poet's objectionable 'philosophy to freeze [the] poetry'. Against such an attitude Sir Charles Elton prefaced his twenty pages of excerpts (1814) with a spirited defence of the poet's morality.

The Victorian preoccupation with questions of materialism and evolution led to a heightened interest: 'Yes, Lucretius is modern', Matthew Arnold conceded in 1857 (Arnold 1960: 33). What was increasingly wanted as the century progressed was not Lucretius the poet, but the philosopher (see p. 478, below); few of the later translations aim at, and none achieves, great poetic merit (for the reversal of emphasis, from Lucretius as chiefly poet to chiefly philosopher, see Turner 1973). This is the case with the standard Victorian translation, by the Cambridge classicist H. A. J. Munro. His 1866 prose version was appended to a massive edition and commentary stressing the links to contemporary philosophical and scientific concerns; and while he praised Lucretius as a poet, his own style is an awkward blend of archaisms and prosiness. Even the most ostensibly poetical translation during the second half of the century—W. H. Mallock's 1900 rendering of scattered Lucretian passages into the stanza of FitzGerald's *Rubáiyát*—is not so much an earnest poetic enterprise as an 'experiment' (Mallock 1900: iii) whose purpose, as Vance has perceived, was to expose, by ironic juxtaposition, Lucretius' cumulative thought as incompatible with poetic expression, to reveal him as 'only very incidentally a poet of lyric power: what mattered was the ... detailed explanations of natural phenomena' (Vance 1997: 105).

Virgil

By the end of the eighteenth century Virgil's reputation was in decline, as he came to be regarded as merely derivative of his ostensible Greek models. In just over a hundred years, we slide from Dryden's confident assertion that Virgil is 'the best poet', to the notorious remark of Coleridge's, a touchstone of Romantic attitudes: 'If you take from Virgil his diction and metre, what do you leave him?' Translations of Virgil by the major Romantics are consequently scarce; Wordsworth's aborted translation of the *Aeneid*—composed, uncharacteristically, in heroic couplets of lofty diction—is the only major example. Wordsworth sought to improve on Dryden's version, which he thought unfaithful both to Virgil's sense and enjambed cadences. Coleridge criticized the work in progress, especially its overwrought latinity, and wondered why his friend had 'wasted [his] time on a work so much below [him]' (see Wordsworth 1998: 163). Wordsworth abandoned the work after three books, publishing no more than an excerpt in a classical journal in 1832. A translation with a scholarly bent appeared in 1825, when Robert Hoblyn, 'late Student of Christ Church, Oxford', brought out a blank verse translation of the first *Georgic* aimed at correcting the 'too paraphrastical' versions of predecessors whom he does not name, striving for scholarly—and in this case particularly agricultural—accuracy (Hoblyn 1825: i–vii).

Victorian poets, attuned to the *lacrimae rerum* note in Virgil, tended to express greater sympathy: Tennyson's paean 'To Virgil'—'Thou majestic in thy sadness'—points to the vein of tender melancholy that the Victorians found congenial to their own attitudes. But mining that vein did not usually extend to translating; that was left largely to scholars and amateurs. No major poets touched the *Eclogues* or the *Georgics*. William Sewell, Fellow of Exeter College, Oxford, in the preface to his 1854 verse translation of the *Georgics*, stressed the importance of preserving 'the *strictest grammatical accuracy* in translation of classical poets' (Sewell 1854: v). The prevalence of such an attitude led A. H. Palmer to apologize for his father Samuel's posthumous translation of the *Eclogues* that made 'no pretension to the scholarly accuracy of the present day' (Palmer 1883: xiv). Palmer's rhymed couplets can claim, however, an easy freedom in drawing out sense from verse to verse, and considerable success in approaching certain aspects of Virgilian sound effects, including the intricate play of assonance and alliteration:

> You thought the airy pine
> Sigh'd 'Tityrus,' and the dishevell'd vine
> And vacant grove; and could his name recall
> Syllabled in the fountain and the fall.
> (Palmer 1883: 21)

The lawyer Sir Charles Bowen won praise for his 1887 *Eclogues*, with its idiosyncratic metre (for a discussion, see Gransden 1996: xxviii–xxix); R. D. Blackmore of *Lorna Doone* fame translated the *Georgics* (1871); and the virtuoso parodist Charles Stuart Calverley made an assured and witty blank verse translation of the *Eclogues*.

Victorians produced a succession of notable translations of the *Aeneid*. The Irish physician and classical scholar James Henry, after an earlier attempt at Books I–II, published in 1853 versions from the first half of the *Aeneid* rendered mostly in two-stress lines ranging from four to seven syllables, with acute accents inserted to indicate where the stress is meant to fall:

> Ánd in mány a clóse-hand fíght
> In the dárkness of the níght
> Full mány of the Dánai
> Dispátch to Orcus dówn
> (Henry 1853: 68–9)

The measure can achieve an impressive force, but does not lend itself to Virgil's subtle modulations, and the relentless thudding makes reading at long stretches hard.

The most influential Victorian translator was the Oxford scholar John Conington, the first Corpus Professor of Latin. The renown of his *Aeneid* (1866) is perhaps an index of what readers by the nineteenth century had come to expect of a translation: the praise it received is often tellingly linked to the translator's scholarly powers. 'Professor Conington's prolonged commentatorial study of Virgil,' wrote a reviewer in *Fraser's Magazine* (January 1867), 'has given him freedom and power, in bringing out the meaning of his author, which has enabled him, on the whole, to keep remarkably close to the original.' Vaunted accuracy aside, the other outstanding feature of Conington's *Aeneid* is its metre: the ballad measure of Sir Walter Scott's *Marmion*. The resulting rapidity, so appreciated by reviewers, often produces a disconcertingly jaunty Virgil. These verses, translating the lines at the end of Book XII where the enraged Aeneas is about to kill Turnus, trip too lightly over Virgil's impacted Latin ('Pallas | immolat et poenam scelerato ex sanguine sumit') with its thick, smacking m's and hissing sibilants:

> Soon as his eyes had gazed their fill
> On that sad monument of ill,
> Live fury kindling every vein,
> He cries with terrible disdain:
> 'What! in my friend's dear spoils arrayed
>   To me for mercy sue?
> 'Tis Pallas, Pallas guides the blade:
> From your cursed blood the injured shade
>   Thus takes the atonement due.'
>   (Conington 1866: 478)

Against the rapidity of Henry and Conington plod the gangly fourteeners of William Morris's 1876 version. Its opening lines demonstrate its reliance on archaisms and line-padding tautologies:

> I sing of arms, I sing of him, who from the Trojan land
> Thrust forth by fate, to Italy and that Lavinian strand
> First came: all tost about was he on earth and on the deep
> By heavenly might for Juno's wrath, that had no mind to sleep:
> And plenteous war he underwent ere he his town might frame.
>   (Morris 1876: 1)

The use of compound epithets and kennings, and a certain rough-hewn feel, have reminded critics of Anglo-Saxon verse (Gransden 1996: xxix; Burrow 1997: 34). Yet it has something in common with its predecessors: not just the metrical experimentation typical of the era, but also the implication that Virgil can be improved by rendering him in metres suggestive of oral folk literature: 'Most Victorian Virgils are influenced by the prevalent belief that the "primary" epic of Homer was superior to the "secondary", literary, epic of Virgil' (Burrow 1997: 34).

Horace

Horace, less obviously ardent than Catullus, suffered some neglect from Romantic poets and their Victorian successors. As the end of the century approached, there are signs of greater interest in Horace among poets: Hopkins, for instance, made memorable translations of two odes, to which he brought characteristic verbal compression; the result has a density analogous to Horace's:

> Kings herd in on their subject drones
> But Jove's the herd that keeps the kings –
> Jove of the Giants: simple Jove's
> Mere eyebrow rocks this round of things.
> (Hopkins 1990: 100)

The third line of that stanza—with its sudden brevity, its analepsis, and its precipitous enjambement—contribute to a majestic severity. And A. E. Housman in the last years of the nineteenth century published one of the most accomplished translations in the language, a version of IV.7, 'Diffugere nives'. His third stanza approaches the headlong enjambement and the gloomy accumulation of u's ('interitura simul | pomifer Autumnus fruges effuderit') that haunts the original:

> Thaw follows frost; hard on the heel of spring
> Treads summer sure to die, for hard on hers
> Comes autumn with his apples scattering.
> (Housman 1997: 118)

Generally, however, the more renowned poets of the century keep their distance from Horace. Though Wordsworth claimed Horace as his 'great favourite' (Carne-Ross and Haynes 1996: 38), that affection enters his verse concretely only in the form of a single early translation of the Bandusia ode and in a few reminiscences in his own poems (such as the sonnets on the River Duddon). Byron is typical of those who, unable to separate Horace from memories of schoolmasters' stringency, left him behind in the schoolroom after one or two juvenile efforts. The very rigour and emphasis of Latin education in the nineteenth century may have inhibited, rather than encouraged, translation: the 'dark age' of translations from Latin, as two critics have pointed out, occurs in 'exactly the era in which the prestige of the classics was at its highest' (Poole and Maule 1995: xlv).

This gloomy judgement perhaps deserves, in Horace's case, some qualification, since scholars and talented amateur poets made notable contributions to Horatian translation throughout the century. Horace's most prominent translator in the period was a scholar. The translations in John Conington's 1863 edition of the Odes stand out for their metrical variety, from the trochaic lines in the Leuconoe ode, to the alternation of long and short lines meant to suggest asclepiads, to the imitation of the unique instance of ionic *a minore* in III.12: 'How unhappy are the maidens who with Cupid may not play' (Conington 1863: 82). Contemporary critics rightly took him to task for rendering Horace's signature metre, the alcaic, into quatrains of alternately rhymed tetrameter—too common, too tame an English measure for the alcaic's complex shifts of rhythm and tempo—but in general Conington manages to build and vary stanzas in ways that suggest the shape and heft of the odes.

The other outstanding virtue of Conington's Horace is a faintly damning one: his accuracy. Time and again he succeeds in compacting all or nearly all of the sense of Horace's very dense stanzas into commensurate stanzas of his own. Consider his handling of a typically packed passage, the last stanza of the Soracte ode (I.9):

> Sweet too the laugh, whose feign'd alarm
> The hiding-place of beauty tells,
> The token, ravish'd from the arm
> Or finger, that but ill rebels.
> (Conington 1863: 12)

'The hiding-place of beauty', to take one instance, brings out with impressive economy both 'latentis ... puellae' and 'intimo ... ab angulo'. Impressive, that is, to those who have Latin and can appreciate it for the exercise that it is. But it is hard to imagine anyone unfamiliar with the Latin making poetic sense of a phrase like 'finger, that but ill rebels', let alone warming to the energy of flirtatious resistance that animates the original. To set Conington's translation beside Dryden's—

> The pleasing whisper in the dark,
> The half unwilling willing kiss,
> The laugh that guides thee to the mark,
> When the kind Nymph wou'd coyness feign,
> And hides but to be found again,
> These, these are joyes the Gods for Youth ordain

—is to feel the gulf between a poet's powers on the one hand, and an accomplished scholar's knack for making shrewd trots on the other. The Mozartian flutter at the end of one famous line—'si parcent puero fata superstiti'—in Conington's version lands with a lethal thud, the scholar's beloved *thus*: 'Would fate but spare the sweet survivor thus' (Conington 1863: 78). When the schoolman's instincts lead him to Latinisms like 'horrent' mountains or archaisms like 'I bid the unhallow'd crowd avaunt!' (Conington 1863: 25, 69), he is reduced to 'the style of no period, writing of actions and emotions that take place nowhere' (Carne-Ross and Haynes 1996: 41).

With Horace, as with Catullus, a number of amateurs enter the field, including Gladstone and Martin once again; the Irish lawyer Sir Stephen de Vere; and the brothers James and Horatio Smith, whose *Horace in London* (1813) transplanted the poet to Regency England (where the Soracte ode begins 'See Richmond is clad in a mantle of snow' (Carne-Ross and Haynes 1996: 217)) and encouraged him to speak in his more jocular registers. Perhaps most notable among these amateurs is Charles Stuart Calverley, whose renderings of fifteen odes are charged with both verbal energy and pictorial vividness. He had translated some verses from Tennyson's *In Memoriam* into Horatian alcaics; reversing that transaction, he rendered Horace's alcaics, including these lines from the Soracte ode, into *In Memoriam* stanza:

> One dazzling mass of solid snow
> Soracte stands; the bent woods fret
> Beneath their load; and, sharpest-set,
> With frost, the streams have ceased to flow.
> (Calverley 1862: 160)

Horace's Satires and Epistles, attempted perhaps less often than the Odes, supplied the occasion for one of the bright moments of nineteenth-century translation: a spry and elegant version, published posthumously in 1845 by the cleric Francis Howes, whose assured couplets recall the ease and polish of the best eighteenth-century verse. When he writes of 'Jove, with burly scowl | (As limners paint him) and inflated jowl' (Howes 1845: 38), the parenthesis is an interpolation, inserted with a confident obliqueness that a Conington could never venture. Later in the same poem he writes that a thrifty man 'wisely studies to confine | His wishes there, while nature draws the line' (Howes 1845: 39), where the perching of 'confine'—at that boundary where the poet draws his poetic line—happily suggests something of the rhetorical inventiveness of the original. Where Pope had tended to take Horace's colloquial diction up several rhetorical notches—as in the inversions and lofty phrases of his rendering of the opening lines of I.6, 'Nil admirari'—Howes, on the other hand, maintains a low-key, easygoing elegance. Where colloquial verve is called for, he charms: ' "My friend, how d'ye do?" 'asks the infamous pest from I.9, ' "And pray," he cried, "how wags the world with you?" ' (Howes 1845: 74).

Propertius, Ovid, Juvenal, Martial

The period's few translations of Propertius are unremarkable. Sir Charles Elton in his 1814 anthology gives twenty elegies in rhymed couplets. Charles Moore in 1870 published a full translation, but his genteel couplets too often smooth over the cragginess of the original: so the violent crackling of 'spirantisque animos et vocem misit: at illi | pollicibus fragiles increpuere manus' fizzles into unruffled primness: 'Her bony fingers rattled in mine ear, | Though was her wrath still warm, her accents clear'(Moore 1870: 128). S. G. Tremenheere, in the introduction to his solid but unremarkable *The Cynthia of Propertius* (1899), justly lamented his inability to convey, in symmetrical rhymed couplets, the variety and antiphonal character of the original elegiac couplets.

Though Ovid's influence can be felt in poets as diverse as Keats, Tennyson, Browning, and Arnold, no major poets translated him: the Romantics found him too glib, the Victorians, too bawdy, as recent critics have asserted (Martin 1998: xxxii–xxxiii; Vance 1988). Arthur Hugh Clough's rendering—not published until 1974—of eight lines out of the *Ars Amatoria* is emblematic of the dearth. Almost all the translators attracted to Ovid in the period are either very minor figures or otherwise unknown to literary history (see Gillespie and Cummings 2004: 213–15).

A number of translations from Juvenal appeared during the Romantic period; his supposed masculinity and moral vehemence (as against the genial tolerance of Horatian satire) appealed especially to conservatives who felt British institutions threatened by Jacobinism, French mores and politics, foreigners, and feminism (Dyer 1997: 51–6). So Arthur Murphy recast Satire 13 (1791) in contemporary terms, pining for the days of good King Alfred, when 'From France no agent of a desp'rate band | Could spread his froth and venom through the land' (Winkler 2001: 284), echoing here Pope's 'Epistle to Dr Arbuthnot' (l. 320); and the Whig politician Henry Richard Vassal Fox, in his 1799 *Imitations*, substituted Scots for the loathsome Greeks that Juvenal deplored in Satire 3. Many others throughout the century tried their hand at individual satires (for a survey, see Winkler 2001).

Two of the leading Romantic poets embarked on Juvenalian sallies. Wordsworth produced, in the last decade of the eighteenth century, an imitation of some hundred lines out of Satire 8, in which he takes aim at George III, the hapless Duke of York, and a slew of loutish noblemen. James I and Raleigh stand in for Nero and Seneca, the burghers of Calais for the Decii, William the Conqueror for Romulus. The version is very free, especially the first twenty-eight lines, which 'have no parallel in Juvenal' (Wordsworth 1981: 935); but his couplets catch something of Juvenal's balance of formal loftiness and colloquial spleen. For all its virtues, Wordsworth nevertheless refrained from publishing the piece. Byron, too, came to repudiate his own imitation of Juvenal, *English Bards and Scotch Reviewers*, published in various versions from 1808 to 1812 (see further Stabler 1995). *Quarterly Review* editor William Gifford had already made his name as a satirist in English verse by the time he turned to translations of Juvenal (1802) and Persius (1821). Both versions are vigorous and acerbic, though slightly tamer than the originals: Gifford wanted his translation to appear 'refined with the age' (Gifford 1802: lxiii). His Juvenal became one of the most widely praised and influential translations of the century—Byron read it in preparing to write 'English Bards'—and it survived, with slight revisions, into the twentieth century in Everyman's Library. Other complete versions were made by the clergyman William Heath Marsh (1804) and Byron's friend Francis Hodgson (1807).

The nineteenth century's 'prevalent condemnation' of Martial (Sullivan 1991: 304) helps to account for the relative paucity of translations of his epigrams. Byron englished a handful of 'those nauseous epigrams of Martial', as did George Lamb. Henry George Bohn oversaw the compilation of the first complete English Martial, by various hands and from various time periods, in 1860. Sullivan (1991: 304–5) considers Bohn's edition a courageous challenge to the prevailing morality; nevertheless, the most obscene epigrams are rendered not in English but in the Italian of Graglia, 'who has been rather dextrous in refining impurities' (Bohn 1860: iv). George Augustus Sala's salacious *Index Expurgatorius* (1868) contained ribald translations of only those epigrams ordinarily bowdlerized. Late in the century Robert Louis Stevenson, who in the *British Weekly* (13 May 1887) had discerned in Martial, behind the bawdiness, 'a kind, wise, and self-respecting gentleman', made a number of translations which were published posthumously.

Reminiscences and Adaptation

Many of the best instances of nineteenth-century translation from Latin verse occur as reminiscences or adaptations within original poems. The first twelve lines of Wordsworth's 'To—Upon the Birth of her First-Born Child, March, 1833' elegantly translate Lucretius V, 222–7:

> Like a shipwrecked Sailor tost
> By rough waves on a perilous coast,
> Lies the Babe, in helplessness
> And in tenderest nakedness.
> (Wordsworth 1981: 734)

Byron in *Hints from Horace* rewrites the *Ars Poetica* as he crosses swords with contemporary literary rivals. In this period Tennyson's verses, perhaps more than any other poet's, come rich in passages that transform lines of Latin verse into English poetry. Though 'Frater Ave atque Vale', which conflates the themes of two Catullan poems, one joyous, one mournful (31 and 101), is not a translation, its English answers to the sonority of Catullus' Latin as few strict translations have ever done: 'Sweet Catullus' all-but-island, olive silvery Sirmio' (Tennyson 1987: III, 71; cf. 'Paene insularum, Sirmio, insularumque'). The lines in his dramatic monologue 'Lucretius' asserting the need for 'No larger feast than under plane or pine | With neighbours laid along the grass, to take | Only such cups as left us friendly-warm' (Tennyson 1987: II, 717) transform a passage from Book II of *De Rerum Natura*, while simultaneously echoing lines from a Horatian ode. Well over a score of Latin phrases are so adapted and woven seamlessly into the tight fabric of the English poem. And in 'To the Rev. F. D. Maurice' Tennyson not only translates and adapts phrases from Horace (from at least three different odes and one satire), but also Horatian metre (the alcaic), genre (sympotic invitation poem), and attitudes (tolerance, balance, rural retreat). The resulting poem comes closer to Horace than any translation, strictly defined, in the nineteenth century. In an age of scholar-translators, much of the best translation from Latin verse is half-hidden: embedded in, incorporate with, original English verse.

LIST OF SOURCES

Translations

Bohn, Henry George, ed. (1860). *The Epigrams of Martial Translated into English Prose, each accompanied by one or more Verse Translations, from the Works of English Poets, and Various Other Sources*. London (Bohn).

Byron, George Gordon, Lord (1980–93). *The Complete Poetical Works*, ed. Jerome J. McGann, 7 vols. Oxford (Vol. 1 contains *English Bards and Scotch Reviewers*, *Hints from Horace*, and the imitations of Martial).

C[alverley], C[harles] S[tuart] (1862). *Verses and Translations*. Cambridge.

—— (1908) *The Idylls of Theocritus and the Eclogues of Virgil*. London.

Carne-Ross, D. S., and Haynes, Kenneth, eds. (1996). *Horace in English*. London.

Conington, John (1863). *The Odes and Carmen Saeculare of Horace*. London.

Conington, John (1866). *The Aeneid of Virgil*. London.
—— (1870). *The Satires, Epistles, and Art of Poetry of Horace*. London.
Drummond, William (1808). *The First Book of T. Lucretius Carus of the Nature of Things*. Edinburgh.
Elton, Sir Charles (1814). *Specimens of the Classic Poets from Homer to Tryphiodorus*. London.
Gaisser, Julia Haig (2001). *Catullus in English*. London.
Gifford, William (1802). *The Satires of Decimus Junius Juvenalis*. London.
—— (1817). *The Satires of Decimus Junius Juvenalis, and of Aulus Persius Flaccus*. London.
Good, John Mason (1805). *The Nature of Things: A Didactic Poem Translated from the Latin of Titus Lucretius Carus*. London.
Gransden, K. W., ed. (1996), *Virgil in English*. London.
Henry, James (1845). *The Eneis: Books I and II Rendered into English Blank Iambic* [Virgil]. London.
—— (1853). *My Book*. Dresden.
Hoblyn, Robert (1825). *A Translation of the First Book of the Georgics of Virgil, in Blank Verse, with Notes, Critical and Explanatory*. London.
Hopkins, Gerard Manley (1990). *The Poetical Works*, ed. Norman H. Mackenzie. Oxford.
Housman, A. E. (1997). *The Poems*, ed. Archie Burnett. Oxford.
Howes, Francis (1845). *The Epodes, Satires, and Epistles of Horace*. London.
Landor, Walter Savage (1969). *Poems*, ed. Stephen Wheeler, Vols. 13–16 of *The Complete Works of Walter Savage Landor*, ed. T. Earle Welby, 16 vols. New York.
Mallock, W. H. (1900). *Lucretius on Life and Death in the Metre of Omar Khayyám*. London.
Martin, Christopher, ed. (1998). *Ovid in English*. London.
Martin, Theodore (1861). *The Poems of Catullus*. London.
Moore, Charles Robert (1870). *The Elegies of Propertius*. London.
Moore, Thomas (1867). *The Poetical Works*. London.
Morris, William (1876). *The Aeneids of Virgil*. London.
Munro, H. A. J. (1866). *T. Lucreti Cari De Rerum Natura Libri Sex, with Notes and a Translation*. Cambridge.
Nott, John (1795). *The Poems of Caius Valerius Catullus in English Verse*, 2 vols. London.
Palmer, Samuel (1883). *An English Version of the Eclogues of Virgil*. London.
Poole, Adrian, and Maule, Jeremy, eds. (1995). *The Oxford Book of Classical Verse in Translation*. Oxford.
Sewell, W. (1854). *The Georgics of Virgil, Literally and Rhythmically Translated*. Oxford (first pub. 1846).
Stoneman, Richard, ed. (1982). *Daphne into Laurel: Translations of Classical Poetry from Chaucer to the Present*. London.
Sullivan, J. P., and Boyle, A. J., eds. (1996). *Martial in English*. London.
Tennyson, Alfred (1987). *The Poems of Tennyson*, ed. Christopher Ricks, 2nd edn., 3 vols. Harlow.
Winkler, Martin M. (2001). *Juvenal in English*. London.
Wordsworth, William (1981). *The Poems*, ed. John O. Hayden. New Haven, CT.
—— (1997). *Early Poems and Fragments, 1785–1797*, ed. Carol Landon and Jared Curtis. Ithaca, NY.
—— (1998). *Translations of Chaucer and Virgil by William Wordsworth*, ed. Bruce V. Graver. Ithaca, NY (The Cornell Wordsworth).

Other Sources
Arnold, Matthew (1960). *On the Classical Tradition*, ed. R. H. Super. Ann Arbor, MI.
Burrow, Colin (1997). 'Virgil in English Translation', pp. 21–37 in Charles Martindale, ed., *The Cambridge Companion to Virgil*. Cambridge.
Byron, George Gordon, Lord (1980–93). *Childe Harold's Pilgrimage*, Vol. 2 of *The Complete Poetical Works*, ed. Jerome J. McGann, 7 vols. Oxford.
Dyer, Gary (1997). *British Satire and the Politics of Style*. Cambridge.
Gillespie, Stuart, and Cummings, Robert (2004). 'A Bibliography of Ovidian Translations and Imitations in English.' *T&L* 13: 207–18.
Gordon, Cosmo Alexander (1985). *A Bibliography of Lucretius*, 2nd edn. Winchester.
Kelley, Paul (1983). 'Wordsworth and Lucretius' *De Rerum Natura*.' *N&Q* 30: 219–22.
Mallock, W. H. (1878). *Lucretius*. Edinburgh.
Mustard, Wilfred P. (1904). *Classical Echoes in Tennyson*. London.
Nitchie, Elizabeth (1930). 'Virgil and Romanticism.' *Methodist Review* 113: 859–67.
Smith, F. Seymour (1930). *The Classics in Translation: An Annotated Guide to the Best Translations of the Greek and Latin Classics into English*. London.
Stabler, Jane (1995). 'The Genesis of Byron's *Hints from Horace*.' *T&L* 3: 47–65.
Sullivan, J. P. (1991). *Martial: The Unexpected Classic*. Cambridge.
Tennyson, Hallam (1897). *Alfred, Lord Tennyson: A Memoir by his Son*. London.
Turner, Frank M. (1973). 'Lucretius Among the Victorians.' *Victorian Studies* 16: 329–48.
Vance, Norman (1988). 'Ovid in the Nineteenth Century', pp. 215–31 in Charles Martindale, ed., *Ovid Renewed: Ovidian Influences in Literature and Art from the Middle Ages to the Twentieth Century*. Cambridge.
—— (1993). 'Horace and the Nineteenth Century', pp. 199–216 in Charles Martindale and David Hopkins, eds., *Horace Made New*. Cambridge.
—— (1997). *The Victorians and Ancient Rome*. Oxford.

5.5 Greek and Latin Prose

Stuart Gillespie

History and Historical Biography

William Wordsworth read extensively in the classical historians, and the role of translations in his reading is typical for university-educated men in the nineteenth century. He refers in letters to a wide range of Latin historians, and owned the works of others. Most of these he seems to have read indifferently in Latin or English, whereas he knew the Greek historians exclusively in translation. The translations Wordsworth used, however, were by no means always contemporary ones: some, such as North's Plutarch and Savile's Tacitus, went back as far as the Tudor period (Worthington 1970: 14–17). Specialized nineteenth-century scholarship increasingly demanded use of the originals, but such was the prestige of the classics that English versions for those without Latin, or without Greek (a more numerous class), were in constant demand. What translations were in their hands?

On some occasions, they, like Wordsworth, supplied themselves with historical English renderings, for reading purposes and not on account of literary-historical interests. The poet A. H. Clough in 1859 revised the 'Dryden' Plutarch *Lives* of 1683–6, which he felt could easily be polished into greater readability than was achieved by the brothers Langhorne's eighteenth-century version, then standard. Clough was right: his revival, which although begun as a potboiler eventually engrossed him, gave this version a new lease of life in terms of publication history, continuing to this day, though it did not deter other Victorian translators from further attempts at Plutarch's *Lives* (such as Stewart and Long in 1880–2). Thomas Hobbes's 1629 Thucydides was revised too, and reappeared in print half a dozen times between 1810 and 1850. Later in the period, historical translations became so much an object of interest in their own right that publishers issued series of them: W. E. Henley's 'Tudor Translations' of 1892 onwards, for instance, included Thomas Heywood's Sallust and Philemon Holland's Suetonius.

Fresh renderings came from a wide variety of translators. The Victorian gentleman-amateur played his part: the 1874 Thucydides of Richard Crawley, the director of a life assurance company, for example, was not only admired in its own day but reprinted in standard paperback series through the twentieth century. New renderings by academic classicists proliferate, more so as time goes on: George Rawlinson's elaborate Herodotus (1858–60), dedicated to Gladstone; Benjamin Jowett's Thucydides (1881), possessing some of the original's high seriousness; Evelyn Shuckburgh's large-scale Polybius (1889). Such multi-volume monuments were intended for libraries, though these would have included certain private collections. At a less exalted level, series of classics in English included many popular (and often admirable) translations. Henry Bohn's Classical Library (see p. 165, above) is the best known, and for the historians, as in other fields, probably the most comprehensive, extending as it does to less major figures such as (in a single volume) Justin, Cornelius Nepos, and Eutropius. But it was not the only such venture, nor the first. At a humbler level again are the versions in series intended purely for educational use, often extending to only the commonly set portion of a text (e.g. two or three books of Livy).

Some ancient historians were frequently translated in this period, others only rarely, and the reasons for this can sometimes be readily inferred. A single Suetonius translator (Thomson 1796) as against a dozen of Tacitus is in line with the two writers' relative prestige in the period, the latter's notably enhanced by Gibbon's *Decline and Fall of the Roman Empire*. No doubt the objectionable content of some of Suetonius' stories and the perceived challenge of Tacitus' style reinforced this disparity. Caesar's five translators against Sallust's ten, on the other hand, may merely reflect Caesar's less demanding Latin: he was well respected later in the nineteenth century (see Vance 1997: 76), but easily managed by readers with a basic command of the language. Livy's pedagogical uses ensured a steady stream of versions, many anonymous—'by a graduate-scholar' (1830) or 'a first-classman' (1879). But perhaps the most striking feature overall is the large number of renderings of even the more voluminous of the Greeks. In the years 1790–1900 the two major versions of Thucydides mentioned above (1874 and 1881) are preceded by three complete ones; Herodotus is translated in full no less than seven times; and new treatments of Xenophon, including the first single-handed complete works (by H. G. Dakyns, 1890–7), are more frequent still. Plutarch translations exemplify the accelerating rate of production towards 1900: new *Lives* (complete and abridged/selected) reach double figures in the years 1880–1900, easily surpassing the rest of the century's total, and there is a complete *Moralia* in 1882–8.

Once again, a basic explanation is not far to seek. The 'impartial narratives' of the Greek historians were lauded by Thomas Arnold at the expense of Roman history (half of it 'if not totally false, at least scandalously exaggerated', he wrote in 'The Use of the Classics', 1844), and later Victorian tastes confirmed the preference. The critical, and in some respects quasi-scientific analysis brought to bear on ancient history had found the Romans wanting; even Tacitus was felt more valuable for his style than anything else. But the ancient Greek historians, like their countrymen in the other arts, were confirmed as the models of gravity, rectitude, and purity which the English-speaking world sought. Their translators, then, though some had proselytizing ambitions, were following rather than moulding contemporary views.

Rhetoric and Oratory

Oratory lay so much at the heart of the educational curriculum by the end of the eighteenth century that it tended to subsume other classical literature. But nineteenth-century pedagogical developments, including a declining interest in rhetoric and the restriction of classical training to a small élite, reduced the centrality of classical oratory as time passed. Cicero observed that poets have the nearest affinity to orators, and so it is that the admiration shown for him by, for example, Shelley (see Behrendt 1995) can be said to fall within a long tradition in which classical orators were highly valued for their stylistic and rhetorical qualities, whether in themselves or as models for emulation. But while some later nineteenth-century readers considered Cicero's *De Oratore* a worthwhile study for the preacher, Anthony Trollope's popular *Life of Cicero* of 1880 evinced a more typical dismay at the apparent manipulativeness and insincerity of the art (Rosner 1986: 160, 166; for Trollope's interest in Cicero, and the reception of his biography, see Vance 1997: 78–9). Instead, Cicero retained the period's interest largely as a historical witness and autobiographical writer. More than twice as many English and American editions of him found a market in the nineteenth century as in the eighteenth, but there was no especially durable or distinguished translation, and little change in the relative numbers of editions in Latin and in English (a ratio of about 2:1; see Rosner 1986: 159). Quintilian's *Institutio Oratoria*, whose admirers included De Quincey, Macaulay, and John Stuart Mill (Harding 1961: 104), was translated as a whole only once in the period, though admittedly J. S. Watson's 1856 Bohn attained great durability.

Of the Greek orators and rhetors, Demosthenes, a standard upper-school author (see Clarke 1959: 81), and Longinus, his eighteenth-century prestige apparently undiminished, fared better. But many of the translations are literal versions for pedagogic purposes, and the standard mid-eighteenth-century rendering of Demosthenes by Thomas Leland was reprinted until as late as the 1850s. By this time, its replacement, C. R. Kennedy's judiciously annotated and rather stately version, had begun to appear. J. H. Freese contributed Isocrates' *Orations* to Bohn's Classical Library in 1894, but whereas R. C. Jebb's Greek *Selections from the Attic Orators* (1876) led to a companion volume and went into further editions, Freese's English text did not.

Prose Fiction

This brief survey begins with the fables of Aesop, touching first on their Latin verse rendering by Phaedrus. Phaedrus was popularly set in schools on account of his easy Latin and uncontentious subject matter. He was translated in 1809 by Sir Brooke Boothby, whose lively verse rendering, in a manner not dissimilar to Christopher Smart's earlier one, was prefaced by a long essay reviewing scholarship and opinions on the classical fabulists. But Smart's work deservedly established itself as standard following its first posthumous publication in 1831, with reprints in Bohn's Classical Library and other series, and apparently little call for further full versions of Phaedrus other than classroom texts.

With direct translations of Aesop the picture is different, and examples much more numerous. The continuing tradition of political and satirical use of the Aesopic fables is one reason: G. F. Townsend's 1866 version, for example, was an appropriation of Samuel Croxall's eighteenth-century one, with new, right-wing 'applications'. The legacy of historical translations was influential and enduring, perhaps because of readers' childhood memories of them, so that many nineteenth-century Aesops turn out to be revisions of L'Estrange's, or Croxall's, or to carry what would have been long-familiar woodcuts and engravings. The scholarly problem of distinguishing the sources of the Aesopic collection was addressed by Thomas James in 1848 by presenting a free translation which he claims reflects the various styles of the Greek and Latin writers on whom Aesop drew. These questions of origins and authenticity were also in the minds of later scholars and translators. A mixture of verse and prose renderings emerges in growing numbers towards, and especially just into, the twentieth century, within which two clearly related trends are obvious: the increasingly prevalent assumption that the stories are for children rather than adults, and the increasing rarity of translations without illustrations. Aesop's tales are detectable here and there behind the thought of a wide range of nineteenth-century figures, from George Eliot to Karl Marx, at a level sometimes well beyond mere proverb lore, as they deploy or reclaim for their own purposes a specific fable (for examples including Marx on the Body's Members see Patterson 1991: 152–6). Almost all of these figures' knowledge, where at all direct, will derive from one of the translations or another, first read in childhood.

For the Renaissance the Greek novel consisted only of Heliodorus, Achilles Tatius, and Longus, and translations were usually from secondary sources. By the eighteenth century the canon had expanded to take in Chariton and Xenophon of Ephesus, and translations became more scholarly, yet in 1803 C. V. Le Grice was still claiming to be the first to translate Longus directly from the Greek. One of the most striking phenomena with the Greek novel in this period is a rash of printings of Longus' *Daphnis and Chloe* in and around the 1890s. Some of these are revisions of Le Grice, others reprints of historical versions such as Angel Day's or George Thornley's. The *fin-de-siècle* interest in Longus centres, as it has at other times (see Barber 1988), on what is seen as the book's sensitive portrayal of emergent sexual knowledge, as is confirmed by the many illustrations and frequent appeals to young lady readers—disapproving Victorian attitudes were losing ground. But in the later nineteenth century overall, Rowland Smith's portmanteau Bohn volume containing his versions of the three ancient Greek novels known to the Renaissance, versions more accurate than readable, was probably the most familiar form of the material.

Of the Roman novelists, Petronius' *Satyricon* bears often-remarked resemblances to the realist prose fiction that George Gissing and others were developing, but this does not mean it was frequently translated. W. E. H. Lecky condemned it as 'one of the most licentious and repulsive works in Roman literature' (Lecky 1897: 215). Before the very end of the century, when 'decadent' tastes perhaps lie behind two or three partial translations (such as Peck 1898) and reprints of earlier ones, the sole new version is Walter Kelly's of 1854. Kelly was a regular Bohn hand, and an eye to the market may explain why this Bohn production collects the fragmentary novel into a volume of largely innocuous classical material with the catchpenny label of 'Erotica'. Similar tactics on another publisher's part lie behind the attribution of a 1902 translation to Oscar Wilde: it was in reality by an obscure literary figure, Alfred Richard Allison (see Boroughs 1995).

Apuleius' translators compensated for Petronius' relative scarcity. Within *The Golden Ass* it was the Cupid and Psyche story that captivated the nineteenth century, Keats's 'Ode to Psyche' (1820) being the most famous manifestation of the taste. But Keats was a latecomer: before him there had been several English attempts on the tale (some of them 'reworkings' rather than translations), including in the 1790s those by Thomas Taylor (in prose, 1795; later complete *Metamorphoses*, 1822) and Hudson Gurney (in verse, 1799). The translations were often patently sentimental or otherwise distorting: Taylor's silently but severely edited text was a vehicle for Platonist allegory, while Pater found in the story 'the ideal of a perfect imaginative love, centered upon a beauty entirely flawless and clean'. The version in Pater's novel *Marius the Epicurean* (1885) is in an other-worldly English prose deriving from William Adlington's sixteenth-century rendering (a rendering also used by Keats, along with Mary Tighe's much-reprinted poem *Psyche* of 1805). Elizabeth Barrett Browning composed a few fragmentary verse translations of various passages, and three more extensive retellings in verse were made by William Morris (a characteristically romantic and wistful treatment in *The Earthly Paradise*, 1868–70), Sir Lewis Morris (a Tennysonian handling in his *Epic of Hades*, 1877), and Robert Bridges (*Eros and Psyche*, 1886, with its morally reflective Psyche an embodiment of purity). In addition to the complete *Golden Ass* versions of the 1890s, Sir George Head clumsily bowdlerized the whole in 1851, while the Bohn of 1853 collects historical Apuleian translations and other material.

Treatises, Dialogues, Letters

Classical philosophy is the subject of § 11.1, below, but the moral treatises of Cicero, together with his letters, are discussed here. In both cases older renderings, particularly the eighteenth-century work of William Guthrie and William Melmoth, held sway well into the nineteenth century. Cicero's exalted standing as moralist—'a shining pattern of virtue to an age of all others the most licentious and profligate', wrote Conyers Middleton, in a biography also being reprinted well beyond 1800—was reflected particularly in the dozens of English versions of selected treatises. The largely literal ones by the prolific writer and translator Charles Yonge became the best-known renderings of the moral treatises, many of them issued in the Bohn Classics. A first group was published in 1848, with other texts translated in successive new editions and collected editions until Yonge's death in 1891. Yonge, a professor at Queen's College, Belfast, also edited portmanteau editions, which collected together historical translations of some treatises with his own renderings of others. Cicero's letters were important to the Victorians for their historical documentary role and for his personality, and were often issued along with a biography such as Middleton's in a volume of 'life and selected letters'. Nineteenth-century readers were presented with a number of translations of the letters over time, beginning with William Heberden (the younger)'s of the *Ad Atticum* (1825) and concluding with Evelyn Shuckburgh's complete but stylistically more sophisticated and challenging one of 1899–1900. That other great Latin epistolary writer, the younger Pliny, was less well served by Victorian translators, many of whose potential readers seem (to judge by the reprint record) to have been content with Melmoth's highly respected older version; but one or two new treatments (such as Lewis 1879) did appear later in the Victorian era.

Two Greek writers complete this survey. Lucian was not a moralist but a rhetorician, and his aim was not to reform society, merely to amuse it. But from Thomas Francklin's ponderous though durable late eighteenth-century versions (reprinted 1887) onwards, this period's English Lucianic dialogues very largely omit to amuse, and Lucian's surprising popularity with nineteenth-century translators seems to rest on an unexamined assumption of moral seriousness. There were at least fourteen separate translations of selected dialogues from Francklin's attempts to 1900 (Foster 1918: 81–2). Few translators had the stamina for the whole collection, but two such (Williams 1888 and Anon. 1895) are responsible for late Victorian productions aiming at literal accuracy.

Like Lucian's dialogues, Theophrastus' *Characters* had been influential on English writers of earlier eras; in this period, however, Theophrastus was translated only infrequently, even though the set of Greek texts had recently been completed with the recovery and printing of the final two items in his collection of sketches in 1786. Isaac Taylor (writing as Francis Howell) in 1824, followed by the great Greek scholar Richard Jebb in 1870, both offered a plain, equable, rather anonymous English version.[1] It was left to the next translator, J. M. Edmonds in the twentieth century, to undertake an archaizing version, with the special justification in Theophrastus' case that it was in the hands of Elizabethan authors that the 'character' was domesticated. In spite of some appearances to the contrary, Theophrastus' translations had no great importance for nineteenth-century English writers. George Eliot, as a Greek reader, would not have been wholly dependent on English texts for the knowledge of the *Characters* which underlies her *Impressions of Theophrastus Such* (1879). For most of her contemporaries, his significance was indirect, largely part of the long story of the novel's development.

LIST OF SOURCES

Translations
Anon. (1831). *The Characters of Theophrastus*. London.
Anon., ed. (1853). *The Works of Apuleius*. London (Bohn; reprints historical translations).
Anon., ed. (1895). *Lucian Literally and Completely Translated*. Privately printed for the Athenian Society.
[Allison, Alfred Richard] (1902). *The Satyricon of Petronius: A New Translation with Introduction and Notes*. Paris.

[1] Reissues of the 'Howell' translation in 1831 and 1866 omit this name, and are sometimes (as by Foster 1918: 116) supposed different works, but all three are identical.

Boothby, Sir Brooke (1809). *Fables and Satires, with a Preface on the Esopean Fable*, 2 vols. Edinburgh.
Clough, Arthur Hugh, ed. (1859). *Plutarch's Lives: The Translation called Dryden's; corrected from the Greek and revised*, 5 vols. London.
Crawley, Richard (1874). *History of the Peloponnesian War* [Thucydides]. London.
Dakyns, H. G. (1890–7). *The Works of Xenophon*. Edinburgh.
Edmonds, J. M. (1929). *The Characters* [Theophrastus]. Cambridge, MA (Loeb).
Francklin, Thomas (1780). *The Works of Lucian*. London.
Freese, J. H. (1894). *The Orations of Isocrates*. London (Bohn).
Gurney, Hudson (1799). *Cupid and Psyche* [Apuleius]. London.
Head, Sir George (1851). *The Metamorphoses* [Apuleius]. London.
Heberden, William (1825). *The Letters of Marcus Tullius Cicero to Titus Pomponius Atticus*. London.
Howell, Francis, pseud. [Isaac Taylor] (1824). *The Characters of Theophrastus*. London.
James, Thomas (1848). *Aesop's Fables: A New Version, Chiefly from Original Sources*. London.
Jebb, R. C. (1870). *The Characters of Theophrastus*. London.
Jowett, Benjamin (1881). *Thucydides Translated into English*, 2 vols. Oxford.
Kelly, Walter K. (1854). *Erotica: The Elegies of Propertius, the Satyricon of Petronius Arbiter, and the Kisses of Johannes Secundus*. London (Bohn).
Kennedy, Charles Rann (1841). *Translation of Select Speeches of Demosthenes*. Cambridge.
—— (1852–63). *Demosthenes*, 5 vols. London (Bohn).
Le Grice, C. V. (1803). *Daphnis and Chloe, A Pastoral Novel, Now first selectly translated into English from the original Greek* [Longus]. Penzance.
Lewis, John Delaware (1879). *The Letters of the Younger Pliny literally translated*. London.
Peck, Harry Thurston (1898). *Trimalchio's Dinner*. New York.
Rawlinson, George (1858–60). *The History of Herodotus: A New English Version*, 4 vols. London.
Shuckburgh, Evelyn S. (1889). *The Histories of Polybius*, 2 vols. London.
—— (1899–1900). *The Letters of Cicero*, 4 vols. London (Bohn).
Smith, Rowland (1855). *The Greek Romances of Heliodorus, Longus, and Achilles Tatius*. London (Bohn).
Stewart, Aubrey, and Long, George (1880–2). *Plutarch's Lives*, 4 vols. London (Bohn).
Taylor, Thomas (1795). *The Fable of Cupid and Psyche* [Apuleius]. London.
Thomson, Alexander (1796). *The Lives of the First Twelve Caesars* [Suetonius]. London.
Townsend, G. Fyler (1866). *The Fables of Aesop, Translated ... by S. Croxall, with New Applications ... by the Rev. Geo. Fyler Townsend*. London.
Watson, John Selby (1856). *Quintilian's Institutes of Oratory ... Literally Translated*. London (Bohn).
Williams, Howard (1888). *Lucian's Dialogues*. London (Bohn).
Yonge, C. D. (1848). *The Academic Questions, Treatise de Finibus, and Tusculan Disputations of M. T. Cicero literally translated*. London (Bohn).
—— [with Barham, Francis] (1853). *The Treatises of M. T. Cicero*. London (selections, with further treatises included in subsequent printings).

Other Sources
Barber, Giles (1988). *Daphnis and Chloe: The Markets and Metamorphoses of an Unknown Bestseller*. London.

Behrendt, Stephen C. (1995). 'Shelley and the Ciceronian Orator', pp. 167–81 in Don H. Bialostosky and Lawrence D. Needham, eds., *Rhetorical Traditions and British Romantic Literature*. Bloomington, IN.

Boroughs, Rod (1995). 'Oscar Wilde's Translation of Petronius: The Story of a Literary Hoax.' *English Literature in Transition 1880–1920* 38: 9–49.

Clarke, M. L. (1959). *Classical Education in Britain 1500–1900*. Cambridge.

Foster, F. M. K. (1918). *English Translations from the Greek: A Bibliographical Survey*. New York.

Harding, Harold F. (1961). 'Quintilian's Witnesses', pp. 90–106 in Raymond F. Howes, ed., *Historical Studies of Rhetoric and Rhetoricians*. Ithaca, NY.

Lecky, W. E. H. (1897). *History of European Morals from Augustus to Charlemagne*, 12th edn., 2 vols. London (first pub. 1869).

Merrill, Elizabeth (1970). *The Dialogue in English Literature*. New York (first pub. 1911).

Patterson, Annabel (1991). *Fables of Power: Aesopian Writing and Political History*. Durham, NC.

Rosner, Mary (1986). 'Reflections on Cicero in Nineteenth-Century England and America.' *Rhetorica* 4/2: 153–82.

Vance, Norman (1997). *The Victorians and Ancient Rome*. Oxford.

Worthington, Jane (1970). *Wordsworth's Reading of Roman Prose*. New Haven, CT.

6

Literatures of Medieval and Modern Europe

6.1	German *David Constantine*	211
6.2	French *Peter France*	230
6.3	Italian *Ralph Pite*	246
6.4	Spanish and Portuguese *Anthony Pym and John Style*	261
6.5	Early Literature of the North *Andrew Wawn*	274
6.6	Modern Scandinavian *Robert E. Bjork*	286
6.7	Celtic *Mary-Ann Constantine*	294
6.8	Literatures of Central and Eastern Europe *Peter France*	308

6.1 German

David Constantine

In the eighteenth century the great majority of translations were from the classical languages and from the modern Romance languages, above all French. While these continued to bulk large, the period covered by the present volume saw an increasing interest in the other literatures of Europe, from modern literature to the writings of the Middle Ages and the folk literature of countries from Portugal to Serbia. While some particular literary genres, such as popular fiction and drama, ballads and folk tales, or religious and historical writing, are dealt with in Chapters 8–11, below, the present chapter surveys the mainstream of translations from the languages of medieval and modern Europe, giving particular emphasis to new discoveries. Perhaps the most striking episode in this story is the British and American awakening to the value of German literature.

Introduction and Historical Overview

Translation is just one important current in the vast and complex dealings between Britain and America and Germany in this period of colossal social change. For example, we might set the eighty translations of German books into English recorded in 1850 alongside the quarter of a million Germans a year who, throughout the 1850s, after the failure of the 1848 revolution, emigrated to the USA; not that these two figures stand in any meaningful relationship, only that they are factors in the making of the nations and their identities in that age. And the essentially humane exchanges effected by translation within the worldwide cosmopolitan Republic of Letters may be contrasted with the ever more inhumane competition among the capitalist and imperialist powers.

The basic bibliographical information about translation out of German into English has been amply collected by Morgan (1938), Morgan and Hohlfeld (1949), and Hathaway (1935). The arrival and presence of German authors in Britain and the United States, through whose agency, in what magazines, through which publishing houses: all this is exhaustively presented in their work, with figures, tables, graphs, and some critical commentary; as a source of material for ideas and arguments these volumes are indispensable. Order was imposed upon the plethora by Walter Schirmer in 1947. He divided up this whole epoch of translation into three periods, and though these compartments are by no means watertight, they are a convenience and do have some *raison d'être*.

The first of Schirmer's periods really begins on 21 April 1788 with Henry Mackenzie's lecture to the Royal Society of Edinburgh on recent German drama.

Much that had come in before then was either accidental and incidental or had merely reflected or confirmed trends and enthusiasms already established among the British reading public. Thus Gellert's *The Life of the Swedish Countess of G.* and Gessner's *The Death of Abel* appealed to the same tastes as Richardson and Thomson respectively. Wieland, so French in taste, had scarcely felt like an import from Germany when J. Richardson translated his *Agathon* in 1773. Goethe's *Werther*, first englished by way of French in 1779, though in fact a radically new thing, was in that guise scarcely recognized as such. Mackenzie on the other hand opened the way to something quite potently new. Having no German himself, he drew his material and his enthusiasm from two substantial French anthologies of the 1780s. Above all other works, he commended Schiller's *Die Räuber* (The Robbers) to British readers, especially to the youthful among them, calling it 'one of the most uncommon productions of untutored genius that modern times can boast' (cited in Schirmer 1947: 8).

In the group formed in Edinburgh after Mackenzie's lecture, the so-called first 'German Class', there was one important translator, Alexander Tytler (on whom see further pp. 63–5, above), and Walter Scott. Other groups dedicated to the study and translation of German works formed shortly afterwards: in London, around Edward Ash ('Monk' Lewis becoming an associate); in Bristol, around Thomas Beddoes, attracting Coleridge and Southey; in Liverpool (Rose Lawrence, Felicia Hemans, and later Anna Swanwick); and, very importantly, around William Taylor in Norwich (Harriet and James Martineau). Taylor, sympathetic to the ideals of the French Revolution, valued the revolt present to the eye of faith in the plays of *Sturm und Drang*; and through his correspondence and conversations with Southey he encouraged such tendencies in Coleridge and Wordsworth, then still youthful and hopeful. He viewed the German *Aufklärung* (Enlightenment) as the beginning of the end of prejudice, bigotry, and narrow nationalism, and in that spirit translated Lessing's *Nathan der Weise* (1791) and Goethe's *Iphigenie* (1793). He undertook the former, so he tells us in his introduction, in March 1790 'when questions of toleration were much afloat', and had it printed the following year for distribution among his friends. His plain blank verse reads well, both here and in *Iphigenie*. But all that humanizing tendency in the German imports was halted in the reactionary later 1790s and replaced with harmless sentimentality, religiosity, and Gothic horror. German literature, in the latter part of this first period, fed the Gothic *Schauerromantik* of Ann Radcliffe, 'Monk' Lewis, and Walter Scott, its radical edge all lost. Taylor, to his credit, tried again. He put the remaining copies of his *Nathan* on sale through a London publisher in 1805, a time, so he fondly believed, when the topic (toleration) was 'acquiring a fresh interest'.

The initiator of the second period was the émigrée Madame de Staël, whose essay on Germany, *De l'Allemagne*, barred from distribution in Paris by Napoleon, was published in London in 1813, and at once translated there. Again, as so often, Germany came to England via France. De Staël's effect on the British understanding of Germany was profound. We owe her, for good and ill, the notion of Germany as the 'land of poets and thinkers' and of these as the vanguard of all humanity. Concretely, she directed attention away from texts which, in their British application at least, had become merely sensational and modish, and on to the great achievements of Weimar Classicism and German Romanticism. Thomas Carlyle, really only interested in literature as a medium of moral teaching and wise ideas, derived directly from her, and he championed and translated Goethe accordingly. Between 1822 and 1832 he wrote half a dozen important essays on Goethe, urging him upon the British public, and translated the two parts of the novel *Wilhelm Meister* (1824, 1827), and the story 'Das Märchen' (1832). This was a powerful advocacy, through criticism and translation, of a living foreign writer, an act of faith. Add to that his *Life of Schiller* (1825), his essays on the *Nibelungenlied*, early German literature, Luther, and Novalis, and his translations of and introductions to stories by Musäus, Fouqué, Tieck, Hoffmann, and Jean Paul (in *German Romance*, 4 vols., 1827): a colossal labour. It was in this period that the academic study of German at Britain's new universities got under way—at University College (1828) and King's College (1831) in London—through the efforts of such people as Henry Crabb Robinson, friend and memorialist of the English Romantics, translator of Arndt and Lessing for the British press, and Carlyle's predecessor in the mission to import Goethe.

In the third period, beginning with the death of Goethe in 1832, although the number of literary translations increased and in Britain and America the reputations of Goethe, Schiller, Lessing, and Hoffmann were consolidated, and Heine's (through Charles Leland and Edgar Bowring) was established, the interest shifted even more from literature to ideas (many of the translations of history, philosophy, and the like are discussed in Ch. 11, below). Carlyle's reading of literature for its ideas certainly encouraged this trend; but it is also the case that contemporary German literature was either too avant-garde for appreciation at home or abroad (e.g. the plays of Büchner) or, after *Aufklärung*, Romanticism, and the whole Goethe period, often enfeebled, especially in prose fiction, and not worth importing. Fontane, the first German novelist of European stature, writing as the century closed, was not amply and well translated into English until the 1960s. But there was, until the 1880s, a great openness to German writing on religion (Schleiermacher, Strauss), philosophy (Feuerbach, Hegel), historiography (Ranke), and education and the idea of a cultured society (Humboldt). Matthew Arnold's writings on the latter topic were influenced by his admiration of Goethe as a humane teacher.

It is remarkable how much translation in this period was done and published outside London. Indeed, for the importing of German literature (except drama) and ideas into Britain, London was a less vital centre than, in their different heydays, Edinburgh, Liverpool, Manchester, Bristol, Norwich, or Coventry. America too, by the end of the century, through translators such as Charles Timothy Brooks (his Schiller, Goethe, Jean Paul), George Henry Calvert (the Goethe–Schiller correspondence), and Charles Leland (Heine), had made a large contribution to the number and variety of German works that could be read in the English tongue (see § 1.2, above). It is also worthy of note that in America and in

Britain many of the translators, and among the best, were women. Some of these at least should be noted at once: Rose Lawrence (Goethe's *Götz von Berlichingen*), Frances Anne Head (Klopstock's *Messias*), Anna Swanwick (*Faust*), to whom we must add Sarah Austin and George Eliot for the part they played, through translation, in the history of ideas. Margaret Fuller of Boston was known in her day as 'the Yankee Corinna', after the heroine of the novel by the Germanophile Madame de Staël—on whom, as a translator and in the free exchange of ideas between nations, she consciously modelled herself.

In the transmission and criticism of literature in the nineteenth century, magazines such as *Blackwood's*, the *Athenaeum*, and the *Westminster Review* were of the utmost importance (see Ch. 4, above); John Gibson Lockhart, for instance, made it his business to give extensive publicity to modern German literature in *Blackwood's* in 1817–25 (see Macbeth 1935: 146–65). Furthermore, in the course of the century some publishing houses, most notably Henry Bohn's (see pp. 8–9, above), made translations a major part of their output. In 1887 Bohn's Standard Library was offering a twelve-volume Goethe (including the autobiography *Dichtung und Wahrheit*, the conversations with Eckermann, and, in a further two volumes, the correspondence with Schiller); Heine's poems; Lessing's plays and his *Laocoon*; a six-volume Schiller (not just the plays, also the poems, the histories, and the aesthetic and philosophical letters); and a good deal of Jean Paul, Friedrich Schlegel, August Wilhelm Schlegel, and Leopold von Ranke. Americans usually had to wait—often not very long, given the absence of copyright protection—for their own edition of works already published in Britain; but in America too literary periodicals such as the *North American Review* (see pp. 21–2 and 146, above) were effective transmitters of the literature and ideas of Germany.

The Republic of Letters was not coterminous with any nation state, and if there was free exchange in the former, the latter had their doubts about things coming in from 'abroad'. Britain always seems especially ridiculous in this respect. Most translations of Goethe came with disclaimers, sighings, and health warnings, and with much omitted too, as being unfit for British hearts and minds. But then Goethe was that glorious thing, a stumbling block, and a large section of his German public too, whom he came rightly to despise, never tired of telling him how immoral he was.

Translations of Medieval Literature

European Romanticism, and the scholarship accompanying it, resurrected the culture of medieval Europe for present needs, and translations were necessary to that recovery (on this topic, see also pp. 231–3, below). They fed various forms of more or less persuasive medievalism, including that of the Pre-Raphaelites. As far as Germany is concerned, Edgar Taylor and Sarah Austin began it with their *Lays of the Minnesingers or German Troubadours* in 1825. This handsome and useful book of translations and commentary set two dozen of the Germans in a context of contemporaries in Provence and other parts of Europe. Walter Alison Phillips's *Selected Poems of Walther von der Vogelweide* (1896) deserves a mention, not for its quality (his abilities as a translator being limited by his abilities as a poet) but because it presents a bowdlerized Walther as an act of deliberate opposition to *fin-de-siècle* corruption (Swinburne, Wilde, Symons). Phillips addresses his poet thus in his dedicatory sonnet:

> Thy song still lives, though thou art gone to dust,
> And still the sharp lash of thy scornful tongue
> May scourge the feeble rhymesters of our day,
> Who sing a love half sicklied into lust,
> And, for the springs of beauty, grope among
> The iridescent fountains of decay.

Edmund Gosse, in his *Studies in the Literature of Northern Europe* (1883), offered a dozen of Walther's poems in very readable English verse, placing them in an essay on their author.

In the field of romance, meanwhile, Hartmann von Aue's *Der arme Heinrich* was paraphrased, as *Henry the Leper*, by Dante Gabriel Rossetti in 1846–7. This long poem in a sort of amiable *Knittelvers* (rough four-beat rhyming couplets) first saw the light of day in Rossetti's collected works after his death. The same romance made another appearance in Longfellow's imitation, *The Golden Legend* (1851). Some decades later, Jessie L. Weston, author of *From Ritual to Romance*, did a verse *Parzifal* (1894), dedicating it to 'the memory of Richard Wagner whose genius has given fresh life to the creations of medieval romance'. And in 1899 she did an abridged prose *Tristan and Iseult*, in two attractive little volumes in a series, published by David Nutt, of Arthurian romances 'unrepresented in Malory's *Morte d'Arthur*'.

Promotion by Carlyle (his review of Karl Simrock's translation of it into modern German), and later Wagner's operas, stimulated translations of the heroic poetry of the *Niebelungenlied*, the first being by Jonathan Birch (an early and quite lively translator of *Faust*) in 1848, in a verse form close to the original. Another was William Nanson Lettsom's, in 1850, also verse. Lettsom's 2,459 quatrains all read much like this one, the 504th:

> Now had the fearless giant all his weapons donn'd,
> Bound on his head a helmet, and in his monstrous hond
> A shield unmeasur'd taken; open the gate he threw,
> And his teeth grimly gnashing, at Siegfried fiercely flew.

The English that medieval German literature passed into in those days is indeed peculiar. Margaret Armour wrote verse of her own and contributed four volumes to the complete Heine published by Heinemann (Leland 1891–1905); but for her *Fall of the Nibelungs* (1897, in the Everyman Library) she used a prose which though accurate was as archaic in its way as Lettsom's verse.

Religious Works

Salomon Gessner's prose epic *Der Tod Abels* (The Death of Abel), first published in 1758, first translated into English by Mary Collyer in 1761, had run through twenty-eight British editions by 1793, and for a further two decades it was regularly reprinted, in towns and cities all over Britain, in Blackburn, for example, Salford, Bungay, and Gainsborough. There was said to be a copy in every household and in every school. This seems unlikely, but the work's sentimental religiosity must have satisfied some British need. Other translators—W. C. Oulton (1811), Frederic Shoberl (1813), and Julius de Benham-Yakobi (1853)—offered new versions; in 1840 a certain M.B.C. translated Mrs Collyer's English prose into blank verse; and William Henry Hall (masquerading in some editions as 'a lady') wrote a *Death of Cain*, in five books, after the manner and as a sequel to *The Death of Abel*, in 1790.

Mrs Collyer herself, encouraged by the extraordinary success of her Gessner, began on Klopstock next, his *Der Messias*, but fell ill and died. Her husband Joseph continued and completed the work and was, so he says, 'frequently fill'd with sensations too big, too sublime for utterance' (Collyer and Collyer 1763: preface). This rhapsody was in prose. Klopstock, much influenced by Milton, had written his twenty cantos on the redemptive passion of Christ in hexameters, which metre, he hoped, would lend his epic all the dignity that Homer, likewise treating the dealings of gods and men, had lent to his. Carlyle damned the Collyers in the introduction to his translation of *Wilhelm Meister* (1824), and two years later Frances Anne Head, in her translation, largely put matters right. Her *Messiah*, which abridges Klopstock's by about a quarter but says clearly where the cuts have been made and summarizes the missing argument, is at least as readable as the original, and that by virtue of its blank verse. She did as Surrey had done 300 years before in his *Aeneid* IV: moved foreign hexameters into English iambic pentameters, as a medium for an epic poem. She quite properly attaches herself, in tone and lineation, to Milton; and, as translations often do, rides along on the memory of a great native achievement. Georg Heinrich Egestorff, a grammarian and a translator of Ewald von Kleist, also did a *Messias* in 1826; but is far less successful than Frances Head, who in her 'Translator's Preface' writes in the third person singular, masculine.

We might also mention in this context of devotional writings Susanna Winkworth's translation in 1854 of the *Theologia deutsch*, a late fourteenth-century text (see further pp. 446–7, below). William Blake, like his fellow Romantics in Germany, drew on the mystic Jakob Boehme, reading him in the translation done by Ward and Langcake between 1763 and 1781. There was to be almost no new translation of Boehme in the nineteenth century, though Charlotte Ada Rainy compiled a quite brief *Thoughts on the Spiritual Life* from his writings in 1896.

Translating Goethe

In 1824, introducing his own translation of Goethe's *Wilhelm Meister* (discussed on pp. 78–9, above) and disregarding many fine achievements, Carlyle characterized the 'literary intercourse' between England and Germany to date as 'slight and precarious'. He wrote: 'Our translators are unfortunate in their selection or execution, or the public is tasteless and absurd in its demands; for, with scarcely more than one or two exceptions, the best works of Germany have lain neglected, or worse than neglected, and the Germans are yet utterly unknown to us' (Carlyle 1899: XXIII, 3). His particular interest was Goethe, not so much neglected as hideously badly served. He cited *Werther*: 'The English reader ought to understand that our current version of *Werter* is mutilated and inaccurate: it comes to us through the all-subduing medium of the French; shorn of its caustic strength; with its melancholy rendered maudlin; its hero reduced from the stately gloom of a broken-hearted poet to the tearful wrangling of a dyspeptic tailor' (XXIII, 16). That is not a very accurate characterization of Goethe's hero, but certainly the version via the French, done by Daniel Malthus or Robert Graves in 1779, was very inadequate. (The autobiographical *Dichtung und Wahrheit* suffered similarly. The first English version, appearing in England and America in 1824, was abridged and added to after the whim of the translator; and he was translating from a French version, whose author had also taken liberties.)

The first English translator of *Die Leiden des jungen Werther* omitted and altered as he pleased. Using a French text already cut on moral grounds, he cut it further for English readers yet more likely to be offended, and said so in his preface. But he also omitted or obscured, without announcing it, much else that actually constitutes Werther's character and the social context in which he loves and dies. He reduces the long effusions to nearly nothing and hacks away realistic details, as though only plot mattered; but even in that—rendering the bare story—he makes numerous errors, some at very critical moments (Lotte's 'dem ich so gut als verlobt bin' ['to whom I am as good as engaged'] becomes 'to whom I am engaged'). We must damn the version as Carlyle did. The French and the English translators in this case were ignorant, careless, arrogant, and manipulative readers, and no good could come of their collusion; the second only compounds the bad practice of his predecessor. R. D. Boylan's version in 1854, the first (according to the publisher, Henry Bohn) to come directly from the German, was a satisfactory and long overdue replacement.

I. Currie, in his preface to Rose Lawrence's *Götz*, said of *Werther* that it was 'a work beautiful in its separate parts, though in its general tendency unfavourable to virtue and happiness'. Such disquiet had been very volubly expressed in Germany twenty-five years earlier. The publication of *Die Wahlverwandtschaften* (Elective Affinities) in 1809 was described by one critic as the emptying of another chamber pot upon the German public; and many were of that view. Carlyle had this reputation to contend with when he championed Goethe in England. Bohn, publishing the two offending novels together in his Standard Library in 1854, concedes, with reference to *Elective Affinities*, there translated for the first time, by James Anthony Froude (who had enough worries and wished to remain anonymous), that 'exceptions may be taken to some of the statements contained in this production of Goethe'. He concedes the same about *Werther*; but then covers himself by quoting Carlyle (preface to *Wilhelm Meister*), whose disciple Froude was: 'Fidelity is all the merit a translator need aim at . . . In many points, it were to be wished that Goethe had not so written; but to alter anything is not in the translator's commission. The literary and moral persuasions of a man like Goethe are objects of a rational curiosity, and the duty of a translator is simple and distinct.'

Beginnings of Theatre Translation

There were compendious English anthologies of German theatre, similar to the French anthologies drawn on by Mackenzie; *The German Theatre*, for example, in six volumes (1801–6), by Benjamin Thompson; or Thomas Holcroft's serial publication *The Theatrical Recorder* (1805–6). Much good literature must wait to be translated. Kleist's *Schroffenstein* made a sort of appearance in 'Monk' Lewis's *Mistrust*, a 'feudal Romance', included among his *Romantic Tales* in 1808, but Büchner (along with Kleist the century's best) had to wait, as he did in Germany, until the twentieth century for his due. Contrariwise, much that is very bad does get translated and is consumed abroad long beyond its shelf-life at home. August von Kotzebue, born 1761, assassinated 1819, is such a case. To Carlyle in 1824, in the preface to his *Wilhelm Meister*, he epitomized the lamentable state of translation from German into English: 'Kotzebue still lives in our minds as the representative of a nation that despises him.' But this was partly, perhaps largely, because theatre needs material, to do as it pleases with, for its own immediate ends. Then, as now, translators supplied the theatres with texts that could be rewritten and adapted by the theatre's own professionals (see § 8.2, below). So Kotzebue's *Menschenhass und Reue* metamorphosed into *The Stranger* (1798, a work of many hands), and in that shape did very well, as did his *Die Spanier in Peru* as Sheridan's *Pizarro* (with music by Michael Kelly) in 1799. Then it became a musical, with a libretto by F. Reynolds. Kotzebue's *Das Kind der Liebe*, adapted by Elizabeth Inchbald as *Lovers' Vows* in 1798, survived in the memory by becoming the play the Bertram family rehearses in *Mansfield Park*. Lessing's *Minna von Barnhelm*, fitter to survive, did so for a while as *The Disbanded Officer* (James Johnstone's version of 1786) or *The School for Honor* (probably by Robert Harvey, in 1799).

Alexander Tytler, working on Schiller's *Die Räuber*, published an *Essay on the Principles of Translation* in 1791. His strategy was to go for equivalence of effect, employing means appropriate to his native language (see pp. 63–5, above). Had there been no French translation Tytler might never have been alerted to Schiller's play. In his preface (p. xviii), however, he is as scathing as Carlyle would later be about the weakness of French as a language of translation:

The English Translator's opinion of that version is, that it is perhaps as good as the language of the translation will admit of: But as the French language in point of energy is far inferior to our own tongue, and very far beneath the force of the German, he owns he is not without hopes that his translation may be found to convey a more just idea of the striking merits of the original.

Tytler used the Mannheim stage version (1782) for his translation, and claimed, pre-empting criticism, that it was 'one of the most truly moral compositions that ever flowed from the pen of genius'. His German was not first-class; L. A. Willoughby

(1921) found seventy-five occasions on which he 'comes more or less to grief'. All the same, his *The Robbers* reads well, has energy, autonomy, pace, and drive. It was enough to superexcite Coleridge (reading it at midnight in Cambridge, in the autumn of 1794): 'My God! Southey! Who is this Schiller? This Convulser of the Heart? Did he write his tragedy amid the yelling of Fiends? ... I tremble like an Aspen Leaf' (letter to Robert Southey, cited in Holmes 1989: 79). He composed a sonnet on it.

Anna Barbauld, visiting Edinburgh in 1794, read a translation of Bürger's ballad 'Lenore' by William Taylor (whose literary adviser she was) to an assembly in the house of Dugald Stewart. Walter Scott, though not present himself, was nonetheless inspired by reports of the occasion to attempt translations of his own. 'Monk' Lewis, visiting in the winter of 1798–9, interested himself in Scott and found a publisher for his version of Goethe's historical drama, *Götz von Berlichingen* (Scott 1799). Lewis is the 'Gentleman of high literary eminence' whose encouragement Scott acknowledges in the preface. He says of his own translation: 'Literal accuracy has been less studied ... than an attempt to convey the spirit and general effect of the piece. Upon the whole, it is hoped the version will be found faithful.' In fact, it is riddled with egregious errors, two or three per page. Several make no English sense; others make a nonsense of the context. There are besides many strange literalisms and a great deal of archaizing—such stuff as 'Zounds!' and 'He sate the curvetting steed' (this last a gratuitous addition). 'Schloss' he translates, typically, as 'Gothic castle'. Generally, he omits, amplifies, rewrites, reorders (the scenes of Act II, for example) much as he pleases or by his poor grasp of the language is obliged. Years later, writing to Goethe himself (9 July 1827), Scott looked back on his endeavour with a nice mix of feelings: 'I still set a value on my early translation because it serves at least to show that I know how to select an object of admiration although from the terrible blunders into which I fell from imperfect acquaintance with the language it was plain I had not adopted the best way of expressing my admiration.'

Lewis included Scott's version of Bürger's 'Der wilde Jäger' and his very prolix rendering of Goethe's 'Der untreue Knabe' in his *Tales of Wonder* (1801); but really Scott was no translator. His version of *Götz* is very much inferior to Rose Lawrence's, published in the same year. One of the Liverpool circle, a friend of Felicia Hemans, Mrs Lawrence (née D'Aguilar) makes relatively few errors, omits and adds far less, and 'upon the whole', is faithful in both letter and spirit to the original. Unsurprisingly, her version got and gets far less recognition than Scott's.

Coleridge's *Wallenstein*

When Coleridge began to learn German in 1796—being already familiar, through translations, with some ballads and with *Die Räuber*—he had in mind to translate 'all the works of Schiller' (Coleridge 2001: 167). In Germany then (mostly Göttingen, September 1798–July 1799) he flung himself with characteristic gusto into an eccentric mastering of the language, conversed in a vile accent with all and sundry, bought German books (many poets) by the hundredweight, and embarked on a life of Lessing (see pp. 107–9, above). But Schiller, much better known in England, was for any publisher a more attractive proposition. After the first German performances of the historical trilogy *Wallenstein* in January and April 1799, the texts of the three plays, authenticated by Schiller, were sent to the English publisher John Bell, to be translated. From Bell they passed to Matthew Longman, who gave Coleridge the commission. He began the second of the plays, *The Piccolomini*, in early February 1800, finishing it a month later, and Longman brought it out, as a separate publication, at the end of April or the beginning of May. He sustained this speed of work on the third play, *The Death of Wallenstein*, and finished it probably on 22 April; both parts were then issued together in early June, which was before the complete original had appeared in Germany. Though Coleridge had intended to translate the prologue play, *Wallensteins Lager*, he never did, declaring it to be lax in style and moreover unnecessary. The translations were taken into Bohn's Library in 1846 with alterations (in the light of the printed texts) by G. F. Richardson and with *Wallensteins Lager* done by James Churchill.

Coleridge was under pressure to do the translations quickly; on them and his other commitments he was, he complained, working fourteen hours a day. Translation itself he described as 'irksome & soul-wearying Labor' (Coleridge 2001: 168); the lukewarm or hostile reviews discouraged him further. He made £50 on the task, Longman lost £250. But after his return from Malta (1806) his interest and pride in his work revived. In a characteristic procedure he annotated three of his own copies, making a commentary on Schiller which overlapped with his study of Shakespeare. He quoted from these translations in his Shakespeare lectures and made further use of them elsewhere in his meditations and his writing. In all this he is a good example of how translation may work vitally in the writer's own development, and enrich the national literary stock.

Coleridge was more than competent to translate Schiller's plays and could have done so very strictly; but he had needs of his own, and asserted them in the act of translating. In his two prefaces he is self-denying; but in his footnotes, almost amounting to a commentary, he is critical and self-assertive. And in translating he omits, expands, and slants as he sees fit. He illustrates perfectly the principle of *compensation*. This is usually understood as doing here what you were unable to do there; but in practice any literary translation is from start to finish one long act of compensation. Coleridge seems to allude to this—to the need for compensation—in his second preface: 'Translation of poetry into poetry is difficult, because the Translator must give a brilliancy to his language without that warmth of original conception, from which such brilliancy would follow of its own accord' (Coleridge 2001: 621). In pursuit of the liveliness of the original a translator must unceasingly deploy all those resources of his native language that might help. He must know and exploit what the native language has achieved already in comparable projects. Blank verse, for example, a new resource in German, was long established in English. Coleridge could refer to Shakespeare for experience in that verse; also for the convention that prose would suit best in certain less lofty scenes.

In addition he had his own poetic language, a plain speaking, a naturalness, that had come of his association with Wordsworth (it shows in *Piccolomini* I.iv, in the voice of Max). These then are the resources for a continual compensation: the poet/translator's own liveliness, his own achievement to date, and the total achievement of the national language, into which he knowingly taps.

Coleridge is richly exemplary. Often in translating Schiller—at *Piccolomini* II.iv.82–129, for example—he moves into pleasing verse which is all his own. He did the same, frequently, when translating Stolberg, Hagedorn, Friederike Brun, poets he bought in Germany, sometimes acknowledging a source in translation, sometimes not. Translation easily slides over into plagiarism. He made use of his Schiller in his Shakespeare lectures; but much larger and unacknowledged use, there and elsewhere, of A. W. Schlegel, Schelling, and Kant. He ingested the foreign texts, made them his own. The spirit of this procedure might be sovereign (when his self-confidence was high) or abject (when his genial spirits failed).

Goethe's *Faust*

Goethe published his *Faust. Part I* in 1808. Madame de Staël having directed British attention to it, there was wide agreement that only Coleridge would be capable of translating it. He thought so himself, and proposed it to John Murray in late summer 1814; Murray offered him £100, but their negotiations came to nothing. Thereafter he continued in the role of the man who ought to have translated *Faust*. Shelley, addressing the text early in 1822 and contemptuous of the translation he was reading it in, wrote to his friends the Gisbornes: 'Ask Coleridge if the stupid misintelligence of the deep wisdom and harmony of the author does not spur him into action'; and in April, unhappy with his own attempt, he concluded: 'No one but Coleridge is capable of this work' (Shelley 1964: II, 376, 407). Coleridge himself had begun to find reasons not to do it. Mary Gisborne noted in her journal for 25 June 1820, having been with him the previous evening: 'He should like to translate the Faust but he thinks that there are parts which could not be endured in English by the English, and he does not like to attempt it with the necessity of the smallest mutilation' (Shelley 1964: 376). By 1833 he was calling it 'vulgar, licentious and most blasphemous' (Holmes 1999: 367).

Byron had no such qualms. He relished *Faust*, so far as he was able to, and wished he could read it in German. 'Monk' Lewis read out bits in extempore translation at the Villa Diodati in the late summer of 1816, just after the notorious *Frankenstein* evening, but when that sort of subject still possessed the company. *Faust* seemed a magnificent ghost story.

Shelley knew *Faust* even before 1822. He had done a strange translation of more than 1,000 lines of it; quite when is uncertain, but it has been tentatively dated to the period between May 1815 and July 1816 (Shelley 1986–2002: XXI, 476). He translated the dedicatory poem ('Zueignung'), 'Prologue in Heaven', and Part I as far as line 1213. The manuscript in the Bodleian Library is a fair copy; that is, Shelley went to the trouble of copying out fair what he had done elsewhere in rough, which surely means he thought it worth preserving. In his translation he mirrored Goethe's lines, giving each new one an initial capital letter but making no attempt to turn them into verse or even into intelligent English. He worked from word to word, setting down what is often only the first dictionary meaning regardless of whether in the context that made sense, and following the German syntax and word order. The result is neither accurate—he makes scores of basic errors—nor readable as any sort of autonomous English. It needs the German, but is a poor reflection of it. So what was he doing? The few alterations in the fair copy are corrections or improvements, so he had *some* interest in accuracy and effect. The usual view is that he was teaching himself German through the medium of a text he was disposed to admire. He would be familiar with such literal construing and such literal cribs from his learning of Latin and Greek. Doubtless then his interest lay primarily in that direction: to acquire the foreign language. Still, the exercise is intriguing, the more so since it somewhat resembles the German poet Hölderlin's more thorough and purposeful preoccupation with Pindar in the early summer of 1800. Cleaving as close to the Greek as Shelley does to the German, Hölderlin did more than 2,000 lines of Pindar, likewise in fair copy, in the strict intention of learning what his own vernacular might be poetically capable of. It cannot be claimed that Shelley in *his* literal rendering of a foreign text either intentionally or accidentally gained so much. Nevertheless, there are moments when by this mechanical procedure a strange poetry materializes. 'Wonder is of belief the most loved child', for example; 'My sorrow sounds to unknown multitudes'; or 'See all the workcraft and the seeds' (Shelley 1986–2002: XXI, 155, 123, and 133, respectively, corresponding to lines 663, 23, and 217).

Shelley was next closely concerned with *Faust* in Pisa, during the last year of his life. He reread the text with Claire Clairmont, who was there to see Byron and her daughter but also passionately involved with Shelley. She had herself begun 'germanizing' the year before and her understanding of the language was better than his. She seems to have tutored him in it, and they read Schiller and then Goethe together. She copied lines from *Faust* into her journal, among them some (1856 ff.) perhaps because they seemed to characterize Shelley. In March 1822 she began translating Goethe's autobiography *Dichtung und Wahrheit*, sending sheets to Shelley as she finished them. Byron, thinking he and Goethe had much in common, had said he would pay £100 to anyone who would translate it for him. Shelley employed a subterfuge so that he, Byron, should not know that his erstwhile mistress was the translator. In the event, when Claire made herself known and when it came to paying, he thought the thing not worth what he had offered, and churlishly demurred. Claire gave up the work, and all that she had done of it is lost.

Reading *Faust* with Claire (and also with Richard Gisborne), Shelley was impelled to translate some of it when he received, in January 1822, a copy of a version in English with illustrations by August Moritz Retzsch. In this book, published in 1820, Retzsch's line drawings (engraved by Henry Moses) were linked, and the whole play summarized, by translated excerpts largely in plain prose but with occasional eruptions into verse by George Soane. Shelley thought the translations 'miserable'; or, later (having tried it himself), 'not bad, & faithful enough—but how weak! how incompetent to represent Faust!' (Shelley 1964: ii, 376; 406–7). But Retzsch's illustrations affected him strongly: 'I am never satiated with looking at them... I never perfectly understood the Hartz Mountain scene, until I saw the etching.' It made his brain 'swim round' merely to touch the page on the opposite side of which the scene in Marthe's summer house was depicted (Shelley 1964: II, 406). It is hard to see why, looking at it now; but we must think of him as trying to translate not only Goethe's verse but also the sensations excited by Retzsch's own translation of it into imagery.

Shelley settled, for his own attempt, on two scenes: 'Prologue im Himmel', which Soane had not versified at all; and 'Walpurgisnacht' of which he had only versified two short sections (for these translations see Shelley 1970: 748–62). Shelley had already admitted (to T. J. Hogg, 22 October 1821) that in *Faust* there were some scenes 'which the fastidiousness of our taste would wish erased' (Shelley 1964: II, 361); and the two he chose to translate were of that kind, the first in its entirety (because of its blasphemous levity) and the second in some gross and obscene parts.

In the same notebook, and probably at the same time, Shelley was translating some scenes from Calderón's *El mágico prodigioso*. These, he said (and the manuscript seems to corroborate it), gave him very little trouble; but *Faust* was a different matter. He took five or six pages of hard and intricate drafting to get out a version of the Archangels' Chorus in the 'Prologue in Heaven', and even then was so dissatisfied that he appended a note on his failure and a literal version of the lines so that readers could assess it themselves. His note reads: 'Such is a literal translation of this astonishing chorus; it is impossible to represent in another language the melody of the versification; even the volatile strength and delicacy of the ideas escape in the crucible of translation, and the reader is surprised to find a *caput mortuum*' (Shelley 1970: 749). There he alludes to his own grave doubts about the very possibility of translation as he had expressed them only a year before in *A Defence of Poetry*: 'it were as wise to cast a violet into a crucible that you might discover the formal principle of its colour and odour, as seek to transfuse from one language into another the creations of a poet' (Shelley 1988: 280).

Shelley's errors in the two scenes are legion. Though far better equipped than he had been when he cribbed his way from line to line, still his German was not up to it. He gets individual words and phrases wrong: 'Muhme'/'my old paramour'; 'die Gesichter schneiden'/'intercept the sight'; 'Junker Voland'/'young Voland'; 'der ist eben überall'/'far above us all in his conceit'; but also entire passages, notably lines 4100ff. (the pedlar witch's speech).

Nonetheless, the scenes stand in a vital relation to the original and have autonomous poetic life, and on those two grounds—always a requirement—Shelley's translation may be called a success. Supplying a literal version of the Archangels' Chorus, he offered a marker of relative failure at the outset, then to do better elsewhere. In that scene and in 'Walpurgisnacht', where Goethe's medium for the dialogue is rhyming lines (often octosyllabics or even shorter), Shelley opts mostly for blank verse. It gives him more freedom in getting closer to the sense, and also encourages his tendency to expand. This strategy, common in Shelley's day and usually only a weakness, is in his case (as in Coleridge's *Wallenstein*) the means to some necessary autonomy. Thus (Goethe's ll. 4039–40): 'Where the blind millions rush impetuously | To meet the evil ones; there might I solve | Many a riddle that torments me.' But he has other successes by a close simplicity: 'The melancholy moon is dead'; 'a pound of pleasure with a dram of trouble' (Goethe's ll. 3991, 4049). And there are longer passages, quite close and accurate and in a tone of his own, Goethe's ll. 4060–71, for example, and the chilling Nightmare Life-in-Death vision of Gretchen.

How he (and his editors) dealt with things 'which the fastidousness of our taste would wish erased' is amusing and instructive. Goethe's ll. 3976–7 he gave as 'The child in the cradle lies strangled at home, | And the mother is clapping her hands', either not knowing or not wishing to convey their true sense, which is violent abortion and death of child *and* mother. Goethe's l. 3961, 'Es f—t die Hexe, es stinkt der Bock' (= 'the witch farts, the billy-goat stinks': there was a dash in most German editions till quite recently), he avoided altogether with two energetic but wholly independent lines: "Twixt witches and incubi, what shall be done? | Tell it who dare! tell it who dare!' Four later quatrains (again shot with dashes in the German editions) went missing entirely between Shelley's fair copy and the first publication. Perhaps it was Mary Shelley, perhaps John Hunt who decided against them. They make up a short interlude in which Faust and Mephistopheles dance with two witches. The manuscripts show that Shelley worked hard at Mephisto and his partner, and tried out various obscenities to match those of Goethe, among them 'a woman's services' (from *Lear*) and 'You might as well put the devil in hell' (from the *Decameron*, tenth tale, third day). In fair copy he toned it all down, and inserted some crosses and dashes, in Goethe's manner. But the first three printings (1822, 1824, 1839) retained only the stage direction: 'FAUST dances and sings with a girl, and MEPHISTOPHELES with an old Woman'; and later editions still omit the lewd exchange between the latter two.

Shelley quotes from his own translation in a letter to Byron of 3 May 1822, speaking of his domestic situation at that time (Claire's daughter Allegra had died): 'But Nature is here as vivid and joyous as we are dismal, and we have built, as Faust says, "our little world in the great world of all" as a contrast with rather than a copy of that divine example' (Shelley 1964: ii, 405). In the notebook containing the drafts of his *Faust* there are more than a dozen sketches of sailing boats, two or three on the pages immediately after 'Walpurgisnacht'. In June 1822 Shelley sent Gisborne this poignant coda to the whole involvement with Goethe's text. He writes of their boating off Lerici: 'We drive along this delightful bay in the evening wind, under the summer moon, until earth appears another world. Jane brings her guitar, and if the past and the future could be obliterated, the present would content me so well that I could say with Faust to the passing moment, "Remain, thou, thou art so beautiful" ' (Shelley 1964: II, 435–6). Three weeks later he was drowned.

Faust. Part II was published in 1832, shortly after Goethe's death. By 1874, according to Edgar Bowring (1853: preface), translations of *Faust* were 'almost endless'. Shelley's fragments have a quite exceptional interest; it will be sufficient here simply to note three of the best complete versions that followed: Anna Swanwick's in 1849 (in Bohn's Standard Authors the following year); Theodore Martin's in 1865; Bayard Taylor's, both parts, published in London and Boston in 1871 (the first appearance of *Part II* in America). All three of these are in verse and in their day enjoyed considerable success. At the same time *Faust* experienced some lively reincarnations, most notably in 1866, in John Halford's 'Free and Easy' adaptation: *A Grand Operatic Extravaganza: Faust and Marguerite; or the Devil's Draught*; and again in the winter of 1885–6, as a melodrama with Henry Irving as Mephisto, nearly 400 performances. *Faust* fed a sort of resurgence of Gothic horror; Rossetti was attracted to Lilith, who briefly appears in the *Walpurgisnacht*: his painting 'Lady Lilith', the accompanying sonnet 'Body's Beauty', and the long poem 'Eden Bower' are tributes in her direction.

It is worth saying a bit more about one earlier version, Abraham Hayward's of 1835 (with preliminary extracts in the *Foreign Quarterly* of that year), because it raises issues of general interest. Hayward prefaced his translation with a detailed critical survey of the efforts of some of his predecessors in England and France, and chiefly, because they were so poor, of Lord Francis Leveson-Gower's in 1823. He demonstrated conclusively—it was an easy thing to do—that the hapless lord, though very given to translating from German, was quite incompetent in the language. In brief, says Hayward (1833: xi–xii), 'Lord F. Gower's translation is about as unfaithful as a translation can be... He has hardly construed any two consecutive pages aright.' His most famous mistake? Rendering 'und lispeln englisch [= 'like angels'], wenn sie lügen' as 'and lisp in English when they lie'. The serious issue is accuracy.

Castigating his predecessors, Hayward determined to be above all else accurate; and to that end he used prose as his medium, not verse. He did so the more readily because, like Carlyle (who reviewed this version approvingly), he was under the misapprehension that *Faust* mattered most as the vehicle of Goethe's ideas. Seize the ideas; and prose will be the best, most accurate, way of conveying them. Hayward (1833: viii–ix) said of *Faust* that 'it teems with thought, and has long exercised a widely-spread influence by qualities wholly independent of metre and rhyme'. Metre and rhyme can therefore be dispensed with. He annotated his own translation with reasons for his decisions and with further explanations of the prose sense of the original. And in his manner of translating, cleaving close to the German, he intrudes on another discussion already long under way among translators: whether to domesticate a text or to point up its foreignness. Carlyle joins him here too, having in his own translation of *Wilhelm Meister* arrived at a style known by his detractors as Anglo-Teutonic. Two things then: ideas are what matter; and the domestic audience must shift towards the foreign text, not demand that it come all the way to them. Leveson-Gower, hopelessly inaccurate but rhyming quite fluently and nicely, provoked Hayward into a prose that is close to the original in sense and in its foreign tone. Carlyle, all for ideas, all for moving the British towards the Germans, felt corroborated.

Lyric Poetry

Throughout the period, translations of German lyric poetry had an existence in British anthologies and magazines. For editors of the latter, a few poems were no doubt agreeable fillers of small spaces. In America, too, from about 1840, the magazines sustained, as Lillie Hathaway (1935: 15) puts it, 'a mild unobtrusive interest in the lyric'. But three poets, Goethe, Schiller, and Heine, the three best representatives of German poetry, as the British nineteenth-century readership believed (Hölderlin's poems had to wait many years for readers, at home and abroad), were very well served, all by the same translator, Edgar Bowring. (They all found many other interpreters, notably Heine, whose poems attracted translators of the calibre of Elizabeth Barrett Browning and James Thomson, as well as appearing in full-scale versions by Theodore Martin and Charles Leland, among others.) Bowring's three volumes, each more copious than the last, are a vast and admirable achievement.

Bowring had two principles: completeness and fidelity. So in two cases at least, Schiller and Heine, Bowring's British public got all the poems then available in Germany; and of Goethe, impossibly abundant, they got a very generous selection (440 pages). This principle of completeness overrode the usual reluctance to import irreligion and immorality. So the strongly anti-Christian strain in German classicism is well represented, in Schiller's 'Götter Griechenlands' and in Goethe's 'Die Braut von Korinth', for example. And Bowring includes five of Goethe's 'Roman Elegies', and not the least offensive either. In his preface to Heine, he makes the customary nervous disclaimer: 'There are doubtless many poems written by Heine that we could wish had never been written, and that one would willingly refrain from translating.' But the principle of completeness obliges him; and besides, he is not answerable for Heine's opinions. So we get 'Deutschland. Ein Wintermärchen' entire (Bowring indicating where the German censor had previously intervened), 'Die schlesischen Weber' (once banned), 'Das Sklavenschiff'; all things which, if taken seriously, would make Britons as uneasy as Germans. Add to them several late poems of savage blasphemy, and Bowring may be said to have been both complete and faithful. The specific fidelity he prided himself on was to sense and to verse forms and metres. 'Metre for metre, line for line, and word for word', was his promise: 'as close and literal an adherence to the original as is consistent with good English and with poetry' (1853: vi). Bowring's successes and his overall failure are equally obvious. He reads Heine closely, understands very well that irony, discrepancy, the mixing of tones, are of the essence in that poetry. He rarely misses them, and that is a success. His failure, to be expected, is that the mix works less delicately, less subtly, or less shockingly harshly than it does, to suit the occasion, in Heine himself. An English reader would note the mix, perhaps without quite feeling it. Bowring's fidelity to metre pays off best in his rendering of regular rhyming stanzas, trochaic or iambic; least well with hexameters, though he was anxious to demonstrate that they *ought* to work in a language (English) 'so closely allied in origin and construction to the German' (Bowring 1851: vi). By the strictest standards—those of a viable and vital poetry—these translations, like most translations of any lyric poetry, must be said to fail. They are astonishingly inventive and skilful, really quite adept; but still tend, except in the case of Heine at his most *outré*, towards a conventional poetic language. This is simultaneously the reason for their success, and the ground for judging them a failure.

The books (Heine especially) *were* successful because in their diction and tone they allude all along to an unadventurous norm of poetic language, the expected, what a public will accept as poetic, a sort of pointer towards what is really so. This is a disposition in the public to which a translator like Bowring ministers, and on which, for his success, he actually relies. For Schiller's poetry of ideas, and for the ballads of all three German poets, this unexceptionable, expected, poetic language will do very well; and in the case of the ballads, interest in what happens next hurries the reader on over language not in itself very exciting but all the while simulating the native and familiar language for such a task. The more lyrical the poem, the harder the translator's job, the more, in his own shortcoming, he will rely on the expected language, and thus the greater his failure; at the same time, by virtue of that expected language, he has success with an audience not actually wishing to be seriously unsettled. It is a complicity of translator and unlively readership. Bowring's translations—a considerable achievement, they did great service—could stand alongside much if not most of what was being published in the magazines at the time by writers in native English.

LIST OF SOURCES

Translations
Armour, Margaret (1897). *The Fall of the Nibelungs*. London.
Birch, Jonathan (1839). *Faust: A Tragedy* (with 29 engravings after Moritz Retzsch). London.
—— (1848). *Das Nibelungen Lied, or, Lay of the Last Nibelungers*. Berlin.
Bowring, Edgar Alfred (1851). *The Poems of Schiller*. London.
—— (1853). *The Poems of Goethe*. London (Bohn).
—— (1859). *The Poems of Heine*. London.
Boylan, R. D. (1854). *Novels and Tales by Goethe, Translated Chiefly by R. D. Boylan*. London (Bohn; contains Boylan's *Werther* and *Elective Affinities* translated by J. A. Froude).
Brooks, Charles Timothy (1842). *Songs and Ballads* [Uhland, Körner, Bürger, and others]. Boston, MA.
—— (1856). *Faust*. Boston, MA.
—— (1862). *Titan: A Romance* [Jean Paul], 2 vols. Boston, MA.
—— (1865). *Hesperus* [Jean Paul], 2 vols. Boston, MA.
Calvert, George Henry (1845). *Correspondence between Schiller and Goethe, 1794–1805*. New York.
Carlyle, Thomas (1899). *Works*, 30 vols. London.

Coleridge, Samuel Taylor (2001). *Plays*, Part 1 (includes *The Piccolomini* and *Wallenstein's Death* [Schiller]. Princeton, NJ (Vol. 16, III, Part 1 of the Princeton *Collected Works* of Coleridge).
Collyer, Joseph, and Collyer, Mary (1763). *The Messiah* [Klopstock]. London.
Collyer, Mary (1761). *The Death of Abel* [Gessner]. London.
Egestorff, Georg Heinrich (1826). *Messiah* [Klopstock]. London.
Fuller, Margaret (1839). *Conversations with Goethe in the Last Years of his Life. Translated from the German of Eckermann*. Boston, MA.
Hayward, Abraham (1833). *Faust: A Dramatic Poem by Goethe*. London.
Head, Frances Anne (1826). *The Messiah: A Poem by F. T. Klopstock*, 2 vols. London.
Lawrence, Rose (1799). *Gortz of Berlingen with the Iron Hand* [Goethe]. Liverpool.
Leland, Charles (1864). *Book of Songs* [Heine]. New York.
—— (1891–1905). *The Works of Heinrich Heine*, 12 vols. London (Vols. 1–8 translated by Leland, all prose).
—— (1893). *The Family Life of Heinrich Heine* [letters]. London.
Lettsom, William Nanson (1850). *The Fall of the Nibelungers*. London.
Leveson-Gower, Lord Francis (1823). *Faust: A Drama, by Goethe*. London.
Lewis, M. G. et al. (1801). *Tales of Wonder* [ballads by Goethe, Schiller, Bürger, and others]. London.
—— (1808). *Romantic Tales*, 4 vols. London.
[Malthus, Daniel] (1779). *The Sorrows of Werter: A German Story* [Goethe]. London (translation also attributed to Robert Graves).
Martin, Theodore (1865, 1886). *Faust. I and II*. London.
Phillips, Walter Alison (1896). *Selected Poems of Walther von der Vogelweide*. London.
Rainy, Charlotte Ada (1896). *Thoughts on the Spiritual Life* [Boehme]. Edinburgh.
Scott, Walter (1799). *Goetz of Berlichingen with the Iron Hand* [Goethe]. London.
Shelley, Percy Bysshe (1970). *Poetical Works*, ed. Thomas Hutchinson and corrected by G. M. Matthews. Oxford (first pub. 1905).
—— (1986–2002). *The Bodleian Shelley Manuscripts*, ed. Donald H. Reiman, 23 vols. in 24. New York.
Swanwick, Anna (1850). *Faust*. London (Bohn).
Taylor, Edgar, and Austin, Sarah (1825). *Lays of the Minnesingers*. London.
Taylor, Bayard (1871). *Faust Parts I and II*. Boston, MA.
Taylor, William (1791). *Nathan the Wise: A Dramatic Poem* [Lessing]. Norwich.
—— (1793). *Iphigenia in Tauris: A Tragedy* [Goethe]. London.
Tytler, Alexander Fraser (1792). *The Robbers: A Tragedy* [Schiller]. London.
Weston, Jessie (1894). *Parzifal*, 2 vols. London.
—— (1899). *The Story of Tristan and Iseult*, 2 vols. London.

Other Sources
Crick, Joyce (1985). 'Some Editorial and Stylistic Observations on Coleridge's Translation of Schiller's *Wallenstein*.' *Publications of the English Goethe Society* 54: 37–75.
Frantz, Adolf Ingram (1949). *Half a Hundred Thralls to Faust: A Study Based on the British and American Translators of Goethe's Faust*. Chapel Hill, NC.
Hathaway, Lillie V. (1935). *German Literature of the Mid-Nineteenth Century in England and America as Reflected in the Journals 1840–1914*. Boston, MA.
Heinemann, William (1882). *A Bibliographical List of the English Translations and Annotated Editions of Goethe's Faust*. London.

Holmes, Richard (1974). *Shelley: The Pursuit*. London.
—— (1989). *Coleridge: Early Visions*. London.
—— (1999). *Coleridge: Darker Reflections*. London.
Macbeth, Gilbert (1935). *John Gibson Lockhart: A Critical Study*. Urbana, IL.
Morgan, B. Q. (1938). *A Critical Bibliography of German Literature in English Translation, 1481–1927*. Stanford, CA.
—— and Hohlfeld, A. R. (1949). *German Literature in British Magazines 1750–1860*. Madison, WI.
Schirmer, Walter F. (1947). *Der Einfluß der deutschen Literatur auf die englische im 19. Jahrhundert*. Halle.
Shelley, P. B. (1964). *Letters*, ed. F. L. Jones, 2 vols. Oxford.
—— (1988). *Shelley's Prose*, ed. David Lee Clark. London.
Stark, Susanne (1999). *'Behind Inverted Commas': Translation and Anglo-German Relations in the Nineteenth Century*. Clevedon.
Tytler, Alexander Fraser (1978). *Essay on the Principles of Translation*, ed. Jeffrey F. Huntsman. Amsterdam (first pub. 1791).
Webb, Timothy (1976). *The Violet in the Crucible: Shelley and Translation*. Oxford.
Willoughby, L. A. (1921). 'English Translations and Adaptations of Schiller's *Robbers*.' *MLR* 16: 297–315.

6.2 French

Peter France

In the nineteenth century even more than in the eighteenth, French was the principal source language for translation into English. The main reason for this was the continuing prestige of French culture, but ease of access also played a part. Many British people visited France or acquired some knowledge of French language and literature from teachers and governesses. Because of this, translation from French was perhaps not so *necessary* as from Russian or Sanskrit, except in the form of classroom cribs, which became common in the period. Writing on French literature in the major journals, critics might quote whole poems or paragraphs in the original. By the same token, most British or American writers of the period are more likely to have been influenced by French texts read in the original than by translations. But one can easily exaggerate the linguistic proficiency of the average reader when faced with a sizeable and difficult text in French. There was a large market for translations of French history, philosophy, travel writing, and the like (discussed more fully in Ch. 11, below). And very importantly, French was the major source of material for popular culture, from stage melodrama and serialized thrillers to edifying stories for children (discussed in Ch. 8, below).

For more sophisticated readers, French literature was a familiar field, and therefore potentially less interesting than the literatures of Germany, Scandinavia, or the East, many of which were discovered for the first time in the nineteenth century. Another factor working against France was a deep-rooted national sentiment of distrust or hostility, reinforced by the experiences of revolution and war. It was commonplace for critics to denounce French immorality. In a famous philippic in the *Quarterly Review* for 1834, John Wilson Croker wrote of the 'turpitude' of contemporary French drama; two years later he described novelists such as Hugo, Balzac, Dumas, and Sand as 'still more immoral than the dramatists' (Croker 1836: 66). More controversy was to follow, from the uproar in 1866 over the Francophile Swinburne's *Poems and Ballads* (see also Robert Buchanan's denunciation of Swinburne's Baudelairean immorality in *The Fleshly School of Poetry*, 1872) to the trial in 1888 of Henry Vizetelly for publishing pernicious French novels. Yet the very dangers imputed to French literature heightened its appeal to some readers and writers, particularly in the last two decades of the century (on which see Campos 1965: 139–92). And even before the audacities of realism, naturalism, and decadence, readers of all kinds found much to admire and enjoy in French literature, from the romances of chivalry to the wit of Voltaire or the effusions of Bernardin de Saint-Pierre.

A World of Romance

Medieval literature had been largely forgotten in France, but the tide began to turn after 1750 with collections such as that of Le Grand d'Aussy. His *Fabliaux ou contes du XIIe et du XIIIe siècle* provided material for an English prose collection (Anon. 1786), several times reissued, and for the versified *Fabliaux or Tales* of Gregory Lewis Way, first published in 1796. Such collections grouped together stories of different kinds and origins, rather in the manner of Boccaccio's *Decameron*. It is not surprising, then, that Marguerite de Navarre's sixteenth-century *Heptaméron* became popular with translators, six different versions appearing between 1846 and 1896.

What medieval and Renaissance France offered was above all a body of stories corresponding to Walter Scott's vision of chivalry. In their original form, these texts might be quite disparate—epic *chansons de geste* such as *Huon de Bordeaux* (reissued in 1895 in the sixteenth-century translation of Lord Berners) or *Les Quatre fils Aymon* (translated by William Hazlitt the younger in 1851), merry *fabliaux*, historical chronicles, fabulous romances in verse or prose—but translators tended to treat them similarly as good stories, adapting them for new audiences, including children. Some translations, it is true, remained close to the original, notably for the chronicles. The scrupulous version of the ever-popular Froissart by Thomas Johnes of Hafod was often reprinted throughout the century, though readers with a taste for the antique might prefer reprints of Lord Berners's translation. In many cases, though, narratives were not so much translated as reworked, whether in prose or in verse. The *Song of Roland* was retold in English prose by Anne Marsh (1854) on the basis of a French abridgement, whereas the Irish judge John O'Hagan (1880) offered an incomplete and leisurely poem in a metre modelled on Coleridge's *Christabel*, and the American Léonce Rabillon (1885) an archaizing text in unrhymed decasyllables. The lays of Marie de France, which had figured in earlier anthologies, provided a starting point for the much expanded *Lays of France* (1872) by the Francophile poet Arthur O'Shaughnessy.

A particular favourite was *Aucassin et Nicolette*, a chivalric fourteenth-century love story mixing prose and verse. Walter Pater praised its graceful simplicity in his *Studies in the History of the Renaissance* (1873), giving lengthy extracts in English, and there were four different translations in the 1880s. Unlike the versions of the late eighteenth century, these were quite exact renderings, particularly that of F. W. Bourdillon (1887). Andrew Lang prefaced his much reprinted translation with the remark: 'I have attempted, if not Old English, at least English which is elderly, with a memory of Malory' (Lang 1887: xvi), and his prose does read like pastiche Malory, with a characteristically *fin-de siècle* fondness for inversion ('Therein I seek not to enter...').

Lang also translated and imitated some shorter old French poems in a conventional poetic idiom in his *Ballads and Lyrics of Old France* (1872), but medieval and Renaissance lyric poetry was less popular than romance with translators and readers. In 1835, however, Louisa Stuart Costello had given a modern dress to some thirty poets from the troubadours to Henri IV in her *Specimens of the Early Poetry of France*. She devotes a good deal of space to Renaissance poetry, which also figures prominently in *The Early French Poets*, published in 1846 by Dante's translator Henry Cary. Thereafter, however, Ronsard and his contemporaries, though popular with the literati, were not much translated until about 1900.

The poet who found most favour, although dismissed by Costello as 'scarcely readable and quite unworthy of translation' (1835: 159), was the attractively disreputable François Villon. In the 1870s, his lyrics achieved wide currency in several evocatively archaic translations by Swinburne. One of the most striking is his version of the 'Ballade des pendus' in which the poet lends his voice to the dead men hanging on a gibbet. In translation, death like sex presented Victorian writers with difficulties. When Housman translated Horace's Ode IV.7, he turned Horace's 'pulvis et umbra sumus' ('we are dust and shade') into 'we are dust and dreams', softening and even sentimentalizing the fact of death. Evasiveness before these two animal facts is a chronic Victorian debility, though not just Victorian and not always a debility. Swinburne, for example in the choruses of *Atalanta in Calydon*, treats death diffusely not to evade it but apprehend it, glancingly at first but with cumulative force. For Villon he prefers the poetry of direct statement:

> Men, brother men, that after us yet live,
>   Let not your hearts too hard against us be;
> For if some pity of us poor men ye give,
>   The sooner God shall take of you pity.
> Here are we five or six strung up, you see,
> And here the flesh that all too well we fed
> Bit by bit eaten and rotten, rent and shred,
>   And we the bones grown dust and ash withal;
> Let no man laugh at us discomforted,
>   But pray to God that he forgive us all.
>   (Swinburne 1904: III, 152; for further
>   discussion see pp. 11–12, above)

At about the same time Dante Gabriel Rossetti published three simpler Villon translations. His rendering of the end of the *rondeau* 'Mort, j'appelle de ta rigueur' is poetically effective even if it fails to convey the ambiguity of the French 'mort' ('death', but primarily 'dead'):

> Deux estions et n'avions qu'un cuer;
> S'il est mort, force est que devie,
> Voire, ou que je vive sans vie
> Comme les images, par cuer
>   Mort![1]
>
> Two we were, and the heart was one;
> Which now being dead, dead must I be
> Or seem alive as lifelessly
> As in the choir the painted stone,
>   Death!
>   (Rossetti 2003: 120)

[1] The refrain effect of 'Mort' disappears from modern editions, which usually place a full stop after 'cuer' and make 'Mort' the first word of a final stanza which reprises the first.

There was a François Villon Society, created to promote the full-scale translation of the poems by the polymath John Payne, who imitates the verse forms of the original in a heavily archaic style, but with a certain flourish (Payne 1878; on Payne and Villon, see Wright 1919: 57–63). Echoed in modern times by Théodore de Banville, Villon was a model for the fixed-form poetry of *ballades* and *rondels* which flourished in Britain around 1880 (for this development see Dale 1954: 103–25).

Two Renaissance prose writers had never gone out of favour: Rabelais and Montaigne. For these the nineteenth century was generally content with the old translations. The Rabelais of Urquhart and Motteux (1653–94) continued to be published, sometimes in a bowdlerized form, and was not displaced by the relatively accurate, but archaizing *Five Books and Minor Writings* of W. F. Smith (1893). Montaigne was read in revised versions of Charles Cotton's translation of 1685–6, which was given a new lease of life by W. C. Hazlitt's edition of 1877; the text, revised by the editor's father William Hazlitt the younger, was closer to Cotton's than that given in eighteenth-century editions. In 1886, however, it was challenged by the first reappearance for some 250 years of John Florio's Montaigne of 1603; the vogue fed from 1892 by the publisher David Nutt's 'Tudor Translations' ensured that Florio would become the 'classic' Montaigne by 1900.

Classical Literature

The writings of France's classical period offered fewer discoveries. Existing translations continued to be published, sometimes with revisions, and they were joined by new versions, many of them literal translations catering for a school audience. While the French were assiduously discovering and translating Shakespeare, there was little new *theatrical* English translation of the French classical playwrights, and almost none of their successors Marivaux and Beaumarchais. Towards the end of the century, however, we see some substantial translations addressed to the studious reader (e.g. van Laun 1875; Boswell 1889–90).

Other authors of the classical period proved more attractive. La Fontaine, surprisingly neglected before 1800, was several times translated in the nineteenth century; a particularly popular version was that published in 1841 by the American abolitionist Elizur Wright, whose sprightly version nevertheless misses much of La Fontaine's subtlety. Pascal's apologia, the *Pensées*, and his anti-Jesuit *Provinciales*, both appealed enough to the religious concerns of nineteenth-century England to be retranslated several times; successive versions of the *Pensées* followed the progress made in France towards editing a satisfactory text of this unfinished work. The end of the century saw two new versions of La Bruyère's *Caractères*: the more accurate (van Laun 1885) is closer to the original than its eighteenth-century predecessors, but rather lacklustre. And the neatly cynical maxims of La Rochefoucauld attracted several new translations which competed (none very successfully) with the much reprinted version of 1749.

There was only one nineteenth-century translation of the greatest early French novel, Madame de La Fayette's *La Princesse de Clèves*, a clear, dignified version by the American Thomas Sergeant Perry (1892). By far the most popular novels, however, were Fénelon's *Télémaque*, a favourite with French teachers, and Le Sage's *Gil Blas*, hailed by Walter Scott as one of the great story books. In both cases an old translation was challenged by new ones. Smollett's *Gil Blas* (1755) fought off the competition of Martin Smart (1807), who deplored Smollett's coarseness, but it was partly replaced by the wordier version of B. H. Malkin (1809); in 1886 Henri van Laun produced a translation that is more accurate than Smollett's, if less racy. For *Télémaque* too there were new prose versions, which sought to replace the standard Hawkesworth text of 1768, notably a good clear version edited by Francis Fitzgerald (1792). The really striking phenomenon was the flurry of verse translations of Fénelon's prose 'epic'; there were at least six of these, usually considerably amplified, including three by clergymen, and one by the anonymous author of *Five Months in the Royal Lunatic Asylum, Glasgow*.

Other eighteenth-century texts that were several times retranslated include Gresset's mock-heroic poem *Vert-Vert*, Marmontel's edifying *Contes moraux*, Hamilton's swashbuckling pseudo-memoirs of the comte de Grammont, and the writings of such radical *philosophes* as Helvétius and Holbach. Of the front-line Enlightenment figures, there was surprisingly little translation of Diderot until very late in the century, and Montesquieu was largely represented by older translations. Rousseau attracted more interest; there were new versions of his *Du contrat social* (see p. 493, below), while his *Confessions*, of which the first (anonymous) translations of 1783 and 1790 were much reprinted throughout the century, was the subject of an impressive new anonymous translation in the 1890s (see France 1986).

Voltaire was by far the most popular of the *philosophes*. While earlier translations continued to be used, notably those in the *Works* edited in 1761–5 by Tobias Smollett and Thomas Francklin, and the theatrical adaptations of Aaron Hill, there were many new renderings of such favourites as the *History of Charles XII*, the *Philosophical Dictionary*, and the epic *La Henriade* (of which Charlotte Brontë dutifully translated one canto at school). In particular, we begin to see the modern concentration on Voltaire's philosophical tales, above all *Candide*. Editions of the tales usually recycled older versions, but there were new translations such as Robert Bruce Boswell's slightly bowdlerized and ponderous volume (1891) and an attractive complete edition by the prolific American translator William Walton (1900).

Modern Poetry and Poetic Drama

Compared with novels and historical writing, French poetry appealed to a small audience, and even these readers generally felt, in the early part of the century at least, that English poetry had little to learn from its superficial and artificial French counterpart. In cases where French poetry was a source of inspiration, in Swinburne for instance, this did not necessarily depend on or result in translation, since most readers of poetry had enough French to read the original texts.

Poetic translation did go on, however, either as an agreeable exercise for men and women of letters, or to reach the less well educated—an aim stated by Henry

Carrington in the introduction to his anthology (Carrington 1900). In almost all cases, translators attempted to echo the form of the original, though they often used blank verse to translate rhyming alexandrine couplets. Some English translators chose to put French prose into verse, as in a translation of Hugo's *Angelo*, prefaced by a thoughtful discussion of French and English verse (Coe 1880). Chateaubriand was following a French tradition when he used prose, albeit rather odd prose, for his foreignizing version of *Paradise Lost* (1836); conversely his prose *Atala* had the strange fortune of being translated into rhyming octaves (Gerard 1873).

Few of these metrical translations were done by poets of any note (Rossetti and Swinburne reserved their efforts for earlier poetry), and few strike the present-day reader as more than dutiful at best. In this typical version of the first stanza of Lamartine's 'L'Isolement' the translator has attempted to match the long lines of the original, while changing the ABAB rhyme scheme to AABB:

> Often beneath the mountain, beside the old oak shade,
> At the hour of the setting sun my listless length is laid.
> Upon the changing tablet of the plain that lies below,
> With soft, yet melancholy thoughts, my careless look I throw.
> (Smith 1852: 3)

As well as occasional slim volumes devoted to a particular poet, some translations were published in periodicals such as *Blackwood's*, *Fraser's*, or *Bentley's*, or in the aesthetic journals of the 1890s. These might subsequently, in the rare cases where a modern poet (e.g. Hugo or Béranger) had gained classic status, be gathered into collected volumes. In addition, the later part of the century saw the publication of three single-author anthologies of French poetry. Harry Curwen's fluent *Echoes from the French Poets* (1870), devoted to nineteenth-century writers, gave pride of place, rather surprisingly, to the scandalous Baudelaire. Half of Henry Carrington's *Anthology of French Poetry* (limited edition 1895, expanded 1900) was devoted to the nineteenth century. But it was the obscure William John Robertson (1895) who offered the best collection of recent poetry, with a fair number of poems by Nerval, Baudelaire, Mallarmé, Verlaine, Rimbaud, and others in translations which give at least some idea of the form and feel of the originals.

By the end of the century, three poets from the Romantic period had emerged as schoolroom classics: Victor Hugo, Alphonse de Lamartine, and Alfred de Musset, but Musset's poetry, as opposed to his plays, was not much translated. Others too, including Alfred de Vigny, Marceline Desbordes-Valmore, and Gérard de Nerval, might be known and admired in the original (for Nerval see Lang 1889), but provoked little translation. To judge by the number of publications—a dozen collections by different translators over the century—the most popular French poet in Britain was the songwriter Pierre-Jean Béranger, who has almost disappeared from view (his songs are discussed in § 9.2, below). Walter Bagehot, in a balanced assessment in the *National Review* (1857), described him as 'the essential Frenchman' with his mastery of light 'social poetry', but little depth

(Bagehot 1879: II, 261–98). Thackeray's rollicking translation of 'Le Roi d'Yvetôt' is included in *Béranger's Poems in the Versions of the Best Translators* (Walsh 1888: 72–5).

Lamartine, with his strong religious and ethical themes, was perhaps the first French Romantic poet to win acceptance in Britain and America (see Lombard 1961). Readers and translators flocked in the first instance to his prose (history, memoirs, travel writing, edifying stories), but by 1870 there were upward of ten English volumes of his poetry, mostly slim and none distinguished, including three versions of parts of his long epic poem of the tribulations of a parish priest, *Jocelyn*. For Hugo, the story is similar. His novels, and to a lesser extent his plays, made him a celebrity from about 1830, but at first there were few translations of his lyric or epic verse. One of the these was *Songs of the Twilight* (1836), a metrical translation by the prolific G. W. M. Reynolds of *Les Chants du crépuscule*, which had appeared only the previous year. Reynolds's versions were reissued, along with others by Andrew Lang, Edwin Arnold, Edward Dowden, and many obscure translators in two large anthologies of Hugo's poetry (Williams 1885; Bettany 1890) which came out in the years following the great man's death. Part of the appeal of the *Chants du crépuscule* had been its reference to recent political events; the same was even more true of the satirical *Les Châtiments*, eight of which were vigorously translated by the Chartist W. J. Linton for inclusion in his journal the *English Republic* in 1853–4 (reproduced by Brian Rigby in his contribution to James 1986: 75–101).

Hugo's romantic verse dramas attracted more translators, even if some (e.g. Coe 1880) were aware that to British ears Hugo's theatre appeared wildly bombastic. The main plays were translated at least once, sometimes being adapted for the stage. *Hernani*, the most popular of them, can serve as an example. After its famously tumultuous première in Paris in 1830, it was quickly translated in heroic couplets by Francis Leveson-Gower (Egerton), future Earl of Ellesmere, and performed before Queen Adelaide at Bridgewater House in 1831. There was also an adaptation for Drury Lane, James Kenney's *The Pledge, or, Castilian Honour* (1831), followed later in the century by two closer versions in run-of-the-mill blank verse by the novelist and poet Mrs Newton Crosland (1887) and by R. Farquharson Sharp (1898). Crosland's translation also figures in a Bohn *Dramatic Works* (1887), and soon afterwards there was a luxurious collected *Dramas* (Burnham 1895), where *Hernani*, like the other plays, is rendered in archaic, undramatic prose.

Later in the century, British literary opinion was more sympathetic to French poetry, particularly after 1880 (see Dale 1954). But whereas Hugo and Béranger were widely appreciated, the Parnassians and symbolists appealed to a circle of Francophiles such as Andrew Lang, W. E. Henley, or George Saintsbury, who had little need for translation. In 1879, however, Arthur O'Shaughnessy collaborated with the French poet Catulle Mendès to produce an article on 'Recent French Poets' in the *Gentleman's Magazine*, illustrated with translations from a number of Parnassian and symbolist poets (O'Shaughnessy 1879), and eleven years later there was a copiously illustrated article on the now largely forgotten Sully Prudhomme (Prothero and Prothero 1890).

Charles Baudelaire was much talked of, but before 1900 had few translators. One of the first was Richard Herne Shepherd, with a group of three poems in 1869—this includes the shockingly explicit 'A Carcass', which jars with the rest of the volume. Thereafter, Baudelaire is quite prominent in the 1870 anthology by Harry Curwen, who later produced a separate volume (Curwen 1894) containing over fifty skilful metrical versions, eschewing Baudelaire's more challenging work, but still the most impressive selection of the poet in English before Arthur Symons's prose poems of 1905. There are also eight of the prose poems in the American-French Stuart Merrill's elegant attempt to acclimatize this French genre in English, *Pastels in Prose* (1890).

The *Yellow Book* milieu of the 1890s was deeply involved in contemporary Parisian culture, and translations of symbolist poetry appeared in 'decadent' journals such as *The Savoy*, *The Dial*, and *Bibelot* (see Roy 1960). This was the context for the most imaginative nineteenth-century versions of new French poems, the Mallarmé and Verlaine of Arthur Symons (see Symons 1902: I, 205–19) and the Rimbaud, Verlaine, and Baudelaire of Oscar Wilde's protégé John Gray. Gray's version of Rimbaud's 'Sensation' catches well the sensuality of the original:

> Par les soirs bleus d'été, j'irai dans les sentiers,
> Picoté par les blés, fouler l'herbe menue:
> Rêveur, j'en sentirai la fraîcheur à mes pieds.
> Je laisserai le vent baigner ma tête nue.
>
> I walk the alleys trampled through the wheat,
> Through whole blue summer eves, on velvet grass.
> Dreaming, I feel the dampness at my feet;
> The breezes bathe my naked head and pass.
>
> (Gray 1998: 36)

Of the modern poets, Verlaine was the most popular, receiving the honour of a separate volume, in the plangent *Poems of Paul Verlaine* of the American Gertrude Hall (1895). Significantly, there were also a number of translations from the Belgian Émile Verhaeren at the very end of the century. The discovery of the new writing of Flanders culminated in the vogue for the poetic theatre of Maurice Maeterlinck, several of whose plays were translated, and in some cases performed, between 1890 and 1900, with different versions of *Pelléas et Mélisande*, both attractively simple, by Erving Winslow (1894) and Laurence Alma Tadema (1895). The symbolist poetic drama of his greater French near-contemporary Paul Claudel remained untranslated until well into the new century.

Modern Fiction

Much non-fictional prose was translated from French during this period (see § 11.2 and § 11.3, below). Alongside works of history and historical memoirs, this included such personal writings as the searchingly introspective diaries of Henri-Frédéric Amiel in the frequently reprinted translation of Mrs Humphry Ward

(1885), and the frank journal of Marie Bashkirtseff, published posthumously in 1889 and translated three times before 1900. But the mass of translations from French was made up of novels and short stories. (At the same time the French were translating and retranslating the novels and stories of Sterne, Scott, Poe, Dickens, and many others.) A major new development was the widespread use of French material for popular fiction, often serialized: thrillers, detective stories, Gothic horror, or science fiction. This is discussed in § 8.1, below, with reference to writers such as Sue, Gaboriau, and Verne, all of whom receive only brief mention here.

The books that are well known today were by no means always those most prominent in translation at the time. Benjamin Constant's *Adolphe*, for instance, although it received a good translation only three months after the original publication in 1816 (Walker 1816: see Courtney 1975), quickly disappeared from view. The novels of Stendhal, written for what he called 'the happy few' and posterity, remained virtually untranslated before 1900. On the other hand the sentimental tale *Picciola* (1836) by Xavier Saintine (Joseph-Xavier Boniface) and Xavier de Maistre's *Voyage autour de ma chambre* (1794), much in demand as a schoolroom classic, were both translated several times; both appeared alongside Homer's *Iliad* in 1844 in Smith's Standard Library.

There was in fact a marked taste in the early nineteenth century for touching or edifying stories from France, for instance those of Mme de Genlis (discussed in Vol. 3 of this *History*). While many of Chateaubriand's non-fictional works were translated, from his travel writing to his defence of Christianity, it was his tragic tale *Atala*, with its exotic North American setting, which attracted most translators. Several different versions appeared from 1802 until the end of the century, including one in verse (Gerard 1873) and a luxurious volume illustrated by Gustave Doré (Harry 1867).

Equally exotic, and even more popular, were two short novels of Bernardin de Saint-Pierre, *La Chaumière indienne* and above all the tragic idyll *Paul et Virginie*; these were repeatedly published in translation, sometimes with Sophie Cottin's tear-jerking adventure story *Élisabeth, ou, Les Exilés de Sibérie*. Bernardin attracted interesting translators; the first version of *Paul et Virginie*, based on the 1788 text, was made by Daniel Malthus (1789), disciple of Rousseau and father of the population theorist, and this was soon followed by the fluent free translation of the full 1789 text by Helen Maria Williams (1795). Williams, working in Paris 'amidst the horrors of Robespierre's tyranny', found 'the most soothing relief in wandering from my own gloomy reflections to those enchanting scenes of the Mauritius' (pp. iii–v). Perhaps her text, embellished with original sonnets, struck a similar chord, for it became immensely popular with British readers.

Chateaubriand's contemporary Mme de Staël was well received in Britain, particularly on account of her opposition to Napoleon. Her novels found several translators, even if *Delphine* was dismissed by Sidney Smith as 'dismal trash' (see George Saintsbury's introduction to Lawler 1894). *Corinne* was twice translated in the year of publication (1807), though these translations were displaced in 1831 by Isabel Hill's much reprinted version, in which the poetic prose of the heroine's 'improvizations' is translated in verse.

According to Patricia Thomson, 'of all French writers, George Sand made the most impression in England in the 1830s and 1840s' (Thomson 1977: 11; for the USA see Joyaux 1965). British commentators were sharply divided in their views of her scandalous life and her novels, but since they almost all read her in French, this did not at first result in a great deal of translation. The challenging *Lélia* was never translated in the nineteenth century, and even the more acceptable novels took some years to appear in English. In 1847, however, *The Works of George Sand* appeared under the editorship of the radical Matilda M. Hays. The intention of publishing a complete works was thwarted by 'inadequate support on the part of the reading public', and only six volumes were published, containing eight novels translated by Hays, her fellow radical Eliza Ashurst, and a reforming clergyman, Edmund R. Larken. This collection was not unfairly criticized in the *Westminster Review* as being confined to 'harmless' works and falling short of the 'magic' of Sand's style (cited by Michael Tilby in Classe 2000: 1223–7). Croker's *Quarterly Review*, meanwhile, thundered against a man of the cloth being involved in translating this '*semivir obscoenus*'—and Larken was duly reprimanded by Archbishop Whateley. Thereafter, the translation of Sand's novels continued fairly steadily in Britain and particularly in America, special favourites being the rustic novels *La Mare au diable* and *La Petite Fadette*, both translated at least four times before 1900.

As we saw, medieval literature was above all a storehouse of romances for English-language translators. So too, in modern fiction, there was a marked preference for adventure stories, sometimes military, and generally with a historical or exotic setting. The two great providers were Hugo and Alexandre Dumas *père*. Their novels were almost all translated very soon after original publication, the major titles generally being done at least twice; by 1900 they had been reissued, often in abridged or altered form, in scores of reprints, both popular and luxury publications, many of them illustrated. Dumas in particular became a staple author of the various 'railway libraries' that flourished in the second half of the century. The 1880s and 1890s saw several collected editions of the romances of both authors in Britain and especially in the United States, often recycling existing translations.

Hugo's early novel *Notre-Dame de Paris*, first published in 1831, was rapidly englished by William Hazlitt the younger, whose translation of 1833 was based on the soon-to-be-superseded first edition; it is preceded by a 'literary and political' preface where the lawlessness of the old regime in France is likened to the 'regime of conquest' which underlies modern British society. The same year saw a rival translation by the prolific Frederic Shoberl, who gave the novel the title (detested by Hugo) by which it has been best known in English, *The Hunchback of Notre Dame*, and whose text, based on the definitive edition, was the basis of many subsequent versions. Then, some thirty years on, Hugo's greatest novel *Les Misérables* received two separate translations in the year of its publication (1862): the 'authorized' English translation by Lascelles Wraxall, and a competing version by the American Charles E. Wilbour, both of them frequently reissued or recycled. Among later translations of these two novels, one should also note those by Isabel

Hapgood, better known for her translations of Russian fiction. All these publications were the work of reputable translators, who strove to give a faithful account of the original, making few cuts (which was emphatically not the case with some of Hugo's other translators, abridgers, and adapters). As was noted by critics of the day, however, they generally failed to match the antithetical and often laconic vigour of the original (see Lebreton-Savigny 1971: 15–16).

Dumas had less prestige than Hugo, perhaps, but he was even more popular. In the words of his bibliographer, 'no translated foreign romance has had so many editions published in the English-speaking world as "Les trois mousquetaires" ' — so many that a full description of them would require a whole volume (Munro 1978: 79). Dumas's masterpiece was published in France in 1844, after being issued in serial form and rapidly pirated in Belgium. Using a mixture of the official and the pirated editions, three different English versions came out in 1846, *The Three Guardsmen* by the American Park Benjamin, and two British versions, an incomplete anonymous one and the 'full and excellent' one of William Barrow (Munro 1978: 81). These were followed in 1853 by the translation of William Robson, whose text was the basis of most later editions, including a shortened 'new translation' published by the very productive Henry Llewellyn Williams in 1893. Other works had a similar history, if on a more modest scale. *Le Comte de Monte-Cristo*, for instance, received an admirably full anonymous translation in 1846, very soon after its original publication; this was reissued in serial form in the *London Journal*, and was recycled in countless later editions. Several of these early translations were sufficiently effective to be reissued in Oxford World's Classics 150 years later.

On a smaller scale, such historical tales as Vigny's *Cinq-Mars*, Prosper Mérimée's *Colomba*, *Carmen*, and *Chronique du règne de Charles IX*, and later in the century the patriotic 'national novels' of the Alsace duo Émile Erckmann and Alexandre Chatrian, all found favour with publishers, translators, and readers looking for entertaining but respectable French fiction. The Erckmann–Chatrian Library, published by the firm of Ward, Lock, and Tyler, contained seventeen titles, including the best-seller *The Conscript*, translated by H. W. Dulcken, who is credited on the title page with a Ph.D. (1871, but first anonymously translated by a different hand in 1865). Unusually, an Erckmann–Chatrian novel was serialized in the *Cornhill Magazine* in 1871–2.

As the example of Erckmann–Chatrian suggests, there was also adventure in modern life. The resounding success of Eugène Sue's serialized thrillers in French and in English in the middle years of the century is discussed together with detective fiction on pp. 375–8, below. Sue had a relatively brief period of glory, whereas that other explorer of the mysteries of the modern world, Honoré de Balzac, was slower to make his mark in translation, particularly in Britain (for a fuller account see Michael Tilby in Classe 2000: 98–102). Partly the trouble was his reputation for immorality, partly the sheer size of his output, partly his vigorous and idiosyncratic style, which often defeated the efforts of his translators. Nevertheless, after an early period around 1840 in which short texts and abridgements were published in journals, a fair number of full-scale translations appeared between 1850 and

1880, always some twenty or thirty years behind the original French publication. There was almost no retranslation until the last decade of the century, but then the floodgates were opened.

Between 1885 and 1900 there were three complete, or nearly complete, translations of *La Comédie humaine* (Wormeley 1896; Ives 1895–1900; Marriage 1895–8). All have been criticized by later commentators as wooden, insensitive, or inaccurate, and the quality does vary within each collection, particularly those done by several hands, but generally these translators did a vital job well, giving the public access to the enormous Balzacian oeuvre. Even when a more famous translator, Ernest Dowson, tried his hand in 1896 at *La Fille aux yeux d'or*, which was too scandalous to be included in two of the collections, he was less convincing than E. P. Robins, working for the limited American edition. The Dent edition, a risky venture by a young publishing house, directed by George Saintsbury and largely translated by Ellen Marriage (for four 'bolder' titles it seems that she used the pseudonym James Waring), continued to be reissued and read over the following century.

In 1881, launching a series of 'some of the very best and newest French novels', the publishing firm of Vizetelly (see pp. 42–4, above) claimed that London publishers fought shy of new French fiction. Thanks partly to Vizetelly, the last decades of the century disproved this amply—and this was even more the case in the USA. In addition to the collections of Hugo, Dumas, and Balzac, French novels of all kinds were translated in considerable quantities, sometimes in specialized collections. Some of the writers who most attracted publishers have now virtually vanished from sight in the English-speaking world—the Swiss Victor Cherbuliez, the king of romance Georges Ohnet, and the prolific author of adventure stories Gustave Aimard—while others, such as the crime writer Émile Gaboriau and the more reputable novelists Paul Bourget, Pierre Loti, and Alphonse Daudet, no longer shine as brightly as they did. Daudet in particular, with a large output ranging from the meridional entertainments of *Lettres de mon moulin* or *Tartarin de Tarascon* to his more ambitious naturalistic and psychological novels, was endlessly translated, notably the shocking *Sapho*, issued as a 'realistic novel' by Vizetelly in 1886, two years after an instant American translation done by Myron A. Cooney 'from the author's advance sheets'. French fiction could be hot property.

Of the currently acknowledged masters, Flaubert made a slowish start. In 1886, nearly three decades after the original publications and following earlier American translations, Vizetelly issued a *Madame Bovary* by Karl Marx's daughter Eleanor (Marx-Aveling 1886) and a version of *Salammbô* by J. S. Chartres. These are reasonably accurate renderings, but make little attempt to match Flaubert's highly worked style. The first versions of *L'Éducation sentimentale*, *La Tentation de saint Antoine*, and *Bouvard et Pécuchet*, all done in the 1890s by the barrister D. F. Hannigan, while following Flaubert's meaning closely, are stylistically inept.

Flaubert's disciple Guy de Maupassant was more fortunate, particularly in America. Translated by a variety of hands, several volumes of novels and short stories appeared in rapid succession between 1887 and 1900. One or two of these received added lustre from the prefaces of well-known men of letters, Henry James

(Sturges 1891) and Arthur Symons (Anon. 1899), for while naturalism appealed to the popular audiences of Vizetelly, it also interested the literary avant-garde who at the same time found inspiration in various strands of French aestheticism and decadence, from Théophile Gautier to the Goncourt brothers and Joris-Karl Huysmans. All of these attracted translators and publishers, Gautier's novels proving particularly appealing. There were two translations of *Mademoiselle Maupin*, and three different editions of *One of Cleopatra's Nights, and Other Fantastic Romances*, translated by Lafcadio Hearn, a champion of the new French literature (Hearn 1886). The year 1900 saw the appearance in New York of a 24-volume *Works of Théophile Gautier*.

The British fortunes of Émile Zola provide a fitting conclusion to this story. It was in fact in the United States that Zola's novels had first been published in English, most of them taken from the twenty volumes of his Rougon-Macquart series, an epic and often scandalously sordid depiction of French society under the Second Empire. Several of these translations were the work of a woman, Mary Neal Sherwood, writing under the pseudonym of John Stirling. In the distinctly partisan view of Henry Vizetelly's son Ernest, these were 'for the most part ridiculous, full of errors, and so defaced by excisions and alterations as to give no idea of what the books might be like in translation' (Vizetelly 1904: 243–4). However that may be, they were popular enough for Vizetelly to launch his own British series. Between 1884 and 1888 he published eighteen Zola titles in anonymous translations; these were all given the subtitle 'a realistic novel', signalling that this was adult fare, and in addition they were lightly expurgated in accordance with the likely sensibilities of readers. But this did not prove enough to stave off the attacks of Members of Parliament and the National Vigilance Association. In 1888–9 Vizetelly was twice brought to court for publishing obscene material, found guilty, imprisoned, and ruined (for a fuller account see p. 54, above, and Vizetelly 1904: 242–99).

The forces responsible for bringing Vizetelly to court were strong enough to force his son into further expurgations of the offending works, but they could not prevent the spread of such dangerous material. French naturalism made a strong if ambiguous impact on English literature in the 1880s and 1890s, and more than 100 men of letters had signed a petition in favour of Zola and Vizetelly (see Frierson 1925: 70–1). It is not surprising therefore that in 1894–5, the Lutetian Society (on which see Merkle 2003) produced a handsome edition (limited, and therefore not open to prosecution) of six of Zola's major novels, unexpurgated and generally well translated by prominent writers including Arthur Symons, Ernest Dowson, and Havelock Ellis (Dowson 1894–5). Immoral French fiction, which had so outraged Croker in 1836, retained its power to challenge British and American values.

LIST OF SOURCES

Translations
Fuller listings will be found in *CBEL 3* IV, 103–27, and for particular authors in Classe 2000 and France 2000.

Anon. (1786). *Tales of the Twelfth and Thirteenth Centuries, from the French of Mr le Grand*. London (reissued as *The Feudal Period Illustrated by a Series of Tales Romantic and Humorous*, ed. W. C. Hazlitt, London, 1873).
Anon. (1846). *The Count of Monte Cristo* [Dumas], 2 vols. London.
Anon. (1899). *Boule de Suif* [Maupassant]. London.
Barrow, William (1846). *The Three Musketeers* [Dumas], 2 vols. London.
Bettany, G. T., ed. (1890). *Victor Hugo: Select Poems and Tragedies*. London.
Boswell, Robert Bruce (1889–90). *The Dramatic Works of Jean Racine: A Metrical English Version*. London (Bohn).
—— (1891). *Zadig and Other Tales* [Voltaire]. London (Bohn).
Burnham, I. G. (1895). *The Dramas of Victor Hugo*, 4 vols. Philadelphia.
Carrington, Henry (1900). *Anthology of French Poetry*. London (expansion of limited edn. of 1895).
Coe, Ernest Oswald (1880). *Angelo* [Hugo]. London.
Costello, Louisa Stuart (1835). *Specimens of the Early Poetry of France*. London.
Curwen, Harry (1870). *Echoes from the French Poets: An Anthology*. London.
—— (1894). *Some Translations from Charles Baudelaire*. London.
Dowson, Ernest, *et al.* (1894–5). *Nana* (tr. V. Plarr); *L'Assommoir* (tr. A. Symons); *Pot-Bouille* (tr. P. Pinkerton); *La Curée* (tr. A. Teixeira de Mattos); *La Terre* (tr. E. Dowson); *Germinal* (tr. H. Ellis) [Zola]. London (limited edn.).
Gerard (1873). *Atala: A Love Tale, in Six Cantos of Verse* [Chateaubriand]. London.
Gray, John (1988). *The Poems of John Gray*, ed. Ian Fletcher. Greensboro, NC.
Harry, James Spence (1867). *Atala* [Chateaubriand]. London.
Hays, Mathilda M., *et al.* (1847). *The Works of George Sand*, 6 vols. London.
Hazlitt, William (1833). *Notre-Dame: A Tale of the 'Ancien Régime'*. London.
Hearn, Lafcadio (1886). *One of Cleopatra's Nights, and Other Fantastic Romances* [Gautier]. London.
Hill, I[sabel] (1831). *Corinne, or, Italy* [de Staël]. London.
Ives, G. B., *et al.* (1895–1900). *The Human Comedy* [Balzac], 53 vols. Philadelphia (limited edn.; earlier limited edns. in 11 and in 22 vols.).
Johnes, Thomas (1803). *Sir John Froissart's Chronicles*, 4 vols. London.
Lang, Andrew (1887). *Aucassin and Nicolete*. London.
Lawler, D[ennis] (1894). *Corinna, or, Italy* [de Staël]. London (first pub. 1807).
Marriage, Ellen, *et al.* (1895–8). *The Human Comedy* [Balzac], 40 vols. London (collection directed by George Saintsbury).
Marx-Aveling, E[leanor] (1886). *Madame Bovary: Provincial Manners* [Flaubert]. London.
O'Shaughnessy, Arthur W. E. (1879). 'Recent French Poets' (by Catulle Mendès, with translations by Arthur O'Shaughnessy). *Gentleman's Magazine* 245: 478–504 and 563–88.
Payne, John (1878). *The Poems of Master Francis Villon of Paris*. London (limited edn.; 2nd edn. 1881).
Pollock, Walter Herries (1880). *The Poet and the Muse* [Musset]. London.
Prothero, E., and Prothero, R. E. (1890). 'The Poetry of Sully-Prudhomme, with Translations in English Verse'. *English Illustrated Magazine* 7: 669–78.
Robertson, William John (1895). *A Century of French Verse*. London.
Robson, William (1853). *The Three Musketeers* [Dumas], 2 vols. London.
Rossetti, Dante Gabriel (2003). *Collected Poetry and Prose*, ed. Jerome McGann. New Haven, CT.

Shepherd, Richard Herne (1869). *Translations from Charles Baudelaire*. London (new edn. 1879).
Smart, Martin (1807). *The Adventures of Gil Blas of Santillana* [Le Sage], 4 vols. London.
Smith, James T. (1852). *Translations from the Meditations of Lamartine, together with Fugitive Pieces*. New York.
Sturges, Jonathan (1891). *The Odd Number: Thirteen Tales by Guy de Maupassant*. London.
Swinburne, Algernon Charles (1904). *Poems*, 6 vols. London.
Symons, Arthur (1902). *Poems*, 2 vols. London.
van Laun, Henri (1875). *The Dramatic Works of Molière*, 6 vols. Edinburgh.
—— (1885). *The Characters of Jean de la Bruyère*. London.
—— (1886). *The Adventures of Gil Blas de Santillana* [Le Sage], 3 vols. Edinburgh.
[Walker, Alexander] (1816). *Adolphe* [Constant]. London.
Walsh, William S., ed. (1888). *Béranger's Poems in the Versions of the Best Translators*. London.
Walton, William (1900). *The Whole Prose Romances of François-Marie Arouet de Voltaire*, 3 vols. London.
Way, Gregory Lewis (1796). *Fabliaux or Tales, Abridged from the French Manuscripts of the XIIth and XIIIth Centuries by M. Le Grand*, 2 vols. London.
Wilbour, Charles E. (1862). *Les Misérables* [Hugo], 2 vols. New York.
Williams, Helen Maria (1795). *Paul and Virginia* [Bernardin de Saint-Pierre]. London.
Williams, Henry Llewellyn, ed. (1885). *Selection, Chiefly Lyrical, from the Poetical Works of Victor Hugo*. London (Bohn).
Wormeley, Katharine Prescott (1896). *The Comedy of Human Life* [Balzac], 40 vols. Boston, MA (the first 12 vols. published in London 1886–91 as *Balzac's Novels in English*).
[Wraxall, Lascelles] (1862). *Les Misérables* [Hugo], 3 vols. London.
Wright, Elizur (1841). *The Fables of La Fontaine*. Boston, MA.

Other Sources
Bagehot, Walter (1879). *Literary Studies*, 2nd edn. London.
Campos, Christophe (1965). *The View of France, from Arnold to Bloomsbury*. London.
Classe, Olive, ed. (2000). *Encyclopedia of Literary Translation into English*, 2 vols. London.
Clements, P. (1985). *Baudelaire and the English Tradition*. Princeton, NJ.
Courtney, C. P. (1975). 'Alexander Walker and Benjamin Constant. A Note on the English Translator of *Adolphe*.' *French Studies* 29: 137–50.
[Croker, John Wilson] (1834). 'State of the French Drama.' *Quarterly Review* 51: 177–212.
—— (1836). 'French Novels.' *Quarterly Review* 56: 65–131.
Dale, E. Hilda (1954). *La Poésie française en Angleterre, 1850–1890*. Paris.
France, Peter (1986). 'Rousseau's *Confessions* in English.' *Franco-British Studies* 2: 27–39.
——, ed. (2000). *The Oxford Guide to Literature in English Translation*. Oxford.
Frierson, W. C. (1925). *L'Influence des naturalistes français sur les romanciers anglais*. Paris.
James, A. R. W. (1986). *Victor Hugo et l'Angleterre*. Liverpool.
Joyaux, George (1965). 'French Fiction in American Magazines: 1800–1848.' *Arizona Quarterly* 21: 28–40.
Lang, Andrew (1889). *Letters on Literature*. London.
Lebreton-Savigny, Monique (1971). *Victor Hugo et les Américains (1825–1885)*. Paris.
Lombard, C. M. (1961). 'Lamartine in America and England (1820–1876): A Check List.' *Bulletin of Bibliography* 23: 103–6.
Merkle, Denise (2003). 'The Lutetian Society.' *TTR* 16/2: 73–101.

Monod, S. (1950). 'Les Fortunes de Balzac en Angleterre.' *Revue de littérature comparée* 24: 188–210.
Munro, Douglas (1978). *Alexandre Dumas père: A Bibliography of Works Translated into English to 1910*. New York.
Roy, G. Ross (1960). 'A Bibliography of French Symbolism in English-Language Magazines to 1910.' *Revue de littérature comparée* 34: 645–59.
Thomson, Patricia (1977). *George Sand and the Victorians: Her Influence and Reputation in Nineteenth-Century England*. London.
Vizetelly, Ernest (1904). *Émile Zola: Novelist and Reformer*. London.
Wright, Thomas (1919). *The Life of John Payne*. London.

6.3 Italian

Ralph Pite

Introduction

The second half of the eighteenth century saw a marked revival of interest among British readers in Italian literature (especially the work of Dante and Petrarch) and a corresponding increase in the number of translations. Generally speaking, Augustan culture had been distinguished by its preference for French neo-classical over medieval or Renaissance models, but now Italian writers regained the importance they had last enjoyed in the seventeenth century thanks to the developing cult of sensibility. As it gave priority to feeling over ratiocination, sensibility destabilized Augustan hierarchies. The primitive and the excessive were preferred over the measured and the refined, and the claims of subjective experience were given greater respect. In that context both Petrarch and Dante were revalued: Petrarch's self-communing sonnets were attractive because they combined romantic plangency with elaborate wordplay and the contortions of emotional double-bind, while Dante's Hell violated the elegiac melancholy of Virgil's underworld, introducing instead feelings of horror, fury, and love.

The sections of Dante's *Commedia* most popular with his eighteenth-century readership and most frequently translated were *Inferno* XXXIII, the Ugolino episode, and, gradually eclipsing it as the century went on, *Inferno* V, the Paolo and Francesca episode (see Ellis 1983; Tinkler-Villani 1989; Pite 1994). Canto XXXIII hinted at cannibalism (a father eating his dead sons) and Canto V depicted adulterous love. In both, Dante highlights the intensity of his own response; he swoons when Francesca finishes her tale, and when Ugolino falls silent, he bursts out in furious indignation against those who condemned father and children alike to an agonizing death. These episodes remained celebrated into the Romantic period. Coleridge remarked in a lecture on Dante given in 1818 that *Inferno* V and XXXIII 'are so well known and rightly so admired' that he would not discuss them in detail. Leigh Hunt's *The Story of Rimini* (1816) is a long-winded retelling of Canto V, whose influence on the style of Keats's early poetry was considerable. Byron also translated Canto V; Shelley (who translated ll. 1–51 of *Purgatorio* XXVIII, plus one or two of Dante's then little-known minor poems) collaborated with his friend Thomas Medwin in producing a version of *Inferno* XXXIII (see Toynbee 1909; Havely 1998, 49–70).

The year 1785 saw the appearance of Henry Boyd's two-volume translation of the *Inferno* (published with a 'Specimen of a New Translation of Ariosto's *Orlando Furioso*'). Though little known now and easily disparaged, Boyd's work received good reviews; he went on to complete *The Divina Commedia of Dante Alighieri* in

1802. Boyd frequently expanded Dante's Italian and he created a uniformly sublime poem out of the original. Nonetheless, his version assisted in the gradual release of Dante from his confinement in anthologies and selections.

This opening up of Dante's work coincided with renewed attention to Petrarch. Although Boyd produced a version of Petrarch's *Trionfi* in 1807, it was more usual, until the very end of the nineteenth century, to see Petrarch as a sonneteer (see Brand 1957). Biographical studies were frequent. In 1784, for instance, A. F. Tytler produced his *Essay on the Life and Character of Petrarch*, publishing an expanded *Historical and Critical Essay* in 1810. Tytler's book included translations, and there were others, nearly all from the sonnets. *Sonnets, and Odes Translated from the Italian of Petrarch* (1777) is attributed to John Nott (see Fiske 1882: 41), who also translated Catullus and who published a larger selection, *Petrarch Translated*, in 1808; Francis Wrangham also published a number of translations, and James, late Earl of Charlemont, produced *Select Sonnets* (1822). Susannah Dobson was exceptional in translating Petrarch's Latin treatise *De Remediis Utrisque Fortunae* as *Petrarch's View of Human Life* (1791 and 1797). The biographical works and the translations that accompanied them established Petrarch as a bard of sensibility. In 1839, he was placed alongside Byron and Sterne in an anonymous polemic against the cult of feeling: *Thoughts on What has been Called Sensibility of the Imagination*.

Immortal Tasso

Something similar happened to Tasso's reputation. His *Gerusalemme liberata* had been translated almost as soon as it was written. Fairfax's famous 1600 translation continued to be reprinted throughout the eighteenth and nineteenth centuries. Meanwhile, new versions began to appear: the most successful was John Hoole's 1763 version, which reached its third edition in 1783 and its eighth by 1803. Even so, the first half of the nineteenth century showed a notable increase in the number of translations. From 1818 onwards, when John Higgs Hunt's version appeared, until the 1850s, versions of *Jerusalem Delivered* appeared steadily: by J. H. Wiffen (1824), C. L. Smith (1851), and several others. The versions by Hunt, Wiffen, and Smith all went into several editions alongside regular reprints of Fairfax and Hoole.

In 1763, Hoole had justified his presentation to the public of a new translation by saying that for all his fame Tasso remained little read. He was a reputation and a legend as much as a writer. And this continued: the Romantic poets, Byron and Shelley in particular, found in the story of Tasso's unrequited love, persecution, and madness an attractive emblem for their own misfortunes. Goethe's frequently translated play *Torquato Tasso* (1790) had established the myth more widely. Similarly, J. H. Wiffen's translation begins with a lengthy 'Life of Tasso', repeating the sad history, and closes with an 'Envoi', composed by Wiffen himself and addressed to Tasso's harp. 'Whisper of me to the few | I love', Wiffen pleads, and to those

> who reverence the wrong'd soul that planned
> Thy world of sound, with archangelic hand. . . .

> Yet was he wretched whom all tongues applaud, –
> For peace he panted, for affection pined:
> (Wiffen 1830: 500)

Mary Howitt's 'The Record of Poetry' in *The Desolation of Eyam* (1827) spoke of 'Immortal Tasso' as 'A wretched maniac, fettered, crushed to earth'.

John Black's *Life of Torquato Tasso* (1810) had taken issue with the more discreet and loyal accounts of Tasso's life written by his fellow Italians. Its defiant frankness laid claim to Tasso, as if only the honest, impartial English could see and tell the truth about him, as if only they had the truly feeling heart to sympathize with such a man. The many translations that followed were patriotic too, though they developed a different version of Tasso—one that made him less supine and more of a crusader. During a period of religious revival and imperial expansion, Tasso's story of Oriental despots being overthrown by Christian knights attracted a new audience.

Wiffen chooses Spenserian stanzas (instead of the original's *ottava rima*) and he feels the need to defend that choice. William Stewart Rose's widely respected translation of Ariosto (discussed below) had opted for *ottava rima*, but the Spenserian stanza was in Wiffen's view much better adapted to 'the sublime and solemn march, the spirit and genius of Tasso' (Wiffen 1830: ii). There is a patriotic feeling at work here, coupled with a desire to remove Tasso's poem from the flippant atmosphere of Byron's *ottava rima* poems, *Beppo* (1818) and *Don Juan* (1819–24). These had Italian sources themselves—in Luigi Pulci's *Morgante maggiore*, for instance, parts of which Byron translated while working on *Don Juan*. Wiffen, however, needed to ensure that Tasso remained 'sublime and solemn', uncontaminated and glorious, when translated into English. Spenserian stanzas fitted with the unironic idealism of the translation's historical moment.

When, for instance, near the opening of the poem, Godfrey is rousing his crusaders to set off for the Holy Land, Hoole's version reads:

> We fight to conquer Sion's hallow'd town;
> To free from servile yoke the Christian train
> Oppress'd so long, in slavery's galling chain:
> To find in Palestine a regal seat,
> Where piety may find a safe retreat;
> Where none the pilgrim's zeal shall more oppose,
> To adore the tomb, and pay his grateful vows.
> (Hoole 1763: I, 11–12)

Wiffen gives the same passage as follows.

> But far more glorious were our aims,—we vowed
> The noble walls of Sion to obtain,
> And work redemption for the Faithful, bowed
> Beneath subjection's ignominious chain;
> Founding in Palestine a purer reign
> Where Piety may rest, and Peace recline

>   In full security, and none restrain
>   The freeborn pilgrim, passing o'er the brine,
>   From offering holy vows at meek Messiah's shrine.
>   (Wiffen 1830: 7)

Leigh Hunt remarked in 1846 that Hoole was 'below criticism', and his couplets are crudely functional at times. The comparison brings out, nonetheless, Wiffen's grandiose style: 'ignominious' translates Tasso's 'indegno' perfectly well but is less punchy than Hoole's 'galling'. Wiffen's 'purer reign' and Hoole's 'regal seat' translate Tasso's 'novo regno'; similarly Tasso has no adjective for 'voto' (vows)—Wiffen makes them 'holy', Hoole makes them 'grateful'. Wiffen is determined to emphasize the sacred meaning of events. His crusade will 'work redemption for the Faithful' and not simply 'free from servile yoke'. Partly as a result of this, his translation becomes cluttered and weighty. Tasso's seriousness grows solemn.

The slant of Wiffen's translation is repeated in Benjamin Disraeli's *Tancred, or, The New Crusade* (1847), the third novel in his Young England trilogy, which evokes a similar idea of Tasso and refashions the plot of *Gerusalemme liberata* in striking ways. Disraeli reworks Tasso's story as a heroic romance offering inspiration to Victorian Christians (see O'Connor 1998). Another illustration of the same tendency can be found in the treatment of Tasso's early, romantic work *Aminta*. Leigh Hunt's *Amyntas: A Tale of the Woods* (1820) possesses Hunt's characteristic gracefulness; after Hunt, however, the poem was left untranslated until 1900. That side of Tasso—melancholic, sensuous, amatory—was displaced by a more muscular Christian poet.

Cary's Dante and Rose's Ariosto

The other major Italian epics, by Dante and Ariosto, were translated in the same period. For Ariosto's *Orlando furioso*, William Stewart Rose's translation, the only complete one done in the period, established itself as a classic. Like Leigh Hunt, Rose despised Hoole's translation. Its heroic couplets were, he said, 'the measure most opposite to that of Ariosto' because their pointedness and homogeneity ran counter to Ariosto's variety, his 'gallery of cabinet pictures...each of which is often only in harmony with itself' (Rose 1823–31: I, xi–xii). When he chose *ottava rima*, Rose was less anxious about invoking Byronic flippancy than about showing too much fidelity to the original—'so religious, some may think so superstitious, an observance of my author's text'. He countered this possible criticism by avoiding any hint of translationese; the result was a fluent, readable, eminently English version, one that quoted Milton when appropriate—'In the same strain of Roland will I tell | Things unattempted yet in prose or rhyme' (I, 3)—and one that could become on occasion plainly nationalistic. 'The account given here of [Merlin's] death does not vary from the ancient romancers' relations, except in that Ariosto has changed the scene from Britain, *the original seat of all sorcery and chivalry*, to France' (I, 97, *emphasis added*; on this subject later in the century, Reynolds 2001 is extremely useful). Rose was a friend of Walter Scott and dedicated the translation to him. Scott had translated the opening of Ariosto's poem in *Rob Roy* (1817) and invoked the Italian poet several times elsewhere in the Waverley Novels as a model of his own practice. Rose's version implies Scott's politics and aims to achieve Scott's facility in writing, even though, in the privacy of his journal, Scott mocked Rose's translation.

Henry Cary's version of Dante assimilated the original with equal success. His *The Vision of Dante*, first published complete in 1814, appeared in a new, much larger format edition in 1819 and again in 1831 and 1844, when Cary made many additions to the notes. It was read very widely, thanks in part to Coleridge's advocacy. Keats's *Hyperion* poems were influenced by its style, and its reputation grew (on the publication history, see p. 141–2, above, and Crisafulli 2003). Later in the century many more Dante translations appeared (discussed later in this section), but Cary's remained the classic version.

During the Romantic period, Dante was increasingly admired for the distinctness of his imagery, for the concision and precision of his comparisons, and for his 'combining', as Hazlitt put it in his 1818 *Lectures on the English Poets*, 'internal feelings with external objects' (Hazlitt 1930–4: V, 18). In Cary's translation, English blank verse (reminiscent in places of Milton but closer in its colloquiality to William Cowper, especially his 1791 translation of Homer) responds within its own structure to the patterns of Dante's *terza rima*.

In *Inferno* XIV, 28–30, for example, Dante compares the flakes of fire raining down on the damned to snowflakes in the Alps:

> Sovra tutto 'l sabbion, d'un cader lento,
> piovean di foco dilatate falde,
> come di neve in alpe sanza vento.

Cary translates the tercet in the following lines. Keats, when reading them, underlined the last two in his copy:[1]

> O'er all the sand fell slowly wafting down
> Dilated flakes of fire, as flakes of snow
> On Alpine summit, when the wind is hush'd.
> (Cary 1814: I, 58)

In the last line of the original, plain diction creates striking clarity and a nearly unpoetic directness. An unusually steady rhythm holds back reading that otherwise would hurry forward. Steadiness is achieved too through the lack of enjambement. Each element in the scene is dispassionately compiled and a comparison found without display or pomp.

Cary's writing imitates much of this restraint. Repeating the word 'flakes' might seem ungainly but it does reflect the parallel between 'di foco' and 'di neve' in the original—the unnerving parallel that initiates the simile. 'Dilated' too appears troublingly more remote from common usage than 'dilatate' is in Italian; the word

---

[1] The volumes are held in a private collection; the annotations are reproduced in Robert Gittings, *The Mask of Keats: A Study of Problems* (1956).

sounds more grandiose in English perhaps and in blank verse it becomes evocative of Milton's Latinisms (Milton uses the word four times in *Paradise Lost*), yet it is precise too and quasi-scientific. Cary achieves through the clash between 'wafting' and 'Dilated' (a clash highlighted by the lineation) something of the shocking simplicity of Dante's 'piovean', which simply means 'rained down'. Likewise, the stillness Dante engenders through the steadiness of the final line is imitated in Cary's half-line 'when the wind is hush'd.' Cary's alliteration ('when' and 'wind') and his assonance ('hush'd' recalls 'summit') assert a closing calm, after the miniature dramas of the previous lines, in which clashes of register and enjambements have drawn the reader on.

One example cannot encompass the complexity of the translation and its relations with Dante's original. Alison Milbank's discussion of the work's political affiliations is most illuminating (Milbank 1998) and Edoardo Crisafulli's study of Cary's version has brought out in it such variety and linguistic ingenuity as to make summarization difficult (Crisafulli 2003). Its quality is not in doubt: the translation was far more accurate than anything published before and Cary went to great lengths in later editions to correct his few errors in meaning. Arguably, his blank verse tended to realign Dante's (and the reader's) relation to narrated events, making it less spontaneous and the events less threatening. His style can be seen as making the poem more 'sublime and steady', like Wiffen's Tasso, and it was criticized from the outset for producing too stately a version of Dante. Even so, Cary's concern to stay as close as possible to Dante's sense created at times a remarkable English equivalent to Dante's laconic style. The translation successfully reflected Dante's reluctance to 'develop character' and his desire instead 'never to employ more than a stroke or two of his pencil, which he aims at imprinting almost insensibly on the hearts of his readers'.

A Changing Image of Italy, 1790–1860

The analysis of Dante just quoted was made by the Italian poet and scholar Ugo Foscolo, in the *Edinburgh Review* of 1818. Foscolo was living in London at the time, exiled from Italy after Napoleon's defeat in 1814 when northern Italy was returned to Austrian control. Foscolo wrote influential essays in English on Petrarch and Tasso during the 1820s and published an edition of the *Commedia* too (Corrigan 1969 reprints the essay on Petrarch and illuminates its context.) Though Foscolo died in poverty, he was a leading member of the Italian expatriate community in London, whose presence profoundly influenced the translation of Italian literature into English.

Italian had been a fashionable accomplishment since the late eighteenth century, when the popularity of Italian opera made the language popular and drew Italians (musicians and librettists) into the country. Numerous operas were published, usually in the original with an English translation attached. Generally speaking, it was not until the 1790s that translated versions began to stand alone. This change may reflect the taste for *opera seria*, which developed around the turn of the century, as well as a desire fully to naturalize the form. Lorenzo da Ponte's works began to be translated: *Iphigenia in Tauride* (1796), *The Island of Pleasure* (1801), and *The Rape of Proserpine* (1816), among many others (see pp. 420–4, below). Metastasio's dramas continued their triumphant career (see Vol. 3 of this *History*); for instance, Mozart's *La clemenza di Tito*, whose libretto was adapted from Metastasio, gave rise to Robert Jephson's *Conspiracy, a Tragedy* (1796), *The Clemency of Titus* by 'A Lady' (1828), and J. Ford's *Titus Vespasian* (1836). Some full-length translations accompanied this critical acclaim: John Hoole produced Metastasio's *Works* (1767), expanded in 1800 as *Dramas and Other Poems*. More usually, however, translations of Metastasio were occasional and consciously amateur. *Translations Chiefly from the Italian of Petrarch and Metastasio* (1795) by Thomas Le Mesurier is a characteristic example. Translation was sometimes designed to accompany a reading of the original text. (Coupling Petrarch with Metastasio was typical here.) Or, translating famous Italian lyric poems became a proof of refinement. Metastasio in particular, whose writing was relatively easy for the foreign reader, was translated very often in this way. Louisa Stuart Costello's *Songs of a Stranger* (1825) contains some of the best examples.

In Foscolo's case, widespread knowledge of the Italian language encouraged the publication of his works in the original rather than in translation. His novel *Ultime lettere di Jacopo Ortis*, first published in Milan in 1802, appeared in London in 1811, 1814, 1817, and 1818, the first translation, *Letters of Ortis*, by 'F.B.' appearing in 1814. Similarly, and this is more curious perhaps, a complete translation of Petrarch's *Canzoniere* did not appear until as late as 1854; an edition of *The Sonnets, Triumphs and Other Poems* came out in 1859, translated by various hands. In other words, because of the fashion for Italian, translation of many of the most popular Italian writers was less frequent than one might expect. More difficult writers were translated entire; the Italian lyric poets—Metastasio, Berni, Casti, Sannazaro, Sacchetti, and many others—were translated patchily. Translation at this time aimed more to celebrate familiar originals than to make them available.

One of the shorter poems frequently translated was Vincenzo Filicaia's sonnet 'Italia, O Italia'. It appeared in *Fraser's Magazine* (February 1835) as 'To Prostrate Italy', in a translation by Father Prout, and James Percival's 'Juvenilia' (in his 1859 *Poetical Works*) included 'Sonnet to Italy' based on the same original. Neither translation is especially distinguished, but they illustrate the growing connection between translation and Risorgimento feeling. In this vein, Macaulay had done a version of Filicaia's 'The Deliverance of Vienna' in 1828 (Macaulay 1866: I, 582–6). And one sonnet by the Renaissance Italian poet Gabriello Chiabrera was translated repeatedly for similar reasons—it was an opportunity to mourn the loss of Italy's 'martial zeal' during the Roman period and to bemoan its present corruption. Aubrey de Vere's version, 'The Italian People' in his *Song of Faith* (1842), is characteristic:

> We, day by day,
> To dalliance, and sweet sound, and idle dance,
> Contented give our dastard souls away;
> Prize of triumphant Force, each robber-despot's prey!

Wordsworth had translated several of Chiabrera's *Epitaffi* thirty years earlier while working on his own *Essays on Epitaphs*. For him, Chiabrera's poems perfectly exemplified the simplicity, sincerity, and heartfelt sentiments that were essential to the form of the epitaph.

This may suggest that the cause of Italian reunification dovetailed in England with a wider desire to recover integrity. It led, certainly, to a reassessment of the Italian tradition. Some Italian poetry was already a byword for decadent elaboration, notably the work of Marino: Foscolo in 1819 claimed that Tassoni 'was almost the only Italian poet of the era in which he flourished, who withstood the general corruption of taste introduced by Marino' (Foscolo 1819: 512), and Edmund Gosse, as late as the 1890s, disapproved of the 'Marini-like [sic] subtleties' he found in Christina Rossetti's verse (Gosse 1893: 217). In the 1830s and 1840s, the same dislike began to extend to Metastasio who fell rapidly from favour: Bulwer Lytton writing in the *Monthly Chronicle* for 1838 (I, 50) condemned him as part of 'a feeble and ephemeral school of the Italians', and G. H. Lewes (following Hegel) and Ruskin attacked his work on similar grounds. Increasingly ambiguous feelings surrounded Ariosto too, whose playfulness and languor could not be made over so easily into something more moral.

Translation focused on prose as Risorgimento fervour increased. Manzoni's classic *I promessi sposi* appeared in a succession of translations and new editions from Charles Swan's 1828 version onwards. His ode to Napoleon was translated by Gladstone in 1861. Similarly, Joseph Mazzini's essays and lectures, including the much read *On the Duties of Man*, were promptly reproduced in English versions: a six-volume *Life and Writings* came out in 1864–70. From comparable motives, English translators returned to Italian historians and political theorists: Machiavelli's *History of Florence and of the Affairs of Italy... together with The Prince*, an anonymous translation, was published (by Bohn) in 1847, after a gap of more than fifty years. The most recent previous translation of *The Prince* in 1810 by J. Scott Byerley (using the pseudonym John Scott Ripon) had been undertaken for different reasons: 'shewing the close analogy [with] the actions of Buonaparte'. Even so, it was not until the end of the century that Ninian Hill Thomson's devotion to Machiavelli assigned him the scholarly attention he deserved. A translation of *The Prince* appeared in 1882, with new editions in 1897 and 1913, and Thomson also translated his *Discourses on the First Decade of Titus Livius* (1883) and his *History of Florence* (1906).

Francesco Guicciardini, a historian contemporary with Machiavelli, was more palatable to the Victorians. His *Storia d'Italia* had been translated several times in the sixteenth and seventeenth centuries; in 1821, it was published in London in the original, adapted 'per uso degli studiosi della lingua italiana'. By the mid-century, attention focused on Guicciardini's *Temporal and Spiritual Power of the Pope* (1860), translated by J. Fowle, and on his *Maxims* (1845), translated by Emma Martin. Martin found parallels between Guicciardini and Pascal, Bacon, and others, elevating the author into a European pantheon. This did credit to the Italians and lent credence to their aspirations to nationhood, while Guicciardini's hostile account of the papacy chimed with the anticlerical views of Mazzini and other Italian republicans (on this subject, see Fraser 1992 and, for its wider context, Bullen 1994).

Thomas Roscoe can be seen pursuing a comparable agenda in his *Italian Novelists* (1825), a remarkable four-volume collection of Italian prose fiction, some fairly well known (Boccaccio, Machiavelli's 'Belphagor', Cinthio's source for Shakespeare's *Othello*) and some obscure. Roscoe's preface argues that Italian stories 'exhibit not unfrequently curious pictures of the history, manners and feelings of the people' and that such realism will help correct 'the too prevalent taste for the Gothic or romantic fiction'. When translating Albergati Capacelli, a late eighteenth-century writer, Roscoe sees him, along with Maffei, Pindemonti, and the dramatist Alfieri, as the predecessors of, 'such names as Foscolo, Manzoni, Monti, who have... infused a nobler and better spirit into the decaying energies of their national literature' (Roscoe 1836: I, iii–iv; IV, 131).

In the drama too, a similar pattern can be found. Carlo Goldoni's operas and comedies had enjoyed a considerable vogue during the mid- to late eighteenth century (see Vol. 3 of this *History*). The anonymous *The Four Nations*, a comic opera based on Goldoni's *La locandiera*, appeared in 1809, and *Love, Honor, and Interest: A Comedy* by John Galt in 1814. From then on, however, Goldoni received little attention. Although his collected works were translated into French in 1822, an English *Comedies of Goldoni* had to wait until 1892 and even then was far from complete. By contrast, Alfieri's heroic tragedies, brought to notice in England by Byron, remained current. Charles Lloyd's famous translation of the *Tragedies* (1815) prompted instead of restraining further translations. *Philip the Second* was perhaps the most popular of the plays among English audiences. It was translated by Fanny Holcroft in 1805, by L. T. Bergner in 1809, and again by C. O. Childe in 1844. The durability of his reputation was linked to Alfieri's personal notoriety. Another version of the complete plays (based on Lloyd's work) appeared in 1876, for instance, nearly coinciding with a reprint of Alfieri's *Memoirs*, first translated anonymously in 1810.

Rossetti

Sympathies with Italian patriots encouraged the native English Risorgimento poetry of Felicia Hemans, Elizabeth Barrett Browning, Swinburne, and many others (on this relation, especially among women, see Chapman and Stabler 2003). Risorgimento writing established too a stock image of the Italian expatriate revolutionary, like Signor Fosco in Wilkie Collins's *The Woman in White* (1860). Partly in reaction against this stereotype and this tradition, Dante Gabriel Rossetti produced a drastically revisionist translation of Dante and others in *The Early Italian Poets* (1861), reissued in an expanded form as *Dante and his Circle* (1872). The fervour, commitment, and robustness of Risorgimento taste were replaced in his work by a renewed focus on the inner life and the involutions of romantic love. Like Roscoe, Rossetti brought into English many hitherto unknown Italian writers, seeking to unsettle the received literary canon in the same way that he and his colleagues in the Pre-Raphaelite Brotherhood challenged Academic painting. In both forms, Rossetti went behind the well established to find the 'primitive'— genuine, fresh, and neglected.

These ambitions coincided with the medievalism of William Morris and Ruskin's praise of the gothic, and as with Victorian medievalism more widely, pursuit of the primitive was combined with pursuit of the ideal. Rossetti's translations have been frequently criticized for an excessive artifice that both ennobles and stifles the original. Modernist criticism—from T. S. Eliot to George Steiner— made him into a prime example of the contrived. Jacopo da Lentino's 'Canzonetta' begins, for example:

> Meravigliosamente
> un amor mi distringe
> e mi tene ad ogn'ora.
> Com'om che pone mente
> in altro exemplo pinge
> la simile pintura,
> così, bella, facc'eo,
> che 'infra lo core meo
> porto la tua figura.

Rossetti translates:

> Marvellously elate,
> Love makes my spirit warm
> With noble sympathies;
> As one whose mind is set
> Upon some glorious form,
> To paint it as it is;—
> I verily who bear
> Thy face at heart, most fair,
> Am like to him in this.
>   (Rossetti 2003: 243)

Rossetti's 'With noble sympathies' is the only positive insertion into the original and, arguably, 'Marvellously elate' cleverly imitates the impressiveness of 'Meravigliosamente', which commands a whole line in the original. Yet 'elate', 'noble', and 'verily' all contribute to the elevated diction of Rossetti's version and its consequent loss of directness. It aims to impress and it loses Lentino's appearance of self-confidence.

Examples of this tendency could be multiplied. Unfortunately perhaps, it is in his versions of Dante's *La vita nuova*, for which he is best known, that he writes in his most ornate style. Antique diction—'I wis', 'pilgrim-folk', etc.—creates a sacred, secret space for the expression of intense feeling (Rossetti 2003: 285, 290). Even so, modernism's hostility to Rossetti was partisan and out of sympathy with his sensibility. Critics like Steiner and Eliot undervalued (or simply ignored) how many unknown Italian poets Rossetti brought into English, creating a Pre-Raphaelite canon of Italian poetry. Moreover, his ornateness was discriminating. In his versions of Franco Sacchetti's light-hearted ballads and of Cecco Angiolieri's violent ill temper, Rossetti's style became much more immediate and energetic.

After Rossetti

In conjunction with his many paintings on Dantean themes—such as *Dante's Dream*, *Beata Beatrix*, and *Beatrice Meeting Dante at a Marriage Feast and Denying him her Salutation*—Rossetti's poems helped significantly to realign the English perception of Dante, making him less the severe moralist or indignant patriot and more like Petrarch or Tasso, the wounded, tortured lover. Translations of the *Commedia* continued to be produced regularly in the second half of the century in both prose and verse (for Charles Eliot Norton's prose version see p. 122, above). Henry Wadsworth Longfellow's 1865–7 translation into blank verse was the first to rival Cary's in popularity. Many others were hampered by their effort to reproduce Dante's *terza rima* in English, a technical feat that is nearly impossible (see pp. 66–7, above; and for some examples, Griffiths and Reynolds 2005). Longfellow's sacrifice of rhyme allowed him to follow Dante's word order more closely, so that for example at the close of *Purgatorio* IV he captures the original's fascination with exotic places and the world's vast extent. Dante had written:

> e dicea; 'Vienne omai: vedi ch'è tocco
> meridian dal sole, e a la riva
> cuopre la notte già col piè Morrocco.
> (ll. 136–8)

Longfellow's translation reads:

> And saying: 'Come now; see the sun has touched
> Meridian, and from the shore the night
> Covers already with her foot Morocco.
> (Longfellow 1865–7: II, 261)

Elsewhere, though, Longfellow's writing can be casual—again in *Purgatorio* IV, Dante's l. 103, 'Là ci traemmo; ed ivi eran persone' becomes 'Thither we drew; and there were persons there' (Longfellow 1865–7: II, 261)—and the ease of the writing affects the emotional range of the translation so that the narrator's feelings lose their characteristic, labile intensity.

Meanwhile, Dante's work was invoked in nineteenth-century visions of an urban hell. James Thomson's 'The City of Dreadful Night' (1874) and George Gissing's *The Nether World* (1889) both assume familiarity with Dante's *Inferno*. But another writer was a nearer source of inspiration, particularly for Thomson. Two epigraphs to Thomson's poem came from Giacomo Leopardi, the Italian Romantic poet, whose work was slowly becoming better known. Thomson himself translated *Twelve Dialogues* (1893), a selection from Leopardi's *Operette morali*, which had already appeared complete as *Essays and Dialogues* (1882), translated by Charles Edwardes. Although French and German translations of Leopardi's poems appeared in 1880 and 1878 respectively, an English translation did not appear until a little later, in 1887.

Leopardi's influence in English literature was significant at this time, though it was more a matter of a pervading tone than the result of particular works being translated. His nihilistic melancholy produced a heroic stance in his poetry, comparable to Nietzsche's philosophy, and his denial of any unifying truth that might give meaning to life manifested itself in the provisional, quasi-fragmentary status of his works. These qualities made him very similar to the guilt-stricken and despairing Dante whom Rossetti painted; furthermore, rather like Rossetti's stylistic artifice, Leopardi's thought set at a distant remove the ideal forms of feeling and belief that he yearned after. Arguably, he was 'translated' most effectively via Thomson's imitations.

This cultural context also left its mark on J. A. Symonds's 1878 version of Michelangelo's sonnets, 'now for the first time translated into rhymed English'. Symonds returned to Michelangelo's original manuscripts, previously available only in versions altered by the artist's great-nephew. Censoring Michelangelo's more extreme utterances was, according to Symonds, thoroughly misguided. It was, first, over-cautious: 'Nothing is more clear', he wrote in his introduction, 'than that Michelangelo worshipped Beauty in the Platonic spirit, passing beyond its personal and specific manifestations to the universal and impersonal' (Symonds 1878: 13). Secondly, it erased Michelangelo's distinctive plangency. When Symonds translated the original versions—with all their homosexual implications and political venom—he refused to tone them down:

> S' i' amo sol di te, signor mio caro,
> quel che di te più ami, no ti sdegni;
> che l'un dell'altro spirto s'innamora.

The last line here was heightened in Symonds's version to 'Souls burn for souls, spirits to spirits cry!' (Symonds 1878: 132–3). Michelangelo is being incorporated into a Pre-Raphaelite aesthetic.

Symonds's advocacy of Michelangelo may be related to a wider improvement in Petrarch's status at the end of the century, which is revealed by the sudden increase in translations. Richard Garnett published a set of translations, *Dante, Petrarch, Camoens* (1896); A. Crompton produced *One Hundred Sonnets of Petrarch* (1898); and there was an anonymous *Selections from the Canzoniere* (1891). Concurrently, professional scholarship began to have a greater bearing on translation, as it sought to fill in the background of famous literary figures. In Petrarch's case, there was a polemic edge to such work as literary scholars, eager to vindicate the discipline in which they worked, found a literary scholar lurking even in Petrarch, previously viewed mainly as a poet of sensibility and feeling. Maud Jerrold's still worthwhile study *Francesco Petrarca: Poet and Humanist* (1909) authoritatively established this new image.

Likewise, Boccaccio received renewed attention; the full range of his output was brought into view via a series of translations, most notably the unexpurgated *Decameron* of John Payne (1886), published under the auspices of the François Villon Society (on which see p. 233, above). Payne's Boccaccio, self-consciously antique and sometimes precious, moulds Boccaccio's original to suit the assumptions of nineteenth-century medievalism, especially that of William Morris. Before this, there had been many versions of individual stories from the *Decameron* since the Romantic period: Keats's 'Isabella, or, The Pot of Basil' (1818) and *A Sicilian Story* (1820) by 'Barry Cornwall' are well known; Elizabeth (or Eliza) Sotheby's *Patient Griselda. A Tale* (1798) deserves to be. Translations of the whole collection had been hampered by the indecency of several stories, and part of the interest for late nineteenth-century readers of Boccaccio lay in his transgressing of Victorian taste. He was a respected, 'classic' writer, a worthy object of study, and an outrage to conventional morality.

As in the English novel at the end of the century, a wish to disrupt the authority of the centre led to an interest in provincial life. Hardy's novels and American local colour fiction contributed to that trend. Osgood and McIlvaine, the publisher of Hardy's first collected edition in 1895–6, began to publish at about the same time translations of Giuseppe Verga's Sicilian novels: *I Malavoglia (The House by the Medlar Tree)* (1890) and *Master Don Gesualdo* (1893), translated by Mary A. Craig, both appeared under their imprint. This coincided with the rediscovery of Goldoni, seen now as a distinctively Venetian writer. Eleonora Duse, the famous actor and wit, published her 'verbatim' translation of Verga's *Cavalleria rusticana* in one volume with Goldoni's *La locandiera* in 1894. The rehabilitation led eventually to Goldoni's inclusion in the repertoire of Lady Gregory's Abbey Theatre in Dublin, and to D. H. Lawrence's 1920s translations of Verga.

One general feature can be found in these later nineteenth-century translations from Italian: where Ruskin found in Dante 'the central man of all the world', his successors tried to recover subjectivity, even eccentricity. Their translations went in search of the variety—the isolated consciousnesses, the hidden and sometimes despairing experience—articulated within Italian literature.

LIST OF SOURCES

Translations
'B., F.' (1814). *Letters of Ortis* [Foscolo]. London.
Boyd, Henry (1785). *A Translation of the Inferno of Dante Alighieri, in English Verse*, 2 vols. Dublin.
—— (1802). *The Divina Commedia of Dante Alighieri consisting of Inferno—Purgatorio—and Paradiso*, 3 vols. London.
—— (1807). *The Triumphs of Petrarch*. London.
Cary, Henry Frances (1805–6). *The Inferno of Dante Alighieri, with a Translation in English Blank Verse*, 2 vols. London.
—— (1814). *The Vision, or, Hell, Purgatory, and Paradise of Dante Alighieri*, 3 vols. London.
Cliffe, Francis Henry (1893). *The Poems of Leopardi*. London.
Cornwall, Barry, pseud. [Bryan Waller Proctor] (1820). *A Sicilian Story, with Diego de Montilla, and other poems* [Boccaccio]. London.

Craig, Mary A. (1890). *I Malavoglia (The House by the Medlar Tree)* [Verga]. New York.
—— (1893). *Master Don Gesualdo* [Verga]. London.
de Vere, Sir Aubrey (1842), *A Song of Faith, Devout Exercises and Sonnets* [Chiabrera]. London.
Duse, Eleonora (1894). *Verga's 'Cavalleria Rusticana' and Goldoni's 'La Locandiera'*. London.
Griffiths, Eric, and Reynolds, Matthew, eds. (2005). *Dante in English*. London.
Homer, Philip Bracebridge (1790). *Poems Translated from the Italian of Metastasio*. London.
Hoole, John (1763). *Jerusalem Delivered: An Heroic Poem, Translated from the Italian of Torquato Tasso*, 2 vols. London.
—— (1783). *Orlando Furioso* [Ariosto], 5 vols. London.
—— (1791). *The Orlando of Ariosto, Reduced to XXIV Books, the Narrative Connected, And the Stories Disposed in a Regular Series*, 2 vols. London.
Hunt, Leigh (1816). *The Story of Rimini*. [Dante]. London.
—— (1820). *Amyntas: A Tale of the Woods* [Tasso]. London.
—— (1846). *Stories from the Italian Poets: with Lives of the Writers*, 2 vols. London.
Le Mesurier, Thomas (1795). *Translations Chiefly from the Italian of Petrarch and Metastasio*. Oxford.
Lloyd, Charles (1815). *The Tragedies of Vittorio Alfieri*, 3 vols. London.
Longfellow, Henry Wadsworth (1865–7). *The Divine Comedy of Dante Alighieri*, 3 vols. Boston, MA.
Lyell, Charles (1835). *The Canzoniere of Dante Alighieri including the Poems of the Vita Nuova and Convito*. London.
Macaulay, Thomas Babington (1866). *Works*, ed. Lady Trevelyan, 8 vols. London.
Nott, John (1808). *Petrarch Translated, in a Selection of his Sonnets and Odes*. London.
Payne, John (1886). *The Decameron of G. Boccacci*, 3 vols. London (limited edition for the François Villon Society).
Piozzi, Mrs, et al. (1785). *The Florence Miscellany*. Florence.
Roscoe, Thomas (1836). *The Italian Novelists... from the Earliest Period down to the Close of the Eighteenth Century*, 4 vols. London (1st pub. 1825).
Rose, William Stewart (1823–31). *Orlando Furioso* [Ariosto], 8 vols. London.
Rossetti, Dante Gabriel (2003). *Collected Poetry and Prose*, ed. Jerome McGann. New Haven, CT.
Swan, Charles (1828). *The Betrothed Lovers* [Manzoni], 3 vols. Pisa.
Symonds, J. A. (1878). *The Sonnets of Michelangelo Buonarroti and Tommaso Campanella, Now for the First Time Translated into Rhymed English*. London.
Thomson, James (1893). *Twelve Dialogues* [Leopardi]. London.
T[homson], N[inian] H[ill] (1882). *The Prince* [Machiavelli]. London.
[Venturi, Emilie H.] (1862). *The Duties of Man* [Mazzini]. London.
Wiffen, J. H. (1830). *The Jerusalem Delivered of Torquato Tasso*, 3rd edn., 2 vols. London (first pub. 1824).
Wrangham, Francis (1817). *A Few Sonnets Attempted from Petrarch in Early Life*. Lee Priory, Kent.

Other Sources
Brand, C. P. (1957). *Italy and the English Romantics: The Italianate Fashion in Early Nineteenth-Century England*. Cambridge.
Bullen, J. B. (1994). *The Myth of the Renaissance in Nineteenth-Century Writing*. Oxford.
Chapman, Alison, and Stabler, Jane, eds. (2003). *Unfolding the South: Nineteenth-Century British Women Writers and Artists in Italy*. Manchester.

Corrigan, Beatrice, ed. (1969). *Italian Poets and English Critics, 1755–1859: A Collection of Critical Essays*. Chicago, IL.
Crisafulli, Edoardo (2003). *The Vision of Dante: Cary's Translation of 'The Divine Comedy'*. Market Harborough.
Cunningham, G. F. (1955–6). *The Divine Comedy in English: A Critical Bibliography*, 2 vols. Edinburgh.
Ellis, Steve (1983). *Dante and English Poetry: Shelley to T. S. Eliot*. Cambridge.
Fiske, Willard (1882). *A Catalogue of Petrarch's Books*. Ithaca, NY.
Foscolo, Ugo (1819). 'Narrative and Romantic Poems of the Italians.' *Quarterly Review* 42: 486–556.
Fraser, Hilary (1992). *The Victorians and Renaissance Italy*. Oxford.
Gosse, Edmond (1893). 'Christina Rossetti.' *Century* 24: 211 ff.
Havely, N. R., ed. (1998). *Dante's Modern Afterlife: Reception and Response from Blake to Heaney*. Basingstoke.
Hazlitt, William (1930–4). *The Complete Works*, ed. P. P. Howe, 21 vols. London.
Milbank, Alison (1998). *Dante and the Victorians*. Manchester.
O'Connor, Maura (1998). *The Romance of Italy and the English Political Imagination*. Basingstoke.
Pite, Ralph (1994). *The Circle of our Vision: Dante's Presence in English Romantic Poetry*. Oxford.
Reynolds, Matthew (2001). *The Realms of Verse 1830–1870: English Poetry in a Time of Nation-Building*. Oxford.
Tinkler-Villani, V. (1989). *Visions of Dante in English Poetry: Translations of the 'Commedia' from Jonathan Richardson to William Blake*. Amsterdam.
Toynbee, Paget (1909). *Dante in English Literature from Chaucer to Cary (c.1380–1844)*, 2 vols. London.

6.4 Spanish and Portuguese

Anthony Pym and John Style

New translations of complete books from Spain and Portugal would perhaps reach some 200 titles in the nineteenth century, if we use a narrow conception of literature (see the various partial catalogues by Hills 1920, Pane 1944, O'Brien 1963, Rudder 1975, and Sousa 1992 for Camões). These translations were initially motivated in part by the presence of a largely bilingual British commercial colony in Portugal, and then by the growth of travel to the Iberian peninsula. Specific impetus, however, came from the cultural impact of the Peninsular wars of 1808–14, in particular the influence of Robert Southey. The number of new translations then sank to a point of relative insignificance and only really revived in the 1870s, when changes in the publishing industry created a demand for popular novels, including those of Iberian naturalism. Before 1880, the average age of the texts translated was just over 200 years, and most of the translators were men. After 1890, the average age was just under 50 years, and most of the translators were women. Here we shall approach those very different dynamics chronologically.

Southey and the Peninsular Wars

Of the figures associated with English Romanticism, Robert Southey was by far the most receptive to Iberian cultures. His connection with the peninsula was established through his uncle and patron the Revd Herbert Hill, chaplain of the British trading community in Lisbon (see Cabral 1959). Hill called his nephew to Lisbon in 1795, a visit reflected in Southey's *Letters Written during a Short Residence in Spain and Portugal*. With those letters we find notes on Iberian literature and versions of poems by Quevedo, Lope de Vega, and Luis de León, among others, rendered with a Romantic freedom that receives tenuous justification: 'I have always done justice to the originals by annexing them' (Southey 1797: I, 3). Southey again sailed for Portugal in 1800 with the intention of collecting material to write his history of that country, returning to England in 1801 and settling in the Lake District, where his 14,000-volume library at Keswick Hall contained a collection of Portuguese and Spanish texts probably unique in England. In 1803 he published translations of poems by Camões, but his interests were soon to turn elsewhere.

Southey's influence on English letters became explicitly political when he gave voice to those who would have Britain side with Spain against the Napoleonic regime. He engaged Wordsworth and his circle in the cause (see Buceta 1923, 1924). The alliance with one of Britain's traditional enemies was indeed made, and

Portugal was brought into the coalition. The war of attrition waged by the Spanish guerrillas and the Spanish-Portuguese-British army under Sir Arthur Wellesley eventually drove the French army out of the Iberian peninsula. The sustained military presence on Iberian soil raised awareness of contemporary Spain and Portugal, to the extent that English letters began to see the Iberian peninsula as a part of the European landscape, worthy of greater attention. Byron visited the peninsula in 1809; both he and Shelley translated some poetry from Spanish. However, the project of converting a traditional enemy into a contemporary ally required more than a few literary conversions and visits. A large-scale translation project could significantly help change perception of the Iberian other.

The number of translations rose following the Peninsular wars. It was also reinforced by a number of re-editions. For example, Mickle's 1776 version of Camões's *Os Lusíadas* (discussed in Vol. 3 of this *History*) reached its seventh edition in 1807, its eighth and ninth in 1809. There was, however, a certain reductionism at work in the choice of texts. Thanks in part to the common opposition to Napoleon, British eyes were disposed to see the Spanish and Portuguese cultures as belonging to a single space at a time when, as now, the cultures themselves insisted quite emphatically on their differences. This conflation continued long into the nineteenth century. Very little attention was paid to Iberian languages other than Portuguese and Spanish, thus presenting an image of centralized nations, and there were relatively few translations of Iberian writers who were politically liberal and thus usually Francophile (many of them exiled in France and later in Britain). Further selective blindness grew as the very positive values projected on Portuguese and Spanish culture were contradicted by awareness of the economic and military decline of the Iberian present. The translations that responded to the Peninsular wars were mostly of medieval or sixteenth-century texts. The authors most translated in the nineteenth century were Cervantes, Camões, and Calderón, writers of the sixteenth and seventeenth centuries, representing the age when Portugal and then Spain were still world superpowers. Indeed, some of the translations implicitly sought to take over the mantle of empire, as is suggested by the work of Southey, both before and during the wars.

Southey turned his attention to medieval epic and romance. He translated a Portuguese version of the famous medieval romance as *Amadis of Gaul* (1803) and abridged Anthony Munday's sixteenth-century version of *Palmerin of England* (1807). More influential, however, was his *Chronicle of the Cid* (1808), created from the medieval Spanish prose chronicle and drawing on popular ballads. Southey did not work from the fourteenth-century *Poema del mio Cid*, but he did present John Hookham Frere's translations from it as an appendix, albeit not naming Frere (the translations were eventually included in Frere's *Works*, 1874).

There were at least seven other versions of the Cid story in the nineteenth century, but Southey's remained the most popular and deserves some attention. Its prose is archaizing, and reminiscent of the Authorized Version in rhythm, syntax, and diction. This is rather an elegant solution to the problem of translating a twelfth-century text, which could not be done in twelfth-century English (Spanish has changed much less than English over the centuries). The solution was nevertheless strongly ideological. Southey placed the value of the Hispanic cultures in the medieval past, well before any conflict with British imperial interests. He sought not only 'those heroic remembrances which are the strength and glory of a nation' (letter to Walter Savage Landor, 19 December 1821, in Southey 1965: II, 231), but also the conversion of a distant past into a call to action. In 1808 he claimed to 'hold up the war [against Napoleon] as a crusade on the part of us and the Spaniards (I love and vindicate the crusades)' (letter to Grosvenor C. Bedford, 17 November 1808, in 1849: III, 187). Nothing better, then, than to have the archetypal crusader sounding like an English Bible. At the same time, however, the biblical tone is combined with the flatness of medieval narrative, producing occasional comic effects that Southey presumably did not seek:

Now it behoves that ye should know whence he came, and from what men he was descended, because we have to proceed with his history. (Southey 1808: 2)

At this time it came to pass that there was strife between Count Don Gomez the Lord of Gormaz, and Diego Laynez the father of Rodrigo; and the Count insulted Diego and gave him a blow. (Southey 1808: 3)

A rather different tone informs Frere's translations from the epic poem, where we find an attempt to imitate the irregular versification of the Spanish. A later translator, John Ormsby, would regard Frere's version as 'bordering on vulgarity' and 'provoking an air of condescension' (1879: 3, 4), as he cleared the ground for his *Cid* in 1879 (Ormsby made much the same critique of previous versions of *Don Quijote*, which he also translated). Ormsby's *Cid*, mixing verse with narrative prose, selected a sanitized Romantic register that remains pedagogically serviceable. A full scholarly verse rendition of the medieval poem would not appear until the three-volume translation and critical edition by the American millionaire Archer Milton Huntington, published in 1897–1903.

Ballads and Poetry

While Southey gave himself wholeheartedly to Spanish epic prose, which he found could be 'exquisitely poetical', he considered the verse ballads 'made in general upon one receipt' and at times 'completely prosaical' (letter to Walter Scott, 6 November 1808, in Southey 1849: III, 178). Despite notable collections such as Lord Strangford's versions of Camões's lyrics in 1803, some decades would pass before Iberian verse was consistently rendered in English verse.

In 1823 Thomas Roscoe translated Sismondi's four-volume *Historical View of the Literature of the South of Europe*, which included versions of Camões, Bernardes, and da Cunha (from Portuguese) and Santillana, Hurtado de Mendoza, and Villegas (from Spanish). The same year also saw the publication of J. H. Wiffen's translations of the sixteenth-century poet Garcilaso de la Vega and, with rather more impact, John Gibson Lockhart's *Ancient Spanish Ballads, Historical and Romantic* (1823). Based on Depping's 1817 editions of the source texts, Lockhart's collection includes Moorish as well as sixteenth-century ballads and passages from *The Cid*. All the translations are presented with a scholarly introduction, suggesting an antiquarian approach to popular culture, in line with Walter Scott's work on Scottish border ballads (for further discussion of Lockhart's ballads, see p. 435, below).

Following Lockhart, John Bowring's *Ancient Poetry and Romances of Spain* evinces ethnographical inspiration, drawing on Moorish as well as troubadour sources in order to present a popular culture considered 'interesting, because it is truly national' (Bowring 1824: vi). Bowring chooses shorter metres close to his sources, managing well enough to preserve the external rhyme scheme. Here are the first lines of his version of Jorge Manrique's thirteenth-century 'Coplas' ('Ode'):

> Awake, awake, my sleeping soul!
> Rouse from thy dreams of hope and fear
> And think, and see
> How soon life's busy moments roll,
> How soon the hour of death draws near,—
> How silently!
>
> (1824: 235)

Lockhart and Bowring effectively opened the way for a more self-assured poetic voice. Henry Wadsworth Longfellow visited Spain on a study journey in 1826–9 and did his own version of Manrique ('Verses for his Father's Death'), as well as sonnets by Lope de Vega and Francisco de Aldana. His Manrique rendition begins:

> Oh let the soul her slumbers break
> Let thought be quickened, and awake,
> Awake to see
> How soon this life is past and gone,
> And death comes softly stealing on,
> How silently!
>
> (Longfellow 1845: 655)

Longfellow also experimented with the boundaries between translation and original creation, interestingly incorporating lines from a Spanish ballad in his poem 'The Secret of the Sea', which explicitly refers to Count Arnaldos.

Longfellow's major contribution to awareness of Iberian verse was his *The Poets and Poetry of Europe* (1845). This massive anthology (on which see p. 29, above) functions rather like a grand tour of the literary Continent, bringing together existing translations rather than creating new ones. The result, admits Longfellow, is 'a collection, rather than a selection' (Longfellow 1845: v). The introduction to Spanish literature is remarkable in that it mentions some of the various languages of Spain (Valencian, Galician, Leonin, Catalan, Majorcan, although not Basque). Yet it is in keeping with the general focus of the day in that the actual translations are almost all from standard Spanish (Castilian) and are heavily focused on a heroic Hispanic past, having almost nothing to show for the eighteenth or nineteenth centuries (just ten pages, out of a total of ninety-five). The volume includes translations by Frere, Bowring, Byron (the Moorish ballad 'Woe is me, Alhama'), Lockhart, Wiffen, Roscoe, Shelley (fragments from Calderón), Bryant, and others, as well as anonymous versions found in the *Edinburgh Review*, the *Quarterly*

Review, *Fraser's Magazine*, and similar publications. Longfellow himself translates Manrique, a song by López Maldonado, and a sonetta by Vega Carpio. The Portuguese section is rather shorter (just thirty-six pages) and includes translations by Strangford, Roscoe, Bowring, and Adamson. In all, the volume is a remarkable piece of research, selflessly presenting the translations of others.

A very different approach is found in James Kennedy's *Modern Poets and Poetry of Spain* (1852). For Kennedy, Spanish poetry is not exotic or 'Moorish'; it displays 'simplicity of expression and propriety of thought' of the kind that one finds, claims the translator, only in English literature (vii–ix). One might thus expect a simple exercise in domestication. Full rhymes and similar metres are indeed used throughout, imposing a certain homogeneity on a 'modern' Spain that dates from the late eighteenth century, running from Jovellanos to Zorilla. The selection is nevertheless as interesting for its politics as it might be for its verse. Included here are the voices of Spanish exiles, particularly Francophiles like Jovellanos and Moratín, whose positions had been marginalized by the alliance against Napoleon. Kennedy's selection emphasizes external views of Spain's contemporary decline and its relations with Britain. We find Arriaza and Quintana writing on the Battle of Trafalgar; Martínez de la Rosa writing about Spain from London in 1811; Espronceda doing the same from London in 1829.

These voices would prove a minor counterweight to the heroic historical Iberia. From Portuguese, one also notes Edgar Prestage's 1894 translation of Antero de Quental's sonnets of 1881, possibly carried out on a suggestion from Richard Burton. For the rest, the most translated writers were Cervantes, Camões, and Calderón, from the sixteenth and seventeenth centuries.

Cervantes

The English nineteenth century saw full versions of *Don Quijote* by Mary Smirke (1818), Alexander James Duffield (1881), John Ormsby (1885), and Henry Edward Watts (1888), as well as numerous anonymous renderings and revisions or re-editions of previous translations. Smirke is mentioned only as the 'editor' of a translation ostensibly pieced together from previous versions, yet the selection reads well as a new version. First published in a luxurious edition to accompany her husband's illustrations to the text, the translation ran to seventeen editions and actually outlived her husband's illustrations (an 1877 revision has fifty plates by Sir John Gilbert). Alexander J. Duffield's translation was published at the expense of the translator and was accompanied by a book on Quixote criticism. The translation was reviewed by an anonymous contemporary as 'pretentious, uncouth, ungrammatical, and weighed down with obsolete words' (Anon. 1885: 267); it had no second edition. John Ormsby's version, which the same review praised as having precisely the opposite values, remains philologically sound and ran to ten editions. Watts's scholarly annotated translation appeared in a restricted edition in 1888 'intended for a limited circle of students and lovers of Cervantes' and was republished in a smaller format in 1895, complete with index and maps. All these versions nevertheless proved less popular than the previous translations by Jarvis (1742, with seventy-nine editions in the nineteenth century, including revisions) and Smollett (1755, with twenty).

This preference for the earlier translations might be attributed to the ageing of Cervantes' text, which was becoming a classic (and being reappraised as such in Spain) at the same time as its comic variants were entering popular culture. Pane (1944: 72) lists some ten 'unidentified' nineteenth-century translations in addition to those we have mentioned, then gives a long list of adaptations like *The Spirit of Cervantes, or, Don Quixote Abridged* (1820), *Stories and Chapters from Don Quixote, Versified* (c.1830) or *The Story of the Don, Rewritten for our Young Folks* (1870). Such popular renderings of the text might draw on the energy of Shelton's 1612 version, or more especially on the confidence of Motteux or Smollett in the eighteenth century, who did not flinch from a little bawdiness or popular language. The nineteenth-century translators, however, showed considerable reluctance to adopt a contemporary voice. If the text was a classic, it was not to be confused with the comedy of popular adaptations. The narrative voice thus had to be situated firmly in the past. The contact with popular culture was not the only aspect of the text that suffered as a consequence.

The language spoken by Don Quixote should be that of the romances he has been reading, and thus of an age earlier than the narrator. To attribute archaic language to the narrator is to risk losing the fundamental distinction between narrator and hero. However, to make the narrator speak contemporary language would mean compromising the work's classical status. How this problem was handled can be seen in the 'Author's Preface', where the Spanish has the author speak to the reader in the intimate second person *tú*, while a discussion between the author and a literary friend is in the formal second person *vos*. Most versions done in the seventeenth and eighteenth centuries render this as *thou* (informal) as opposed to *you* (formal); all those of the twentieth century lose this distinction by using *you* throughout (since *thou* is now archaic rather than informal). At which point did this transition occur? The use of *you* throughout (i.e. an informal *you*) can actually be found in eighteenth-century versions by Motteux/Ozell (1762) and Kelly (1769). But the new versions of the nineteenth century generally resisted the transition:

Smirke (1818)	READER, thou wilt believe me, I trust, without an oath
Jarvis (1809, 1824)	You may believe me, without an oath, gentle reader
Jarvis/Clark (1864–67)	You may depend upon my bare word, reader, without any farther security
Jarvis/Johannot (1870)	Loving reader, thou wilt believe me, I trust, without an oath
Ormsby (1885)	IDLE READER: thou mayest believe me without any oath
Watts (1888)	IDLE READER; thou canst believe me without an oath

Smirke, Ormsby, and Watts all prefer the archaic *thou*, which by this stage was expressing anything but an intimate relation with the reader. They accorded the text the decorum deemed appropriate for a world classic. On the other hand, we find revisions of the seventeenth-century Jarvis version straddling the divide (one with *you*, the other with *thou*), and a more extensive revision, by J. W. Clark for a popular version sold in parts in 1864–7, also with *you*. Note also the problematic renderings of Cervantes' naming of the reader as *desocupado* (un-busy): 'idle reader' is slightly humorous but possibly a little insulting for a classic of world literature. Ormsby and Watts nevertheless risk the humour, placing philological literalism above consistency in the narrative voice.

Cervantes' theatre was far less translated than his *Quijote*. One notes *Persiles and Segismunda* rendered by Louise Dorothea Stanley in 1856, *Galatea* by G. W. J. Gyll in 1867, *Numantia* and *The Commerce of Algiers* by Gyll in 1870, and *Numantia* by James Y. Gibson, 'Magistrate in Zululand', in 1885. The last-mentioned play, about the heroic defence of a Spanish town under siege, lent itself to a certain imperial parallelism. Gibson's 1885 translation is in heroic verse, in full archaic battledress ('In very sooth...'), and related most tenuously to the valour of British imperialism: 'we have ventured to link the name of Gordon with that of Cervantes [since] this Quixotism, what is it but the sublime of imprudence' (Gibson 1885: xvii). Similar heroism is to be found in Gibson's work on the Cid ballads (1887). Indeed, the strategy of imperial parallelism might be traced back to Southey's manipulation of the Spanish crusades; a comparable case is that of the Portuguese poet Luís de Camões.

Camões

Camões's epic poem *Os Lusíadas* (1592) sings the heroism of Vasco da Gama and the Portuguese colonies in India. The text most clearly served the British tendency to place Iberian virtues in the distant past. That is no doubt why there were re-editions of Mickle's translation in the years of the Peninsular wars. There were also significant new translations throughout the century.

In a systematic comparison of these translations, Ramos and Lousada (1992) reveal shifts of various kinds. The earlier versions tended to highlight commercial aspects and the racial superiority of Europe. Following Fanshawe's initial translation in 1655, Mickle's long-lived version in rhyming verse, first published in 1776, appealed to the principle that 'None but a Poet can translate a Poet' in order to justify significant changes to the poem. Frequent amplifications focus on exotic details and eroticism, in constant capital letters. This was the vision of heroic Portugal that was to serve the period of the Peninsular wars. Thomas Moore Musgrave, on the other hand, translating in 1826, chose blank verse and omitted licentious details. His version was followed in 1853 by Edward Quillinan's translation in *ottava rima*, published posthumously with notes by the scholar and translator John Adamson. The following year, in 1854, Sir T. L. Mitchell published a closer literal version, albeit toning down erotic details and using the occasional Gallicism or archaism in order to give the text an erudite tone. In 1878 John James Aubertin was the first translator to have his version published alongside an edition of the original. His translation follows the original closely, imitating the syntactic inversions of the Portuguese. In 1880, marking the third centenary of Camões's death, Robert ffrench Duff's version of *Os Lusíadas* used prosodic expansion (adding a ninth line to the *ottava rima*) for the purposes of highlighting detail. Quite a different intention was at work, however, in Richard Francis Burton's rendition, also of 1880, where numerous archaisms and the workings of alliteration and rhyme are used to amplify not only heroism but also the highly lyrical moments:

> Thou, only thou, pure Love, whose cruel might
> obligeth human hearts to weal and woe,
> thou, only thou, didst wreak such foul despight.
> (III, 119, 1–3)

These same devices mark Burton's versions of Camões's lyric poetry, published in 1884 and by far the most complete translation in the nineteenth century. This is not to say Camões's verse had been entirely overlooked: Lord Strangford translated some thirty-seven poems in 1803, Aubertin rendered seventy sonnets in 1881, Garnett gave a further selection of sonnets in 1896, and the numerous translators of smaller selections were often those who worked on *Os Lusíadas* or translated from Spanish as well: Southey, Adamson, Bowring (two poems in his *Ancient Poetry and Romances of Spain*), Roscoe, Quillinan, Lady Wilde, and Duff (for a detailed bibliography of these and more, see Igreja 1992). Although Burton and Aubertin stayed relatively close to Camões, many of the earlier translators were engaged in the business of Romantic re-creation, highlighting the lyricism of Camões as a love-torn poet.

As that particularly Romantic reading of Camões's verse waned, there were corresponding changes in renditions of his epic. Ramos and Lousada (1992: 45) find that the earlier translations of *Os Lusíadas* (Fanshawe, Mickle and Musgrave) highlight the heroic role of the individual hero, Vasco da Gama. From the mid-nineteenth century, however, the renditions tended to emphasize the heroic role of the Portuguese *people*. Ramos and Lousada cite the following renditions of the line 'Que eu canto o peito ilustre Lusitano' (I, 3, 5), literally 'That I sing the illustrious Lusitanian breast'. The variations show a shift of narrative focus:

Fanshawe (1655)	For to a Man recorded in this Peece
Mickle (1776)	A nobler Hero's deeds demand my lays ... Illustrious GAMA, whom the waves obey'd
Musgrave (1826)	I sing th'illustrious Lusitanian Chief
Quillinan (1853)	I sing the illustrious Lusian heart so bold
Mitchell (1854)	I sing the illustrious valour Lusitanian
Aubertin (1878)	I sing a daring Lusitanian name
Burton (1880)	The noble Lusian's stouter breast sing I
Duff (1880)	I will chant the praise	of Lusian chiefs
Hewitt (1883)	Since I rehearse the noble Lusian breast

These few lines also illustrate a growing tendency to stay closer to the words in the source. At the same time, an archaizing translationese persists right through to the end of the nineteenth century. This was certainly a marked strategy in Burton's renditions, in keeping with the kind of classicization we have noted in versions of *Don Quijote*.

The translators of Camões (studied by Ferreira 1992) included remarkably few people entirely operating within English-speaking countries. Musgrave was in Lisbon in 1819–1820 as an agent for a shipping company. Richard Harris was a member of the British community in Porto and published his translations in the community's journal *The Lusitanian*. Quillinan was brought up in the Porto colony and fought in the Peninsular wars. Lieutenant Colonel Sir Thomas Livingstone Mitchell fought in the Peninsular wars then went to Australia, translating Camões during a return voyage. Aubertin was a railway engineer who had worked in Brazil before living in Portugal for several years; the second edition of his bilingual *Lusiads* was dedicated to Luís I of Portugal and was well received by the Portuguese critics. Robert ffrench Duff, from an English family that had resided in Portugal for many generations, was responsible for a paper factory, only turning to translation when approaching his seventieth year. His version (1880) was dedicated to King Fernando II of Portugal and printed at the National Printing Office in Lisbon. Of James Edwin Hewitt we know little except that he moved: he published one translated canto of *Os Lusíadas* in Lisbon in 1881, then the first two cantos in Rio de Janeiro in 1883, 'with a letter from the great American poet, Henry W. Longfellow'. Considerably more mobile, Burton probably started working on *The Lusiads* while in Goa in 1846, although he completed much of his version during his time as British consul in Brazil. In the preface he states that one of his principal qualifications for the task is his itinerant status: 'None but a traveller can do justice to a traveller' (1880: ix). The phrase might clearly apply to a good many other translators as well. Burton, however, was paraphrasing the more traditional precept Mickle had used when prefacing his 1776 version of Camões: 'None but a Poet can translate a Poet.' Both traveller and poet presumed to occupy much the same intercultural space.

Calderón

The seventeenth-century Spanish playwright Pedro Calderón de la Barca has long held a stronger position in world literature than might be believed from his translations into English. Notwithstanding interest by poets of the order of Shelley, whose scenes from *El mágico prodigioso* (The Mighty Magician) were published posthumously in 1824, Calderón's presence in the English nineteenth century is limited (though stronger than that of Lope de Vega for instance). A melodrama is noted as having been translated by Fanny Holcroft in the *Theatrical Recorder* of 1805, a small anonymous version of *La vida es sueño* (Life is a Dream) is mentioned as being published in Edinburgh in 1830, and John Oxenford's blank verse translation from the same play appeared in the *Monthly Magazine* in 1842, but book-length translations of Calderón would come only in the second half of the century.

The two-volume collection by the barrister Denis Florence McCarthy (1853) advertises itself as 'principally in the metre of the original', retains effective rhyme schemes, uses archaic diction ('thee' and 'doth'), and does not always avoid

Romantic excess. The translations are nevertheless accompanied by extensive notes and introductions. Richard Chenevix Trench published versions of two Calderón plays in 1856 (claiming they had remained unpublished for eighteen years). Most of his rendition is prose narrative interspersed with fragments in rhymed verse, clearly as a pedagogical introduction to Calderón more than anything that could be staged. On the other hand, Edward FitzGerald's versions of 1853 are presented as 'freely translated', arguing that 'an exact translation would be bombastic' (vi). FitzGerald's translations are mostly melodrama in unrhymed verse and contemporary diction, curiously accompanied by an apology: FitzGerald points out that he has not touched any of Calderón's 'famous plays' (v). (This defence was later contradicted when the same translator published versions of two of Calderón's better-known plays in 1865.) In his preface to *The Mighty Magician*, FitzGerald nevertheless notes that this translation is 'not for acting' (1865: 67). The verse is indeed closer to Calderón, with effective rhyme schemes and contemporary diction (no 'thou's). Here is Cyprian's opening speech:

> This is the place, this the sequester'd spot
> Where, in the flower about and leaf above,
> I find the shade and quiet that I love,
> And oft resort to rest a wearied wing;
> And here, good lads, leave me alone, but not
> Lonely, companion'd with the books you bring.
> (FitzGerald 1865: 3)

Compare this with the greater economy of Shelley's earlier version:

> In the sweet solitude of this calm place,
> This intricate wild wilderness of trees
> And flowers and undergrowth of odorous plants,
> Leave me; the books you brought out of the house
> To me are ever best society.
> (Shelley 1970: 731–2)

As Norman MacColl later observed in his edition of Calderón's Spanish texts (1888), both FitzGerald and McCarthy struggled against not just different systems of versification, but also the grandiloquence of Calderón, which often sounds bombastic in English. On the other hand, notes MacColl, other parts of Calderón are extremely simple and appear unacceptably bald in English. Shelley, at least, took the liberty of editing out both extremes.

Naturalism

The dominance of translations from a distant Iberian past was only really broken with the advent of European naturalism in the novel and the theatre. Iberian naturalism built on *costumbrista* traditions, absorbing the international movement led by Zola into a moment of national soul searching. This provided exotic colour for the growing lending libraries in industrialized countries, which were generating new demands for literature. Among the novelists whose works were taken up in the 1880s and 1890s were Galdós, Valdés, Echegaray, and Pardo Bazán from Spanish, and Eça de Queirós and Júlio Dinis (pseudonym of Joaquim Gomes Coelho) from Portuguese. Many of these translations were first published in the United States, whereas in the previous decades American editions had usually followed or coincided with publication in Britain.

This new translation regime was marked by relatively short time-gaps between the sources and the translations. There were also changes in the cultural identity of translators. As the publishing houses became the main drive behind the importation of literature, translators tended to lose much of their independence and personal input, assuming an industrial status well removed from the gentlemanly amateur work of previous generations. Many translators of novels were women, as were quite possibly most of their readers. The language of translations, especially dialogue, was brought closer to vernacular norms, and text length could be adjusted to meet publishers' specifications.

The most prolific translator of the last decade of the century was perhaps the American Mary Jane Serrano. Between 1889 and 1900 she translated some thirteen novels from Portuguese and Spanish (Eça de Queirós, Pardo Bazán, Alarcón, Galdós, Valera), in addition to work from French (see Hartman 1999). Produced at an industrial rate (seven of her translated novels are listed as being published in 1891 alone), Serrano's translations are generally straight renditions, retaining some Spanish proverbs but simplifying details and side-stepping many fast balls, sometimes out of visible haste. For example, in her version of Alarcón's story 'Moors and Christians' (1891*b*), she uses the term as 'Moorish' to render both 'moro' (Muslim) and 'morisco' (a Muslim baptized under Christian rule), which leads her to speak of a Moorish town that had previously been Moorish. Comparing Serrano's American version of Galdós's *Doña Perfecta* with a previous translation by an acronymous 'D.P.W.' published in London in 1880, we find the American translator refusing traces of Spanish ('Uncle Licargo' and 'gentleman' instead of D.P.W.'s 'Tio Licurgas' and 'señorito'), economizing on details ('beasts' instead of 'saddle horses'), and editing out foreign expressions ('terribly cold' instead of 'cold enough for three thousand devils'). On the other hand, in Serrano's version of Emilia Pardo Bazán's *Morriña* (Homesickness) we find occasional strains of a New York Jewish mother in a Spanish setting: 'Ah, there comes old Contreras already' (1891*a*: 5), indicating both calque from the Spanish and possible colour from the translator's specific location. Serrano nevertheless claimed that a translator should be 'absolutely selfless, content to live a reflected intellectual life' (1897: 168). That was a position that few translators before 1880 would have taken, given their personal engagement with the source cultures. Serrano's deliberate abnegation might be seen as reflecting the growing professionalism of translators towards the close of the century (see § 3.1, above).

LIST OF SOURCES

Translations
Aubertin, J. J. (1878). *Os Lusíadas de Luiz de Camões: The Lusiads of Camoens*, 2 vols. London.
—— (1881). *Seventy Sonnets of Camoens*. London.

Bowring, John (1824). *Ancient Poetry and Romances of Spain*. London.
Burton, Richard Francis (1880). *Os Lusíadas (The Lusiads)* [Camões], ed. Isabel Burton. London.
—— (1884). *Camoens, the Lyricks: Sonnets, Canzons, Odes and Sextines*. London.
Clark, J. W., ed. (1864–7). *The History of Don Quixote* [Cervantes]. London (rev. of Jarvis's translation).
Duff, Robert ffrench (1880). *The Lusiad of Camoens, Translated into English Spenserian Verse*. Lisbon.
Duffield, A. J. (1881). *The Ingenious Knight, Don Quixote de la Mancha* [Cervantes], 3 vols. London.
FitzGerald, Edward (1853). *Six Dramas of Calderon*. London.
—— (1865). *The Mighty Magician; Such Stuff as Dreams are Made of* [Calderón]. Bungay.
Garnett. R. (1896). *Dante, Petrarch, Camoens: CXXIV Sonnets*. London.
Gibson, J. Y. (1885). *Numantia: A Tragedy* [Cervantes]. London.
Hewitt, J. E. (1883). *The First Canto of the Lusiad* [Camões]. Rio de Janeiro.
Huntington, Archer M. (1897–1903). *Poem of the Cid*, 3 vols. New York.
Kennedy, James (1852). *Modern Poets and Poetry of Spain*. London.
Lockhart, J. G. (1823). *Ancient Spanish Ballads, Historical and Romantic*. Edinburgh.
Longfellow, H. W. (1845). *The Poets and Poetry of Europe*. Philadelphia, PA.
McCarthy, Denis Florence (1853). *Dramas of Calderon, Tragic, Comic, and Legendary*, 2 vols. London.
Mickle, William Julius (1776). *The Lusiad, or, The Discovery of India. An Epic Poem* [Camões]. Oxford.
Mitchell, Sir T. L. (1854). *The Lusiad of Luis de Camoens, Closely Translated*. London.
Musgrave, Thomas Moore (1826). *The Lusiad: An Epic Poem* [Camões]. London.
Ormsby, John (1879). *The Poem of the Cid*. London.
—— (1885). *The Ingenious Gentleman Don Quixote of La Mancha* [Cervantes], 4 vols. London.
Prestage, E. (1894). *Sixty-Four Sonnets* [Quental]. London.
Quillinan, Edward (1853). *The Lusiad of Luis de Camoens. Books I to V*. London.
Serrano, Mary J. (1891*a*). *Morriña (Homesickness)* [Pardo Bazán]. New York.
—— (1891*b*). *Moors and Christians and Other Tales* [Alarcón]. New York.
—— (1896). *Doña Perfecta* [Galdós]. New York.
Shelley, Percy Bysshe (1970). *Poetical Works*, ed. Thomas Hutchinson and corrected by G. M. Matthews. Oxford (first pub. 1905).
[Smirke, Mary] (1818) *Don Quixote de la Mancha* [Cervantes]. London.
Southey, Robert (1797). *Letters Written during a Short Residence in Spain and Portugal, with Some Account of Spanish and Portuguese Poetry*, 2 vols. Bristol.
—— (1808). *The Chronicle of the Cid*. London (contains Frere's verse translation).
Strangford, Viscount (1803). *Poems from the Portuguese of Luis de Camoens*. London.
Trench, R. C. (1856). *Life's a Dream; The Great Theatre of the World* [Calderón]. London.
W., D. P. (1880). *Doña Perfecta: A Tale of Modern Spain* [Galdós]. London.
Watts, H. E. (1888). *The Ingenious Gentleman Don Quixote of La Mancha* [Cervantes], 5 vols. London.
Wiffen J. H. (1823). *The Works of Garcilasso de la Vega*. London.

Other Sources
Anon. (1885). 'Ormsby's Don Quixote.' *Atlantic Monthly* 56: 265–9.
Buceta, Erasmo (1923). 'El entusiasmo por España en algunos románticos ingleses.' *Revista de filología española* 10: 1–25.

—— (1924). 'Traducciones inglesas de romances en el primer tercio del siglo XIX. Nota acerca de la difusión del hispanismo en la Gran Bretaña y en los Estados Unidos.' *Revue hispanique* 52: 459–555.
Cabral, Adolfo de Oliveira (1959). *Southey e Portugal 1774–1801: Aspectos de uma biografia literaria*. Lisbon.
Ferreira, Isabel Simoes de (1992). 'Apontamento biográfico aos tradutores de *Os Lusíadas*', pp. 69–74 in M. L. Machado de Sousa, ed., *Camões em Inglaterra*. Lisbon.
Hartman, Kabi (1999). 'Ideology, Identification and the Construction of the Feminine in *Le Journal de Marie Bashkirtseff*.' *The Translator* 5: 61–82.
Hills, Elijah Clarence (1920). 'English Translations of Spanish Plays.' *Hispania* 3: 97–108.
Igreja, Maria Eugénia (1992). 'A lírica de Camões em língua inglesa', pp. 101–27 in M. L. Machado de Sousa, ed., *Camões em Inglaterra*. Lisbon.
O'Brien, Robert (1963). *Spanish Plays in English Translation: An Annotated Bibliography*. New York.
Pane, Remigio Ugo (1944). *English Translations from the Spanish 1484–1943: A Bibliography*. New Brunswick, NJ.
Ramos, Iolanda Freitas, and Lousada, Isabel Cruz (1992). 'Traduções de *Os Lusíadas* em Inglaterra', pp. 13–67 in M. L. Machado de Sousa, ed., *Camões em Inglaterra*. Lisbon.
Rudder, Robert S. (1975). *The Literature of Spain in English Translation: A Bibliography*. New York.
Serrano, Mary Jane (1897). 'A Plea for the Translator.' *The Critic* (25 September), 167–8.
Sousa, Maria Leonor Machado de, ed. (1992). *Camões em Inglaterra*. Lisbon.
Southey, Robert (1849). *The Life and Correspondence of Robert Southey*, ed. C. C. Southey, 6 vols. London.
—— (1965). *New Letters of Robert Southey*, ed. Kenneth Curry, 2 vols. New York.

6.5 Early Literature of the North

Andrew Wawn

The Emergence of a Poetic Canon

The preface to Sir Edmund Head's pioneering translation of *Víga-Glúms saga* notes that 'The Sagas...were composed for the men who have left their mark in every corner of Europe, and whose language and laws are at this moment important elements in the speech and institutions of England, America, and Australia' (Head 1866: vii). With the cultural centrality of Old Icelandic sagas so confidently asserted, it is small wonder that nineteenth-century translators across the English-speaking world had begun to make them more accessible. Old northern poetry generated similar enthusiasm. In the introduction to their *Corpus Poeticum Boreale*, Guðbrandur Vigfússon and Frederick York Powell express the wish that their labours as editors and translators in Oxford might encourage 'Englishmen and Americans to...turn to the [old northern] rock from which we are hewn' (1883: cxvii). John Kemble had made a similar claim about *Beowulf* almost half a century earlier: it was a 'fine poem' that celebrated 'the exploits of one of our own forefathers', and deserved more prominence in an age in which 'a little more attention seems to be paid to the old feeling of England than heretofore' (Kemble 1837: v). In each case the message was clear. It was time for Victorian citizens on both sides of the Atlantic fully to acknowledge and celebrate their old northern cultural heritage—Old English and Old Norse—and translators bore the responsibility of helping them to do so.

The vigorous tradition of translation in evidence by 1900 developed from a virtual standing start in 1790. At that time there were English translations of only a handful of pieces drawn from the extensive corpus of Old Icelandic prose and verse. There was no version of the poetic *Edda*, nor of any of the forty or so *Íslendingasögur* (sagas of Icelanders—the so-called 'family sagas'), nor of the sixteen *konungasögur* (kings' sagas) that make up Snorri Sturluson's *Heimskringla*, nor of the two dozen *fornaldarsögur* (legendary sagas), nor of the many *riddarasögur* (sagas of chivalry). As for Old English poetry, though British scholars warmed to the idea of a native tradition of early heroic verse, by 1790 there had been little interest in specific pieces, apart from *The Battle of Maldon* and *The Battle of Brunanburh* (see Frank 1993). *Beowulf* remained unedited and untranslated, its fate still in the hands of Grímur Thorkelín, the Copenhagen-based Icelandic scholar of *Edda* and saga who had discovered (in 1786) and transcribed (by 1791) the long neglected manuscript in London. His pioneering but unreliable edition and Latin translation of the poem eventually appeared in 1815.

This is not to say that old northern literature lacked dedicated British and North American enthusiasts in 1790. Material from seventeenth- and eighteenth-century

Latin compendia, and text editions with Latin translations, gradually trickled down into the popular consciousness through précis, paraphrase, and review (see Fell 1996). Bishop Thomas Percy and Thomas Gray played a major part in this dissemination (see Clunies Ross 1998, 2001; also Vol. 3 of this *History*). Percy's *Five Pieces of Runic Poetry* (1763), as well as offering original texts, established the canon of translated Old Icelandic poems from which the defining images of the old north were derived. Three of the pieces were included in Percy's companion work, *Northern Antiquities* (1770); and all five appeared in the 1809 reprint. As a group the poems presented an exuberant vision of Viking Age values: zest for life, love of battle, defiance of death, a coherent spirituality, and respect for the verbal arts.

Percy knew Thomas Gray, a fellow old northernist, the example of whose haunting poetic paraphrases 'The Fatal Sisters' (based on 'Darraðarljóð' from *Njáls saga*) and 'The Descent of Odin' (the eddic 'Baldrs draumar'), both published in 1768, further encouraged native English poets to engage with the pagan gods and Viking chiefs of the north. The year 1790 alone saw the publication of three such pieces: William Williams's 'The Hervarer Saga: A Gothic Ode', Frank Sayers's *Dramatic Sketches of Northern Mythology*, and the second edition of Hugh Downman's 'The Death Song of Ragnar Lodbrok' (1781). Such pieces lay comfortably along the grain of late eighteenth-century fascination with the sublime and the Gothic (see Shippey 1998). Verse after verse presented formulaic images of shattered shields, fateful spears, and jet-black ravens wading up to their beaks through 'ensanguin'd' battlefields. Without the haunting spareness of Percy's prose responses and the austere good taste of Gray's poetic sensibility, eighteenth-century poetasters and paraphrasers were often seduced but rarely inspired by the eddic muse.

Shades and Shadows

Sir Walter Scott owned copies of the Percy volumes, and knew many of the satellite poetic paraphrases, including those by his friend Anna Seward ('Herva. At the Tomb of Argantyr. A Runic Dialogue', 1796, and 'Harold's Complaint: A Scandinavian Ode', 1810). He was also aware, however, that virtually none of these enthusiastic translators 'understood the original Icelandic, but contented themselves with executing their originals from the Latin version, and thus presenting their readers with the shadow of a shade' (Scott, *Edinburgh Review*, October 1806: 212). Indeed, sometimes even the 'shade' itself could distort the old northern mindset, as with a celebrated mistranslation from the 'Regnar lodbrog' ode. Ragnarr, the putative narrator, notes with wry old northern understatement that the experience of battle 'varat sem biarta brude | I bing hia sier leggia' (Percy 1763: 90). Following Ole Worm's seventeenth-century error, subsequent versions missed the negative ('-at') particle in the verb 'varat', thereby establishing the heady association of battlefield with bedroom: 'The pleasure of that day was like having a fair virgin placed beside one in the bed' (Percy 1763: 34). William Herbert was the first English translator to correct this particular infelicity—'Twas not, I trow, like wooing rest | On gentle maiden's snowy breast' (1804–6: II, 41).

The image of Ragnarr loðbrók, with or without his 'gentle maiden', remained popular throughout the nineteenth century—there were even claims that the Hanoverian royal family was descended from him. Similar esteem extended to mythological and heroic pieces from the poetic *Edda*. The proliferation of translations highlighted the variety of ways in which such poetry could be voiced. Three versions of lines from the end of *Skírnismál* make the point. Skírnir journeys to the land of the giants to woo the giantess Gerðr on behalf of his master Freyr. Where bribery fails, browbeating succeeds, and the messenger returns to Ásgarðr with his mission accomplished. First, William Herbert (1804–6: II, 12–13):

> *Skirner sung.*
> 'Barri is hight the seat of love;
> Nine nights elaps'd, in that known grove
> To brave Niorder's gallant boy
> Will Gerda yield the kiss of joy.'
>
> *Freyr sung.*
> 'Long is one night, and longer twain;
> But how for three endure my pain!
> A month of rapture sooner flies,
> Than half one night of wishful sighs.'

Then, Benjamin Thorpe (1866: 84):

> *Skirnir.*
> Barri the grove is named,
> which we both know,
> the grove of tranquil paths.
> Nine nights hence,
> there to Niörd's son
> Gerd will grant delight.
>
> *Freyr.*
> Long is one night,
> yet longer two will be;
> how shall I three endure.
> Often a month to me
> less has seemed
> than half a night of longing.

And, lastly, Guðbrandur Vigfússon and his amanuensis Frederick York Powell (1883: I, 117):

> *Skirni*. Barra is the name of a peaceful copse we both know; there after three nights' time Gerda will grant her love to Niord's son.
> EIGHTH SCENE.—*Frey* (soliloquising). One night is long, two nights are longer! How can I endure three? A month has often seemed shorter to me tha[n] this half (short) bridal night.

Each translator knew Old Icelandic, and was familiar with the latest European scholarship on his chosen text. Priorities differ, however. Herbert's decorous quatrains and couplets yield to Thorpe's spikier unrhymed stanzas, though neither version signals the alliterative patterns of the original. In the 1883 prose version, the format and stage directions reflect emerging theories concerning the dramatic origin of eddic verse.

The Emergence of Saga

Potential translators of the poetic *Edda* had reason to be grateful for the publication of *Edda Sæmundar hinns fróda* (1787–1828), an authoritative three-volume edition, complete with facing-page Latin translations. The edition took its place in a prestigious text series published under the auspices of the Arnamagnaean Commission in Copenhagen, with Grímur Thorkelín as one of its contributing editors. This series was, however, dominated by saga rather than poetry. The *Íslendingasögur* edited and translated into Latin included *Gunnlaugs saga ormstungu* (1775), *Víga-Glúms saga* (1786), *Eyrbyggja saga* (1787), *Njáls saga* (1809; Latin translation only), *Laxdæla saga* (1826), and *Kormáks saga* (1832). These colourful narratives of the birth and maturation of the early Icelandic commonwealth gradually attracted the attention of Victorian translators. In 1790 English translations of short scenes from just three sagas had been published (by James Johnstone—see Clunies Ross 1998: 167–80, and Thorkelín 1788); by 1900 over two dozen complete sagas were available, the work of a small group of British enthusiasts and their long-suffering Icelandic collaborators—William Morris and Muriel Press (guided by Eiríkr Magnússon), Frederick York Powell, George Dasent, John Sephton, Oliver Elton (supported by Guðbrandur Vigfússon), and Gilbert Goudie (who worked with Jón Hjaltalín). In North America, translators such as Arthur Reeves were drawn primarily (and inevitably) to the Vínland sagas.

The canon of sagas that had emerged by 1900 favoured historical realism over wonder-tale fantasy, the heroism of the Icelandic settlement over the turbulence of the Sturlung Age commonwealth, and native Scandinavian and Icelandic tradition over sagas based on French sources. Sagas relating to real and imagined Viking Age contacts with the British Isles and North America were of particular interest. By 1900 most of the *Íslendingasögur* had been translated into English, whereas few *fornaldarsögur* and hardly any *riddarasögur* had attracted attention. Anglo-Catholic scholars toiled determinedly in translating one or two *Biskupasögur* (Eiríkr Magnússon 1875–83; Elton 1890), while their protestant colleagues favoured bracing tales of righteous pagans.

One such saga became by far the most popular old northern narrative in the nineteenth-century English-speaking world (see Fry 1990; Acker 1992). George Stephens's *Frithiof's Saga* (1839) includes translations both of the original medieval Icelandic text and of Bishop Esaias Tegnér's lively verse adaptation in Swedish, first published in 1825. Stephens was a vicar's son and Chartist's brother from Liverpool, who settled in Stockholm in the late 1830s. *Friðþjófs saga* was the first Icelandic text to which he devoted his formidable philological energies. Set in Sognefjord, Norway, the saga tells of a worthy yeoman's son who becomes a brave

Viking leader and a gifted poet. Surviving many trials and temptations he is chosen as leader of his community, and, in Bishop Tegnér's augmented version, accepts the newly proclaimed Christian faith. The tale, particularly as reinvented by Tegnér and three-dimensionalized by Stephens's peppery commentary, footnotes, and songs, constructs a bracing rather than brutal Viking Age. It valorizes upward social mobility, sexual decorum, brain rather than brawn, nature rather than nurture, and authority legitimized by popular acclaim rather than by official decree (Wawn 2000: 117–41).

The Politics of Translation

The Frithiof story promoted an old northernism with which many Victorians were proud to be associated. The formidable George Stephens, for over forty years professor of English at the University of Copenhagen, counted himself as one of them. He devoted his life to editing and translating old northern texts and runic inscriptions in order to promote his influential political and philological agenda. This had four intersecting strands: (i) all that was best in British life, letters, and language was based on old northern values; (ii) a common culture had united the islands of and the lands bordering the north Atlantic from the third century onwards; (iii) the most authentic extant texts from that unified old north were runic inscriptions; (iv) texts exhibiting the 'folk-tungs' [dialects] of old northern English stand closer to the early common 'Anglo-Scandic' language than do those texts that survive only in the standardized 'book dialects' of Alfredian Wessex and Saga Age Iceland.

Stephens's translations of Old Icelandic prose and Old English verse were heavily informed by these notions. Translation style had a political dimension; old northern texts were to be voiced wherever possible in language of old northern provenance, rather than that of slavish Rome or feudal France. Two examples make the point and mark the problems. First, in *Friðþjófs saga*, Ingibjörg's brothers have sent two troll-maidens to destroy Elliði, the magic ship carrying the eponymous hero to the Orkney Islands. Stephens translated from C. C. Rafn's 1829–30 text (II, 79):

'Two women see I on the back of that Whale; they it is who, with their worst spells and blackest witchcraft, cause this horrible head-storm. Now will we try whether our fortune or their incantations avail the most; steer ye right onward as before; myself, with a dart-club, will bruise these evil demons.' Then sang he this song:

> 'Weird witches see I,
> Two, on the wave there;—
> Helge has sent them,
> Hither to meet us:
> Ellida shall snap a-
> Sunder i' th' middest
> Their backs,—ere o'er billows
> Bounds she right onward.'
> (Stephens 1839: 18)

Stephens's prose seems at times uncertain of its linguistic decorum, as radical philological instinct wrestles with conservative literary training. Thus, while careful attention is paid to the Icelandic word order and to the verse's alliteration, we find 'hamíngja... tröllskapr þeirra' represented by 'fortune... incantations', vocabulary of Johnsonian amplitude.

The second example involves a hitherto unknown Old English poem. In 1860 Stephens edited and translated two newly discovered fragments of an epic lay which, he claimed, belonged to a lost 'saga cyclus' of a quality matching that of *Beowulf*. The inclusion of poems such as *Widsith* in J. J. Conybeare's *Illustrations of Anglo-Saxon Poetry* (1826) and Benjamin Thorpe's *Analecta Anglo-Saxonica* (1834)—volumes that now did for Old English verse what Percy's *Five Pieces* had already done for Icelandic poetry—had already hinted at the existence of a long-lost tradition of vernacular epic poetry in England. To the jubilant Stephens the *Waldere* fragments confirmed these hints. They offered a tantalizing glimpse of an eighth-century English poetic *Edda*. The editor's excitement was self-evident: England '*has had* a hoard of antique National Champion-Ballads no less varied and no less splendid than her Scandinavian kinsmen—even Iceland not excepted' (Stephens 1860: xii). Here, at last, was the decisive proof that *Beowulf* was just '*one of many*' such works (1860: xi).

For the paranoid Copenhagen professor and his Danish 'kinsmen', working not long before the 1863 renewal of the Slesvig-Holsten hostilities with Germany, the fragments would have to be edited rapidly in order to outflank predatory Prussian scholars. They would also have to be translated fastidiously in order to do full philological justice to this major discovery. Stephens duly provides two versions, one unblushingly literal and the other more polished, as in the passage in which the loyal Hildegund addresses her lover Waldere during their last stand against overwhelming opposition (Stephens 1860: 48–51):

'Nalles, ic ðe, wine min,	'Never-was-it—I thee, friend mine,
wordum ciðe ðy,	in-words say-it therefore—
ic ðe ge-sawe	that-I thee saw
æt ðam sweord-plegan,	at the sword-play,
ðurh edwitscype	thro the cowardice
æniges monnes,	of-any man
wig for-búgan,	war bend-from,
oððe on weal fleon,	or on (the-battle-)field flee,
lice beorgan,	thy-lyke (body) to-save,
ðeah-þe laðra fela	tho-that of-loath'd-foes fele (many)
ðinne byrn-homon	thy brinie-hame (harness)
billum heowun.'	with-bills hew'd.'

'Never, dear friend-lord—
I fear not to say it—
saw I thee anywhere
in the heroes' sword-play,
thro the coward qualms
of quailing soldier,

> wend from the warfare,
> flee from the wrong,
> thy life to shelter—
> tho loath'd foes many
> thy brinie-harness
> with bills might hew.'

Each archaism, compound noun, alliterative doublet, or defiance of syntactical convention that recalled the 'Anglo-Scandic', or 'Scando-Gothic' (Stephens despised the term 'Anglo-Saxon') language of the original poem represented a truculent assertion of the continuity of old northern cultural values. In his commentary the translator celebrates those values in characteristically flamboyant prose:

> We sometimes call the founders of the free states in Europe—the Angles and other Northmen, the Goths and the Germans—'Barbarians'... But—establishing such States, and laying down such laws so wise... and balancing the internal governing powers so judiciously, and gradually extirpating slavery itself,—and the while possessing Songs and Sagas whose splendor never will be surpast, Robes and Armour and Tools admirable in beauty, Dragon-Ships glowing with gold and fleet as the falcon:—merely because they had not gone to a Sunday-school or been cowed or crammed to meet some Mandarin Examination-board, *were* these stalwart Men, our Hero-Ancestors... really and of a sooth 'savages' and '*Barbarians*'? (Stephens 1860: xiii)

A similar mindset drove the Orcadian Samuel Laing, whose influential 1844 translation of Snorri Sturluson's *Heimskringla*, deriving from Jacob Aall's 1838 Dano-Norwegian version, was accompanied by a lengthy introductory polemic in which the old Norwegian material world and cultural values were translated and celebrated as painstakingly as the actual sagas. The demonic energy that drove the northmen to the New World is singled out for praise. The Vínland sagas were eagerly translated by protestant North Americans of Scandinavian and north European descent as offering a more congenial foundation narrative than that represented by tales of the Italian Catholic Christopher Columbus (on this see Barnes 2001; Wawn 2001).

Paradigm Shifts

In three important respects George Webbe Dasent's pioneering translation of *Brennu-Njáls saga* marked a pivotal moment in the evolution of old northern literary translation during the nineteenth century. First, *The Story of Burnt Njal* (1861) confirmed the rising status of prose sagas in a century dominated by the novelistic realism of Scott, Dickens, and George Eliot. Secondly, Dasent's translations of both *Njáls saga* and *Gísla saga* helped to relocate the epicentre of the old north from Frithiof's Norway to Njáll's Iceland. And, lastly, Dasent, a devoted pupil of George Stephens in Stockholm in the early 1840s, eventually developed a linguistically less idiosyncratic way of translating sagas than that of his fiery mentor. Dasent's 1842 translation of Snorri's *Edda* was marked by a white-knuckled literalism bordering on transliteration, and had *Burnt Njal*, already under preparation, been published at the same time, its style would surely have been similarly marked. In the event, the translation was allowed to mature in cask over two decades, as Dasent grew in philological confidence and stylistic suppleness.

Dasent and Morris were the dominant saga translators in Britain after 1860. A passage from *Njáls saga* (translated from Ólafur Olavius' edition, *Sagan af Niáli Þorgeirssyni ok sonum hans*, 1772: 118) highlights their contrasting approaches. Gunnarr, hero of the first half of the saga, has been killed by his enemies, but appears in a vision to the sons of his loyal friend Njáll:

Now those two, Skarphedinn and Hogni, were out of doors one evening by Gunnar's cairn on the south side. The moon and stars were shining clear and bright, but every now and then the clouds drove over them. Then all at once they thought they saw the cairn standing open, and lo! Gunnar had turned himself in the cairn and looked at the moon. They thought they saw four lights burning in the cairn, and none of them threw a shadow. They saw that Gunnar was merry, and he wore a joyful face. He sang a song, and so loud, that it might have been heard though they had been further off.   (Dasent 1861: I, 250)

Skarphedin and Hogni were abroad one evening by Gunnar's howe, on the south side thereof: the moonshine was bright but whiles the clouds drew over: them seemed the howe opened and Gunnar had turned in the howe, and lay meeting the moon; and they thought they saw four lights burning in the howe, and no shadow cast from any: they saw that Gunnar was merry, and exceeding glad of countenance: and he sang a song so high that they had heard it even had they been farther off.   (Morris 1910–15: VIII, 49)[1]

Both translators aim for a kind of literalism, retaining coordinate constructions and avoiding intrusive editorializing. Nevertheless Morris's preoccupation with archaisms ('abroad', 'howe', 'thereof', 'whiles') and phrases which mimic Old Icelandic idiom ('them seemed' ('þeim sýndiz'), 'lay meeting the moon' ('sá í moti túnglinv')) contrasts with Dasent's declared preference for the idiomatic language of his own day (see Quirk 1953–5; Cook 2002). In Morris's collaboration with Eiríkr Magnússon, it was the Icelander who produced the unadorned draft translations, whose vocabulary and syntax were then briskly medievalized by Morris (Barribeau 1984). In the event, the philological ingenuity exhibited may help to explain why the Morris/Eiríkr Magnússon translations exercised relatively little popular influence. Unlike Morris's seductive verse rhapsodies on scenes and themes from *Völsunga saga* (*Sigurd the Volsung*) and *Laxdæla saga* ('The Lovers of Gudrun'), the saga translations preached mainly to the converted.

Beowulf

In 1895, just a year before his death, William Morris turned his attention to *Beowulf*. By this time, with the text stabilized, the initially puzzling sequence of narrative events unravelled, the grammar of Old English more securely understood, and a mass of learned commentary available for consultation, translators of the poem had experimented boldly in seeking to capture the poem's alliteration, paratactic syntax, formulaic phraseology, and sinewy patterns of

---

[1] A footnote in Morris's journal of his (1871) Iceland travels. He never translated the whole saga.

variation. Versions of lines from the description of Grendel's approach to Heorot mark the shifting priorities of a representative range of translators. Here is Kemble's text:

> Ðá com of móre
> under mist-hleóþúm
> Grendel gongan
> gódes ẏrre bær
> mynte se mán-scaða
> manna cynnes
> sumne b(e)syrwan
> in sele þam héan
> wód under (wolc)num
> tó þæs þe he wín-reced
> gold-sele gum(e)na
> gearwost wisse
> fættum fáhne.
> (Kemble 1833: 50)

J. J. Conybeare, using Thorkelín's problematic 1815 text, and leaning heavily on the Icelander's unreliable Latin translation, favours the smoothing effect of the initial subordinate 'When' clause, deploys some tonally uncertain noun phrases—'foul assassin' for 'se man scaþa', 'that princely bower' for 'win reced' (Thorkelin 1815: 56), and seems unconcerned about establishing a regular pattern of alliteration:

> When on the moor beneath the hill of mists
> The Grendel came—a heaven-abandon'd wretch;—
> The foul assassin thought in that high hall
> To gorge some human prey. Onwards he pass'd
> In darkness, till right near he might behold
> That princely bower, the nobles' golden seat
> Rich deck'd with many a mead–cup.
> (Conybeare 1826: 46)

John Kemble, working from his own better-edited text, translates more literally and in prose. Conybeare's Thorkelín-derived 'heaven-abandoned wretch' is jettisoned, and some alliteration is signalled:

Then under veils of mist came Grendel from the moor; he bare God's anger, the criminal meant to entrap some one of the race of men in the high hall. He went under the welkin, until he saw most clearly the wine-hall, the treasure-house of men, variegated with vessels.
(Kemble 1837: 30)

Colonel H. W. Lumsden adopts lengthy rhyming couplets that encourage syntactic experiment, as with the dramatically delayed identification of the subject in the first two lines. Alliteration is patchy, and epic dignity is occasionally compromised, as when 'one of the race of men' becomes merely 'some sleeper':

> Down from the moor, 'neath misty fells, bearing the wrath of God,
> Thinking in that high hall to snare some sleeper, Grendel trod.

> Onward he went beneath the clouds, until he could behold
> The goodly-plated house of wine, the heroes' hall of gold.
> (Lumsden 1881: 23)

It was William Morris who, like George Stephens before him, had the philological bravado and political will to signal linguistically the close cultural identification that he felt between an idyllic Anglo-Scandic old north and a reformed Victorian England. Working, as ever, from a literal prose version (supplied on this occasion by Eiríkr Magnússon's Cambridge colleague A. J. Wyatt), Morris relishes the alliterative lifts, unfamiliar compounds, deft archaisms and syntactic inversions:

> Came then from the moor-land, all under the mist-bents,
> Grendel a-going there, bearing God's anger.
> The scather the ill one was minded of mankind
> To have one in his toils from the high hall aloft.
> 'Neath the welkin he waded, to the place whence the wine-house,
> The gold-hall of men, most yarely he wist
> With gold-plates fair colour'd.
> (Morris 1910–15: X, 200)

Coolly received at the time, even by Morris's admirers, *The Tale of Beowulf* may be due for re-evaluation in an age more sympathetic to philological ingenuity and energy.

Coda: A Translation Community

By 1900 many enthusiasts of old northern texts could translate the works for themselves with decent competence. The teaching of Old Icelandic had become well established as a university discipline in both Britain and the United States; learned Icelanders provided postal tuition to far-flung pupils; others taught themselves, working through the graded reading passages in the available grammar books. The development of Old English studies and enthusiasms between 1790 and 1900 followed a similar trajectory (see Hall 2001). Translating old northern literature had thus become democratized as well as politicized. Accordingly, there were many who came to agree with Guðbrandur Vigfússon and Frederick York Powell that 'It were... an excellent thing if every handicraftsman and trader, great or small, had some literary... occupation... for his leisure time.... we can recommend no more delightful study than that of the Old Northern Literature' (1883: I, cxxi).

LIST OF SOURCES

Translations and Originals
Anderson, Rasmus B., and Bjarnason, Jón (1877). *Viking Tales of the North*. Chicago, IL.
Conybeare, J. J. (1826). *Illustrations of Anglo-Saxon Poetry*. London.
Dasent, George Webbe (1842). *The Prose or Younger Edda, Commonly Ascribed to Snorri Sturluson*. Stockholm.
—— (1861). *The Story of Burnt Njal, or, Life in Iceland at the End of the Tenth Century*, 2 vols. Edinburgh.

Dasent, George Webbe (1866). *The Story of Gisli the Outlaw*. Edinburgh.
Elton, Oliver (1890). *The Life of Laurence Bishop of Hólar in Iceland (Laurentius Saga) by Einar Haflidarson*. London.
Head, Sir Edmund (1866). *Viga-Glum's Saga: The Story of Viga-Glum*. London.
Herbert, William (1804–6). *Select Icelandic Poetry*, 2 vols. in 1. London.
Hjaltalín, Jón, and Goudie, Gilbert (1873). *The Orkneyinga Saga*, ed. Joseph Anderson. London (facsimile Edinburgh, 1975).
Kemble, John (1833). *The Anglo-Saxon Poems of Beowulf, The Travellers Song and the Battle of Finnes-Burh*. London.
—— (1837). *A Translation of the Anglo-Saxon Poem of Beowulf*. London.
Laing, Samuel (1844). *The Heimskringla, or, Chronicle of the Kings of Norway*, 3 vols. London.
Lumsden, H. W. (1881). *Beowulf: An Old English Poem*. London.
Magnússon, Eiríkr (1870). *Lilja: The Lily: An Icelandic Religious Poem of the Fourteenth Century*. London.
—— (1875–83). *Thómas saga Erkibyskups: A Life of Archbishop Thomas Becket*, 2 vols. London.
Morris, William (1877 [for 1876]). *The Story of Sigurd the Volsung and the Fall of the Niblungs*. London.
—— (1910–15). *Collected Works*, ed. May Morris, 24 vols. London.
—— and Magnússon, Eiríkr (1869). *The Story of Grettir the Strong*. London.
—— —— (1870). *Völsunga Saga*. London.
—— —— (1875). *Three Northern Love Stories and Other Tales*. London.
—— —— (1891–1905). *The Saga Library*, 6 vols. London.
—— and Wyatt, A. J. (1895). *The Tale of Beowulf*. Hammersmith.
Percy, Thomas (1763). *Five Pieces of Runic Poetry Translated from the Islandic Language*. London.
—— (1770). *Northern Antiquities*, 2 vols. London (repr. Edinburgh, 1809; new edn., ed. J. A. Blackwell, London, 1847).
Press, Muriel (1899). *The Laxdæla Saga*. London.
Rafn, C. C., ed. (1829–30). *Fornaldar Sögur Nordrlanda*, 3 vols. Copenhagen.
Reeves, Arthur Middleton (1890). *The Finding of Wineland the Good*. London.
Sephton, John (1894). 'The Saga of Frithiof the Fearless.' *Proceedings of the Liverpool Literary and Philosophical Society* 48: 69–97.
—— (1895). *The Saga of King Olaf Tryggwason*. London.
—— (1899). *Sverrissaga. The Saga of King Sverri of Norway*. London.
Stephens, George (1839). *Frithiof's Saga: A Legend of Norway*. London and Stockholm.
—— (1860). *Two Leaves of King Waldere's Lay*. Cheapinghaven [Copenhagen] and London.
Thorkelin, Grimr Johnson [Grímur Jónsson Thorkelín] (1788). *Fragments of English and Irish History in the Ninth and Tenth Century, in Two Parts*. London.
—— (1815). *De Danorum rebus gestis secul. III & IV. Poëma Danicum dialecto Anglo-Saxonica*. Copenhagen.
Thorpe, Benjamin (1866). *Edda Sæmundar Hinns Frôða: The Edda of Sæmund the Learned*, 2 vols in 1. London.
Vigfusson, Gudbrand [Guðbrandur Vigfússon] and York Powell, F. (1883). *Corpus Poeticum Boreale: The Poetry of the Old Northern Tongue*, 2 vols. Oxford.
York Powell, F. (1896). *The Tale of Thrond of Gate, Commonly Called Færeyinga Saga*. London.

Other Sources

Acker, Paul (1992). 'Norse Sagas Translated into English: A Supplement.' *Scandinavian Studies* 65: 66–102.

Barnes, Geraldine (2001). *Viking America: The First Millennium*, Cambridge.

Barribeau, James Leigh (1984). 'William Morris and Saga Translation: "The Story of King Magnus, Son of Erling" ', pp. 39–61 in Robert T. Farrell, ed., *The Vikings*. Ithaca, NY.

Clunies Ross, Margaret (1998). *The Norse Muse in Britain, 1750–1820*. Trieste.

—— (2001). *The Old Norse Poetic Translations of Thomas Percy: A New Edition and Commentary*. Turnhout.

Cook, Robert (2002). 'On Translating Sagas.' *Gripla* 13: 107–45.

Fell, Christine (1996). 'The First Publication of Old Norse Literature in England and its Relation to its Sources', pp. 27–57 in Else Roesdahl and Preben Meulengracht Sørensen, eds., *The Waking of Angantyr: The Scandinavian Past in European Culture*. Aarhus.

Frank, Roberta (1993). '*The Battle of Maldon*: Its Reception 1726–1906', pp. 29–44 in Helen Damico and John Leyerle, eds., *Heroic Poetry in the Anglo-Saxon Period: Studies in Honor of Jess B. Bessinger Jr*. Kalamazoo, MI.

Fry, Donald (1980). *Norse Sagas Translated into English*. New York.

Hall, J. R. (1994). 'The First Two Editions of *Beowulf*: Thorkelin's (1815) and Kemble's (1833)', pp. 239–50 in D. G. Scragg and Paul E. Szarmach, eds., *The Editing of Old English*. Cambridge.

—— (2001). 'Anglo-Saxon Studies in the Nineteenth-Century: England, Denmark, America', pp. 434–54 in Phillip Pulsiano and Elaine Treharne, eds., *A Companion to Anglo-Saxon Literature*. Oxford.

Quirk, Randolph (1953–5). 'Dasent, Morris and Problems of Translation', *Saga-Book of the Viking Society* 14/1–2: 64–77.

Shippey, Tom (1998). ' "The Death Song of Ragnar Lodbrog": A Study in Sensibilities', pp. 155–72 in Richard Utz and Tom Shippey, eds., *Medievalism in the Modern World: Essays in Honour of Lesley J. Workman*. Turnhout.

—— and Haarder, Andreas (1998). *Beowulf: The Critical Heritage*. London.

Tinker, Chauncey B. (1903). *The Translations of Beowulf: A Critical Bibliography*. New Haven, CT (repr. 1974).

Wawn, Andrew (2000). *The Vikings and the Victorians: Inventing the Old North in Nineteenth-Century Britain*. Cambridge.

—— (2001). 'Victorian Vínland', pp. 191–206 in Andrew Wawn and Þórunn Sigurðardóttir, eds., *Approaches to Vínland*. Reykjavík.

6.6 Modern Scandinavian

Robert E. Bjork

The motives for translating modern Scandinavian literature into English in the nineteenth century were as varied and complex as the literatures themselves. Translators caught up in the medieval preoccupations of the times, for instance, had ample material to work with in the modern echoes of the Viking Age in such writers as Adam Gottlob Oehlenschläger and Esaias Tegnér. Those interested in promoting conservative social values could find their views reinforced in the early works of such writers as Bjørnstjerne Bjørnson and Marie Sophie Schwartz. And those passionate for radical social change and women's rights had strong allies in such writers as Henrik Ibsen and Fredrika Bremer. The artistic innovations of the Scandinavians attracted some translators; others stumbled unawares upon the beauty of that literature while engaged in everyday business affairs.

Readers turned to translations of Scandinavian literature for similarly complicated and manifold reasons. They wanted to be entertained, educated, challenged, titillated, and even shocked. A New York woman, for example, was rumoured to have committed suicide after reading an Ibsen play, which made Ibsen's plays even more popular. In addition, the current popularity of a particular kind of writing might encourage readers to look for examples of that genre elsewhere, as had happened with satire in the eighteenth century when the translation of Scandinavian literature into English first began.

Denmark

There was an early interest in Ludvig Holberg, the major Enlightenment figure often considered the father of Danish (and Norwegian) literature. His Latin satirical work *The Journey of Niels Klim to the World Underground* (a Danish *Gulliver's Travels*) had come out in an anonymous English translation as early as 1742, but translations of his Danish works began appearing in 1782, and the last of eight came in 1885 from T. Weber, whose uncertain command of English resulted in the amusingly translated plays *The Blue-Apron Statesman* and *Erasmus Montanus, or Rasmus Berg*.

Of the other twenty-seven or so authors translated during the nineteenth century, two are represented by considerably more than fifteen translations, three by four, and twenty-two by just one to three. Hans Christian Andersen towers among all of these, indeed among all Scandinavian authors of the period. Over 200 translations, legitimate and pirated, appeared between 1845 and 1900. Most of these were for children (see pp. 397–8, below), but Andersen's first major work and international success, the autobiographical novel *The Improvisatore, or, Life in Italy*, was not. It was the first of his works translated into English. Depending at first on a German translation because she had not yet mastered Danish, one of the most prominent translators from the Scandinavian languages into English, Mary Botham Howitt, published the two-volume book in 1845 (see her account in Howitt 1889: II, 29). Her translations of two other novels in one volume, *O.T., or, Life in Denmark* and *Only a Fiddler*, also appeared in 1845 but, according to Howitt, were translated from the Danish, as was her version of *The True Story of My Life*, Andersen's autobiography, in 1847. These translations, like all of Howitt's work, have the simplicity of style of everyday speech. Besides Howitt, two other translators worked on Andersen's books for adults. Charles Beckwith-Lohmeyer published his translations of the travel books *A Poet's Bazaar* in 1846 and *Pictures of Sweden* in 1851 as well as the novel *The Two Baronesses* in 1848; Mrs Anna S. Bushby published her versions of the novels *To Be, or Not to Be?* and *Lucky Peer* in 1851 and 1871 and of the travel book *In Spain* in 1864.

Next to Andersen, the poet and dramatist Adam Oehlenschläger claimed most attention from English readers on account of his promotion of Nordic myth and legend. If Holberg is considered the father of modern Danish literature, Oehlenschläger is its renewer after the Age of Rationalism. English readers were first given access to his work through an anonymous translation in 1826 of *The Adventurers*, which was followed rapidly in 1827 by I. Heath's translation of *The Little Shepherd-Boy: An Idyll*. Another anonymous translation appeared in 1840, that of the popular tragedy *Hakon Jarl*, which depicts the clash between paganism and Christianity, and from then to 1888, ten other translators produced interpretations of it and of five other Oehlenschläger works. Three of these were translated twice or more (see Bjork 2005 for details). Among the translators, the most prominent is Theodore Martin, whose clear and natural-sounding translations reflect his wish to capture vividly the impression the works made on him.

Three other Danish authors attracted a modicum of attention in Britain and the United States. A transitional figure between Rationalism and Romanticism, Johannes Ewald intrigued first the prolific and flamboyant George Borrow, an enthusiastic translator of Danish ballads, who attempted to emulate the clarity and directness of Daniel Defoe's prose style. In 1823 he published his translation of Ewald's 'King Christian stood beside the mast', the Danish national anthem (Longfellow published his in 1836), and in 1829 translated Ewald's play *The Death of Balder*, a play that had greatly influenced Oehlenschläger and others and was fundamental to the revival of Old Norse literature. Two of Ewald's other works were made available anonymously in 1867 (*The Story of Waldemar Krone's Youth*) and 1868 (*John Falk*). *King René's Daughter*, a play by Henrik Hertz, the comic dramatist, was translated four times, and the work of Meïr Aron Goldschmidt, a journalist and author of psychological fiction, was translated by both himself and others.

Sweden

Twenty-five Swedish authors were published in English translation during the nineteenth century, starting in 1833. Most were represented by single works but four by eleven or more. Fredrika Bremer, the founder of the Swedish realistic novel and prime mover in the Swedish women's movement, heads this list as far as the number of translations of her work is concerned, but Esaias Tegnér, Sweden's first internationally acclaimed poet, begins it. *Frithiof's Saga*, his masterpiece and a work of obvious interest to anyone drawn to the Viking Age, was translated initially and ornately by the British clergyman William Strong in 1833, then by 1877 by eleven others, including the noted philologists Robert Gordon Latham, who paraphrased the poem in 1838, and George Stephens, who produced a metrical version in 1839 that went into at least four subsequent editions (see pp. 277–8, above, and Benson 1926: 147–57). Similarly, Tegnér's sentimental narrative about Karl XII's war with Russia, *Axel*, was translated six times, once by Latham (1838).

Bremer's works began being translated into English in 1842, and those of the two other most translated authors in 1843 and 1868 respectively. Bremer, Emilie Flygare-Carlén, and Marie Sophie Schwartz were held in high esteem, commanded a large international audience, and paved the way for Selma Lagerlöf, the 1909 winner of the Nobel Prize in Literature. These four authors gave 'the Swedish literary Parnassus...a female face' during the second half of the nineteenth century (Algulin 1989: 102). That face was unique in Scandinavia, and many of the translators who helped create it were women. Pauline Bancroft Flach, for example, translated three of Lagerlöf's novels into mellifluous English between 1898 and 1899 with one of those three (*The Miracles of Antichrist*) also being translated by Selma Ahlström Trotz in 1899. But Bremer's major translator and the dominant translator of Scandinavian literature during the period, Mary Howitt, has routinely been given sole credit for her work whereas her husband William deserves half of it. Wanting to promote the illusion of a joint female production, the Howitts decided to put Mary's name alone on their translations of Bremer (Burman 2001: 206). The amount they published under Mary's name between 1842 and 1863 is prodigious: some two dozen individual titles, plus the eleven-volume *Miss Bremer's Novels* (1843–4) and the four-volume *Fredrika Bremer's Works* (1852–3), all of which bear the stamp of Mary's living, unsentimental English prose style. The first book they turned to in 1842 was the German version of *The Neighbours*, a novel that ranks as one of Bremer's best works. The last, a travelogue, was *Greece and the Greeks* in 1863. During these two decades, they became close friends with Bremer, with whom they coordinated their efforts so that original and translation could be published simultaneously whenever possible (on this collaboration see p. 92, above).

The Howitt name appears on two more Bremer volumes. William published his translation of *Life in Dalecarlia* in 1845 (revised under Mary's name in 1849), and the Howitts' daughter Margaret published her translation of *The Butterfly's Gospel and Other Stories* in 1865. Several anonymous or pirated translations of

Bremer's works appeared between 1842 and 1898, and three other named individuals translated her as well. The most prominent of these is E. A. Friedlænder, who contributed reliable translations of four novels to another collection of *The Novels of Fredrika Bremer* between 1844 and 1849.

Flygare-Carlén was a productive writer who is now relatively obscure, probably because of the melodramatic, non-realistic nature of her work. Her *The Professor and His Favorites* appeared in an anonymous English translation in 1843. Many further anonymous translations of her fiction came out over the next thirty years, but there were also named translators. Howitt translated Flygare-Carlén's debut novel, *The Rose of Tistelön*, in 1844, for instance, and the minor New York novelist and *littérateur* Elbert Perce translated three novels together with Alex L. Krause in 1852 and 1853, then produced translations of three more on his own: *Gustavus Lindorm, or, 'Lead Us Not Into Temptation'* (1853), *The Home in the Valley* (1854), and *The Whimsical Woman* (1854).

Schwartz—now almost completely forgotten—had eleven of her novels translated into English, beginning in 1868 with an anonymous rendition of *The Man of Birth and the Woman of the People*. Annie Wood published her translation of *Gold and Name* as *Elvira, Lady Casterton* in 1874, but it was Selma Borg and Marie Adelaide Brown, accomplished translators also active in Finland-Swedish literature, who translated nine of Schwartz's works between 1871 and 1874 beginning with *Birth and Education* and ending with *Gerda, or, The Children of Work*.

Norway

Although John Chapman introduced modern Norwegian literature to the English-speaking world in 1855 with his privately published translation of the drama *Solomon de Caus* by the poet and playwright Peter Andreas Munch, two other Norwegian authors commanded almost all the attention during the period. From 1858, Bjørnstjerne Bjørnson and Henrik Ibsen occupied centre stage. The major translator from Swedish, Mary Howitt, produced one translation from Norwegian: Bjørnson's first novel, *Synnøvé Solbakken*, a tale about peasant life, was published as *Trust and Trial* in 1858 and was the first of his works to appear in English. An anonymous translation of another peasant tale, *Arne*, appeared in 1860, and Augusta Plesner and Susan Rugeley-Powers published their translation of it in 1866. From then to the end of the century, a large number of Bjørnson's works appeared in numerous English translations. These culminated in Edmund Gosse's thirteen-volume edition of *The Novels of Bjørnstjerne Bjørnson* (1895–1909), ten volumes of which were available before 1900, four of them translated by Gosse himself. Between 1881 and 1883, seven of Bjørnson's works were also published in English under the name of Professor Rasmus Bjørn Anderson of the University of Wisconsin (for details, see Bjork 2005). Having accepted the commission, Anderson passed the work on to Anna Aubertine Woodward, a translator who published her work under the pseudonym Auber Forestier, but for marketing reasons it was his name that appeared on the books (Hustvedt 1966: 168).

The first published translation of an Ibsen play came in 1876 with Catherine Ray's *The Emperor and the Galilean*. The second was T. Weber's transmutation of *A Doll's House* in 1880. Weber was a Danish schoolteacher now infamous for producing the painfully translated *Nora*, 'one of the most sustained specimens of unconscious humour in all literature' (Meyer 1967: 482). The third was Henrietta Frances Lord's 1882 version of *A Doll's House*, likewise entitled *Nora*. It was Ray's work, however, that may have helped inspire that of the foremost Ibsen translator of the century, William Archer, friend of George Bernard Shaw, influential and prolific drama critic, and staunch supporter both of spelling reform in English and of the idea of a British national theatre.

Archer's great knowledge of theatre and staging, his meticulous attention to detail, and his sensitive rendering of Ibsen's Norwegian into a speakable, natural English made his versions a landmark in the history of translation. His first published Ibsen translations appeared in *The Pillars of Society and Other Plays* (1888): *Ghosts* was loosely based on the much inferior, amateurish work of Henrietta Frances Lord, who published her version of the play in 1885; and *The Pillars of Society* was a revision of Archer's unpublished translation that originally bore the title *Quicksands*. By 1891, he had published the five-volume *Ibsen's Prose Dramas*, to which his wife Frances contributed translations of *The Wild Duck* and *The Lady from the Sea* and his brother Charles of *Lady Inger of Østråt* and *Rosmersholm*. Of lesser importance as a translator of Ibsen than Archer but still significant is Eleanor Marx-Aveling, Karl Marx's youngest daughter (on whom see pp. 129–30, above). In Ibsen, she saw a realistic depiction of social problems that could help lead to their solution, and she produced translations of *The Enemy of Society*, *The Lady from the Sea*, and *The Wild Duck* between 1888 and 1890.

Dominant as Bjørnson and Ibsen were, two other Norwegian authors also merit our attention. Jonas Lie, now regarded as the founder of the Norwegian novel, and Alexander Kielland, considered along with Lie and Bjørnson as one of the major realistic prose writers of the so-called Modern Breakthrough in Norway, began appearing in English in 1873. Nine translators worked on Lie from that date; six on Kielland from 1883. Prominent among these are William Archer, who contributed an important translation of Kielland's *Tales of Two Countries* in 1891, and his friend Hans Lien Brækstad, a bookseller from Trondheim, then a journalist and Norwegian specialist in London, who produced respectable translations of both Lie and Bjørnson between 1890 and 1899.

Iceland

In 1818, Ebenezer Henderson, a Scottish agent of the British Bible Society who had spent two years in Iceland, published a translation of Jón Þorláksson's poem 'Iceland to the British and Foreign Bible Society' (Henderson 1818: II, 317–20). Þorláksson was the great translator of Milton's *Paradise Lost* into *fornyrðislag* metre, and Henderson's translation was the first item of modern Icelandic literature published in English. The next did not appear for forty-four years. In 1862, Andrew James Symington published two more translations in his *Pen and Pencil Sketches of Faröe and Iceland*: his own of Bjarni Thorarensen's 'The Remembrance of Iceland' and Ólafur Pálsson's of Jón Árnason's 'Icelandic Stories and Fairy Tales'. Árnason—the major collector of Icelandic fairy tales and folklore—is considered to be the Grimm of Iceland and attracted more translators than anyone else. George Powell and Eiríkr Magnússon produced a large collection of Árnason's *Icelandic Legends* (1864), which helped pave the way for Icelandic studies in England.

Besides the well-known figure Eiríkr Magnússon, William Morris's collaborator in saga translation, two other translators deserve mention. Sir William Craigie, the Scottish lexicographer who eventually became Editor-in-Chief of the *Oxford English Dictionary*, published translations of a handful of poems and some specimens of folklore from 1895 to 1896 (for details, see Bjork 2005). And Mrs Disney Leith included numerous translations in her *Original Verses and Translations* (1895) and *Three Visits to Iceland* (1897). She was cousin to Swinburne, with whom she wrote the novel *Children of the Chapel* (1864) while she still bore her maiden name, Mary Gordon.

Finland

Finland's was the last of these northern literatures to be translated into English (for translations of the folk epic *Kalevala* see pp. 432–4, below). Beginning in 1872, seventeen books appeared. In addition, *Finland: An English Journal Devoted to the Cause of the Finnish People* published eight poems and short stories between 1899 and 1900. Virtually all the material translated was the work of the two luminaries of the golden age of Finland-Swedish literature and of national Romanticism, Johan Ludvig Runeberg and his disciple Zacharias Topelius. In 1878, Eiríkr Magnússon and E. H. Palmer published their translation of Runeberg's *Lyrical Songs, Idylls and Epigrams*, and Marie A. Brown followed with her translation of the narrative poem *Nadeschda* in 1879. In between times, she published books on Sweden, Norway, and *The Icelandic Discoverers of America* (1888). Topelius' work emerged in much more profusion than Runeberg's, however. The first novel of *The Surgeon Stories*, entitled *Gustav Adolf and the Thirty Years' War*, came out in 1872 in Selma Borg's and Marie A. Brown's translation; Brown then produced the whole series between 1882 and 1884. The six novels constitute a historical epic, told by a veteran of the Russian–Swedish War of 1808–9 and ranging over formative events for Finland during the seventeenth and eighteenth centuries.

This account of the history of English translations of Scandinavian literature in the nineteenth century dispels two commonly held assumptions. First, the profusion of such translations gives the lie to the notion that little appeared in English before 1900, a notion probably derived from the fact that, excepting Andersen, Ibsen, and perhaps Bjørnson, none of the authors translated remained popular long into the twentieth century. Secondly, the diversity of the works and genres translated and the varied backgrounds and motivations of the translators belie the idea that the attraction of the Nordic literatures for the English-reading public came simply from a fascination with the Viking Age and those who were heir to it. That fascination was very real, but it was just one of many reasons for both translators and readers to turn their attention northwards.

LIST OF SOURCES

For a complete list of translations except for H. C. Andersen, see Bjork 2005. For a list of translations of Andersen's works, see Bredsdorff 1950.

Translations
Anderson, Rasmus Bjørn (1881–3). *Works of Björnstjerne Björnson*, 5 vols. Boston, MA (seven novels actually translated by Anna Aubertine Woodward).
Archer, William, et al. (1890–1). *Ibsen's Prose Dramas*, 5 vols. London.
Borrow, George (1823). 'Sea-Song: From the Danish of Evald', *Monthly Magazine* 56: 437.
—— (1826). *Romantic Ballads, Translated from the Danish*. Norwich.
—— (1889). *The Death of Balder* [Ewald]. London (translated in 1829).
Brækstad, Hans Lien (1890). *A Gauntlet* [Bjørnson]. London.
—— (1897). *Niobe* [Lie]. London.
—— (1899 [1898]). *Paul Lange and Tora Parsberg* [Bjørnson]. London.
Brown, Marie Adelaide (1883–4). *The Surgeon's Stories* [Topelius]. Chicago, IL.
Chapman, John (1855). *Solomon de Caus: A Lyric Drama* [Peter Andreas Munch]. London.
Friedlænder, E. A., et al. (1843–9). *The Novels of Fredrika Bremer*, 11 vols. London.
Gosse, Edmund, ed. (1895–1909). *The Novels of Bjørnstjerne Bjørnson*, 13 vols. London.
Henderson, Ebenezer (1818). *Iceland, or, The Journal of a Residence in that Island during the Years 1814 and 1815*, 2 vols. Edinburgh.
Howitt, Mary Botham (1843–4). *Miss Bremer's Novels*, 11 vols. London.
—— (1845a). *The Improvisatore, or, Life in Italy* [H. C. Andersen]. London.
—— (1845b). *Only a Fiddler, and O.T., or, Life in Denmark* [H. C. Andersen]. London.
—— (1847). *The True Story of My Life: A Sketch* [H. C. Andersen]. London.
—— (1852–3). *Fredrika Bremer's Works*, 4 vols. London.
Martin, Theodore H. (1850). *King René's Daughter: A Danish Lyrical Drama* [Hertz]. London.
—— (1854). *Correggio: A Tragedy* [Oehlenschläger]. London.
—— (1857). *Aladdin, or, The Wonderful Lamp: a Dramatic Poem in Two Parts*. [Oehlenschläger]. London.
Marx-Aveling, Eleanor (1888). *An Enemy of Society* [Ibsen], in Havelock Ellis, ed., *Ghosts; An Enemy of Society*. London (rev. William Archer as *An Enemy of the People* in Archer 1890–1, Vol. 2).
—— (1890a). *The Lady from the Sea* [Ibsen]. London.
—— (1890b). *The Wild Duck: A Drama in Five Acts*, in Vol. 2 of *The Prose Dramas of Henrik Ibsen*, 3 vols. New York.
Perce, Elbert (1853). *Gustavus Lindorm, or, 'Lead Us Not Into Temptation'* [Flygare-Carlén]. New York.
—— (1854a). *The Home in the Valley* [Flygare-Carlén]. New York.
—— (1854b). *The Whimsical Woman* [Flygare-Carlén]. New York.

Other Sources

Aaltonen, Hilkka (1964). *Books in English on Finland: A Bibliographical List of Publications Concerning Finland until 1960, Including Finnish Literature in English Translation*. Turku.

Afzelius, Nils (1951). *Books in English on Sweden: A Bibliographical List*, 3rd edn. Stockholm.

Algulin, Ingemar (1989). *A History of Swedish Literature*, tr. John Weinstock. Stockholm.

Benson, Adolph B. (1926). 'A List of English Translations of the *Frithiofs Saga*. A Restrospect at the Centenary.' *Germanic Review* 1: 142–67.

Bjork, Robert E. (2005). 'A Bibliography of Modern Scandinavian Literature (Excluding H. C. Andersen) in English Translation, 1533–1900, and Listed by Translator.' *Scandinavian Studies* 77: 105–42.

Bredsdorff, Elias (1950). *Danish Literature in English Translation with a Special Hans Christian Andersen Supplement: A Bibliography*. Copenhagen.

Burman, Carina (2001). *Bremer: En biografi*. Stockholm.

Grönland, Erling (1961). *Norway in English: Books on Norway and by Norwegians in English 1936–1959: A Bibliography Including a Survey of Norwegian Literature in English Translation from 1742 to 1959*. Oslo.

Howitt, Mary B. (1889). *Mary Howitt: An Autobiography*, ed. Margaret Howitt, 2 vols. London.

Hustvedt, Lloyd (1966). *Rasmus Bjørn Anderson: Pioneer Scholar*. Northfield, MN.

Meyer, Michael (1967). *Henrik Ibsen*. London.

Mitchell, P. M., and Ober, Kenneth H. (1975). *Bibliography of Modern Icelandic Literature in Translation, Including Works Written by Icelanders in Other Languages*. Ithaca, NY.

6.7 Celtic

Mary-Ann Constantine

Introduction

The years 1790–1900 cover a crucial period in the histories and literary histories of the Celtic-speaking countries, with rather different Celtic 'revivals' at the end of each century. The period also saw the growth of scholarly interest in the relationship between the languages and countries involved: on the Goidelic side of the family, Irish, Scots Gaelic, and Manx, and on the Brittonic side, Welsh, Breton, and Cornish (the last named, effectively dead as a spoken language during this period, would be revived in the twentieth century). Partly as a result of the success and scandal surrounding James Macpherson's 'Ossian' poems of the 1760s (discussed in Vol. 3 of this *History*), there was widespread interest, inside and outside the countries themselves, in the imaginative possibilities of a Celtic past (if not always of a Celtic future). Translation into English played a fundamental role in shaping these ideas.

The concept of the 'Celtic' has been comprehensively deconstructed in recent years (see Chapman 1992; James 1999), and one should be clear from the outset that the translation of these languages and literatures for an English-speaking world does not imply the uncovering of some homogeneous Celtic culture. At the beginning of the nineteenth century, religious and political allegiances were far more persuasive than any sense of kinship between the Celtic countries as a whole: there was little love lost, for example, between Catholic Ireland and nonconformist Wales, and antiquarians fought each other in print over claims to indigenous primacy. This did change over the century as the work of scholars filtered into national consciousness: exchanges and alliances between the Celtic countries proliferated, and 'ancient' cultural institutions (some of them resting on rather shaky foundations) were dusted down and revived. Notions of innately 'Celtic' characteristics were further consolidated in the synthesizing work of writers such as Ernest Renan and Matthew Arnold, both of whom produced influential descriptions of the melancholy, spiritual 'Celt', based on a highly uneven knowledge of translated texts (Renan 1928; Arnold 1962; see Bromwich 1965; Sims-Williams 1986).

This raises perhaps the single most important issue of all, the nature of the relationship between the languages involved in the translation process. For all of the Celtic languages except Breton, translation into English meant translation into the language of a dominant ruling culture, albeit a culture in which Celtic speakers were themselves to a greater or lesser degree implicated. Under such conditions, perennial questions of 'loyalty' in the translation process take on a necessarily political edge. In what follows some attempt has been made, while surveying the translations, to note the kinds of tensions, contradictions, and ironies that resulted from this unequal relationship.

Ireland

In 1789 Ireland provided a quietly understated response to the Ossian controversy with Charlotte Brooke's *Reliques of Irish Poetry*. The collection, as much a homage to Thomas Percy's *Reliques of Ancient English Poetry* (1765) as a reply to Macpherson, presents several poems whose heroes (such as Oisín himself) have their counterparts in the Ossianic oeuvre, but studiously avoids confrontation with the Scottish work. It opens with some strong narrative pieces from the medieval Ulster and Fenian cycles (the hero stories of Cú Chulainn and Finn mac Cumaill); modern poems include the work of the blind bard Carolan (1670–1738), who remained a favourite with translators throughout the following century. The Irish texts are printed separately, with contributions from scholars including Sylvester O'Halloran and Joseph Cooper Walker, from whose *Historical Memoirs of the Irish Bards* (1786) some of the poems are derived.

Brooke puts these into conventional eighteenth-century dress—odes, heroic couplets, and, with a little more flair, ballad metre. Her comments on the act of translating, though hedged with the necessary feminine diffidence, show an awareness of the technical difficulties of turning Irish into English, for example the abundance of synonyms, or the diffusion of force caused by the necessary unpacking of dense description: 'one compound epithet must often be translated by two lines of English verse... just as that light which dazzles, when flashing swiftly on the eye, will be gazed at with indifference, if let in by degrees' (Brooke 1789: vi). She sees her own translations as benign mediators between Irish and English culture—'sweet ambassadresses of cordial union' (vii)—and insists on the value and antiquity of the native tradition. Despite their 'tendency to inflated paraphrase' (Welch 1988: 40), Brooke's translations mark a significant moment in bringing the results of antiquarian research into the fuller view of the English-speaking literary world.

The upheavals of the 1790s, culminating in the Act of Union in 1800, further politicized the business of translation. Scholarly and literary interest in Irish continued in various centres from Cork to Belfast, but no collection followed Brooke's lead in exploring the warrior tales and heroic narratives of the Middle Ages. Instead, the main perception of Irish through English in the early decades of the century was decidedly lyric, typified by the dreamy, melancholy song-poems of Thomas Moore, whose popular *Irish Melodies* appeared in ten volumes between 1807 and 1834. These were translations of an unusual kind, being essentially textual evocations of traditional Gaelic music—'interpreting in verse the touching language of my country's music' (Moore 1854: vii). Yet even this sentimental lyric mode had a political undertow, and several of Moore's most famous poems allude to his involvement with the patriot movement of the 1790s. The lyric 'Oh breathe not his name, let it sleep in the shade', for example, commemorates his college friend Robert Emmet, hanged for his part in the failed insurrection of 1803.

The next major publication of translations after Brooke was James Hardiman's *Irish Minstrelsy*, whose title acknowledges Walter Scott's earlier collection of national song. It appeared in 1831, in two solid volumes, with texts in Irish type and facing-page translations by Thomas Furlong, John D'Alton, Edward Lawson, Henry Grattan Curran, and William Hamilton Drummond. Hardiman's introduction makes great play with the antiquity of the Irish literary record, but the anthology in fact contains relatively little medieval material; this was largely a problem of scholarship, since knowledge of Old and Middle Irish was still in its infancy, but the avoidance of the Fenian and other early narrative material used by Brooke is noticeable. The two volumes, in four sections, introduce the 'Remains of Carolan', 'Sentimental Songs', 'Jacobite Relics', and 'Odes and Elegies'; tentative translations of earlier texts are included in the notes.

The presence of the Irish texts, coupled with Hardiman's nationalist agenda, made the *Irish Minstrelsy*—'that king-book', as Douglas Hyde put it (1893: 103)—a source of contention and inspiration for decades to come. But the English translations are now best remembered for provoking Samuel Ferguson to write a series of highly critical articles, with his own translations, in the *Dublin Magazine* in 1834. Ferguson's position as a translator is characteristic of the compounded ironies of the traffic between the two cultures and languages at this period. 'A Northern Protestant who had been deeply affected by the Belfast radical spirit and its enthusiasm for the Gaelic past' (Welch 1988: 92), Ferguson, like Brooke, framed his Irish patriotism within the context of the empire, and saw translation as a form of mediation (Cronin 1996: 108). His translations are noted for a lively accuracy, with some of his lyrics now classics in their own right:

> Put your head, darling, darling, darling,
> Your darling black head my heart above;
> Oh, mouth of honey, with the thyme for fragrance,
> Who, with heart in breast, could deny you love?
> (Ferguson 1865: 216)

Lyrics such as these were appreciated by a subsequent generation of writers for their 'destabilizing effect on English' (Cronin 1996: 111), and helped the movement towards a distinctive literary Anglo-Irish. But Ferguson's own aim was rather to give a country losing touch with its native language (and he took it for granted that Irish would not survive much longer) a sense of historical depth, to allow people in Ireland to '*live back* in the land they live *in*' (cited in Welch 1988: 92). In his influential collection *Lays of the Western Gael* he also published adaptations and retellings of medieval myth and legend, for which Yeats in 1886 gave him 'full-hearted thanks; he has restored to our hills and rivers their epic interest' (Yeats 1970: 30). And though Ferguson himself took pains to dissociate his translations from any political bias 'lest, by any means, the Nationalists should claim him for their own', Yeats was adamant: 'We claim him through every line' (43).

One of the best-known literary figures of nineteenth-century Ireland is the poet James Clarence Mangan, whose translations and adaptations (or 'perversions', as he himself put it) from Irish and other languages are flamboyantly unscholarly, and have a kind of selfish brilliance. Like Ferguson, Mangan drew on Hardiman's collection for his Irish texts, but he also (since his knowledge of Irish seems to have been at best weak) worked from literal translations supplied by friends and colleagues (Lloyd 1987: 85–95): his work appeared in Dublin journals, and in John O'Daly's *Poets and Poetry of Munster* (1849). His best-known poem is a version of 'Roisin Dubh', the first verse of which appeared in Thomas Furlong's translation thus:

> Oh! my sweet little rose, cease to pine for the past,
> For the friends that come eastward shall see thee at last;
> They bring blessings – they bring favors which the past never knew,
> To pour forth in gladness on my Roisin Dubh.
> (Hardiman 1831: I, 255)

In Mangan this becomes altogether more mysterious, and politically charged:

> O, my Dark Rosaleen,
> Do not sigh, do not weep!
> The priests are on the ocean green,
> They march along the Deep.
> There's wine... from the royal Pope,
> Upon the ocean green;
> And Spanish Ale shall give you hope,
> My Dark Rosaleen!
> My own Rosaleen!
> Shall glad your heart, shall give you hope,
> Shall give you health, and help and hope,
> My Dark Rosaleen!
> (Mangan 2003: 236)

Written during the ravages of the Famine, Mangan's reinterpretations of Irish poetry take a fiercely nationalist stance. 'Dark Rosaleen' picks up on the native tradition of the *aisling*, in which Ireland is presented as a suffering woman, an interpretation of the original poem favoured earlier by Hardiman and rejected by Ferguson. Mangan's interpolations are unequivocal: 'And gun-peal, and slogan cry | Wake many a glen serene'. A comparison of the three versions by Furlong, Ferguson, and Mangan of 'The Mourner's Soliloquy in the Ruined Abbey of Timoleague' by John Collins again shows how Ferguson played down, and Mangan played up, potentially nationalist and anti-English elements (Hardiman 1831: 235–43; Ferguson 1865: 190–4; Mangan 2003: 247–50). But Mangan was more than a propagandist: his spacious clarity, wit, and often unnerving use of rhyme and rhythm were a genuinely revolutionary response to the conventionally stolid (and usually florid) poetic idiom of the day.

The Jacobite and lyric interests of Hardiman's *Minstrelsy* continued in the 1840s with translations by Edward Walsh appearing in his *Reliques of Irish Jacobite Poetry*

(1844) and *Irish Popular Songs* (1847). In 1852 W. H. Drummond's *Ancient Irish Minstrelsy*, though stiff and rather dated in tone, introduced some of the later Ossianic lays, while Standish Hayes O'Grady brought a long-overdue element of comedy to the translated corpus with the robust heroic couplets of *The Adventures of Donnchadh Ruadh Con-Mara* (1853). In 1860 the young George Sigerson, following Mangan, contributed a range of translations for the second series of *Poets and Poetry of Munster*. Sigerson's work would culminate nearly forty years later in his important *Bards of the Gael and the Gall*, which offered, for the first time, a real sense of the depth and variety of the Irish poetic tradition by including much hitherto untranslated medieval material, and by attempting where possible to retain the metrical forms of the originals. Between Sigerson's earlier publications of 1860 and Douglas Hyde's work of the 1890s, however, there was surprisingly little translation activity from Irish at all.

Douglas Hyde's book of folk tales, *Beside the Fire*, marks a resurgence of interest in Irish culture, and a new approach to translation. Hyde deliberately used a highly idiomatic English, modelled on the speech of 'three-fourths of the people of Ireland', an Irish-English haunted by Gaelic syntax and idiom (Hyde 1890: xlvii). A volume of lyrics, *Love Songs of Connacht*, went a step further, providing texts and commentary in both languages on facing pages, with the English firmly subordinate to the Irish, deliberately written *through* it in a way that drew attention to its 'translatedness' ('This is the place to put down another little song of the same sort. It was some woman who gave love to a tailor who made it.' Hyde 1893: 37). Hyde's discussions of the difficulties in translating are linguistically perceptive and deeply politicized, with the process framed as a struggle: 'there are no two Aryan languages more opposed to each other in spirit and idiom' (Hyde 1890: xlvii). Yet his vigorous promotion of the Irish language through English in this way had its own ironies: because his poems and stories were widely read in newspapers such as the *Nation* and the *Weekly Freeman*, they encouraged the development of a distinct Irish-English idiom rather than the language he was fighting to keep alive (see Cronin 1996: 137). Hyde's work was a major inspiration to the Anglo-Irish movement at the turn of the century, and directly influenced Augusta Gregory, W. B. Yeats, and J. M. Synge.

Alongside the literary translations ran a parallel and sometimes overlapping tradition of scholarly edition and translation from early and middle Irish, which gathered momentum as the century progressed (see France 2000: 175–8). These mainly appeared under the auspices of various scholarly societies, and included Theophilus O'Flanagan's influential translation of the Deirdre story in the *Transactions of the Gaelic Society of Dublin* (1808), John O'Donovan's *Annals of the Four Masters* (1851), Eugene O'Curry's posthumously published *On the Manners and Customs of the Ancient Irish* (1873), and Jeremiah Curtin's *Myths and Folk-lore of Ireland* (1890). Towards the end of the century, however, an increasing number of editions came from continental scholars such as Rudolf Thurneysen, Ernst Windisch, Arbois de Jubainville, and Kuno Meyer. As translations, the influence of many of these texts was limited by their editors' overwhelmingly philological interest in the material and the 'forbidding literalness' of their approach (Cronin 1996: 133)—a tradition which, with rare exceptions like Robin Flower, had a long life into the next century. Works of popularization, such as Standish James O'Grady's *History of Ireland: Heroic Period* (1878) and *History of Ireland: Cuchullain and his contemporaries* (1881), translated the scholarly idiom for a more general readership, and through these combined labours, as well as through the imaginative retellings of the Literary Revival, the early Irish textual corpus came gradually into more general view. Its unparalleled richness and variety would ensure Ireland's prominence in the emerging discipline of Celtic Studies, and continue to inspire Irish literature of both languages into the twentieth century.

Wales

Nothing appears to me so strangely unaccountable as that no English Literary Gentleman should have applied himself to the acquisition and study of the Welsh language during so long a period that the two nations have been so amicably united. It is the primitive language of their own Country... (National Library of Wales MSS 13121B: 480)

This is the stonecutter Edward Williams, better known as the Welsh bard Iolo Morganwg, writing some time around 1805. The claim, typically, is somewhat overstated; indeed, as Iolo himself acknowledges shortly after, the historian Sharon Turner had studied Welsh to good effect for his *Vindication of the Genuineness of the Ancient British Poems of Aneurin, Taliesin, Llywarch Hen and Merdhin* (1803). But there is truth in Iolo's accusation of English indifference (or, worse, hostility) to matters Welsh, and it was a situation he spent much of his life trying to remedy.

Ossian was a large part of the problem: after a mid-century enthusiasm for Wales and its antiquities largely inspired by Thomas Gray's *The Bard* (1757), the Macpherson controversy had left the Welsh under a cloud of suspicion covering all Celtic claims to cultural antiquity (see Constantine 2004). Welsh scholars were roused to transcribe, edit, and publish a literary heritage neglected at home and ignored or belittled abroad. In 1792 the lexicographer William Owen (later William Owen Pughe) published *The Heroic Elegies of Llywarç Hen*, giving literal translations of the short gnomic stanzas associated with the figure of Llywarch the Aged, thought at the time to be a sixth-century prince and poet; here is a characteristic example:

> The tops of the ash glisten, that are white and stately,
> When growing on the top of the dingle:
> The breast rackt with pain, longing is its complaint.
> (Owen 1792: 13)

The poetry, however, was overshadowed by a lengthy introduction, anonymously written by Iolo Morganwg, who worked closely with the unsuspecting Owen for nearly twenty years, using him as a conduit for many of his forgeries.

The introduction set out the poetic philosophy of the Ancient British Bards in elaborate detail, and included several pages of 'translated' Bardic triads, the three-line epigrammatic verse forms which Iolo, a gifted medievalist, faked by the hundred. More spurious triads appeared three years later in his own volume of *Poems, Lyric and Pastoral*, among them perhaps his best known:

> The three primary and indispensable requisites of poetic genius are,
> An eye that can see Nature;
> A heart that can feel Nature;
> And a resolution that dares follow Nature.
>   (Williams 1794: 176)

This volume also contains translations of the renowned fourteenth-century poet Dafydd ap Gwilym, whom Iolo had already successfully mimicked in a dozen forgeries published in 1789.

Between 1801 and 1807 Iolo Morganwg and William Owen produced three large volumes of edited Welsh texts, known as *The Myvyrian Archaiology* (after Owain Myfyr, the bardic name of their sponsor, Owen Jones). Covering everything of note from the sixth-century Taliesin to the late medieval Poetry of Princes, the collection is prefaced by an essay in English, written by Iolo, defending the authenticity of the Welsh manuscript tradition (a claim which holds reasonably well for the material of the first two volumes, less so for the last, which contains much of his own invention). Though many of these pieces were not published in translation until later, the volumes became a useful quarry for writers and antiquaries, and translations were disseminated through journals and through networks of scholars and friends: Robert Southey, for example, incorporated much genuine and spurious lore into his 'Welsh' epic *Madoc* (1804).

In 1828 T. J. Llewelyn Pritchard published a little volume entitled *The Cambrian Wreath*. It was an explicitly low-cost venture, aimed at a popular readership, and containing selections from English writers like Gray, Southey, and Hemans, as well as translations by various authors from a wide chronological span. These include a liberal sprinkling of Iolo's bardic pieces, and the author's own rather excitable versions of the sixth-century *Gododdin*, of which this couplet is typical:

> While chiefs with the glow of resentment were blushing,
> Mid death-shrieks of women, and dreadful blood-gushing.
>   (Pritchard 1828: 81)

Then in 1834 came Arthur James Johnes's undistinguished *Translations into English Verse from the Poems of Davyth ap Gwilym*, which again included some of Iolo's forgeries.

Though primarily concerned with the poetic tradition, William Owen also laboured for many years at translating medieval Welsh prose. His work was never published, and it was Lady Charlotte Guest's *Mabinogion*, appearing between 1838 and 1849, which brought the classic tales to an English audience. Guest (on whom see further pp. 102–3, above) had learned Welsh, but was assisted by scholars whose literal translations formed the basis of her still highly readable versions. In the splendid 1849 edition, which has illustrations, facsimiles, Welsh text, translations, and notes, pride of place is given to the romances, with extracts from their analogues in French and English. From one of these, 'Peredur the Son of Evrawc', Matthew Arnold took his illustration of the Celts' gift for 'natural magic':

And he saw a tall tree by the side of the river, one half of which was in flames from the root to the top, and the other half was green and in full leaf. (Guest 1849: I, 344)

The romances are followed by various 'native' tales, including the 'Four Branches of the Mabinogi' (from which, via a scribal error, Guest took her title) and 'The Tale of Taliesin', a later folk tale about the legendary wonder-child and poet whose name is synonymous with Welsh bardic tradition.

It was a nineteenth-century Taliesin, the bardically named son of Iolo Morganwg, who helped to perpetuate more modern myths by preparing many of his father's papers for publication. *The Iolo Manuscripts*, which included translations, is a compendium of law, history, genealogy, poetry, and fable, all purporting to be a faithful transcript of earlier texts. This book, like the *Myvyrian Archaiology*, fed the druidic speculations and sceptical deconstructions of scholars such as Edward 'Celtic' Davies, Thomas Stephens, and D. W. Nash (whose own translation of 'The Battle of the Trees' would provide the kernel for Robert Graves's *The White Goddess*). Further selections from the Iolo Morganwg papers, with translations, appeared in John Williams's *Barddas*, with predictable consequences for the general perception of Wales as a land of tradition and mystical solemnity. The legacy of Welsh bardism also had consequences for the development of a Celtic identity in Brittany and Cornwall, both of which adopted many of its structures and ceremonies in their revivals.

Another unconventional but irresistible interpreter of Wales and the Welsh was George Borrow, who claimed to have learnt the language as a boy from a groom in East Anglia, and to have translated thousands of lines of Dafydd ap Gwilym while articled to a solicitor in Norwich. These translations were not published, but Borrow's version of Ellis Wynne seventeenth-century classic *The Sleeping Bard* appeared in 1860, rapidly followed by the extraordinary performance of *Wild Wales*, in which the author strides the length of Cambria reciting medieval stanzas and explaining difficult place names to awestruck peasants in their native tongue. Since each 'instructive' encounter adds to the reader's knowledge of the history, literature, language, and customs of Wales, the whole book can be taken as a kind of translation—indeed, many of the dialogues, supposedly taking place through Welsh, are written in a deliberately translated Cambro-English. It is, as John Davies points out, a fantastically skewed representation, in love with a medieval past and oblivious to social realities (Davies 1999); and because Borrow is naturally provocative (and perhaps because he is not Welsh himself), the differences between the two languages and cultures, often played down in Welsh writing at this period, are a constant leitmotif.

In Wales however, partly as a result of the cultural insecurity that followed the Blue Books Report of 1847 (which had criticized the Welsh for their loose morals), the tendency was rather to minimize difference. Towards the end of the century English readers received a milder (and much meeker) dose of Wales in two anthologies, John Jenkins's *The Poetry of Wales* (1873), and Edmund O. Jones's *Welsh Lyrics of the Nineteenth Century* (1896), both characterized by what M. Wynn Thomas calls an 'anxious Britophilia' (1999: 120). James Harris's English version of Daniel Owen's novel *Rhys Lewis*, missing the sceptical humour of the original, did little to challenge these bland representations of late Victorian Wales.

In Ireland throughout this period translation is tangled in a situation of open conflict; in Wales one constantly picks up a note of hurt bafflement at the English failure to understand. Thomas Stephens's enlightened work *The Literature of the Kymry* (which contains many reliable literal translations of the early poems) opens with the quietly sardonic comment: 'On the map of Britain, facing St George's Channel, is a group of counties called Wales, inhabited by a people, distinct from, and but very imperfectly understood by, those who surround them' (Stephens 1849: v). Charlotte Guest's *Mabinogion* apart, it is not certain, in the confusion of forged and real traditions, that a century's worth of translation did much to improve matters.

Scotland and Man

In Scotland the Ossian controversy had stimulated the hunt for oral and literary 'remains' which might be used to prove or disprove the authenticity of Macpherson's translations. A major work to result from this activity was John Francis Campbell's *Popular Tales of the West Highlands*, which, as Douglas Hyde noted in 1890, put Scots Gaelic well ahead of Irish in the collection and documentation of the oral literature of its people. Campbell's collection broke new ground for folklore research, providing exact transcriptions and details of informant and provenance, supplied from a wide network of trained Gaelic speakers. The translations of the tales and lays retain many dialect words and closely follow the style and syntax of the original. Besides testifying further to the shared culture of Irish and Scottish Gaelic speakers, Campbell's work showed that parts of the Highlands and Islands still possessed a thriving, if un-Macphersonian, Fenian tradition. It also paved the way for a highly significant and influential collection of translations of Gaelic traditional lore, Alexander Carmichael's *Carmina Gadelica*, which appeared at the end of the century. The search for manuscripts was also fruitful, one of the most important finds being the early sixteenth-century Book of the Dean of Lismore, which was edited and translated by W. F. Skene and Thomas MacLauchlan in 1862. This is a valuable, if idiosyncratic, early record of the bardic poetry of eulogy and elegy that survived until the forced disintegration of the clans in the mid-eighteenth century. Another edition of the Dean's Book appeared, with a wide range of translated 'genuine' Ossianic texts, in Alexander Cameron's posthumous *Reliquiae Celticae*.

The country that produced Burns was unlikely to neglect its lyrics, and there were various attempts throughout the century to capture something of the Gaelic tradition in both English and Scots. Alexander Campbell, in *Albyn's Anthology*, set Gaelic airs and songs to English or Scots verse translations supplied by 'eminent authors' such as James Hogg and Walter Scott. These 'imitations' were accompanied by Gaelic texts and literal translations, which at least had the virtue of making the gentrification process transparent. Robert Munro's *Minor Poems and Translations* (1843) merely retreads Ossianic ground in a fulsome and uncritical style; a wider range of texts, including poems by Duncan Ban Macintyre (1724–1812), can be found in *Selections from the Gaelic Bards* by Thomas Pattison. In the four volumes of *The Modern Scottish Minstrel* Charles Rogers rounds up the 'gems' of (mostly nineteenth-century) Scottish song. Though predominantly Scots and English, each volume includes some attempt to 'adapt, by means of suitable metrical translations, the minstrelsy of the Gaël for Lowland melody' (Rogers 1855–7: I, v). The difficulty of the task is recognized in an endearing introduction to Robert Mackay's (Rob Donn's) 'The Song of Winter', in which the translator complains of 'a style peculiar to the Highlands, where description runs so entirely into epithets and adjectives, as to render recitation breathless, and translation hopeless' (Rogers 1855–7: I, 311).

Whereas Gaelic Scotland's literary tradition, oral and written, could be recovered and revived by writers and scholars fluent in a still-living language, this was not the case on the Isle of Man where, during the nineteenth century, Manx went into rapid decline. Translation into English bears all the marks of a salvage operation. A. W. Moore's *Carvalyn Gailckagh* is a selection of the Manx 'carvals' or hymns described enthusiastically by George Borrow on an expedition to the island in 1855. They are mostly eighteenth century, and written, according to their editor, 'by men who had the Manx Bible [1722] in their hands, and who were under the influence of strong religious enthusiasm' (Moore 1891: iv). A companion volume, *Manx Ballads and Music*, extended the range of texts but was equally modest in its claims for Manx tradition; in the preface T. E. Brown laments that 'the songs are so few in number, and in quality, so trifling, so unromantic, so unpoetical, and so modern' and attributes the absence of bardic poetry to 'the football position of the Island, kicked about from Celt to Norseman, from English to Scot' (Moore 1896: x). Moore is also somewhat disparaging, but the collection, with its plain literal translations, has aged surprisingly well. It opens with a fragment of an Ossianic lay, 'Fin as Oshin', and includes a lively range of children's songs and a version of the European 'Hunting the Wren' song of great value to folklorists.

Cornwall and Brittany

By 1790 Cornish was no longer spoken as a living language, and all translation work of this period has an archaeological flavour. Surviving written Cornish is confined to a handful of texts, most of them from the later Middle Ages and on religious themes. In 1826 and 1827 Davies Gilbert published two early and rather unreliable translations by the seventeenth-century antiquary John Keigwin of the poem on the Passion, *Pascon agan Arluth*, and the Creation drama *Gwreans an bys*. Both texts were re-edited and translated by Whitley Stokes, who also translated the early sixteenth-century play *The Life of Saint Meriasek, Bishop and Confessor* in 1872. Edwin Norris's *The Ancient Cornish Drama* gave a reliable edition and translation of the cycle of plays known as the *Ordinalia*, written at the same period as the Passion poem. Dry as some of these translations are (and they do little justice to the flashes of humour and beauty in the originals: see Murdoch 1993), they were vital in waking an interest in the Cornish language which would lead, in the twentieth century, to its revival on a small scale as a spoken tongue.

Breton at this period was very much alive, and spoken widely all over Breizh-Izel (Lower Brittany); with virtually no surviving manuscript literature, its chief wealth was an abundant oral tradition. Its impact on an English readership, however, was slight. The very few translations of Breton folk tales, such as the anonymous *Breton Legends*, are clearly taken from French-language rewrites (in this case Émile Souvestre's *Le Foyer breton* of 1844), which do little to reflect Breton patterns of speech. The plainer style of Mrs A. E. Whitehead's *Dealings with the Dead* may be closer to the folk-tale mode, but again comes mediated through Anatole Le Braz's *La Légende de la mort* (1893). The ballad tradition, if anything, fared still worse. The nineteenth century saw several translations from Hersart de la Villemarqué's *Barzaz-Breiz*, an ingenious compendium of songs and ballads whose Breton originals were conflated and rewritten to form a romanticized history of the Breton people from druidic times onwards. The first edition, published in 1839, met a quick response in Louisa Stuart Costello's tour account *A Summer among the Bocages and Vines* (1840), but the major translation into English (of a sort) was Tom Taylor's *Ballads and Songs of Brittany*. Though La Villemarqué did include Breton texts in his collection, and though Taylor claims to be following these 'originals' in his translations (Taylor 1865: xviii), the resulting verse owes more to the romantic minstrelsy of devotees of Scott than to any Celtic language (see Constantine 1996: 179–88). Shorter selections followed, one in 1870 by the wonderfully named Headmaster of Hipperholme Grammar School, F. Fleay, and one in 1886 by Henry Carrington. Between them they left the Breton ballad tradition as pale and enervated as any respectable Victorian heroine:

> 'Twas pity still to see her weeping salt salt tears and sair
> On the threshold of the manor, she that was so douce and fair,
> For her foster-brother's good ship looking ever o'er the foam,
> Her only living comfort, longing sore for it to come.
> (Taylor 1865: 110)

The process of translation into Victorian English can be read as a coercion to Britishness, a quashing of internal difference: the conventional dictates of nineteenth-century verse do much to mask the real diversity of the originals. In this respect, with notable exceptions, it may be that the most important translations of the time were the crabbed literal editions of the scholars, which have often had a more productive afterlife in the works of later writers (one thinks of Seamus Heaney's *Sweeney Astray*). Yet by the time this period closes, all the Celtic-speaking countries had, to a greater or lesser degree, experienced a revival of interest in their languages and literatures which did much to improve their confidence, and helped slow the rate of language loss. Mediation through English played a significant part in the process of rediscovering and forging (in various senses of the word) cultural links—and in creating, for better *and* for worse, a new 'pan-Celtic' identity.

LIST OF SOURCES

Translations
Anon. (*c.* 1860). *Breton Legends*. London.
Borrow, George (1860). *The Sleeping Bard, or, Visions of the World, Death, and Hell* [Ellis Wynne]. London.
—— (1862). *Wild Wales: Its People, Language and Scenery*, 3 vols. London.
Brooke, Charlotte (1789). *Reliques of Irish Poetry*. Dublin.
Cameron, Alexander (1892). *Reliquiae Celticae*, 2 vols. Inverness.
Campbell, Alexander (1816–18). *Albyn's Anthology, or, A Select Collection of the Melodies and Vocal Poetry Peculiar to Scotland and the Isles*. Edinburgh.
Campbell, John Francis (1860–2). *Popular Tales of the West Highlands*, 4 vols. Edinburgh.
Carrington, Henry (1886). *Breton Ballads*. Edinburgh.
Davies, Edward (1804). *Celtic Researches, on the Origin, Traditions & Language of the Ancient Britons*. London.
Drummond, William Hamilton (1852). *Ancient Irish Minstrelsy*. Dublin.
Ferguson, Samuel (1834). 'Hardiman's *Irish Minstrelsy* I–IV', *Dublin University Magazine* (Vol. 3, no. 16, 456–78; Vol. 4, no. 20, 152–67; Vol. 4, no. 22, 447–67; Vol. 4, no. 23, 514–42).
—— (1865). *Lays of the Western Gael, and Other Poems*. London.
Fleay, F. (1870). *The Master Pieces of the Breton Ballads*. Halifax.
Guest, Charlotte (1849). *The Mabinogion: from the Llyfr Coch o Hergest, and Other Ancient Welsh Manuscripts*, 3 vols. London.
Hardiman, James (1831). *Irish Minstrelsy, or, Bardic Remains of Ireland*, 2 vols. London.
Harris, James (1888). *Rhys Lewis, Minister of Bethel: An Autobiography* [Daniel Owen]. Wrexham.
Hyde, Douglas (1890). *Beside the Fire: A Collection of Irish Gaelic Folk Stories*. London.
—— (1893). *Abhráin Grádh Chúige Connacht, or, Love Songs of Connacht*. Dublin.
Keigwin, John (1826). *Mount Calvary, or, The History of the Passion, Death and Resurrection, of our Lord and Saviour, Jesus Christ*, ed. Davies Gilbert. London.
—— (1827). *The Creation of the World with Noah's Flood, written in Cornish in the Year 1611 by Wm Jordan*, ed. Davies Gilbert. London.
Mangan, James Clarence (2003). *Selected Poems*, ed. Jacques Chuto *et al*. Dublin.
Moore, A. W. (1891). *Carvalyn Gailckagh*. Douglas, IOM.
—— (1896). *Manx Ballads and Music*. Douglas, IOM.
Moore, Thomas (1854). *Irish Melodies*. London (the first two numbers of *Irish Melodies* appeared in 1807, with seven further numbers between then and 1834).
Nash, D. W. (1858). *Taliesin, or, The Bards and Druids of Britain*. London.
Norris, Edwin (1859). *The Ancient Cornish Drama*, 2 vols. Oxford.

Owen [Pughe], William (1792). *The Heroic Elegies and Other Pieces of Llywarç Hen*. London.
Pattison, Thomas (1866). *Selections from the Gaelic Bards*. Glasgow.
Pritchard, T. J. Llewelyn (1828). *The Cambrian Wreath: A Selection of English Poems on Welsh Subjects, Original and Translated from the Cambro British*. Aberystwyth.
Rogers, Charles (1855–7). *The Modern Scottish Minstrel, or, The Songs of Scotland of the Past Half-Century*. Edinburgh.
Sigerson, George (1897). *Bards of the Gael and Gall: Examples of the Poetic Literature of Erin*. London.
Skene, W. F. and MacLauchlan, Thomas, eds. (1862). *The Dean of Lismore's Book: A Selection of Ancient Gaelic Poetry*. Edinburgh.
Stephens, Thomas (1849). *The Literature of the Kymry*. Llandovery.
Stokes, Whitley (1860–1). 'The Passion: A Middle Cornish Poem', *Transactions of the Philological Society*, Appendix, 1–100.
—— (1864). *Gwreans an bys: The Creation of the World*. London.
—— (1872). *The Life of Saint Meriasek, Bishop and Confessor*. London.
Taylor, Tom (1865). *Ballads and Songs of Brittany*. London.
Walsh, Edward (1844). *Reliques of Irish Jacobite Poetry*. Dublin.
—— (1847). *Irish Popular Songs*. Dublin.
Whitehead, Mrs A. E. (1898). *Dealings with the Dead: Narratives from 'La Légende de la mort en Basse Bretagne'*. London.
Williams, Edward ('Iolo Morganwg') (1794). *Poems, Lyric and Pastoral*, 2 vols. London.
—— (1848). *Iolo Manuscripts*, ed. Taliesin Williams. Llandovery.
Williams, John ('Ab Ithel') (1862–74). *Barddas*, 2 vols. Llandovery.

Other Sources
Arnold, Matthew (1962). 'On the Study of Celtic Literature', pp. 291–395 in *Lectures & Essays in Criticism*, ed. R. H. Super. Ann Arbor, MI (first pub. 1867).
Bromwich, Rachel (1965). *Matthew Arnold and Celtic Literature: A Retrospect, 1865–1965*. Oxford.
Chapman, Malcolm (1992). *The Celts: The Construction of a Myth*. London.
Constantine, Mary-Ann (1996). *Breton Ballads*. Aberystwyth.
—— (2004). 'Ossian in Wales and Brittany', pp. 67–90 in Howard Gaskill, ed., *The Reception of Ossian in Europe*. London.
Cronin, Michael (1996). *Translating Ireland: Translation, Languages, Cultures*. Cork.
Davies, John (1999). 'George Borrow's Wales.' *Planet* 134: 61–7.
France, Peter, ed. (2000). *The Oxford Guide to Literature in English Translation*. Oxford.
Glen, Duncan (1991). *The Poetry of the Scots: An Introduction and Bibliographical Guide to Poetry in Gaelic, Scots, Latin and English*. Edinburgh.
James, Simon (1999). *The Atlantic Celts: Ancient People or Modern Invention?* London.
Jones, Owen, et al., eds. (1801–1807). *The Myvyrian Archaiology of Wales, Collected out of Ancient Manuscripts*, 3 vols. London.
Lloyd, David (1987). *Nationalism and Minor Literature: James Clarence Mangan and the Emergence of Irish Cultural Nationalism*. Berkeley, CA.
Murdoch, Brian (1993). *Cornish Literature*. Cambridge.
Renan, Ernest (1928). 'La Poésie des races celtiques' [reprinted from *Revue des deux mondes*, 1854], pp. 375–456 in Ernest Renan, *Essais de morale et de critique*. Paris.

Sims-Williams, Patrick (1986). 'The Visionary Celt: The Construction of an Ethnic Preconception.' *Cambridge Medieval Celtic Studies* 11: 71–96.
Thomas, M. Wynn (1999). *Corresponding Cultures: The Two Literatures of Wales*. Cardiff.
Thomson, Derick (1989). *An Introduction to Gaelic Poetry*, 2nd edn. Edinburgh.
Welch, Robert (1988). *A History of Verse Translation from the Irish, 1789–1897*. Gerrards Cross.
Yeats, W. B. (1970). 'The Poetry of Sir Samuel Ferguson', pp. 29–53 in Roger Mc Hugh, ed., *Davis, Mangan, Ferguson? Tradition and the Irish Writer: Writings by W. B. Yeats and by Thomas Kinsella*. Dublin.

6.8 Literatures of Central and Eastern Europe

Peter France

The Beginnings: John Bowring

In 1821, introducing the first of his series of anthologies of poetry from Central and Eastern Europe, John Bowring wrote that Russia had recently 'emerged, as it were instantaneously, from a night of ignorance' (Bowring 1821–3: I, v). This is a sizeable error: there is a formidable body of medieval Russian literature, which was little known in Russia before 1800 and largely neglected in the West until the late nineteenth century. But Bowring's pardonable ignorance here is symptomatic of a more general lack of awareness of the literatures of Central and Eastern Europe at the beginning of the nineteenth century. Writers who composed in Latin (such as Sarbiewski, Copernicus, Comenius) were read, and might be translated, but the vernacular literatures of Russia, Poland, Hungary, and other Central and Eastern European countries were more or less *terra incognita* until about 1820, when it was Bowring himself who began the process of discovery.

We can therefore conveniently place the revelation of Central and Eastern European literature between two Russian anthologies, Bowring's and the much fuller one produced by Leo Wiener in 1902–3 under the title *An Anthology of Russian Literature from the Earliest Period to the Present Time*. Wiener, a Russian-born professor at Harvard, whose two volumes include writing from the tenth century to Chekhov, could look back over nearly a century of translation and commentary. His anthology includes much poetry translated by hands other than his own, very few of them well known. These translations are not noticeably better than those of Bowring (some indeed are by Bowring), but their range and abundance suggest that the latter's pioneering initiative had not gone unheeded. Over the same period, the literatures of Russia's western neighbours also began to attract attention.

Brought up as a merchant, Bowring travelled widely and had a passion for languages. In addition to the French, Italian, Spanish, Portuguese, Dutch, and German he acquired in his early years, it has been claimed (*DNB1*) that he had some knowledge of Swedish, Danish, Russian, Serbian, Polish, and Bohemian, as well as studying Arabic, Magyar, and Chinese. The depth and accuracy of his knowledge are highly questionable—a hostile George Borrow, whose own philology was idiosyncratic, described him as 'slightly acquainted with four or five of the easier dialects in Europe' (Borrow 1923–4: VI, 315)—but he clearly worked in part from original texts, with much help from native informants or from translations into French or German. *DNB1* suggests that he had early schemes for 'writing the history and giving translated specimens of the popular poetry, not only of the

Western, but of the Oriental world'. What survives of this grandiose design is impressive enough: a series of seven anthologies (including Russian, Serbian, Polish, Magyar, and Czech), all translated by himself and published between 1820 and 1832 (much later in his career he published translations of the great Hungarian poet Sandór Petőfi). The anthologies are by no means confined to 'popular poetry' (i.e. ballads etc.), and they helped to establish a British canon for the poetic literatures in question—for instance, a much fuller Polish anthology by Paul Soboleski (1881) incorporates some of Bowring's translations.

Bowring's ambition, he declares in the preface to his *Poetry of the Magyars* (Bowring 1830: viii), is 'one of benevolence'; he has 'never left the soil of [his] native country but with the wish to return to it, bearing fresh olive branches of peace and fresh garlands of poetry' (Bowring 1830: viii). He notes the indulgence with which his 'attempts' have been received, and some indulgence may indeed have been necessary for publications that were remarkable more for quantity than for quality. Nevertheless, his achievement was considerable (for an appreciation see Sova 1943) and was honoured by numerous learned societies in the lands he had brought to the attention of his countrymen.

Insofar as he had a theory of translation, it was purportedly one of respect for his source texts. In his Czech anthology he states: 'I have always refrained from attempting to *adapt* them to English taste, and the occasions are very few in which I have wandered even from the phraseology of the original' (Bowring 1832: 85). Generally, though, the demands of metre and rhyme seem to have led this not particularly gifted writer to produce translations which, however interesting, are not distinguished. Here, for instance, is his rendering of the opening lines of the eighth poem in the Polish Renaissance poet Jan Kochanowski's sequence *Treny* (Laments), which he was the first to reveal to anglophone readers:

> My gentle child! and art thou vanished? – Thou
> Hast left a dreary blank of sadness now;
> Our house though full is desolate and lone
> Since thy young spirit and its smiles are gone.
> (Bowring 1827a: 51)

The exclamation and question of the first line come from the translator here, as does the doubling up 'desolate and lone' and 'thy young spirit and its smiles', while the 'dreary blank of sadness' is a Romantic overtranslation of Kochanowski's plainer original ('emptiness').

In addition to his books, Bowring contributed both translations and reviews to the journals of the day. While Central and Eastern Europe were not among their central concerns, some, such as the *North American Review* in the USA and the *Athenaeum*, the *Westminster Review*, and the *Foreign Quarterly Review* in Britain, devoted a fair amount of space to this unfamiliar material (see Phelps 1960; Brewster 1954: 46–50). As well as reviews of new writing, this coverage extended to new translations of literary texts. The first separate publications of translations from Adam Mickiewicz, for instance, were preceded by extracts in the *Foreign Quarterly Review* (for this journal's coverage of Russian and Polish literature see Curran 1961).

Some idea of the likely interest of the journal-reading public in Eastern European writing can be gained from the fact that Bowring's *Poetry of the Magyars* (1830) was reviewed in no fewer than twenty-five periodicals (Czigány 1969: 34–5). There was an audience for this new material, then, though also hostility: a long satirical review in *Fraser's Magazine* (May 1830), not content with attacking Bowring as the first editor of Bentham's *Westminster Review*, mocks the exoticism fed by his translations, as in this parallel-text parody by one John Churchill:

Te Pikke Megge	*The Pious Maiden*
Hogy, wogy, Pogy!	Holy little Polly!
Xupumxe trtzááá bnikttm.	Love sought me but I tricked him.
Pogy, wogy hogy!	Polly little holy!
Bsduro plgvbz ettnsttm.	You thought of me, 'I've nicked him'.
Wogy hogy Pogy!	Little holy Polly!
Mlésrz vbquógp fvikttm.	I'm not to be your victim.

Following Bowring, then, in the journals and elsewhere, there was a certain amount of translation from the languages of Central and Eastern Europe. Most of this was done by obscure individuals, the exception being George Borrow, even if his translations remained virtually unknown in their day. Like Bowring (with whom he once hoped to collaborate on a Scandinavian volume), Borrow travelled widely and gained some knowledge of a great range of languages. Two volumes published in St Petersburg in 1835, *The Talisman* and *Targum*, contain translations from some thirty languages, including Russian, 'Malo Russian' (Ukrainian), and Polish. Among the Polish texts are two by Mickiewicz, whose Romantic outsider status seems to have appealed to Borrow (see discussion in Hyde 1999: 82–92). But it is the Russian contribution which is most notable, including some remarkable versions of folk tales and several poems by Pushkin, who came on the scene too late to figure in Bowring.

Ballads and Nationalism

One recurrent interest, seen in Bowring and Borrow and throughout the century, is in folk songs, ballads, and other traditional oral material from Eastern Europe. There are collections of this kind for all the major languages of the region, in some cases several different volumes. The songs of Serbia, for instance, attracted a good deal of attention, particularly at times when the Serbian struggle for independence was in the news (the years 1875–9 saw five publications on the subject in significant journals). As for books, following Bowring's *Servian Popular Poetry* (1827), one can cite the following collections: *Serbski Pesme, or, National Songs of the Serbs* (1861) translated via the French by Owen Meredith (the poetic pseudonym of the younger Bulwer Lytton); *Popular Tales* (1874), *Kossovo* (1881, a compilation of oral epics), and *Serbian Folk-Lore* (1899), all by E. L. Mijatovich; and *Songs of Liberty and Other Poems* (1897) by R. U. Johnson. In addition, the translations published by J. G. Lockhart in a review article in the *Quarterly Review* (January 1827) were in fact by Lockhart himself, who like Bowring had been attracted by the German translation of poems in the great Serbian folk-song collection of Vuk Karadžić. Lockhart describes this poetry as 'minstrelsy'—a reference to his father-in-law Sir Walter Scott's versions of the ballads of his own country. As a young man, Scott had been interested in foreign ballads, translating several from the German, but also (via the Italian and Goethe's German) a traditional Serbian song 'Hasanaginica' ('The Wife of Hasan-aga'), which before the end of the nineteenth century had appeared in a dozen different English translations (on Serbian ballads in English see Subotić 1932: 222–66).

Serbian folk poetry reached Britain principally through German, then, and the British interest in East European folk literature is part of the wider movement, inspired above all by Herder, which led to the collection—and in many cases the translation—of the literature of the 'people' from all over Europe and beyond (see § 9.3, below) and to the production of a copious ballad literature in countries of Western Europe. Later in the century, for instance, we find Jeremiah Curtin, who by this time worked in the American Bureau of Ethnology, publishing a volume of *Myths and Folk-Tales of the Russians, Western Slavs and Magyars* (1890) alongside volumes devoted to the folklore and mythology of Ireland, North America, and elsewhere.

In the case of Eastern Europe, however, the interest was not simply anthropological or poetic. As some of the titles quoted above suggest, there were political motives in play as well. For this was the time when the peoples of Central and Eastern Europe were emerging into nationhood, liberating themselves from the power of the Ottoman Empire, Russia, or Austro-Hungary. The struggle of the Greeks attracted most attention in the West, but other peoples followed suit. All this had implications for literature and for literary translation. By 1830, writes J. P. T. Bury, 'philologists and historians, poets and journalists, had played their part in rekindling the national spirit of Greek and Serb' (Bury 1960: 213). To publish a translation of the national folk epics of the Serbs was therefore implicitly to offer support to the cause of Serbian independence. Similarly, when the exiled Mickiewicz's *Konrad Wallenrod* was twice translated into English in one year (Cattley 1841; Jablonski 1841), it is clear from the translators' introductions that they were alive to what a later translator of the same poem called the 'undercurrent of political meaning' and 'the utterances of a Pole against Russian tyranny' (Biggs 1882: xiii).

Since the Napoleonic wars and the Congress of Vienna, the affairs of Central and Eastern Europe had become more familiar to the western reader—and the journals leave little doubt about the openness of some readers to the foreign. For Russia in particular, this was partly a question of self-interest; as early as 1823, Bowring had written: 'The statesman will do well to study the tendency and the character of that fountainhead whose waters will spread over generations of men, and over the widest empire in the world' (Bowring 1821–3: II, vii). Events in the Crimea were to add a new impetus to find out more about the hostile new power in the east; paradoxically, perhaps, 'the Crimean War did miracles for Turgenev's fortunes in Britain, as indeed for those of Russian culture in general' (Waddington 1995: 2).

Poland, Hungary, and Beyond

It was in the second half of the century that the translation of individual books began to increase from a trickle to a broad stream, with a new predominance of prose fiction. The major presence was that of Russia, but there were popular translations from other countries, notably Poland (which at this time had no existence on the map, having been swallowed up by its neighbours). For most of the century, Mickiewicz, living in exile in Paris, was the best-known Polish writer. His patriotic poem *Konrad Wallenrod*, excerpted by Borrow in his unpublished *Songs of Scandinavia*, was translated in its entirety by four different hands; the first version, by Leon Jablonski (1841), is in prose, with substantial explanatory notes, and with the songs done into verse by a 'lady of Edinburgh'. Cattley's translation, published in the same year, attempts to imitate Mickiewicz's metres and rhymes, but the basic narrative appears in plodding octosyllabic couplets. Maude Ashhurst Biggs in 1882 chose rather to use blank verse for the narrative, but this freedom did not lead to distinction, any more than with her version of Mickiewicz's epic masterpiece, *Pan Tadeusz*. Nevertheless, the limp, archaizing verse of her *Master Thaddeus* reads quite easily and is accompanied by full explanatory notes.

Mickiewicz was thus fairly well known to English-speaking readers, as were one or two other writers such as the poet Zygmunt Krasinski, whose allegorical *Undivine Comedy* received three separate translations in the United States. But the great popular success at the end of the century was the novelist Henryk Sienkiewicz, who was to win the Nobel Prize for Literature in 1905. Many of Sienkiewicz's novels, including the Roman epic *Quo Vadis?* and the great Polish historical trilogy *With Fire and Sword*, *The Deluge*, and *Pan Michael*, were published in the USA in rapid succession in the 1890s in translations by Jeremiah Curtin. *Quo Vadis?* was also translated by two other hands in the same decade. Curtin's texts are broadly faithful to the originals, if stylistically unimpressive; they did service for many years.

Another central European success story was that of the Hungarian novelist Jókai Mór (or Maurus), many of whose works were englished by various translators in the last two decades of the century. His compatriot Kálmán Mikszáth was being translated at the same time, and there were versions of a variety of isolated works by Hungarians, Czechs, Poles, Romanians, and even Bulgarians during the second half of the nineteenth century, while Georgian writings, by Ilya Chavchavadze, Sulkhan-Saba Orbeliani, and Shota Rustaveli, began to be translated by Marjory and Oliver Wardrop in the 1890s (for more details see pp. 554–5, below). But it was Russian literature which from about 1840 dominated translation from Central and Eastern Europe.

Russian Literature: Pushkin

Donald Davie once declared that 'the awakening of the Anglo-Saxon people to Russian literature—something which happened to all intents and purposes between 1885 and 1920—should rank as a turning-point no less momentous than the discovery of Italian literature by the generations of the English Renaissance' (Davie 1990: 276). While the high point of this revolution straddles the periods dealt with by this volume and its successor, the basic canon of classic Russian literature in translation was in place by the end of the nineteenth century, and a number of major translations had already been made. In 1886 the Russian novel was described to western readers in the influential French work by Melchior de Vogüé, *Le Roman russe*, and in December of the following year Matthew Arnold, in his article 'Count Leo Tolstoi' in the *Fortnightly Review*, wrote: 'The Russian novel has now the vogue, and deserves to have it.' At the same time, the London publisher Henry Vizetelly was advertising in his publications a list of 'Vizetelly's Russian novels' including Gogol's *Dead Souls* and *Taras Bulba*, Lermontov's *A Hero of our Time*, Tolstoy's *Anna Karenina* and *War and Peace*, and Dostoevsky's *Crime and Punishment*.

If Pushkin, the Russian national poet, occupied only a modest place in the vogue for things Russian, this was due to the difficulty of making his verse interesting in translation (Flaubert is reputed to have said to Turgenev, who had shown him some French translations: 'Il est plat, votre poète'). As we have seen, Borrow was a pioneer here, and his achievement has been praised (see for example Cross 1993: 209–21). Like Bowring and many other translators, he is often led by his desire to replicate the prosody of the original and by the relative shortness of English words to a kind of doggerel with repeated phrases and added adjectives adulterating the simplicity of the original. In the opening lines of his fairly close translation of 'The Black Shawl', for instance, his echoing of the rhyme and ternary metre of Pushkin's text produces a somewhat childish effect in English:

> On the shawl, the black shawl with distraction I gaze,
> And on my poor spirit keen agony preys.
>
> When easy of faith, young and ardent was I,
> I lov'd a fair Grecian with love the most high.
>
> The damsel deceitful she flattered my flame,
> But soon a dark cloud o'er my sunshine there came.
> (Borrow 1923–4: XVI, 29)

Borrow was succeeded as a translator of Pushkin by Thomas Budge Shaw, a professor of English in St Petersburg, who in 1845 published three articles about the poet in *Blackwood's Magazine*, with a substantial selection of lyrics, diligently replicating the forms of the original, reasonably accurate in meaning, but with much conventional padding.

Much later in the century, there were larger but otherwise unnoteworthy selections of Pushkin's verse by Ivan Panin (Boston, 1888) and C. E. Turner, a long-standing resident of St Petersburg who had written and lectured on Russian literature in Britain, and whose centenary volume of 1899 includes a version of the drama *Boris Godunov*. The verse novel *Eugene Onegin* found its only nineteenth-century translator in 1881, the otherwise obscure Lieutenant Colonel H. Spalding.

Although mocked by Vladimir Nabokov in the introduction to his own translation of the work, Spalding's version, done from Russian rather than from French, remains quite close to the original in form and content, and has a certain vigour and unforced directness. But it was Pushkin's prose, in particular the novel *The Captain's Daughter* and the short story 'The Queen of Spades', both repeatedly translated, that was the principal centre of attraction (for a listing of versions see Line 1972: 27–9).

Turgenev and the Novel

The predominant approach to Russian fiction at this time was as a window on an unknown and fascinating world. Stress was laid on the realistic qualities of the prose, whether that of a Gogol or a Dostoevsky. Thus Gogol's fantastic prose epic *Dead Souls* appeared first (in an 1854 travesty by Krystyn Lach-Szyrma) as *Home Life in Russia, by a Russian Noble*, and Frederick Whishaw's early translation of *Crime and Punishment* was described on the title page as a 'Russian realistic novel'. These early translators tended to be less interested than their successors in the stylistic qualities of their authors.

Anglo-American novelists possessed a justifiable confidence in their native resources for much of the nineteenth century, but the search for new and more realistic techniques eventually brought some authors to consider the possibilities that Russian writing appeared to hold out. It is significant that the year of Henry James's essay 'The Art of Fiction' (1884), questioning the Anglo-Saxon novel tradition, also sees him recommending Turgenev's manner as 'always the most fruitful' for the English novelist (see Turton 1992: 45–7). Russian fiction was often associated with French realism or naturalism, but it owed a good deal of its popularity with critics to a 'spiritual' dimension which set it apart from the disreputable work of Balzac or Zola. Because the French translations were first in the field, however, many English authors and critics came to the novels through them rather than through the renderings discussed here.

Easily the best-known Russian writer until about 1885 was Turgenev, who acquired a formidable reputation, particularly in America, where translations of many of his works were issued in the 1870s and 1880s by the publisher Henry Holt. His effects on American authors began with a surge of interest within an influential group of New England writers including William Dean Howells and Henry James in the 1870s. In Britain, a total of some sixty translations of Turgenev appeared in book form or in journals in the years between 1854 and 1900, in addition to Constance Garnett's fifteen-volume collection. He visited England several times, and came to be recognized by some of its writers as 'Europe's greatest novelist'—though a story is told of him insisting the company toast George Eliot rather than himself under that sobriquet when the pair met in 1878. To James, who wrote about the Russian master's work on several occasions and was aware of the inadequacies of some of the translations, Turgenev was the 'novelist's novelist', the supreme exponent of an independent art of fiction. Differing accounts are offered of his influence on James, perhaps because it is so thoroughly absorbed: on his approach to plots and themes in the tales; on certain of his fictional heroines; on his subject matter and overall development (see variously Lerner 1941; Phelps 1956: 59–87; Turton 1992: 58–100). Gissing too acknowledged the power of Turgenev's example, and its likely effects include his avoidance of the most aggressive forms of naturalism (see Waddington 1995: 61–2). Turgenev's impact was to be still more obvious on writers of the Edwardian period such as George Moore, Arnold Bennett, and John Galsworthy.

But the early translators saw Turgenev, as they saw his fellow novelists, primarily as a source of information about Russian life. Thus his first work to be translated, in 1855, the *Sportsman's Sketches*, was given the title *Russian Life in the Interior, or, The Experiences of a Sportsman* by its 'editor' J. D. Meiklejohn. Like many nineteenth-century English renderings of Russian works, this was made from a French one. Since Turgenev lived in France and worked with some of his translators, these French translations possessed a kind of authority; more generally, it was often claimed, with little justification, that the novels of Turgenev and Tolstoy were better suited to the elegance of French than to plainer English.

Turgenev's most important champion in Britain was William Ralston, a senior employee of the British Museum and a translator of Russian folk tales and folk songs. He published vigorous attacks on the inadequate renderings of such translators as Rowland Crawley (*Smoke*, 1868) and C. E. Turner (*On the Eve*, 1871). Ralston himself translated Turgenev's novel *Liza* (1869, a version of *Dvoryanskoe Gnezdo*, literally *A Nest of Gentlefolk*), and there were abortive plans for him to collaborate with the author on a political novel (see Waddington 1995: 45–7). The most important of Turgenev's translators, however, were Constance Garnett and her American rival Isabel Hapgood. Garnett brought out her edition of the *Novels* in 1894–9, whereas Hapgood's, in sixteen volumes, was published in 1903–4, with an introduction by Henry James.

Hapgood's translations from Russian have not worn particularly well, but they were numerous and in their day influential (her translation of the Orthodox Service Book has been seen as her masterpiece). She was one of the early translators of Gogol and Tolstoy, and it is a sign of the popularity of things Russian that her versions of Gogol's *Dead Souls* and *Taras Bulba* were immediately reissued without acknowledgement by the enterprising publisher Vizetelly, who contented himself with having them slightly revised (and improved, it must be said). But among the different versions of *A Nest of Gentlefolk*, her translation, while accurate enough on the whole, now seems laboured, particularly in the dialogue passages, when compared with both Garnett's and Ralston's. The latter, starting from an 'absolutely literal' version, had had help from Russian friends, including the author; his rendering remained a close one, written in plain English which still reads quite well. He is not shy of using Russian names and keeping occasional words in the original, and in places offers explanatory footnotes. Garnett, whose Turgenev was her first major undertaking, had already established the easy and elegant style—sometimes discreetly modifying or simplifying the Russian—that was to win her such success in the coming decades with her Chekhov and Dostoevsky. It is not surprising that her Turgenev remained a standard text well into the twentieth century (see p. 14, above).

Tolstoy and Dostoevsky

Tolstoy had many translators. The main point to note is that the two different sides of his work—the great novels and the moral or religious pamphlets—became known in English all together in the 1880s (see Jones 1995: 10–11). Before then there had been only an isolated version of the autobiographical *Childhood and Youth* by the German writer Malwida von Meysenbug in 1862, and in 1878 a translation of *The Cossacks* by the American Eugene Schuyler, also the first translator of Turgenev's *Fathers and Children*. From about 1885, however, interest in Tolstoy outstripped that in Turgenev, and some of his works came out in several competing English versions, once again often done partly or wholly from the French (for a listing see Line 1972: 31–52).

At the close of the century Tolstoy had a strong connection with England, where his disciples Vladimir Chertkov and Aylmer Maude settled on their move from Moscow in 1897. Chertkov and his British associates in the Tolstoyan community known as the Purleigh Brotherhood not only published Russian texts by the Master that had been banned or mutilated by the censor in Russia, they also produced numerous translations, mainly of short and edifying pamphlets by Tolstoy priced so as to appeal to a popular audience (see Holman 1988). It was as part of this campaign that Aylmer Maude's wife Louise (née Shanks), who had lived for forty years in Russia, made a remarkable translating debut with Tolstoy's late novel *Resurrection*. With the author's approval and cooperation, *Resurrection* was published simultaneously in Russian and English in 1899–1900. The English version came out in the labour magazine *Clarion* and in thirteen 'pocket parts' costing a penny each from the Brotherhood Publishing Company. The translation was a great success, and was often reprinted. Aylmer Maude notes in the preface to the revised 1902 edition (Maude 1902: xxii) that his wife donated £150 from her English royalties to help the Tolstoyan Dukhobor community in North America (though when the Dukhobors discovered what was in the novel they returned the money).

More than twenty years later Aylmer and Louise Maude were to bring to completion their Centenary Edition of the works of Tolstoy, but at the turn of the century their efforts in this direction were thwarted by Chertkov's exclusive claim to 'first publication' (Jones 1995: 13). Meanwhile it was primarily in America that the great fictional works received their first translations, few if any of them very satisfactory. The leading spirit was a prolific man of letters, Nathan Haskell Dole, who between 1886 and 1894 produced translations of *War and Peace*, *Anna Karenina*, and many shorter texts. It is not clear how much Russian Dole knew; it seems that he made use of French translations, and it was no doubt because of this that his successor, Leo Wiener, advertised his *Complete Works of Count Tolstoy* (1904–5) as 'translated from the original Russian'. But Dole had done enough to give many American readers their first taste of Tolstoy. In 1899 his translations were issued together with others, including *Childhood, Boyhood, Youth* and *Life* by Isabel Hapgood, in *The Complete Works of Lyof N. Tolstoï*, which was published in a variety of formats.

There were translations of other Russian fiction, notably Mikhail Lermontov's romantic series of linked tales, *A Hero of Our Time*, which was englished on five occasions before 1900, the last version being a bilingual edition (for these see Reid 1986). But the only other figure to make a serious impression on the English-speaking world was Dostoevsky. He figured prominently alongside Tolstoy and Turgenev in Vogüé's *Le Roman russe*, but was less translated than them and made less of an impression—his heyday came with the translations of Constance Garnett, beginning with *The Brothers Karamazov* in 1912. The first of his works to be translated was *Notes from the House of the Dead*, rendered as *Buried Alive* by Marie von Thilo in 1881. Thereafter, the main translator was Frederick J. Whishaw, who had lived some years in Russia and was also the author of over sixty adventure stories, several of them on Russian themes. Having completed his work on Dostoevsky, he wrote a book of memoirs called *Out of Doors in Tsarland: A Record of the Seeings and Doings of a Wanderer in Russia* (1893), which as its title suggests is as remote as one could imagine from the world of *Crime and Punishment*.

Whishaw translated rapidly. Between 1886 and 1888 he produced half a dozen titles, including *Crime and Punishment* (published without the translator's name in 1886), *The Idiot*, *Insult and Injury*, and *The Gambler*; all of these figured in 'Vizetelly's Russian novels' with the subtitle 'a Russian realistic novel', and for the most part they were published more or less simultaneously in the United States. The translations bear the marks of haste; Whishaw cuts corners, simplifies Dostoevsky's syntax, and tones down his 'extravagance', rather as Constance Garnett was to do, though in her case with greater accuracy and a much greater sense of style. Nevertheless, even if they were not enough to launch a Dostoevsky cult, these translations did service for some thirty years, and some of them were being reprinted in Dent's Everyman's Library until well into the twentieth century. It is noticeable, however, that unlike Tolstoy Dostoevsky was represented in nineteenth-century Britain and America by a limited group of works, excluding some of those that later came to seem the greatest: *Notes from Underground*, *The Possessed* (*The Devils*), and *The Karamazov Brothers* remained untranslated until after 1910.

Russian literature, and in particular the Russian novel, made greater inroads into the consciousness of English-speaking readers than the other Central and Eastern European literatures, which with a few exceptions such as Mickiewicz or Sienkiewicz were largely represented in translation by ballads and folk tales. In all cases, moreover, the translation work can best be described as pioneering. Some of the translators had a shaky knowledge of the source languages, and with the exception of Constance Garnett's Turgenev and perhaps Louise Maude's *Resurrection*, none of their work achieved a lasting place in the English-language canon. Nevertheless, these enthusiasts, addressing a journal-reading public anxious to know more of this dark continent, laid the foundations of an awareness of Eastern European cultures which was to flourish in the following century.

LIST OF SOURCES

For more complete listings of book-length translations see *CBEL*3 IV, 183–96, 201–6, and for Russian, Line 1972. Shorter translations are listed for all Central and Eastern European countries in Lewanski 1967; for Hungarian and Serbian material see also Czigány 1969 and Mihailovich and Matejic 1984 respectively. Separate discussions and bibliographies for all the languages mentioned here will be found in France 2000: 190–221, 582–98.

Translations

Biggs, Maude Ashurst (1882). *Konrad Wallenrod: An Historical Poem* [Mickiewicz]. London.
—— (1885). *Master Thaddeus, or, The Last Foray in Lithuania* [Mickiewicz]. London.
Borrow, George (1923–4). *Works*, ed. Clement Shorter, 16 vols. London.
Bowring, John (1821–3). *Specimens of the Russian Poets*, 2 vols. London.
—— (1827a). *Specimens of the Polish Poets, with Notes and Observations on the Literature of Poland*. London.
—— (1827b). *Servian Popular Poetry*. London.
—— (1830). *Poetry of the Magyars, Preceded by a Sketch of the Language and Literature of Hungary and Transylvania*. London.
—— (1832). *Cheskian Anthology: Being a History of the Poetical Literature of Bohemia with Translated Specimens*. London.
Cattley, H. (1841). *Konrad Vallenrod: An Historical Tale* [Mickiewicz]. London.
Curtin, Jeremiah (1890a). *With Fire and Sword: An Historical Novel of Poland and Russia* [Sienkiewicz]. Boston, MA.
—— (1890b). *Myths and Folk-Tales of the Russians, Western Slavs and Magyars*. Cambridge, MA.
—— (1896). *Quo Vadis? A Narrative of the Time of Nero* [Sienkiewicz]. Boston, MA.
Dole, Nathan Haskell, ed. (1899). *The Complete Works of Lyof N. Tolstoï*, 12 vols. New York.
Garnett, Constance (1894–9). *The Novels of Ivan Turgenev*, 15 vols. London.
Hapgood, Isabel F. (1886). *Taras Bulba* [Gogol]. New York.
—— (1888). *Tchitchikoff's Journey, or, Dead Souls* [Gogol]. New York.
—— (1903–4). *The Novels and Stories of Iván Turgénieff*, 16 vols. New York.
Jablonski, Leon (1841). *Conrad Wallenrod: An Historical Poem* [Mickiewicz]. Edinburgh.
Maude, Louise (1902). *Resurrection* [Tolstoy], rev. edn. London (first pub. 1899).
Ralston, W. R. S. (1869). *Liza* [Turgenev]. London.
—— (1872). *The Songs of the Russian People, as Illustrative of Slavonic Mythology and Russian Social Life*. London.
—— (1873). *Russian Folk-Tales*. London.
Shaw, Thomas B. (1845). 'Pushkin, the Russian Poet.' *Blackwood's Edinburgh Magazine* 57: 657–8; 58: 28–43, 140–56 (includes translations).
Spalding, H. (1881). *Eugene Onéguine: A Romance of Russian Life in Verse* [Pushkin]. London.
Turner, C. E. (1871). *On the Eve: A Tale* [Turgenev]. London.

—— (1899). *Translations from Poushkin: In Memory of the Hundredth Anniversary of the Poet's Birthday*. St Petersburg.
[Whishaw, Frederick J.] (1886). *Crime and Punishment: A Russian Realistic Novel* [Dostoevsky]. London.
—— (1887). *The Idiot* [Dostoevsky]. London.
Wiener, Leo, ed. (1902–3). *Anthology of Russian Literature from the Earliest Period to the Present Time*, 2 vols. New York.

Other Sources
Alexeyev, M. P. (1964). 'William Ralston and Russian Writers of the Later Nineteenth Century.' *Oxford Slavonic Papers* 11: 83–93.
Brewster, Dorothy (1954). *East–West Passage: A Study in Literary Relationships*. London.
Bury, J. P. T. (1960). 'Nationalities and Nationalism', pp. 213–45 in J. P. T. Bury, ed., *The New Cambridge Modern History*, Vol. 10. Cambridge.
Cross, Anthony (1993). *Anglo-Russica: Aspects of Cultural Relations between Great Britain and Russia in the Eighteenth and Early Nineteenth Centuries*. Oxford.
Curran, Eileen M. (1961). 'The *Foreign Quarterly Review* on Russian and Polish Literature.' *Slavonic and East European Review* 40: 206–19.
Czigány, Magda (1969). *Hungarian Literature in English Translation Published in Great Britain, 1830–1968: A Bibliography*. London.
Davie, Donald (1990). *Slavic Excursions: Essays on Russian and Polish Literature*. Manchester.
France, Peter, ed. (2000). *The Oxford Guide to Literature in English Translation*. Oxford.
Holman, Michael J. de K. (1988). 'Translating Tolstoy for the Free Age Press: Vladimir Chertkov and his English Manager Arthur Fifield.' *SEER* 66: 184–97.
Hyde, George (1999). ' "Language is First of All a Foreign One": George Borrow as a Translator from Polish.' *SEER* 77: 74–92.
Jones, W. Gareth, ed. (1995). *Tolstoi and Britain*. Oxford.
Lerner, Daniel (1941). 'The Influence of Turgenev on Henry James.' *SEER* 20: 28–54.
Lewanski, Richard C., ed. (1967). *The Slavic Literatures*, Vol. 2 of *The Literatures of the World in English Translation: A Bibliography*, ed. George B. Parks and Ruth Z. Temple. New York.
Line, M. B. (1972). 'A Bibliography of Russian Literature in English Translation to 1900 (Excluding Periodicals)', pp. 7–75 in M. B. Line, A. Ettlinger, and J. M. Gladstone, eds., *Bibliography of Russian Literature in English Translation to 1945*. Totowa, NJ.
Mihailovich, Vasa D., and Matejic, Mateja (1984). *A Comprehensive Bibliography of Yugoslav Literature in English, 1593–1980*. Columbus, OH.
Phelps, Gilbert (1956). *The Russian Novel in English Fiction*. London.
—— (1960). 'The Early Phases of British Interest in Russian Literature.' *SEER* 36: 418–33; 38: 415–50.
Reid, Robert (1986). 'The Critical Uses of Translation (Lermontov's *A Hero of our Time*).' *Essays in Poetics* 11/2: 55–90.
Sova, Miloš (1943). 'Sir John Bowring (1792–1872) and the Slavs.' *SEER* 21: 128–44.
Subotić, Dragutin (1932). *Yugoslav Popular Ballads: Their Origin and Development*. Cambridge.
Turton, Glyn (1992). *Turgenev and the Context of English Literature, 1850–1900*. London.
Waddington, Patrick, ed. (1995). *Ivan Turgenev and Britain*. Oxford.

7

Eastern Literatures

7.1	**Arabic** *Wen-chin Ouyang*	323
7.2	**Persian** *Dick Davis*	332
7.3	**Literatures of the Indian Subcontinent** *Harish Trivedi*	340
7.4	**Chinese** *Lauren Pfister*	355
7.5	**Japanese** *Anne Commons*	363

7.1 Arabic

Wen-chin Ouyang

Introduction

Nineteenth-century British Orientalism was distinguished by an increasingly nuanced knowledge of the Orient and the expansion of curiosity into areas outside biblical and classical studies. The Orient, which in previous centuries primarily meant the home of the 'other' to the Christians, had been a landscape of fuzzy contours that might stretch all the way from Morocco to China; knowledge of the Orient and Orientals had come mainly from sources written in Latin or other European languages, and the majority of English translations of Oriental works were from other European languages.

The expansion of the British Empire to India, which brought greater numbers of Britons into direct contact with the cultures of the Orient in the nineteenth century, and an increasingly secular world view led to what has been called an 'Oriental Renaissance' (Schwab 1984). The study of the Orient came to be driven by the desire to know everything about the diverse habitats and 'original' inhabitants of the empire. More important, perhaps, was the opening up of British culture to influences from the Orient. Already in the eighteenth century, this burgeoning openness had found expression in popular Orientalism, which took the form of fascination with Oriental paintings, clothes, music, interior decoration, and garden design; most significant for the history of translation was the vogue for 'Oriental tales' initiated by Antoine Galland's translation of the *Alf layla wa-layla* into French, *Les Mille et une nuits* (1704–17). By the end of the century, however, a more informed interest was made possible in part through works such as Robert Heron's translation of Carsten Niebuhr's *Beschreibung von Arabien* (*Travels through Arabia and Other Countries in the East*, 2 vols., 1792). Moreover, nineteenth-century Orientalism in Britain was informed by an expertise in Oriental languages and direct access to the Orient, whether through travel or original Oriental works. William Jones, founder of Oriental Studies in Britain, together with his contemporary Silvestre de Sacy, the greatest of French Arabists, ushered in a new era of Orientalism in Europe. Arabic literature outside *The Thousand and One Nights* began to be read and studied.

Jones (whose work is also discussed below in §§ 7.2 and 7.3 and in Vol. 3 of this *History*) attempted to translate pre-Islamic Arabic poetry into English early in his career. His *Poems, Consisting Chiefly of Translations from the Asiatick Languages* (1772) contained an important 'Essay on the Poetry of Eastern Nations' that betrays his rather sketchy understanding of Arabia, Arabic poetry, its history and development. Even so, his prose translation of the canonical pre-Islamic

Mu'allaqāt (1782–3) has been praised as 'an admirable version of the seven great odes of pagan Arabian' (Arberry 1943: 16; for further details see Vol. 3 of this *History*). The same critic also describes it as 'polite, latinized, and little suggestive of the wild vigour of the original Arabic' (Arberry 1946: 28). More crucially, however, it is full of mistakes and 'pastoral' misreadings. Jones's rendition of the first line of Labīd's ode reads:

Desolate are the mansions of the fair, the stations in Minia, where they rested, and those where they fixed their abodes! Wild are the hills of GOUL, and deserted is the summit of RIJAAM. (Jones 1807: X, 59)

This is more accurately translated by Alan Jones as:

There is almost no trace of those abodes, either brief halting-places or longer encampments, at Mina, and Ghawl and Rijam have become desolate. (Jones 1998: 88)

Even more than Jones, Joseph Carlyle emphasized the pastoral in his verse translation of 1796. He believed that Labīd's ode, even in translation, 'must give pleasure to any person of true taste, by its picturesque descriptions, appropriate images, and simple delineation of pastoral manners' (Carlyle 1796: 5).

Pre-Islamic poetry, it must be said, is notoriously difficult to translate. Its rigid mono-rhyme scheme and strict metrical symmetry have no equivalent in English. And its references to pre-Islamic desert landscape and animals, and Bedouin lifestyle, make its language alien even to native speakers of Arabic today. Sir Charles James Lyall, an Oxford graduate and colonial officer stationed in India for many years, who devoted his career to editing and translating pre-Islamic Arabic poetry and medieval commentary on this poetry (most of which would be published in the first two decades of the twentieth century), had plans to retranslate the seven odes. He never fully realized his rather ambitious project, but fragments appeared in his *Translations of Ancient Arabian Poetry* (1885) and in periodicals. He was clearly a better Arabist than Jones and his renditions in verse were more sensitive to the original Arabic. The same line from Labīd's ode is translated:

Effaced are her resting-places—where she stayed but a while and where she dwelt long in Mina: desolate are her camps in Ghaul and er-Rijam. (Lyall 1877: 84)

There is no explicit mention of a woman in the line, but her presence may be inferred since it is part of the love prelude of an Arabic ode. Lyall is more attentive to nomadic lifestyle, and no 'mansion' or 'station' is inserted in the desert landscape of pre-Islamic Arabia. His translations read better too. It is a pity that he did not complete his project, for the various other nineteenth-century translations of the *Mu'allaqāt*, literal versions done for students (such as Johnson 1893), were devoid of literary value.

The value of Jones's translation lay in making pre-Islamic Arabic poetry available in English for the first time while also presenting it as beautiful and sublime. His translation, though largely forgotten today, left its imprint on a whole generation of Romantics in Europe, including Goethe. The persona of the 'Arab of the Bedouin tribes' cuts a romantic figure in Book V of Wordsworth's *Prelude*, while Tennyson's 'Locksley Hall' echoes the sensibilities and motifs found in the *mu'allaqa* of Imrū' al-Qays. Jones's appreciation of Arabic poetry was in line with his enthusiasm for the study of the history, arts, and sciences of 'eastern' nations—an enterprise he believed would enrich western knowledge and expression.

Knowledge of Oriental languages was in growing demand in the nineteenth century. In addition to colonial officers and employees of such institutions as the East India Company, adventurers, travellers, scholars, or the intellectually curious learned Oriental languages through travel or at the growing number of academic institutions which provided tuition in these languages. Arabic and Persian were among the subjects for which professorships were established. Moreover, genuine Arabic texts were now used to teach the language. (The first text of *The Thousand and One Nights*, Calcutta I, was compiled for the purpose of teaching Arabic at Fort William College.) Collecting manuscripts, making them accessible to students of Arabic, and translating them into English became a priority. The Oriental Translation Fund, founded in 1828, published its first series of translations from 1829 to 1871; in 1891 it became attached to the Royal Asiatic Society of Britain and Ireland and began a new series. The Fund saw its mission as complementary to the work of the academy. Even though its focus was not on literature, it nevertheless sponsored the translation of a classical Arabic literary masterpiece, the eleventh-century *Maqāmāt* or *Assemblies of al-Harîri* (Vol. 1 by Thomas Chenery, 1867; Vol. 2 by F. Steingass, 1898). However, this was no more than a literal translation intended as a companion to the Arabic text (edited and published by Steingass in 1897) for students of language. (For translations of the Qur'ān, see pp. 466–7, below.)

The Thousand and One Nights

The fascination with *The Thousand and One Nights* began with Galland's popular and influential French translation. For almost a century translations of his translation, rather than of an Arabic text, were made into other European languages, especially English (for a full discussion, see Vol. 3 of this *History*). The first English translation with serious literary ambitions, that of Jonathan Scott, was based on Galland's work. Scott was, however, not entirely faithful to Galland in his six-volume *Arabian Nights Entertainments* (1811). He integrated into the work, especially in Volume 6, stories from other Arabic sources not found in Galland. Such interpolation was very much in the spirit in which Galland rendered the Arabic stories into French, since Galland included stories which he read in other manuscripts or heard from oral sources.

The liberal attitude towards the text during the early stages of the *Nights* industry has made it practically impossible to identify an authentic original text. In fact, the history of the text is so intricately woven into the history of its translation that it is impossible to discuss the former without the latter. Although the tales incorporated into the book now known as *The Thousand and One Nights* had been in circulation for centuries, they were given little attention in medieval Arabic sources, and not all of them were considered part of the work familiar to us today. The written version of *The Thousand and One Nights* took on its present form primarily during the eighteenth and nineteenth centuries, due largely to the interest Europeans showed in it. Part of this interest was triggered by the perception that Galland's text, which included only 282 nights' worth of stories, was incomplete.

The obsession with finding the complete text that accurately reflects the title, fanned by the fascination with the exotic world of the Orient, prompted an earnest search for Arabic *Nights* manuscripts and created a lucrative market for manuscript hunters and suppliers. Consequently, or subsequently, a series of Arabic texts were put together and published. There are at least twenty-two Arabic manuscripts (most of them now in European libraries) of the *Nights* of either Egyptian or Syrian origin that are known to have survived to the present day. We now have four sets of *Nights* texts in print, all published in the first half of the nineteenth century: Calcutta I (1814–28), Breslau (1824–39), Bulaq (1835), and Calcutta II (1839–42). With the publication of these four texts, translation of the *Nights* gained momentum despite some lingering suspicions regarding the work's sources and status. During the same period three English translations of the *Nights* appeared: Edward William Lane's in 1839–41; John Payne's in 1882–4; and Richard Burton's in 1885–8. All these translations were beset by problems relating to the uncertain status of the *Nights* texts, the notions of translation operative in the nineteenth century, the difficulties involved in translating from Arabic into English, and the ideology and personal taste of the translators. None relied on one single Arabic text. Lane worked primarily with the Bulaq text, using Calcutta I and Breslau only as secondary texts. Payne and Burton on the other hand, relied mainly on Calcutta II and used sparingly Calcutta I, Bulaq, and Breslau.

Lane, Payne, and Burton

Edward William Lane, the leading Arabist of the nineteenth century, made several lengthy visits to Egypt. During his first sojourn (1825–8), he formed the opinion that the stories of the *Nights* reflected and illustrated a way of life that still continued in Cairo even in his time. He announced his intention to translate the stories from Arabic. Upon hearing this, Henry Torrens, a British civil servant in India who had translated the first fifty nights from Calcutta II, gave way to him. Lane's translation appeared in monthly parts from 1838 to 1841 and was later bound in three volumes. In 1859 his nephew, Edward Stanley Poole, issued a revised edition. Lane intended his translation to be an extension of his *Account of the Manners and Customs of Modern Egyptians* (1836) and provided copious footnotes on every aspect of life portrayed in the work. The footnotes were so extensive that they were later published as a separate work under the title *Arabian Society in the Middle Ages: Studies from The Thousand and One Nights* (1883). These heavy footnotes, while cumbersome, have not provoked as much controversy as his distortions of the Arabic.

Lane's language is seen by some as 'simple, accurate and formal in style' with 'an elegance which is at times at odds with the rowdy, earthly, inelegant and bawdy styles and contents which make up many of the *Nights*' tales' (Sallis 1999: 50) and by others as 'grandiose and mock-biblical', 'pompously high-flown', and 'peppered with Latinisms' (Irwin 1994: 24). Whether influenced by his own Victorian morality or by the taste and market of his time, he edited the stories, expurgating or rewriting sections he thought unsuitable for family reading. 'In cases where he found whole stories to be obscene', Irwin complains, 'he omitted them altogether' (Irwin 1994: 25). Some very good stories disappeared from his version, and so did most of the poetry. This is not a full translation of the *Nights*; it amounts only to about two-fifths of the original. Lane also discards the division into nights as the organizing principle of the stories. Instead, he divides his text into thirty chapters, each chapter comprising one full- or medium-length story followed by extensive notes and one or more short pieces. More fundamentally, he omits the frame story: the role of Sheherazade practically disappears, and Lane usurps the role of the storyteller, destroying in the process the structure of the original beyond recognition.

Unlike Lane, who concentrated on Arabic, John Payne was a gifted linguist who translated from many languages. He seems to have learnt Arabic, Persian, and Turkish without having ever set foot in the Orient. He had ambitions as a poet and a literary translator, and thanks to his independent means he was able to devote himself to these activities. He began translating Calcutta II in 1876 or 1877 and completed the work in six years; his translation was published in nine volumes between 1882 and 1884. He then went on to translate additional stories from Calcutta I and Breslau; the results were published as *Tales from the Arabic* in 1884–9. When a copy of Zotenberg's manuscript of 'Zayn al-Asnam' and 'Aladdin' became available, he also translated these (Irwin 1994: 27).

Praised recently as 'the best full English version', one that aimed to 'establish the *Nights* as literature and not as social commentary' (Sallis 1999: 54), Payne's work did not expurgate the text and included, albeit in an understated fashion, the sexually explicit passages (names of sexual organs are translated as 'commodity', 'kaze', 'catso', and 'coney'). He was able to escape charges of obscenity due to his membership of the François Villon Society, which funded the publication, since he was able to plead that the Society's publications were intended for subscribing members only. He also translated all the poetry, but here his translation, like his own poetry, was awkward and inelegant. He does not provide any equivalent to the rhymed prose that is so much part of the charm of the original. Payne's language has inspired diverse reactions. According to one critic, it 'shows an uncomplicated attempt at the scholarly and accurate rendition of his chosen material' (Sallis 1999: 54); according to another, it is 'a tortured, impossible prose, laboriously constructed out of archaic and rare words and turns' (Gerhardt 1963: 80). Like Lane, he too did away with the formal division of nights, so that his translation is 'really a new compilation, created on an inclusive rather than a selective principle' (Sallis 1999: 54). It is a rarity because only 500 copies were printed. This may partially explain why Burton's translation eclipsed it, even though Burton depended heavily on Payne.

Richard Francis Burton was already famous as an author, adventurer, and explorer when he started translating the *Nights*. When he learned in November 1881 that Payne was proposing to undertake a new translation, he wrote to him immediately and offered to help, claiming that he had been working on a translation since 1852. Later, with Payne's approval, he decided to produce his own translation. His ten-volume edition of the main corpus of the *Nights* was published in 1885, followed by his six-volume *Supplemental Nights* (1886–8). The volumes include Payne's *Tales from the Arabic* and Galland's orphan stories. Burton's dependence on Payne is incontrovertible. His borrowings from Lane are less obvious. His 'translation' of 'The Porter and the Three Ladies of Baghdad' is a word-for-word transplantation of Lane's earlier translation. To his critics, Burton's rendition is 'dated' and 'unreadable' (Knipp 1974: 49), 'careless' (Gerhardt 1963: 88), and 'erratic' (Sallis 1999: 55). However, the most controversial aspect of his version is not his translation but his authorial presence in the notes, which he made the vehicle for his obsessions: racism, sexism, anti-Christian prejudice, and preoccupation with sex (see Irwin 1994: 33). On occasion he even tampers with the text in order to make it suit the purpose of his annotations (see Gerhardt 1963: 91), especially where Oriental eroticism is concerned. Where Payne understates, he exaggerates. The Arabic passage describing the Queen's adultery in the frame story is closer to Payne's rendition than to Burton's. Payne keeps the tone relatively low-key:

Then the queen called out, 'O, Mesoud!' And there came to her a black slave, who embraced her and she him. Then he lay with her, and on like wise did the other slaves with the girls. And they ceased not from kissing and clipping and clicketing and carousing until the day began to wane. (Payne 1882–4: I, 3)

Burton adds many elements not found in the original Arabic to heighten the dramatic effect:

But the Queen, who was left alone, presently cried out in a loud voice, 'Here to me, O my lord Saeed!' and then sprang with a drop-leap from one of the trees a big slobbering blackamoor with rolling eyes which showed the whites, a truly hideous sight. He walked boldly up to her and threw his arms round her neck while she embraced him as warmly; then he bussed her and winding his legs round hers, as a button-loop clasps a button, he threw her and enjoyed her. On like wise did the other slaves with the girls till all had satisfied their passions, and they ceased not from kissing and clipping, coupling and carousing till day began to wane. (Burton 1885: I, 6)

To his admirers, however, Burton's copious notes provide valuable information and insight into the world of the Orient. He also gives the most faithful rendition, in some ways, of the Arabic text. He retains the formal division into nights, preserving the structure of the text; he often reproduces the rhymed prose of the

Arabic original, and even if his translation of poetry is jarring and laborious, it expresses the complex contents of the Arabic poems. When he sticks to Calcutta II, he gives a very faithful translation. He respects the word order and phrasing of the original more scrupulously than Payne, and he does not expurgate (Gerhardt 1963: 88). Unlike Lane, who judiciously selected stories for translation, 'Burton provided a full edition of the tales, even to the point of including in the supplementary volumes variants of tales he had already translated . . . His judgement of the respective merits and failings of individual tales was on the whole good, and he had a much saner view of the likely history of the formation of the corpus of the *Nights* than Lane had' (Irwin 1994: 36).

Today, these nineteenth-century translations of the *Nights* are overshadowed by the more accessible and shorter twentieth-century renditions, such as those of N. J. Dawood (1954) and Hussain Haddawy (1990). Their 'datedness' may have rendered them obsolete for most contemporary readers, but their value as historical documents and cultural artefacts cannot be overlooked. Moreover, these translations are also a storehouse of the various notions, even theories, and practices of translation of the time. The stylistic devices which create the rhythms and nuances in Arabic prose and poetry are hard to capture in English; literal translations more often than not lead to awkward sentence structures, if not obscurity and redundancy. The historical layers and registers of Arabic presented equally nagging problems. How could nineteenth-century English be used to represent accurately the medieval Arabic of the *Nights*? The *Nights* is narrated in what is conventionally known as Middle Arabic, a language pitched somewhere between the high language of the élite and the colloquial speech of the common people. The registers of the Arabic language, however, can vary in each story and from one story to another, reflecting differences in gender, class, and education. How were the subtle nuances of the Arabic registers to be conveyed in English? The use of archaic English by Lane, Payne, and Burton—'thee' and 'thou,' phrases such as 'Hoist up!', and sentences such as 'Thou art foul of favour and it befitteth not that thou wear rich clothes' (Payne 1884–9; II, 291)—is their attempt to give *The Thousand and One Nights* a kind of 'literariness' and to convey its 'ancientness', even though the linguistic registers in Arabic do not work in the same way as they do in English.

The nineteenth-century translators of the *Nights*, just like their critics today, grappled with the question of how to represent the Orient. Their works, like those of their critics, were necessarily coloured by their ideology, experience, and taste. Scholars of the *Nights* have begun to look at how these factors have influenced the translators and shaped their 'texts', though much work needs to be done before a clearer picture can emerge. The influence of these translations on nineteenth-century English writing too has yet to be fully assessed. And although English scholarship has begun to look at the influence of the *Nights* on the narrative strategies of English fiction, from Oriental tales to English novels, the impact of the style of these translations on nineteenth-century writing remains to be investigated.

LIST OF SOURCES

Translations

Burton, Richard F. (1885–6). *A Plain and Literal Translation of the Arabian Nights Entertainments Now Entitled the Book of the Thousand Nights and a Night*, 10 vols. 'Benares' (Stoke Newington).

—— (1886). *The Perfumed Garden of the Cheikh Nefzaoui: A Manual of Arabian Erotology*. 'Cosmopoli' (London).

—— (1886–8). *Supplemental Nights to the Book of the Thousand Nights and a Night*, 6 vols. 'Benares' (Stoke Newington).

Carlyle, Joseph D. (1796). *Specimens of Arabic Poetry*. Cambridge.

Chenery, Thomas (1867). *The Assemblies of Al Harîri*, Vol. 1. London.

Johnson, Frank E. (1893). *The Seven Poems Suspended in the Temple of Mecca*. Bombay.

Jones, Sir William (1807). *Works*, 13 vols. London.

Lane, Edward William (1839–41). *The Thousand and One Nights Commonly Called, in England, The Arabian Nights' Entertainments*, 3 vols. London.

Lyall, Sir Charles James (1885). *Translations of Ancient Arabian Poetry Chiefly Prae-Islamic*. London.

—— (1877). 'The Mo'allaqah of Lebid'. *Journal of the Asiatic Society of Bengal* 46: 61–96.

Payne, John (1882–4). *The Book of the Thousand Nights and One Night*, 9 vols. London.

—— (1884–9). *Tales from the Arabic of the Breslau and Calcutta (1814–18) Editions of the Book of the Thousand Nights and One Night Not Occurring in the Other Printed Texts of the Work*, 3 vols. London.

—— (1889) *Alaeddin and the Enchanted Lamp: Zein ul Asnam and the King of the Jinn*. London.

Scott, Jonathan (1811). *The Arabian Nights' Entertainments*, 6 vols. London.

Steingass, F. (1898). *The Assemblies of Al Harîri*, Vol. 2. London.

Torrens, Henry (1838). *The Book of The Thousand Nights and One Night*, Vol. 1 (no more published). Calcutta.

Other Sources

Ahmed, Leila (1978). *Edward W. Lane: A Study of his Life and Works and of British Ideas of the Middle East in the Nineteenth Century*. London.

Ali, Muhsin Jassim (1981). *Scheherazade in England: A Study of Nineteenth-Century English Criticism of the Arabian Nights*. Washington, DC.

Arberry, A. J. (1943). *British Orientalists*. London.

—— (1946). *Asiatic Jones: The Life and Influence of Sir William Jones (1746–1794) Pioneer of Indian Studies*. London.

—— (1960). *Oriental Essays: Portraits of Seven Scholars*. London.

Cannon, Garland Hampton (1990). *The Life and Mind of Oriental Jones: Sir William Jones, the Father of Modern Linguistics*. Cambridge.

Caracciolo, Peter L., ed. (1988). *The Arabian Nights in English Literature: Studies in the Reception of the Thousand and One Nights into British Culture*. New York.

Gerhardt, Mia (1963). *The Art of Story-Telling: A Literary Study of the Thousand and One Nights*. Leiden.

Irwin, Robert (1994). *The Arabian Nights: A Companion*. London.

Jones, Alan (1998). 'Sir William Jones as an Arabist', pp. 67–89 in Alexander Murray, ed., *Sir William Jones 1746–1794: A Commemoration*. Oxford.

Kabbani, Rana (1994). *Imperial Fictions: Europe's Myths of Orient*. London.

Knipp, C. (1974). 'The Arabian Nights in England: Galland's Translation and its Successors.' Journal of Arabic Literature 5: 44–54.
Meester, Marie E. de (1915). Oriental Influences in the English Literature of the Nineteenth Century. Heidelberg.
Said, Edward (1978). Orientalism. New York.
Sallis, Eva (1999). Sheherazade through the Looking Glass: The Metamorphosis of the Thousand and One Nights. Richmond.
Schwab, Raymond (1984). The Oriental Renaissance: Europe's Rediscovery of India and the East, 1680–1880, tr. Gene Patterson-Black and Victor Reinking. New York (original French edn. 1950).
Sharafuddin, Mohammed (1994). Islam and Romantic Orientalism: Literary Encounters with the Orient. London.

7.2 Persian

Dick Davis

Introduction

The translation of Persian literature into English during the nineteenth century involved a number of specific circumstances which had far-reaching effects both on the choice of authors to translate and on the nature of the translations themselves. The circumstances can be considered under two broad headings: (1) political and (2) moral and religious.

The political circumstances are relatively easy to formulate. Outside the scholarly world (and often even within it) British interest in Persian in the late eighteenth and nineteenth centuries derived primarily from the fact that the lingua franca of the courts of Moghul India was Persian. The increasing British presence in India during the period meant that any official of the East India Company, and later of Her Majesty's government or the Indian Army, who wished to have an entrée to these courts had perforce to learn at least some Persian. The acquirement of Persian was seen as a step to administrative advancement, and while the language was studied as a means of communication and diplomatic negotiation, the texts chosen for the most intense scrutiny tended to be those which it was felt gave an insight into the customs and modes of thinking of the Persian-speaking aristocracy of northern India. These naturally became the texts set in examinations in Persian that British administrators had to pass, and they in turn became the texts that were most frequently translated, as cribs for the examinees if nothing else. Despite the often difficult relations between the British and the indigenous populations there was a sense, widely attested on both sides, that the British were more able to achieve some kind of intellectual *modus vivendi* with Indian Muslims than with Hindus; the fact that Persian literature formed the basis of Muslim Indian *belles-lettres* encouraged the translation of texts that were considered central to this tradition. That Sa'dī (12th century CE) was by far the most frequently translated Persian author in the late eighteenth and early nineteenth centuries is due largely to the fact that his works formed the literary basis of the education of any self-respecting Persian-speaking Muslim in India, and that quotations from them were a minimal mark of cultural standing in such circles. This predilection for Sa'dī among translators was further increased by the fact that his works, especially the *Gulistān*, a compendium of moralizing tales arranged under various headings (e.g. 'On the manners of kings', 'On the manners of dervishes', 'On love and youth'), were thought to give a unique insight into the morals and customs of Asian Muslims.

Sa'dī, Ḥāfiẓ, and Rūmī

The first version of Sa'dī's compendium was made by Francis Gladwin (*The Gûlistân of Sâdy*, 1806). He had preceded this translation with that of another work then believed to be by Sa'dī, but now considered not to be part of his oeuvre, the 'Pandnāmeh' (literally 'Book of Advice'), which appeared as the *Compendium of Ethics* (1788); this was the first complete Persian work to receive an English translation. Gladwin's *Gûlistân* was reprinted in 1822 and then in 1856 with a preface by Emerson (who also translated a number of short Persian lyrics, via a German translation); this later edition enjoyed a considerable vogue among American Transcendentalists. This work is a prosimetrum (prose interspersed with verses, like the *De Consolatione Philosophiae* of Boethius, and the *Vita nuova* of Dante; the form is considerably more common in Persian literature than in the West), but Gladwin translates the whole text as prose and does not indicate which parts are in verse.

The popularity of Sa'dī, and his ubiquity in the examinations of British officials in India, are suggested by the spate of translations of the *Gulistān* which followed on from this pioneering version: these include Dumoulin (1807), Ross (1823), Eastwick (1852), Platts (1873) and Rehatsek (1888). With the possible exception of Rehatsek's version, all the above translations were almost certainly made with the help of an Indian translator, or 'monshee'. The use of a literate native informant was an accepted part of the process of translation of works from Asian languages in the nineteenth century, but these individuals were almost never named, or even acknowledged as having existed, when the works were published. Rehatsek was something of a special case; he settled in India, but as a Hungarian he had an at best oblique relationship with the British presence there and was considered something of an eccentric recluse. His great gift for languages, and his preference for Asian rather than European company, give his translations from Persian a unique authority; he also translated the *Bahāristān* of Jāmī (15th century CE). His *Gulistan or Rose Garden of Sa'di* is, as regards its general accuracy and fidelity to nuance and shifts of authorial tone, arguably the best nineteenth-century translation of a Persian work into English (despite the fact that like Gladwin he translates the verse as prose), and this is the more remarkable when one remembers that his first language was not English. However, the 1888 version of the *Gulistān* was not printed under Rehatsek's name but as the work of Richard Burton, and Rehatsek's version of the *Bahāristān* (1887) was also attributed to the same flamboyant source. The two works were published as Burton's by the Kama Shastra Society, which specialized in 'oriental erotica' and was based supposedly in Benares (Banaras) but actually in the somewhat less exotic town of Stoke Newington. It is virtually certain that Burton had nothing to do with these versions, and indeed whether he knew any Persian or not is a moot point (see Yohannan 1977: 179–80). When the earnestly well-meaning Edwin Arnold (once relatively famous for his poem on the life of the Buddha, *The Light of Asia*) produced *The Gulistan of Sadi* in 1899, he stopped at the end of Book IV; Book V is the one entitled 'On Love and Youth'.

That Arnold should stop his *Gulistan* before Book V, and that Saʿdī and Jāmī should be published in their late Victorian English versions by a company specializing in limited editions of 'oriental erotica', brings us to the second of the particular circumstances attending the translation of Persian literature during the nineteenth century: the moral and religious problems that many such works were thought to pose for anglophone readers. The situation is best indicated by what was, until FitzGerald's *Rubáiyát of Omar Khayyám*, the best-known English translation of a short Persian poem: Sir William Jones's late eighteenth-century version of a ghazal by Ḥāfiẓ (Hafez), the first line of which reads in his version 'Sweet maid if thou wouldst charm my sight'. The difficulty with this line is that Ḥāfiẓ's poem is almost certainly addressed to a boy. The lack of gender markers for personal pronouns in Persian (the same word is used for 'he' and 'she', and, as in English, there is no gender differentiation in the word for 'you' either) means that a love poem can apparently be to or about a person of either sex, unless there are specific indications in the poem to the contrary (e.g. a reference to a boy's sprouting moustache, or to a girl's breasts). However, the fall-back assumption, if such indications are absent, is that a medieval Persian lyric poem is addressed to a boy; the pervasive convention within which such poems were written was one of pederasty, and it is the heterosexual poems that can be considered deviant from the convention (we are speaking here only of lyric verse: medieval Persian narrative love poems almost always celebrated heterosexual relationships). Saʿdī has many lyric poems that are clearly addressed to boys, as does Ḥāfiẓ (14th century CE), the most famous of the Persian lyric poets, and so do their many imitators. Such verse was rarely translated in the nineteenth century, because it was thought offensive, or, if it was translated, it was usually quietly bowdlerized, as in Jones's 'Sweet maid if thou wouldst charm my sight'. This means that what many Persians consider to be one of the great glories of their literature, the *dīvān* (lyric) poetry, is virtually unrepresented in English until the closing decades of the nineteenth century. Apart from the pervasive pederasty, it must be admitted that the rhetoric of medieval Persian lyric verse can be extremely difficult to render convincingly in English. Indicative of this is the fact that the history of Persian scholarship in English is littered with failed attempts to produce a tolerable Ḥāfiẓ; most of the serious attempts to do this (e.g. the complete versions by Wilberforce-Clarke in 1891 and Payne in 1901) have produced almost unreadable results. Ḥāfiẓ is a highly ambiguous poet, and it is often difficult to tell whether we are reading about literal or spiritual intoxication, carnal or celestial love, or both. Wilberforce-Clarke is laboriously insistent in his translation and notes that only spiritual matters are meant, and his versions of the poems are relentlessly tedious. Payne's attempt to reproduce the metres and rhyme schemes of the originals frequently results in bizarrely incoherent English. Translations of selections from Ḥāfiẓ include John Nott's relatively staid renderings (1787) and the very ripe prose version by Justin Huntly McCarthy (1893).

A further problem in the work of many Persian poets, and one that is often related to the frequency of pederastic references, is that much of their verse has a Sufi (Islamic mystical) tinge to it, if it is not outright Sufi in content. Some poets, e.g. Ḥāfiẓ and 'Irāqī, often combine the two relatively unfamiliar subjects for a western reader (Sufism and pederasty) in the one poem. Although translations of Persian Sufi verse have proved very popular in the twentieth century, this was not the case in the nineteenth century, and it was not until relatively late in the century that Sufi poetry began to be translated with any frequency into English; its apparent antinomianism, as well as its penchant for pederastic anecdotes, proving too much of a barrier. Selections from Rūmī's *Mathnawī* (13th century CE), considered to be the greatest of Persian mystical poems, and certainly one of the longest, were translated by Redhouse (1881) and Whinfield (1887). Whinfield also translated another significant mystical work, the short verse treatise by Shabistarī, *Gulshan-i rāz* (1880). In 1898 Reynold Nicholson, who was to devote much of his life to establishing the critical text of Rūmī's *Mathnawī* on which all subsequent editions have been based, published translations of a selection of Rūmī's shorter lyrics (*Selected Poems from the Divani Shamsi Tabriz*).

Edward FitzGerald

The reputation that Persian verse acquired during the Victorian period for occasionally dealing with homosexual subject matter perhaps contributed to the composition of what was to become the most famous translation of Persian into English ever made, FitzGerald's *Rubáiyát of Omar Khayyám* (1859). FitzGerald's homosexual orientation, whether or not he ever acted on it, seems very clear from his life and friendships, as well as from his rather disastrous marriage (the disaster occurred, his wife said, because her husband could never resist taking up with 'any embryo Apollo'). FitzGerald was born into a wealthy Anglo-Irish family in 1809; he attended Trinity College, Cambridge, where he became friends with Tennyson and Thackeray. After graduation he returned to the county he had grown up in, Suffolk, though he kept his distance from most of his family. He lived simply, and his modest wealth enabled him to live as a quiet country gentleman. His main interests were literary, and his enthusiasm for translation was probably sparked by his meeting a young man of considerable linguistic talent, Edward Cowell, who taught him first Spanish and then, beginning in 1852, Persian (on FitzGerald's attitude towards translation see pp. 101–2, above).

The Persian book they first worked on together was Jāmī's allegory *Salamān and Absāl*, a peculiar choice for a number of reasons. Jāmī's Persian is quite difficult, especially for a beginner, and the tale is not one that has much obvious appeal to an uninformed western taste. It involves a king who is disgusted by sex but who nevertheless wishes to have progeny; he achieves this by magical means, but then to his horror his son is almost seduced by the woman sent to nurse him. The son represents the human soul, the woman represents the wiles of the physical world; the woman is burnt to death and the son/soul emerges unscathed from her snares. It may be that the poem's implicit misogyny appealed to FitzGerald (he had bad relations with both his mother and his wife), and the vivid descriptions of the beleaguered pure young man may also have been a factor in his liking for the story.

He produced a (severely cut) verse translation of it in 1856; this was also the year of FitzGerald's divorce.

In the same year Cowell sailed for India, and his parting gift to FitzGerald was a copy he had made of a manuscript in the Bodleian of a number of quatrains purportedly by the eleventh-century poet, mathematician, and astronomer 'Umar (Omar) Khayyām. Almost immediately, probably as a way of keeping in touch with his friend, FitzGerald began work on translating the quatrains, and he sent frequent letters to Cowell detailing his progress and asking his former teacher for advice. These letters demonstrate, contrary to what many have claimed, that FitzGerald was a good Persianist by this time, and that when he changed or compressed the meaning of his originals (which he frequently did—he wrote of his 'mashing together' of the stanzas), he did so with full knowledge of what he was doing. The letters also make it abundantly clear that he felt he had found a soul mate in Khayyām (how many of the poems are actually by Khayyām is another matter; quite likely virtually none of them are, but this is irrelevant to FitzGerald's achievement). As he wrote to Cowell, 'In truth I take old Omar more as my property than yours: he and I are more akin, are we not? You see all [his] *Beauty* but you can't feel with him in some respects as I do' (FitzGerald 1980: II, 305).

In the Persian the quatrains are discrete entities; each is an entirely self-sufficient poem. It was FitzGerald who made, as he put it in a letter to Cowell, 'a very pretty Eclogue ... tessellated out of [Khayyām's] scattered quatrains' (FitzGerald 1980: II, 294), arranging a selection of the poems so that they form a quasi-narrative depicting a day in the life of a hedonistic religious sceptic. In doing this FitzGerald took a hint from Louisa Costello, who had also arranged a number of Khayyām's quatrains into a narrative sequence in an anthology she had published in 1845 (*The Rose Garden of Persia*; Costello did not know Persian, and her translations were from European, mainly German, versions). But where Costello looked chiefly for Sufi or pious quatrains to translate, the themes that especially interested FitzGerald were religious scepticism and a kind of defiant Epicureanism. We may also remark that there are no women in his poem: the 'Sáki' (cup-bearer) is certainly a boy, a Ganymede, in the Persian originals, and presumably FitzGerald knew this; stanza 19 (of the first edition) with its implicit comparison of an adolescent boy's moustache to the grass on which the lovers lean, reinforces this homoerotic element, as do the references to Hyacinth (stanza 18) and to the 'Angel Shape' (stanza 13), referred to as 'he'.

Four editions of the poem appeared in FitzGerald's lifetime, the first three (1859, 1868, 1872) anonymously, and a fifth (1889) was made from a corrected copy of the fourth edition of 1879 found among his papers after his death. The first edition remained largely unsold until Dante Gabriel Rossetti came across it at a reduced price and bought copies for Ruskin, Swinburne, and Browning, all of whom were enthusiastic. The first, second, and third editions differ considerably from one another, with FitzGerald adding quatrains, cancelling others, and revising still others (for details see FitzGerald 1997). The fourth and fifth editions differ mainly in minor matters such as punctuation. Most readers have preferred the first edition, though some of the poem's best-known stanzas only occur in later editions. The work achieved enormous popularity (its heyday was around the time of the First World War), and it has been estimated that it is the most widely sold book of poetry ever to have been published in English. (On the poetry of the *Rubáiyát*, see further pp. 79–80, above.)

Later in life FitzGerald worked on a translation of 'Aṭṭār's *Manṭeq al Ṭayr* (12th century CE; 'The Bird-Parliament' was FitzGerald's working title for this), but his dissatisfaction with his version is indicated by the fact that he never attempted to publish it. As with his version of Jāmī, he cuts the poem drastically (and shows virtually no understanding of its highly complex structure). This translation was first published after his death in his posthumous *Letters and Literary Remains* (1889).

Narrative and Epic Poetry

FitzGerald's version of Jāmī and his attempt to produce a version of 'Aṭṭār are among the relatively few nineteenth-century translations of medieval Persian narrative poems. Besides these, three narratives by Niẓāmī (12th century CE) were very indifferently translated: *Lailí and Majnún* by Atkinson (1836), *The Sikandar Nama* by Wilberforce-Clarke (1881), and *In Persia's Golden Days* by Griffiths and Rogers (1889). One reason for this relative dearth and for the lack of success of the few attempts that were made may be that the rhetoric of these poems was considered by the Victorians to be, in the main, tiresomely prolix and hyperbolical (this is also certainly the reason why one whole major genre of Persian verse, the court panegyric, was completely ignored by nineteenth-century translators, and this latter situation has not changed much to this day). The one important exception to this relative neglect of Persian narrative verse by translators in the nineteenth century is the interest that was shown in the major Persian epic of the tenth and eleventh centuries CE, the *Shāhnāma* of Firdausī (Ferdowsi).

Although Firdausī's poem had been known by reputation from the seventeenth century onwards, it was Sir William Jones who first devoted serious attention to it; he planned to write a tragedy based on one of its sections. In 1788 Joseph Champion brought out a version of the opening section, translated into fluent heroic couplets, and he intended to translate the whole poem (the work is immensely long; the standard modern edition by Bertels, published in Moscow in 1966–71, runs to nine volumes). Unfortunately, Champion's mental health gave way before he could continue work on his translation. In 1814 James Atkinson published *Soohrab*, a translation of the poem's most famous incident, and this too was in heroic couplets. The following year saw the privately printed translation of extracts from the *Shāhnāma* by Stephen Weston; he does not translate with anything like the competence of Atkinson, but his preface is significant as it makes some attempt to place the poem within the milieu and conventions that produced it.

In 1832 Atkinson followed up on the relative success of his *Soohrab* and published an abridged translation of what he implied was the whole poem, *The Sháh Námeh of the Persian Poet Firdausí*, and this was reprinted a number of times throughout the nineteenth century. This translation is into prose, with a few episodes rendered as verse. It is by no means 'complete', as it breaks off around two-thirds of the way through the poem, with the advent of Sekandar (Alexander the Great). Samuel Robinson's book of translated extracts from the *Shāhnāma*, published privately in 1823 and revised and reissued in 1876, deserves mention. Robinson's model would seem to have been that of the poetry of the Bible as rendered in the King James version, and Macpherson's Ossian too may have been an influence, as the lines are lineated as verse but have no regular metrical stress. Another 'complete' (and in reality very incomplete) version by Alexander Rogers into barely competent heroic couplets was published in 1907. Atkinson's version remained the most popular throughout the nineteenth century and had a demonstrable influence on Matthew Arnold's 'Sohrab and Rustum' (1853), which was based on an incident in the poem, although Arnold's main source was Jules Mohl's mid-nineteenth-century French version of the *Shāhnāma*. Atkinson's *Sháh Námeh* was finally superseded by the nine-volume blank verse translation of Arthur and Edmond Warner (1905–25).

LIST OF SOURCES
Translations
Arnold, Edwin (1899). *The Gulistan, Being the Rose-Garden of Shaikh Sà'di: The First Four Babs, or 'Gateways'*. London.
Atkinson, James (1814). *Soohrab: A Poem Freely Translated from the Original Persian of Firdousee*. Calcutta.
—— (1832). *The Sháh Námeh of the Persian Poet Firdausí*. London.
—— (1836). *Lailí and Majnún: A Poem from the Original Persian of Nazámi*. London.
Champion, Joseph (1788). *The Poems of Ferdosi*, Vol. l (no more published). London.
Costello, Louisa Stuart (1845). *The Rose Garden of Persia*. London.
Dumoulin, James (1807). *The Goolistan of the Celebrated Musleh-ud-Deen of Shirauz, Surnamed Sheikh Sadi*. Calcutta.
Eastwick, Edward (1852). *The Gulistan, or, Rose-Garden of Muslihu'd-din Sadi of Shiraz*. London.
FitzGerald, Edward (1856). *Salámán and Absál: An Allegory Translated from the Persian of Jámí*. London (subsequent edns. in 1868, 1872, and 1879).
—— (1889). 'A Bird's-Eye View of Faríd-Uddín Attar's Bird-Parliament', pp. 430–82 in Vol. 3 of Edward FitzGerald, *Letters and Literary Remains*. London.
—— (1997). *Rubáiyát of Omar Khayyám*, ed. Christopher Decker. Charlottesville, VA (a critical edition of the first four versions of the text).
Gladwin, Francis (1788). *A Compendium of Ethics, Translated from the Persian of Sheikh Sadi of Shiraz*. Calcutta.
—— (1806). *The Gûlistân of Sâdy*, 2 vols. Calcutta.
—— (1865). *The Gulistan or Rose Garden . . . with an Essay on Saadi's Life and Genius, by James Ross, and a Preface by R. W. Emerson*. Boston, MA.
Griffiths, Robert, and Rogers, Alexander (1889). *In Persia's Golden Days* [Niẓāmī]. London.
McCarthy, Justin (1893). *Ghazels from the Divan of Hafiz*. London.
Nicholson, Reynold (1898). *Selected Poems from the Divani Shamsi Tabriz* [Rūmī]. Cambridge.

Nott, John (1787). *Select Odes from the Persian Poet Hafez*. London.
Payne, John (1901). *The Poems of Shemseddin Mohammed Hafiz of Shiraz*. London.
Platts, John (1873). *The Gulistan, or, Rose-Garden*. [Sa'dī]. London.
Redhouse, James (1881). *The Mesnevi ... of Mevlana ... Jelalu-'d-Din, Muhammed, er-Rumi*. London.
[Rehatsek, Edward] (1887). *The Behâristân (Abode of Spring)* [Jāmī]. 'Benares' (Stoke Newington, published under the name of Richard Burton).
[——] (1888). *The Gulistan, or, Rose-Garden of Sa'di*. 'Benares' (Stoke Newington, published under the name of Richard Burton).
Robinson, Samuel (1876). *Sketch of the Life and Writings of Ferdusi*. London.
Rogers, Alexander (1907). *The Shah-Namah of Fardusi*. London.
Ross, James (1823). *The Gulistan, or, Flower-Garden* [Sa'dī]. London.
Warner, Arthur G., and Warner, Edmond (1905–25). *The Sháhnáma of Firdausí*, 9 vols. London.
Weston, Stephen (1815). *Episodes from the Shah Namah, or Annals of the Persian Kings* [Firdausī]. London.
Whinfield, E. H. (1880). *Gulshan i Raz: The Mystic Rose-Garden of Sa'd ud din Mahmud Shabistari*. London.
—— (1887). *Masnavi i Ma'navi ... Translated and Abridged* [Rūmī]. London.
Wilberforce-Clarke, H. (1881). *The Sikandar Nama, e Bara, or, Book of Alexander the Great* [Niẓāmī]. London.
—— (1891). *Diwan-I-Hafiz*, 2 vols. Calcutta.

Other Sources
Arberry, A. J. (1956). *FitzGerald's Salaman and Absal: A Study*. Cambridge (includes two versions of FitzGerald's translation and a literal translation by Arberry).
Beard, Michael (1982). 'Translations of Classical Persian Literature', pp. 443–7 in Vol. 8 of *Encyclopaedia Iranica*, ed. Ehsan Yarshater. London.
FitzGerald, Edward (1980). *The Letters of Edward FitzGerald*, ed. Alfred McKinley Terhune and Annabelle Burdick Terhune, 4 vols. Princeton, NJ.
Heron-Allen, Edward (1899). *Edward FitzGerald's Rubá'iyát of Omar Khayyám with their Original Persian Sources*. London.
Loloi, Parvin (2004). *Hâfiz, Master of Persian Poetry: A Critical Bibliography: English Translations Since the Eighteenth Century*. London.
Yohannan, John D. (1977). *Persian Poetry in England and America: A 200-Year History*. Delmar, NY.
—— (1982). 'Persian Influences in English and American Literature', pp. 140–3 in Vol. 8 of *Encyclopaedia Iranica*, ed. Ehsan Yarshater. London.

7.3 Literatures of the Indian Subcontinent

Harish Trivedi

Introduction

The history of translation into English from the Indian languages is inextricably entwined with the history of British rule in India. It has even been suggested that India under colonial rule was in a state of 'translation', but that theoretical and ideological formulation is perhaps a little too facile if not also counter-productive. To use the term 'translation' in this way, to deploy it 'under erasure' as the postmodernist phrase goes (Niranjana 1992: 48), is to do a double disservice: to mitigate the far-reaching effects of colonialism, on the one hand, as if it were no more coercive and exploitative than translation could ever be, and to strip 'translation' of its defining constituent element, that of a bilingual transaction, on the other. Without quite conflating or confusing translation with colonialism, it should still be possible and useful to read one in the light of the other, in order to enrich our understanding of both 'history' and 'translation'.

Though the British had been travelling to India since before the founding of the East India Company in 1600 and some of them thereafter had begun to stay in the country for a number of years at a time (as notably Sir Thomas Roe, ambassador at the court of the Moghul emperor Jahangir from 1615 to 1618), it was not until the 1770s that translations of any Indian texts were published in English. By then, the British were not merely traders but effectively administrators of substantial parts of India who needed to know more about the people they ruled. Not confident enough yet to wish to impose their own civilization, values, or even language on the Indians and treading cautiously on Indian sensibilities, the first major translation project the British undertook was to render manuals of Hindu laws from their traditional sources in Sanskrit into English, so as to be able to govern the natives by their own codes and conventions but without, in the process, having to depend blindly on the Sanskrit pandits (see Teltscher 1997: 195–202).

The first translation of such a text into English was *A Code of Gentoo* [i.e. Hindu] *Laws* (1776) by Nathaniel Brassey Halhed, except that it had been done not from the original Sanskrit but from a version in Persian, the official or court language of India under Muslim rule until it was replaced by English in 1837. Two of the best-known Britons connected with India in the late eighteenth and early nineteenth centuries, Sir William Jones and Lord Macaulay, had both gone out to assist in this vital and long-running project of legal codification and administration, Jones as a judge of the Supreme Court of Bengal at Calcutta (1783–94) and Macaulay as the Member for Law in the Council of the Governor-General (1834–8).

Meanwhile, some Britons had acquired a knowledge of Sanskrit, hard-won not only because the language was classically complex but also because no one in caste-regulated India would initially teach these *mlechchhas* or unclean foreigners the sacred language of the gods, the *deva-bhasha*. They included not only jurists and administrators but also missionaries with their different and scrupulously segregated agenda; the East India Company did not officially permit any British missionaries to enter India until 1813, so that they might not with their solicitous proselytizing get in the way of the primary objective of conquest and territorial gain. The mutually distinct, but sometimes mixed, motives of these various groups inspired the early translations from Sanskrit into English, with the 'discovery' of purely literary texts often constituting an incidental gain.

The first non-legal Indian text to be translated into English was the *Bhagavad Gītā* (literally, The Song sung by God; popularly the *Gītā*) in 1785 by Charles Wilkins, as *The Bhagvat-Geeta, or, Dialogues of Kreeshna and Arjoon*. Comprising a dialogue in about 700 couplets between the warrior hero Arjuna and his charioteer Lord Krishna in the middle of a battlefield just when the war is about to commence, this was a text at once both religious and secular, both scriptural and literary; it forms a small part of the foundational epic the *Mahābhārata* and has proved to be the Indian text most frequently translated into English, with over 300 versions so far. Having surveyed the two armies and finding kinsmen and friends arrayed on both sides, Arjuna refuses to fight, whereupon Krishna says to him (II, 2–3):

Whence, O Arjoon, cometh unto thee, thus standing in the field of battle, this folly and unmanly weakness? It is disgraceful, contrary to duty, and the foundation of dishonour. Yield not thus to unmanliness, for it ill becometh one like thee. Abandon this despicable weakness of thy heart, and stand up. (Wilkins 1785: 33)

Wilkins here raises *kaṣmala*, i.e. misapprehension, to 'unmanly weakness' (though 'unmanliness' used later for *klaibya* is accurate), edits out a reference to such misapprehension not leading to heaven (so as to prevent his readers from confusing this heathen heaven with the Christian heaven?), adds instead 'contrary to duty' which in a footnote he explains as 'Contrary to the duty of a soldier', turns the simple 'you' to 'one like thee', and omits Krishna's rousing address to Arjuna here as 'foe-conquering'. On the other hand, so as to enhance readability, he spells out 'crisis' as 'this field of battle' and breaks down long compounds and sentences into smaller units. His translation of the epic *Mahābhārata* remained far from complete but he did publish the *Hitopadeśa* (1787), a version of the witty moral fables better known as the *Pañcatantra* which had already been in circulation in Europe as received through indirect translations from its Arabic version.

The next Sanskrit text to be translated was a work that ranks as probably the best literary work ever composed in Sanskrit, the play *Abhijñānaśākuntalam* (literally, The Recognition of Shakuntala; popularly, *Śakuntalā*) by the poet and playwright Kālidāsa (4th century CE). It was rendered into English as *Sacontala, or, The Fatal Ring: An Indian Drama* (1789) by Sir William Jones (discussed more fully in Vol. 3 of this *History*), who proved to be the key pioneering figure in transmitting Sanskrit texts into English and propagating and 'theorizing' them generally; he came to be called 'Oriental' Jones. His translation is idiomatic and fluent, and does not either 'domesticate' or at every step gloss references embedded in an alien culture and mythology, as evidenced in the very first speech in Act I:

Charioteer: When I cast my eye on that black antelope, and on thee, O king, with thy braced bow, I see before me, as it were, the God Mahesa chasing a hart, with his bow, named pinaca, braced in his left hand. (Jones 1807: IX, 380)

The only concession Jones makes here to his reader is to name 'the God Mahesa' (another name for Shiva) while in Sanskrit he is elliptically the One with the Pinaka. Earlier, among 'Persons of the Drama', Jones had identified the king as 'Emperor of India', perhaps to emphasize the representative character of the text, while most other translations as well as Sanskrit editions identify him as merely the 'king of Hastinapur', a small kingdom. In any case, hardly any more widely typical Indian texts could have been chosen to be the first works to be translated into English than these three by Halhed, Wilkins, and Jones, though their choice was very likely guided by the recommendations of the Sanskrit pandits who acted as the native informants and unacknowledged collaborators in translation.

Early Impact: An Oriental Renaissance?

In a prefatory statement that he contributed to Wilkins's version of the *Bhagavad Gītā*, the Governor-General of the day, Warren Hastings, pronounced the text to be 'of great originality; of a sublimity of conception, reasoning, and diction, almost unequalled', while its author 'soar[ed] far beyond all competitors in this species of composition'. The discovery and dissemination of such works would help the British, he said, to think better of the Indians and 'teach us to estimate them by the measure of our own'. Texts such as these 'will survive', Hastings went on to prophesy, 'when the British dominion in India shall have long ceased to exist, and when the sources which it once yielded of wealth and power are lost to remembrance' (in Wilkins 1785: 11–12, 14). This was almost to concede the empire morally even before it had been quite consolidated materially. A similar admission of Indian equality if not superiority was made by Jones when, in his own preface to *Sacontala*, he called Kālidāsa 'the Shakespeare of India'; and he had already, in 1786, declared that the Sanskrit language was 'of wonderful structure, more perfect than the Greek, more copious than the Latin, and more exquisitely refined than either' (Jones 1807: III, 34).

Once the early Sanskrit translations reached Europe, the excitement caused there was no less remarkable, especially as the discovery of the Orient coincided with and fed into the rise of Romanticism. Jones's translation of *Śakuntalā* and the volumes of *Asiatick Researches* edited by him which also contained translations by diverse hands were repeatedly reprinted, and further translated into other European languages including especially German. (After reading Georg Forster's translation of Jones's *Sacontala* into German, Goethe wrote an ecstatic quatrain in 1791 which concluded, 'When I mention Śakuntala, everything is said.') Of the major English poets of the period, Coleridge, Byron, Shelley, and Keats all registered a new consciousness of India, and not only in their poetry. Byron, for example, wanted to extend his Grand Tour as far as India but the East India Company denied him permission; he wrote a poem titled 'Stanzas to a Hindoo Air', and deployed several Indian images in his poems including, humorously, a key image from the *Gītā* in *Don Juan*, IX, st. 75 (see Trivedi 1995: 85).

Similarly, Shelley toyed with the idea of going to India to seek employment with the East India Company, and in *Prometheus Unbound* imagined, as did several of his contemporaries, that the Vale of Kashmir had been the site of the Edenic paradise (see Drew 1987: 231–82). In what turned out to be far the most popular poem of the age, *Lalla Rookh: An Oriental Romance* (1817), Thomas Moore described in four cantos his eponymous heroine and her suitor in disguise travelling from Delhi via Lahore to 'Cashmere' (Kashmir). And the soporifically meditative Coleridge identified with the Indian god Vishnu who awoke only 'once in a million years for a few minutes', while he quizzically wondered about the sacred texts of India: 'What are | These Potentates of inmost Ind?' (see Drew 1987: 185–8).

The initial impact of the translations from Sanskrit was altogether so great that Raymond Schwab entitled his book on the subject *The Oriental Renaissance*. Just as the rediscovery through translations of Greek and Roman literature had given Europe a deeper and more cohesive understanding of itself, the discovery of the Orient made through translations, Schwab says, now profoundly challenged Europe by forcing it to revise its very definition of the world:

> the world, in the sense that we know it, dates from this period ... The writings deciphered by the orientalists made the world, for the first time in human history, a whole ... For so long merely Mediterranean, humanism began to be global ... a whole buried world arose to unsettle the foremost minds of an age.   (Schwab 1984: 4, 8)

Similarly, J. J. Clarke has written of an 'Oriental Enlightenment' not only in terms of the 'strong fascination' that the East has exercised over the West since the discovery of the Orient but also, more problematically, as an 'encounter between Asian and Western thought' (Clarke 1997: 5).

In fact, following the first impact of the translated Oriental texts, there had soon begun a strong European reaction against it. Friedrich Schlegel may have written in 1803 that 'Everything, yes, everything without exception has its origin in India' (quoted in Schwab 1984: 71), but when Coleridge cited in 1815 Schelling's statement, 'now we hear of nothing but the language and wisdom of India' (quoted in Drew 1987: 185), it was in a tone of some exasperation. In contrast to the enthusiastic incorporation of India in their poems by the major Romantic poets, Robert Southey, Poet Laureate, had written an 'epic' poem virulently hostile to the Hindu gods and customs, *The Curse of Kehama* (1810), which featured a scene of suttee and a rebellion by the people against a tyrannical Indian king.

On the whole, however, there can be few comparable instances in history of a handful of translated texts from one language producing such a sudden, unsuspected, and widely unsettling effect, in both positive and negative ways, on not only another literature but a whole civilization. If the effect did not last—and the claim of another renaissance is vastly exaggerated—it was because of a whole variety of larger factors which always attend on literature and translation and circumscribe their production and influence. In the Indian case, the discovery of Sanskrit literature lost some of its shine in the years immediately succeeding the death of Jones when the British finally defeated and killed in battle the dreaded Tipu Sultan in 1799, and then won another crucial victory against the combined forces of the Moghul emperor, the Marathas, and the French at Delhi in 1803. Hitherto regarded as the expression of another comparable civilization, works of Indian literature were now increasingly seen as curious productions of a subject race. Another major factor which militated against a more positive response to 'Hindoo' literature was a strong Christian backlash. The reception of the early Oriental translations would prove, if proof were needed, that literary translation is seldom merely literary or translation, especially in the colonial context.

Retrospectively the most influential view of just what was going on in the late eighteenth and nineteenth centuries in the name of translations and discovery of the Orient is that of Edward Said in his *Orientalism* (1978) which, among other things, has served to stand on its head the very meaning of the term. Said's view that the West produced in this period a body of motivated misknowledge of the Orient so as to be able to dominate and rule it better is ideologically overdetermined, textually hazy, and patently partial, and yet there can be no denying the more general historical fact that Oriental translations and the impact they had ran parallel to the colonial enterprise and were shot through with what Nigel Leask has called, in a broader sense, the 'anxieties of empire' (Leask 1993: 3).

The Canon: Religious and Classical

As the nineteenth century unfolded—and the 'long nineteenth century' in the context of translations from India can plausibly be seen to have a trajectory extending from Halhed in 1776 to Tagore in 1912—the activity of translating from Sanskrit seemed at first to diminish; it was only in the second half of the century, when the study of the language had become well established as an academic discipline in Britain and Europe as well as India, that translations from Sanskrit were undertaken systematically as part of a grand collective project. By then, historical and archaeological 'discoveries' (or, more accurately, revelations and recoveries) had also stimulated a parallel interest in Buddhism and Jainism, the two other old religions of India, whose sacred literature was to be found not in Sanskrit but in

Pali and Prakrit, respectively. Another ancient language of India, Tamil, gradually achieved recognition, and so, finally, did some of the modern 'vernaculars' from which a few texts were eventually translated. On the whole, however, throughout the nineteenth century, the parameters of selection of texts remained religious and classical, and the norms for translating them, scholarly and even recondite.

While the early policy of the East India Company required all those serving it to acquire a working knowledge of one or more modern Indian languages, which they were trained to acquire at the College of Fort William set up for this purpose at Calcutta in 1800, most translations of significant texts continued to be from Sanskrit. However, as British rule became more confident and hegemonic, a demand arose for the British not to have to learn the Indian languages but for Indians to be taught English instead. The introduction of western education in India, beginning in the 1810s and gathering strength as more schools and colleges on the western pattern were set up in various parts of India, seemed to accord with this new trend. When an allocation of £10,000 per annum was made by the British government in India to support local education, the long-running controversy between the so called 'Orientalists' and the 'Anglicists' regarding whether to promote indigenous or western learning came to a head.

This was the issue decisively settled by Lord Macaulay in his 'Minute on Indian Education' submitted to the Governor-General on 2 February 1835, a text that has come to be seen in postcolonial discourse as more important perhaps than any single pronouncement by even a governor-general or viceroy. In this 'Minute', Macaulay first dismissed all Oriental literature as being useless and even absurd, especially when judged by European standards; he claimed that all the Orientalists he had spoken to in England or India 'could not deny that a single shelf of a good European library was worth more than the whole native literature of India and Arabia'. Secondly, he sought to reverse the direction in which translation between India and Britain had flowed so far. By teaching English to Indians instead, the British would form 'a class who may be *interpreters* between us and the millions whom we govern; a class of persons, Indian in blood and colour, but English in taste, in opinions, in morals, and in intellect' (*emphasis added*; Macaulay 1972: 41).

While Macaulay's sweeping dismissal of all Oriental literature and learning was a triumphalist assertion of the western Renaissance and Enlightenment vis-à-vis the East, his project of cloning brown Englishmen placed the translator's menial burden squarely on Indian shoulders. In one stroke of governmental decision-making, the liberal cultural need to translate Indian literature into English was replaced by the pragmatic politics of translating the Indians themselves into Englishmen. Macaulay's recommendations were implemented as government policy in 1837. The first three universities on the western pattern were set up in 1857 in Calcutta, Bombay, and Madras, where English language and literature and the western sciences were taught to the Indians. Remarkably, the only classical languages taught in the Indian universities and colleges were those already prevalent, mainly Sanskrit and Persian (and not Latin or Greek as later in the other British colonies which lacked classical languages of their own). This provision kept open a channel for studying and translating from classical Indian literature.

In the first half of the nineteenth century, the most notable and prolific follower of the example set by Jones and Wilkins was Horace Hayman Wilson, who, during his extended stay in India (1808–32), spent a year at the holy seat of ancient learning, Banaras, improving his Sanskrit and collecting manuscripts. He translated a play entitled *Uttara Rama Cheritra, or, Continuation of the History of Rama* (1826) by Bhavabhūti (7th–8th century CE), a dramatist who ranks second only to Kālidāsa, and a work of prose fiction, *The Dasa Kumara Charita, or, Adventures of Ten Princes* (1846) by Daṇḍin (7th century CE). He also translated a selection of hymns from the oldest and the most venerated religious text in Sanskrit, the *Ṛg Veda Saṁhitā* (1850) as well as a complete translation of the *Viṣṇu Purāṇa*, somewhat grandly subtitled *A System of Hindu Mythology and Tradition* (1840).

One of the most delightful and enlightening of Wilson's numerous translations is *The Mégha Dúta, or, Cloud Messenger*, a poem of nearly 500 lines by Kālidāsa in which a lover implores a cloud to carry a message to his separated wife across a thousand miles of varied Indian landscape—which, like the wife herself, is lovingly and even erotically described. Wilson's translation now contracts the original, mostly to edit out some erotica, and now expands it, so as to render it 'intelligible to the *English* reader' whom he seems to treat with solicitous care. His fluent iambic pentameter couplets are generously supplemented with detailed notes, which are a compendium of comparative references to western classics such as Horace, Lucretius, Shakespeare, and Milton as well as to a wide range of other Sanskrit texts and contemporary British accounts of Indian landscape and culture.

Altogether, *The Cloud Messenger* is an outstanding example of poetic translation and scholarly commentary, of Orientalism at its best in its first (pre-Macaulay) flush. A characteristic moment is verse II, 21 where the languishing wife is at last reached and described:

> There, in the fane, a beauteous creature stands,
> The first best work of the Creator's hands;
> Whose slender limbs inadequately bear
> A full-orbed bosom, and a weight of care;
> Whose teeth like pearls, whose lips like *Bimbas* show,
> And fawn-like eyes still tremble as they glow.
> (Wilson 1868: 153)

Here, the 'fane' is Wilson's own mildly archaicizing addition, the *Bimba* is explained as '*Bryonia grandis*' which 'bears a red fruit', the 'first best' is to be compared with 'the last and best, | Of all God's works' (*Paradise Lost*, IX, 896), while the 'weight of care' is in fact Wilson's euphemistic substitution for the weight of the ample hips of the heroine, traditionally considered erotically desirable in India. At the same time, Wilson calls this passage 'perhaps the most pleasing part of this elegant little poem', robustly defends it against 'the illiberal and arrogant criticism' of a certain Mr Pinkerton who had opined generally 'that the climate of

India, while it inflames the imagination, impairs the judgment', and finally pronounces his own verdict: 'we have few specimens either in classical or modern Poetry, of more genuine tenderness or delicate feeling' (Wilson 1868: 152).

Wilson left India in 1832 on being appointed the first Boden Professor of Sanskrit at Oxford, a particularly well-paid lifelong appointment endowed by Lieutenant Colonel Joseph Boden, who had made his money in India in the service of the East India Company, to promote his belief, as he put it, that 'a more general knowledge and critical knowledge of the Sanskrit language will be a means of enabling his countrymen to proceed in the conversion of the Natives of India to the Christian Religion' (quoted in Chaudhuri 1996: 211). On Wilson's death in 1860, the appointment of a successor was hotly and even acrimoniously contested between Friedrich Max Müller, then universally acknowledged to be the best western scholar of Sanskrit, and Sir Monier Monier-Williams, with the latter claiming that though he might not be the candidate best suited 'to secure a worldwide reputation for the Sanskrit chair', he was the better man for 'aiding, by means of Sanskrit, the diffusion of Christianity in India', which had been 'the one object of the Founder'. He won by polling 833 votes of the Convocation against 610 cast for Max Müller (Chaudhuri 1996: 213–18).

The bitterly disappointed Max Müller, who suspected that his being a German had also been a factor in his defeat, persevered to compete his six-volume edition of the *Ṛg Veda*, of which he also translated a selection. He now planned to gather together a team of translators to make available the major sacred texts of all religions; the twenty-four volumes of the Sacred Books of the East (SBE), later expanded to fifty, were published by the Oxford University Press with funds made available by the university and the Government of India. Coming at the end of the century, the SBE (fully discussed in § 10.3, below) remains the crowning achievement of Oriental translation into English in the nineteenth century, in its cogent conceptualization, its rigorous scholarly standards, and its mammoth proportions. The translators came from all over Europe where, after the initial British discoveries, Indology had flourished more vigorously than in Britain itself, thus giving the lie to the Foucauldian-Saidian formulation that knowledge was (colonial) power.

At the same time, the SBE did have a palpable ideological design, and it was in Max Müller's conception hardly less Christian than Boden might have wished for. It included only religious texts, indeed only the scriptures, studiously keeping out several major works which had a strong claim to being religious and literary at the same time. Thirty-three of the volumes were devoted to the religions of India (twenty-one to Hinduism, nine to Buddhism, two to Jainism) and yet these did not include either the *Rāmāyaṇa* or the *Mahābhārata*, the two great epics of Indian civilization in which Rama and Krishna, the two great gods of the Hindu pantheon, are major characters though neither yet fully sacralized as God, or the *Bhagavata Purāṇa* which again has a different and more godly Krishna as its hero—each so profoundly originary and influential in Indian culture that it has been said that all of Indian literature, at least until the middle of the nineteenth century, comes out of these two and a half books. The only clearly literary work to be translated in the series was an epic biography of the Buddha by Aśvaghoṣa, *Buddhacarita* (1st century BCE), here rendered twice, from the original Sanskrit and also from an early translation into Chinese (Vols. 49 and 19, respectively).

For the rest, nearly all the Indian books translated were arcane, dull, and even in the original venerated more in name than through being actually read and used. As Max Müller explained in his introduction to the first volume, the texts were meant to be of use mainly to theologians and missionaries and therefore did not omit 'what seems tedious and repulsive' (quoted in Chaudhuri 1996: 332). Already in 1856 Max Müller had written in a letter: 'India is much riper for Christianity than Rome or Greece were at the time of St Paul', and now in 1879 as the first volumes of the SBE were published, he wrote in another letter: 'Of one thing I feel very certain, that this translation of *The Sacred Books of the East* . . . will do a great deal towards lifting Christianity into its highest historical position' (quoted in Chaudhuri 1996: 306, 334). The SBE volumes continue to have a shelf or more to themselves in most respectable libraries of the anglophone world, where they repose undisturbed by anyone except the specialist scholar.

Popular Translations

At more or less the same time that the SBE were making their stately progress, a number of other translations were published which represented somewhat different strands of Indian literature and indeed proved highly popular. Far the most enchanting and widely circulated of any Oriental text to be published in translation in the nineteenth century was of course Edward FitzGerald's *The Rubáiyát of Omar Khayyám* (on which see § 7.2, above). FitzGerald had been introduced to the Rubáiyát by his friend Edward Cowell, who was a professor of history in the Presidency College, Calcutta, before becoming professor of Sanskrit at Cambridge. Cowell himself is best remembered for his translation from Sanskrit of Aśvaghoṣa's life of the Buddha in the SBE (1894) and his co-translation in prose with F. W. Thomas of a Sanskrit epic biography of a king, *Harṣacarita* (1897) by his court poet Bāna Bhatta (7th century CE), which abounds in so many puns that just twelve lines of translated text on one particular page, for example, require nine footnotes each beginning 'Or . . .' (Cowell and Thomas 1993: 100). Cowell also edited a major work, *The Jataka, or, Stories of the Buddha's Former Births* (1895–1907), translated from Pali by various hands.

The most popular version of the life of the Buddha was produced, however, by Sir Edwin Arnold, who had served in India as the Principal of the Deccan College, Poona, from 1856 to 1861. His *The Light of Asia, or, The Great Renunciation . . . being the Life and Teachings of Gautama, Prince of India and Founder of Buddhism*, published in 1880, had already gone into its fiftieth edition by 1889; it is not strictly a translation, and yet it is not an original work either, with the main Indian source for it being yet again the master text for Buddha's life, the *Buddhacarita*. It thus belongs to a whole category of English texts which are closely based on one or more Indian sources and offer an amalgamated re-creation, 'pseudo-translation', or 'transcreation' of them, a sub-genre inaugurated in fact by Sir William Jones in his nine 'Hymns' to various Hindu gods and goddesses.

Among the works Edwin Arnold clearly translated from Sanskrit were *The Book of Good Counsels: from the . . . Hitopadesa* (1861), earlier translated in part by Charles Wilkins; *The Song of Songs* (1875), a rhymed translation of the *Gīta-Govinda*, a devotional-erotic poem about the love of Krishna and Radha by Jayadeva (12th century CE), first translated in literal prose as an exercise by Sir William Jones in 1792; and the *Song Celestial* (1885), a remarkably fluent and lucid version of the *Bhagavad Gītā* which proved quite as popular as *The Light of Asia*. In a huge colonial irony, this was the version in which Mahatma Gandhi first read this work while a student in London in the late 1880s; he was later to say in his autobiography: 'I have read almost all the English translations of it, and I regard Sir Edwin Arnold's as the best. He has been faithful to the text, and yet it does not read like a translation.' Gandhi went on to read the *Gītā* in the original, to adopt it probably as the key text of his life and 'a book of daily reading', and even to publish his own commentary on it. Meanwhile, he also read in London *The Light of Asia*, 'and I read it with even greater interest than I did the *Bhagavadgita*. Once I had begun it I could not leave off' (Gandhi 2002: 62–3).

One other Sanskrit text which in its English version achieved high and abiding popularity (or at least universal name recognition and curiosity) was the *Kāma Sūtra*, a treatise on sex and the civic conventions governing its place in society, by Vātsyāyana (3rd century CE). It was first translated by Richard Burton in 1883 and published 'for private circulation' by the 'Kama-Sastra Society of London and Benares', a society which had just one member other than Burton himself, his friend and collaborator in the translation, F. F. Arbuthnot (Grant 2005: 511). This ruse was adopted not only to get around the Obscene Publications Act of 1857 and the prevailing climate of prudery at the high noon of the Victorian age but also so as to contain (and paradoxically reinforce) the image of India, in a central Orientalist stereotype, as a brazenly licentious and depraved society, as seen for example in much temple architecture (now routinely used as illustrations in reprints of this somewhat arid and elaborately taxonomical text). Of all the cultural differences between Britain and India that various translators had to negotiate, this contrast in the attitudes towards sex and its representation was perhaps the sharpest and the most problematic. In his translation of *Śakuntalā*, Jones had already come up against it, and had decided to turn the ample hips of the heroine into 'elegant limbs', even exchanging them at another point for 'graceful arms', while moderating her breasts drooping under the wilting fever of love into a drooping neck; he had also gallantly mopped up all her perspiration, perhaps not knowing that it is seen in Sanskrit as a primary sign of erotic interest and excitement (see Telstcher 1997: 214; Bassnett and Trivedi 1999: 7). Another strategy employed to cope with what were seen as shockingly explicit passages was, of course, simply to omit them, or to translate them into Latin, as Max Müller did even with an epic simile in the *Bṛhadāraṇyaka-upaniṣad* in which the sexual act is described in terms of the sacred ritual of a *yajña* or fire-offering. The classical languages of the West were never far away from the minds of the British translators of Indian literature; Jones had translated *Śakuntalā* first into Latin and subsequently into literal and then idiomatic English. The literary template for translating Indian texts into English was unmistakably classical.

The apparent bowdlerization of Indian texts by western translators is routinely regarded as an act of blatant Orientalism. However, it is possible to look at it from a different, even contrary, point of view. Conscious of the wide discrepancy in attitudes in this regard between the East and the West, the Orientalist translators toned down the potentially more offending passages not so much to traduce the Indian texts as to protect them against a knee-jerk rejection by the prudish and sanctimonious western reader. Wilson's note to the verse describing the heroine of *The Cloud Messenger* (cited above) in what are, from the point of view of Indian aesthetics, unexceptionable and even conventional terms, is a strategically wise example of such a procedure.

Non-classical Literatures

The classical bias of British translators may in part explain why nearly all the Indian literature translated into English throughout the nineteenth century came from the classical Indian languages, Sanskrit, Pali, and Prakrit. (Indeed, the first two histories of Indian literature, by Albrecht Weber (1852) and Moriz Winternitz (1907–22), confined themselves almost entirely to Sanskrit literature.) But the older languages were all safely dead, and another reason for an exclusive focus on them might have been that there was no live charge to their literature; that to study and to translate them did not in any significant way impinge on, and was conveniently bracketed off from, the pragmatic and dirty business of ruling India. To concentrate on the ancient glories of Indian literature also offered a justification for ruling India for, following Hegel, it was argued that India represented an early stage in human development and had thereafter remained static and outside history, in contrast with the history of the West, which had been one of enlightened rise and progress (see Leask 1993: 107). Thus viewed, there was nothing worthwhile in contemporary Indian culture and literature and it became the moral duty of the British to redeem India from all its contemporary ills and to civilize it.

It was only slowly and sporadically, therefore, that works from any living Indian language began to be translated into English. The language that had been most flagrantly ignored was perhaps Tamil, a Dravidian language of South India which had a literary history nearly as long as that of Sanskrit, except that it had continued to flourish as a living language. Though a pioneering anthology had come out as early as 1794, *Specimens of Hindoo Literature, consisting of Translations from the Tamoul Language, of some Hindoo Works of Morality and Imagination* by E. N. Kindersley, not much of significance followed it for the succeeding half-century, until

Tirukkura̱l, a didactic work of maxims in couplets, was translated by the Revd G. U. Pope as *The 'Sacred' Kurral of Tiruvalluva-Nayanar* (1886), the inverted commas around 'Sacred' signalling Pope's missionary scepticism.

From the other modern languages of India, over a dozen of which had emerged broadly speaking around 1000 CE and had a rich and continuous literary history since then, hardly anything was translated into English until the last quarter of the nineteenth century, but for a stray selection here and there. Thus, as Kindersley had for Tamil, Colonel Thomas Duer Broughton put together *Selections from the Popular Poetry of the Hindoos* (1814), representing Hindi poets mainly of the seventeenth and eighteenth centuries whose verses he had heard the (mainly) Brahmin soldiers in the Bengal Army quote from memory when 'talking upon any subject' (Broughton 2000: 38–9). In contrast with the ancient Sanskrit scriptures which many Hindus may have sworn by but hardly any actually read, versions of the *Rāmāyaṇa*, the *Mahābhārata*, the *Gītā*, and the *purāṇas*, which were not regarded as mere translations from the Sanskrit but as original and foundational texts in each of these languages, were in fact read with reverence, often as a part of daily worship, and even the illiterate masses knew numerous lines and passages from them by heart through the sheer frequency of their evocation in common discourse. Perhaps the most outstanding of such texts was the *Ramacharitamanas*, the story of Rama as retold by Tulsi Das (1532–1623) in Hindi, the most widely spoken language of India; it was translated into English in 1883 as *The Rámáyana of Tulsi Dás* by F. S. Growse.

Growse was a member of the Indian Civil Service whose job it was, as a district officer, actually to go into the hinterland and communicate in the local language with the masses. He and his colleagues thus had their ear to the ground, like the later missionaries who, having failed to knock down high Brahminic Hinduism frontally, were now trying to nibble away at it from the margins by working among the poor and lowly sections of the society. Unlike the Orientalists in colleges and universities in both Britain and India in their Sanskrit ivory towers, both these groups had a more intimate empirical knowledge of what India at large was about, and of its emotional imaginary as manifested in its living languages. Thus another ICS officer, William Waterfield, translated episodes from a seventeenth-century oral folk epic, the *Alha*, from a dialect of Hindi, in the *Calcutta Review* (1875–6), and another civil servant, William Crooke, editor of the *North Indian Notes and Queries*, published in that journal between 1891 and 1896 over 250 folk tales 'recorded from the lips of peasants ... and literally translated', ostensibly by himself but in fact in collaboration (as usual, only indirectly acknowledged) with a native informant, Pandit Ram Gharib Chaube (Naithani in Crooke and Chaube 2002). These can be seen as belated but worthy attempts to set alongside the ancient India of religious and classical literature the present-day India of popular and folk orature.

Just how topical and politically subversive the vernaculars could be when translated into English was demonstrated to explosive effect in the case of an enormously popular Bengali play, *Nil-Darpana* (1860) by Dinabandhu Mitra, anonymously translated the same year as *Nil Darpan, or, The Indigo Planting Mirror*. It showed British planters coercing Indians to cultivate indigo on extortionate terms, with one of them (named 'P. P. Rogue' in the original but in the edited English version given the sweeter name of 'Rose') raping an Indian woman who then dies, as do three other peasants. The publisher, the Revd James Long, had been working as a missionary in India for over twenty years and had constantly advocated that vernacular literature 'already in circulation among the native population should be translated [into English] for the information of those to whom it was of importance to understand native feelings' and for their own good (quoted in Rao and Rao 1992: 120). In the absence of an identifiable translator, Long was now prosecuted for libel and sentenced by the presiding judge to a fine of 1,000 rupees and one month's imprisonment, in a classic case of shooting the messenger—even though this messenger was well meaning and a fellow Briton.

Conclusion

As the nineteenth century drew to a close, the main institutional site of Oriental scholarship and translation into English moved from Britain to the USA just as European, especially German and French, Indological researches had already overtaken comparable efforts in Britain. The Harvard Oriental Series distinguished itself from the Sacred Books of the East by publishing, among other things, many more literary texts including plays by Rājaśekhara, Śūdraka, and Bhavabhūti as well as the classic anthology of Sanskrit poetry, the *Subhāṣitaratnakoṣa* compiled by Vidyākara. Meanwhile, as Indians grew more competent and confident in their use of English, the English translation of one of the key ancient Indian texts, which is also by far the longest, the *Mahābhārata*, was undertaken and accomplished by an Indian, Kisari Mohan Ganguly (1887–96). While Ram Mohun Roy, a pioneering reformer, had already translated five *upaniṣads* between 1815 and 1819, a concerted Indian effort was now directed towards producing translations of Indian texts by the Indians themselves, a patriotic and counter-Orientalist endeavour facilitated by the setting up of a number of Indian publishing houses and research institutes such as the Chowkhambha Sanskrit Series Office established in Banaras in 1892.

This development could be described as an instance of collective self-translation in an endeavour to project more fully the wealth of Indian literature on Indian terms. However, it is doubtful whether, at the end of the century, any translations from India had a notable popularity or visibility in Britain; on the contrary, the excitement of discovery felt at the beginning of the century had almost entirely cooled off. It was, as it happened, momentarily renewed through the phenomenal success of a single slim volume of poems translated by the author, *Gitanjali* (i.e. Song Offering; 1912), which won Rabindranath Tagore the Nobel Prize for Literature the following year and a reputation in the West as a sage-poet, a wise man from the East writing in a spiritual-mystical vein.

Eventually, if translations into English from India led to any kind of a renaissance at all, it was paradoxically through their impact on the Indians themselves. Through the rediscovery and translation of the ancient writings of India, whether religious, philosophical, or literary, many Indians of the 'interpreter' class that Macaulay had envisaged now read these works in English and began to claim a kind of cultural seniority and superiority over the British, and to challenge the self-professed justification by the British of their rule over India as a civilizing mission. A widely influential text which greatly helped to fuel anti-British feeling was the *Annals and Antiquities of Rajasthan* (1829–32), a wide-eyed retelling by Colonel James Tod of proud sagas composed by native bards one of whom he called 'the Rajput Homer, the Indian Ossian' (Keay 1988: 195). This work served as a source book for a spate of militant narratives of medieval Indian glory, ostensibly against an earlier foreign conqueror, the Muslims, but metaphorically against the British. Beginning in the last quarter of the nineteenth century, by when a significant number of Indians had learnt to read English, such cultural nationalism prepared the ground for and fed into the political nationalism that was to emerge at the beginning of the twentieth century and to lead in 1947 to Independence. Initially meant to serve as an instrument of more effective colonization, translations of Indian works into English, as appropriated by the Indians themselves, eventually contributed in a significant measure to nationalist resurgence and decolonization.

LIST OF SOURCES

Towards the end of the nineteenth century, several major series of editions and translations of texts from the classical Indian languages were initiated. These include Friedrich Max Müller's Sacred Books of the East (Oxford, 1879–1910, 50 volumes), the Harvard Oriental Series (Cambridge, MA, 1891–; 62 volumes by 2002), and the Chowkhambha Sanskrit Series (Banaras, 1892–, in several sub-series of unnumbered volumes).

Translations
Anon. (1860). *Nil Darpan, or, The Indigo Planting Mirror* [Mitra]. Calcutta.
Arnold, Sir Edwin (1880). *The Light of Asia, or, The Great Renunciation (Mahâbhinishkramana), being The Life and Teachings of Gautama, Prince of India and Founder of Buddhism (as Told in Verse by an Indian Buddhist)*. London.
—— (1861). *The Book of Good Counsels: from the . . . Hitopadesa*. London.
—— (1875). *The Song of Songs* [Jayadeva]. London.
—— (1885). *The Song Celestial* [the *Bhagavad Gītā*]. London.
Broughton, Thomas Duer (2000). *The First Published Anthology of Hindi Poets*, ed. Imre Bangha. Delhi (first pub. as *Selections from the Popular Poetry of the Hindoos*, 1814).
Burton, Richard, and Arbuthnot, F. F. (1883). *The Kamasutra of Vatsyayana*. London.
Cowell, E. B., ed. (1895–1907). *The Jātaka, or, Stories of the Buddha's Former Births*. Oxford.
—— and Thomas, F. W. (1993). *The Harṣa-Carita of Bāṇa*. Delhi (first pub. 1897).
Growse, F. S. (1883). *The Rāmáyana of Tulsi Dás*. Allahabad.
Halhed, Nathaniel Brassey (1776). *A Code of Gentoo Laws*. Calcutta.
Jones, Sir William (1807). *Works*, 13 vols. London.

Kindersley, E. N. (1794). *Specimens of Hindoo Literature, consisting of Translations from the Tamoul Language, of some Hindoo Works of Morality and Imagination*. London.
Pope, G. U. (1886). *The 'Sacred' Kurral of Tiruvalluva-Nayanar*. London.
Wilkins, Charles (1785). *The Bhagvat-Geeta, or, Dialogues of Kreeshna and Arjoon*. London.
——. (1787) *The Hitopadesa*. Calcutta.
Wilson, Horace Hayman (1826). *Uttara Rama Cheritra, or, Continuation of the History of Rama* [Bhavabhūti]. Calcutta.
—— (1840). *The Vishnu Purána: A System of Hindu Mythology and Tradition*. London.
—— (1846). *The Dasa Kumara Charita, or, Adventures of Ten Princes* [Daṇḍin] London.
—— (1850). *Rig-Veda-Sanhita*. London.
—— (1868). *The Mégha Dúta, or, Cloud Messenger* [Kālidāsa], ed. Kedar Nath Tarakaratna. Calcutta (first pub. 1813).

Other Sources
Bassnett, Susan, and Trivedi, Harish, eds. (1999). *Post-colonial Translation: Theory and Practice*. London.
Chaudhuri, Nirad C. (1996). *Scholar Extraordinary: The Life of Friedrich Max Müller*. New Delhi (first pub. 1974).
Clarke, J. J. (1997). *Oriental Enlightenment: The Encounter between Asian and Western Thought*. London.
Crooke, William, and Chaube, Pandit Ram Gharib (2002). *Folktales from Northern India*, ed. Sadhana Naithani. Santa Barbara, CA.
Drew, John (1987). *India and the Romantic Imagination*. Delhi.
Gandhi, M. K. (2002). *An Autobiography, or, The Story of my Experiments with Truth*. Ahmadabad (first pub. 1927).
Grant, Ben (2005). 'Translating "The" *Kamasutra*.' *Third World Quarterly* 26: 509–16.
Keay, John (1988). *India Discovered*. London.
Leask, Nigel (1993). *British Romantic Writers and the East: Anxieties of Empire*. Delhi (first pub. 1992).
Macaulay, Thomas Babington (1972). *Selected Writings*, ed. John Clive and Thomas Pinney. Chicago, IL.
Niranjana, Tejaswini (1992). *Siting Translation: History, Post-structuralism, and the Colonial Context*. Berkeley, CA.
Rao, Amiya, and Rao, B. G. (1992). *The Blue Devil: Indigo and Colonial Bengal, with an English Translation of Neel Darpan by Dinabandhu Mitra*. Delhi.
Said, Edward (1978). *Orientalism*. London.
Schwab, Raymond (1984). *The Oriental Renaissance: Europe's Rediscovery of India and the East 1680–1880*, tr. Gene Patterson-Blach and Victor Reinking. New York (original pub. 1950).
Teltscher, Kate (1997). *India Inscribed: European and British Writing on India, 1600–1800*. Delhi (first pub. 1995).
Trivedi, Harish (1995). *Colonial Transactions: English Literature and India*. Manchester (first pub. 1993).

7.4 Chinese

Lauren Pfister

The Beginning of Chinese Studies

Early English translations of Chinese literature had to face monumental linguistic and bibliographical obstacles. Not only were Chinese grammatical principles little understood in Europe and North America at the beginning of the nineteenth century, but the massive literary collection of nearly 3,600 books within the 'four treasuries' of the imperial library (*Sì kù quánshū*) was still largely unknown and inaccessible to Europeans. The fact that this situation was dramatically reversed by the year 1900 had very much to do with the unusual roles taken up by Protestant Christian missionaries as well as a few outstanding consular figures who established a new sinological tradition within English-speaking institutions of higher education. It was remarked already in mid-century that without the missionary involvement in the study of Chinese linguistics as well as of canonical and popular literature, later developments in consular, military, educational, and mercantile areas would have been greatly hindered. A discussion of Chinese literature in translation must therefore begin by explaining how its foreignness was overcome for an anglophone audience.

Without question the lexicographical watershed was the multi-volume trilingual dictionary (1815–22) produced by Robert Morrison (on whom see Cranmer-Byng 1967). Providing both Cantonese and Mandarin vocabulary (characters and transliterated sounds, but without indication of tonal differences) with English equivalents, Morrison illustrated phrases related to these characters by reference to many works from the Ruist ('Confucian') canon, following precedents in imperial authorized dictionaries and other sources. Though his renderings of these passages were regularly criticized by James Legge, who nonetheless employed both Morrison's transliteration system and his dictionary for the first edition of his *Chinese Classics* (1861–72), Morrison's dictionary had set a pioneering precedent. Legge built on this precedent by providing a more advanced alternative: at the very end of each volume of the *Chinese Classics* he prepared a dictionary of classical terms, illustrating the nuances of each term by references to classical passages. Further advances in precision, both in lexicography and in translation, appeared in the dictionaries of John Chalmers, who provided not only modern Chinese–English tomes, but also English renderings and explanations from two standard classical dictionaries, a version of the Qīng court's authorized *Concise Kang Hi* [Kāng Xī] *Dictionary* (1877) and a classical Hàn dynasty lexical dictionary and thesaurus, the *Shuō wén* (1882). This brought new information about ancient etymology and rhyming schemes to English readers, and so opened new doors for further sinological research into classical and poetic literature. By the end of the century a massive lexicographical effort by Herbert A. Giles resulted in a multilingual dictionary, which was not only a *tour de force* in providing numerous dialectal instances of each term but also added Japanese and Korean pronunciations to the Chinese transliterations. In addition, Giles developed and refined Thomas Wade's system of transliteration, so that the Wade–Giles system was destined to become a standard transliteration for much of the twentieth century. All these lexicographical works provided necessary information to make literature accessible to translators and their audiences.

Traditional Chinese bibliographical understanding became accessible only later, the most significant advance being Alexander Wylie's study published in 1867 with the unassuming title *Notes on Chinese Literature*. Far more than mere notes, Wylie provided the first genuine insights for English readers into the system of the imperial library, that is, the four 'treasuries' of the scriptures (*jīng*), histories (*shǐ*), masters (*zǐ*), and *belles-lettres* (*jí*). Through this work foreign missionaries, officials, scholars, and other readers could begin to understand the overriding authority given to Ruist traditions, especially in the first and third major categories, and they could sense the emphatic importance of the dynastic histories. Much later, in 1898, Herbert Giles added another research tool of similar significance, the first Chinese biographical dictionary, which included more than 2,500 entries as well as a useful appendix which added to the personal names their sobriquets and status of canonization in the Ruist temple.

In 1790 the President of the Royal Asiatic Society, Sir William Jones, presented his audience with information about the language and literature of China (see Fan 1946), but academic circles in England would remain far behind their French counterparts in scholarly production until branches of the Society were established, first in Hong Kong (1847) and then the 'North China Branch' in Shanghai (1857). In fact, the academy and universities in Britain and America did not have much to offer in sinology until well into the latter half of the nineteenth century; before that, Protestant missionaries living along the eastern Chinese seaboard were the primary source for literary activity of many sorts, supplemented by a few scholarly minded merchants and some government officials.

The Macartney Expedition to Beijing in 1793 was a failure, even though it stimulated an 11-year-old boy, George Staunton, to take up the challenge of translating the Qīng legal code (published in 1810). British scholars and translators were unable to match the expertise and productivity of contemporary French scholars such as Abel Rémusat and Stanislas Julien. Besides Staunton, the other exception to this rule was John Francis Davis, whose literary works consisted initially of translations of a novel (*The Three Dedicated Rooms*, 1815) and a drama (*An Heir in his Old Age*, 1817), later followed by additional translations of novels and 'Chinese moral maxims' (1822). By the end of the 1820s, Davis offered English renderings of selected poetry, a popular novel (*The Fortunate Union*, 1829), and several theatrical pieces including *The Sorrows of Han: A Chinese Tragedy* (1829). A compilation of further translations appeared much later in a work entitled

Chinese Miscellanies: A Collection of Essays and Notes (1865). Davis was notably indebted to Morrison's scholarship. By the 1820s he deliberately abandoned literal translations, preferring to write in a more fluent English acceptable to a more general readership. Foreignness in the text was marked by occasional explanatory notes; he also indicated in a few places where he had dropped passages he considered tedious or repetitive. He would later become the head of the East India Company and the first Governor of Hong Kong.

Nevertheless, when John Robert Morrison, the son of the Protestant missionary, wrote in the *Chinese Repository* of 1838 about the 'facilities' for studying Chinese language and literature in English-speaking countries, the majority of these materials were not in English. Chinese language and literature were still largely *terra incognita* to the English-speaking world.

One of the ways this ignorance was overcome was through journals published on the east coast of China, the first of this kind being the *Chinese Repository* (1832–51) edited in succession by two American missionaries, Elijah Bridgman and Samuel Wells Williams. Coordinating a group of the earliest Protestant missionaries and merchants associated with the East India Company and other mercantile organizations, they produced a magazine which sought to inform an English-reading public living in China and abroad about the Chinese world. Certainly, close connections between missionaries, merchants, and some governmental and military figures existed, but this did not prevent a few sympathetic missionaries (including Bridgman) and merchants from being invited by Qīng officials to observe the destruction of English merchants' opium caches in the run-up to the first Opium War. Though the *Chinese Repository* regularly described the various institutions connected with English persons living within or near China as well as many of their parallel Chinese institutions, it also became a medium for promoting various kinds of Chinese literature in translation. In addition to the translations of current political documents (imperial edicts, public correspondence from local officials, and treaty conditions), there also appeared selections of popular religious tracts, passages from the Ruist scriptures, translations of texts for children and students (the *Trimetrical Classic*, *Thousand Character Classic*, and essays and stories on filial piety), as well as summaries of Chinese novels, plays, biographies of various mythological and imperial figures, and renderings from the major philosophical writings of representative Ruist scholars (particularly Zhū Xī).

Only occasionally were these translators associated with the British military or government (as, for example, Thomas Wade); the vast majority of the literary pieces were produced by the editors and other missionaries, including a Prussian missionary who later became a British colonial official, Charles Gutzlaff; the American missionaries Walter Lowrie and J. L. Shuck; and the prolific translator and cultural commentator from the London Missionary Society, William H. Medhurst. So influential were these writings that James Legge included the *Chinese Repository* within the annotated bibliography of the first volume of his *Chinese Classics* (1861). In subsequent bibliographical notes he would add the titles of two other relevant journals: the Société Asiatique's *Journal asiatique*, founded along with the Société in 1822, and another notable missionary journal, the *Chinese Recorder*, started in 1868. All the major advances in translating Chinese literature were anticipated by initial summaries or selected renderings within the pages of the *Chinese Repository*. This exploration of Chinese literature in English translations was later extended through more focused studies found within the *Chinese Recorder* and some contemporary academic journals also published in China, especially the journal published in Shanghai by the North China Branch of the Royal Asiatic Society and the first English-language journal specializing in sinology, the *China Review* (initiated in Hong Kong in 1872). These matters set the course for a growing sophistication in literary translation, anticipating the thoroughly academic productions of the French journal started in 1890, *T'oung Pao*.

The Major Translators

The most prominent translator of Chinese literature into English, particularly regarding the Chinese classical canon, was James Legge, the Scottish nonconformist missionary posted in Hong Kong by the London Missionary Society (for fuller accounts of his work see Pfister 1994, 2004; Girardot 2002). Though most famous for his monumental work on the Ruist scriptures, the *Chinese Classics*, Legge started his publishing career in 1843 by editing a two-volume translation of a popular Cantonese novel written in the 1820s and initially translated into English by his Chinese friend and later pastoral colleague Ho Tsun-sheen. That novel, *The Rambles of the Emperor Ching Tih in Këang Nan: A Chinese Tale*, which had first been summarized by Gutzlaff in the *Chinese Repository*, introduced Legge to the distinctive format of Chinese novels as well as the Chinese world view that in 1850 he was to study in his quest for the best Chinese terms to translate the biblical concept of God and related theological words. Later, with the help of a team of Chinese readers, he explored numerous popular works and religious tracts, and began research into imperial worship in Beijing and Ruist canonical literature. Some of the latter materials he was able to study in depth because he regularly taught them to Chinese students at the Anglo-Chinese College in Hong Kong.

Consequently, it was appropriate that he initiated his *Chinese Classics* in 1861 with translations and commentaries of the *Four Books*, presenting them in the order of his own focus of attention, that is, the teachings of the Chinese sage, Master Kǒng (whom he regularly called 'Confucius', following Jesuit precedents) in the *Analects*, followed by the *Great Learning*, the *Doctrine of the Mean*, and finally in a second volume, the *Mencius*, the first three titles being his own precedent-setting creations. This arrangement did not follow the order of the authorized version of the *Four Books* created by Zhū Xī, which placed the *Analects* in the third place after the shorter works and before the far lengthier *Mencius*, suggesting that Legge was driven by missionary concerns about the putative religious status of Master Kǒng in the imperial cult rather than a desire to be strictly literal in his translations. Nevertheless, he did present the edited versions of the *Great Learning* and the *Doctrine of the Mean* as prepared by Zhū Xī and authorized by the Qīng imperial house, even though he knew that 'old text' versions existed in the *Book of Rites*. English versions of those alternative texts he saved for his later publication of the *Book of Rites* (1885) in the series Sacred Books of the East, which appeared after he had become a professor at Oxford (see p. 467, below). Significantly, Legge at that time was even willing to change the name of the title of the Aristotelian-sounding 'Doctrine of the Mean' to a more informed rendering, the *State of Equilibrium and Harmony*, but his previous title had already become so much of a standard that he had to relegate this change to a footnote in his revised edition of the *Four Books* (1893).

Creating a wide range of classical translations was Legge's strategy for more than thirty-five years. Multiple renderings of a single work were published, ranging for example from a more or less imitative archaic terseness in his first edition of the *Four Books* to a relatively more flowing contemporary English in a 'modern' series of the *Chinese Classics* (1865–76). His metrical *Book of Poetry* (1876) offered an alternative to his strictly prose renderings made in 1871 (*Chinese Classics*) and later also in 1879 (*Sacred Books of China*). Here his views about the form of poetic translation varied with his translating goal: should he be philologically more precise, or aesthetically more creative? In the former he chose to render all plant names in a strictly Latin form following scientific nomenclature, while in the metrical version most of them were given more generic English names. In the former he rarely indicated the wide variety of dialects existing in the *Book of Poetry*, while in the metrical version he rendered some in Scottish Doric, others in Latin, and put prayers into the English of the King James Bible; in a few cases he even gave two versions of the same poem. Here we sense the boldness of Legge's translation art, anticipating a number of modern approaches, but one should stress that he preferred philologically precise translation, making use of Chinese commentaries in accordance with interpretative principles learned at university and seminary, even allowing his English renderings at times to be disrupted by awkward phrasing or an eccentric neologism. Finally, it is to be noted that Legge's translation of certain key terms was influenced by Scottish realist philosophy, while his strong Christian interests prompted him to search for traces of the divine in the Ruist scriptures. As a consequence, the word *dào* was variously translated as 'principle', 'truth', and 'way', depending on the context, and *shàngdì* was regularly rendered as 'God'.

How did Legge handle textual problems where the original was unclear or perhaps corrupt? First, he identified and followed the best modern version of the text, which was part of the extensive series totalling 188 books edited by Ruǎn Yuán in the *Huáng Qīng jīngjiě* (Scriptural Exegesis of [Scholars under the] August Qīng, 1829); this was printed in Chinese at the top of the page most of the time. Second, when textual alternatives were known, he placed them among his various footnotes to the passage, which appeared normally beneath the English rendering. If the problem was even more significant, such as the corruptions he identified in the *Book of Historical Documents*, he dealt with it by citing indigenous Ruist commentators, often also discussing it in his extensive prolegomena. Furthermore, if there was no clear consensus about the content of the text, Legge relied on the imperially authorized paraphrases, found always with the term *rì jiǎng* or 'daily lectures' in their titles, to provide a gloss for the passage. In this way he could highlight problems without allowing the translation to fall into complete incoherence.

In addition to these features of his translations in the *Chinese Classics*, Legge included at the end of each prolegomenon an annotated working bibliography of Chinese texts and a list of foreign-language texts consulted during the eleven years of his translation process. Besides the nearly 200 Chinese titles there were also journals, previous translations, interpretative and historical works, and lexicographical aids. Though nearly half of all the foreign-language texts were in English, he also included thirteen in French, nine in Latin, and two each in German and Russian. Nineteen works by academics were included and twenty-six by missionaries (including nine by Catholic and two by Russian Orthodox authors). His concern was to sum up previous scholarship in both Chinese and foreign settings, in order to set a new standard for comprehensiveness in the study of Chinese literature, if not also to establish a more justified rendering for each classical text. Beyond these bibliographical matters, Legge added at the back of each volume several indexes (for subjects and proper names) as well as a dictionary of classical terminology including citations to the Ruist scripture.

While Legge set the scholarly standard for Chinese classical literature, Herbert Giles, his counterpart at Cambridge University during the last decade of the century, was a consummate popularizer. Not always philologically precise, Giles pressed instead for translations that were readable and attractive. Though some argue that Giles's greatest sinological contributions were his dictionaries, he also produced a series of translations intended to inform a broader public about Chinese literature. These started with *Strange Stories from a Chinese Studio* (1880), leading on to *Gems of Chinese Literature* (1884) and the rhymed renderings of *Chinese Poetry in English Verse* (1898). In addition, he presented the story of the early Buddhist pilgrimage of Fǎxiǎn and cleverly rendered the creative and sometimes sarcastic text associated with the ancient Daoist philosopher Zhuāngzǐ, capturing many of its wordplays and much of its sceptical power, entitling the work *Chuang tzu: Mystic, Moralist and Social Reformer* (1889). In another notable case Giles struggled sceptically with the textual problems inherent in the Daoist classic the *Lao tzu*, prompting a thorough response by the more conservative Legge (Legge 1888). While Giles doubted the text's historical reliability and authorship, Legge adhered to traditional claims about its textual coherence and authorship by Lǎozǐ. Later scholarship has vindicated Giles's critical assessments.

A propitious sign of future developments in English translations of Chinese literature was also evident at the end of the century. An overseas Chinese scholar educated in Scotland, Ku Hung-ming, offered an alternative popular rendering of the *Analects* as *Discourse and Sayings of Confucius* (1898) with a lively flair, suggestive scholarly comparisons, and seemingly flawless idiomatic English. He was a forerunner of a number of major ethnically Chinese translators in the twentieth century.

By the end of the nineteenth century, then, English translations of Chinese literature had attained a new breadth and a rich variety of styles and genres. Earlier ground-breaking philological and bibliographical works had made this possible, and these advances in turn prepared the necessary grounds for even more solid etymological and philological studies in the future, so with better translation tools great advances in translation could be made in the twentieth century.

LIST OF SOURCES

Translations
Davis, John Francis (1815). *San-Yu-Low, or, The Three Dedicated Rooms*. Canton.
—— (1817). *Laou-seng-urh, or, 'An Heir in his Old Age': A Chinese Drama*. London.
—— (1822). *Chinese Novels . . . to which are added Proverbs and Moral Maxims . . . prefaced by Observations on the Language and Literature of China*. London.
—— (1829). *The Fortunate Union: A Romance* [Mǎ Zhìyuǎn], 2 vols. London.
—— (1829). *Han Koong Tsew, or, The Sorrows of Han: A Chinese Tragedy*. London.
—— (1865). *Chinese Miscellanies: A Collection of Essays and Notes*. London.
Giles, Herbert A. (1877). *Record of the Buddhistic Kingdoms* [Fǎxiǎn]. London.
—— (1880). *Strange Stories from a Chinese Studio* [Pú Sōnglíng], 2 vols. London.
—— (1884). *Gems of Chinese Literature* [ed. Wú Chǔcái and Wú Tiáohòu]. London.
—— (1889). *Chuang tzu: Mystic, Moralist and Social Reformer*. London.
—— (1898). *Chinese Poetry in English Verse*. London.
[Ho] Tkin Shen [Ho Tsun-Sheen] (1843). *The Rambles of the Emperor Ching Tih in Këang Nan: A Chinese Tale* [Hé Mèngméi], ed. James Legge. London.
Ku Hung-ming (1898). *The Discourse and Sayings of Confucius: A New Special Translation Illustrated with Quotations from Goethe and Other Writers*. Shanghai.
Legge, James (1861–72). *The Chinese Classics with a Translation, Critical and Exegetical Notes, Prolegomena, and Copious Indexes*, 5 vols. in 8. Hong Kong.
—— (1876). *The She King, or, The Book of Poetry*. London (the 'metrical version' produced by Trübner; the volume was also issued as Vol. 3 of *The Chinese Classics*).
—— (1879–91). The Sacred Books of the East, ed. F. Max Müller. Vol. 3: *The Texts of Confucianism, Part I: The Shu King, The Religious Portions of the Shih King, The Hsiao King* (1879); Vol. 16: *The Texts of Confucianism, Part II: The Yi King* (1882); Vols. 27–8: *The Texts of Confucianism, Parts III and IV: The Li Ki* (1885); Vols. 39–40: *The Texts of Taoism, Parts I and II* (1891). Oxford (these six volumes are also headed 'Sacred Texts of China', Vols. 1–6).

Other Sources
Barrett, Timothy (1989). *Singular Listlessness: A Short History of Chinese Books and British Scholars*. London.
Chinese Recorder (1868–1949). Fuzhou.
Chinese Repository (1832–51). Canton.
China Review (1872–1903). Hong Kong.
Cranmer-Byng, J. L. (1967). 'The First English Sinologists: Sir George Staunton and the Reverend Robert Morrison', pp. 247–60 in Frederick Sequier Drake, ed., *Symposium on Historical, Archaeological and Linguistic Studies on Southern China, South-East Asia and the Hong Kong Region*. Hong Kong.
Fan, T. C. (1946). 'Sir William Jones's Chinese Studies.' *Review of English Studies* 22: 304–14.
Giles, Herbert A. (1898). *A Chinese Biographical Dictionary*. London.
—— (1892). *A Chinese–English Dictionary*. London.

Girardot, Norman J. (2002). *The Victorian Translation of China: James Legge's Oriental Pilgrimage*. Berkeley, CA.

Honey, David B. (2001). *Incense at the Altar: Pioneering Sinologists and the Development of Classical Chinese Philology*. New Haven, CT.

Legge, James (1888). 'A Critical Notice of "The Remains of Lao Tsze, Retranslated" by Mr. Herbert A. Giles.' *China Review* 16: 195–214.

Liu Jiahe and Shao Dongfang (2000). 'A Critical Assessment of James Legge's Translations of the *Book of Historical Documents* and the *Bamboo Annals*.' *Bulletin of the History and Philology Institute of the Academia Sinica* 71: 681–726 (Chinese text) and 737–44 (English abstract).

Morrison, Robert (1815–22). *A Dictionary of the Chinese Language, in Three Parts*. Macau.

Neumann, Karl Friedrich (1847). 'Die Sinologen und ihre Werke.' *Zeitschrift der Deutschen Morgenländischen Gesellschaft* 1/2: 91–128.

Pfister, Lauren F. (1990). 'Serving or Suffocating the Sage? Reviewing the Efforts of Three Nineteenth Century Translators of *The Four Books*, with Special Emphasis on James Legge (A.D. 1815–1897).' *Hong Kong Linguist* 7: 25–56.

—— (1994). 'James Legge', pp. 401–22 in Chan Sin-wai and David E. Pollard, eds., *An Encyclopedia of Translation: Chinese–English, English–Chinese Translation*. Hong Kong.

—— (1997). 'James Legge's "Metrical Book of Poetry".' *Bulletin of the School of Oriental and African Studies* 60/1: 64–85.

—— (2001*a*). 'Chinese, Translation of Theological Terms into', pp. 118–22 in J. M. Y. Simpson and J. F. A. Sawyer, eds., *Concise Encyclopedia of Language and Religion*. Amsterdam.

—— (2001*b*). 'Translation and its Problems', pp. 734–9 in Antonio S. Cua, ed., *Encyclopedia of Chinese Philosophy*. New York.

—— (2004). *Striving for 'The Whole Duty of Man': James Legge and the Scottish Protestant Encounter with China*, 2 vols. Frankfurt am Main.

Ting, Joseph C. (1951) 'British Contribution to Chinese Studies.' Ph.D. diss. School of Oriental and African Studies, University of London.

Wang, Elizabeth Te-chen (1976). 'The Beginning of Chinese-Studies in the English-Speaking World.' *Chinese Culture: A Quarterly Review* 17/1: 1–62.

Wylie, Alexander (1867). *Notes on Chinese Literature, with Introductory Remarks on the Progressive Advancement of the Art, and a List of Translations from the Chinese into Various European Languages*. Shanghai.

7.5 Japanese

Anne Commons

The end of Japan's self-imposed isolation in the late 1850s allowed foreign visitors to visit freely many parts of the country for the first time in over 200 years. Various western interests quickly established themselves in Japan, which also became a popular tourist destination. Accounts of life in Japan and textbooks for learning the language began to appear, as did the first English translations of Japanese literary works. These nineteenth-century translations concentrated largely on earlier texts, from major classical works to folk tales from both written and oral sources, a reflection both of the evolving canon of national literature as envisaged by Japanese scholars at the time and of the contemporary western interest in Japan. The first overview of Japanese literature to be published in a European language was Sir Ernest Mason Satow's 1874 article in *Appleton's American Cyclopaedia*, while major literary translations into English were made by William George Aston, Basil Hall Chamberlain, and to a lesser extent Frederick Victor Dickins. Aston and Chamberlain also produced the earliest major scholarly accounts of Japanese literature in English.

Aston spent twenty-five years in the consular service in Japan and Korea. He was a founding member of the Asiatic Society of Japan in Yokohama in 1872 and published many articles in its *Transactions*. These were mostly historical and philological essays but also included his earliest published work on Japanese literature, a summary and partial translation of the tenth-century *Tosa Diary* (1875). The works for which Aston is remembered today, however, are those published after his retirement in 1889. His complete translation of the eighth-century state history *Nihon shoki* in 1896 remains today the standard English version of the text. His other significant contribution was his 400-page *History of Japanese Literature* (1899), the first extensive survey of the field to be written in English. Aston acknowledges his debt to Satow and to the first history of Japanese literature to be published in Japanese, Mikami Sanji and Takatsu Kuwasaburō's *Nihon bungakushi* (1890). His *History*—itself translated into Japanese in 1908—incorporates summaries of and translated excerpts from a number of literary texts from the earliest times to the late nineteenth century, many appearing in English translation for the first time. Having cautioned his readers in the preface that 'it is not possible to do justice to Japanese literature by translation' due to the vast cultural differences involved (Aston 1899: vii), Aston attempts to overcome these obstacles by providing historical and cultural background in his commentary. He discusses stylistic features of the genres covered, particularly poetry and nō, using both Japanese and western terminology, and renders Japanese poems in blank verse. He includes works by Japanese writing in classical Chinese, and in the seventh chapter of the *History*, entitled 'Tokio Period (1868–1900)', he comments on the work of leading contemporary authors such as Tsubouchi Shōyō, Ozaki Kōyō, and Higuchi Ichiyō. This chapter also includes a rare example of contemporary Japanese literature in English translation: a 'new style poem' by Shioi Ukō. Aston's *History* was reprinted many times—nine times in the United States alone between 1899 and 1937 (Kornicki 1991: 71)—and was read by a number of modern poets, including Laurence Binyon and Ezra Pound (see the bibliography maintained by Ewick 2004).

Basil Hall Chamberlain arrived in Japan in May 1873 and soon took up a post teaching English at the Naval Academy. He published what he termed his 'first literary effort' (Chamberlain 1939: xii), a rhymed translation of the nō play *The Death Stone*, in the *Cornhill Magazine* in 1876. This was the first full translation of a nō play into English (an almost-complete translation of *Takasago* had appeared the previous year in F. V. Dickins's *Chiushingura*). Chamberlain, like Aston, served as President of the Asiatic Society of Japan and presented a record twenty-seven papers at its meetings. These included translations of classical texts from a variety of genres—poetry, prose fiction, drama, and critical writing—and analyses of stylistic features of Japanese literary texts. Chamberlain's first book-length publication was his *Classical Poetry of the Japanese* (1880), which includes translations of sixty-six poems from the eighth-century anthology *Man'yōshū* (c.759) and fifty from the tenth-century imperially commissioned anthology *Kokinshū* (c.905), along with four nō and two kyōgen, the short comic plays presented with nō in a traditional performance. The book marks the first sizeable collection of Japanese poetry in English translation and indeed 'the first knowledgeable study of Japanese poetry in a European language' (Ewick 2004: D.5.a). After a discussion of the difficulties of translating Japanese poetry, Chamberlain opts to follow the example of 'the best translators of Western classical poetry' (Chamberlain 1880: 29) and render Japanese poems in rhymed English verse. He translates thirty-one-syllable poems—the standard classical form—as quatrains; longer poems he sometimes leaves intact and sometimes breaks into a series of four-line stanzas.

One of these thirty-one-syllable poems is *Kokinshū* V: 294, composed by the ninth-century poet Ariwara no Narihira on an autumnal scene of red maple leaves floating down the Tatsuta River: 'chihayaburu kamiyo mo kikazu Tatsutagawa karakurenai ni mizu kukuru to wa'. It may be rendered in English as 'Even in the age | of the awesome gods | such a thing was unheard of: | the waters of the Tatsuta River | tie-dyed Chinese crimson.' Chamberlain preferred rhyme and was very willing to pad lines:

> E'en when on earth the thund'ring gods held sway
> Was such a sight beheld? — Calm Tatsta's flood,
> Stain'd, as by Chinese art, with hues of blood,
> Rolls o'er Yamato's peaceful fields away.
> (Chamberlain 1880: 122)

It should be noted that rhyme, although frequently used in early translations, is not a feature of classical Japanese poetry or of nō.

Chamberlain's other book-length translation from the Japanese was his *Ko-ji-ki, or, Records of Ancient Matters* (1883), a translation of the monumental myth-history *Kojiki*. Although Aston's *Nihongi* and Chamberlain's *Ko-ji-ki* are the earliest full translations of those works, excerpts from both appear in Satow's 'The Revival of Pure Shintō', along with an account of the National Learning (*kokugaku*) movement and extracts from texts by several of its scholars, including Kamo no Mabuchi and Motoori Norinaga. The considerable difficulty of early texts like *Nihon shoki*, *Kojiki*, and *Man'yōshū*, particularly given the relatively few editions and commentaries available in Aston and Chamberlain's time, makes their accomplishments as translators all the more noteworthy, despite their sometimes condescending attitudes toward the material.

The contemporary western interest in folklore is evident in the 1888 publication of Chamberlain's *Aino Folk-Tales* by the Folk-Lore Society in London. The short tales and accounts of Ainu beliefs translated in this text were collected by Chamberlain—by this time professor of Japanese and philology at the Imperial University in Tokyo—on a trip to Ezo (now Hokkaidō) in 1886, and all but one were making their first appearance in any foreign language. Although Chamberlain in his introduction warned his readers of the 'hideous indecencies' of some of the stories, he was at pains to present unexpurgated renditions of the accounts passed on to him 'for the sole perusal of the anthropologist and ethnologist' (Chamberlain 1888: 5). In *Ko-ji-ki*, by contrast, he rendered indelicate phrases in Latin.

Frederick Victor Dickins, a naval physician who was also a founding member of the Asiatic Society of Japan, produced several historically significant translations. These include translations of two texts very popular in Japan, the thirteenth-century poetic anthology *Ogura Hyakunin isshu* (One Hundred Poets, One Poem Each) and the 1748 Takeda Izumo puppet play *Kanadehon chushingura* (Forty-Seven Model Rōnin). Dickins's version of the former (Dickins 1865) is not only the first English translation of *One Hundred Poets, One Poem Each*, but the first English translation of any Japanese literary work. Dickins took some liberties with the forms of the texts he translated: although he would later abandon the use of rhyme, his earliest translations of thirty-one-syllable Japanese poems were four- to eight-line rhyming stanzas. These include the *Kokinshū* poem given earlier, which Dickins translated as follows in his *Hyak nin is'shiu, or, Stanzas by a Century of Poets*:

> O Tatsta! when th' autumnal flow
> I watch of thy deep ruddy wave —
> E'en when the stern gods long ago
> Did rule, was ne'er beheld so brave,
> So fair a stream as thine, I vow.
> 			(Dickins 1866: 11)

This translation is in five lines, in imitation of the five-phrase form of the original poem; in his later, revised versions of these translations, Dickins settled on the five-line format as standard, and it has been employed by a number of subsequent translators of the thirty-one-syllable form (Sato 2000: 237–8).

Dickins's *Chiushingura, or, The Loyal League* (1875) is a novelistic English rendering of *Forty-Seven Model Rōnin*, and includes in an appendix the first substantial English translation of a nō play, *Takasago*, almost all of which is presented in rhyming quatrains. Dickins also produced the first English translation of the tenth-century *Tale of the Bamboo-Cutter* (1888), a text largely overlooked by medieval Japanese critics but which was gaining prestige in nineteenth-century Japan through the influence of the western concept of the novel (see Shirane 2000: 6).

The 1880s also saw the first substantial translation of the eleventh-century *Tale of Genji*, the pinnacle of classical Japanese prose narrative, which had been reinterpreted in the nineteenth century as 'the world's first realistic novel' (Shirane 2000: 8). The first seventeen chapters of the *Genji* were translated into English by the statesman Suematsu Kenchō (1882), in an attempt to establish Japan's position on the global literary stage.

The range of contexts in which Japanese literary translations were being published—from the scholarly tomes of Aston and Chamberlain to the mass media—is suggested by the appearance of anonymous translations of three kyōgen and one nō in the magazine *Chrysanthemum* (Yokohama) in 1882 and the publication in 1891 of an illustrated translation of *Tosa Diary* by Flora Best Harris which had earlier appeared in the newspaper *Japan Mail* (Yokohama).

Early modern prose works translated at this time included some by authors whose work had been censored or suppressed in the early nineteenth century, notably Ryūtei Tanehiko, whose *Ukiyo gata rokumai byōbu* (Six-Panelled Screen of the Floating World, 1821) was translated anonymously as *Account of a Japanese Romance* (1867). The German translation of this text by August Pfizmaier in 1847 was the earliest translation of Japanese fiction into any European language and influenced later translations of the work (see Inada 1971: 7).

Along with major classical texts, a large number of popular tales were translated into English. The earliest collection of such stories was A. B. Mitford's *Tales of Old Japan*, first published in 1871 and subsequently reprinted many times. Mitford's book, which was extremely widely read, includes in an appendix a detailed account of a *seppuku* or ritual suicide; however, although it seems intended for an adult audience, a number of its stories were later retold in English-language collections aimed at younger readers. The twenty-eight-volume Japanese Fairy Tale Series, published in the 1880s in Tokyo and London, included not only short, anonymous tales such as 'Little Peachling' (14th–16th centuries) and 'Crackling Mountain' (c. 16th century), both of which had first appeared in *Tales of Old Japan*, but also versions of myths from *Kojiki* such as 'The Eight-Headed Serpent' and 'The White Hare of Inaba'. Translators of the tales included Chamberlain and James Hepburn, the American missionary better known for compiling the first

Japanese–English dictionary in 1867. A similar mixture of popular tales and bowdlerized myths appears in Susan Ballard's *Fairy Tales from Far Japan* (1898).

Although the writings of Lafcadio Hearn were hugely influential in shaping western images of Japan, his output of literary translation—for which he was heavily reliant on the assistance of native speakers of Japanese—was less than that of Aston or Chamberlain. His books, produced at the rate of almost one per year in the 1890s, include reminiscences, essays on Japanese folklore and religion, and some translations of popular tales, legends, poems, and songs. The sources for many of the tales he translates are unidentified, but his *Shadowings* (1900) includes stories from the tale collections *Konjaku monogatari* (12th century) and *Jikkinshō* (13th century). Although Hearn wrote mainly for a general rather than scholarly audience, he did present his translations of 'Three Popular Ballads' to the Asiatic Society of Japan in 1894 (*Transactions of the Asiatic Society of Japan*, Vol. 22).

As noted earlier, little of the literature being produced in Japanese in the late nineteenth century was translated at the time. One exception is Arthur Lloyd's *Kiri-Hitoha* (*Far East Magazine*, Tokyo, 1897–8), a partial translation of Tsubouchi Shōyō's 1896 play of the same title. Lloyd also produced English versions of several German translations of Japanese works, including *Poetical Greetings from the Far East* (1897), an English rendering of Karl Florenz's 1894 German translation of fifty-eight poems taken mostly from *Man'yōshū* and *Kokinshū*.

The massive social changes undergone by Japan in the second half of the nineteenth century are scarcely to be seen in the literary texts translated at the time, which tended to depict traditional Japan while denying its modernity. Nonetheless, the pioneering studies of Aston, Chamberlain, and others not only made Japanese literature accessible to English-speaking readers—including poets and writers working in English—for the first time, but also laid the groundwork for an ever-expanding field of study and translation of Japanese literature in the twentieth century.

LIST OF SOURCES

Translations
Anon. (1867). *Account of a Japanese Romance* [Ryūtei Tanehiko]. Yokohama.
Aston, W. G. (1875). 'An Ancient Japanese Classic.' *Transactions of the Asiatic Society of Japan* 3/2: 121–30.
—— (1896). *Nihongi: Chronicles of Japan from the Earliest Times to A.D. 697*. London.
—— (1899). *A History of Japanese Literature*. London.
Chamberlain, Basil Hall (1876). 'The Death-Stone: A Lyric Drama from the Japanese.' *Cornhill Magazine* 34: 479–88.
—— (1880). *The Classical Poetry of the Japanese*. London.
—— (1883). 'Ko-ji-ki, or, Records of Ancient Matters.' *Transactions of the Asiatic Society of Japan* 10, Supplement.
—— (1888). *Aino Folk-Tales*. London.
—— et al. (1885–8). *Japanese Fairy Tales*, 28 vols. Tokyo.
Dickins, F. Victor (1865). 'Translations of Japanese Odes, from the *H'yak nin is'shiu* (Stanzas from a Hundred Poets).' *Chinese and Japanese Repository* 3: 137–9, 185–7, 249–51, 296–9, 343–5, 389–94, 438–43, 484–7, 537–8.

—— (1866). *Hyak nin is'shiu, or, Stanzas by a Century of Poets*. London.
—— (1875). *Chiushingura, or, The Loyal League*. Yokohama.
—— (1888). *Taketori no Okina no Monogatari: The Old Bamboo-hewer's Story*. London.
Hearn, Lafcadio (1900). *Shadowings*. Boston, MA.
Lloyd, Arthur (1897). *Poetical Greetings from the Far East*. Tokyo.
Mitford, A. B. (1871). *Tales of Old Japan*. London.
Satow, Ernest Mason (1875). 'The Revival of Pure Shintō.' *Transactions of the Asiatic Society of Japan* 3/1: 1–98.
Suematsu, Kenchō (1882). *Genji Monogatari; The Most Celebrated of the Classical Japanese Romances*. London.

Other Sources
Bowring, Richard (1991). 'An Amused Guest in All: Basil Hall Chamberlain (1850–1935)', pp. 128–36 in Sir Hugh Cortazzi and Gordon Daniels, eds., *Britain and Japan 1859–1991: Themes and Personalities*. London.
Chamberlain, Basil Hall (1939). *Things Japanese*, 6th edn. London (first pub. 1890).
Ewick, David (2004). *Japonisme, Orientalism, Modernism: A Critical Bibliography of Japan in English-Language Verse, 1900–1950* (**http://themargins.net/bib/contents.htm**).
Inada, Hide Ikehara (1971). *Bibliography of Translations from the Japanese into Western Languages from the 16th Century to 1912*. Tokyo.
Kornicki, Peter (1991). 'William George Aston (1841–1911)', pp. 64–75 in Sir Hugh Cortazzi and Gordon Daniels, eds., *Britain and Japan 1859–1991: Themes and Personalities*. London.
Sato, Hiroaki (2000). 'Japanese Poetry', pp. 237–41 in Peter France, ed., *The Oxford Guide to Literature in English Translation*. Oxford.
Satow, Ernest Mason (1874). 'Language and Literature of Japan', pp. 547–65 of *Appleton's American Cyclopaedia*, Vol. 9. New York.
Shirane, Haruo (2000). 'Introduction: Issues in Canon Formation', pp. 1–27 in Haruo Shirane and Tomi Suzuki, eds., *Inventing the Classics: Modernity, National Identity, and Japanese Literature*. Stanford, CA.

8
Popular Culture

8.1	**Popular Fiction** *Terry Hale*	371
8.2	**Popular Theatre** *Terry Hale*	382
8.3	**Children's Literature** *David Blamires*	394

8.1 Popular Fiction

Terry Hale

In the nineteenth century various sub-genres of the novel experienced a spectacular growth. The opening decade of the century was dominated by the Gothic novel, the staple fare of the circulating libraries until it was displaced by the emergent forms of the historical novel and pioneer fiction. In the mid-century, the rise of the 'mysteries and miseries' school of fiction anticipates other new developments such as the Victorian sensation novel and what can be broadly labelled detective fiction. Finally, towards the end of the century, the scientific romance emerged, a form combining visionary speculation and high adventure and resembling the genre which would later come to be called science fiction (this term did not come into general usage until the 1930s). Translation played a crucial role in the emergence of these various sub-genres, even though much of it was of a hidden or concealed nature; adaptation, plagiarism, imitation, pseudo-translation, and false attribution are as much in evidence as translation in the strict sense of the word.

The Gothic Novel

The Gothic novel or tale of terror flourished in the late eighteenth and early nineteenth centuries with such works as Ann Radcliffe's *The Mysteries of Udolpho* (1794), M. G. Lewis's *The Monk* (1796), Mary Shelley's *Frankenstein* (1818), and Robert Maturin's *Melmoth the Wanderer* (1820). It has tended to be portrayed by modern commentators as an essentially British cultural phenomenon, rooted in a range of ideas developed by eighteenth-century British (as opposed to continental) intellectuals (for a useful overview of this line of enquiry, see Clery 2000). From the outset, however, British Gothic was also heavily marked by the work of continental writers, intellectuals, and playwrights. Horace Walpole's *The Castle of Otranto*, which had inaugurated the genre in 1764, owed a great deal to French models (see Hale 2001: 152–4). And in the years just preceding the period covered by this volume, the four writers who bridge the gap between Walpole's singular experiment and Radcliffe's best-sellers of the 1790s were all translators: Charlotte Smith, Sophia and Harriet Lee, and Clara Reeve.

Over about twelve years beginning in 1788, Smith wrote eight Gothic novels of her own, but her career as a Gothic novelist had begun a few years earlier. In 1785, she had published a translation of the Abbé Prévost's *Histoire du Chevalier des Grieux et de Manon Lescaut* as *Manon L'Escaut, or, The Fatal Attachment*. Though Smith's version follows the plot of Prévost's novel fairly accurately, her transformation of the aesthetics and the ideology of the text is so radical that

Manon Lescaut becomes a fledgling Gothic novel. The translator reworks the gender implications of the text, refusing to conform to Prévost's portrait of Manon Lescaut as a subject for male sexual fantasy. Moreover, by incorporating into her translation elements drawn from Burke's theories of the sublime, she introduces themes later explored by the Gothic but alien to the early eighteenth century. For example, a relatively simple sentence in the original, 'L'effort qu'elle faisait pour se cacher était si naturel, qu'il paraissait venir d'un sentiment de modestie', is embellished by the addition: 'and the expression of *grief and terror* impressed on features *delicate, regular and animated*, made her the most interesting figure I had ever seen' (*emphasis added*; see Hale 2002a: 18–21 for a further discussion of this passage).

Two years later, Smith brought out *The Romance of Real Life*, a three-volume selection of tales drawn from the early volumes of Gayot de Pitaval's *Les Causes célèbres*, a long sequence of criminal trial reports that first began to appear in 1735. Here again, given that the Gothic novel almost by definition revolves around some form of criminal activity, she anticipates future developments. British writers would continue to ransack French trial reports for inspiration throughout almost the entirety of the nineteenth century, not least Wilkie Collins in the 1860s; the eighteenth-century Douhault case, for example, provided the central idea for *The Woman in White* (see Hyder 1939).

In the same period just preceding 1790, Sophia Lee had drawn on French sources in much the same way as Smith, producing in 1783–5 an adaptation of Prévost's sprawling historical novel *Le Philosophe anglais: Histoire de Cleveland* as *The Recess, or, A Tale of Other Times*. Lee's rewriting of Prévost is even more far-reaching than that of Charlotte Smith, perhaps because her experience of the theatre had given her the confidence to intervene more overtly. But for both authors the paramount issue remains the transformation of gender issues to appeal to the burgeoning female readership for such works. In view of the popularity of *The Recess*, it is not surprising that the author looked to France for a source for her next novel, *Warbeck: A Pathetic Tale*, which is based on Baculard d'Arnaud's *Varbeck*.

Clara Reeve made similar use of Baculard d'Arnaud in *The Exiles, or, Memoirs of the Count de Cronstadt*, as did Harriet Lee in *Kruitzner, or, The German's Tale*, which was quickly judged by contemporaries as the most memorable contribution to *The Canterbury Tales*, a five-volume collection of Gothic stories jointly written with her elder sister Sophia. Even by this date, the influence of Baculard d'Arnaud was still not entirely played out in Britain or further afield. *The Recess* provided Rossini with the plot for his 1815 opera *Elisabetta regina d'Inghilterra* (Summers 1964: 473–4); Byron (with due acknowledgement) appropriated Harriet Lee's *Kruitzner* as the basis of his tragedy *Werner* in 1822 (see Motter 1935); while Mary Shelley published a version of *The Fortunes of Perkin Warbeck* as late as 1830.

In this way translation and adaptation allowed the sentimental adventure stories of Prévost and his ablest successor Baculard d'Arnaud to be given a fresh topical interest for a new British readership. Historians of the Gothic novel often contrast this early phase of 'sentimental' Gothic writing, primarily the work of female authors, with a later phase, ushered in by M. G. Lewis's *The Monk*, a graphic and violent novel, which is termed 'the tale of terror'. *The Monk* is probably best described as a tapestry of borrowings, though in most cases Lewis improves the material he has to hand. This is also true of his translation of Heinrich Zschokke's *Abällino der grosse Bandit*, one of the most popular novels of the period dealing with the figure of the romantic outlaw, as *The Bravo of Venice*. In this instance Lewis acknowledges the existence of a source text, perhaps because of the widespread accusations of plagiarism that had been levelled at him in the past, but does not go so far as to name the author. Lewis's version shortens the text, changes the names of many of the characters, and heightens dramatic effect (see Brown 2004: 23–4).

Lewis was not alone. In both Britain and France there was a fashion for German literature. In 1807, the *Critical Review* complained: 'So great is the rage for German tales, and German novels, that a cargo is no sooner imported than the booksellers' shops are filled with a multitude of translators, who seize with avidity and without discrimination, whatever they can lay their hands upon' (cited in Varma 1968*a*: viii). This is an exaggeration, but a surprising number of German Gothic novels were translated by German émigrés in London such as the Revd G. F. Wedderburn, pastor at Ludgate Hill, or the Revd Peter Will, Lutheran minister of the German Chapel at the Savoy (see Varma 1968*b*). The effect of these translations was clearly to be seen. Of the seven 'horrid' novels referred to by Jane Austen's Isabella in Chapter 6 of *Northanger Abbey*, two are translations from the German, two pseudo-translations, while a fifth, perhaps qualifying as an imitation pseudo-translation, is entitled *The Orphan of the Rhine* (Eleanor Sleath was the author). If the translation, appropriation, and rewriting of eighteenth-century French sentimental adventure stories was responsible for the first wave of Gothic fiction in Britain, the second wave was stimulated by the translation, appropriation, and rewriting of the German *Schauerromane* (see Hale 2002*b*).

Pioneer Novels and Westerns

Chateaubriand's *Atala* and *René*, both of which were quickly translated and repeatedly reprinted (see also p. 238, above), provided the initial model for what was to become the 'western' or 'pioneer' novel in North America. Caleb Bingham's 1802 translation of *Atala* adapted certain aspects of Chateaubriand's novel to suit North American sensibilities: the author's Catholicism was largely neutralized, familiar Indian words were used, and the erotic elements were toned down or removed (see Schwarz in Bingham 1930: 8–9). Without Chateaubriand, Fenimore Cooper's romanticization of the American landscape would hardly have been possible. But an important stage in the further development of the genre is marked by the work of the Austrian-American writer 'Charles Sealsfield' (i.e. Carl Postl, 1793–1864), perhaps the outstanding figure on the very active scene of German-language publishing in the USA in the 1830s and 1840s.

In his later works, Sealsfield wrote almost exclusively in German, but he always insisted on his American citizenship. It is an open question whether he should be seen as a German author who was profoundly affected by America, an American who had a tremendous vogue in Germany (and encouraged widespread migration), or a German-American who was appreciated by other German-Americans (see Cazden 1984: 386). His main innovation was to introduce a note of realism into the pioneer novel that was quickly imitated by an entire school of European writers; he went further than Cooper in his rejection of romanticism in favour of political critique. The tone was set in his first novel, written in somewhat defective English, and published anonymously as *Tokeah, or, The White Rose* (1829), a work which attributes the suffering of the Cherokee Indians to the depredations caused by white colonizers (see Billington 1981: 136).

The boom in western novels would henceforth be largely driven by such expatriate Europeans. Dozens of German, Austrian, Swiss, French, and British writers produced a body of thrilling, but uneven, accounts of life in a mythical Far West. The German and French authors included Friedrich Armand Strubberg, the author of some sixty novels dealing largely with the experiences of German immigrants and the westward expansion; Friedrich Gerstäcker, who exploited the theme of German migration but also glorified the lawlessness of the period; Balduin Möllhausen, perhaps the most popular German author of the 1860s and 1870s; Karl May, sometimes claimed to be the most read German author since Goethe, and one of the few authors of such fictions never to have set foot in North America; and Gustave Aimard (i.e. Olivier Gloux), the most popular of the French authors of westerns.

These expatriate writers were extremely prolific and were widely translated in an international exchange where translation into English was only one element. As with the Gothic novel, the tasks of translation and authorship often coexisted. Gustave Aimard's main British translator, for example, was Percy Bolingbroke St John, himself the author of a number of westerns together with various serials published in the *London Journal* in the 1850s and 1860s, while the translation of Gabriel Ferry's *Costal l'Indien* was undertaken by the famous author of adventure fiction Captain Mayne Reid, at a time when his own career as a writer started to fall into decline. His translation, an extremely free one, appeared in Britain under the title *A Hero in Spite of Himself* (1861).

Not all of these authors were translated into English to an equal extent. On the one hand, Sealsfield's novels of the 1830s and 1840s were first published in Europe in German, but appeared in pirated English translations in the United States almost simultaneously, further pirated, abridged, or rewritten versions being published in the following years. Karl May, on the other hand, despite being translated into twenty other languages, remained virtually unknown in both Britain and the United States (see Sammons 1998: 9; Billington 1981: 341). Collectively, however, the authors and translators of such fictions created a range of powerful myths about North America that often had a great impact on the lives of those who consumed them.

Crime, Mystery, and Detective Fiction

Writing in *Blackwood's Magazine* in 1890, a critic noted: 'The French are our masters in criminal romance' (Shand 1890: 219). Though the writer does not entirely dismiss the contribution to the genre made by British novelists (e.g. Edward Bulwer Lytton, M. E. Braddon, Charles Dickens, and Wilkie Collins), he believes that the detective novel came of age with Honoré de Balzac and Eugène Sue in the Paris of the 1840s and did not reach full maturity until the 1860s and 1870s with the arrival on the literary scene of Émile Gaboriau and, slightly later, Fortuné du Boisgobey. This is not a view entirely shared by twentieth-century historians of the genre (for instance the influential Haycraft 1941), but it is one that few British authors of the period would have contested, though some might have given more prominence to the work of Edgar Allan Poe.

Historically, the memoirs of supposedly real detectives represent one of the earliest manifestations of detective fiction. This form of 'fiction' was ushered into existence by the publication of the four volumes of Vidocq's *Mémoires* (1828–9). This life of Eugène-François Vidocq falls into two parts, the first describing his colourful early adventures against the background of Revolutionary Europe and the second relating his career as a professional detective and eventually head of the Brigade de Sûreté. By 1827, Vidocq had negotiated a generous advance from a Parisian publisher for an autobiography. The resultant book, though largely written by two ghost writers (and including much extraneous matter), was a sensation.

The *Mémoires* were quickly translated into English, the first British edition being published in 1829 with the first American edition following in 1834; the identity of the translators is unknown. Various other editions were issued at intervals, and Vidocq was imitated by a host of British and American writers throughout the nineteenth century. In Britain, 'Waters' (i.e. William Russell) was Vidocq's most prolific early disciple; his *Experiences of a Detective Police-Officer* recounting the cases of a supposedly real Scotland Yard detective was serialized in *Chambers's Edinburgh Journal*, beginning in July 1849, pirated in book form by an American publisher in 1852, and followed by more than a dozen similar collections by 'Waters'. In America, Chandos Fulton published in 1891 a detective novel under the title *The Vidocq of New York* (it concerns Thomas F. Byrnes, who commanded the New York City detective bureau from 1880 to 1895). Though direct references to Vidocq are few and far between, the indebtedness of the authors concerned is very considerable. The first-person narrative form, the determination and adroitness of the detective, the reliance on disguise and dissimulation, the urban setting, the fascination with low life—all these themes and characteristics are to be found in large measure in Vidocq's *Mémoires*.

Before the memoirs-of-a-real-life-detective formula had become an identifiable sub-genre, Eugène Sue's *Les Mystères de Paris* had introduced a number of fresh elements to the detective story. This massive *feuilleton* (it was serialized in *Le Journal des débats* over an eighteen-month period from June 1842 to October 1843) chronicles the adventures of Prince Rodolphe, who is scouring Paris for his long-lost daughter. Rodolphe's quest brings him into contact not only with the dangerous working-class criminals of the *faubourgs*, but also with the gilded vice of the fashionable boulevards. Unlike Vidocq (and his ghost writers), Sue was not only an experienced author, he also had a good ear for dialogue (the use of slang is among the book's most remarkable features), a remarkable ability to develop a dramatic situation, and a pronounced political and social agenda. Effectively, with *Les Mystères de Paris* Sue simultaneously dethroned Dumas, Balzac, and Frédéric Soulié as the leading French serial novelist of the period.

Even before Sue's serial had reached a conclusion, British and American publishers were vying to bring out a translation (on Sue's British reception, see Chevasco 2003). There were no less than six different translations, mostly anonymous, on sale in London alone at one moment, each catering for a different segment of the market, ranging from William Dugdale's closely printed one-volume edition (1844), sold from his shop in the notorious Hollywell Street, to Chapman and Hall's elegant three-volume edition (1845), accompanied by over a hundred illustrations (on this translation see pp. 72–3, above). As with the real-life detective memoir, Sue's *feuilleton* energized popular fiction elsewhere. Principal among his English admirers was G. W. M. Reynolds, author of *The Mysteries of London* (1845–8) and its sequel *The Mysteries of the Court of London* (1849–56). Issued in weekly penny instalments, these two works, heady mixtures of radical politics and Gothic sensationalism, represent not only one of the most profitable literary ventures of the century (the sales figures approached 40,000 copies a week) but also one of the longest novels in the English language (see James 1963: 46–7; Mighall 1999: 28). Given the dominance of Reynolds's penny dreadful, it is hardly surprising that other writers tended to shy away from the word 'mystery'. But this is not to say that they did not imitate the genre. Indeed, M. E. Braddon's first novel, *Three Times Dead* (1860), like G. R. Sims's *Rogues and Vagabonds*, first serialized in 1879, is an urban mysteries novel in the manner of Sue, even if it covers its traces.

In North America, the impact of Sue's serial was even greater. Published in 1848, Ned Buntline's (i.e. Edward Zane Carroll Judson) *The Mysteries and Miseries of New York* is perhaps the most socially and stylistically faithful of the numerous American rewritings of *Les Mystères de Paris*, the novel focusing on the financial and sexual victimization of a seamstress at the hands of a gang of young swells. George Lippard's sensational accounts of aristocratic immorality in the large cities have proved to be the most enduring, however. *The Quaker City, or, The Monks of Monk Hall: A Romance of Philadelphia Life, Mystery, and Crime* (1845) is reputed to have sold 60,000 copies in its first year, making it the most popular American novel prior to *Uncle Tom's Cabin* (Reynolds 1995: vii). Like Lippard's other work in this vein, it represents a skilful blending of social critique, an urban setting, and the demonic energy of the Gothic novel (the main plot centres on the seduction of a merchant's daughter by a rake and his murder by her brother).

But the impact of French fiction on the development of the detective story does not begin and end with Vidocq and Sue. *Burton's Gentleman's Magazine*, for instance, nowadays mainly remembered because of Edgar Allan Poe's association with it, was saturated with French fiction, though relatively few items formally signal themselves as translations. As Poe's editorial control of the magazine increased, the number of hybrid pieces (i.e. American rewritings of French anecdotes and other material) tended to increase rather than decrease. This underlying translational background of *Burton's* is especially significant in view of the centrality of Poe's 'The Murders in the Rue Morgue' in the history of the detective story.

Poe's stories were translated into French by Charles Baudelaire and were soon imitated. By the early 1860s, Émile Gaboriau in particular was writing lengthy *romans judiciaires* which clearly depend on ratiocination, the most famous titles being *L'Affaire Lerouge, Le Crime d'Orcival, Le Dossier No. 113, Les Esclaves de Paris*, and *Monsieur Lecoq*. The first American translation of Gaboriau (*The Widow Lerouge* by Fred Williams and George A. O. Ernest) was published in Boston by Estes and Lauriat more than a decade before there was an English edition. The same Boston publisher had issued all of Gaboriau's detective stories in translation by 1880. By this time, in addition, at least one adaptation had also been published. Dr John B. Williams, a popular American author, had transposed *L'Affaire Lerouge* to New York where it was published as a serial in *Saturday Night* in 1868 under the title *Who Was Guilty? or, The Harlem Mystery* (see Johannsen 1950: II, 114). Henry Llewellyn Williams likewise transposed *Le Dossier No. 113* to New York where it appeared as *Warrant No. 113, or, The Mystery of the Steel Safe*.

In England, the same phenomenon can be observed. Erskine Boyd published a version of *L'Affaire Lerouge* under his own name in the late 1870s as *A Desperate Deed* in a penny periodical (it was quickly appropriated by an American pirate who issued it as a dime novel in 1881; see Johannsen 1950: II, 114). As late as 1885, the more respectable Charles Gibbon published a plagiarism of the same novel under the title *A Hard Knot*. Other authors of the period would later acknowledge their debt explicitly. In a later preface to his best-selling *The Mystery of a Hansom Cab* (1886), Fergus Hume explains that, having decided to abandon the theatre in favour of the novel, 'I enquired of a leading Melbourne bookseller what style of book he sold the most of. He replied that the detective stories of Gaboriau had a large sale; and as, at this time, I had never even heard of this author, I bought all his works—eleven or thereabouts—and read them carefully. The style of these stories attracted me, and I determined to write a book of the same class; containing a mystery, a murder, and a description of low life in Melbourne' (Hume 1982: 8). One of the most remarkable aspects of the development of the English detective story in the late nineteenth century is the deliberate manner in which British authors set out to imitate French detective fiction. 'My first detective story', writes Major Arthur Griffiths in his memoirs, 'was *Number 99*, written in the manner of Gaboriau, whom I studied closely, together with [Du] Boisgobey, Eugène Chavette, and A. K. Green' (Griffiths 1907: 400). Other authors are more reticent about their sources. Robert Louis Stevenson discreetly alludes to Du Boisgobey on a number of occasions, but the references are only intelligible to the initiated. Conan Doyle's immense debt to Gaboriau receives only the curtest of acknowledgements in his autobiography (Doyle 1924: 74).

By the mid-1880s, Gaboriau and Du Boisgobey were available in English translation in shilling editions published by Vizetelly, who then focused their attention on translating more minor authors of *romans judiciaires*, including works by Alexis Bouvier, Adolphe Belot, and Jules Mary. With the widespread availability of translations of Gaboriau, British and American writers were forced to greater efforts of originality. In New York, Anna Katherine Green established her credentials as Gaboriau's leading American disciple with *The Leavensworth Case* (1878), while in Chicago, Lawrence L. Lynch (i.e. Emma Murdoch van Deventer) reworked the portrayal of gender in the detective story by the extensive use of cross-dressing (see for example *Shadowed by Three*, 1879). Both writers enjoyed considerable popularity with women readers on both sides of the Atlantic in the final two decades of the century. In Britain, meanwhile a host of popular authors contributed short stories to the shilling illustrated monthlies. Though the *roman judiciaire* underwent an enormous process of domestication, there can be little doubt that the whodunit of the 1920s and 1930s, especially in the hands of a writer such as Agatha Christie, ultimately derives—via a process of translation and adaptation—from this French source.

Science Fiction

When Hugo Gernsback published the first issue of his landmark science fiction magazine *Amazing Stories* in 1926, a drawing of Jules Verne's tomb at Amiens adorned the title page (see Smyth 2000: 1). It is a useful reminder that much of the nineteenth-century impetus towards the creation of the science fiction genre originated in France. If science fiction, especially in its American manifestation, was one of the most important branches of twentieth-century popular literature, the principal constituents of the genre (narratives of fantastic voyages, utopian fiction, the *conte philosophique*, political satire, and the Gothic novel) were all either specifically French or were revived with a new topicality by French writers in the late eighteenth and early nineteenth centuries.

For one commentator at least 'the modern style in futuristic fiction' begins with Sébastien Mercier's 1771 *L'An deux mille quatre cent quarante* (Clarke 1979: 15). This Enlightenment fantasy rapidly made its way into English in a version by William Hooper entitled *Memoirs of the Year Two Thousand Five Hundred* and gave rise to a new genre of *Zukunftsroman* (novel of the future) in Germany, Denmark, and the Netherlands. Not every author shared Mercier's optimism, however. Cousin de Grainville's *Le Dernier Homme* of 1805, an apocalyptic vision of a failing solar system, introduced the theme of the 'last man' into British fiction. An English translation appeared the year after French publication. Though almost entirely forgotten today, over the course of the next thirty years Cousin de Grainville's novel gave rise to a surprising range of works by artists, poets, and novelists both in France as well as Britain and North America. Mary Shelley's *The Last Man* (1826) is indebted to both Mercier and Cousin de Grainville, as her publisher, Colburn, shrewdly noted (Seymour 2000: 360).

If Mercier, Cousin de Grainville, and other more obscure practitioners are familiar only to literary specialists, the same is not true of Jules Verne. From his first meeting with the publisher P.-J. Hetzel in October 1862, Verne's success seemed assured. Hetzel brought out a revised version of *Cinq semaines en ballon* barely a month after this initial encounter between the two men. It was followed the next year by the *Voyage au centre de la terre*, which cemented the author's reputation, while the serialization of *De la terre à la lune* in 1865 trebled the circulation of the *Journal des débats*. By the time *Le Tour du monde en quatre-vingts jours* was being serialized in *Le Temps* a decade later, British and American interest in Phileas Fogg's progress were so great that details were cabled by correspondents to their newspapers back home (Clarke 1979: 93).

Verne's major novels, such as *Vingt mille lieues sous les mers* or *Le Tour du monde en quatre-vingts jours*, all received two or more different translations very soon after publication, many of these figuring in one of three series, the Jules Verne Library of Ward, Lock, & Tyler, Routledge's Every Boy's Library, and Sampson Low's 'authorized and illustrated' edition of Jules Verne's Works. One of the early British translators was W. H. G. Kingston, who himself wrote more than a hundred stories for boys; he was also an early contributor to the *Boy's Own Paper*, where Verne's novels continued to be serialized after his death. The editorial interventions of Edward Roth, who translated a number of Verne's works for the American market, were so considerable that his translations bear 'little resemblance to the original' (Costello 1978: 132).

In fact, Verne was probably treated in a more cavalier fashion by his translators than any other major French novelist of the nineteenth century. Part of the problem was that he was initially viewed in Britain solely as an author of children's literature, as indeed he was in France. But Verne also prided himself on his knowledge of contemporary scientific and technological developments. The *Voyage au centre de la terre*, for example, was planned as a geological epic. The author was not only familiar with the main accounts of scientific expeditions to Iceland, he was also conversant with the debate concerning the scientific challenge to Creationism represented by works such as Sir Charles Lyell's *Principles of Geology*. When Verne prepared a new illustrated edition of the novel in 1867, he incorporated the latest information about human fossil remains (see Costello 1978: 83–4). Material of this kind tended to suffer most in the English translations. Descriptive passages concerning flora, fauna, local customs, and geographical or geological information were often excised in the interests of driving on the narrative or, in some cases at least, because the material was contentious. In addition to substantial cuts, additions were also made and, in some cases, 'the sense of whole episodes altered' (Costello 1978: 125).

Altered in this way, shorn of their more didactic features, Verne's thrilling tales offered a model for writers in the English-speaking world. In this, science fiction resembles the other popular sub-genres discussed above. All of these had a rich and varied progeny in English and American literature of the nineteenth and twentieth centuries. And all of them, as we have seen, were largely the product of inter-cultural exchange. Given the cultural dominance of France at the beginning of the nineteenth century, it is not surprising that writers looked to Paris for literary inspiration. But the importation of foreign material was by no means confined to faithful translation; adaptation, transposition, rewriting, and imitation played an equally significant role. The history of each of these sub-genres shows a first generation of imaginative rewritings of key texts followed by subsequent refinement by later writers who often had scant knowledge of the foreign works from which the tradition stemmed.

LIST OF SOURCES

Translations and Imitations
For further information on translations of Sue, see Chevasco 2003; for a Verne bibliography, see Gallagher 1980.

Anon. (1829). *Memoirs of Vidocq, Principal Agent of the French Police until 1827*, 4 vols. London.
Anon. (1844). *The Mysteries of Paris* [Sue]. London.
Anon. (1845). *The Mysteries of Paris* [Sue], 3 vols. London.
Bingham, Caleb (1930). *Atala, or, The Love and Constancy of Two Savages in the Desert* [Chateaubriand], ed. William Leonard Schwarz. Stanford, CA.
Buntline, Ned, pseud. [Edward Zane Carroll Judson] (1848). *The Mysteries and Miseries of New York: A Story of Real Life* [Sue]. New York.
Hooper, William (1772). *Memoirs of the Year Two Thousand Five Hundred* [Mercier], 2 vols. London.
Hume, Fergus (1982). *The Mystery of a Hansom Cab* [Gaboriau]. New York (first pub. 1886).
Kingston, W. H. G. (1875). *The Mysterious Island* [Verne], 3 vols. London.
Lee, Harriet (1797). *Kruitzner, or, The German's Tale* [Baculard d'Arnaud], in Vol. 4 of Harriet and Sophia Lee, *The Canterbury Tales*, 5 vols. London.
Lee, Sophia (1783–5). *The Recess, or, A Tale of Other Times* [Prévost], 3 vols. London.
—— (1786). *Warbeck: A Pathetic Tale* [Baculard d'Arnaud]. London.
Lewis, M. G. (1805). *The Bravo of Venice* [Zschokke]. London.
Reeve, Clara (1788). *The Exiles, or, Memoirs of the Count de Cronstadt* [Baculard d'Arnaud], 3 vols. London.
Reid, Mayne (1861). *A Hero in Spite of Himself* [Ferry], 3 vols. London.
Reynolds, G. W. M. (1845–50). *The Mysteries of London* [Sue], 6 vols. London.
—— (1849–56). *The Mysteries of the Court of London* [Sue], 8 vols. London.
Smith, Charlotte (1785). *Manon L'Escaut, or, The Fatal Attachment. A French Story* [Prévost], 2 vols. London.
—— (1787). *The Romance of Real Life* [Gayot de Pitaval], 3 vols. London.
'Waters', pseud. [William Russell] (1852), *The Recollections of a Policeman* [Vidocq]. New York (as *Experiences of a Detective Police-Officer*, London, 1856).
Williams, Fred., and Ernest, George A. O. (1875). *The Widow Lerouge* [Gaboriau]. Boston, MA.
Williams, Henry Llewellyn (1884). *Warrant No. 113, or, The Mystery of the Steel Safe* [Gaboriau]. New York.

Other Sources
Billington, Ray Allen (1981). *Land of Savagery, Land of Promise: The European Image of the American Frontier in the Nineteenth Century*. New York.

Brown, Phillip (2004). 'M. G. Lewis and the Violence of Translation: A Study of Ideological Transformation in the Translation Process.' MA diss. University of Hull.

Cazden, Robert E. (1984). *A Social History of the German Book Trade in America to the Civil War*. Columbia, SC.

Chevasco, Berry Palmer (2003). *Mysterymania: The Reception of Eugène Sue in Britain, 1838–60*. Berne.

Clarke, I. F. (1979). *The Pattern of Expectation, 1644–2001*. London.

Clery, E. J. (2000). *The Rise of Supernatural Fiction*. Cambridge.

—— (2002). 'The Genesis of "Gothic" Fiction', pp. 21–39 in Jerrold E. Hogle, ed., *The Cambridge Companion to Gothic Fiction*. Cambridge.

Costello, Peter (1978). *Jules Verne: Inventor of Science Fiction*. London.

Doyle, Arthur Conan (1924). *Memories and Adventures*. London.

Gallagher, Edward J. (1980). *Jules Verne: A Primary and Secondary Bibliography*. Boston, MA.

Griffiths, Arthur (1907). *Fifty Years of Public Service*. London (first pub. 1904).

Hale, Terry (2001). 'Translation, Adaptation, Appropriation: The Origins of the European Gothic Novel.' *Anglistica* 55: 145–71.

—— (2002a). 'Translation in Distress: Cultural Misappropriation and the Construction of the Gothic', pp. 17–38 in Avril Horner, ed., *European Gothic: A Spirited Exchange, 1760–1960*. Manchester.

—— (2002b). 'French and German Gothic: The Beginnings', pp. 63–84 in Jerrold E. Hogle, ed., *The Cambridge Companion to Gothic Fiction*. Cambridge.

Haycraft, Howard (1941). *Murder for Pleasure: The Life and Times of the Detective Story*. New York.

Hyder, C. K. (1939). 'Wilkie Collins and *The Woman in White*.' *PMLA* 54: 297–303.

James, Louis (1963). *Fiction for the Working Man, 1830–50*. Harmondsworth.

Johannsen, Albert (1950). *The House of Beadle and Adams and its Dime and Nickel Novels: The Story of a Vanished Literature*, 2 vols. Norman, OK.

Mighall, Robert (1999). *A Geography of Victorian Gothic: Mapping History's Nightmares*. Oxford.

Motter, T. H. Vail (1935). 'Byron's "Werner" Re-estimated: A Neglected Chapter in Nineteenth Century Stage History', pp. 243–75 in Hardin Craig, ed., *Essays in Dramatic Literature: The Parrott Presentation Volume*. New York.

Reynolds, David S. (1995). Introduction to George W. Lippard, *The Quaker City, or, The Monks of Monk Hall: A Romance of Philadelphia Life, Mystery, and Crime*. Amherst, MA.

Sammons, Jeffrey L. (1998). *Ideology, Mimesis, Fantasy: Charles Sealsfield, Friedrich Gerstäcker, Karl May, and Other German Novelists of America*. Chapel Hill, NC.

Seymour, Miranda (2000). *Mary Shelley*. London.

Shand, A. Innes (1890). 'Crime in Fiction.' *Blackwood's Edinburgh Magazine* 148: 172–89.

Smyth, Edmund J. (2000). 'Verne, SF, and Modernity: An Introduction', pp. 1–10 in Edmund J. Smyth, ed., *Jules Verne: Narratives of Modernity*. Liverpool.

Summers, Montague (1964). *A Gothic Bibliography*. New York.

Varma, Devendra P. (1968a). Introduction to Lawrence Flammenberg, *The Necromancer, or, The Tale of the Black Forest*. London.

—— (1968b). Introduction to the Marquis of Grosse, *Horrid Mysteries*. London.

8.2 Popular Theatre

Terry Hale

Introduction

In October 1884, Henry Arthur Jones, flush with the success of writing a sequence of colourful melodramas for the Princess's Theatre in Oxford Street, seized upon the pretext of an inaugural address to deliver a sustained attack on the state of the English theatre:

> It is a matter of every-day newspaper comment that managers cannot obtain satisfactory original plays of home-growth, and it is a fact that the manager of our leading comedy theatre has only produced one original play of English authorship for the last eight years, and is now contemplating a revival of a French adaptation; while, if at the end of any recent year, we have turned to the summary of plays produced during the previous twelve months, we must have been forced to confess that... the harvest of good, sound, ripe grain... has been miserably small. (Jones 1885: 281–2)

In short, Jones argues that the London stage is dominated, and has been for some considerable time, by ephemeral productions, mainly translations or adaptations of French plays, entirely lacking 'serious import'.

Worse still, the London stage had proved incapable of nurturing a strain of independent English dramatic writing. Jones quotes with approval the assessment of a contemporary critic: 'With Sheridan we may say that the history of the English drama closes.' Since Sheridan's *School for Scandal* had been first performed more than a hundred years previously, while the playwright himself had died in 1816, Jones was effectively arguing that the English stage had not produced a single playwright of stature during the course of the nineteenth century to 1884.[1] Many would have agreed with him.

His analysis hinges on a single point: the British public has been exposed to the extravagances of popular entertainment, mainly of French origin, for so long that their taste, and not only their taste but also that of theatre managers and actors, has become utterly corrupted. The success of such popular fare 'confirms the public in their carelessness and in their natural taste for pretentious superficial work. It confirms the manager in the hideous belief that pecuniary success can only be won by more and more consulting the more debased taste of his patrons... It lowers the tone of endeavour for all' (284). In a word, originality is sacrificed in the search for novelty.

Any overview of translation in relation to the British theatre in this period (for the position in America see p. 24, above) must deal with the question of

---

[1] Jones's argument here ignores Sheridan's Irish birth and the fact that in later years he devoted himself to the translation of Kotzebue.

whether the latter really was as dependent on foreign sources as contemporaries believed. This question has a number of different facets. First, how great a proportion of the plays produced were translated or adapted (the distinction between translation and adaptation is particularly difficult to maintain in the case of popular drama)? Second, across which languages and in which directions did the translations move? Third, what types of play were translated? Fourth, did playwrights alter or manipulate French texts for domestic consumption, and if so, how extensive and intrusive were their interventions? More generally, did the legitimate and illegitimate theatres (these terms are explained below) on the one hand and the London and provincial theatres on the other operate in the same manner with regard to the translation market? Finally, why did the system work in the manner it did? Were commentators like Jones correct to say that translation and adaptation arrested the development of British playwriting?

The Growth of the London and Provincial Theatre

Between 1800 and 1850, the population of London almost trebled. Not surprisingly, the period also witnessed a large growth in new theatres and places of entertainment, not only in the outlying regions but also in the very heart of the West End. In 1800, only three theatres were legally permitted to mount 'legitimate' drama (i.e. plays that relied on spoken dialogue) in the city of Westminster: Covent Garden, Drury Lane, and, in a more restricted manner, the Haymarket. That monopoly had been established by the Licensing Act of 1737 and was lifted with the Theatres Act of 1843.

Though the patent theatres had a legal monopoly on legitimate drama, there was nothing to prevent 'illegitimate' forms of theatre (involving mime, dancing, or music) from being mounted elsewhere. In the early 1770s, the Haymarket experimented successfully with puppet shows, which were then enjoying something of a vogue, while in the 1780s the Royal Circus had been mounting dramatic entertainments which combined the traditions of the stage with those of the circus (Moody 2000: 17–24). After the turn of the century, the competition intensified. In 1806, the Olympic and the Sans Pareil (renamed the Adelphi in 1819) both opened in the Strand. Both theatres were at pains to divest themselves of the trappings of illegitimate theatre, especially with regard to the performance of spoken dialogue without musical accompaniment (except for songs). In 1809, the Lyceum, which had been mounting performances even before 1800, was granted a licence which placed it in much the same situation as the Haymarket. A second wave of building work saw the opening of, among others, the Strand Theatre in 1832, the St James's Theatre in 1835, and the Princess's Theatre in 1840. The terms 'Legitimate Drama' and 'Illegitimate Drama' were popularized after they appeared as characters in a burlesque by J. R. Planché in 1838.

Outside the West End, where building costs were high, the theatre boom was even more noticeable. South of the Thames, the Royal Circus was transformed into the Surrey Theatre in 1810 while the vast Coburg Theatre (the Old Vic, as it became known later), which could accommodate an audience of more than 3,000, opened in 1818. The same phenomena may be observed in the larger provincial towns and cities throughout Britain. By 1866, it is estimated that around 5,000 different venues were in operation across the country. The total seating capacity of the London theatres, meanwhile, had reached more than 52,000 (Davis 2000: 199). Although the abolition of the patents in 1843 did not lead to the outbreak of theatre-building which some had prophesied (the next major wave did not occur until the 1880s), the Victorian theatre was undoubtedly the dominant popular art form of the century, and the demand for new play texts was correspondingly high.

Repertoire

The predominant kinds of drama on the nineteenth-century British stage were essentially French imports. The main exception to this rule, and even this is but a partial exception, concerns the work of the German playwright August von Kotzebue. Following productions of Kotzebue's *Menschenhass und Reue* and *Die Spanier in Peru, oder, Rollas Tod* in London—the former in an adaptation by Benjamin Thompson, as *The Stranger*, at Drury Lane in 1798, and the latter in a version by Richard Brinsley Sheridan generally known simply as *Pizarro* at the same theatre the following year—a 'Kotzebue mania' (as contemporary journalists referred to it) swept through the British theatre (see Moody 2000: 51, and for translations of *Die Spanier in Peru* see Hushan 2004). The fad was not limited to Britain; the American William Dunlap translated several plays for the New York theatre. *The Stranger*, essentially an exercise in sentimentalism (an erring wife obtains her husband's forgiveness by a life of atonement), became one of the most popular plays of the nineteenth century. *Pizarro*, however, is a more complex work, especially in Sheridan's reworking of the material. Though the main interest—the human interaction between the principal characters—remains the same, Sheridan treats the story of Pizarro's conquest as a metaphor for Anglo-French relations. In this reading of the play, Pizarro comes to stand for Napoleon who is about to embark on the subjugation not of the peaceful and orderly Peruvians but of his peaceful and orderly neighbour across the English Channel (see Donohue 1970: 139).

If this account of *Pizarro* is correct, the play's popularity with a British audience is hardly surprising. However, Kotzebue's play was based on Marmontel's 'roman poétique' *Les Incas*. Though Anglo-French relations might be strained by political events, the cultural voice of France still dominated cultural relations, even when that voice was mediated through a German playwright. In the case of *Pizarro*, Sheridan's work as translator involved not only an appeal to British patriotism but also a considerable rewriting of the play in terms of the conventions of British spectacular theatre (including an entirely new conclusion).

If Sheridan's *Pizarro* became an exercise in British Romantic theatre, elsewhere on the Continent Kotzebue was seen mainly as a purveyor of melodrama, a genre first introduced to the London stage in the early years of the new century and one which rapidly established itself as the dominant form for the next sixty years. It was not until the opening decades of the twentieth century that melodrama, after numerous transformations, would finally die a lingering death on the British stage.

One of the most influential early French exponents of the melodrama was the prolific Guilbert de Pixerécourt. It was one of Pixerécourt's melodramas, *Coelina, ou l'Enfant du mystère*, that was the first such work to make the transition to the London stage in a version by Thomas Holcroft entitled *A Tale of Mystery* (1802). Coelina, the orphaned heroine of the play, has two suitors, Trugelin, a scheming and unprincipled villain, and Stéphany, the son of her guardian, with whom she shares a reciprocal affection. It quickly transpires that Trugelin is prepared to go to any length in order to wed Coelina. When thwarted in his plans, he fabricates a story that she is the product of a bigamous union; Dufour, her guardian, believing this to be true, expels her from his house. The latter repents, however, when he learns that a mysterious mute stranger who has recently turned up again, Francisque Humbert, was the victim of a violent attack organized by Trugelin eight years earlier. Trugelin's character is now revealed in its true light; he is tracked down and captured amidst wild Alpine scenery. By the end of the play, Coelina is reunited with her lost father (Francisque Humbert) and her future husband (Stéphany).

Such a plot is clearly reminiscent of the English Gothic novel, and there can be little doubt that *Coelina*, which is partly based on a French novel of the same title published two years earlier by Ducray-Duminil, essentially represents a reworking, though in a contemporary setting, of themes developed by British authors such as Ann Radcliffe. But melodrama was, above all, about spectacle, and though the Alpine trappings of the Gothic novel (amongst other conventions) may have found their way into *Coelina*, all manner of other sensational events and situations, including natural disasters, would impose themselves subsequently on the melodrama.

It would be wrong to see sensational and rapid action, accompanied by a predictable range of stock characters, as being the only defining characteristics of melodrama. As Charles Nodier commented in 1841, in a preface to an edition of plays by his old friend Pixerécourt, what bound the entire enterprise together was a shared social morality. For Nodier, the early melodrama was nothing less than a cultural representation of the aims of the French Revolution, a dramatization of aristocratic excess and popular virtue rewarded (Brooks 1985: 43). This moral dimension was, from the outset, strongly visual, placing 'a heavy reliance on emotional semiology to carry content and moral point of view' (Booth 1981: 60). In other words, in addition to the creation of powerful incidents and effects, melodrama could eschew the intrusive use of language in favour of mime, gesture, and physical action. Holcroft actually expunges much of the dialogue to be found in the original play, substituting 'a silent dramaturgy of pantomime' (Moody 2000: 90), and so intensifying the dumbness of Francisque Humbert in the original.

British playwrights quickly began flocking to Paris intent on bringing back plays of this type for the London theatres. Nor was it only Pixerécourt whose work was plagiarized or imitated, though some of his plays—notably *La Peste de Marseille*, *L'Homme à trois visages*, and *Charles le Téméraire*—spawned four versions each (see Rahill 1967: 115). A number of works by Louis Caigniez, Jean Cuvelier de Tyre, Jean-Baptiste Hapdé, and Anne Mélesville—to name but four lesser French melodramatists of the same period—equally found their way to the British stage. 'We are not over scrupulous whence we derive our entertainment', remarks, with some justification, a character in J. R. Planché's *The Brigand Chief* (1829), 'whether by sly plagiarism, or open theft—by translation, adaptation, or any other channel accessible to dramatic ingenuity' (cited in Moody 2000: 80–1). On the basis of Allardyce Nicoll's bibliography of the nineteenth-century drama, Rahill claims that 'fully half of the plays written in England during the period [1800–50] must have been suggested by Parisian models and many were literally adapted by English authors' (Rahill 1967: 115). Tolles puts the proportion in the case of melodrama in the first quarter of the century even higher, claiming that 'almost all the melodramas produced on the English stage before 1825 were based on French pieces or on novels and tales' (Tolles 1940: 22).

As the century progressed, the melodrama underwent various transformations. Having learned to translate and adapt French melodrama to suit British requirements, the next step was, of course, the production of domestic melodramas. Murder and crime exercised a perennial fascination, and here once again French sources predominated. Edward Fitzball's *Jonathan Bradford, or, The Murder at the Roadside Inn* (1833) is clearly appropriated from *L'Auberge des Adrets* (1823) by Antier, Lacoste, and Chapponier; George Dibdin Pitt's *Sweeney Todd, or, The Fiend of Fleet Street* (1847), now regarded as an archetypal British urban legend, was probably suggested by an incident recounted in Peuchet's *Mémoires tirés des archives de la police de Paris* (1838). Dennery and Grangé's *Les Bohémiens de Paris* (1843), one of many plays hurriedly rushed into production in the wake of the astonishing success of Eugène Sue's serial *Les Mystères de Paris*, gave rise to three British productions almost immediately: C. Z. Barnett's *The Bohemians of Paris, or, The Mysteries of Crime* (1843) at the Surrey; Edward Stirling's *The Bohemians, or, The Rogues of Paris* (1843) at the Adelphi; and, at Sadler's Wells, William Moncrieff's *The Scamps of London* (1843), the first version to relocate the action to the British capital. It resurfaced again twenty-five years later, now in a version by Dion Boucicault, as *After Dark: A Tale of London Life* (1868) at the Princess's Theatre. Boucicault's version incorporates a clever piece of staging in which the hero is left bound to the tracks on the London Underground (here, for once, there is no French source: the scene is borrowed from a recent American play) but is otherwise little more than a reworking of the Moncrieff version (see Booth 1965: 169–70).

The most accomplished British dramatist of the second half of the nineteenth century, and the major practitioner of the 'well-made play', was Tom Taylor. Taylor's master was the French playwright Eugène Scribe, whose work was characterized by its meticulous construction, plausible plotlines, the careful spacing and preparation of effects (so as to keep the audience in a state of expectation), clever dialogue, and the neat binding together of the various threads of the action. In one form or another, most of Scribe's four hundred or so plays (many written in collaboration) made their way to Britain; besides Taylor, J. R. Planché was one of the most adept of Scribe's adapters.

Between 1853 and 1865, Taylor wrote some twenty plays for the Olympic Theatre which collectively not only represent the apogee of his achievement as a playwright but are also indicative, in the words of his principal biographer, 'of the widespread French influence on the English drama of the day' (Tolles 1940: 114). *Still Waters Run Deep* (1855), one of his most successful plays, exemplifies his work as translator/adapter. The source text in this case was a novella by Charles Bernard, *Le Gendre* (1841). In Bernard's version, the action revolves around a wedding dowry owed by the Bailleuls to the mild-mannered Chaudieu following his marriage to their daughter Alphonsine. Mme Bailleul, who is much younger than her husband, has invested part of the sum with a M. Laboissière, director of an enterprising scheme to operate a steamship line using 'bateaux inexplosibles' (fire-proof boats). The main reason for Mme Bailleul's behaviour is that she has been having a clandestine love affair with Laboissière, though he is by now clearly more interested in Alphonsine. When Mme Bailleul tries to break off her relationship with him and recover the money invested in his scheme, he threatens to send her love letters to her husband. In despair, Mme Bailleul turns to her son-in-law for help. Chaudieu, in the role of the reluctant hero, plays his part with quiet aplomb. By the end of the novella, Chaudieu has firmly established himself as the head of his own household, respected and obeyed by both his wife and his mother-in-law.

Taylor's adaptation rapidly established 'a tenacious hold on public favour... which few Victorian pieces can equal' (Tolles 1940: 138). First, he relocates the action to London or, more precisely, Brompton. Second, he neatly avoids the moral problem (as far as a British audience was concerned) of portraying on stage a mother and daughter involved in an adulterous rivalry by changing the relationship to aunt and niece (needless to say, neither of the adulterous flirtations is consummated). Third, the focus of Taylor's version is exclusively on the domestic hearth of Chaudieu (now called John Mildmay) and his wife. Indeed, all the elements which serve to place the original in its historical and cultural context are expunged (e.g. duelling). What Taylor offers his audience is a domestic comedy, perhaps the setting for which the well-made play was best suited, which moves seamlessly from one carefully modulated domestic confrontation to the next before concluding with the reassuring reassertion of the authority of the paterfamilias.

It was a trick Taylor would pull off many times in his career, for instance with *The Ticket-of-Leave Man* (1863), a melodrama on the contemporary theme of low life (reworked from a minor play by Edouard Brisebarre and Eugène Nus). If Taylor learned the lesson of stagecraft from Scribe, that lesson was in turn passed on to successors such as T. W. Robertson, Henry Arthur Jones, Arthur Wing Pinero, and, later, Coward and Rattigan.

Copyright

At the beginning of the nineteenth century, British playwrights, like other authors, enjoyed only limited protection with regard to the copying of their works, while there was no statutory protection for stage productions. The 1833 Copyright Act regularized some of these anomalies, particularly by providing British dramatists with the sole right, though only for a limited period, to authorize performance of their works. This legislation, however, did not extend the same rights to foreign authors and dramatists, though the work of British authors had benefited from the same copyright protection on the other side of the channel as that of their French colleagues since 1810 (Nowell-Smith 1968: 19). Even when, after protracted negotiations, Britain passed the International Copyright Act of 1852, the main purpose of which was to enforce a reciprocal convention with France, the provisions of the agreement were so badly drafted that they generally failed to meet their objectives as far as the theatre was concerned. (On the copyright of translated texts, see further pp. 55–6, above.)

In *The Eighth Commandment* (1860), Charles Reade was candid about his own debt to French theatre before the 1852 legislation; he was not, however, as candid about his subsequent practice: despite representations to the contrary, he continued to pirate French plays even after the copyright protection came into force, even if he did pay for some of his subsequent adaptations. Of his own plays performed in the early 1850s, he freely admits that *The Ladies' Battle* (1851) was 'a close version' of a play by Scribe and Legouvé; *Angelo* (1851) was an 'abridged version' of Victor Hugo's play of the same title; *A Village Tale* (1852) was 'an adaptation' of George Sand's charming pastoral *Claudie*; *Art* (1855) was 'an adaptation' of L. P. N. Fournier's *Tiridaté*; while *The Courier of Lyons, or, The Attack upon the Mail* (1854), one of Reade's most successful theatrical ventures, was 'a free version' of *Le Courrier de Lyon* by Eugène Moreau, Paul Siraudin, and Alfred Delacour (Reade 1860: 14).

As Reade himself comments, the intention of the 1852 Act 'was not to prevent foreign authors' ideas being *taken*, but *stolen*'. Accordingly, during the course of a visit to Paris in 1851, he called upon the French playwright Auguste Macquet in order to negotiate with him the English rights to a drama called *Le Château de Grantier*. Much to Macquet's astonishment (he had been for many years the principal ghost writer for Alexandre Dumas and was fully conversant with both publishing and theatrical practices), Reade bought the rights from him for £40. Reade's indebtedness to the French stage also includes his 1868 novel *Foul Play* (written, apparently, in collaboration with Dion Boucicault), based on a French melodrama entitled *Le Portefeuille rouge*.

Emile Zola's *L'Assommoir* (1877) rapidly made its way into English in the form of various novelistic and stage adaptations. Though Reade's *Drink* was by no means the first such version, it was undoubtedly the most financially successful. Walter Gooch, the lessee of the Princess's Theatre, was so worried by the rawness of the play (the English version retains the French setting and does little to tone down the most striking scenes) that he decided to go into partnership with Reade in order to share the risks. The production is claimed to have netted Reade more than £20,000 in royalties.

If for most of the century the British copyright law was ineffective in protecting foreign authors, it nonetheless offered legal protection to those who officially (through the payment of a modest sum in exchange for the British rights) pirated their works. In other words, the new legislation created a market in what we would term today 'secondary rights' or rights of exploitation. Foreign dramatists might be powerless to act, but British playwrights could look after their own interests.

Translation Practices

Like most young men of his rank (Reade was born into the landed professional class and educated privately prior to winning a scholarship to Magdalen College, Oxford), the future author of *The Cloister and the Heath* had an excellent knowledge of French. Indeed, such was his command of the language that in 1859 he even wrote a two-act play, *Le Faubourg Saint-Germain*, in the language. His experience of the French theatre dated back to the late 1840s, when he was a frequent visitor to Paris hunting down violins (these could be resold in London at a substantial profit). His first work to be staged publicly was his heavy-handed version of Scribe and Legouvé's *La Bataille des dames*.

Reade saw the play during the course of a trip to Paris in March 1851. The chances are that, having seen the play and recognized its possibilities, he returned several times to the theatre, scribbling down lines in pencil during the performance, memorizing other passages and jotting them down in the interval, until he was able to piece together a working copy of some kind. British playwrights had been assembling working copies of the texts of French plays in this manner at least since Thomas Holcroft had come to Paris to learn by heart Beaumarchais's *Le Mariage de Figaro*, which was staged in London in 1784 as *The Follies of a Day*.

The process was extremely laborious. Perhaps the most complete description is the fictional example found in M. E. Braddon's *Eleanor's Victory* (1863). Richard Thornton, the hero of the novel, is in Paris to prepare an English version of a melodrama currently being staged at the Porte Saint-Martin called *Raoul l'empoisonneur*. His task goes much further than simply noting down the text, however. He explains: 'I'm over here to pick up the music, sketch the scenery and effects, and translate the play. Something like versatility there, I think, for five-and-thirty shillings a week' (Braddon 1863: 40). Richard, whose normal situation is that of 'assistant scene-painter and second-violinist at a transpontine theatre' (p. 41), has been selected for the task only because the main dramatist at the theatre does not understand French. In addition to his standard remuneration, he expects no more than £5 from the lessees of the London theatre where the translation is to be staged.

Not all playwrights were as intent on producing straightforward facsimile versions of French plays as Braddon's Richard Thornton. As J. R. Planché noted in 1872, 'The crime [reliance on French sources], if it be one, carries its own punishment along with it—a poor bald, literal translation fails, and a clever, spirited one, succeeds' (Planché 1872: I, 246). In the case of Charles Reade, the introduction of broad, farcical elements would seem to have been one route to box-office success. But perhaps the playwright with the surest touch, as we have already seen, was Tom Taylor, whose reworking of material, both in terms of content and structure, was always very considerable. The nature of the final production, however, by no means rested with the playwright alone. As the promptbooks of the period clearly show, deletions of material, not only of new works but also of established plays, were common; more generally, the Victorian theatre squeezed everything, whatever its origins, into the box with which it felt comfortable: melodrama (and its various sub-genres), burlesque, extravaganza, well-made play, etc.

Attribution

The first two decades of the nineteenth century gave rise to miscellaneous kinds of illegitimate drama. For more than half-a-century, this more or less unregulated explosion (successive lord chamberlains seem not to have taken the slightest interest in the issue of nomenclature) gave rise to the most outlandish descriptions of the fare on offer as advertised by playbills: 'new grand pantomimical drama', 'original originality', 'ludicrous quizzical comical nautical burlesque burletta', even 'burlesque tragedy'. But if theatres were very good at promoting their wares by the use of an essentially meaningless nomenclature, they were very poor at providing any genuine information as to their provenance. Playbills and other printed sources rarely, if ever, point to the fact that a work is a translation or adaptation of a foreign play; they do not always even divulge the name of those responsible for making the translation or adaptation.

Even in the mid-century, matters did not noticeably improve. Tom Taylor described *Still Waters Run Deep* as 'an original comedy', even though the play was a stage adaptation of a French novella. In doing so, he had no qualms. For Taylor, it was quite legitimate for a play to be described as 'new' or 'original' simply on the strength of the fact that the source material had undergone modification (see Tolles 1940: 116). Despite his vocal support of copyright legislation, Charles Reade behaved in exactly the same manner.

This gives rise to very considerable difficulties for the student of translation practice in the nineteenth century. Though earlier scholars have succeeded in identifying a significant proportion of the original source texts of nineteenth-century plays, especially with regard to major figures, the process is far from complete. In many cases, it is likely that the source text will never be identified.

Take for example the case of George R. Sims, the author of *The Lights o' London* (1881), one of the most successful melodramas of the period with a stage history stretching through to the 1930s. In his bibliography of the English drama, Allardyce Nicoll lists nearly fifty plays attributed to Sims, all of which at first sight seem so firmly anchored in the Victorian experience as to exclude any suggestion of foreign influence. But a close reading of Sims's autobiography, *My Life: Sixty*

Years' Recollections of Bohemian London (1917), reveals the extent to which his stage career revolved around the processes of translation and adaptation. In 1879, for example, the actor Charles Wyndham engaged Sims to adapt a French play on behalf of the Royalty Theatre. This unidentified play Sims transformed into a three-act comedy called *Crutch and Toothpick*. For this work, he was paid £50 on receipt of manuscript and a further fee of £1 for each performance to a maximum of £150 (Sims 1917: 73). Sims's adaptation obviously served its purpose, for two years later he received another commission of the same kind for the Royalty Theatre. This time it would seem that the choice of original text was left to Sims and the work had to be completed at short notice. Though Sims hints at the main changes he wrought with the French text, he again fails to provide any clues as to its identity: 'So I went home—it was then Saturday afternoon—worked day and night on the French play, and by midday on Wednesday I had completed the three-act comedy which I called *The Member for Slocum*. I made the hero a member of Parliament and the heroine a lady of pronounced views on the equality of the sexes, temporarily separated from her husband and devoting herself vigorously to a campaign for women's rights' (Sims 1917: 114). Significantly, when Sims wrote *The Lights o' London*, or rather the earlier novel on which the play is based, he adopted the conventions of the French 'miseries and mysteries' school.

But if playwrights such as Reade and Sims, who achieved distinction in other fields, have left some trace of the sources they used, and the way they approached the translation or adaptation process, there are hundreds of lesser figures for whom we are thrown back on supposition and guesswork.

Conclusion

The denunciation of popular theatre was a favourite Romantic pastime. In 1802, in his preface to the *Lyrical Ballads*, Wordsworth had castigated an age whose degraded taste sought pleasure in 'silly German tragedies'. Henry Arthur Jones's 1884 inaugural lecture presented a substantially similar case against the popularity of French drama. Certainly, the nineteenth century was a period in which British playwrights engaged in a project involving adaptation and rewriting on a large scale; however, it is implausible to maintain that the importation of foreign plays single-handedly held back the flowering of British dramatic talent. Translation and adaptation have repeatedly stimulated the development of other art forms.

Perhaps the respective prestige of French and English was partly at issue. If French was the dominant language of cultural exchange throughout the early and mid-nineteenth century, as was surely the case, English would progressively assume that mantle during the course of the twentieth century. We might, therefore, expect a more fluid situation to have arisen during the closing decades of the nineteenth century with regard to the theatre. Arguably, this is exactly what we do find. The prestige of the British theatre began to rise again. A tradition of native drama largely independent of foreign sources began to emerge (e.g. Wilde, Shaw, Barrie, Pinero). The ascendant status of the British playwright found recognition in the International Copyright Act of 1886 and the American Copyright Act of 1891. Finally, though translations and adaptations from French by no means came to a halt, a small but influential audience began to demand productions of more challenging or experimental work by dramatists such as Ibsen. With the publication of *The Renascence of the English Drama* in 1895, Henry Arthur Jones effectively retracted his criticisms of a decade earlier.

LIST OF SOURCES

Translations and Adaptations
Barnett, C. Z. (1843). *The Bohemians of Paris* [Sue; Dennery and Grangé]. London.
Dunlap, William (1800). *Pizarro in Peru, or, The Death of Rolla* [Kotzebue]. New York.
Holcroft, Thomas (1802). *A Tale of Mystery* [Pixerécourt]. London.
Moncrieff, William (1843). *The Scamps of London* [Sue; Dennery and Grangé]. London.
Planché, J. R. (1833). *Gustavus the Third, or, The Masked Ball* [Scribe]. London.
—— (1835). *The Jewess* [Scribe]. London.
Reade, Charles (1851*a*). *The Ladies' Battle, or, Un Duel en Amour* [Scribe and Legouvé]. London.
—— (1851*b*). *Angelo* [Hugo]. London.
—— (1854). *The Courier of Lyons, or, The Attack upon the Mail* [Moreau, Siraudin, and Delacour]. London.
—— (1855). *Art* [Fournier]. London.
—— (1991). *Drink* [Zola; Busnach and Gastineau], ed. David Baguley. London, Ontario (first performed 1879).
Sheridan, Richard Brinsley (1799). *Pizarro* [Kotzebue]. London.
Stirling, Edward (1843). *The Bohemians, or, The Rogues of Paris* [Sue; Dennery and Grangé]. London.
Taylor, Tom (1855). *Still Waters Run Deep: An Original Comedy in Three Acts* [Charles de Bernard]. London.
—— (1863). *The Ticket-of-Leave Man* [Brisebarre and Nus]. London.
Thompson, Benjamin (1800). *The Stranger* [Kotzebue]. London.

Other Sources
Booth, Michael (1965). *English Melodrama*. London.
—— (1981). *Victorian Spectacular Theatre, 1850–1910*. London.
Braddon, M. E. (1863). *Eleanor's Victory*, 3 vols. London (repr. 1996).
Brooks, Peter (1985). *The Melodramatic Imagination: Balzac, Henry James, Melodrama and the Mode of Excess*. New York (first pub. 1976).
Davis, Tracy C. (2000). *The Economics of the British Stage, 1800–1914*. Cambridge.
Donohue, Joseph W., Jr. (1970). *Dramatic Character in the English Romantic Age*. Princeton, NJ.
Hushan, Helga (2004). 'The Extraordinary Case of Kotzebue's English Spaniards in Peru: Competing Versions or Perversions', pp. 359–74 in Sabine Coelsch-Foisner and Holger Klein, eds., *Drama Translation and Theatre Practice*. Salzburg.
Jones, Henry A. (1885). 'The Dramatic Outlook.' *English Illustrated Magazine* 2: 280–9 and 341–52 (repr. in his *The Renascence of English Drama*, 1895).
Kinne, Willard Austin (1939). *Revivals and Importations of French Comedies in England, 1749–1900*. New York.

Moody, Jane (2000). *The Illegitimate Theatre in London, 1770–1840*. Cambridge.
Nicoll, Allardyce (1955). *A History of English Drama*, Vol. 4: *Early Nineteenth Century*, rev. edn. Cambridge.
Nowell-Smith, Simon (1968). *International Copyright Law and the Publisher in the Reign of Queen Victoria*. Oxford.
Planché, J. R. (1872). *Recollections and Reflections*, 2 vols. London.
Rahill, F. (1967). *The World of Melodrama*. University Park, PA.
Reade, Charles (1860). *The Eighth Commandment*. London.
Sims, George R. (1917). *My Life: Sixty Years' Recollections of Bohemian London*. London.
Tolles, Winton (1940). *Tom Taylor and the Victorian Drama*. New York.

8.3 Children's Literature

David Blamires

The nineteenth century displays an amazing variety of children's books in English translation, many of which have become classics. German and French material predominates, with French in several instances providing a conduit for a German text. The publishers Joseph Cundall and James Burns are important for their role in introducing German tales in the 1840s, but many other major publishers quickly joined in. The number of translators was very large, many remaining anonymous; women were particularly active in this area. The quality of translation varies greatly, as do the methods of the translators. They often took liberties with their source texts, modifying and abridging as well as adapting details to suit British prejudices and attitudes. They were more interested in providing useful, readable new books than in introducing their child readers to the specifics of foreign ways of life. Most translations served their period and were then forgotten or replaced, but a very few have achieved classic status for themselves: Edgar Taylor's pioneering version of the Grimms, the first anonymous translation of *Struwwelpeter*, M. A. Murray's *Pinocchio*.

Fairy Tales

Apart from such quintessentially English tales as 'Jack the Giant-Killer', 'Tom Thumb', and 'Dick Whittington', most of the fairy tales known to nineteenth-century English children came from abroad. The eighteenth century brought a large number of fairy tales from France. Antoine Galland's *Les Mille et une nuits*, translated from the Arabic, immediately gained currency as *The Arabian Nights' Entertainments* (see Vol. 3 of this *History* for further discussion). Fairy tales from these sources remained popular throughout the nineteenth century despite strong competition from Germany, especially the Brothers Grimm, and from Andersen and Norwegian folk tales.

The seventeenth-century author Mme d'Aulnoy was the leading writer of literary fairy tales, combining traditional plots with fanciful themes of her own and adding artful descriptions and contemporary allusions. Her eighteenth-century popularity continued into the nineteenth century. Much-abbreviated texts appeared in *Mother Bunch's Fairy Tales* between 1799 and 1825. Early in the century individual tales, usually greatly abridged, were published as chapbooks. Such productions, lacking any mention of d'Aulnoy as author or of any adapter, continued to c.1860. However, in 1855 d'Aulnoy's reputation was restored by J. R. Planché's translation of the complete corpus of her fairy tales except for

'Prince Marcassin' and 'Le Dauphin'; these latter two were excluded because they 'could not, without considerable alterations in their details, have been rendered unobjectionable to the English reader' (Planché 1855*a*: xi–xii). The two stories exemplify the animal bridegroom theme, and the sexual implications seem to have been distasteful to the translator. Nearly forty years later, however, another translation by Miss Annie Macdonell and Miss Lee (1892) did include 'Prince Marcassin' and 'The Dolphin'.

The story collection of Charles Perrault, now more highly esteemed than d'Aulnoy and closer to the oral sources of his day, had been translated by Robert Samber in 1729 as *Histories, or, Tales of Past Times* and included 'Little Red Riding-Hood', 'Cinderella', 'Puss in Boots', 'The Sleeping Beauty', and 'Bluebeard'. Samber's translation, lightly revised by 'G. M., Gent' (Guy Miège) in 1768, was reprinted until *c.*1830. In 1858 J. R. Planché followed up his success with Mme d'Aulnoy by producing *Four and Twenty Fairy Tales*, which included six tales by Perrault and the rest by half a dozen other French eighteenth-century authors. Even more than was the case with Mme d'Aulnoy, individual tales of Perrault's circulated widely in chapbook format. The chapbooks tended to dispense with the original verse morals, but because Perrault's texts were short, there was no need to publish abridgements of the stories. Instead there were various versified adaptations.

A few of D'Aulnoy's and Perrault's contemporaries were occasionally included in collections of fairy tales. Mademoiselle Lhéritier's 'The Discreet Princess' was often appended to Perrault's tales without any indication of her authorship. Count Anthony Hamilton's tales suited a more adult taste, being long, extravagant, and parodying the fashion for literary fairy tales. His most famous tale, translated as 'The Four Facardins' by M. G. Lewis, was the leading item in Lewis's *Fairy Tales and Romances* (1849). Like the foregoing, the influential educational writer Mme Le Prince de Beaumont (known above all for her 'Beauty and the Beast') occupied a permanent place in nineteenth-century anthologies of fairy tales and was often republished in chapbook format.

While English versions of *The Thousand and One Nights* published during the eighteenth century were aimed at an adult readership, Richard Johnson, using the pseudonym of the Revd Mr Cooper, produced an abridged version for children under the title *The Oriental Moralist* (1791/2). The nineteenth century saw several new translations appear (see § 7.1, above). It is not always easy to judge what is meant for children and what for adults. There are full-text editions of 'Aladdin' designed for children as well as slightly bowdlerized and severely abridged versions. The two different editions of the traditional anonymous eighteenth-century *Arabian Nights' Entertainments* published by Milner (1843) and Milner and Sowerby (1859) were probably read by both adults and children, being cheap and convenient. Needless to say, chapbooks and toybooks of individual stories abounded, the latter copiously illustrated in colour.

Towards the end of the eighteenth century a new source for fairy tales became available in Germany. In 1791 there appeared *Popular Tales of the Germans*, which presented anonymously five tales by J. K. A. Musäus. The identity of the anonymous translator, mistakenly thought until recently to be William Beckford, is not known (Butler 1999: 30). This suave translation introduced 'Richilda' (a version of the Snow White story told from the viewpoint of the stepmother), 'The Books of the Chronicles of the Three Sisters', and 'Legends of Number Nip' (the capricious mountain spirit Rübezahl); each of these was included in a new translation by J. T. Hanstein (published anonymously) entitled *Select Popular Tales from the German of Musaeus* (1845). The Rübezahl legends proved popular and crop up in a variety of places, most notably in the anonymous *Legends of Rubezahl, and Other Tales* (1845) and Mark Lemon's *Legends of Number Nip* (1864). In *Fairy Tales* (1868) Lemon also produced a version of 'The Chronicles of the Three Sisters', which was Musäus' best-known children's tale, being frequently included, in different formats and translations, in general collections of fairy tales.

The dominant fairy-tale collection in the nineteenth century in Britain was undoubtedly that of the Grimms, and the most influential translation (for better or for worse) was Edgar Taylor's, first published as *German Popular Stories* in two volumes (1823–6), with striking etchings by George Cruikshank that were much admired by Ruskin. Reprinted many times throughout the century, it held its own against more accurate and comprehensive translations because of its readability. Taylor adapted his source material where it conflicted with English notions of sexual and social propriety (e.g. in 'The Frog Prince' and 'The Fisherman and his Wife'), and he added a few tales that did not belong to the Grimms' collection. His selection is based on the first two German editions, while the Grimms continued to revise and expand their texts through another five.

As later translators got to work, new selections were made and the corpus extended. Fourteen tales were included by W. J. Thoms in his *Lays and Legends of Germany* and thirty-two in the anonymous *Household Tales and Traditions* of 1845. John Edward Taylor, a relative of Edgar Taylor, translated thirty-six more tales in *The Fairy Ring*. The first more or less complete collection was the anonymously translated *Household Stories* of 1853. Matilda Davis produced *Home Stories*, while another nameless translator included several stories in *Grimms' Goblins* of 1861, a collection that included tales by d'Aulnoy, Wilhelm Hauff, and others as well as the Grimms. *Household Tales and Popular Stories* of 1862 also printed the Grimms and Hauff together. Mrs H. B. Paull translated another large selection for *Grimms' Fairy Tales* (1872), and in 1882 Lucy Crane provided the texts for her more famous brother Walter's illustrations in *Household Stories*. The first scholarly translation of the complete corpus was made by Margaret Hunt in *Grimms' Household Tales* (1884). (For an excellent analysis of these, see Sutton 1996.) Further translations were made between 1890 and 1900 by Ella Boldey; Mrs H. B. Paull and Mr L. A. Wheatley; L. L. Weedon and Beatrice Marshall. Several publishers exploited the Grimms' popularity, commissioning new illustrations as well as new translations, but none achieved the longevity of Edgar Taylor's.

The vogue for the German Romantics took in Fouqué's *Undine* (first translated 1818) and *Sintram* (translated 1820) and Chamisso's *Peter Schlemihl* (translated 1824), all of which later became standard reading for children. Somewhat later the fairy tales of Wilhelm Hauff joined this company. One of his most famous tales, 'The Cold Heart', was published twice in 1844, once by C. A. Feiling, once anonymously, to be followed by the anonymous *Select Popular Tales* (1845). Hauff's literary tales used both German and Oriental materials and enjoyed great popularity. New translations were made by Percy E. Pinkerton (1881), S. Mendel (1886), and L. Eckenstein (1893). Two favourite tales were 'Dwarf Nose' and 'Little Mook'. Clemens Brentano's much quirkier fairy tales were not translated until the end of the century, when Kate Freiligrath Kroeker, daughter of the political poet Ferdinand Freiligrath, produced two volumes. Jacob and Wilhelm Grimm's namesake, the unrelated Albert Ludwig Grimm, who composed his own fairy tales in a more expansive style, also had some books translated. *Lina's Märchenbuch* appeared as *Fairy Tales* (Anon. 1827) and contained 'The Black Guitar', 'The Two Foundlings of the Spring', and 'The Three Brothers, or, The Avenging Cudgel'. His later *Tales from the Eastern-Land* (Anon. 1847b) proved engaging enough to be reprinted by different publishers.

Ludwig Bechstein, the Grimms' chief rival in collecting traditional tales, did not figure among English books until *The Old Story-Teller* was published (Anon. 1854). Although this was reissued with the new title *As Pretty as Seven* (c.1870), Bechstein's stories never gained the ready popularity of the Grimms'; they were not sufficiently different in character from those of the Grimms, which had already had thirty years to secure their position. Four stories by the little-known J. J. Rudolphi were published in *The King of the Swans, and Other Tales* (1846). Richard von Volkmann-Leander's attractive *Dreams by a French Fireside*, written in periods of respite during the Franco-Prussian War, was translated twice within a brief timespan, by M. O'Callaghan (1886) and J. Raleigh (1890), and deserves to be more widely known.

Meanwhile, in the middle of the century, came a sudden flood of translations of Hans Christian Andersen, who had been producing a steady stream of tales for children in Danish since 1837. Four selections, by three different translators, were issued by three different publishers in 1846. Mary Howitt, who had already translated three of his novels, produced from Danish *Wonderful Stories for Children*. Caroline Peachey translated, also from the original, *Danish Fairy Legends and Tales*, which was twice enlarged, in 1852 and 1861. Charles Boner, however, did *A Danish Story Book*, *The Nightingale and Other Tales*, and, in 1848, *The Dream of Little Tuk, and Other Tales* from German editions. Three further translations, all anonymous, had appeared in 1847, another came in 1848, and Madame de Chatelain's *Tales and Fairy Stories*, probably from the German, in 1852. Further editions of Andersen appeared every few years throughout the rest of the century. Translations by H. W. Dulcken (1864 and 1866), Peachey, Plesner, Ward and others (1870), and an anonymous collection published by Ward, Lock, and Tyler (1876) flooded the market. Brian Alderson is rightly critical with regard to the accuracy, style, and tone of most of these nineteenth-century translations, which miss Andersen's conversational immediacy and satirical humour; he regards Nisbet Bain's translation of 1893 as best capturing Andersen's 'sound' (Alderson

1982: 6). Not until 1914 was the complete canon of 155 tales available in a translation by W. A. and J. K. Craigie, revising Dulcken and adding new items of their own. Only a small proportion of Andersen's tales can be regarded as fairy tales in the narrow sense (e.g. 'The Tinder Box', 'The Little Mermaid', 'The Snow Queen'), but translations of his work vastly extended the range of children's reading with such tales as 'The Ugly Duckling', 'The Little Match Girl', and 'The Steadfast Tin Soldier'.

During the 1840s more Scandinavian material entered the orbit of children's books. While Andersen was, for the most part, inventing his tales, the Norwegians P. C. Asbjørnsen and J. I. Moe were collecting traditional folk tales, as the Grimm brothers had done. Their *Popular Tales from the Norse*, translated by George Webbe Dasent (1842), went into a second, enlarged edition in 1859. Dasent later translated another collection by Asbjørnsen as *Tales from the Fjeld* (1874). Further translations of Norwegian folk tales were made by H. L. Brækstad and by Abel Heywood, the latter of whom translated 'The Husband who was to Mind the House' (Dasent's title) in Lancashire dialect as 'Th' Mon ut Wanted to manage th' Heause'. All the translations succeeded in capturing the directness and humour of the originals, but Dasent's *Popular Tales*, which contained much ancillary material, justifiably became the standard version and was reprinted with modern illustrations in 1969.

Other areas of Europe made a much smaller impact with their fairy tales. Apart from three tales included in Thomas Keightley's *Tales and Popular Fictions* (1834), the Italian Straparola figures only in *The Nights of Straparola*, translated by W. G. Waters (1894), which was clearly designed for adults. Basile's *Pentamerone* (the earliest European collection consisting entirely of fairy tales) fared rather better. A translation made by John Edward Taylor (1848) was revised and excerpted by Helen Zimmern (1893) for Unwin. The same publisher issued *Finnish Legends for English Children* by R. Eivind (1893) and *Fairy Tales from Finland* by the Swedish-speaking Zacharias Topelius, translated by Ella R. Christie (1896). In the 1890s the indefatigable folklore scholar Joseph Jacobs produced *Indian Fairy Tales*, *Celtic Fairy Tales*, and *More Celtic Fairy Tales* in editions for children that parallel his *English Fairy Tales* and *More English Fairy Tales*. Jacobs's collections have become classics of their kind, comparable with the series of 'colour' *Fairy Books* edited by Andrew Lang (1889–1910), each of which presents a varied anthology of tales from around the world. These collections can safely be assigned to the category of children's literature, but there are many others published in the 1880s and 1890s that belong more appropriately to the field of folklore. Russian fairy tales, for example, were not published for children until the twentieth century, although some scholarly collections appeared in the late nineteenth.

Moral, Religious, and Didactic Tales

The earliest children's books were designed to socialize as well as amuse their readers; they provided models of behaviour and belief that were to be emulated or avoided.

The fables of Aesop and Phaedrus had proved enduringly popular in this regard, likewise Fénelon's *Télémaque*, of which an abridged English version was published in 1805. (See Vol. 3 of this *History* for previous translations of these texts.) From the late eighteenth century onwards there had been a constant flow of material dealing with contemporary, mainly middle-class family life and inculcating appropriate behaviour. One of the most popular collections of such stories, published originally in magazine format, was Arnaud Berquin's *L'Ami des enfants* (1782–3), which first appeared in English as *The Children's Friend* (1783–6), translated by M. A. Meilan. Several further editions appeared during the nineteenth century as well as a selection entitled *The Looking-Glass for the Mind*, first published in 1787. The work of Berquin's German contemporary C. G. Salzmann, *Moralisches Elementarbuch*, narrating episodes in the life of a single middle-class family, was translated and adapted to fit English circumstances by Mary Wollstonecraft as *Elements of Morality* (1790). This went through numerous editions in Britain and America.

Behind most of these Enlightenment writers stands the figure of J. J. Rousseau and his *Émile*. While this was not a book for children, one of his most notable followers, Madame de Genlis, tutor to the children of the Duke of Chartres, wrote specifically for them. *Tales of the Castle, or, Stories of Instruction and Delight*, translated by Thomas Holcroft, had appeared in 1785, and *The Palace of Truth* was published in 1819. Her *Theatre of Education* (1781) contained twenty-four comedies that became a staple of English girls' schools, some being expressly designed for 'the children of Shop-keepers and Mechanics' (see Vol. 3 of this *History* for a fuller discussion).

Early in the nineteenth century several more German books were translated, often with no indication of their author's name. Among these was G. E. Fischer's *Gustavus, or, The Macaw* (1814), which had the subtitle 'A story to teach children the proper value of things'. From F. A. Krummacher came selections from his *Parables*, one translated by F. Shoberl (1824), another by Miss F. Johnston (1839), and *The Little Dove* translated by Ann Steinkopff (1828), which is based on episodes from the real life of Adelbert, Count von der Recke-Volmerstein. This latter work was republished in mid-century, and a new translation also appeared, with the title *Alfred and the Little Dove*. In 1829 Harvey and Darton published F. S. Meyer's *Little Swiss Seppeli*, but with no mention of the author's name. Perhaps the most extraordinary success was enjoyed by F. W. Carové's *The Story without an End*, first translated by Sarah Austin, one of the most distinguished translators of the day, in 1834. This sentimental tale, which anticipates Andersen's 'Thumbelina', was republished *c.*1840 and 1864. It was later lavishly illustrated with fifteen colour plates by Eleanor Vere Boyle (1868) and issued as a miniature book with illustrations by Aimée G. Gifford (1899).

During the early nineteenth century several German writers provided books with a strong moral or religious message for children. The most prolific was Christoph von Schmid, author of the constantly reprinted *Basket of Flowers*, the tale of a poor girl wrongly accused of the theft of a ring but later proved innocent.

It was translated into English at least five times. The first translation was made from a French version by an American Episcopal priest, G. T. Bedell (1833), and like many other first translations it was the one most widely reprinted, right into the twentieth century, often with no reference to Schmid. The first translation from the German was by William Drugulin (1848), but it had little resonance, probably because it originated in Germany. In its original German form Schmid's book was insufficiently Evangelical for the English public, so additions and alterations had to be made; no reference was ever made to the fact that Schmid was a Catholic. *The Basket of Flowers* was a best-seller, probably because it was constantly given as a Sunday School reward book. Several other books by Schmid profited from the fame of this one: *Little Henry* (1823), *The Easter Eggs* (1829), *Christmas Eve* (1843). This list, which is not exhaustive, only gives the date of first translation (most were frequently republished; for further details on Schmid, see Renier 1972 and Blamires 1994).

The writer C. G. Barth is the nearest Protestant counterpart to Schmid. *Setma, the Turkish Girl* and *Woodrof, the Swedish Boy*, which appeared in one volume in 1838, display an earnest missionary zeal and show how prayer and persistence in adversity are ultimately rewarded. Further editions of *Setma* came in 1853 and an undated one from the Religious Tract Society. A composite volume entitled *Winter Evening Stories* was published c.1844 including *The Young Tyrolese* and *The Wanderer*.

Robinsonades

Defoe's *Robinson Crusoe*, though not written for children, quickly became popular among them in abridged and adapted formats. It also gave rise to imitations in other languages. One of the most successful was J. H. Campe's *Robinson der Jüngere*, translated by the author as *Robinson the Younger* (1781–2). In thirty episodes a father retells Defoe's story didactically and interactively to a small group of children, eliciting varied responses and questions. An anonymous translation from a French version entitled *The New Robinson Crusoe* (1788) continued to be reprinted and abridged up to 1827. Campe's book gained a new readership when another translation was made by R. Hick (1855) from a later German edition. As Campe modified Defoe in form and details, so his text was also freely adapted.

Though Campe's book was read for more than eighty years after its first appearance in English, its fame was overtaken by another German Robinsonade, which has become an English classic: *The Swiss Family Robinson*. This story of a father, mother, and four boys shipwrecked on an uninhabited island combines gripping adventure with instruction in practical domesticity and natural history. The first English version was made in 1814, conjecturally by William Godwin, from Isabelle de Montolieu's French translation of Johann David Wyss's German original (1812–13). Each of these texts consisted of only a part of the whole, which was not published in its entirety in German until 1826–7. Numerous further texts of *The Swiss Family Robinson* were published throughout the nineteenth century, modernizing the language or adding to Godwin's text, sometimes using a later German edition or the later French translations of Élise Voïart and 'Pierre-Jules Stahl' (pen-name of P. J. Hetzel) as their base. The textual and publishing history of *The Swiss Family Robinson* is extraordinarily complicated and provides a further example of the role of French in mediating German literature during the eighteenth and nineteenth centuries. Remarkably, the book is better known in the English-speaking world than in Switzerland or Germany.

France produced two further Robinsonades that made an impact in English. Madame Mallès de Beaulieu's *Le Robinson de douze ans* (1818) was anonymously translated as *The Young Robinson* (1825, second edition) with the subtitle 'an interesting narrative of a French cabin boy who was shipwrecked on an uninhabited island'. A sequel to the events of *The Swiss Family Robinson* was written by Adrien Paul and translated as *Willis the Pilot* (1857).

History, Adventure, and Contemporary Life

Linked with the Robinsonades and infused to some degree with didacticism are several books dealing with historical themes and adventure. J. H. Campe's *Polar Scenes, exhibited in the Voyages of Heemskirk and Barenz to the Northern Regions* (Anon. 1821) follows the success of his earlier books about America (1799, 1800a, 1800b), which were translated by Elizabeth Helme. Two French works from this period enjoyed great success in translation. Madame Cottin's *Elizabeth, ou Les Exilés de Sibérie* (tr. Anon. 1808) owes its Europe-wide popularity to the combination of an exemplary love story with the heroine's Christian fortitude in walking from Siberia to Moscow to plead with the Emperor for a pardon for her father, an exiled Polish nobleman; it was often reprinted alongside translations of Bernardin de Saint-Pierre's *Paul et Virginie*. In a different way J. P. C. de Florian's *William Tell* also pleads the cause of the victims of tyranny and adds a youthful love story. It was first translated by William B. Hewetson in 1809 and again, rather freely, by Barbara Hofland in 1823 (see Blamires 1995).

From the middle of the century several books by the German writer Gustav Nieritz were translated. The most popular seems to have been *Der junge Trommelschläger*, a story about the horrors of the Napoleonic wars, translated by different hands as *Duty and Affection* (Anon. 1850, wrongly attributed to the non-existent Gustav Moritz), *The Little Drummer* (1859), and *The German Drummer Boy* (new edition, 1883). Other translations were *The Ratcatcher's Magic Whistle, or, The Children of Hameln* (Anon. c.1873), a retelling of the Pied Piper story; *The Exiles of Salzburg* (Anon. c.1888), a story about the protestants expelled by the Archbishop of Salzburg, and *Menzikoff, or, The Danger of Wealth* (Anon. c.1895), which focuses on the rise and fall of the favourite of Peter the Great. Though Nieritz's books were taken up largely for their strong Protestant themes, they introduced British children to a broad range of European history. More adventure material without the moral ballast was provided by Friedrich Gerstäcker in such books as *The Little Whaler* (1857).

While most translated authors were male, several women writers, usually dealing with themes from contemporary life, began to emerge. A work by Amalie Schoppe was translated by Susan Cobbett in 1860, *Henry and Mary, or, The Little Orphans*. Marie Nauthusius' *Tagebuch eines armen Fräuleins* (1854), the story of an impoverished young Christian lady who is forced to become a governess, was translated five times into English in scarcely more than a dozen years (1857–69). The first was an anonymous American translation entitled *Louisa von Plettenhaus* (1857). Of the two British translations *The Diary of a Poor Young Gentlewoman* (1860) was made by M. Anna Childs but with no indication of the German author's name, while *Step by Step, or, The Good Fight* (also 1860) appeared anonymously. *Christfried's First Journey, and Other Tales* (c.1871) was also published without Nauthusius' name. A few books by Ottilie Wildermuth were also translated into English, the most popular being *The Holidays at Bärenburg Castle*, first translated by either Mary or William Howitt in 1861; it is particularly interesting for its detailed descriptions of German life. However, the enduring success in this more realistic mode was Johanna Spyri's *Heidi*, a complex, subtle tale of a Swiss orphan girl whose vigorous personality transforms the character of her crusty grandfather, the peasant boy Peter in her Alpine home district, and Klara, the sick girl in Frankfurt to whom she is sent as a companion. Published in German in 1880–1, *Heidi* remains popular today. The first (British and anonymous) translation (1882–4) was deservedly displaced by two extremely successful American versions: Louise Brooks (1885) and Helen B. Dole (1889), the latter still in print in 2000. Dole aimed particularly at retaining the Swiss character and names of the original (for further details see O'Sullivan 2004).

After all this German material we have to note one French work: Hector Malot's *Sans famille* (1877–8), translated by May Laffan with the title *No Relations* (1880). As soon as it was known in English, abridgements and adaptations of the French were made as a language-learning tool for the school market (see Steel 1995: 90–1). And of course many other popular French novelists such as Alexandre Dumas *père* and Jules Verne were frequently read by young people as well as adults (for fuller discussion see pp. 238–40 and 379, above).

Fantasy

The vein of fantasy is strong in children's writing, and several classics of European literature have made their mark here. Spain made virtually no impact through its children's books, but adaptations of *Don Quijote* proved perennially entertaining for English children. An edition abridged from Charles Jarvis's translation was published in 1778 and reissued in 1806. A short verse toy book version illustrated by Percy Cruikshank appeared c.1855. Other adaptations for children were made by M. Jones (1871), C. L. Matéaux (c.1872), and 'Sir Marvellous Crackjoke' (1872). A version by Judge Parry, based largely on Thomas Shelton's 1612 translation, appeared in 1900 and is best known for its illustrations by Walter Crane.

One outstanding book from the German Romantics specially written for children is E. T. A. Hoffmann's *Nussknacker und Mausekönig* (Nutcracker and

Mouse King), which has had a chequered history in translation. The embedded fairy tale of 'The Hard Nut' was engagingly translated from the German as 'The History of Krakatuk' in 1833 (the translation has been attributed to Thackeray), but the first complete version did not appear until 1847, when the French adaptation of Alexandre Dumas *père* was translated into English. Dumas's version was used as the basis of Tchaikovsky's ballet and thus dominated the English reception of Hoffmann's story. The first complete translation from the German was made by Major Alexander Ewing in *The Serapion Brethren* (1886), and it was followed in 1892 by a second, specifically for children, by Ascott R. Hope, published in Unwin's Children's Library series. Ewing's careful scholarly translation keeps close to the original in style and vocabulary, while Hope tends to simplify and gives the children English names.

Unwin's Children's Library issued several other translations, among them *Tales from the Mabinogion* (1892), taken from Lady Charlotte Guest (see pp. 300–1, above), and Standish O'Grady's *Finn and his Companions* (1892, taken from Irish legends), but its major coup was *The Story of a Puppet, or, The Adventures of Pinocchio* (1892) by Carlo Collodi, translated by M. A. Murray. This was the first appearance in English of the great Italian children's classic whose popularity remains undimmed more than a century later. Mary Alice Murray's translation has stood the test of time and is still in print. It faithfully conveys the directness, ironic humour, and pathos of the original as Collodi leads Pinocchio through the twists and turns of his captivating story.

Picture Books

Illustration was significant in children's books throughout the nineteenth century, but around the mid-century with a few particular authors the image became the leading element. Heinrich Hoffmann both drew the pictures and composed the verses for his *Struwwelpeter, or, Shock-Headed Peter*, and the combination of immediately recognizable pictures and comic horror stories in verse exercised an extraordinary influence in Britain and the United States from its first appearance in English in 1848. The pictures were taken over directly from the German editions. The first translation, published in Leipzig with no name, became the standard version as far as the verses are concerned. Eight different British translations were published between 1848 and 1910, since when no new ones have been made (for further details see O'Sullivan 2000). The pictures remained those of Hoffmann. The book became so popular in Britain that it gave rise to numerous parodies. Another book of Hoffmann's, *King Nut-Cracker, or, The Dream of Poor Reinhold*, partly reminiscent of E. T. A. Hoffmann's story, was translated by J. R. Planché (1855*b*) but was hardly a success. Then, riding, as it were, on the back of *Struwwelpeter*, Adolf Glassbrenner and Theodor Hosemann's *Lachende Kinder* (1850) was translated by Madame de Chatelain, noted for her interest in German material, as *A Laughter Book for Little Folk* (*c*.1851), though it was Hosemann's pictures that were the focus. Hosemann was one of the best German illustrators of the day, but in this book he chooses to imitate Heinrich Hoffmann's naïve style.

An earlier and more traditional picture book was *The Child's Picture and Verse Book: Commonly Called Otto Speckter's Fable Book* (1844), Mary Howitt's translation of fables by Wilhelm Hey, illustrated by Otto Speckter. Another translation was made by Henry W. Dulcken (1858). Speckter's work was not always well reproduced. The younger German artist Oscar Pletsch, who is noted for scenes of domestic and rural harmony, was represented by at least seventeen books published in Britain between 1862–75. Typical of his work are *Little Lily's Alphabet* (1865) and *Buds and Flowers of Childish Life* (1870).

During the last third of the nineteenth century the major figure was Wilhelm Busch, an artist and poet with a mordant sense of humour. His most famous work, *Max und Moritz*, was first translated in the United States in 1871, with a different translation being published in 1874 in London and Munich. Several other books by Busch also appeared. The first was *A Bushel of Merrythoughts* (1868) with the verses adapted by W. H. Rogers, reprinted in a slightly different form as *A Book of Merry Thoughts* in the *Books for the Bairns* (1900). *Die fromme Helene* was translated by John MacLush as *Pious Jemima* (1872), and in the same year *Schnurrdiburr oder die Bienen* was turned by W. C. Cotton into *Buzz a Buzz, or, The Bees*. Several other short items were presented with colour illustrations as *Fools Paradise* (1872, reprinted 1883), while a further collection was translated by H. W. Dulcken as *Hookeybeak the Raven, and Other Tales* (1878). Busch's witty and sardonic words have not translated into English as memorably as Heinrich Hoffmann's, but his skilful drawings make their impact still.

A considerable number of fairy-tale collections, fantasies, adventure stories, and comic books have become enduring classics and are still widely read today in nineteenth-century translations, though some of these are, by today's standards, misleading.

LIST OF SOURCES

Translations
Anon. (1791). *Popular Tales of the Germans* [Musäus]. London.
Anon. (1808). *Elizabeth, or, The Exiles of Siberia* [Cottin], 2nd edn. London.
Anon. (1821). *Polar Scenes* [Campe]. London.
Anon. (1825). *The Young Robinson* [Mallès de Beaulieu]. London.
Anon. (1827). *Fairy Tales* [A. L. Grimm]. London.
Anon. (1844). *Popular Tales* [Hauff]. Rugeley and London.
Anon. (1845a). *Legends of Rubezahl, and Other Tales* [Musäus]. London.
Anon. (1845b). *Select Popular Tales of Wilhelm Hauff*. London.
Anon. (1846). *The King of the Swans, and Other Tales* [Rudolphi]. London.
Anon. (1847a). *The History of a Nutcracker* [Dumas/E. T. A. Hoffmann]. London.
Anon. (1847b). *Tales from the Eastern-Land* [A. L. Grimm]. London.
Anon. (1848). *The English Struwwelpeter, or, Pretty Stories and Funny Pictures for Little Children* [Heinrich Hoffmann]. Leipzig.
Anon. (1850). *Duty and Affection* [Nieritz]. Edinburgh.
Anon. (1854). *The Old Story-Teller* [Bechstein]. London.
Anon. (1860). *Step by Step, or, The Good Fight* [Nauthusius]. London.

Anon. (*c*.1871). *Christfried's First Journey, and Other Tales* [Nauthusius]. London.
Anon. (*c*.1873). *The Ratcatcher's Magic Whistle, or, The Children of Hameln* [Nieritz]. London.
Anon. (*c*.1888). *The Exiles of Salzburg* [Nieritz]. London.
Anon. (*c*.1895). *Menzikoff, or, The Danger of Wealth* [Nieritz]. London.
Austin, Sarah (1834). *The Story without an End* [Carové]. London.
Bedell, G. T. (1833). *The Basket of Flowers* [Christoph von Schmid]. Philadelphia, PA.
Boner, Charles (1846). *A Danish Story Book* [Andersen]. London.
Brækstad, H. L. (1880). *Northern Fairy Tales* [Asbjørnsen and Andersen]. London.
—— (1881). *Round the Yule Log* [Asbjørnsen]. London.
—— (1887). *Fairy Tales from the Far North* [Asbjørnsen]. London.
Brooks, Louise (1884). *Heidi: Her Years of Wandering and Learning* and *Heidi: How She Used What She Learned* [Spyri]. Boston.
Chatelain, Madame de (*c*.1851). *A Laughter Book for Little Folk* [Glassbrenner/Hosemann]. London.
Childs, M. Anna (1860). *The Diary of a Poor Young Gentlewoman* [Nauthusius]. London.
Cobbett, Susan (1860). *Henry and Mary, or, The Little Orphans* [Schoppe]. London.
Crane, Lucy (1882). *Household Stories* [Grimms]. London.
Dasent, George Webbe (1842). *Popular Tales from the Norse* [Asbjørnsen and Moe]. Edinburgh.
—— (1874). *Tales from the Fjeld* [Asbjørnsen]. London.
Davis, Matilda (1855). *Home Stories* [Grimms]. London.
Dole, Helen B. (1899). *Heidi's Years of Learning and Travel* and *Heidi Makes Use of What She Has Learned* [Spyri]. Boston.
Dulcken, Henry W. (1858). *Picture Fables* [Hey/Speckter]. London.
—— (1864). *Stories and Tales* [Andersen]. London.
Eckenstein, L. (1893). *The Little Glass Man and Other Stories* [Hauff]. London.
Ewing, Alexander (1886). *The Serapion Brethren* [E. T. A. Hoffmann], 2 vols. London.
[Godwin, William?] (1814). *The Family Robinson Crusoe* [Wyss]. London.
[Hanstein, J. T.] (1845). *Select Popular Tales from the German of Musaeus*. London.
Helme, Elizabeth (1799). *The Discovery of America* [Campe]. London.
—— (1800*a*). *Cortes, or, The Discovery of Mexico* [Campe]. London.
—— (1800*b*). *Pizarro, or, The Conquest of Peru* [Campe]. London.
Hewetson, William B. (1809). *William Tell, or, Swisserland Delivered* [Florian]. London.
Hick, R. (1855). *Robinson the Younger, or, The New Crusoe* [Campe]. London.
Hofland, Barbara (1823). *William Tell, or, The Patriot of Switzerland* [Florian]. London.
Hope, Ascott R. (1892). *Nutcracker and Mouse King* [E. T. A. Hoffmann]. London.
Howitt, Mary (1844). *The Child's Picture and Verse Book: Commonly Called Otto Speckter's Fable Book* [Hey/Speckter]. London.
—— (1846). *Wonderful Stories for Children* [Andersen]. London.
Howitt, Mary or William (1861). *The Holidays at Bärenburg Castle* [Wildermuth]. London.
Hunt, Margaret (1884). *Grimms' Household Tales*. London.
Jacobs, Joseph (1892). *Indian Fairy Tales*. London.
—— (1892). *Celtic Fairy Tales*. London.
—— (1894). *More Celtic Fairy Tales*. London.
Keightley, Thomas (1834). *Tales and Popular Fictions*. London.
Laffan, Mary (1880). *No Relations* [Malot]. London.
Lemon, Mark (1864). *Legends of Number Nip* [Musäus]. London.

Lemon, Mark (1868). *Fairy Tales* [Musäus]. London.
Lewis, M. G. (1849). *Fairy Tales and Romances* [Hamilton]. London.
Macdonell, Annie, and Lee, Miss (1892). *The Fairy Tales of Madame d'Aulnoy*. London.
Mendel, S. (1886). *Tales by Wilhelm Hauff*. London.
Murray, M. A. (1892). *The Story of a Puppet, or, The Adventures of Pinocchio* [Collodi]. London.
O'Callaghan, M. (1886). *Dreams by a French Fireside* [Volkmann-Leander]. London.
Oxenford, John, and Feiling, C. A. (1844). *Tales from the German* [Hauff]. London.
Paull, Mrs H. B. [1872]. *Grimms' Fairy Tales*. London.
[Peachey, Caroline] (1846). *Danish Fairy Legends and Tales* [Andersen]. London.
Pinkerton, Percy E. (1881). *Longnose the Dwarf and Other Fairy Tales* [Hauff]. London.
Planché, J. R. (1855*a*). *Fairy Tales by the Countess d'Aulnoy*. London.
—— (1855*b*). *King Nut-Cracker, or, The Dream of Poor Reinhold* [Heinrich Hoffmann]. London.
Raleigh, J. (1890). *Dreams by a French Fireside* [Volkmann-Leander]. London.
St A., J. H. (1857). *The Basket of Flowers* [Christoph von Schmid]. London.
Steinkopff, Ann (1828). *The Little Dove* [Krummacher]. London.
[Taylor, Edgar] (1823–6). *German Popular Stories* [Grimms], 2 vols. London.
Taylor, John Edward (1846). *The Fairy Ring* [Grimms]. London.
Thoms, W. J. (1834). *Lays and Legends of Various Nations* [Grimms]. London.
Wheelock, Lucy (1889). *Swiss Stories for Children and Those Who Love Children* [Spyri]. London.
Wollstonecraft, Mary (1790). *Elements of Morality* [Salzmann]. London.

Other Sources
Alderson, Brian (1982). *Hans Christian Andersen and his Eventyr in England*. Wormley.
Blamires, David (1994). 'Christoph von Schmid's Religious Tales for Children: German and English Versions.' *Bulletin of the John Rylands University Library of Manchester* 76/3: 69–82.
—— (1995). 'Politics, Religion and Family Values in English Children's Versions of the William Tell Story.' *New Comparison* 20: 61–74.
—— (2001). 'The Reception of Musäus's Fairytales in English up to 1900.' *New Comparison* 31: 23–34.
Butler, G. P. (1999). 'Beckford and Musäus: A Likely Pair?', pp. 24–35 in Eoin Bourke, Roisin Ni Néill, and Michael Shields, eds., *Schein und Widerschein. Festschrift für T. J. Casey*. Galway.
Gumuchian (1979). *Les Livres de l'enfance du XVe au XIXe siècle*, 2 vols. London (first pub. 1930).
Hill, Ruth A., and de Bondeli, Elsa (1937). *Children's Books from Foreign Languages: English Translations from Published and Unpublished Sources*. New York.
Macdonald, Duncan B. (1937). 'A Bibliographical and Literary Study of the First Appearance of the *Arabian Nights* in Europe.' *Library Quarterly* 2: 387–420.
McLean, Ruari (1976). *Joseph Cundall: A Victorian Publisher*. Pinner.
Moon, Marjorie (1976). *John Harris's Books for Youth 1801–1843*. Cambridge.
O'Sullivan, Emer (2000). ' "Anything to me is sweeter…": British Translations of Heinrich Hoffmann's *Struwwelpeter*.' *Princeton University Library Chronicle* 62/1: 59–71.
—— (2004). 'The Little Swiss Girl from the Mountains: Heidi in englischen Übersetzungen', pp. 139–62 in Schweizer Institut für Kinder- und Jugendmedien, ed., *Johanna Spyri und ihr Werk—Lesarten*. Zurich.

Renier, Anne (1972). *The Basket of Flowers by Christoph von Schmid: A Checklist of Copies in the Renier Collection*. Stroud.
Roscoe, S. (1973). *John Newbery and his Successors 1740–1814*. Wormley.
St John, Judith (1975). *The Osborne Collection of Early Children's Books: A Catalogue*, 2 vols. Toronto.
Skrine, Peter (1994). 'Johanna Spyri's *Heidi*.' *Bulletin of the John Rylands University Library of Manchester* 76/3: 145–64.
Steel, David (1995). 'Hector Malot, *Sans Famille* and the Sense of Adventure.' *New Comparison* 20: 75–95.
Sutton, Martin (1996). *The Sin-Complex: A Critical Study of the English Versions of the Grimms' Kinder- und Hausmärchen in the Nineteenth Century*. Kassel.

9
Texts for Music and Oral Literature

9.1	**Hymns** *J. R. Watson*	411
9.2	**Opera, Oratorio, Song** *Denise Gallo*	420
9.3	**Oral Literature** *Kenneth Haynes*	430

9.1 Hymns

J. R. Watson

The nineteenth century is a high point in the translation of hymns into English. The principal examples were from Latin and from German, although Greek hymns were not far behind, and there were some translations from Danish and other languages. The activity was remarkable: Julian's *Dictionary of Hymnology* lists 133 translations of the 'Dies Irae', 38 of 'Adeste fideles', 37 of 'Vexilla regis prodeunt', and 34 of 'Veni sancte Spiritus', together with 68 of 'Ein' feste Burg ist unser Gott'. These hymns made up a surprisingly large component of some hymn books: the 1875 edition of *Hymns Ancient and Modern* contained 462 hymns, of which 143 were from Latin, 10 from Greek, and 13 from German.

Translation, in the intense religious climate of the nineteenth century, could never be a neutral activity. While the sea of faith was on the ebb, as Matthew Arnold saw, the religious energy of the Victorian Church continued unabated, all the more intensely because of the threats it perceived in secularism, science, and rationalism. In this context, the translation of hymns was more than the provision of new texts for the people to sing. It was an ideological statement. Anglo-Catholics, or 'Puseyites' as they were sometimes called (after E. B. Pusey), were ranged against Evangelicals, 'High Church' against 'Low Church'. Latin and Greek hymns tended to be Anglo-Catholic; German ones protestant.

German Hymns

It was Thomas Carlyle, from outside this English in-fighting, who produced the first great hymn translation of the nineteenth century from the German. Carlyle had been working on a history of German literature, and cherished hopes of writing a separate book on Luther, 'the great German Lion'. His essay entitled 'Luther's Psalm' was published in *Fraser's Magazine* in 1831. In it he translated Luther's rendering of Psalm 46, 'Ein' feste Burg ist unser Gott', a text 'probably never before printed in England'. The translation is bold, matching the rough and strong consonants of Luther's lines, the 'cht's and the 't's, and the hard 'a' vowel sounds:

> Mit unsrer Macht ist nichts gethan,
> Wir sind gar bald verloren.

Carlyle adds his own image of battle to make up for the less harsh English: for 'verloren' (lost) there is 'down-ridden':

> With force of arms we nothing can,
> Full soon were we down-ridden.
> (Carlyle 1899: II, 163)

The language is deliberately inverted: it would be possible to see Carlyle's unusual style as evidence of his impatience with the Church of 1831, preoccupied as it was with its problems over Roman Catholic emancipation and looking for help from what John Keble had recently called (in the preface to *The Christian Year*, 1827) 'the *soothing* tendency in the Prayer Book'. Carlyle's translation turns its back on the idea that religion should soothe: religion for Carlyle was a fight, and Luther, like Christ in the hymn, was the 'proper Man'.

Carlyle's translation could be sung to Luther's tune as it kept close to his metre. A similar fidelity was found in *Sacred Hymns from the German* (1841), by Frances Elizabeth Cox. Cox's book printed the German and English texts opposite each other, to allow the reader to compare the two. Her principles of translation were similar to those of Carlyle:

> It is hoped that the translations will be found to give not only a faithful version, but, so far as the English language will admit, a close expression of the style and character of the originals, the metre having been retained, in order to keep up the resemblance as much as possible. (Cox 1841: vii–viii)

Cox liked to use quantitatively similar words, such as 'confidence' for 'Zuversicht'. This is the first verse of a hymn by Christian Fürchtegott Gellert:

> Jesus lebt, mit ihm auch ich: Jesus lives! no longer now
> Tod, wo sind nun deine Schrecken?   Can thy terrors, Death, appal me;
> Er, er lebt und wird auch mich   Jesus lives! and this I know,
> Von den Todten auferwecken: From the dead he will recall me;
> Er verklärt mich in sein Licht;   Brighter scenes will then commence;
> Diese ist meine Zuversicht.   This shall be my confidence.
> (Cox 1841: 35)

Cox managed to avoid the awkwardness of the German first line, and she was faithful to the metre, using words such as 'own' and 'all' as fillers. But a line such as 'Brighter scenes will then commence' suggests that her effort to render the German faithfully sometimes led her into the stilted and artificial. This may also have been the result of her laudable attempt to follow the German trochaic metre, something in which Catherine Winkworth (on whom see also p. 126, above) allowed herself more freedom.

Winkworth, like Cox, had had her attention drawn to German hymns by C. K. J. von Bunsen, the scholarly Prussian diplomat and man of letters. It was Bunsen's selection of German hymns, *Versuch eines allgemeinen evangelischen Gesang- und Gebetbuch, zum Kirchen- und Hausegebrauch*, which inspired Winkworth to produce *Lyra Germanica* (first series, 1855; second series, 1858), a book which signalled a great new awareness of German hymnody: five of its hymns were printed in *Hymns Ancient and Modern* in 1861. The two volumes contained hymns such as 'Now thank we all our God', 'Deck thyself, my soul with gladness', 'All my heart this night rejoices', 'Christ the Lord is risen again'. *The Chorale Book for England*, which followed in 1863, contained 'Praise to the Lord, the Almighty, the King of Creation' and 'Jesu, priceless treasure'.

Writing to her fellow translator, Richard Massie, Winkworth gave some insights into her practice:

With regard to form, I should claim more latitude than you find it necessary to allow yourself. But a hymn that sounds popular and homelike in its own language must sound so in ours if it is to be really available for devotional purposes, and it seems to me allowable for this object to make such alterations in the metre, as lie in the different nature of the language; that is, especially, to substitute in most cases single for double rhymes and in some few cases to adopt an iambic measure for a trochaic. I think the change to iambic measure adds dignity and force occasionally where the trochaic melts into too great softness.
(Shaen 1908: 181)

Winkworth's success as a translator was owing to her ability to get round the awkwardness of the literal meaning of the German. She translated the following hymn by Georg Neumark twice:

> Wer nur den lieben Gott lässt walten
> Und hoffet auf ihn allerzeit,
> Den wird er wunderbar erhalten
> In allem Kreuz und Traurigkeit.
> Wer Gott, dem Allerhöchsten, traut,
> Der hat auf keinen Sand gebaut.

The first translation was in the 1855 *Lyra Germanica*, using a truncated form of Neumark's metre, and beginning:

> Leave God to order all thy ways,
> And hope in him whate'er betide.
> (Winkworth 1855–8: I, 152)

The first line makes much of the German 'lässt', turning the verb 'walten' ('prevail') into 'order thy ways', but loses 'nur' ('only'). The second version, Hymn 134 in *The Chorale Book for England*, not only uses Neumark's metre (and tune), but is more faithful to the original:

> If thou but suffer God to guide thee,
> And hope in him through all thy ways.

This keeps 'nur' as 'but', and throws the emphasis more on 'guide' rather than 'suffer', which receives less stress, as it should; while the second line translates the original 'Und hoffet auf ihn allerzeit' very simply. The last two lines of the verse (the same in both translations), by contrast, show how Winkworth could take the original and modify it with an appropriate freedom. The man 'Der hat auf keinen Sand gebaut' ('who has built on no sand') becomes:

> Who trusts in God's unchanging love
> Builds on the rock which cannot move.
> (Hymn 134)

This is a free rendering, using the parable to avoid the difficulty of fitting the literal translation into the verse. It was this knowledge of when to depart from the original and when to stick with it that marked out Winkworth's hymns. As Bunsen noted with delight, they sounded natural in English: 'her really wonderful translations seem to promise to effect what hitherto has proved impossible—namely, to *naturalize* in England the German *Hymns*, the most immortal literary fruit of the Reformation' (Shaen 1908: 139).

This is a reminder that German hymns were associated with protestantism. It is found most clearly in Richard Massie's *Martin Luther's Spiritual Songs* of 1854. Massie, a Cheshire vicar, prefaced his translations with a long preface which nailed his colours to the mast: 'For my own part, the longer I live, the more I learn to bless God for the Reformation and the Reformers' (1854: xiii). Luther was the greatest of the reformers because 'he was the first to lay the axe to the root of the tree' and because he was 'a man of faith'. This sense of Luther's pre-eminence was further enhanced by the title of a popular series of little books, *Hymns from the Land of Luther*, by two sisters, Jane Laurie Borthwick and Sarah Laurie Findlater. Other women translators included Eleanor, Lady Fortescue (*Hymns, Mostly Taken from the German*, 1843), Catherine Hannah Dunn (*Hymns from the German*, 1857), Henrietta Joan Fry (*Hymns of the Reformation by Dr M. Luther and Others from the German*, 1845), and Jane Montgomery Campbell, who translated the robust and jolly harvest hymn by Matthias Claudius, 'Wir pflügen und wir streuen' ('We plough the fields and scatter', printed in C. S. Bere, *A Garland of Song, or, An English Liederkranz* of 1862).

Latin and Greek Hymns

Most of the translators of German hymns were women, which is an indication of the educational provision of the time. These brilliant young women linguists were excluded from the universities. Their German was acquired through local classes for ladies and (occasionally) from study in Germany itself (Shaen 1908: 15 ff.). The translation of Latin and Greek hymns, on the other hand, was almost entirely done by men, most of whom were in holy orders. As the products of the public schools and of Oxford and Cambridge, they had spent years of their lives writing verse in Greek and Latin and in classical metres; the gradual introduction of hymns into the worship of the Church of England during the first half of the nineteenth century was in part owing to this Oxford/Cambridge male-dominated clerical society and its discovery of pre-Reformation hymnody.

Latin hymns also suited those who wanted the Church of England to become more 'Catholic', who stressed its unbroken continuity with the Church of St Peter, and who wanted it to have authority over its own affairs rather than being subject to government interference. Greek and Latin were a link with the early Church, both in the earliest times and in the Middle Ages. While the rediscovery of monastic hymns may be said to be a part of the medieval dreaming of the nineteenth century, the spread of translated hymns from the classical languages also satisfied a craving for Apostolic or Primitive Christianity. It was an attempt to get back to a world before the Reformation. To this end John Henry Newman produced a selection of texts, *Hymni Ecclesiae* (1838), from the Roman and Paris breviaries.

The new hymnody was in touch with ancient rituals and seasonal splendours: with the lighting of the lamps, or the seven 'O's of Advent which form the structure of 'O come, O come Emmanuel'. It made use of the breviaries, either from Rome or Milan or Paris, or from pre-Reformation England, such as those from Sarum, York, and Hereford. One of the earliest translators to use these was Richard Mant, who published *Ancient Hymns from the Roman Breviary, for Domestic Use* in 1837. His hymn 'Bright the vision that delighted', entitled 'Hymn commemorative of the "Thrice Holy" ', was characteristic of the emphasis on splendour in worship.

One of those who followed Newman into the Roman Catholic Church was Edward Caswall. Caswall's *Lyra Catholica* (1849) contained 'Bethlehem! of noblest cities', from Prudentius; 'Jesus, the very thought of thee', from a twelfth-century text beginning 'Jesu, dulcis memoria'; and 'Come, thou Holy Spirit, come', from a thirteenth-century text, 'Veni, sancte Spiritus', attributed to Pope Innocent III. Caswall's images resemble those of early Italian painting, as in 'Bethlehem, of noblest cities' ('O sola magnarum urbium', 'O alone—incomparable—of great cities') where he writes of the nativity star:

> By its lambent beauty guided,
>   See, the eastern kings appear;
>   See them bend, their gifts to offer, —
> Gifts of incense, gold, and myrrh.
>   (1849: 55)

'Lambent', meaning 'shining with a soft clear light', is Caswall's addition to the Latin, which is simple and unadorned:

> Videre postquam illum magi
>   Eoa promunt munera,
> Stratique votes offerunt
>   Thus, myrrham et aurum regium.

Caswall often responds to and amplifies images of light, as in the Advent hymn:

Vox clara ecce intonat	Hark! an awful voice is sounding
Obscura quaeque increpat:	'Christ is nigh!', it seems to say;
Pellantur eminus somnia	'Cast away the dreams of darkness,
Ab aethere Christus promicat.	O ye children of the day!'
	(1849: 46)

'Awful' is an odd translation for 'clara', though appropriate for Advent. It may be Caswall's attempt to bring in 'increpat', which can mean 'chides' as well as 'makes a noise'. Keble preferred 'Give ear! The voice rings clear and true', which takes care of 'clara' but adds its own gloss. 'Thrilling' is the adjective that appears most frequently in English versions, though there is one strangely artificial rendering from the *Hymnarium Anglicanum* of 1844 beginning 'In music, lo, yon orb appears to rise' (though this is not so bizarre as the Chaucerian 'Hark, hark, the voice of chanticleer' by J. Wallace in 1874). As sometimes happened with Latin hymns, the text was altered in a rewriting of the *Roman Breviary*, in this case to 'En clara vox redarguit'. Mant's version of this began 'Hark, a voice of warning, hark', in an admonitory mood like that of Caswall, but Newman translated that first line quite differently with 'Hark, a joyful voice is thrilling'.

The most effective translator of Latin and Greek hymns was John Mason Neale. His *Mediaeval Hymns and Sequences* (1851) included versions of 'Pange lingua gloriosi' ('Sing, my tongue, the glorious battle') and 'Vexilla regis prodeunt' ('The royal banners forward go'), attributed to Venantius Fortunatus, and the hymn for Palm Sunday, 'Gloria, laus, et honor' ('All glory, laud, and honour'). Neale's translations have an extraordinary assurance:

> Jerusalem the golden!
>   With milk and honey blest,
> Beneath thy contemplation
>   Sink heart and voice opprest:
> I know not, oh I know not
>   What social joys are there,
> What radiancy of glory
>   What light beyond compare.
>   (Neale 1851: 57)

This hymn (from the *De Contemptu Mundi* of Bernard of Morlaix, or Cluny) was one of the few occasions when Neale departed from the Latin metre, 'because our language, if it could be tortured to any distant resemblance of its rhythm, would fail to give any idea of the majestic sweetness which invests it in Latin' (Neale 1851: 69). The Latin text shows how closely he followed Bernard (even the touching repetition of 'nescio, nescio') in everything except this complex metre, with what Neale described as 'a dactylic hexameter, divided into three parts ... a tailed rhyme, and feminine leonine rhyme between the two first clauses':

> Urbs Syon aurea, patria lactea, cive decora,
> omne cor obruis, omnibus obstruis, et cor et ora.
> Nescio, nescio, quae iubilatio, lux tibi qualis,
> Quam socialia gaudia, gloria quam specialis.

In his *Hymns of the Eastern Church* (1862) Neale noted that 'there is scarcely a first or second-rate hymn of the Roman Breviary which has not been translated' and that 'of many we have six or eight versions' (1862: xi). But, he went on, there had been little use of Greek hymns. Although Keble had published one of the earliest known hymns, 'Hail, gladdening light', in 1834, it was Neale who pioneered the more extensive use of Greek hymns, with 'The day is past and over', 'A great and mighty wonder', 'The day of resurrection', and 'O happy band of pilgrims'. His note on 'the second Epoch' of Greek hymnody, the age of the Iconoclasts, made it clear where he stood with respect to the Reformation:

Till Calvinism, and its daughter Rationalism, showed the ultimate development of Iconoclastic principles, it must have been well-nigh impossible to realize the depth of feeling on the side of the Church, or the greatness of the interests attacked by their opponents... The supporters of Icons, by universal consent, numbered amongst their ranks all that was pious and venerable in the Eastern Church. (1862: 15–16)

This Tractarian link between beauty and religion is found most clearly in Robert Bridges' *Yattendon Hymnal*, published in four parts (1895–9). Bridges had been brought up on *The Christian Year*, 'a book regarded in my family as good poetry, and given to us on Sunday to learn by heart' (Ritz 1960: 10); at school he thought of himself and his friends as Puseyites. His hymnal was beautifully printed, in contrast to the serviceable ordinariness of *Hymns Ancient and Modern*, which, said Bridges, 'when it is opened fills the sensitive worshipper with dismay' (Ritz 1960: 130). He used many standard translations in the book, including those of the 'Dies irae' and the 'Stabat mater', but included his own from both Latin and German, and also from the Greek ('O gladsome light, O grace', an alternative to Keble's 'Hail, gladdening light'). In the case of the Latin hymns, he printed the Latin text next to the English, so that the tune could be used for either. He was bold in the use of archaisms or unusual words, provided that they allowed the metre and rhyme to be preserved:

Jesu, Thou King of highest hest,	Jesu, rex admirabilis
Whose triumph hath the world possest,	Et triumphator nobilis
Exceeding sweetness unexprest,	Dulcedo ineffabilis
All-loving loved and loveliest.	Totus desiderabilis.

(Hymn 32)

Bridges allowed himself some freedom. Paul Gerhardt's 'Nun ruhen alle Wälder' had been closely translated by Catherine Winkworth as 'Now all the woods are sleeping', but Bridges preferred:

> The duteous day now closeth,
> Each flower and tree reposeth,
>   Shade creeps o'er wild and wood:
> Let us, as night is falling,
> On God our Maker calling,
>   Give thanks to him, the Giver good.
>   (Hymn 83)

The convoluted syntax is typical of Bridges's work in translation. He was determined not to pander to current taste, to a kind of utterance which 'seems designed to make the worldly man feel at home, rather than reveal to him something of the life beyond his knowledge' (Bridges 1899–1900: 63). He was referring to music here, but his whole aim in the *Yattendon Hymnal* was to raise the standard of taste in worship, often by new translation.

Hymns from Other Sources

The two great resources for hymn translators in the nineteenth century were texts from Latin and German, with Greek as a less common alternative. There were very few translations from French in hymn books, although the dramatic 'Est-ce vous que je vois, ô mon Maître adorable' by Jacques Bridaine appeared in the 1889 *Supplement* to *Hymns Ancient and Modern*, translated by T. B. Pollock as 'My Lord, my Master, at thy feet adoring'. In the same volume there was also a translation from Danish by A. J. Mason, 'O Jesu, Blessèd Lord, to Thee' ('O Jesu, söde Jesu, dig', by Thomas Kingo). Other translations from the Danish were made by Sabine Baring-Gould for R. F. Littledale's *The People's Hymnal* of 1867 (Watson and Trickett 1988: 270), of which the best known is 'Through the night of doubt and sorrow' ('Igjennem Nat og Traengsel', by Bernhard Severin Ingemann). Although there seems to have been little significant translation of Welsh texts, other Celtic discoveries were made, and there appeared translations of work attributed to two great saints. 'I bind unto myself today', known as 'St Patrick's Breastplate' or *Lorica*, was a versification made by Cecil Frances Alexander in 1889 from an earlier prose translation; and in 1897, to mark the 1300th anniversary of the death of St Columba, Duncan MacGregor translated two sections of a hymn beginning 'In Te, Christe, credentium miserearis omnium' ('Have mercy, Christ, have mercy | On all that trust in thee'). The second of these contains the startling line in verse 2 'Christ the red Cross ascended', and both hymns bring into worship not only the traditional monastic celebration of Christ as Creator and Redeemer but also the world of earth and sky, the beauty of the northern landscape. These hymns, from so many different origins, were taken into mainstream hymn books. In them can be seen the competing richness of many traditions, serving different purposes but greatly increasing the variety available in worship.

LIST OF SOURCES

The standard reference work is still John Julian, *A Dictionary of Hymnology* (1892, revised 1907), now in process of revision. Many hymns that were translated appeared individually in hymn books throughout the century.

Translations
Anderson, John (1847). *Geistliche Lieder: Hymns from the German of Dr Martin Luther*. London.
Bere, Charles S. (1862). *A Garland of Song, or, An English Liederkranz*. London.
Bevan, Frances (1895–7). *Hymns of Ter Steegen, Suso, and Others* (first and second series). London.
Borthwick, Jane Laurie, and Findlater, Sarah Laurie (1854–62). *Hymns from the Land of Luther* (first, second, third, and fourth series). Edinburgh.
Bridges, Robert, and Wooldridge, H. E. (1895–9). *The Yattendon Hymnal*, 4 pts. Oxford.
Carlyle, Thomas (1899), 'Luther's Psalm', pp. 160–4 in Vol. 2 of *Critical and Miscellaneous Essays*. London (first pub. in *Fraser's Magazine* in 1831).
Caswall, Edward (1849). *Lyra Catholica*. London.
Cox, Frances Elizabeth (1841). *Sacred Hymns from the German*. London (2nd edn. 1864).
Dunn, Catherine Hannah (1857). *Hymns from the German*. London.
Fortescue, Eleanor Lady (1843). *Hymns, Mostly Taken from the German*. London.
Fry, Henrietta Joan (1845). *Hymns of the Reformation by Dr M. Luther and Others from the German*. London.

MacGregor, Duncan (1897). *Saint Columba: A Record and a Tribute*. Edinburgh.
Mant, Richard (1837). *Ancient Hymns from the Roman Breviary, for Domestic Use*. London.
Massie, Richard (1854). *Martin Luther's Spiritual Songs*. London.
—— (1860). *Lyra Domestica*. London.
Neale, John Mason (1851). *Mediaeval Hymns and Sequences*. London (2nd edn. 1862).
—— (1862). *Hymns of the Eastern Church*. London.
—— (1865). *Hymns, Chiefly Mediaeval, on the Joys and Glories of Paradise*. London.
Newman, John Henry (1838). *Hymni Ecclesiae*. London.
Stokes, Whitley (1866). *Goidilica . . . with eight Hymns from the Liber Hymnorum*. Calcutta.
—— (1887). *The Tripartite Life of Patrick*. London.
Walker, George (1860). *Hymns Translated or Imitated from the German*. London.
Winkworth, Catherine (1855–8). *Lyra Germanica* (first and second series). London.
—— (1863). *The Chorale Book for England*. London.

Other Sources
Bridges, Robert (1899–1900). 'A Practical Discourse on Some Principles of Hymn-Singing.' *Journal of Theological Studies* 1: 40–63.
Chadwick, Owen (1970–1). *The Victorian Church*. London.
Daniel, Hermann Adalbert (1841–56). *Thesaurus Hymnologicus*, 5 vols. Halle (Vol. 1) and Leipzig (Vols. 2–5).
Jenkyns, Richard (1980). *The Victorians and Ancient Greece*. Oxford.
Litvack, Leon (1994). *J. M. Neale and the Quest for Sobornost*. Oxford.
Luff, Alan (1990). *Welsh Hymns and their Tunes*. Carol Stream, IL.
Macdonald, Frederic W. (1899). *The Latin Hymns in the Wesleyan Hymn Book*. London.
Milgate, Wesley (1982). *Songs of the People of God: A Companion to The Australian Hymn Book / With One Voice*. London.
Phillips, C. S. (1937). *Hymnody, Past and Present*. London.
Raby, F. J. E. (1953). *A History of Christian Latin Poetry*, 2nd edn. Oxford (first pub. 1927).
Ritz, Jean-Georges (1960). *Robert Bridges and Gerard Manley Hopkins, 1863–1889: A Literary Friendship*. London.
Shaen, Margaret J. (1908). *Memorials of Two Sisters: Susanna and Catherine Winkworth*. London.
Tennyson, G. B. (1981). *Victorian Devotional Poetry: The Tractarian Mode*. Cambridge, MA.
Trench, Richard Chenevix (1849). *Sacred Latin Poetry*. London.
Wackernagel, C. E. P. (1841). *Das deutsche Kirchenlied von Martin Luther bis auf Nicolaus Herman und Ambrosius Blaurer*. Stuttgart.
Watson, J. R. (1997). *The English Hymn*. Oxford.
—— (2002). *An Annotated Anthology of Hymns*. Oxford.
Watson, Richard, and Trickett, Kenneth, eds. (1988). *Companion to Hymns and Psalms*. Peterborough.

9.2 Opera, Oratorio, Song

Denise Gallo

Rising literacy and the growing importance of amateur musicianship merged to encourage one of the most significant relationships in the arts of the nineteenth century: words and music. Vocal genres such as opera, oratorio, and art song enjoyed immense popularity; furthermore, musical adaptations of literary works also strengthened the bonds between text and music. Novels, poems, and stage plays inspired operas, while the Bible continued to provide material for oratorios and *azioni sacre*, operas in sacred trappings permitted during penitential seasons when theatres were closed. Composers culled published collections of verse for song texts, often setting some complete cycles of poems as a single opus to maintain the integrity of the original grouping. Not only were vocal compositions enjoyed in theatres and concert halls, but, because of the immense popularity of the piano and the rising middle class's new financial capability to own an instrument, piano-vocal reductions of larger works were standard fare for home entertainment. Indeed, familiarity with these repertories and the ability to perform them were considered as essential to an individual's social and cultural development as was familiarity with their literary sources.

Opera

Although English aristocrats and the mercantile class had supported opera throughout the eighteenth century, the patronage that encouraged it in continental Europe was absent; hence, a national tradition would not emerge until the twentieth century. Meanwhile, American composers, especially those writing operas, had to contend with the prejudices of their own countrymen who deemed their works inferior to European art music. Therefore, many early nineteenth-century composers contented themselves with adapting foreign operas into English-language versions. These, of course, required translations.

Vocal texts are translated either for comprehension or for performance. Although the former usually attempts to render the meaning of the original text, it does not match the syllabic stresses or rhythms of the original language or melodic line. Therefore, texts in the former category are inherently unsingable, even sections set as recitative. Performance translations, rendered specifically to be sung, must respect as much as possible the work's original musical and poetic elements, placing textual meaning second. Although genres with dialogue rather than recitative, such as the French *opéra comique* or German *Singspiel*, can employ literal translations for spoken sections, their arias, duets, trios, and choruses require performance translations. Unfortunately, the original meaning of singable translations is often obscured by heavy-handed poetry. The following excerpts from translations of Arsace's aria 'Ah! quel giorno ognor rammento' from Rossini's *Semiramide* (I.v) demonstrate the point. The first, translated by Manfredo Maggione for an 1854 performance by the Royal Italian Opera in London but published as well in the United States, is an almost literal translation appearing in the dual-language libretto sold to audiences:

> Ah! That day I e'er remember,
> Of my glory and great content.
> When I could from the barbarians
> Both preserve her life and honor.
> In these arms I bore her off
> From the vile oppressor's grasp,
> And I felt against my heart
> The quick throbbings of her own.
> (Maggione 1854: 3)

On the other hand, Charles Lamb Kenney's translation for an undated English-language performing edition based on a British production maintains the aria's rhythmic sense. Kenney, however, like other nineteenth-century translators, attempts to compensate for the change from a foreign language to the vernacular by employing stilted verse and archaic vocabulary:

> Live this day, in mem'ry shining,
> All its glories for aye enshrining;
> When from barb'rous foes insulting,
> I thy honour, thy life did wrest,
> From th'oppressor, when I tore thee,
> In my arms I fondly bore thee
> 'Gainst my heart, wildly exulting,
> Thine responded joy opprest.
> (Kenney c.1872: 80)

Throughout the nineteenth century, critics and audiences often complained that singing translations were distortions of the original libretti, for translators concocted texts that fitted pre-existing musical lines but altered the sense of the original or detracted from its poetry.

In the broadest sense, nineteenth-century translation of opera into English included parodies and pastiches. More than simply a textual or vocal rendering of a foreign work, these at one and the same time manipulated the original piece to fit the tastes of local audiences and mocked the élitism of the originals, primarily works by Italian and French composers. This love-hate relationship with foreign opera goes back to the days of Joseph Addison's *Spectator* reviews of operas in eighteenth-century London (see Fenner 1994: 66). By the early nineteenth century, such criticism abounded, but there appeared to be no common target. 'It will be remembered', Edward Sterling wrote in 1828, 'that, in recitative, many an insignificant dialogue will pass, which, in words, appears intolerable' (quoted in Fenner 1994: 592). Others resented the intrusion of arias: 'Just as you begin to take interest in the plot, your enjoyment is interrupted by a song', Edward Holmes commented (quoted in Fenner 1994: 593). In America, more radical adaptations were standard fare for minstrel troupes (discussed in Cockrell 1997 and Mahar 1999) featuring 'performers' named Signor Big-nees, Crotchiatio, Cavetino, and Madame Big Gourd in operas such as *Lend-her-de-sham money* (*Linda di Chamounix*), *Lucy-do-lam-her-more* (*Lucia di Lammermoor*), and *The Gas Ladder* (*La gazza ladra*). In addition to cultural and aesthetic comment, the minstrels of the Jacksonian democracy satirized European arts as examples of élitist culture. Nevertheless, foreign opera provided the repertory for a majority of works on British and American musical stages with works such as *The National Guard* (Auber's *La Fiancée*); *The White Lady* (Boïeldieu's *La Dame blanche*); *The Libertine* [also *Don Juan*] and *Tit for Tat* (Mozart's *Don Giovanni* and *Così fan tutte*); and *The Turkish Lovers* and *Cinderella* (Rossini's *Il turco in Italia* and *Cenerentola*). Despite nationalistic prejudices, English-speaking audiences enjoyed keeping abreast of contemporary continental culture.

Audiences actually preferred adaptations over operas performed in strict translation; indeed, the latter works were often the butt of critical reproach. As one British reviewer suggested, 'The fault of the vocal music we think generally to be in the quantity of words which are forced into the air (song), and which necessarily break up ... the softness and continuous flow of the music' (quoted in Fenner 1994: 597). William Ayrton agreed, commenting on the 'superabundance of words' necessary to a performing translation: 'It requires some skill, we confess, to restrain a translation within the syllabic compass of the original, but this ought to be done; for, unless accomplished, a sort of *chattering* will be produced, wholly at variance with musical effect' (quoted in Fenner 1994: 597). In his review of *The Turkish Lovers*, William Hazlitt stated that he preferred a work in the original because, in translation, certain phrases, when repeated in ensembles, sounded 'half-English, half-nonsense', trivializing the intended musical effect (quoted in Fenner 1994: 596).

Many composers and musicians made their reputations by adapting foreign works; two of the most famous, on both sides of the Atlantic, were the Englishmen Henry Rowley Bishop and Michael Rophino Lacy. Although his works are now commonly considered hack jobs, Bishop answered the needs of the contemporary stage with adaptations of operas by Mozart, Rossini, Boïeldieu, and Weber, among others. Honest about his manipulations of foreign works, Bishop advertised them as featuring selections from the operas of the original composer with the addition of his own 'new musick'. As musical director of Covent Garden from 1810 to 1824, his works, along with those of his contemporary Lacy, remained staples in that theatre's repertory until the 1840s. Lacy was not a composer but a theatre musician and actor. The main period of his activity in opera was from 1827 to 1833; while Bishop was centred primarily at Covent Garden, Lacy worked between that theatre and Drury Lane, translating the texts and arranging the scores he adapted. Like Bishop, he often took liberties with a score. A case in point is Lacy's adaptation of Rossini's *La Cenerentola*, produced in English as *Cinderella, or, The Fairy and the Little Glass Slipper*. Although he did employ sections of the original libretti by Jacopo Ferretti, Lacy reintroduced elements from the original fairy tale, thus bringing the work closer to a source with which the majority of his audience would be familiar. He also altered the original score by employing selections from three other operas by Rossini. The end result was decidedly one of the most popular operas on the contemporary English-speaking stage (Lacy 1994: xxiv).

Another author whose adaptations became famous was W. S. Gilbert, who transformed foreign operas into English burlesques or 'travesties'. His first was *Dulcamara, or, The Little Duck and the Great Quack* (1866), a parody of Donizetti's *L'elisir d'amore*. Although the work was less than successful, it was followed by others, among them *Robert the Devil, or, The Nun, The Dun, and The Son of a Gun* in 1868 (Meyerbeer's *Robert le diable*) and *The Pretty Druidess, or, The Mother, The Maid, and The Mistletoe Bough* in 1869 (Bellini's *Norma*). Belcore's entrance in *Dulcamara* offers a vivid demonstration of how Gilbert manipulated the original libretto to suit English humour. Instead of using the march that Donizetti had written for the character's entrance, Gilbert wrote a new text to 'Johnny comes marching home' to usher the sergeant onstage. Belcore's first air, set to the aria 'La tremenda ultrice spada' borrowed from Bellini's *I Capuleti e i Montecchi*, is peppered with typically British phrases:

> Also, Yah! Pshaw! Phew! Ugh! Pish! Tosh! Pooh! Bah!
> (aside) The only interjection that I know,
> Except, 'alas', which don't my meaning show.
> (Gilbert 1866: 7)

Gilbert's burlesques and the American minstrel shows relied on one significant factor: their audiences needed to be familiar with the original operas in order to comprehend the humour. To ensure this, minstrel troupes frequently followed travelling opera companies throughout the United States, performing black-faced versions of the musical works to which audiences had just been treated.

By the reign of Queen Victoria, the fashion changed to opera sung in Italian; indeed, works in French, German, Russian, and even English would be translated into Italian before they could be presented on the Covent Garden stage. Even though some travelling companies continued to perform operas in English throughout the United States, the arrival of noted European singers employed by industrious impresarios such as P. T. Barnum and Max Maretzek enticed audiences to original-language productions for which dual-language libretti became the standard editions. These could be purchased before a performance so that audience members could study the plot in advance; however, it was possible to read the translation and follow the original language during the opera, for house lights were still kept on during performances. Thus, with the decline of adaptations during the second half of the nineteenth century and the acceptance of original-language productions, patrons on both sides of the Atlantic came to think of opera as a foreign art form.

Selections from operas became, along with art songs and ballads, the standard fare for parlour entertainment. These pieces required singing translations, but because the pieces were out of their original context, translators (or poets, as some preferred to be identified) were often less careful about preserving the exact sense of the original text. The translators' task was to fit these famous melodies with sets of words that amateur singers could manage easily; music arrangers often had a role in preparing these pieces by adjusting note values to fit the English syllabification. One such popular piano-vocal selection was an arrangement of Manrico's 'Sconto col sangue mio' from *Il trovatore*, in which he swears on his blood his eternal love for Leonora before he is put to death. Identified only as the music of Verdi but not by the title of the opera from which it was taken, the text became 'Ah! I have sigh'd to rest me!' Other pieces of operatic sheet music were marketed by the fame of the singers who had performed them. Thus, 'At length a brilliant ray', a fairly faithful translation of 'Bel raggio lusinghier' from *Semiramide* published in the 1860s by Oliver Ditson in Boston, was promoted on the fame of Miss Adelaide Kemble, the popular English soprano who had sung the piece. These piano-vocal arrangements featured simplified versions of the original melodies with little or no vocal ornamentation suggested. While some selections contained the original foreign-language text as well as the translation, many contained only the English lyrics; therefore, the translators were credited on the sheet music, not the original librettists. Such treatment, in many ways, took these pieces out of the realm of opera and into that of the art song.

Oratorio

In his musical memoirs of 1862, Henry F. Chorley noted, 'The English people (since Handel's time, at least) have always cultivated a taste and relish for choral singing' (Chorley 1984: I, 59). Hence, composers of oratorios found their work in this genre readily accepted. Also, because oratorio is formally and structurally similar to opera (both employ recitative, aria, and chorus), composers were given the opportunity to experiment in an area in which they could be respected along with their continental counterparts. With a large number of amateur choral groups, oratorios in English were in demand. Only professional choirs and, in the United States, certain areas with immigrant populations (such as Moravian communities in Pennsylvania) were able to perform oratorios in German, French, and Italian. Nevertheless, some of these compositions from European repertories became popular and therefore required English texts.

A prominent case of oratorio translation is that of Mendelssohn's *Elijah* (1846; see Edwards 1976). Because the composer felt uncomfortable setting English texts, even though the work was to première in England, the original libretto was written in German by Julius Schubring, the librettist for Mendelssohn's other oratorio, *St. Paul* (1836). When the composition was completed, William Bartholomew translated *Elijah* into English. It quickly became one of the most popular oratorios in England and the United States; indeed it was performed before Queen Victoria and Prince Albert. Although it was not premièred in English, William Ball translated *St. Paul* and it was published by Novello of London. Subsequently, it also became a favourite, particularly at music festivals throughout England and in Boston, New York, and Baltimore. Because these two works became standard English oratorios, their original translations were considered authoritative. Thus, they were not subject to the same vagaries as operas, where numerous theatre translators would offer different versions of the same original text.

Rossini's *azione sacra Mosè in Egitto* also became a favourite oratorio in England and the United States as *Moses in Egypt*. One version, published by the former Mozart librettist Lorenzo da Ponte (and perhaps translated by him), was issued in conjunction with a performance at St Patrick's Church in New York in 1832. Rather than producing a text in forced poetic rhymes and rhythms, the translator chose a prose rendering. Moses's aria 'Eterno, immenso, incomprensibil Dio' (I. ii) thus becomes:

> O God, eternal, great, inscrutable, who still watchest over the safety of thy servants, and showerest down blessings on thy people; thou who art holy, just and great ... now show thy mercy; and again to the wonder of Egypt, restore the light which thou hast taken.
>
> ([Da Ponte?] 1832: 11)

Despite the archaic syntax and 'thou', used not only in this prayer but throughout the libretto, the translation is accurate and easily read. Yet another popular oratorio that eventually found its way into English translation was Louis Spohr's *Die letzten Dinge* (1826). Its success on the Continent spread to England, where it was performed in the original German at the Norwich Music Festival in 1830. The following year, it was published in an English translation by Edward Taylor as *The Last Judgment*, and as such it remained one of the most frequently performed oratorios well into the twentieth century.

Oratorio selections, too, found their way into home entertainment editions; however, since the most popular numbers were the choruses, keyboard arrangements for pianos and parlour pump organs were usually instrumental solos with the four-part harmonies represented in choral accompaniments. While texts were sometime included, they were not as significantly represented as they were in sheet music of opera selections.

Song

Perhaps the genre most representative of nineteenth-century aesthetics was the art song, for it provided examples of the all-important link between words and music in arrangements that were, for the most part, accessible to amateur musicians. British and American composers wrote songs, but, because of prejudices in favour of Europeans, works by composers such as Schubert, Schumann, Mendelssohn, Berlioz, Duparc, and Debussy in many ways set the genre standards. More than with opera, translators of German *Lieder* and French *mélodies* and *chansons* attempted to retain the integrity of the poems they put into English.

Frederic W. Root, a composer associated with the Christian Scientists in America, translated and published English versions of some of the German and French classic songs in his series *Best Songs of the Great Composers* (1885). In one of these songs, based on the melody of Schubert's 'Ständchen' (D. 889), Root returned the text to its origins in Shakespeare's *Cymbeline*, 'Hark! Hark! The lark!' Other translations of *Lieder* that were originally settings of some of Germany's finest poets, such as Heine, Goethe, and Eichendorff, were treated with respect by translators who revered the original poetry. French songs as well appeared in sheet music, such as a translation by Theodore T. Barker of Victor Hugo's 'La Captive', set by Berlioz; it was published as *Le Captive: The Captive*, and its arrangement was specified 'as sung at the New York Music Festival, 1881'. Later in the nineteenth century, songs by other European composers would be made available in translation. For example, 'Blumendeutung', a German text set by the Czech composer Anton Dvořák, was adapted by Louis C. Elson and published as 'Language of Flowers' in 1882. These selections served a dual purpose for English-speaking audiences. They not only introduced them to the classics of the European art song repertory but also gave them access to some of the finest poets of the eighteenth and nineteenth centuries.

In most cases, translators were silent partners in the production of musical arrangements and adaptations. For this reason, Robert B. Brough, translator of the songs of the French political *chanson* writer Pierre-Jean de Béranger, offers a rare glimpse into the philosophy behind rendering a text into a new language. Although he began his career as a singer in what today might be called a cabaret, Béranger became one of the best-known and most respected composers of political song in France. For the most part employing existing popular melodies, he wrote new texts. These parodies were such powerful political tools that their author suffered imprisonment twice. Béranger composed songs through the early 1830s, and Brough's translations were published some twenty years later. In the preface to his edition, Brough wrote that his aim was to translate Béranger into 'passable English verse, with careful editing and annotations' (Brough 1856: ix). Beyond functioning simply as a conduit from one language to another, Brough noted that his task had actually been a long-standing literary ambition. He also considered the practical side of dedicating one's time to such a task: 'the labour of carefully digesting, and reproducing in another language, the life's work of a very old man (never at any time an idler) could not possibly meet with adequate pecuniary compensation; and "labours of love", on an extended scale, are luxuries that a working author must be chary of indulging in' (1856: xiv–xv). Yet, because Brough felt that the song's political messages were still urgent, he undertook the project. He 'endeavoured to adhere to the author's meaning and form of expression as nearly as possible' and, by preserving the exact metre, he gave his readers 'an equivalent, in general form and character, of the thing to be translated—namely a song' (1856: xiv). Brough's translations are published as a volume of poems, with no reference to the tunes to which they would have been sung. Yet the musical elements in the verse are respected, as is apparent in this excerpt from his translation of Béranger's most popular song, 'Le Roi d'Yvetôt' (1813):

> It was a king of Yvetot,
> Whom few historians name;
> A sleeper fast, a waker slow,
> No dreams had he of fame.
> By Betty's hand with nightcap crown'd,
> He snored in state—the whole clock round—
> Profound!
> Ha! ha! ha! ha! Ho! ho! ho! ho!
> A kingdom match with Yvetot!
> Ho! ho!
>
> (Brough 1856: 21)

Although Brough must have expected his translations to be read as literature, he took care to maintain the musical form and flow of Béranger's original lyric.

Musical culture had a significant part to play in the dominant currents of nineteenth-century history. Just as revolutionaries fought for liberty and national constitutions, composers and librettists strove to express themselves in the music and languages of their homelands. In a peculiar way, some text translations, especially parodies and pastiches, manifested a different type of nationalism, for through the alteration of works into English, translators and adapters removed them from their parent culture and manipulated them into their own. Despite this seeming need to anglicize continental music to make it palatable, the demand for it was overwhelming. Indeed, vocal genres continued to provide stage, concert, and parlour entertainment for audiences as well as models for British and American composers as they enriched their own national traditions later in the century.

LIST OF SOURCES

The Library of Congress American Memory website offers digitized examples of sheet music from numerous historic sheet music collections. Most of the individual sheet music examples mentioned in this essay were accessed at this site: **http://memory.loc.gov**. To search and to view music scores, select 'Search' and then 'Limit Search to Sheet Music'.

Translations and Adaptations
Anon. (c.1859). *Lucie de Lammermoor. A Grand Opera in Three Acts. The Music by Donizetti, as represented at the Royal Italian Opera, London, and the Academy of Music, New York*. New York
Arnold, Samuel James (1828). *Tit for Tat* [Mozart]. London.
Ball, William (c.1836). *St. Paul: An Oratorio* [Mendelssohn]. London.
Barker, Theodore T. (1881). *Le Captive: The Captive* [Berlioz]. Boston, MA.
Bartholomew, William (c.1847). *Elijah: An Oratorio* [Mendelssohn]. London.
Beazley, Samuel, Jr. (1826). *The White Lady* [Boïeldieu]. London.
Brough, Robert B. (1856). *Béranger's Songs of The Empire, The Peace, and The Restoration*. London.

[da Ponte, Lorenzo?] (1832). *Moses in Egypt, A Sacred Oratorio to be sung in the Catholic Church of Saint Patrick in New York* [Rossini]. [New York].

Elson, Louis C. (1882). *Language of Flowers* [Dvořák]. Boston, MA.

Gilbert, W. S. (1866). *A New and Original Extravaganza, entitled Dulcamara, or, The Little Duck and the Great Quack* [parody of Donizetti]. London.

Kenney, Charles Lamb (*c*.1872). *Semiramide: Opera in Two Acts* [Rossini]. London.

Lacy, M. Rophino (1827). *The Turkish Lovers* [Rossini]. London.

―― (1994). *Italian Opera in English: 'Cinderella' (1831) adapted by M. Rophino Lacy from Gioacchino Rossini's La Cenerentola*, ed. John Graziano. New York (first pub. 1831).

Maggione, Manfredo (1854). *Semiramide: A Grand Opera in Two Acts* [Rossini]. New York.

Planché, James Robinson (1830). *The National Guard* [Auber]. London.

Popcock, Isaac (1817). *The Libertine* [Mozart]. London.

Root, Frederic W. (1885). *Best Songs of the Great Composers*. Cincinnati, OH.

Royer, Alphonse, and Vaez, Gustave (*c*.1861). *Donizetti's Opera Lucia di Lammermoor, Containing the Italian Text, with an English Translation, and the Music of All the Principal Airs*. Boston, MA.

Taylor, Edward (1831). *The Last Judgment: An Oratorio* [Spohr]. London.

Other Sources

Ahlquist, Karen (1997). *Democracy at the Opera: Music, Theater, and Culture in New York City, 1815–60*. Urbana, IL.

Chorley, Henry F. (1984). *Thirty Years' Musical Recollections*, 2 vols. New York (first pub. 1862).

Cockrell, Dale (1997). *Demons of Disorder: Early Blackface Minstrels and their World*. Cambridge.

Edwards, F. G. (1976). *The History of Mendelssohn's Oratorio 'Elijah'*, introd. Sir George Grove. New York (first pub. 1896).

Fenner, Theodore (1972). *Leigh Hunt and Opera Criticism: The 'Examiner' Years, 1808–1821*. Lawrence, KS.

―― (1994). *Opera in London: Views of the Press, 1785–1830*. Carbondale, IL.

Krehbiel, Henry Edward (1980). *Chapters of Opera Being Historical and Critical Observations and Records Concerning the Lyric Drama in New York from its Earliest Days Down to the Present Time*. New York (first pub. 1909).

Lawrence, Vera Brodsky (1995–9). *Strong on Music: The New York Music Scene in the Days of George Templeton Strong*, 3 vols. Chicago, IL.

Loney, Glenn, ed. (1984). *Musical Theatre in America: Papers and Proceedings of the Conference on the Musical Theatre in America*. Westport, CT.

Mahar, William J. (1999). *Behind the Burnt Cork Mask: Early Black Minstrelsy and Antebellum American Popular Culture*. Urbana, IL.

Maretzek, Max (1968) *Revelations of an Opera Manager in 19th-Century America: Crochets and Quavers & Sharps and Flats*, introd. Charles Haywood. New York (first pub. 1855).

Mussulman, Joseph A. (1967). 'Mendelssohnism in America.' *Musical Quarterly* 53: 335–46.

Parsons, James, ed. (2004). *The Cambridge Companion to the Lied*. Cambridge.

Preston, Katherine K. (1993). *Opera on the Road: Traveling Opera Troupes in the United States, 1825–60*. Urbana, IL.

Sadie, Stanley, and Tyrrell, John, eds. (2001). *The New Grove Dictionary of Music and Musicians*, 20 vols. London.

Smith, William Charles (1955). *The Italian Opera and Contemporary Ballet in London, 1789–1820: A Record of Performances and Players*. London.

Smither, Howard E. (2000). *A History of the Oratorio*, Vol. 4: *The Oratorio in the Nineteenth and Twentieth Centuries*, Chapel Hill, NC.
Temperley, Nicholas (1966). 'The English Romantic Opera.' *Victorian Studies* 9: 293–301.
—— (1989). 'Musical Nationalism in English Romantic Opera', pp. 143–57 in Nicholas Temperley, ed., *The Lost Chord: Essays on Victorian Music*. Bloomington, IN.
Tunley, David, ed. (1994–5). *Romantic French Song 1830–1870*, 6 vols. New York.
White, Eric Walter (1983). *A History of English Opera*. London.
—— (1983). *A Register of First Performances of English Operas and Semi-Operas from the 16th Century to 1980*. London.

9.3 Oral Literature

Kenneth Haynes

Two works published in the 1760s had a large influence on how oral narrative poems would be assembled and translated in the nineteenth century: the Ossianic writings of James Macpherson and Thomas Percy's *Reliques*. They fed an appetite across Europe for 'primitive' literature (a taste which had also been stimulated by discussions of Homer's epics). However, although Macpherson and Percy supplied prominent examples of the two main kinds of oral narrative poetry, the epic and the ballad, the status of their works as oral literature is equivocal. How precisely Macpherson adapted his Gaelic sources has been the subject of dispute for centuries (see further Vol. 3 of this *History*), and Percy regularly improved and revised the old ballads he found in manuscript (see Groom 1999: 145–92). Moreover, although notions of 'oral tradition', 'oral poems', and even, at the end of the century, of 'oral literature' were available in this period (instances are documented by the *Oxford English Dictionary*), the methods by which oral traditional poetry was composed and transmitted, as well as the complex relation of written texts to oral literature, were not well understood until the twentieth century. Even so, significant scholarship on folklore and ballads was first accomplished in the Victorian period.

In the nineteenth century, nationalism transformed and replaced primitivism as the current which most influenced how oral works were edited and translated, and as with primitivism, it both shaped and was shaped by oral literature. The role of Germany was central. The works of Macpherson and Percy were enthusiastically read by Klopstock, Herder, Goethe, and others, and perhaps had an even greater impact among Germans than in Britain. Herder in particular wove together many threads that insisted on the intimate connection of a people, its language, and its art. He celebrated Ossian and Percy in an influential essay of 1773; he collected the folk songs of many peoples; indeed, it was due to him that the word *Volkslied* became a familiar term. Herder's emphases on the *Volk*, on organic history, and on culture as uniquely expressive, even constitutive, of national identity, became central tenets of German nationalism. From Herder as well as from the German literature, and especially the historical drama, which he influenced, these tenets became influential also in Britain; Scott, Coleridge, Carlyle were among the most influential mediators. The consequence for both the editing and the translating of oral literature was profound: an oral epic was understood to be a national epic; ballads were heard as expressions of the soul of a people.

Oral Epics

Homer was the constant point of reference for oral epics. The classical scholar F. A. Wolf had argued in his *Prolegomena ad Homerum* (1795) that the text we now have of the Homeric epics was radically unlike the original poems; the illiterate Homer had composed ballads (like those of the early Germans and other primitive peoples) not unified into an epic whole until the time of Pisistratus. Another great textual scholar, Karl Lachmann, argued influentially in the second quarter of the nineteenth century that the *Iliad* consisted of sixteen layers that had originally been independent. Their arguments about the unity of the Homeric poems, though neither the beginning nor the end of the Homeric question, were regularly used to support the view that the Homeric epics emerged from oral ballads expressive of the folk genius of a people and later unified into a 'national epic' by a great poet. This process was also discovered in or imputed to the other 'national epics' in world literature. Opinions varied regarding how many such epics were extant— Max Müller counted five (Müller 1862: 318) while the German philologist Heymann Steinthal counted four (see Crawford 1888: xxxix)— but it was in this guise that oral epics were compiled, read, and translated. The equation of oral and national epics lasted until the end of the century; it was expressed at a popular level by Kate Rabb (who counted ten national epics):

As the nation passed from childhood to youth, the legends of the hero that each wandering minstrel had changed to suit his fancy, were collected and fused into one by some great poet, who by his power of unification made this written epic his own. This is the origin of the Hindu epics, the 'Iliad' and the 'Odyssey,' the 'Kalevala,' the 'Shah-Nameh,' 'Beowulf,' the 'Nibelungen Lied,' the 'Cid,' and the 'Song of Roland.' (Rabb 1898: 4)

Rabb also makes evident the implicit third part of the equation: oral epics were understood not only as national or proto-national but as childlike or youthful.

In practice, different aspects of that equation dominated the translation of particular works. The emphasis on orality and the new understanding of the oral genesis of epics had great influence on the translation of Homer (it was also the premiss of Macaulay's best-selling *Lays of Ancient Rome*, 1842). The *Homeric Ballads* of William Maginn appeared bilingually in *Fraser's Magazine* from 1838, and was published posthumously in 1850. Maginn took sixteen short episodes from Homer, mostly from the *Odyssey*, and turned them into ballads. 'Scholars of that time ... favoured a theory that the Homeric poems were composed piecemeal for a popular audience. Maginn decided to put the ballad theory into practice' (Stanford 1976: 170). Gladstone praised them; Matthew Arnold tried to be sympathetic, writing that the *Homeric Ballads* are 'vigorous and genuine poems in their own way' (Arnold 1960: 131). However, Arnold found that Maginn's version was a risible travesty of Homer, and most subsequent readers have concurred (e.g. Stanford 1976: 170 and Steiner 1996: 148). Arnold not only rejected Maginn's attempt to recover the discrete ballads that may have been Homer's source, he also adamantly opposed adopting ballad metres for Homeric translation, as F. W. Newman had done (Arnold 1960: 125–6). His insistence on the nobility of Homer's verse became a primary obstacle to future translators who sought to capture the oral dimension of the Homeric epics (see § 5.2, above).

The 'national' part of the equation was at least as important as the 'oral' in translating the epics of Spain and Finland into English. The *Poem of the Cid*, discovered in 1779, first entered English in an anonymous appendix to Robert Southey's *Chronicle of the Cid* (1808; see pp. 262–3, above). The date is significant:

In 1808, meaningful British support for the Spanish and Portuguese cause was far from assured; Napoleon was not yet regarded as a Manichean demon; and the Spanish themselves were, from the British point of view, politically corrupt, barely civilized, and hopelessly Catholic. In this context, a massive work on the Spanish national hero who helped drive non-Christian invaders from Spanish soil, takes on a decidedly political tone.

(Graver 2001: 153)

In such a context, John Hookham Frere, the unnamed translator, was under a particular pressure to recreate the simplicity and power of this 'Homer of Spain' (Southey 1808: xi) while avoiding what would strike his contemporaries as 'barely civilized' or childlike. He balanced the rude and the civilized by adopting a direct and relatively unliterary diction that avoided archaisms and by his choice of metre, a long line with either six or seven beats. This is a ballad metre, and Frere used it to convey an unadorned heroism:

> We must all sally forth! There cannot a man be spared,
> Two footmen only at the gates to close them and keep guard;
> If we are slain in battle, they will bury us here in peace,
> If we survive and conquer, our riches will increase.
> (Frere 1872: II, 412)

In 1835, a new national epic was added to world literature. Elias Lönnrot compiled the *Kalevala* from a number of Finnish oral sources. Lönnrot set himself the Herderian and patriotic task of forging an authentic national epic from these sources, taking authenticity to mean 'fidelity to lines actually sung by his informants' (Schoolfield 1998: 27). According to his own criteria he largely succeeded, adding relatively few lines of his own to the poem and drawing on oral sources that were to a great extent fixed (in contrast to the oral-formulaic compositions of Serbian singers). Nonetheless, no single episode in the poem corresponds to a single source (Schoolfield 1998: 13, 27). He revised and enlarged the poem in 1850.

In the nineteenth century, translations of the *Kalevala* into English were almost exclusively an American affair. Attention was first directed to the Finnish following the success of Longfellow's American epic, the *Song of Hiawatha* (1855). He was publicly accused of having plagiarized from the *Kalevala*, and the baseless charge was extensively discussed in both England and the United States; the controversy was renewed in 1868 and 1888, when new translations of the *Kalevala* were published.

Because of Longfellow's connection to the poem, public interest in the *Kalevala* was very wide, if unscholarly. John A. Porter's posthumously published partial translation (1868) was made from German, not Finnish. In his introduction, Eugene Schuyler compared it to Longfellow's *Hiawatha*: Porter had chosen to translate into trochaic tetrameter, which called Longfellow irresistibly to mind:

> On the plains of Kalevala,
> On the prairies of Wainola
> Chanting ever wondrous legends
> Full of old time wit and wisdom
> Wainamoinen, ancient minstrel,
> Passed his days in sweet contentment.
> (Porter 1868: 59)

Porter concentrated on the narrative, avoiding mythology and folklore. In contrast, those two aspects of the poem had a particular interest for John Crawford, who published the first complete translation of the *Kalevala* into English in 1888. Though he nowhere says so, he appears, like Porter, to have translated from the German version (see Schoolfield 1988: 30). In his preface, he praises the poem for being 'replete with most fascinating folk-lore' and for its myths 'full of significance and beauty'. He praised it also as a national epic, that is, for representing 'the entire wisdom and accumulated experience of a nation' (Crawford 1888: xlii–xliii). The magic depicted in the poem, that is, the specialized knowledge necessary to defeat evil, particularly attracted Crawford's attention; such passages stirred his imagination, keeping him from flagging when confronted with what one publisher had called the 'uninteresting mythological details and the monotonous repetition' of the original (Porter 1868: v):

> My beloved, helpful mother,
> Go at once to yonder mountain,
> To the store-house on the hill-top,
> Bring my vest of finest texture,
> Bring my hero-coat of purple,
> Bring my suit of magic colors,
> Thus to make me look attractive,
> Thus to robe myself in beauty.
> (Crawford 1888: 415)

Crawford, like Porter, chose to translate into trochaic tetrameters and so like him was metrically reminiscent of Longfellow. Crawford went on further to cement the connection between *Hiawatha* and the *Kalevala* by drawing on Longfellow's poem for some of his lines (Moyne 1963: 102). His translation enjoyed great success, creating 'a far-reaching stir not only in the scholarly world but in the world of general readers as well'; 'hundreds of articles' were published on it, and one magazine devoted an entire issue to it (Moyne 1963: 21).

The only nineteenth-century poet of some renown who seems to have been tempted to translate from the *Kalevala* was Longfellow's successor at Harvard, James Russell Lowell, presumably using an intermediate source; he once called the poem his 'favorite' (Lowell 1893: II, 90). The few pages of his translation were published posthumously by Charles Eliot Norton in 1894. With Lowell, the emphasis in translation is once again placed on the primitive and the childlike:

> Ah, you should not, kindly people,
> Therein seek a cause to blame me,
> That, a child, I sang too often,
> That, unfledged, I twittered only.
> I have never had a teacher,
> Never heard the speech of great men,
> Never learned a word unhomely,
> Nor fine phrases of the stranger ...
> But for this it does not matter,
> I have shown the way to singers.
>   (Lowell 1894: 27)

Ballads

Percy included translations of two Spanish ballads in the *Reliques*, noting their similarities to English ballads. Later, collectors of ballads began to discover other European parallels to English and Scottish ballads, particularly German and Danish. In 1806 the Scottish antiquary Robert Jamieson published his *Popular Ballads and Songs ... with Translations of Similar Pieces from the Ancient Danish Language*; he had discovered not just that ballads in English were sometimes similar to Danish ones, but that sometimes they were obviously derived from the same source. By the time of the second edition of Child's authoritative *English and Scottish Popular Ballads* (1882–98), parallels to English and Scottish ballads could be drawn from more than two dozen languages.

German ballads sparked much excitement. The early collaboration of Walter Scott and M. G. Lewis produced the *Tales of Wonder* (1801), a collection of both original and translated ballads; the ballads that were translated were both literary (Goethe, Bürger) and folk (collected or translated by Herder). The volume included the famous version by William Taylor of Bürger's 'Leonore', a literary ballad drawing on folk sources (see Child, Ballad 272). Lewis praised it highly, calling it 'a masterpiece of translation' and 'far superior' to the German. Taylor took considerable liberty with his original. Seeking to make the ballad more at home in English, he changed the scene from the Battle of Prague under Frederick the Great (1757) to the Third Crusade under Richard I of England, a jump of more than 500 years. He also dropped the original stanza form, adopting instead the English ballad metre, and wrote in an archaic spelling. The resulting version was very popular, attracting the attention of Blake, Byron, Coleridge, Lamb, and Scott; within a year of its first appearance in the *Monthly Magazine* (1796), five translators, including Scott, had made English versions of it (Ehrenpreis 1966: 67–8). Bürger's literary ballad, disguised thus in translation as a folk ballad, excited the interest of many readers in oral ballads. Scott would soon turn to Scottish ballads and publish *The Minstrelsy of the Scottish Border* (1802–3). In 1819, he turned to an old German ballad and translated 'The Noble Moringer' (Scott 1820), extracts from which he later quoted in the introduction to *The Betrothed*, itself inspired by that tale.

This mingling of original and translated works, and of literary and folk ballads, was typical of the literary treatment of ballads. Andrew Lang's *Ballads and Lyrics of Old France* (1872) includes translations not only of Villon, Du Bellay, and Ronsard, but also of French folk songs (from the collection of Nerval) and even of two Greek folk songs that were translated from a French version; his own poetry is also printed.

In addition to the ballads from Germanic countries, those of Spain, Serbia, and Celtic-speaking regions were frequently translated (for Celtic ballads, see § 6.7; for Serbian ballads, pp. 310–11, above). A number of poets throughout the century tried their hands at Spanish ballads, though none of them at length: Robert Southey, John Hookham Frere, M. G. Lewis, Sir Walter Scott, Lord Byron, William Cullen Bryant, and Henry Wadsworth Longfellow (see further Bryant 1973). Notable are the versions by Frere, who freely rendered two ballads at his usual high standard of verse translation; by Byron, whose three translations published with Canto IV of *Childe Harold's Pilgrimage* in 1818 reached a wide public; and by Longfellow, whose travel book *Outre-Mer* (1833) contains a chapter 'Ancient Spanish Ballads' in which some of his own translations were included.

The most successful translation was *Ancient Spanish Ballads* (1823), by the critic and literary editor John Gibson Lockhart, the son-in-law and future biographer of Walter Scott. It was widely and enthusiastically read and reviewed. In the spirit of Scott, Lockhart frequently begins the ballads with great brio:

> To the chase goes Rodrigo with hound and with hawk;
> But what game he desires is revealed in his talk:
> 'Oh, in vain have I slaughtered the Infants of Lara:
> There's an heir in his hall, — there's the bastard Mudara.
> There's the son of the renegade, — spawn of Mahoun,
> If I meet with Mudara, my spear brings him down.'
> (Lockhart 1842: 80)

He does not hesitate to cut lines that do not contribute to the main action or to compress lines in order to heighten the action. In 'Bavieca' Lockhart reduces the sixteen stanzas of the Spanish original to six English stanzas, beginning the story in the midst of the action and compressing the ending, in order to tighten the focus on the Cid and his horse. On the other hand, he does not generally sustain the momentum for the course of an entire ballad since he often falls into the clichés of ballad diction and sometimes inserts gratuitous picturesque detail. Lockhart uses long English lines to translate the ballads, occasionally adding various sorts of internal rhyme.

One of the finest translations of Spanish ballads was published more than sixty years after Lockhart's. Though James Young Gibson's *The Cid Ballads and Other Poems and Translations from Spanish and German* (1887) never had the popular success which its predecessor enjoyed, it has received critical praise from the time of its posthumous publication. Despite the title, many kinds of Spanish ballads are included in his large selection; he translates almost twice as many as Lockhart. He also uses a wide range of metres, though he most often translates into the common English ballad metre. His translations are more literal than Lockhart's, though he willingly and quite skilfully changes narrative or reported speech into dialogue (discussed in Bryant 1973: 230). In translating monologues and dialogues, Gibson is usually more adept than Lockhart, giving more finely individuated voices to speakers.

A year after Lockhart's translation appeared, John Bowring had published his *Ancient Poetry and Romances of Spain* (1824), with a marked preference for literary ballads; it was shortly followed by his version of Serbian ballads, *Servian Popular Poetry* (1827). He was by no means unique in being drawn to ballads from diverse traditions. George Borrow published translations of ballads in *Romantic Ballads: Translated from the Danish* in 1826 and *Targum, or, Metrical Translations from Thirty Languages and Dialects* in 1835. When his remaining translations of ballads were published posthumously, they filled 1,500 pages; a selection, *Ballads of All Nations*, was published in 1927. Borrow was also responsible for stimulating interest in the oral traditions and poetry of the Gypsies, and although only one of his books on Gypsy life, *The Zincali*, took up the question of their literature in translation, and although his grasp on Romani was such that even the title was not quite right ('he should have written *Zincala*', Williams 1982: 140), he was instrumental all the same in encouraging sympathetic interest and future scholarship. The *Journal of the Gypsy-Lore Society* was founded in 1888; the first president of the Society, Charles G. Leland, had co-translated *English Gipsy Songs* (1875).

Folklore and Folk Tales

In addition to oral poetry, oral prose, such as folklore and folk tales, began to be collected and translated in this period: traditions, proverbs, superstitions, jokes, customs, as well as folk tales broadly defined (fairy tales, legends, fables, tall tales, etc.). One main impetus was the *Kinder- und Hausmärchen* of the Grimm brothers, first translated as *German Popular Stories* by Edgar Taylor in 1823 but later more commonly known as *Grimms' Fairy Tales*. In contrast to earlier collections, the approach was scholarly by the standards of the time: they eschewed literary embellishment and their collection included an introduction and notes. In translation, however, their work was redirected toward children, and was routinely adjusted for that audience (see further p. 396, above).

The London Folk-Lore Society was founded in 1878 and sought to place the study of folklore on a more scholarly footing. From its inception, it was concerned with both British and foreign folklore. It published a journal and sponsored a wide variety of publications, including for example *Portuguese Folk-Tales* in 1882, *The Folk-Tales of the Magyars* in 1889, and *Notes on the Folklore of the Fjort (French Congo)* in 1898. The Society was only one manifestation of a new and wide interest in folk tales at the end of the century. From 1880 to 1900, books covering the folk tales and folklore of Denmark, West Ireland, modern Greece, Georgia, Norway, the Cossacks, Brittany, Korea, and others were published, and although not all were concerned with oral literature as such, they represented a substantial addition to the handful of translated and reported 'popular tales' that had previously appeared. In the same period collections of translated proverbs also became numerous.

Translated fairy tales were widely read in Andrew Lang's dozen fairy books, from the *Blue Fairy Book* of 1889 to the *Lilac Fairy Book* of 1910. Lang served as President of the Folk-Lore Society from 1889 to 1891, and he had brought new anthropological methods to folklore and mythology. However, in contrast to his scholarly activity, Lang's fairy books were aimed at children. He simplified and adapted existing translations of stories, mostly of European origin but also including Asia, Africa, and America. The degree to which the stories were derived from oral literature varies greatly; few works could be more literary than his own adaptation of the story of Perseus from Apollodorus, Pindar, and Simonides ('The Terrible Head'), but on the other hand his versions, heavily reworked, of stories from Steere's *Swahili Tales* or from ethnographic texts published by the Smithsonian Bureau of Ethnology in the United States placed him in closer contact with oral literature. Joseph Jacobs likewise combined scholarly activity (he was the editor of the journal *Folk-Lore* from 1889 to 1900) with writing for children. He adapted existing translations of folklore and tales from Celtic Britain and from India to produce *Celtic Fairy Tales* (1892), *More Celtic Fairy Tales* (1894), and *Indian Fairy Tales* (1892). His avowed goal was to attract children, not appeal to scholars; to transfer, not translate.

Ethnographic Texts

Translations from the songs of North and South American Indians were occasionally made before the nineteenth century. One of the earliest into English appeared in Florio's translation of Montaigne, whose essay 'Of the Cannibals' had quoted a song that was given by Jean de Léri in his account of a voyage to Brazil. A translation from Cherokee that was published in *The Memoirs of Lieut. Henry Timberlake* (1765) is a very early English version of a North American Indian song. However, Timberlake's version is at a great distance from the original for two reasons: first, he did not know Cherokee, and he would have relied on interpreters to make his version; and second, he translated into heroic couplets in ignorance of the original form (see Swann 1992: xiv–xvi). Still, it does seem to relay accurate details of Cherokee warfare (see Clements 1996: 81).

In the nineteenth century, translations from North American Indian languages appear in a variety of sources (for examples see Hollander 1993: II, 953–6 and Day 1951: 185–211), at first sporadically; but by mid-century a wide and general interest in the ethnography of Native Americans was evident, stimulated in part by the work of Henry Rowe Schoolcraft. His major ethnological work was the *Historical and Statistical Information Respecting the History, Condition, and Prospects of the*

Indian Tribes of the United States (1851–7), but his most important work from the point of view of literary translation was probably the *Algic Researches* of 1839, which contained a number of oral narratives from the Ojibwa; Schoolcraft's wife Jane Johnston and her Ojibwa relatives were a critical source of information for this work. The translation became famous with the success of Longfellow's *The Song of Hiawatha* (1855), which acknowledged its debt to Schoolcraft; when *Algic Researches* was revised in 1856, it bore the title *The Myth of Hiawatha*. From at least the early part of the twentieth century, Schoolcraft has been criticized for distorting his sources in the interest of literary sentimentality or decorum. More recently, he has been viewed as excessively drawn to the theme of the 'vanishing Indian': 'he perceived the Indian as afflicted with a deep malaise, characterized by a melancholy as profound as any suffered by a Romantic poet' (Clements 1996: 125). In contrast, it has also been pointed out that he included matter that was not acceptable to the literary sentiment of his day, that his distortions usually took the form of omission rather than fabrication, and that he was himself anxious that the stories not be excessively literary (Schoolcraft 1956: xx–xxi).

It would take another generation before American ethnology became scholarly. The first, and most significant, event in this transformation was the founding of the Bureau of American Ethnology in 1879. Through their Annual Reports, the eight volumes of *Contributions to North American Ethnology* (1877–93), and their series of *Bulletins*, the Bureau covered all aspects of North American ethnology, including translation. Of the large number of translators associated with the Bureau, we might mention Frank Cushing, whose fluent and highly accomplished translations of Zuni material are 'colored by his opinion that Zuni oral narrative resembled Victorian prose' (Clements 1996: 22); Alice C. Fletcher, whose attention was directed to Indian songs (including music), and whose adopted Omahan son, Francis La Flesche, would publish accounts of ritual practice for the Bureau in the next century; and Washington Matthews, the foremost student of the Navajos in the nineteenth century.

The founding of the *Journal of American Folk-Lore* in 1888 was another significant step in promoting greater accuracy in translations. The first issue contained, for example, an early article by Franz Boas (one of the founders of modern anthropology) on certain songs, legends, and ceremonies of the Kwakiutl. The same issue of the journal included an article by Daniel Brinton on 'Lenape Conversations'; in contrast to Boas, Brinton, with his aversion to fieldwork and theoretical enthusiasms, belonged decisively to the nineteenth century. Nonetheless, Brinton's *Library of Aboriginal American Literature* was a major advance: it offered bilingual editions of eight important texts, including translations from the written literatures of the Aztec and Mayan Indians. An early translation from Nahuatl had previously appeared in the appendix to William Hickling Prescott's *History of the Conquest of Mexico* (1843), but this was unusual; before Brinton translations from Central and South American literature into English had been neglected. Another exception is *Ollanta* ('An ancient Ynca drama'), translated by the prolific British explorer and geographer Clements Markham in 1871.

Translations from African and Oceanic literatures were also undertaken in the nineteenth century. Civil servants like George Grey, Edward Shortall, and John White collected and examined the oral legends and traditions of the Maori, while missionaries provided most of the translations from Africa (Henry Callaway from Zulu, Edward Steere and William Ernest Taylor from Swahili).

Oral literature does not disappear in a literate culture, but becomes thoroughly intertwined with written texts. Before the latter part of the nineteenth century, oral stories and ballads were only exceptionally recorded by methods consistent with more scholarly ethnography; more often, they were written and translated with an eye to nationalist or other ideological interests, or made to conform to the literary style of children's books, or turned into sophisticated entertainment; sometimes, too, oral sources were incorporated into high literacy in the form of literary ballads, fantastic stories, and so on. Conversely, written stories and ballads were sometimes transmitted orally and altered in the process. Some written texts were even dismantled in an attempt to extract and recover the oral sources behind the work. The translation of oral literature, that is, involves a double process of translating: first from oral literature to written, and second from one written literature to another.

LIST OF SOURCES

Translations
Borrow, George (1835). *Targum, or, Metrical Translations from Thirty Languages and Dialects*. St Petersburg.
—— (1841). *The Zincali*. London.
—— (1927). *Ballads of All Nations*. London.
Crawford, John Martin (1888). *The Kalevala*, 2 vols. (continuously paginated). New York.
Cushing, Frank Hamilton (1976). *Outlines of Zuñi Creation Myths*. New York (first pub. 1896).
—— (1901). *Zuñi Folk Tales*. New York.
Ehrenpreis, Anne Henry, ed. (1966). *The Literary Ballad*. London.
Fletcher, Alice Cunningham (1900). *Indian Story and Song from North America*. Boston, MA.
Frere, John Hookham (1872). *The Works of John Hookham Frere in Verse and Prose*. London.
Gibson, James Young (1898). *The Cid Ballads and Other Poems and Translations from Spanish and German*. New York (first pub. 1887).
Hollander, John, ed. (1993). *American Poetry: The Nineteenth Century*, 2 vols. New York.
Jamieson, Robert (1806). *Popular Ballads and Songs ... with Translations of Similar Pieces from the Ancient Danish Language, and a Few Originals by the Editor*. Edinburgh.
Lang, Andrew (1872). *Ballads and Lyrics of Old France*. London.
—— (1889–1910). *The Fairy Books*, 12 vols. London.
Lewis, Matthew Gregory (1801). *Tales of Wonder*. London.
Lockhart, John Gibson (1842). *Ancient Spanish Ballads*. New York (first pub. 1823).
Lowell, James Russell (1894). 'Fragments III. Kalevala.' *The Century* 48: 26–8.
Maginn, William (1850). *Homeric Ballads*. London.
Markham, Clements (1871). *Ollanta: An Ancient Ynca Drama*. London.
Matthews, Washington (1897). *Navaho Legends*. New York.
—— (1902). *The Night Chant: A Navaho Ceremony*. New York.

Porter, John A. (1868). *Selections from the Kalevala*. New York.
Prior, R. C. Alexander (1860). *Ancient Danish Ballads*. London.
Schoolcraft, Henry Rowe (1839). *Algic Researches*, 2 vols. New York.
—— (1956). *Schoolcraft's Indian Legends*, ed. Mentor L. Willams. East Lansing, MI.
Scott, Walter (1820). 'The Noble Moringer: An Ancient Ballad, Translated from the German.' *Edinburgh Annual Register, for 1816* 9: 495–501.
Southey, Robert (1808). *Chronicle of the Cid*. London.
Weber, Henry, and Jamieson, Robert (1814). *Illustrations of Northern Antiquities . . . with Translations of Metrical Tales, from the Old German, Danish, Swedish, and Icelandic languages*. Edinburgh.

Other Sources
Arnold, Matthew (1960). *On the Classical Tradition*, ed. R. H. Super. Ann Arbor, MI.
Bryant, Shasta M. (1973). *The Spanish Ballad in English*. Lexington, KY.
Clements, William M. (1986). *Native American Folklore in Nineteenth-Century Periodicals*. Athens, OH.
—— (1996). *Native American Verbal Art: Texts and Contexts*. Tucson, AZ.
Day, A. Grove. (1951). *The Sky Clears: Poetry of the American Indians*. New York.
Finnegan, Ruth (1992). *Oral Poetry: Its Nature, Significance, and Social Context*. Bloomington, IN (first pub. 1977).
Graver, Bruce (2001). 'George Ticknor, Robert Southey, and *The Poem of The Cid*.' *Wordsworth Circle* 32: 151–4.
Groom, Nick (1999). *The Making of Percy's 'Reliques'*. Oxford.
Jolles, Evelyn B. (1974). *G. A. Bürgers Ballade Leonore in England*. Regensburg.
Judd, Neil M. (1967). *The Bureau of American Ethnology: A Partial History*. Norman, OK.
Lowell, James Russell (1893). *Correspondence*, ed. Charles Eliot Norton. New York.
Moyne, Ernest J. (1963). *'Hiawatha' and 'Kalevala'*. Helsinki.
Müller, Max (1862). *Lectures on the Science of Language*, 2 vols. New York.
Rabb, Kate Milner (1898). *National Epics*. Chicago, IL (first pub. 1896).
Ruoff, A. LaVonne Brown (1990). *American Indian Literatures*. New York.
Schoolfield, George C. (1988). 'American Translators of the Kalevala', pp. 26–32 in *The* Kalevala: *Epic of the Finnish People*, tr. Eino Friberg. Helsinki.
—— (1998). *A History of Finland's Literature*. Lincoln, NE.
Stanford, W. B. (1976). *Ireland and the Classical Tradition*. Dublin.
Steiner, George, ed. (1996). *Homer in English*. London.
Swann, Brian (1992). *On the Translation of Native American Literatures*. Washington, DC.
Ticknor, George (1863). *History of Spanish Literature*. London.
Umphrey, George W. (1945). 'Spanish Ballads in English, Part I: Historical Survey.' *Modern Language Quarterly* 6: 479–94.
—— (1946). 'Spanish Ballads in English, Part II: Verse Technique.' *Modern Language Quarterly* 7: 21–34.
Williams, David (1982). *A World of his Own: The Double Life of George Borrow*. Oxford.

10

Sacred and Religious Texts

10.1	Christian Texts *Kenneth Haynes*	443
10.2	The Revised Version of the Bible *David Norton*	451
10.3	Sacred Books of the East *Richard Fynes*	458

10.1 Christian Texts

Kenneth Haynes

From about 1780, in sharp contrast with the first part of the century, a new interest in translating the Bible was widely evident in Britain, prompted in part by recent German biblical criticism. Although this initial enthusiasm did not endure in the face of the French Revolution and the Napoleonic wars (see Sheehan 2005: 241–7), throughout our period, new and revised biblical translations were made quite often in both Britain and America. The most significant of these was the Revised Version of the King James Bible (the subject of § 10.2, below). Devotional texts were also frequently translated, to serve sectarian ends as well as personal needs, and a handful of these endured into the twentieth century. Finally, the massive task of translating the Church Fathers in bulk was largely accomplished at this time, and these translations continue even now to be in use. The focus here is on translation specifically; for the subject of the continued influence of the Bible, especially the King James Bible, on literature and literary discussions in this period, see (for example) Norton 1993 and pp. 14–15, above.

Quantitatively, the translation of Christian texts in a typical year in this period accounted for up to a quarter of all literary translations; this proportion excludes reprints of the King James Bible. Using the search method outlined in Chapter 4, above, we estimated that in 1870, 128 of the 507 total literary translations (that is, after rounding to the nearest percentage, 25 per cent) were Christian texts. Of the 128 we found that some 23 per cent were devotional works; 21 per cent biblical commentaries (an unusually high number, reflecting the twenty-five translations of German biblical commentaries published in Edinburgh that year); 18 per cent were concerned with theology (the Church Fathers are categorized here); 13 per cent were occupied with church history (including the lives of saints); 12 per cent were translations from biblical texts; 8 per cent were prayers, hymns, and the like; the remaining 5 per cent comprised translations of three sermons, two Swedenborgian works, and a few others.

The Bible

A. S. Herbert's *Historical Catalogue of the Printed Editions of the English Bible* lists about 150 new translations and revisions of translations in the period 1790–1900, not counting metrical psalms (and there were more than a hundred of those, often made from existing English versions); William Chamberlin's *Catalogue of English Bible Translations* lists many more. The Bible was seldom translated in its entirety; it was far commoner to translate the New Testament alone, or the Psalms.

The motivations for the translations varied, sometimes reflecting new religious impulses, though sometimes it was the progress of scholarship, especially regarding the text of the New Testament,[1] that provided the impetus.

The Revised Version (1885) was the first great success in a long line of revisions of the King James Bible. John Wesley's revision of the New Testament had been published in 1755, 'for plain, unlettered men, who understand only their Mother Tongue'; it would attain great popularity in the United States (Daniell 2003: 536, 601). In contrast, Noah Webster's revision of the King James Bible (1833), mainly concerned to impose a dignified tone, correct grammar, and insert euphemisms, did not attain even a modest success until later in the century (Daniell 2003: 650–2). Joseph Smith, founder of the Mormons, revised the King James Bible during a period in which he received direct revelation (June 1830 to July 1833); the result was published in 1867. From 1847 to 1856, the American Bible Society worked on a revision of the King James translation, but it was in only a few instances that the text was substantively revised (see Norton 2005: 119–22). In reaction, Baptists in America formed their own society, the American Bible Union, which sought to correct the Greek text of the New Testament as well as revise the translation. One grave matter confronting them was the rendering of βαπτίζω; 'immerse' was preferred to 'baptize' in its earliest editions, but the 1866 New Testament was issued in both an 'immerse' and a 'baptize' form. In England meanwhile, the 'Five Clergymen', as they called themselves, published anonymous revisions of individual books of the New Testament from 1857 to 1861. This work and its subsequent editions 'did much to prepare English public opinion for an authoritative revision' (Herbert 1968: 405). One of those five clergymen, Henry Alford, combined and completed the earlier translations in his New Testament of 1869, in the desire to 'keep open the great question of an authoritative Revision' (Herbert 1968: 418). Hermann Gollancz described his 1880 version of the Hebrew Bible, 'for Jewish families', as a revision of the King James Bible.

The revision of the Catholic 'Douay-Rheims' Bible by Richard Challoner in 1749–50 (discussed in Vol. 3 of this *History*) remained the standard translation for English Catholics throughout the period. Although a number of scholars attempted their own revisions, none met with general success. Francis Kenrick's effort (1849–60) was the only revision on the scale of Challoner's (Paul 2003: 125–6).

New translations were frequent, though sometimes these did not depart greatly from the King James Bible. A New Testament associated with the Unitarians and published in 1808 (it was adapted from a previous translation by Newcombe) was often reprinted in the course of the century, though this did not stop subsequent Unitarians from translating; versions of the New Testament by Unitarians appeared in 1840, by Samuel Sharpe, who would become President of Manchester College, Oxford, and in 1869, by George Noyes, professor at Harvard. The

---

[1] Major textual advances were made by J. J. Griesbach, who revised the Greek text in 1774–5 (it was first used as the basis of an English translation by William Newcombe in 1796); Karl Lachmann, who published the first critical edition of the New Testament in 1831; and Konstantin von Tischendorf, who discovered the *Codex Sinaiticus* in 1859.

Quaker Luke Howard translated a number of Old Testament books. John Nelson Darby, one of the founders of the Plymouth Brethren, was much occupied with translating the Bible. His New Testament was first published as a unit in 1871–2; the Old Testament he did not live to complete, but it was completed and published in 1885, on the basis of his translations into German and French.

The word 'literal' often appeared on the title pages of new translations, but it was not uncommon to see others described as 'modern'. In 1790, the first year of our period, Stephen Street published a 'literal version of the Psalms' while William Gilpin offered a 'modern speech' version of the New Testament. The tension between close and free renderings is particularly intense in biblical translation. Literal translators sometimes insisted that Greek and Hebrew must not be assimilated to English patterns because the truth of the Bible lies in the idiom and word order of the original. In 1845 James M'Farlan published a version of Ezekiel mostly retaining 'the same order of expression which occurs in the Hebrew original'. More famously, Robert Young published a literal translation of the Bible in 1863, 'according to the letter and idiom of the original languages' (Herbert 1968: 411), a version whose language however is at times very odd because of Young's theories about the tenses of the Greek and Hebrew verbs (see Bruce 1961: 132; Paul 2003: 266). Joseph Rotherman translated the New Testament 'according to the logical idiom of the original' in 1872, and a few years later Julia Smith, a Sandemanian, published a literal translation of the Bible in very unnatural English. Toward the end of the century translations into 'modern English', 'in a modern American dress', 'in current and popular idiom', etc., became more frequent. Particularly popular in America was *The Twentieth Century New Testament* (1898–1901), whose translators sought to 'exclude all words and phrases not in current English'.

It was only in the nineteenth century that several ancient translations of the Bible were themselves first translated into English. Two of these were done by Americans. The first English version of the Septuagint was the work of Charles Thomson, formerly the Secretary to Congress; it was published in Philadelphia in 1808. The American Congregational Minister James Murdock translated the New Testament on the basis of the Syriac in 1851, and this work was reissued six or more times. It was also during this period that famous early English translations of the Bible were published: the Wycliffite Bible was printed for the first time in 1850, and Tyndale's New Testament was reprinted several times in the course of the century.

Major poets were not often drawn to translating or paraphrasing the Psalms in the nineteenth century, though some would draw on them powerfully in their own work (Hopkins, for example, in the sonnet 'Thou art indeed just'). Among the minor English poets, the versions by James Montgomery are attractive, with the clarity and metrical skilfulness of his hymns, rather than the diffuse epic and lyric ambitions of his poems. The version by John Hookham Frere is disappointing. He was one of the finest verse translators of the century and moreover knowledgeable about Hebrew, but his translation, instead of being the 'austere and simple poetry' he desired to write (Frere 1872: II, 479), does not often rise above the low standards of contemporary sacred poetry, heaping up synonyms pleonastically ('the last degree | Of deep debasement, ignominy, and scorn, | Oppresses me overwhelm'd and overborne', Frere 1872: II, 484) and sometimes indulging in the typically religiose vocabulary of that poetry.

In sharp contrast, the 1,500 lines of biblical paraphrase which John Clare made in 1841, the year of his escape from the asylum at High Beach, include lively and innovative versions of several psalms, at times combining the colloquial and the archaic powerfully. He moves across a wide range of moods: from awe ('The Lord reigneth now earth is green in his smiles', Ps. 97; Clare 1984: I, 136) and intimate trust ('The Lord my lasting friend shall be', Ps. 91; Clare 1984: I, 134) to affliction ('Lord hear my prayer when trouble glooms', Ps. 102; Clare 1984: I, 137). He had previously imitated a handful of other psalms and was notable in particular for his loving attention to the countryside: 'Moss!... Put on your sattin smoothening green' (Ps. 148; Clare 1989: II, 605). William Barnes's translation of the Psalms lies unpublished in the Dorset County Museum. He did publish a version of the Song of Solomon, paraphrasing from the King James Bible into Dorset dialect; it was one of dozens of versions of the Song of Solomon in provincial dialects commissioned by Prince Louis Lucien Bonaparte, an amateur philologist, from 1858 to 1860 (Norton 1993: II, 256). The third chapter begins: 'By night on my bed I sought him I do love to my soul: I sought en, but noowhere could vind en; I called en, but he never heärd me. I'll rise then, an' goo round the town, in the streets, in the squares, a-seekèn the oone I do love to my soul' (Barnes 1859: 9).

Devotional Texts

Devotional writings both famous and obscure were translated in this period, largely in the second half of the nineteenth century; some of the most famous had never been translated before. The leaders of the Oxford Movement saw translation as a vehicle for their goals. E. B. Pusey undertook to translate and adapt a series of devotional texts for Anglican use. The first volume, *A Guide for Passing Lent Holily* (1844), was a translation of the late seventeenth-century French divine Avrillon. Though it was prefaced with remarks 'vindicating the principle, and pointing out the limits, of his adaptations', Pusey alarmed even some of his friends by choosing to translate a post-Tridentine French Catholic author (Liddon 1894–7: II, 388–90, 393). Further translations of Avrillon followed, as well as of other French devotional writers.

German presented another set of problems. When Susanna Winkworth published her translation of the fourteenth-century mystical work *Theologia Germanica* (1854), she offered it as an antidote to the German theology currently circulating in England. Her style is mildly archaizing; her subtitle is more so ('which setteth forth many fair Lineaments of Divine Truth and saith very lofty and lovely things touching a Perfect Life'). In his preface, Charles Kingsley was at pains to distance the work from pantheism, which he feared incautious readers might take Winkworth's close translation to endorse. Read properly, the translation would make readers more 'manlike' and be of use 'in the family, in the market, in the senate, in the study, ay, in the battlefield itself'. Kingsley also wrote the preface to Winkworth's translation of Tauler's sermons (1857), though he urged the excision of Romanist excrescences from it (see Thorp 1937: 96).

Cardinal Manning edited the first translation of the *Little Flowers* of St Francis of Assisi (1864), made by 'three devoted children' of St Francis: the Marchesa di Salvo, Lady Georgiana Fullerton, and the Revd Mother of the Franciscan convent at Bayswater, whose names do not appear on the title page (Hudleston 1926: vi–vii). The first translation of the books of St John of the Cross was made by the Tractarian convert to Catholicism, David Lewis, whose *Complete Works of Saint John of the Cross* (with a preface by Cardinal Wiseman) was published in 1864 and revised in 1889. Lewis has been highly praised as a translator, and his works have been reprinted in the twentieth century. In addition, he translated most of the works of St Teresa of Avila, as did the Irishman John Dalton. In 1865 Cardinal Manning edited a translation of Teresa's *Life*, which like the *Little Flowers* does not identify the translators.

In contrast to these works, there is a continuous tradition of the *Imitation of Christ* (generally attributed to Thomas à Kempis) in English. In the eighteenth century, John Wesley and Richard Challoner were among its translators. The dozen or so translations of the nineteenth century—all done after 1850—include two metrical versions, Annie Thompson's execrable octosyllabic couplets (1868), and Henry Carrington's iambic pentameter quatrains (1889). Some translators were free: Bishop Goodwin (1860) believed he could 'remove to a great extent the monkish dress' of the original without spoiling it, and the anonymous translator of 1894 cut references to saints and priests. The finest translation may be the one by Stephen MacKenna, who would achieve some fame in the twentieth century for his translation of Plotinus. Though he later regretted that he failed to do justice to the emotional richness of the original (MacKenna 1937: 8), he writes a fairly direct English ('Every man naturally desires knowledge; but what is the use of learning if we have not the fear of God?'), and his anonymous translation went through many editions.

Church Fathers

Pusey, Newman, and Keble oversaw the most important and influential translating enterprise of the Oxford Movement: 'The Library of the Fathers'. The series consisted of forty-eight volumes, published between 1838 and 1888. Only thirteen ancient authors were represented, and two of them, Chrysostom and Augustine, took up twenty-eight volumes. On the title page it was declared that the volumes had been 'translated by members of the English Church'; these translators, some of whom chose to remain anonymous, included a number of Oxford and Cambridge clerics. Their goal was to display continuity between the ancient Church and the Anglican; it was also done in the hope that the Anglican Church would once again value the Fathers, and so steer between the Latitudinarians, cultured despisers of the Fathers, and the Evangelicals, with their often Puritanical suspicion of ecclesiastical tradition. Pusey favoured exact and literal translations (a practice he defended in his preface to the *Confessions* of Augustine), while Newman argued for freer and more idiomatic renderings. Pusey was the main force behind the series, especially after Newman's withdrawal; his activity on its behalf mostly took the form of revising translations made by others. Nonetheless, though the title page announces that his version of the *Confessions* has been 'revised from a former translation', it should be regarded as an independent translation (as he states in the preface, Pusey 1838: xxxii). Along with Pusey's Augustine, Newman's Athanasius and Keble's Irenaeus have been singled out for praise. The series made available works that had not been previously translated, like Gregory's *Morals on the Book of Job*.

In the nineteenth century there appeared half a dozen new translations of Augustine's *Confessions*, the first since the seventeenth century (see Farrar and Evans 1946: 54–5). But an older translation continued to be read: William Watts's very literal version from 1631 was reprinted three times in the nineteenth century (and it was adopted as the Loeb translation in the twentieth). It also had an influence on two nineteenth-century versions of the *Confessions*, those by Pusey (1838) and J. G. Pilkington (1876). Watts's was the 'former translation' which Pusey consulted, and it was also used as a control by Pilkington to check his translation after he had finished it. Pusey's translation has established itself as a kind of classic and has been reprinted many times. However, it is more effective with Augustine's devotional moments than it is with his thought. Compare Augustine's account of how he learned to speak as an infant (I, 8) in Pusey and Pilkington:

> It was not that my elders taught me words (as, soon after, other learning) in any set method; but I, longing by cries and broken accents and various motions of my limbs to express my thoughts, that so I might have my will, and yet unable to express all I willed, or to whom I willed, by the understanding which Thou, my God, gavest me, practise[d] the sounds in my memory. When they named any thing, and as they spoke turned towards it, I saw and remembered that they called what they would point out by the name they uttered. (Pusey 1838: 8)

> for my elders did not teach me words in any set method, as they did letters afterwards; but I myself, when I was unable to say all I wished and to whomsoever I desired, by means of the whimperings and broken utterances and various motions of my limbs, which I used to enforce my wishes, repeated the sounds in my memory by the mind, O my God, which Thou gavest me. When they called anything by name, and moved the body towards it while they spoke, I saw and gathered that the thing they wished to point out was called by the name they then uttered. (Pilkington 1886: 49)

Pusey's desire to be literal and to follow the Latin word order closely has resulted in a jerky English far less competent than Pilkington's to convey complex ideas with clarity. However, his literalism is not without its advantages, as the repetition of 'will' echoes, and even intensifies, Augustine's own emphasis.

The Presbyterian, evangelical publishing house T. & T. Clark in Edinburgh followed the example of the High Anglicans and launched its own series: 'The Ante-Nicene Library'. Its shorter chronological scope reflects a greater concern to limit 'Roman novelties'; it also enabled the selection to be more comprehensive, less partial (even so, only a few of Origen's works were translated in the series). Twenty-four volumes were published between 1866 and 1872, edited by two academics, James Donaldson and Alexander Roberts, and translated by twenty-two men, mostly clerics. The library was highly praised by reviewers for its faithfulness, its refusal to 'tone down' the Fathers; still the sales, even with the essential American market, were 'unspectacular' (Dempster 1992: 45, 47). This series was reprinted in the United States in the mid-1880s and then followed by two series of Nicene and Post-Nicene Fathers, edited by Philip Schaff and Henry Wace; they offered both revised versions of translations that had appeared in the Oxford Library and some new works. Readily available in their day, many time reprinted in the twentieth century, and now freely accessible on a public website, they have exerted a large influence.

LIST OF SOURCES

For further information on biblical translations see Herbert 1968, Chamberlin 1991, and Paul 2003.

Translations
Barnes, William (1859). *The Song of Solomon in the Dorset Dialect, from the Authorised English Version*. London.
Churton, Edward (1854). *The Book of Psalms in English Verse*. Oxford (the 'Cleveland Psalter').
Clare, John (1989). *The Early Poems*, ed. Eric Robinson, 2 vols. Oxford.
—— (1984). *The Later Poems*, ed. Eric Robinson, 2 vols. Oxford.
Darby, John Nelson (1871–2). *The Gospels, Acts, Epistles, and Book of Revelation, Commonly called the New Testament*. London (first pub. in undated parts 1859–67).
—— (1885). *The Holy Scriptures commonly called the Old Testament*. London (first pub. in four parts 1883–5).
Davie, Donald, ed. (1996). *The Psalms in English*. London.
Frere, John Hookham (1872). *The Works of John Hookham Frere in Verse and Prose*, 2 vols. London.
Lewis, David (1864). *The Complete Works of Saint John of the Cross of the Order of Our Lady of Mount Carmel*. London.
—— (1870). *The Life of St. Teresa of Jesus, of the Order of Our Lady of Carmel*. London.
[MacKenna, Stephen] (1896). *The Imitation of Christ* [attributed to Thomas à Kempis]. Dublin.
Manning, Henry Edward, ed. (1864). *The Little Flowers of St. Francis of Assisi*. London.
Montgomery, James (1822). *Songs of Zion, being Imitations of Psalms*. London.
Murdock, James (1851). *The New Testament... A Literal Translation from the Syriac Peshito Version*. New York.
Pilkington, J. B. (1886). *The Confessions... of St. Augustine*. Buffalo, NY (first pub. 1876).
Pusey, E. B. (1838). *The Confessions of S. Augustine*. Oxford.
—— (1844). *A Guide for Passing Lent Holily* [Avrillon]. Oxford.
Pusey, E. B. et al., eds. (1838–88). *Library of the Fathers of the Holy Catholic Church: Anterior to the Division of the East and the West*, 48 vols. Oxford.

Roberts, Alexander, and Donaldson, James, eds. (1866–72). *The Ante-Nicene Christian Library: Translations of the Fathers down to AD 325*, 24 vols. Edinburgh.

Schaff, Peter, and Wace, Henry, eds. (1886–1900). *A Select Library of the Nicene and Post-Nicene Fathers of the Christian Church*, 28 vols. in two series. Buffalo, NY.

Thomson, Charles (1808). *The Holy Bible... translated from the Greek*. Philadelphia, PA.

Winkworth, Susanna (1854). *Theologia Germanica*. London.

—— (1857). *The History and Life of the Reverend Doctor John Tauler of Strasbourg, with Twenty-five of his Sermons (temp. 1340)*. London.

Young, Robert (1863). *The Holy Bible, containing the Old and New Covenants, Literally and Idiomatically Translated out of the Original Languages*. Edinburgh.

Other Sources

Baxter, Lucy (1887). *The Life of William Barnes, Poet and Philologist*. London.

Bruce, F. F. (1961). *The English Bible: A History of Translations*. Oxford.

Chamberlin, William J. (1991). *Catalogue of English Bible Translations*. New York.

Copinger, W. A. (1900). *On the English Translations of the 'Imitatio Christi'*. Manchester.

Daniell, David (2003). *The Bible in English*. New Haven, CT.

Dempster, John A. H. (1992). *The T. &. T. Clark Story: A Victorian Publisher and the New Theology*. Edinburgh.

Farrar, Clarissa P., and Evans, Austin P. (1946). *Bibliography of English Translations from Medieval Sources*. New York.

Herbert, A. S. (1968). *Historical Catalogue of the Printed Editions of the English Bible 1525–1961*. London.

Hudleston, Roger, ed. (1926). *The Little Flowers of St Francis of Assisi in the First English Translation Revised and Amended*. London.

Liddon, Henry Parry (1894–7). *Life of Edward Bouverie Pusey*. 4 vols. London.

MacKenna, Stephen (1937). *Journal and Letters*, ed. E. R. Dodds. London.

Norton, David (1993). *A History of the Bible as Literature*, 2 vols. Cambridge.

—— (2005). *A Textual History of the King James Bible*. Cambridge.

Paul, William E. (2003). *English Language Bible Translators*. Jefferson, NC.

Shaen, Margaret J., ed. (1908). *Memorials of Two Sisters: Susannah and Catherine Winkworth*. London.

Shea, David, and Whitla, William, eds. (2000). *Essays and Reviews: The 1860 Text and its Reading*. Charlottesville, VA.

Sheehan, Jonathan (2005). *The Enlightenment Bible: Translation, Scholarship, Culture*. Princeton, NJ.

Thorp, Margaret Farrand (1937). *Charles Kingsley 1819–1875*. Princeton, NJ.

10.2 The Revised Version of the Bible

David Norton

The first major revision of the King James or Authorized Version of the Bible (1611; KJB) was the Revised Version (1885; RV). The revisers faced in the most acute form the dilemma of all translators, whether to be ruled by the original languages or by their own. With even the smallest letter of the originals being sacred, the Bible has always exerted a unique pressure towards literal rather than literary translation. But the Bible in English was also a literary text; in the words of the RV Old Testament (OT) preface, it was 'an English classic' (p. vi). Moreover, its English, with that of the Prayer Book, had become the inescapable form of religious English, so there was also an extreme stylistic pressure. The revisers had to produce, if possible, a religious and a literary work.

The prime motive for revision was dissatisfaction with the KJB's accuracy, and therefore its reliability as a presentation of religious truth; as one writer put it, 'no man can fully and truthfully expound the Holy Scriptures if he depends altogether upon the authorized Version' (Day 1858: 5–6). This dissatisfaction increasingly focused on the biblical heart of Christianity, the New Testament (NT). Much new evidence for the Greek text had been discovered since 1611, and, besides, the Victorians were confident their understanding of Greek outdid that of their Jacobean predecessors.

Decades of advocacy produced the will necessary for official revision in 1870. A motion 'to report upon the desirableness of a revision of the Authorised Version of the New Testament', amended to include the OT, was approved by the Convocation of Canterbury. A committee then reported that a revision making necessary emendations was desirable, and noted that it did 'not contemplate any new translation of the Bible, or any alteration of the language, except where in the judgment of the most competent scholars such change is necessary' (Hemphill 1906: 30). Rules for this cautious, minimal revision were drawn up. The following concern the scope of the work:

1. To introduce as few alterations as possible into the text of the Authorised Version consistently with faithfulness.
2. To limit, as far as possible, the expression of such alterations to the language of the Authorised and earlier English versions.
4. That the text to be adopted be that for which the evidence is decidedly preponderating; and that when the text so adopted differs from that from which the Authorised Version was made, the alteration be indicated in the margin.

They could hardly be more basic, giving one criterion each for what to change in the translation, the language to use for it, and what to change in the original language texts. However, the seemingly innocuous move from contemplating necessary changes to thinking of changes that are consistent with faithfulness was to prove significant.

The other rules were procedural. Most importantly, the work was to be done twice, first provisionally, then finally. Proposed changes were to be voted on, a simple majority deciding in the first revision, but two-thirds required in the final revision. This enforced the strictest sort of committee translation, with a strong bent towards minimal change.

Independent committees were established for each Testament. In addition, American cooperation was sought and obtained. Thus the largest body of translators ever, ninety-nine, worked on the translation, half of whom were from Episcopalian churches and half from other denominations, a combination which minimized sectarian tendentiousness. Moreover, the American cooperation meant that the RV contained notes of different readings preferred by the Americans.

The NT committee met in the Jerusalem Chamber of Westminster Abbey on four consecutive days each month, working through passages read out from the KJB by the chairman, Charles Ellicott; they attended to proposals for change, first to the Greek, then the translation. The first revision of the NT took 241 meetings, that is, six years of work, the second revision 96 meetings. A further 36 meetings were given to considerations of English phraseology and to consideration of American responses to the work. The final months were devoted to the single question of uniformity in rendering individual Greek words. The work finished on 11 November, 1880, after 407 meetings attended by an average of 15.8 members (Newth 1881: 122–5).

Revising the New Testament

The single most important factor in the NT work was involved in one word from the rules, 'faithfulness':

> some alteration had been proposed in the rendering of the Greek to which objection was made that it did not come under the rule and principle of faithfulness. This led to a general, and, as it proved, a final discussion. Bishop Lightfoot... contended that our revision must be a true and thorough one; that such a meeting as ours could not be assembled for many years to come, and that if the rendering was plainly more accurate and true to the original, it ought not to be put aside as incompatible with some supposed aspect of the rule of faithfulness. (Ellicott 1901: 98–9)

Having made this decision, the committee could not, if it was to be consistent, treat apparently inconsequential aspects of Greek any differently from the cruxes, and it was equally bound to represent, as far as English permitted, all the niceties of the Greek. The Greek decisively overruled considerations of English style. If the KJB was a more literal, often less stylish translation than Tyndale's (see Daniell 1994), then the RV NT continued the tendency.

This is not to say that the revisers believed they were turning their back on 'the sense and spirit of the original' (Ellicott 1901: 98): they were clear as to where the sense and spirit lay, in the smallest details of the eclectic Greek text they created for themselves. They could argue that in this way they avoided tendentiousness and produced truth. Brooke Foss Westcott nicely brings this out, moving from precision in the rendering of prepositions to theological truth:

> Two alterations... each of a single syllable, are sufficient to illuminate our whole conception of the Christian faith. How few readers of the Authorised Version could enter into the meaning of the baptismal formula, the charter of our life; but now, when we reflect on the words, 'make disciples of all the nations, baptising them into (*not* in) the name of the Father and of the Son and of the Holy Ghost' (Matt 28: 19), we come to know what is the mystery of our incorporation into the body of Christ. And as we learn this we enter into St Paul's words, 'the free gift of God is eternal life in (*not* through) Christ Jesus our Lord' (Rom 6: 23). It is indeed most true that the Son of God won life for us, but it is not anything apart from Himself.... Am I then wrong in saying that he who has mastered the meaning of these two prepositions now truly rendered—'*into* the Name', '*in* Christ'—has found the central truth of Christianity? (1897: 62–3)

Occasionally the many accounts of the work and the surviving manuscript material show both the process and the reasoning behind changes. Luke's Gospel describes how at the age of 12 Jesus listened to and questioned the doctors in the temple at Jerusalem, amazing everyone with his understanding and answers. In response to his mother's reproach, he replies, 'wist ye not that I must be about my Father's business?' (Luke 2: 49, KJB). In the RV this becomes, 'wist ye not that I must be in my Father's house?' The KJB's famous phrasing, now placed in the margin, implies that Jesus was beginning his ministry, teaching people, but this does not fit well with a context where the young man is clearly learning, and incidentally impressing with his precocity. So argued David Brown in the first revision, surprising Ellicott, who had supposed that 'no one will propose to change this'. Brown noted that the Greek (literally, as the margin notes, 'in the things of my Father') could mean 'in the business' or 'in the premises of my Father', and that 'premises' was the correct understanding because of the context and because of the later statement during the marriage at Cana that 'mine hour is not yet come' (John 2: 4), implying that the ministry, and therefore doing his Father's business, was yet to begin.

The reading was adopted unanimously, but, at the second revision, Brown supposes that the revisers 'had forgotten... their reason for accepting this rendering of the verse, and restored the Authorised Version, putting the other in the margin' (Blaikie 1898: 229–30). Samuel Newth's notes record that Archdeacon Palmer proposed moving 'in my Father's house' to the margin, and that this was carried 8 to 5 (3: 153^v). Subsequently Dr Field of Norwich circulated a paper to the revisers demonstrating that, in spite of the ambiguity, there are examples in the Septuagint and in classical and patristic Greek of the phrase meaning 'in the house', while there are none for the meaning, 'to be about a person's business'. Moreover, though the Vulgate, Arabic, and Ethiopic are ambiguous, the Syriac has 'in the house of my Father', and various of the Greek Fathers read the verse in this sense (Humphry 1882: 98). Such thorough argument reversed the decision, and a famous answer was again removed from the text in favour of a more probable understanding.

In such ways the religious and scholarly duty typically took precedence over the literary duty. When the NT was greeted with widespread criticism for going beyond necessary changes to make a host of changes that manifested 'pedantic literality' and 'faulty rhythm', the revisers' response was that they had heard all these arguments in committee, and to declare with pride that they had given the English reader 'a copy of the original which is marked by a faithfulness unapproached ... by any other ecclesiastical version' (Westcott 1897: 2, 4). And heard them they certainly had: to give one example, when an English word was, according to their principles, used for the Greek, producing objectionable English, one of the revisers exclaimed, 'we are impoverishing the English language', to whispers of 'hear, hear' from across the table (Hemphill 1906: 79). Yet it is worth noting that, for all that the translators made 36,191 changes (an average of four and a half changes in each verse, Hemphill 1906: 71), there is plenty of evidence that arguments for the KJB's language and understanding did succeed in the first revision, and that KJB readings were sometimes restored during the second revision. 'Pedantic literality' was tempered by a literary consciousness and the lure of the KJB.

Revising the Old Testament

The RV OT has a somewhat different character that owes much to its original text. The revisers judged that the present state of knowledge did not justify a reconstruction, so they adopted the same Masoretic text the KJB translators had used, and varied from it 'only in exceptional cases' (preface v). This removed one major source of change, making the OT appear a lighter, less pedantic revision. It also made it appear more literary, since the bulk of the changes now concerned matters of English expression.

The surviving evidence all points to matters of English predominating in the discussions—and to eventual restraint in making changes: the average of just over one change per verse in Genesis compared with the NT's four and a half is telling (it is about the same as the number of changes made to Genesis in editions of the KJB between 1611 and 1769).[1] Moreover—the same could be said for a lesser proportion of the NT changes—the bulk of the changes are minor matters, spelling, including that of names, and punctuation, and matters of English such as changing 'his', when used as a neuter pronoun, to 'its'. Unless changes are highlighted, as in *The Interlinear Bible*, one can read for long stretches without noticing any difference from the KJB. For example, in Genesis 2, the revisers introduced

---

[1] 1,745 changes in 1,533 verses. Such a count includes every example of repeated changes since this is probably how the NT count was done. There are about 1,600 changes of punctuation and 50 textual changes in the KJB text of Genesis between 1611 and the 1769 Oxford edition which is the basis of most modern KJBs.

fourteen substantive changes as well as four changes to punctuation. Most of the substantive changes are very minor, concerned for example with the definite article or the correct translation of the dual. Overall the result is slightly more literal, even at the expense of clarity, as when the Hebrew name 'Cush' is restored in place of 'Ethiopia' (v. 13), or when a phrase is translated literally as 'in front' (v. 14) despite the fact that the KJB translation 'toward the east' reflects the usual sense.

Almost nothing in the changes to Genesis 2 suggests revision for stylistic purposes, yet in the first revision the desire to rewrite was constantly present, as can be seen in the way they tackled v. 5 ('and every plant of the field before it was in the earth, and every herb of the field before it grew'). The Hebrew presents a problem because it follows 'and all' or 'every', with a negative, 'not yet'. Previous translators going back to the Septuagint had ignored the negative aspect, but the revisers decided to bring it out at the expense of 'every', perhaps judging that 'no plant' was the negative form of 'every plant'. Here is the sequence of suggestions they made (the version adopted is given in bold, interim suggestions in square brackets):

1. Now
2. But
3. **no plant** [shrub] **of the field was yet** [as yet was; yet existed] **in the earth**
4. ground
5. and no herb of the field yet grew
6. as yet was growing
7. had yet grown up
8. Now no shrub of the field was yet in the earth and no herb of the field had yet sprouted forth
9. And when as yet no shrub existed on the earth nor had any herb of the field sprung up
10. And every plant of the field was not yet in the earth, and every herb of the field had not yet sprung up
11. And as yet there was no plant of the field, and no herb of the field as yet sprouted
12. And no shrub [plant] of the field was yet in the earth
13. **and no herb of the field had yet sprung up**
14. Neither was there yet any plant . . . in the earth, nor had any . . . yet grown
15. No plant . . . was yet . . . nor had any . . . yet grown (Wright's notes: 3, adapted)

Only suggestion 10 preserves the Hebrew exactly, but it is obviously unsatisfactory as English. The rest explore different words or phrasings with degrees of looseness in relation to the structure of the Hebrew, showing some desire to rewrite for the sake of rewriting.

There were 1,470 suggestions for change in the first six chapters: a multitude of rejected suggestions is in the very nature of committee translation (and perhaps reflects the mental processes that go on, unrecorded except as occasional manuscript corrections, in the work of individual translators). That so few were eventually made shows the conservatism of the OT revision. This contrasts not only with the RV NT but also with the KJB: in Genesis 2 the KJB translators made twice as many changes to their exemplar.

The American Connection

The OT preface notes that many of the 'points of ultimate difference' between the English and the American revisers were 'changes of language which are involved in the essentially different circumstances of American and English readers' (x). One might casually take this as a reference to differences of vocabulary (grain for corn, etc.), but more was involved. Behind the work of the American revisers lay the hugely influential figure of Noah Webster, both as a lexicographer and as a reviser of the Bible. Amending the language of the Bible, he substituted 'words and phrases now in good use for such as are wholly obsolete, or deemed below the dignity and solemnity of the subject', corrected errors of grammar, and, where possible, euphemized (1833: iv). Webster's example was most effective in producing an anti-archaic spirit in the new world revisers. The English tended to increase the archaism of the text, while most of the American changes were to more modern forms and spellings. So they preferred 'a' and 'my' to 'an' and 'mine' before an aspirated h, 'who' for 'that' or 'which' referring to persons, 'astonished' to 'astonied', and spellings such as 'basin' for 'bason' and 'winevat' for the generally incomprehensible 'winefat'.

After an agreed lapse of time, the Americans published an RV with their preferred readings, the American Standard Version (1901). It may be that the difference between their cautious modernization of language and the RV's staunch conservatism led to the next major committee revision in America being a revision of the American Standard Version, the Revised Standard Version (1952). In England, however, the next major committee version, the New English Bible (1970), was a new translation rather than a revision, deliberately rejecting the hallowed language of the KJB for modern English. But for the work of the Americans, the RV, over-constrained by the pressures of literalism and the KJB's language, might well have proved to be a dead end for the progressive revision of Tyndale's work that had reached its most successful form in the KJB.

LIST OF SOURCES

Translations

Anon. (1834). *Specimen of a Proposed Accurate Translation of the Four Gospels, from the Received Greek Text, on the Basis of the Authorised Version*. London.

Alford, Henry (1869). *The New Testament... after the Authorised Version, Newly Compared with the Original Greek, and Revised*. London.

Bellamy, John (1818). *The Holy Bible, Newly Translated from the Original Hebrew*. London.

Eadie, John (1876). *The English Bible... with Remarks on the Need of Revising the English New Testament*. London.

Five Clergymen [John Barrow, George Moberly, Henry Alford, W. G. Humphry, Charles John Ellicott] (1857). *The Gospel According to St. John, after the Authorized Version. Newly Compared with the Original Greek, and Revised*. London.

The Holy Bible... Being the Version Set Forth A.D. 1611 Compared with the Most Ancient Authorities and Revised (1885). Oxford and Cambridge.
The Interlinear Bible: The Authorised Version and the Revised Version (1910). Cambridge.
Newcome, William (1785). *An Attempt towards an Improved Version... of the Twelve Minor Prophets*. London.
Webster, Noah (1833). *The Holy Bible... in the Common Version, with Amendments of the Language*. New Haven, CT.

Other Sources
Beard, John. R. (1857). *A Revised English Bible the Want of the Church and the Demand of the Age*. London.
Blaikie, William Garden (1898). *David Brown... : A Memoir*. London.
Burges, George (1796). *A Letter to... the Lord Bishop of Ely on the Subject of a New and Authoritative Translation of the Holy Scriptures*. Peterborough.
Burgon, John William (1883). *The Revision Revised*. London.
Chambers, Talbot W. (1885). *A Companion to the Revised Old Testament*. New York.
Daniell, David (1994). *William Tyndale: A Biography*. New Haven.
Day, Henry Thomas (1858). *Bible and Ritual Revision: A Plea for the Revision of the Authorized Version*. London.
Ellicott, Charles John (1870). *Considerations on the Revision of the English Version of the New Testament*. London.
—— (1901). *Addresses on the Revised Version of Holy Scripture*. London.
[Elliott, C. J.] (1881). 'The Revised Version New Testament.' *Edinburgh Review* 154: 157–88.
Hemphill, Samuel (1906). *A History of the Revised Version of the New Testament*. London.
Humphry, W. G. (1882). *A Commentary on the Revised Version of the New Testament*. London.
Johnston, David (1864). *Plea for a New English Version of the Scriptures*. London.
Lightfoot, Joseph Barber (1871). *On a Fresh Revision of the English New Testament*. London.
Newth, Samuel (1881). *Lectures on Bible Revision*. London.
—— (n.d.). 'New Testament Company, Notes of Proceedings, Taken and Transcribed by Samuel Newth.' British Library MS Add. 3,284–6.
Norton, David (1993). *A History of the Bible as Literature*, 2 vols. Cambridge.
—— (2000). 'Imagining Translation Committees at Work', pp. 157–68 in Orlaith O'Sullivan, ed., *The Bible as Book: The Reformation*. London.
Schaff, Philip (1873). *The Revision of the English Version of the Holy Scriptures*. New York.
Scholefield, James (1832). *Hints for an Improved Translation of the New Testament*. Cambridge.
Trench, Richard Chenevix (1858). *On the Authorized Version of the New Testament, in Connexion with some Recent Proposals for its Revision*. London.
Westcott, Brooke Foss (1897). *Some Lessons of the Revised Version of the New Testament*. London.
Wright, William Aldis (n.d.). 'Proposed alterations in the Authorised Version.' Hectographic reproduction of manuscript notes. Cambridge University Library.

10.3 Sacred Books of the East

Richard Fynes

Introduction

The publication by the Clarendon Press between the years 1879 and 1910 of the fifty volumes of the Sacred Books of the East (SBE) translated by twenty-one scholars under the general editorship of Friedrich Max Müller, professor of comparative philology at the University of Oxford, marked a culmination of nineteenth-century linguistic scholarship, and the series provides a useful focus for the discussion of late nineteenth-century western attitudes to the translation of non-Christian religious texts. The fifty years prior to the publication of the first SBE volume had seen great advances in the study and understanding of the Indo-Aryan languages and of classical Chinese. The British Sanskritists H. T. Colebrook and H. H. Wilson, the first holder of the Boden chair of Sanskrit at the University of Oxford, built on the work of Sir William Jones and the eighteenth-century Orientalists (for a fuller discussion see §§ 7.1 and 7.3, above). The systematic study of Buddhism and of the Pali language was initiated by the French scholar Eugène Burnouf and the Norwegian scholar Christian Lassen. Burnouf also advanced the study of Zoroastrianism by working on the manuscripts of the Avesta that had been taken to France in 1771 by Anquetil du Perron. Notable landmarks in the history of translation were Wilson's English translations of the *Viṣṇu Purāṇa* (1840) and of the first book of the *Ṛg Veda* (1850), Burnouf's French translation of the *Bhāgavata Purāṇa* (1840–7), the Latin translation by the Danish scholar Victor Fausböll of the Pali *Dhammapada*, and the commencement in 1841 of his translation of Chinese classics by the Scottish missionary James Legge, later to become professor of Chinese at Oxford and Max Müller's most valued collaborator on the SBE.

Max Müller had conceived the idea of assembling a team of scholars to provide a series of translations of what he saw as the principal texts of the major eastern religions in 1875, when he first broached the idea to Legge. He circulated a prospectus and gained powerful support. In 1877 it was agreed that the Oxford University Press would publish twenty-four volumes at the joint expense of the Press and the Government of India. The terms offered to the translators were sufficiently generous to ensure the engagement of competent scholars: they were to receive £4 per quire of printed text. Max Müller's remuneration was even more generous: he received £100 for each published volume. The first volume appeared in 1879, and by early 1882 fourteen volumes had been published. Max Müller then began to lobby for an extension to the number of twenty-four volumes stipulated in the original agreement. This request was approved, and the fiftieth and final volume in the series was published in 1910, ten years after Max Müller's death: Moriz Winternitz, *A General Index to the Names and Subject-matter of the Sacred Books of the East* (SBE 50).

Max Müller's object was to apply to the study of religion the methods of comparative philology, first developed in the early nineteenth century by Franz Bopp. The SBE volumes were to provide the working data for a new 'science of religion', the method and goal of which were 'to collect all the evidence that can be found on the history of religion all over the world, to sift and classify it, and thus try to discover... the laws which govern the growth and decay of human religion, and the God to which all religion tends' (Müller 1873: 281). Allied to his belief in the comparative method, Max Müller had developed a belief in an evolutionary theory of religion according to which God progressively revealed himself during the process of history (for a full account see Voight 1967: 14 ff.). The publication of the SBE was to be one of the determining steps in this process, which would ultimately lead to the discovery of the very essence of religion: 'These *Sacred Books of the East* will become in future the foundation of a short but universal religion' (Müller 1902: 141). The twenty-four volumes of the initial series were to be divided among texts of the Vedic religion, Zoroastrianism, Buddhism, Confucianism, Daoism, and Islam. In applying the term 'sacred' to this heterogeneous material, Max Müller was claiming the validity of the comparative method that would use the texts as a source for the discovery of religious truth. Codification, law, and texts as a source of authority were key concepts in his understanding of what constituted a sacred text. In his lecture on 'Sacred Books' given as part of the Gifford Lectures at the University of Glasgow in 1888 he stated: 'Sacred Books may be said to be to religion what legal codes are to law' (Müller 1889: 563). This attitude naturally became a determining factor in the selection of texts for translation and is one of the reasons for the number of volumes containing codifications of law.

Revealed literature in Sanskrit: *Vedas, Brāhmaṇas*, and *Upaniṣads*[1]

The *Vedas, Brāhmaṇas,* and *Upaniṣads* are part of a literature that was thought to be uncreated, eternally existent, and revealed to mankind by semi-divine sages. Its *raison d'être* was ritual sacrifice, the central element of which was fire: the *Vedas* consist primarily of hymns to be recited at ritual sacrifices by Brahmins, the hereditary class of sacrificial priests, the *Brāhmaṇas* are voluminous tracts containing instructions and mythological explanations for the performance of sacrifice ritual, and the varied material of the *Upaniṣads* develops from speculation about the relationship between the sacrifice and the universe. No element of this vast literature, which continued to be transmitted predominantly by oral exegesis even after the

---

[1] The system of transliteration for the series adopted by Max Müller and imposed by him on the individual translators was a stumbling block for both its general and its scholarly readership. In the following survey of the individual volumes of the SBE I have reproduced Max Müller's system of transliteration when citing the published titles of the volumes, but in all other cases I have used the system of transliteration now in common use.

development of systems of writing in India in the third century BCE, can be dated with any precision; the oldest parts of the *Ṛg Veda* probably date from *c*.1200 BCE, while the most recent of the 'classical' *Upaniṣads* probably dates from *c*.300 BCE.

The *Upaniṣads* were translated by Max Müller himself in two volumes, in 1879 and 1884 (SBE 1 and 15). He tells in his introduction to the first of these that his 'real love for Sanskrit literature was first kindled by the Upanishads' and states his belief that 'the earliest of these philosophical treatises will always... maintain a place in the literature of the world, among the most astounding productions of the human mind in any age and in any country' (SBE 1: xlv, xlvii). However, he did not value so highly all elements of the *Upaniṣads*, the oldest of which are compilations of earlier material. The *Upaniṣads* have attracted over the centuries a body of diverse interpretation and commentary. One of the dominant schools has been that of Vedānta philosophy, the chief tenet of which is the identity of the individual self (*ātman*) with the impersonal underlying principal of the universe (*brahman*). Max Müller's translation is free from the most zealous over-interpretations of the Vedantic commentators. Nevertheless, it was those elements in the *Upaniṣads* which provided support for and were the foundation for a Vedāntic viewpoint that he chiefly valued and which as a consequence led him to present an over-spiritualized interpretation in parts of his translation. He employed euphemisms when translating the more sensual material in the *Upaniṣads* and left untranslated passages which he judged too frankly sexual for translation.

Given that Max Müller's scholarly reputation rested upon his edition of its Sanskrit text, his selection of hymns from the *Ṛg Veda*, *Vedic Hymns Part I: Hymns to the Maruts, Rudra, Vāya, and Vāta* (SBE 32, 1891), is a disappointment. Based on his earlier translation of hymns to the Maruts published in 1869 with the addition of some further hymns and revisions, the volume does not provide a balanced overview of the 1,028 hymns of the *Ṛg Veda*. The actual purpose of the hymns, their recitation by Brahmin priests at various sacrifices, is nowhere discussed. Indeed, in apparent contradiction to the aims of the SBE, Max Müller had a proprietary attitude to the *Ṛg Veda* and wished to confine its study to the cognoscenti. The reason why hymns to the Maruts, the Vedic storm gods, which, as he conceded, are not the most attractive of the Vedic hymns, formed the main body of his selection was because he 'hoped they would prove attractive to serious students only, and frighten away the casual reader who has done so much harm by meddling with Vedic antiquities' (SBE 33: xxiii).

Hermann Oldenberg, professor of Sanskrit at Kiel University, who had collaborated with Max Müller on the first volume, translated the second volume of Ṛg Vedic hymns in the series, *Vedic Hymns Part II: Hymns to Agni (Mandalas I–V)* (SBE 46, 1897). Oldenberg was more directly engaged in current Vedic research than was Max Müller at that time, so his volume, consisting of hymns to Agni, the Vedic god of fire, has the advantage of greater accuracy. However, the reader lacking a background in Vedic studies is given no help in contextualizing the hymns, since Oldenberg's introduction consists of a single sentence acknowledging Max Müller's assistance.

In overall usefulness, the two volumes of hymns from the *Ṛg Veda* in SBE did not provide an advance on the pioneering translation of the *Ṛg Veda* begun by H. H. Wilson and completed after Wilson's death by E. B. Cowell and W. F. Webster. This, despite inaccuracies that were unavoidable given the pioneering nature of the work, had the virtue of completeness. It is striking that the two SBE volumes contain no translation of *Ṛg Veda* X, 90, the famous *Puruṣa-sūkta*, Hymn to the Cosmic Man, a creation hymn which provides a rationale for the hierarchical structure of Indian society.

Maurice Bloomfield, professor of Sanskrit at Johns Hopkins University, Baltimore, was the translator of *Hymns from the Atharva-Veda together with Extracts from the Ritual Books and the Commentaries* (SBE 42, 1897). Bloomfield's volume, a selection of about one third of the total material of the *Atharva Veda*, provides a useful conspectus of its heterogeneous content of hymns, charms, incantations, spells, and curses and is more accessible than many other volumes in the series, Bloomfield's language, both in his translation and his notes, being direct and in parts even lively.

The *Brāhmaṇa* texts were represented by the five volumes of *The Satapatha-Brâhmana according to the Text of the Mâdhyanindâ School* (SBE 12, 26, 41, and 43–4, 1882–90), translated by Julius Eggerling, professor of Sanskrit at the University of Edinburgh. In the opening paragraphs of his preface to the first volume, Eggerling demonstrates a somewhat disenchanted view of his material and also the extent to which his understanding of non-western religions, like those of other contributors to the SBE, was informed by the ethos of nineteenth-century protestantism (SBE 12: ix). Nevertheless, the remainder of the introduction is informative, the translation sound, and the SBE volumes remain the standard English translation of the *Śatapatha Brāhmaṇa*.

Although it is not considered to be a revealed text, it is convenient to discuss at this point, since it is an attempt to give logical form to the diverse material of the *Upaniṣads*, the *Brahma Sūtra*, commonly known as the *Vedānta Sūtra*. The *Brahma Sūtra* is ascribed to the authorship of Bādarāyaṇa, who lived sometime in the first five centuries CE. This relatively short text, written in the terse, aphoristic *sūtra* style (the basic meaning of *sūtra* is thread), has been the stimulus for a diverse and voluminous commentarial tradition. George Thibaut, Principal of Sanskrit College, Banaras, translated the text with its earliest surviving commentary, that of Śaṅkara (SBE 34, 38). Thibaut's dry but accurate style was well suited to the terseness of both the original text and Śaṅkara's commentary, as it was to his later translation of the same *Brahma Sūtra* presented with the commentary of Rāmānuja, known as the *Śrībhāṣya* (SBE 48).

Sanskrit Texts on Law: Rules for Ritual and Society

'Law' is an inadequate translation of the Sanskrit word *dharma*, which, depending on the context, can mean religion, law, right, duty, morality, nature, society as it should be, the correct performance of ritual, as well as other associated meanings.

Texts dealing with social and ritual duties, the *Gṛhya Sūtras*, the *Dharma Sūtras*, and the *Dharma Śāstras*, were composed and compiled by Brahmin priests and hence present a normative view of society from the point of view of a Brahminical ideology. The earliest of the *Dharma Śāstras* is also the best known in both India and the West: the *Mānava Dharmaśāstra* or *Manu Smṛti*, usually translated as the *Laws of Manu*.

It was their aspect as codices of law that initially led the British governors of the East India Company to encourage the translation into English of the various *sūtras* and *śāstras* which deal with custom and society and with ritual and domestic duties. A defining belief of British Orientalists of the later eighteenth century was that India should be governed according to its own laws and customs; to this end Sir William Jones, the founder of Indological studies (more fully discussed in Vol. 3 of this *History*), published his translation of the *Laws of Manu* in Calcutta in 1794 and was working on a *Digest of Hindu and Mohammedan Laws* at the time of his death in April of that year. Jones believed that his work on Indian law was his most important achievement. The British retained a trust in the utility of English translations of traditional Indian texts on law and custom long after the eighteenth-century heyday of Orientalism. Max Müller, believing that the SBE translations of the ancient lawbooks conferred a 'real benefit' on 'the administrators of the modern laws of India' (Müller 1882: 6), devoted seven volumes of the series to this material. Its western translators are sometimes criticized for replacing, in their search for clarity and definition, a fluid native tradition of disputation and commentary with the inflexibility of fixed texts; the benefits or otherwise of this remain a matter of debate.

The two volumes of *The Grihya-Sûtras* (SBE 29, 1886; 30, 1892) contained Hermann Oldenberg's competent translations of the *Gṛhya Sūtras* with useful introductory material and a less competent translation by Max Müller of the *Yajñaparibhāṣa Sūtras* (ancillary rules for performing a Vedic sacrifice), which was closely based on a German translation he had first published in 1855. Julius Jolly, professor of Sanskrit at the University of Würzburg, editor of the Sanskrit text of the *Mānava Dharmaśāstra*, also produced competent translations of some of the minor *Dharma Śāstras* (SBE 7, 33). Georg Bühler, professor of Indian philology and antiquities at the University of Vienna, prepared translations of the four surviving *Dharma Sūtras*, and the *Mānava Dharmaśāstra* (SBE 2, 14, and 25). Bühler's translations, despite his bowdlerization of some of the more sexually frank passages, which may have been due to Max Müller's editorial control rather than his own reticence, were of a very high standard, and his accompanying notes were scholarly and useful. These volumes remained the standard translations until the last decade of the twentieth century.

Epic Narrative Literature in Sanskrit

The two great epics of Sanskrit literature, the *Mahābhārata* and the *Rāmāyaṇa* (on which see also § 7.3, above), were composed in the period between about the third century BCE and the third century CE from martial narratives edited and expanded by Brahmin priests. Embedded within the narrative structure is material on statecraft, theology, and ethics. The major concern of the two epics is with *dharma*, in the sense of duty. Containing less-focused narratives than the two epics, but presenting accounts of dissolutions and creations of the universe, genealogies of gods and royal dynasties both legendary and historical, are the *Purāṇas* (Tales of Old), the earliest parts of which date from the fourth century CE. Given that this narrative material was of profound importance for the development of Indian culture, that the two epics were translated into nearly all the vernaculars of modern India, and that their stories were known to all through recitation and performance, it was a striking imbalance in the SBE series that Sanskrit narrative literature was represented by only one volume. This consisted of three self-contained episodes from the *Mahābhārata*: *The Bhagavadgîtâ with the Sanatsugâtîya and the Anugîtâ*, translated by Kashinath Trimbak Telang (SBE 8, 1882). Charles Wilkins's 1785 *Bhagavad Gītā* was the first English translation of a Sanskrit text to be published, and by the time of Telang's translation, several further translations into European languages had appeared. Wilkins's translation was a seminal element in the growth of popularity and the heightened status of the *Bhagavad Gītā* within Hinduism during the course of the nineteenth century. By the mid-twentieth century it had received more English translations than any other text originally composed in an Indian language and was established as a 'classic of world spirituality'. Telang's translation played little part in this process, failing to establish either an academic or a popular readership, since it was both inaccurate and so literal as to be in parts virtually unintelligible. The same faults vitiated Telang's accompanying translations, the first in English, of the *Sanatsujātīya* and the *Anugītā*.

Buddhist Texts in Sanskrit

The defining feature of Mahāyāna (Great Way) Buddhism (also known as Northern Buddhism among western scholars) was the compilation of new texts (*sūtras*), which, despite the fact that the earliest of them date from several centuries after the death of the historical Buddha, nevertheless claim his spiritual authority for their innovations, the most important of which is the promulgation of devotion to Boddhisattvas. A Boddhisattva is a human being who takes a vow to work for the salvation of others over a period of countless lifetimes. The Mahāyāna *sūtras* were compiled between the first century BCE and the sixth century CE.

The *Saddharmapuṇḍarīka Sūtra* or *Lotus Sūtra*, compiled sometime between 100 BCE and 100 CE, contains material on the way of life of the Boddhisattva, devotion, the nature of Buddhahood, and the advantages that accrue to those who promulgate the Lotus Sūtra; the Mahāyāna *sūtras* were themselves objects of devotion. Johan Hendrik Caspar Kern of Leiden prepared the SBE translation (SBE 21). He believed that not only the *Lotus Sūtra*, but also the *Upaniṣads*, the *Bhagavad Gītā*, and indeed the whole development of religious thought in India, was initially inspired by and subsequently pervaded by a solar mythology.

Although Kern's remains the only complete English translation of this important text, the reader needs to be aware that it is not unaffected by his mistaken belief, largely discredited even at the time of publication.

The other SBE volume of Mahāyāna texts contained the translations of three scholars: E. B. Cowell, F. Max Müller, J. Takakusu, *Mahâyâna Sûtras* (SBE 49, 1894). Cowell, professor of Sanskrit at Cambridge and Edward FitzGerald's adviser for the *Rubáiyát*, provided a translation of the *Buddhacarita* (Deeds of the Buddha) of Aśvaghoṣa (fl. *c.*120 CE). Aśvaghoṣa's poem on the life of the Buddha is the earliest surviving example of Sanskrit poetry written in the ornate and allusive style known as *kāvya*. Cowell, who published an edition of its Sanskrit text, was alive both to the intrinsic poetical merit of the *Buddhacarita* and to its influence on the succeeding development of classical Sanskrit poetics; he largely succeeded in his aim of producing an intelligible translation which conveyed the poetry and charm of the original. The remainder of SBE 49 consisted of translations of *sūtras* proper. Sanskrit texts of the *Sukhāvatīvyūha* (Description of the Pure Land) *Sūtras* had recently been discovered in Japan. They describe how rebirth in a pure and blissful land can be attained through devotion to the Buddha Amitābha. Max Müller's work on editing and translating these *sūtras* was his final substantial contribution to scholarly research. His lack of mastery of the technical terminology of Buddhist thought was not particularly detrimental to his translations of *Sukhāvatī Sūtras*, since they consist mainly of concrete descriptions of the Pure Land. However, his touch was not so sure in his translations of the *Heart Sūtras*, short texts asserting the truth that everything lacks ultimate existence.

Max Müller was responsible for the genesis of another series of translations, the Sacred Books of the Buddhists. He managed to obtain sponsorship for the expenses of the first three volumes from King Chulalankarana of Siam. J. S. Speyer translated the first volume in the series, a translation from the Sanskrit of the *Jātakamālā*, a collection of popular stories about the Buddha's previous lives: *Jâtakamâlâ: Garland of Birth-stories* (1895). The subsequent history of the series belongs to the twentieth century.

Texts in Middle Indo-Aryan Languages: Pali and Prakrit

Prakrit (*prākṛta*) is the generic term for the Middle Indo-Aryan languages which descended from Old Indo-Aryan as exemplified by Vedic Sanskrit. Pali (*Pāli*) is one of the Prakrits; the other Prakrit of which there were translations in the SBE is known as Ardhamāgadhī.

The basic meaning of Pali is 'text', and the name is applied to and is peculiar to the language of the texts of Theravāda Buddhism (also known as Southern Buddhism among western scholars), the main concentration of whose followers is now in Sri Lanka and the countries of South-East Asia. The Pali canon is divided into three *piṭakas* or baskets, which take their name from the baskets in which the palm-leaf manuscripts were deposited. The *Sutta Piṭaka* contains the Buddha's discourses or *suttas* (Sanskrit *sūtra*); the *Vinaya Piṭaka*, the rules for monastic life and the penalties for their infringement; and the *Abhidhamma Piṭaka*, a scholastic analysis of Buddhist doctrine. Also in Pali are voluminous commentaries on the canon, as well as important works, such as historical chronicles, which stand outside the canon.

The translations from the Pali of Thomas William Rhys Davids, with their scholarly yet accessible introductions and notes, are among the finest volumes in the SBE series. His *Buddhist Suttas translated from the Pâli* (SBE 11, 1881) was the first published English translation of Pali prose, consisting of an anthology of excerpts from seven sermons, chief among them the sermon the Buddha is reported to have delivered on his deathbed, the *Mahāparinibbāna Sutta*. One of the strengths of Rhys Davids's translations is his striving to find English renderings for the many technical terms in Pali. Even though, as he himself foresaw, some of his renderings have not stood the test of time, it was his work which formed the basis for further advances in knowledge. As co-author with Herman Oldenberg, he also translated half of the *Vinaya Piṭaka*, the rules of Buddhist monastic life: *Vinaya Texts Translated from the Pâli* (SBE 12, 17, and 20). The first volume contains a valuable introduction discussing the historical development of the *Vinaya*, which, since its rules give the background to their promulgation, is inextricably linked to and is largely synonymous with the development of early Buddhism. Since the work is concerned with prescribing modes of behaviour for monks and nuns who have abandoned the life of householders, it is inevitably concerned with lapses. Sexual misdemeanours, to which the *Vinaya* takes a pragmatic attitude, and their penalties are discussed in detail. However, Oldenberg and Rhys Davids, either because of their own reticence or Max Müller's editorial direction, felt unable to reproduce these passages, which were either bowdlerized or left untranslated. The final text Rhys Davids translated for the SBE was the *Milindapañha: The Questions of King Milinda: Part I* (SBE 35–6, 1890 and 1894). This is a post-canonical text which is held in high regard among Theravadin Buddhists; it consists of dialogue between a king, Milinda, whose capital was Sāgala in north-west India, and Nāgasena, a Buddhist monk. Rhys Davids considered the Milinda Pañha to be 'the masterpiece of Indian prose' (SBE 12: 232), and his translation does justice to its eloquence, humour, and varied characters and incident. Indeed, Rhys Davids, to a greater extent than most of the other SBE translators, who considered their originals primarily in the light of philological problems, was aware of the literary merits of his originals, and as a consequence his translations are livelier and more elegant than many others in the series.

Volume 10 of the SBE (1881) consists of two translations of verse portions of the Pali canon: F. Max Müller, *The Dhammapada: A Collection of Verses*; V. Fausböll, *Sutta-Nippâta: A Collection of Discourses*. The *Dhammapada* has since received many translations into western languages, and in the twentieth century it became, like the *Bhagavad Gītā*, naturalized in the West as a spiritual handbook. Max Müller's lack of a sound understanding of the technical vocabulary of Pali was detrimental to his translation, and furthermore Fausböll in the introduction to his translation of the *Sutta-Nipāta* stated that he found it impossible 'to find terms exactly corresponding to the varied terminology of Buddhism' (p. xiii). A second edition, in which Fausböll acknowledged the benefit gained from the suggestions of Rhys Davids, was published in 1898, but even so the volume was not representative of the advances in Pali scholarship which had been made by that time.

Just as Pali is peculiar to the texts of Theravāda Buddhism, so the Prakrit known as Ardhamāgadhī is peculiar to the canonical texts of the Śvetāmbara (White Clad) Jains; that is, those Jains whose ascetics wear a white robe. Hermann Jacobi, professor of Sanskrit at the University of Münster, was responsible for the two SBE volumes of translations from this Prakrit (SBE 22, 45). The dry and somewhat abrupt language of Jacobi's pioneering translations, which are peppered with bracketed words and phrases, conveys the difficulties of the originals but not the nature of their more poetical passages.

Avestan and Pahlavi

The *Avesta*, the sacred book of the Zoroastrians, is composed of various texts that were transmitted orally until committed to writing in Sasanian Persia in the fifth to sixth centuries CE. Its language, known as Avestan, is not otherwise attested. All the material is anonymous with the exception of seventeen hymns, the *Gāthās*, composed by the prophet of the religion, Zarathustra (or Zoroaster). The *Gāthās* are the earliest part of the *Avesta*, and their language is closely related to that of the *Ṛg Veda*. The *Avesta* was translated in three volumes, the first two by James Darmesteter (SBE 4, 23), the third, which contains the *Gāthās*, by Lawrence Heyworth Mills (SBE 31). The first volume gives a useful account of the reception in the West of the Avesta and of earlier translations. There have since been translations into European languages of individual parts of the *Avesta*, but the SBE volumes remain the only complete translation.

The five SBE volumes of *Pahlavi Texts* (SBE 5, 18, 24, 37, and 47) are the work of Edward William West, an engineer by training and one of the outstanding Orientalists of the century. *Pahlavi* is an adjective of which the basic meaning is 'Parthian' with the concomitant meaning 'heroic, ancient, and noble'. It is applied to the related dialects of Middle Persian in which Zoroastrian texts were written between the third and ninth centuries CE. West argued, against those who wished to confine the study of Zoroastrianism to the earlier parts of the *Avesta*, that a knowledge of the Pahlavi texts was essential for an understanding of the religion. His achievement is remarkable, given the difficulties of the material on which he was working and the fact that Pahlavi studies were still very much in their infancy.

Arabic Texts

Edward Henry Palmer, professor of Arabic at Cambridge, retained some of 'the nervous energy and rugged simplicity of the original' (SBE 6: lxxix) in his translation of the Qur'ān (SBE 6, 9). His use of a syntax and vocabulary influenced by the King James Bible also lent dignity to his translation. Biblical phraseology had previously been used by the Revd J. M. Rodwell in his translation of 1861, but whereas Rodwell was writing as a Christian apologist, Palmer was writing as an Arabist. His translation contains a valuable introduction to Islam and to the society among which the Prophet Muhammad received and recited the divine revelations which form the Qur'ān. Whereas Rodwell had rearranged its *sūrahs* or chapters into what he considered to be their chronological order, Palmer retained the arrangement of the original.

Max Müller's limited interest in and understanding of Islam was the reason why there were no further translations from Arabic in the series. In his prospectus to the SBE he wrote, 'For Islam, all that is essential is a trustworthy translation of the Koran' (Müller 1876: 4), and he later expressed pleased surprise at the positive reception given to Palmer's translation: 'Professor Palmer's translation of the Qurân... seems to have raised quite a new interest in a work which was often supposed to be unreadable except in Arabic' (Müller 1882: 8).

Chinese Texts

The six SBE volumes entitled *The Sacred Books of China* translated by James Legge, professor of Chinese at Oxford, formed a subset of the SBE series. Lauren Pfister has shown how his translations of *The Texts of Confucianism* (SBE 3, 16, 27, and 28) were informed by his desire to emphasize certain monotheistic elements in early Confucianism, and how in his translations of *The Texts of Taoism* (SBE 39, 40) he presented Daoism from a Confucian standpoint (Pfister 1995: 414 ff.; on Legge see pp. 358–60, above).

Another Chinese work in the series was the translation by Samuel Beal, professor of Chinese at the University of London, of *The Fo-Sho-Hing-Tsan-King, a Life of the Buddha by Asvaghosha Bodhisattva translated from Sanskrit into Chinese by Dharmaraksha, AD 420* (SBE 19, 1883). As is apparent from the title, this text is a Chinese translation of the Sanskrit poem which was translated by Cowell as part of SBE 44. Beal did not know Sanskrit, and so was unable to check the meaning of the Chinese against the Sanskrit original, of which the Chinese is in any case a rather free translation. He was forthright about the difficulties he found in translating the allusive Chinese from a single corrupt manuscript and was diffident in presenting his translation, which he stated was only to be regarded as tentative.

Conclusion

The Sacred Books of the East did not become the foundation of a 'short but universal religion' as Max Müller had hoped. Taken together, the series did not provide a balanced selection of the writings of the major eastern religions on which one could base such a comparative project. There were no translations from Japanese. Islam was represented solely by the Qur'ān; the collections of Sayings of the Prophet (*ḥadīth*) and the writings on Islamic customary law which developed out of them were ignored, as were the rich traditions of Islamic mysticism and philosophy. Even though Max Müller devoted seven volumes to texts on Hindu customary law, he seemed oblivious to the fact that Islamic customary law had been woven into the fabric of Indian society since the twelfth century. Nor did the SBE provide a balanced view of religious traditions within India. Max Müller, in his enthusiasm for the older Sanskrit of the *Vedas* and the *Upaniṣads*, was able to see little merit in the literature of Classical Sanskrit, which he regarded merely as 'pretty poetry'.

The scholarly reception and fate of individual volumes in the series differed. Some, among them those of Max Müller himself, became obsolete shortly after their publication; others remain standard translations in the first decade of the twenty-first century. By and large, the collection, with its dense notes and heavily bracketed translations, did not attain a wide readership in the West, despite the popular interest in eastern religions which continued to develop throughout the twentieth century in Europe and the USA.

For all its imperfections, the SBE is more than a monument to the scholarship of the latter part of the nineteenth century. The series affected the development of some eastern religions, since it made available to an educated lay public material which, since it was written in learned languages, had previously been the sole preserve of priestly classes. Moreover, by inducing so many scholars to work together on a common task, Max Müller stimulated a body of scholarly communication, a discourse in which those working in the areas of concern to the SBE continue to participate.

LIST OF SOURCES

The authors, titles, and dates of the individual volumes of SBE will be found above.

Translations
Burnouf, Eugène (1840–7). *Le Bhâgavata Purâṇa, ou histoire poétique de Krichna*, 3 vols. Paris.
Fausbøll, Viggo Michael (1855). *Dhammapadam*. Hauniae.
Müller, Friedrich Max (1869). *The Sacred Hymns of the Brahmans: Hymns to the Maruts or the Storm-Gods*. London.
—— ed. (1879–1910). *The Sacred Books of the East*, 50 vols. Oxford.
Rodwell, John Medows (1861). *The Koran, the Suras Arranged in Chronological Order*. London.
Speyer, Jacob Samuel (1895). *Jâtakamâlâ: Garland of Birth-stories*. London (Vol. 1 of the series *Sacred Texts of the Buddhists*).
Wilson, Horace Hayman (1840). *The Vishṅu Purâṅa, a System of Hindu Mythology and Tradition*, 5 vols. London.
—— Cowell, Edward Byles, and Webster, W. F. (1850–88). *Rig-Veda-Sanhita: A Collection of Ancient Hindu Hymns*, 6 vols. London.

Other Sources
Müller, Friedrich Max (1873). *Introduction to the Science of Religion*. London.
—— (1876). *The Sacred Books of the East, Translated, with Introductions and Notes, by various Oriental Scholars, and edited by F. Max Müller (Prospectus)*. Oxford (reprinted in SBE 1: xl–xlv).

—— (1882). *Sacred Books of the East: Letter to the Very Rev. the Dean of Christ Church, 18 March 1882*. Oxford.
—— (1889). *Natural Religion: The Gifford Lectures delivered before the University of Glasgow in 1888*. London.
[Müller, Georgina Max] (1902). *The Life and Letters of The Right Honourable Friedrich Max Müller*, 2 vols. London.
Pfister, Lauren F. (1995). 'James Legge', pp. 400–22 in Sin-wai Chan and David E. Pollard, eds., *An Encylopaedia of Translation: Chinese–English, English–Chinese*. Hong Kong.
Voight, Johannes H. (1967). *F. Max Müller: The Man and his Ideas*. Calcutta.

11

Philosophy, History, and Travel Writing

11.1	Greek and Roman Philosophy *Alexandra Lianeri*	473
11.2	Modern Philosophy, Theology, Criticism *Susanne Stark*	481
11.3	Modern History and Socio-political Theory *Ian Patterson*	489
11.4	Exploring the World *Laura Dassow Walls*	498

11.1 Greek and Roman Philosophy

Alexandra Lianeri

The translation of non-fiction (a category invented in the nineteenth century and developed for the use of libraries) is represented in this chapter by philosophy, history, biography, political and social criticism, and the literature of travel and exploration, the last being a capacious genre, combining science with historical and philosophical reflections. Such works accounted for more than a third of the published translations in the years examined in Chapter 4, above, and they include several popular and critical successes, such as the several histories by Guizot or Humboldt's *Cosmos*. The discussion of classical philosophy in this first section, emphasizing the influence of ideas, is meant to complement the discussion in Chapter 5, which treats classical works as literature; Lucretius is discussed in both places.

Greek Philosophy

The selection of texts to be translated privileged Greek over Roman philosophy. This choice was related to a broader tendency in both Britain and America to revive the Greek heritage in the new context of industrial economies, the secularization of religious discourses, and the founding of democratic politics (see further pp. 155–7, above). Though what motivated such a revival was a belief in the continuity between ancient and modern philosophical thought, translations of Greek philosophy had the effect of challenging the continuity which they had initially been called upon to sustain. Far from demonstrating the unity of philosophical reason, they formed a vehicle for debate about religion, political authority, ethics, and democracy.

The Greek text that helped to initiate this debate was the *Nicomachean Ethics*, first in the translation by John Gillies in 1797 and subsequently in other versions; it was one of the most frequently translated philosophical texts of the period. According to Stephen Halliwell, Gillies's work has 'a period refinement too elegant to be authentic' (2000: 378). It nevertheless had a notable popularity (it was reprinted four times), and during the first part of the century it influenced all other translations of the *Ethics*. One reason for this success may have been the text's ideological orientation, which moved Aristotle's thought in the direction of recent apologias for the Christian faith. Following Bishop Butler's attempt to prove the rational basis of religion, Gillies invited his readers to 'observe how nearly the rules discovered by reason and experience... coincide with those precepts which are given in the Gospel' (1797: I, 174). On this view, he sought to dissociate *eudaimonia* from happiness and to identify the 'supreme good' with moral Christian duty. Hence, he not only omitted the last sections of Book VII, which deal with the issue of pleasure, but also transformed several statements linking *eudaimonia* to the condition of 'living well'. A telling example is the translation of Aristotle's discussion of how to define *eudaimonia* (1.4.1–2; 1095ᵃ19). In rendering this passage, Gillies omitted the statement that *eudaimonia* consists of both 'faring well' (εὖ ζῆν) and 'acting well' (εὖ πράττειν); moreover, we subsequently read that only the vulgar relate the good to palpable things, while the learned define *eudaimonia* in terms of 'absolute goodness' (I, 152). The latter phrase was used as the equivalent of the Aristotelian concept of 'good in itself'. Yet the translation, by using the term 'absolute', alluded to a transcendent, divine origin of the good, while for Aristotle the good is a human achievement and lies in the form of life in which doing well and faring well may be found together (MacIntyre 1998: 60).

Thomas Taylor's translation in 1818 did not share Gillies's christianizing tendency; characteristically, it rendered *eudaimonia* by 'felicity' (1818: 8). Yet the translator's obscure and often archaic language alienated both reviewers and readership. The Revd D. P. Chase's translation of 1847 had a more favourable reception, resulting in two reprints. Chase's work followed Gillies in replacing the Aristotelian ethics of virtue with an ethics of (moral) duty. When, for example, he translated the beginning of the *Ethics* (1.1) he rendered the term 'the good' by 'the Chief Good', and instead of Aristotle's idea that every premeditated, deliberate choice (προαίρεσις) aims at the good, the translator wrote that only a 'moral choice' can do so (Chase 1847: 1). In the same vein, Robert William Browne's translation, addressed to students of Greek, also sought to dissociate *eudaimonia* from happiness by downplaying Aristotle's description of the concept in terms of both 'living well' and 'faring well' (Browne 1850: 5).

These translators set out to demonstrate that the Christian notion of moral duty does not merely involve obligation, but also fulfils the rational nature of humanity and is therefore ultimately beneficial for those who pursue it (see Chase 1847: 75). This claim was, however, challenged by the mid-nineteenth-century publication of Alexander Grant's annotated edition of the *Nicomachean Ethics* (1857–8), which encouraged a historicist reading of the Aristotelian text. Grant's work was not a translation, but a critical edition with commentary. He nevertheless offered an interpretation of the *Ethics* that had a profound influence on subsequent translators, especially since he provided several translations of isolated passages in the extended footnotes to the text. The main purpose of Grant's work was 'to exclude religious associations (as being un-Aristotelian) from our conception of the ethical *telos*'. Only then, he argued, would the moderns be able to recognize that this *telos* 'is evidently meant to have a definite relation to the nature and constitution of man' (Grant 1857–8: I, 173). Grant therefore abandoned the use of the terms 'Chief Good' or *summum bonum*, found in previous translations, and rendered the beginning of the *Ethics*: 'every art...act and purpose, seems to aim at some good' (II, 5n.i.i).

After Grant's publication, translators made substantially less use of Christian connotations and allusions. The most significant translators of the period, Robert Williams, Walter M. Hatch, St George William Joseph Stock, F. H. Peters, F. A. Basford de Wilson, S. H. Jeyes, J. E. C. Welldon, and Franklin Harvey, read Aristotle in terms of a secularized ethics which opposed utilitarianism and provided a new ideal of social coherence and order. For example, in the translations of Williams (1869: 5), Peters (1881: 5), and Wilson (1884: 11), Aristotle is dissociated from the view of *eudaimonia* or happiness as a condition of living well *and* faring well. The result was a striking attack on utilitarian ideas of happiness. By omitting the source idea of 'acting well'—and thus rewriting *eudaimonia* in terms of prosperity—and by further implying that such a claim is one which Aristotle himself rejects, the translators claimed at the very outset of the *Ethics* that Aristotle's subsequent arguments should be read as directed against the view which would link *eudaimonia* and a happy life. They could therefore argue that the end of human life was not to be identified with personal happiness but with the advancement of social unity. Man's perfection, as another translator put it, is found 'in a life in a community under the guidance of the State'. Aristotle's ethical enquiry instructs us that 'the study of life' in terms of ethical precepts 'will therefore be a study of civil life' (Hatch 1879: 2).

While none of the other Aristotelian works acquired the eminence of the *Ethics*, there was a notable interest in the *Rhetoric* and the *Poetics*. The most prominent translations of these treatises were by Thomas Taylor (1818) and Theodore A. Buckley (1850), whose version was included in the Bohn Classical Library. Towards the end of the century, the *Rhetoric* was also translated by J. E. C. Welldon (1886) and the *Poetics* by S. H. Butcher (1895). The reading of Aristotle in terms of the ideal of social unity created a renewed interest in the *Politics*, which had hitherto been read in translations by John Gillies (1797; it appeared in the same volume as his *Ethics*) and by Edward Walford (1853). Three new translations of the text appeared after 1870, by W. E. Bolland (1877), Welldon (1883), and Benjamin Jowett (1885). Although Jowett's work did not quite attain the popularity of his Platonic translations, it nonetheless became the most frequently reprinted translation of the *Politics* for the remainder of the century.

Unlike Aristotle, Plato did not attract the interest of many translators, nor did he have a central role in philosophical debates before the 1860s. The first complete English translation of Plato's works, written partly by Floyer Sydenham and partly by Thomas Taylor (1804), had a notoriously negative reception, due to its difficult language as well as Taylor's poor knowledge of Greek and his Neo-Platonist sympathies (see Turner 1981: 371). In 1848 Henry Rogers, writing anonymously in the *Edinburgh Review*, observed that given the 'great genius of Plato', it is surprising to see that 'so little justice has been done [to his works] by English translators' (Rogers 1848: 322).

A notable exception was John Stuart Mill's translation of nine Platonic dialogues, four of which were published in the *Monthly Repository* between 1834 and 1835. Mill combined commentary and translation to produce a free rendering.

His works omitted substantial parts of the dialogues (especially those descriptive of action) and inserted comments into the main body of the text. Their most distinctive feature was the enlistment of Plato in the liberal-democratic cause. This was partly achieved by a reappraisal of the Sophistic movement and the association of Socratic dialectics with the politics of liberal democracy. Hence in his version of the *Protagoras* Mill praised the Sophist's 'political art', but this praise was possible because Mill had downplayed the ambiguous role of τέχνη, which in the original is something that both sustains and undermines the political. Furthermore, by defining the political as a profession of experts, he transformed the source-text idea that the political art stands in a continuum with social life. For example, in his translation of Protagoras' argument about flute-players (372d), Mill introduced 'civilized men' as the equivalent to men reared within laws and society. He also replaced the statement that each of these men is educated to be 'just' as well as a 'maker' or 'craftsman' (δημιουργός) of justice with the assertion that a civilized man 'would appear a perfect master in virtue' (1978: 51). Yet the phrase 'master in' conveys only the idea of one who has expertise in the rules of justice and not one who 'produces' the laws by which justice is determined.

The mid-nineteenth century witnessed a renewal of interest in Platonic studies and translations. In 1818 Shelley had translated the *Symposium* with missionary fervour (see p. 10, above and Webb 1976: 299–300), but it was not published until almost twenty years after his death and seems to have had little influence. A wider audience was reached with a new translation of Plato's works written for the Bohn Classical Library by George Burges, Henry Cary, and Henry Davis between 1848 and 1854. This was followed by J. Llewelyn Davies and David James Vaughn's translation of the *Republic* (1852), which was reprinted four times by the end of the century, as well as William Whewell's *Platonic Dialogues for English Readers* (1859–61). As Frank Turner argues, while none of these translations can lay claim to exceptional value or interest, they nevertheless marked the outset of a new appreciation of Plato, which resulted in nothing less than a fully-fledged 'Platonic revival that far outshone that of the Renaissance' (Turner 1981: 371–2).

One of the most important works in this context was George Grote's *Plato and the Other Companions of Sokrates* (1865). Grote followed Mill's practice of combining commentary with translation. Indeed, although his book is conventionally treated as a scholarly treatise, a careful reading shows that the writer systematically uses translation to sustain his interpretation and analysis. A philosophical radical and utilitarian, Grote deepened and radicalized Mill's assimilation of Plato's text to liberal democracy. By relating Socrates to the Sophistic movement, Grote aimed to endorse the ideal of individual autonomy, without however severing personal liberty from constitutional loyalty (1865: II, 358–9, 362). His translation of Protagoras' concept of the 'maker' or 'craftsman' of justice (see above) maintained the original notion of 'craftsmanship' but nevertheless suppressed the term 'justice'. Grote presented the democratic citizen as 'a craftsman in...endowments' that relate to virtue, but not one who actually institutes justice (1865: II, 44). Grote's *Plato* had a mixed reception, which ranged from wholehearted praise to total rejection. Yet as the first extended rewriting of Plato in terms of modern democratic ideology, this book set up the vocabulary for a far-reaching and enduring debate over Plato's political allegiances.

The most influential nineteenth-century translation of Plato was Benjamin Jowett's *Dialogues of Plato*, first published in 1871 and revised in 1875 and 1892. Jowett also combined translation, analysis, and commentary, but not in continuous prose. His translations, couched in readable and often domesticating language, were said to have made Plato 'an English book' (Abbott and Campbell 1897: II, 7; see also pp. 121–2, above). This is probably the reason why they became remarkably popular for almost half a century, despite repeated criticisms from classical scholars. Jowett aptly captured the philosophical spirit of his time. His thought was well attuned to the retreat of the radicalized liberalism of the early part of the century and to the subsequent conservative and idealist turn of the liberal-democratic movement after the mid-1850s. Under the profound impact of Hegel, Jowett intended 'to represent Plato as the father of Idealism, who is not to be measured by the standard of utilitarianism or any other modern philosophical system' (1892: I, xi). His Plato was, indeed, devoid of allusions to utilitarianism. Yet Jowett's use of the rhetoric of the Authorized Version of the Bible (Turner 1981: 415) and the employment of Hegelian vocabulary, stressing the notions of state authority and social coherence, located the translation within contemporary philosophy and politics. Thus, his translation of the *Protagoras* 326d–e identified justice with the 'state' by using the latter term to render the word *polis*. This rendering enabled him to assert in his commentary that for Plato, as for Hegel, 'the state is the reality of which justice is the idea' (1892: III, vi).

Apart from Jowett's, several other translations of Plato contributed to the late nineteenth-century Platonic revival. These included fourteen translations of the *Apology*, seven of the *Euthyphro*, five of the *Meno*, three translations of the *Gorgias*, the *Philebus*, and the *Theaetetus*, as well as six complete or partial translations of the *Republic* (see Foster 1918; Turner 1981).

The end of the century was also marked by two translations of the Presocratics, who did not play a large role in shaping nineteenth-century culture. These were produced by John Burnet in 1892 and by G. T. W. Patrick, who rendered Heraclitus' fragments in 1889.

Roman Philosophy

During the nineteenth century, Greek philosophy was predominantly related to metaphysical, ethical, and political debates, while the reception of Roman philosophers focused on the questions of science, religion, and civil organization. As Norman Vance points out, the Victorians perceived a special connection between modern advances in science and political reform and the ancient Roman spirit of practical organization and scientific engineering (Vance 1997: 4).

In this context, the Roman who most attracted the philosophical imagination was Lucretius, regarded by many nineteenth-century writers as distinctly modern; in fact, he became the symbol of many versions of modernity. For Matthew Arnold he was associated with modern depression and *ennui*. For others, such as Marx and J. A. Symonds, he was the predecessor of scientific and free-thinking modernity. For J. H. Newman he was a writer who both fiercely denied and profoundly captured the nature of religious experience (see further Vance 1997: 84). In the early part of the century, John Mason Good published a translation in blank verse of *De Rerum Natura* (1805), W. H. Drummond translated the first book of the poem (1808), and Thomas Busby rendered the whole into rhymed couplets (1813). At mid-century John Selby Watson published a literal prose translation which was included, together with Good's verse translation, in the Bohn Classical Library (1851).

Yet the most important translation of the time was produced by the classicist H. A. J. Munro in 1864. This three-volume work included text, prose translation, and commentary and went through four editions, the last published in 1886. Munro had a deep and pervasive interest in comparing *De Rerum Natura* to modern scientific thought. Of Lucretius' conception of the universe he wrote: 'there is much that is striking, much even that may be true, much at all events that Newton accepted, in this description; something too in which he was in advance even of the age of Newton' (1886: 7). While Munro qualified this assertion by stating that the moderns do not care for Lucretius' 'scientific value or truth' but rather for his 'poetical grandeur', he nevertheless related the philosophical qualities of *De Rerum Natura* to its poetic passion: 'if his premises are granted, his arguments are striking and effective, and carried through with the energy of a fanatical conviction. The poetry and pathos and earnest satire...are of a very high order' (1886: 7). Paradoxically, while Munro admired Lucretius as a philosopher-poet, he did not attempt to convey the poetic dimension of philosophical thought. (For an appraisal of translations of Lucretius as poetry, see § 5.4 above.)

Despite Cicero's and Seneca's interest in questions of political organization and civil morality, neither was thought to possess a significant status as a philosopher. The nineteenth century witnessed 'the eclipse of Cicero as a thinker'. He was rarely quoted as an authority and little recommended for edification (Higginbotham 1967: 29). There are relatively few translations of Cicero's political philosophy (his moral treatises and letters are discussed in § 5.5 above). The *Republic* was translated by George William Featherstonhaugh (1829). This was followed by a translation of Cicero's political works, including the *Republic* and the *Laws*, by Francis Foster Barham (1841). This translation was included in the Bohn Classical Library in 1853, with revisions by Charles Duke Yonge. The *Republic* was retranslated toward the end of the century by George G. Hardingham (1884). Seneca's nineteenth-century reception is well summarized by Coleridge's dry rejection of his value as a philosopher: 'you may get a motto for every sect or line of thought or religion from Seneca—yet nothing is ever thought out in him' (quoted in Share 1998: 146). Perhaps the most widely read translation of Seneca in the period is Aubrey Stewart's rendering of the *De Beneficiis* for the Bohn Classical Library (1887).

The Stoic philosophy of Marcus Aurelius was well served by the classical scholar George Long, who translated the *Meditations* from the Greek in 1862; the translation would be frequently reprinted. Matthew Arnold praised it for treating Marcus Aurelius' writings 'as documents with a side of modern applicability and living interest... as food for men, and men engaged in the current of contemporary life and action' (Arnold 1962: 136). An edition of 1869 was dedicated to Robert E. Lee, the defeated Confederate general.

While few of these works remain in use as a translation, they all have a historical value. The nineteenth-century encounter between ancient and modern thought both sustained and challenged modern conceptions of science, religion, ethics, and politics. Thus the translations in question provide a way to appraise the role of antiquity in the development of modern philosophical and political discourses.

LIST OF SOURCES

Translations
Browne, R. W. (1850). *The Nicomachean Ethics of Aristotle*. London.
Buckley, Theodore A. (1850). *Aristotle's Treatise on Rhetoric... Also the Poetic of Aristotle*. London.
Burges, George, Cary, Henry, and Davis, Henry (1848–54). *The Works of Plato: A New and Literal Version*, 6 vols. London.
Burnet, John (1892). *Early Greek Philosophy*. London.
Butcher, S. H. (1895). *Aristotle's Theory of Poetry and Fine Art, with a Critical Text and the Translation of the Poetics*. London.
Chase, D. P. (1847). *The Nicomachean Ethics of Aristotle*. Oxford.
Davies, J. Llewelyn, and Vaughn, David James (1852). *The Republic of Plato*. Cambridge.
Gillies, John (1797). *Aristotle's Ethics and Politics*, 2 vols. London.
Hatch, Walter M. (1879). *The Moral Philosophy of Aristotle*. London (Books VIII–IX of the *Nicomachean Ethics* translated by W. A. Spooner).
Jowett, Benjamin (1885). *The Politics of Aristotle*, 2 vols. Oxford.
—— (1892). *The Dialogues of Plato*, 5 vols. Oxford (first pub. 1871).
Long, George (1862). *The Thoughts of the Emperor M. Aurelius Antonius*. London.
Mill, John Stuart (1978). *Collected Works of John Stuart Mill*, Vol. 11: *Essays on Philosophy and the Classics*, ed. J. M. Robson. Toronto (contains the *Protagoras, Phaedrus, Gorgias, Apology, Charmides, Euthyphron, Laches, Lysis*, and *Parmenides*; the first four were published in the *Monthly Repository* in 1834–5).
Munro, H. A. J. (1886). *T. Lucreti Cari De Rerum Natura Libri Sex, with Notes and a Translation*. Cambridge (first pub. 1864).
Patrick, G. T. W. (1889). *The Fragments of the Work of Heraclitus*. Baltimore, MD.
Peters, F. H. (1881). *The Nicomachean Ethics of Aristotle*. London.
Share, Don, ed. (1998). *Seneca in English*. London.
Stewart, Aurey (1887). *L. Annaeus Seneca on Benefits*. London.
Taylor, Thomas (1804). *The Works of Plato*, 5 vols. London.
—— (1818). *The Rhetoric, Poetic and Nicomachean Ethics of Aristotle*, 2 vols. London.
Welldon, J. E. C. (1886). *The Rhetoric of Aristotle*. London.
Williams, Robert (1869). *The Nicomachean Ethics of Aristotle*. London.
Wilson, F. A. Basford de (1884). *Aristotle's Ethics Books I, II, III, IV, and X, Translated with Notes, Analyses and Questions*. Oxford.

Other Sources

Abbott, Evelyn, and Campbell, Lewis (1897). *The Life and Letters of Benjamin Jowett*, 2 vols. London.

Arnold, Matthew (1962). *Lectures and Essays in Criticism*, ed. R. H. Super. Ann Arbor, MI.

Foster, Finley Melville Kendall (1918). *English Translations from the Greek: A Bibliographical Survey*. New York.

Grant, Alexander (1857–8). *The Ethics of Aristotle Illustrated with Essays and Notes*, 2 vols. London.

Grote, George (1865). *Plato and the Other Companions of Sokrates*, 3 vols. London.

Halliwell, Stephen (2000). 'Classical Philosophy', pp. 375–80 in Peter France, ed., *The Oxford Guide to Literature in English Translation*. Oxford.

Higginbotham, John (1967). *Cicero on Moral Obligation*. London.

MacIntyre, Alasdair (1998). *A Short History of Ethics: A History of Moral Philosophy from the Homeric Age to the Twentieth Century*. London (first pub. 1966).

[Rogers, Henry] (1848). 'The Genius of Plato.' *Edinburgh Review* 87: 321–67.

Stray, Christopher (1998). *Classics Transformed: Schools, Universities, and Society in England, 1830–1960*. Oxford.

Turner, Frank M. (1981). *The Greek Heritage in Victorian Britain*. New Haven, CT.

Vance, Norman (1997). *The Victorians and Ancient Rome*. Oxford.

Webb, Timothy (1976). *The Violet in the Crucible: Shelley and Translation*. Oxford.

Winterer, Caroline (2002). *The Culture of Classicism: Ancient Greece and Rome in American Intellectual Life 1780–1910*. Baltimore, MD.

11.2 Modern Philosophy, Theology, Criticism

Susanne Stark

By far the main source of nineteenth-century translations of modern philosophy was Germany. While Immanuel Kant, Georg Wilhelm Friedrich Hegel, and Arthur Schopenhauer are not the only German philosophers who were translated into English during the nineteenth century, their books were among those most frequently translated and discussed. Other thinkers in the fields of philosophy and theology who became available in English during this period include J. G. Herder and F. D. E. Schleiermacher, as well as the post-Kantian idealists J. G. Fichte and F. W. J. von Schelling. Finally, the translation of Nietzsche began in the last decade of the nineteenth century.

The debates following the publication of Kant's *Kritik der reinen Vernunft* (Critique of Pure Reason) and of his introduction to this work, the *Prolegomena zu einer jeden künftigen Metaphysik* (Prolegomena to Any Future Metaphysics), together with the multiple translations of both texts, mark the beginning of an increased interest in German philosophy among a nineteenth-century English readership. At the same time, the difficulty of Kant's style and the indeterminacy of his meaning restricted the influence of his work (but see pp. 107–8, above, on Kant and Coleridge). It is therefore probably not a coincidence that a high proportion of his translators, including Abbott, Bernard, Hastie, Mahaffy, Meiklejohn, Müller, and Stirling, were academics, professional philosophers, or people with an interest in education who showed an awareness of the need to make Kant more accessible to their students and to a broader readership. Similarly, the translation of Hegel was initiated to a considerable extent by academic mediators including Bosanquet, Dyde, Hastie, and Wallace.

A different picture emerges for Schopenhauer, whose writings were found to be less impenetrable. Two of his most significant translators, Haldane and Saunders, pursued legal and political careers while maintaining their interests in philosophy and their university connections. In the case of the theological and critical ideas of David Friedrich Strauss and Ludwig Feuerbach, a relatively wide dissemination of their ideas was probably encouraged by the fact that their works were translated by, among others, the novelist George Eliot and her biographer Mathilde Blind. The influence of Strauss's radical source criticism of biblical texts in his *Das Leben Jesu* was also increased by the widespread controversy this work provoked (he provided a popular version of his own text, which was also translated). Similarly, the French writer Ernest Renan directed his *La Vie de Jésus* at a broad public, and his work was received with a great deal of orthodox disapproval. Unlike Strauss, however, Renan became known to English readers as a writer who addressed himself to a broad spectrum of theological, historical, and philological issues, and who expressed himself in a variety of genres.

Kant

The translation of Kant's oeuvre, almost all of it written in the eighteenth century, was initiated with a selection of his essays rendered into English in 1798–9 by John Richardson. In 1819 Richardson also became the first translator of the *Prolegomena to Every Future Metaphysic*, which restated in a more accessible way the ideas explored in the *Critique of Pure Reason*, and thus introduced English readers to the concepts of this seminal work even before it was translated. The *Critique of Pure Reason* was often considered to be Kant's most original treatise and it was the work most frequently translated into English in the nineteenth century. Francis Haywood's translation was published in 1838 and complemented by the translator's *Analysis of Kant's Critick of Pure Reason* (1844); notes and explanations were added to the second edition of the translation (1848). Haywood was followed by John Miller Dow Meiklejohn, who translated this work for Bohn's Philosophical Library in 1855, and by Max Müller (1881). Both criticized Haywood for his linguistic inaccuracies. Meiklejohn aimed to be an 'interpreting intellect' rather than a 'dictionary' and rendered the *Critique* fluently; his translation was frequently republished in the nineteenth and twentieth centuries. Max Müller, whose version was also reprinted in the twentieth century, used his competence as a German native speaker to construe Kant's syntax with such precision that his English version would be more intelligible than the German original. All three translators of the *Critique* discussed so far were motivated by the wish to make the 'mazes' of Kant's sentences and the obscurity of the work palatable to English readers, even though George Henry Lewes maintained that this obscurity contributed much to its fascination (Lewes 1871: II, 458). A fourth translator, the philosopher James Hutchison Stirling, did not comment on other English versions in his *Text-Book to Kant* and claimed not to have consulted them in the process of undertaking his rendering of parts of the *Critique*. In the *Text-Book* Stirling combined translation with criticism, commentary, and biography. He was thus comparable to Max Müller, who prefaced his recasting of the work with a book-length introduction to Kant's philosophy by Ludwig Noiré.

The classical scholar John Pentland Mahaffy of Trinity College Dublin devoted the first volume of his *Kant's Critical Philosophy for English Readers* (1872) to an explanation and defence of the *Critique*, while the third volume (1874; Vol. 2 was never published) constituted a new English version of the *Prolegomena*. In 1889 John Henry Bernard, another academic of Trinity College Dublin, collaborated with Mahaffy on a new edition of Mahaffy's book. Three years later Bernard was solely responsible for the first English version, annotated, of the *Kritik der Urteilskraft* (Critique of Judgment). Yet another member of Trinity College Dublin, Thomas Kingsmill Abbott, translated the *Kritik der praktischen Vernunft* (Critique of Practical Reason) in 1879, prefaced with an extensive memoir; it was an enlarged edition of the selections from Kant which he had translated in 1873 under the title *Kant's Theory of Ethics*. His version of Kant's *Introduction to Logic* followed in 1885. Many other translators, including E. B. Bax in his *Handbook of the History of Philosophy* (1886), followed the pattern of combining translation with explanation and criticism. John Watson, for example, attempted to disseminate knowledge about Kant by making extracts from a wide range of his works available to an English readership in 1888, having previously devoted a book-length study to the examination of *Kant and his English Critics* (1881).

Hegel

The Glasgow theologian William Hastie, who published three translations of Kant (1887, 1891, 1900), also played an important role in the reception of Hegel, as did the Kantian scholar Edward Caird. As in the case of Kant, translation and criticism were closely interrelated. Hastie dedicated his 1886 version of Hegel's *Philosophy of Art* (a partial rendering of the philosopher's introduction to his *Vorlesungen über die Ästhetik*) to Stirling, not only a translator of Kant but also the author of *The Secret of Hegel* (1865). In the same year, however, Bernard Bosanquet published a more faithful translation of Hegel's complete text, preceded by a prefatory essay. Similarly, William Wallace, who published *The Logic of Hegel* (1874) and *Hegel's Philosophy of Mind* (1894), which are both part of the *Enzyklopädie der philosophischen Wissenschaften*, complemented his second translation with five introductory essays; he also wrote critical studies of Kant and Schopenhauer. Shortly afterwards, Elizabeth Sanderson Haldane co-translated the *Lectures on the History of Philosophy* and edited selections from a wide range of Hegel's writings entitled *The Wisdom and Religion of a German Philosopher* (1897); she was shaped by the same intellectual environment in Edinburgh as her brother Richard Burdon Haldane, who translated Schopenhauer into English. We see, then, the emergence of networks of British intellectuals dedicated to conveying the significance of German philosophy to English-speaking readers. Their achievements were enhanced by American and Canadian scholars, including Samuel Walters Dyde, William Torrey Harris, John Steinfort Kedney, and J. Macbride Sterrett, who contributed significantly to the dissemination of Hegel's ideas through translation and criticism. Sterrett's preface to his *Studies in Hegel's Philosophy of Religion* (1891) discusses the close interaction between British and American scholars in the transmission of Hegel's thinking.

The most frequently reprinted translation of any of Hegel's works in this period was John Sibree's 1857 rendering of the *Lectures on the Philosophy of History*, which has been described as the most easily comprehensible introduction to the philosopher's system, because its argument is less rigid than that of his metaphysical works. Sibree's version of the *Lectures* was in common use until the middle of the twentieth century. It was his intention to present Hegel 'in a really English form' (Sibree 1861: iv), and he has been criticized for his loose paraphrasing and at times inaccurate rewriting of the author's ideas (Nisbet 1999: xlvii).

Sibree's efforts reflect one of the major problems of translating Hegel, namely the 'insecurity' of the original text, to which a number of nineteenth-century translators referred in their prefaces. In her rendering of the *Lectures on the History of Philosophy*, E. S. Haldane explained to her readers that the difficulty of her task was exacerbated by the fact that most of the treatise was put together from the notes of different lecture courses. She chose to translate from the 1840 version of the text, which had been carefully prepared by C. L. Michelet, one of Hegel's pupils, who attempted to incorporate all available sources, including the notes of students (Haldane 1892–6: I, v–vi). The problems of editorial compilation, which according to Bernard Bosanquet increased the literary deficiencies of Hegel's work, were also discussed by Ebenezer Brown Speirs and J. Burdon Sanderson in the preface to their translation of the *Lectures on the Philosophy of Religion* (Bosanquet 1886: vi; Speirs and Sanderson 1895: v). S. W. Dyde, on the other hand, explained in the introduction to his translation of Hegel's *Philosophy of Right* that editorial notes and additions to the main text by Hegel's students can help to elucidate the author's ideas (Dyde 1896: xiii).

Another crucial problem was the accurate and consistent use of Hegel's terminology. Elizabeth Haldane made it clear that she had decided to give 'recognized symbols' for words which have no satisfactory equivalents in English, while Speirs considered it advisable not to adhere rigidly to any one set of English words. Bosanquet, whose translation of the introduction to Hegel's *Philosophy of Fine Art* was published in the same year as William Hastie's less complete version of the same text, criticized Hastie for the freedom he permitted himself. At the same time he found it necessary to 'interpret philosophical expressions, instead of merely furnishing their technical equivalents' and to complement his rendering of specialized terms by annotations (Bosanquet 1886: vi–vii). S. W. Dyde introduced an index at the end of his volume to illustrate the different English words needed to translate a given German term in different contexts, and he considered it his right as a translator to make Hegel's phraseology less rigid.

Schopenhauer

In contrast to Kant and Hegel, Schopenhauer was initially more successful outside than within his own country. It can be argued that an essay in the *Westminster Review* of 1853 by the critic and dramatist John Oxenford, who was well known for his translations from Spanish, French, and German, contributed significantly to an appropriate recognition of the author's work (Zimmern 1876: v). Schopenhauer was not part of the German professorial establishment; indeed he attempted to subvert it. He popularized philosophy for the general reader and, unlike his academic colleagues, was considered to be an accomplished stylist who wrote clear and readable prose which did not require commentaries or glossaries. According to Thomas Bailey Saunders, one of Schopenhauer's most prolific nineteenth-century translators, the author, 'trained in realities even more than in ideas', was 'an enemy of all philosophic indefiniteness and obscurity' (Saunders

1889: iii); moreover, his English was of such a high standard that he intended to translate Kant into English and Hume into German (Bax 1891: xx–xxi). The characteristics of Schopenhauer's writing contributed significantly to his popularity in Britain. William Wallace, who has already been discussed in connection with Hegel and Kant, also wrote *The Life of Arthur Schopenhauer* (1890). T. B. Saunders added well-informed introductions to his wide range of English renderings of Schopenhauer's works, and was the author of *Schopenhauer: A Lecture* (1901). All his translations were published by Swan Sonnenschein; these editions are noteworthy because they reprint extracts from a considerable number of reviews of Saunders's texts in the British periodical press and thus help to document the author's far-reaching impact. Similarly, Mrs Rudolf Dircks (Sara Hay Dircks, née Goddard) and Ernest Belfort Bax prefaced their versions of Schopenhauer's essays with substantial introductions including biographical material.

Bax is also interesting because, like Wallace, he translated works by Schopenhauer and Kant. Links in the translation of different German philosophers can also be established in the work of the Haldanes. Together with John Kemp, Richard Haldane translated Schopenhauer's earliest and most significant work, *Die Welt als Wille und Vorstellung* (The World as Will and Idea), originally published in 1819. This *magnum opus* is based on a criticism of Kant, whose 'thing-in-itself' Schopenhauer equated with the concept of will, the fundamental reality of the world, to which all matter, organism, and intellect is subordinated. Kemp and Haldane's translation of 1883–6 at times aimed for faithfulness in the rendering of the German text at the expense of fluency in the English prose; it remained the standard version until 1958. Despite the fact that Schopenhauer's other treatises have been described as 'merely corollary to' *The World as Will and Idea*, it was his last publication, *Parerga und Paralipomena* (1851), a collection of essays relating to his own philosophical system, which attained immediate success in Germany and from which the first Schopenhauer translation in Britain was done by Saunders in 1872. The vast majority of nineteenth-century translations from Schopenhauer's work were selections of essays from *Parerga und Paralipomena*; this increased the accessibility of his ideas among a wider readership, some pieces being made available in several versions (Bax 1891; Dircks 1892; Saunders 1872, 1889; Thomson 1896). Bax, for example, emphasized that he did not consult Saunders's work and that he aimed for over-literality rather than paraphrase (Bax 1891: v). What is more, Saunders's and Thomson's choice of the title *Studies in Pessimism* for essays taken from the *Parerga* firmly established Schopenhauer's reputation as a pessimistic philosopher in Britain. While Oxenford had deplored this trait of Schopenhauer's work, Thomson saw it merely as a feature of his realism.

Strauss, Feuerbach, and Renan

Even though David Friedrich Strauss, Ludwig Feuerbach, and Ernest Renan strongly depended on the German philosophical tradition, especially on Hegel's thought, they were best known among British and American readers for their theological ideas and innovative critical approaches. Strauss and Renan became most famous for their works on the life of Jesus entitled *Das Leben Jesu* (1835–6) and *La Vie de Jésus* (1863). Despite this parallel it is questionable whether Renan can be considered a 'French Strauss', as one of his French contemporaries suggested (Plasman 1858). While it cannot be denied that Renan's *Vie de Jésus* was influenced by Strauss's *Leben Jesu*, Strauss's work was less a biography than a piece of searching criticism based on philological scholarship. His approach to the gospel repudiated both the historicity and the supernaturalism of the biblical accounts. Even though Renan also questioned the authenticity of the gospels, he laid greater emphasis on providing his readers with the life story of a humanized Jesus.

Both works were translated into English several times during the nineteenth century. *Das Leben Jesu* was first undertaken by an anonymous translator, but it gained lasting fame through the translation of George Eliot and the enthusiastic reception of the Coventry freethinking circle in which she moved. Eliot, who did not yet publish under her pen-name in 1846, attempted to remain anonymous altogether at first, since she thought it might decrease Strauss's influence if it were known that his treatise had been made available in English by a woman. Her translation was widely acclaimed in the periodical press and has remained in use until the present day (see Stark 1997: 124–5, 129). Renan's *Life of Jesus* was first published (by Trübner in 1864) in an anonymous translation, while a different translation by Charles Edwin Wilbour appeared in New York in the same year. It was again rendered into English in 1897 by William George Hutchison, the Renan translator who covered the widest range of the author's publications and who also complemented his texts with informative introductions. A different anonymous translation was included in *The History of the Origin of Christianity* (1889–90), of which *The Life of Jesus* constituted the first volume. The popular impact of Strauss and Renan was further enhanced by the shorter versions which they provided of their works. These popular editions were subsequently translated into English (Anon. 1865 for Strauss; Anon. 1887 for Renan). An early cheap edition of Renan's original work, published in English in 1865, helped to spread its author's ideas further.

In the light of this wide and varied dissemination of Strauss's and Renan's controversial ideas it is not surprising that their work provoked a plethora of essays and pamphlets criticizing their liberal tendencies and frequently attacking their lack of religious orthodoxy. Ludwig Feuerbach's theology, on the other hand, which was considered on the Continent to have a similarly subversive effect, was less widely discussed in Britain. This was the case even though George Eliot was also responsible for the translation of *Das Wesen des Christentums*, in which Feuerbach sought to anthropomorphize Christian doctrine and to make the supernatural elements of religion part of a historically traceable world. While she disapproved of the excesses of Strauss's critical method, Eliot maintained a great deal of sympathy for Feuerbach's religion of humanity and exercised more freedom in translating his work than in the case of Strauss. In her rendering of Feuerbach, she was determined to improve the author's style and even decided to omit some of his ideas. Moreover, she published *The Essence of Christianity* (1854) under her real name Marian Evans (see further Stark 1997: 131–3).

Strauss and Renan were not exclusively associated with their research on the life of Jesus. It is thus significant that Mathilde Blind, the first biographer of George Eliot, continued Eliot's efforts by publishing *The Old Faith and the New*, in which Strauss ventured to replace Christianity with scientific materialism; the 1874 edition of her translation contains an extended biographical essay. Even though Renan's translators were more obscure, the diversity of his writings which were available in English was greater, and he became known not only as an author of historical, theological, and philological writings but also for his philosophical and political works, his literary production and criticism, his autobiographical writings, and his accomplished style (Hutchison 1897: xxv).

LIST OF SOURCES

Translations

Anon. (1865). *A New Life of Jesus, Written for the Use of the German People* [Strauss]. London.
Anon. (1887). *The Life of Jesus: Abridged People's Edition* [Renan]. London.
Abbott, Thomas Kingsmill (1873). *Kant's Theory of Ethics of Practical Philosophy, Comprising 1. Fundamental Principles of the Metaphysic of Morals. 2. Dialectic and Methodology of Practical Reason. 3. On the Radical Evil in Human Nature*. London.
—— (1879). *Kant's Critique of Practical Reason and Other Works on the Theory of Ethics*. London.
Bax, Ernest Belfort (1883). *Kant's Prolegomena, and Metaphysical Foundations of Natural Science*. London.
—— (1891). *Selected Essays of Arthur Schopenhauer*. London.
Bernard, John Henry (1892). *Kant's Kritik of Judgement*. London.
Bosanquet, Bernard (1886). *The Introduction to Hegel's Philosophy of Fine Art*. London.
Dircks, [Sara] (1892). *Essays of Schopenhauer*. London.
Dyde, Samuel Walters (1896). *Hegel's Philosophy of Right*. London.
[Evans, Marian] (1846). *The Life of Jesus, Critically Examined* [Strauss], 3 vols. London.
—— (1854). *The Essence of Christianity* [Feuerbach]. London.
Haldane, Elizabeth Sanderson, and Simson, Frances H. (1892–6). *Hegel's Lectures on the History of Philosophy*, 3 vols. London.
Haldane, Richard Burdon, and Kemp, John (1883–6). *The World as Will and Idea* [Schopenhauer]. London.
Hastie, William (1887). *The Philosophy of Law* [Kant]. Edinburgh.
—— (1891). *Kant's Principles of Politics, Including His Essay on Perpetual Peace*. Edinburgh.
—— (1900). *Kant's Cosmogony, as in His Essay on the Retardation of the Rotation of the Earth, and His Natural History and Theory of the Heavens*. Glasgow.
Haywood, Francis (1838). *Critick of Pure Reason* [Kant]. London.
Hutchison, William George (1897). *Life of Jesus* [Renan]. London.
Meiklejohn, John Miller Dow (1855). *Critique of Pure Reason* [Kant]. London.
Müller, Friedrich Max (1881). *Immanuel Kant's Critique of Pure Reason. With an Historical Introduction by L. Noiré*, 2 vols. London.
Richardson, John (1798–9). *Essays and Treatises on Moral, Political and Various Philosophical Subjects* [Kant]. London.
—— (1819). *Prolegomena to Every Future Metaphysic* [Kant]. London.

Saunders, Thomas Bailey (1872). *Studies in Pessimism: A Series of Essays* [Schopenhauer]. London.
—— (1889). *Religion: A Dialogue, and Other Essays* [Schopenhauer]. London.
Sibree, John (1861). *Lectures on the Philosophy of History* [Hegel]. London (first pub. 1857).
Speirs, Ebenezer Brown, and Sanderson, J. Burdon (1895). *Lectures on the Philosophy of Religion, Together with a Work on the Proofs of the Existence of God* [Hegel]. London.
Stirling, James Hutchison (1881). *Text-Book to Kant, The Critique of Pure Reason: Aesthetic, Categories, Schematism*. Edinburgh.
Thomson, William M. (1896). *Studies in Pessimism* [Schopenhauer]. London.
Watson, John (1888). *The Philosophy of Kant, as Contained in Extracts From His Own Writings*. Glasgow.

Other Sources
Caird, Edward (1877). *A Critical Account of the Philosophy of Kant, with an Historical Introduction*. Glasgow.
—— (1883). *Hegel*. Edinburgh.
Lewes, George Henry (1871). *The History of Philosophy from Thales to Comte*, 2 vols. London (first pub. 1845–6).
Nisbet, Hugh Barr (1999). 'Translator's Preface' to G. W. F. Hegel, *Political Writings*, ed. Laurence Dickey. Cambridge.
Oxenford, John (1853). 'Iconoclasm in German Philosophy.' *Westminster Review* 3: 388–407.
Plasman, L. C. de (1858). *Les Strauss français: Lettres critiques sur les doctrines antireligieuses de MM. Littré et Renan*. Paris.
Stark, Susanne (1997). 'Marian Evans, the Translator', pp. 119–40 in Susan Bassnett, ed., *Translating Literature*. Cambridge.
Sterrett, James Macbride (1891). *Studies in Hegel's Philosophy of Religion*. London.
Wellek, René (1931). *Immanuel Kant in England, 1793–1838*. Princeton, NJ.
Zimmern, Helen (1876). *Arthur Schopenhauer: His Life and His Philosophy*. London.

11.3 Modern History and Socio-political Theory

Ian Patterson

History

'The spirit of the monarchy was at variance with the spirit of the age,' wrote Hazlitt in his sketch of Coleridge, in 1825 (Hazlitt 1991: 66). By using 'the spirit of the age' as the title of his collection of biographical and critical portraits, he was signalling two things: a new kind of awareness of the historical moment, and an international focus underlying it, derived from the challenges posed to conservative, legitimist thinking by the American and French Revolutions and by German Idealism. The phrase itself appeared in several languages, including the French of Montesquieu, the English of Hume, and the German of Herder; however, it became widespread in English only with the decade of the 1820s, when it became almost indispensable, the mark of a new and consciously historical approach to the workings of society. Characteristically modern approaches to history, economics, and social and political thought date from the first half of the nineteenth century, when they were shaped in a process which involved a great deal of mutual influence among writers in different European languages.

Much of this material was anonymously translated, and much was evanescent: the radical and political press, pamphlets, the weekly or fortnightly press, and the serious quarterlies carried all sorts of translations, usually unattributed, sometimes digests or adaptations rather than strict translations, often making it hard (especially in the case of the radical movements) to assess what part was played in the reception of new ideas by complete, published translations and how far the ground was already prepared by more ephemeral propagandists in the newspapers, journals, and magazines. We cannot consider here all the thousands of works translated into English, but the many translations that fall into these categories not only reveal the marginal output of some relatively well-known politicians, commentators, journalists, and civil servants, who energetically produced translations in their spare time, but also point to an extensive network of ephemeral writing and a Grub Street world of competing publishers, underpaid writers, and professional translators whose output must have totalled millions of words. Familiar figures like Thomas Carlyle, Harriet Martineau, Eleanor Marx-Aveling, or Frederic Harrison as well as almost forgotten names like Hannibal Evans Lloyd, Sarah Austin, David Dundas Scott, William Hazlitt the younger (son of the essayist), and Henry Reeve represent the tip of a huge iceberg, most of which continues to be invisible. In the earlier part of the century especially, many of the most interesting and cosmopolitan of these intellectuals, writers, and translators came not from London but from Edinburgh or from provincial cities such as

Norwich and Liverpool; some of them lived abroad for considerable periods or had been educated in other European countries, most commonly in Switzerland or Germany.

The French and American Revolutions gave a dramatic focus to the issues of power and liberty, monarchy and democracy, and government and society, which were moulding a new historicist outlook in the first decades of the century, an outlook exemplified in Walter Scott's novels. These novels probably had an almost equal impact on European culture, with their popular refractions of contemporary historical and historiographical issues through visions of a recreated past; but certainly the Revolution and the Napoleonic wars that followed it forced the question of history to the centre of the political and intellectual stage. One index of this is the quantity of memoirs of the last days of the *ancien régime* and the first years of the Republic, which were, and continued to be, translated. The most popular of these were regularly reissued; they were followed by numerous lives of Napoleon. One of these, Hazlitt's massive biography of Napoleon (1928–30), consisted of mostly unacknowledged translations, sometimes verbatim and sometimes adapted, of French sources (documented in Robinson 1959). The writer and poet Robert Charles Dallas, best remembered as Byron's editor and memorialist, found time to translate a prodigious amount of French history between 1800 and 1808, including Bertrand de Moleville's *Annals of the French Revolution* (1800–2) in nine volumes; likewise the prolific writer and commentator John Wilson Croker, a founder of the *Quarterly Review*, translated several such works over a period of thirty-seven years.

The fate of the French monarchy led to heated debates and to reconsiderations of European history from the Reformation onwards, by writers such as Lamartine, Alfred de Vigny, Michelet, Guizot, F. C. Dahlmann, von Ranke, Thiers, and Thierry, all of whom were widely published in English translation. Lady Wilde, Oscar Wilde's mother, translated two of Lamartine's works, notably *Pictures of the French Revolution, being Episodes from the History of the Girondists* (1850); and there were many other translations (on Lamartine's reception in Britain and America see pp. 235–6 above). Vigny's historical novel *Cinq-mars* was translated first by William Hazlitt the younger in 1847 and again three years later by William Bellingham.

From a European point of view, England appeared as 'the classic example of historical development... the practical, model example for the new style of historical interpretation' (Lukács 1962: 32), and accounts of English history needed to be read in England, as well as in France or Germany or wherever they originated. There was renewed interest in Cromwell and the English Commonwealth as part of the wider search for theoretical legitimacy for bourgeois power. The civil war of the mid-seventeenth century was widely seen as reflecting contemporary conflicts; as Blair Worden puts it, 'The eighteenth century had for the most part repudiated the nation's Puritan past. The nineteenth century gradually, and with increasing confidence, reclaimed it' (Worden 2000: 127). François-Pierre-Guillaume Guizot, who wrote extensively on the subject, was one of the most frequently and widely translated historians, and his reputation in England was at least as high as it was in France. Shortly before his death he told his friend and translator Henry Reeve how glad he was to have been in all but name a citizen of both countries.

There was lively competition between publishers for editions of Guizot's works, especially his works on the English Revolution and the Commonwealth, and leading translators such as William Hazlitt the younger, Henry Reeve, Robert Black, Sarah Austin, Sir Andrew Scoble, and the historian and dramatist J. W. Cole all produced substantial, and sometimes competing, versions, as did a host of less well-known or unnamed translators. Louise Coutier, who in 1838 was the first to translate Guizot's *Histoire de la révolution d'Angleterre*, claimed in her preface that Guizot 'shows that the French revolution having placed the events of 1688 in a new light, the narrative[s] of Hume and other historians are no longer sufficient to satisfy the present age' and enthusiastically emphasizes that the 'cause of liberty is advocated throughout' in lively and theatrical scenarios. Six years later Hazlitt's translation adds eleven more transcriptions of historical documents and an index, but its main advance on Coutier's version is stylistic. Coutier was French, and her English style, though fluent and effective, was old-fashioned, thirty or forty years out of date. Hazlitt introduces more direct speech, writes more dramatically, and tends to expand on Guizot's text, bringing it in line with the expectations of a popular readership. Eight years later still, Scoble introduces his translation as 'carefully revised and corrected', adds that 'the references have, for the first time, been carefully verified, and the quotations are given, in every instance, from the original authorities', and claims it as 'the only correct, complete, and authorized English edition' (Scoble 1852: vi). The translation itself is similar to Hazlitt's but slightly less melodramatic and less taut, as befits a more scholarly text. Thus, over a period of two decades, Guizot's 1826 text was shaped and reshaped to conform to the developing market for historical texts that brought to life crucial moments of the past (as for example the trial and execution of Strafford). Many of the translators of historical works were also translators of historical novels; William Robson, for instance, who translated Dumas and Balzac, also translated books about the history of the crusades, France, and Garibaldi, as well as writing history and novels himself. Nor were all translations of particularly influential books: Hannibal Evans Lloyd, one of the most prolific writers and translators of the period (he also collaborated with Sarah Austin), translated a dozen works of history, in addition to many other titles.

The liberal dream of a scientific historiography and a scientific study of society developed alongside a belief in democracy and in progress that could be systematically evaluated. These ideas impinged on democrats and anti-democrats alike, as historians and politicians tried to make a new sense out of European history. Active in the revolt against the French King, Charles X, on 26 July 1830, Guizot and Thiers were both deeply committed to ideas about democracy and government, a debate which received further stimulation in England from the writings of Tocqueville and Saint-Simon. Henry Reeve translated Alexis de Tocqueville's *De la démocratie en Amérique* almost as soon as it was published, in

1835 (the second volume appeared in 1840), in the hope, as he put it, 'that this translation may tend to spread in England some of those sound and comprehensive views of the nature and tendency of the democratic element which its author has put forward in France' (Reeve 1835–40: I, xi). He became Tocqueville's lifelong friend and his principal point of contact with the British press and with British politicians; he would go on to produce the translations *On the State of Society in France before the Revolution* (1856) and *American Institutions* (1851). Tocqueville's work was widely read on both sides of the Atlantic, and rival translations claimed his support for different political positions.

The comte de Saint-Simon (on whom see Pankhurst 1952–3) was unable to attract much lasting interest from English translators. Both Carlyle and Mill were briefly enthusiastic about his more radical ideas in the early 1830s: Carlyle translated the *Le Nouveau Christianisme* in 1830 but failed to find a publisher for it; as *The New Christianity* it was eventually published in a translation by the Revd J. E. Smith in 1834. This was the only work of Saint-Simon's to be published in full in English translation, but extracts and digests were frequently published in periodicals. In June 1833, for instance, Robert Owen's *Crisis* published a translation by Mrs Anna Wheeler of a Saint-Simonian manifesto on the emancipation of women, taken from the French periodical *La Femme libre*.

Jules Michelet's work, like Guizot's, was widely translated in the 1840s and 1850s, and again competing versions struggled for market dominance. The polyglot writer and historian Walter Keating Kelly, for example, and G. H. Smith, each produced a *History of France* in 1846, and in the same year Smith and Hazlitt each published a *Life of Luther*. But neither Michelet nor Guizot was as controversial as Leopold von Ranke. His was one of the most influential voices in nineteenth-century historiography, but he did not become associated with any translator in particular; when the Clarendon Press published the six volumes of his *History of England* in 1875, eight separate translators were credited. Translation was central to the ideological battle over his work, as is evident from a comparison of three different versions of his *History of the Popes*. In the translator's preface to the first of these (published by John Murray in three elegant volumes in 1840), Sarah Austin declares her scholarly credentials, emphasizes her belief that 'every translator is bound to fidelity by a duty which he owes to his author', and quotes Goethe's dictum that every translator should regard himself 'as a broker in the great intellectual traffic of the world'. Such integrity is doubly important in a work of objectivity such as Ranke's, which had been betrayed by the 'bad faith' of the French translation of 1838; the translator had effectively reworked the book from a Catholic standpoint, infecting it 'with the sectarian spirit from which the original is so remarkably and so laudably exempt'. To clinch the point, she quotes a letter from Ranke in which he says that he looks to her 'to redress the wrong done me in France'. Seven years later, Foster's translation for Bohn's Library occasionally slips into using 'popery' in place of 'the papacy', but is otherwise unexceptionable, although it is duller and wordier than Austin's intelligent prose. Then four years later in Edinburgh, Blackie published a third translation, with a preface in which the anonymous translator made explicit his view of the book's function, namely to denounce the 'fraud, oppression and cruelty' of the Catholic Church. This was followed by a second, much longer, and rantingly sectarian introduction by the Genevan Calvinist propagandist, J. H. Merle d'Aubigny, designed to ensure that nobody read Ranke's text in any but a spirit of Puritan outrage at the excesses of the papacy.

Political Economy and Social Thought

While historians and reformers argued over the shape and purposes of history, some of the writers most associated with radicalism attracted less attention. Jean-Jacques Rousseau had been much translated during his lifetime (see Vol. 3 of this *History*), but there were few new translations, or even reprints, during the nineteenth century. It was not until John Morley's biography (1873) and Thomas Craddock's *Rousseau as Described by Himself and Others* (1877) helped create a climate sympathetic to the re-examination of his work that much new work was done: two translations of *The Social Contract* appeared in the 1890s, one by R. M. Harrington in 1893, one by H. J. Tozer in 1895. A new edition of *Émile*, edited and abridged by W. H. Payne, was also published in 1893, joining the previous American translation by Eleanor Worthington Booth (1884). At the same time as the French Restoration historians were redefining the development of bourgeois society, the Saint-Simonians and the disciples of Charles Fourier were developing more extensive versions of the cycles of history, looking beyond the defects and contradictions of bourgeois society to new forms of freedom. They sent missionaries 'from Constantinople to Mississippi', as Harriet Martineau put it, preaching government control of industry, new forms of community, and female emancipation. But there was little direct translation of Saint-Simon's writing (beyond short expository pieces in journals by reformers like William Thompson, Anna Wheeler, and the Revd James Elimalet Smith).

Apart from a sketch of his ideas in *Political Economy Made Easy* (1828), presented by the (anonymous) translator to the London Co-operative Society, Fourier's ideas had even less purchase on the book market in Britain, although the Revd John Reynell Morell wrote a *Sketch of the Life of Charles Fourier* in 1849, as an introduction to his translation of *The Passions of the Human Soul* (1850–1). A weekly newspaper, *The Phalanx*, edited by Hugh Doherty, was devoted to advancing the ideas of his followers, but it was in America that Fourier was more appreciated, in a growing society more receptive to social experiment: Emerson among others was attracted to their ideas. Several publishers issued substantial texts and commentaries by translators; among these was Hugh Doherty, who also translated Abel Transon's influential book *Charles Fourier's Theory of Attractive Industry, and the Moral Harmony of the Passions* (1841).

Among the successors to Saint-Simon's rationalist religion, Auguste Comte (who had been Saint-Simon's secretary for seven years) was introduced to an English audience through Harriet Martineau's *The Positive Philosophy of Auguste*

Comte, published in two volumes in 1853. Not so much a translation as a free adaptation and condensation of Comte's work, it went through three editions, the third, with a new introduction by Frederic Harrison, in 1896. Comte's positivism argued for the emergence of a sociological reason for productive and coherent social reorganization, and the systematic aspect of this was what appealed to his supporters. In the latter part of the century, Harrison became the most influential advocate of Comte's thought in England, but Richard Congreve, founder of the Church of Humanity, was the more assiduous translator: between 1858 and 1894, the two of them published *The Religion of Humanity, Essays Political, Social and Religious, The Positivist Library, The Positivist Calendar, The Catechism of Positive Religion*, and many more.

The publications of the International Working Man's Association circulated mainly in newspaper and pamphlet form, but some manifestos were translated by Eugene Oswald in the late 1860s. Despite the interest in the development of European socialism, little of its theory was translated in book form until quite late in the century. Karl Marx's *Das Kapital*, the first volume of which was published in German 1867, did not begin to appear in English for two decades. (An American translation had been planned in 1876, but no suitable translator could then be found.) The first volume of *Capital*, translated by Samuel Moore and Edward Aveling and edited by Friedrich Engels, was published by Sonnenschein in 1887 (the other two volumes had to wait until 1919). At the end of his preface to the first English edition, Engels stressed the role that history played: Marx's 'whole theory is the result of a life-long study of the economic history and condition of England'. Indeed, although a few early pamphlets appeared in America, none of Marx's most important works was available in English until relatively late. Despite the original plan to translate it into five languages in 1848, even the *Communist Manifesto* did not appear in full until 1866 (1883 in New York), although a translation of the first section by Helen McFarlane, writing as 'Howard Morton', had appeared in November 1850 in the *Red Republican*, edited by the Chartist G. J. Harvey (see Stedman Jones 2002: 15 n.). Only in the 1890s did translations of the major works start to become widely available. *The Poverty of Philosophy*, translated by Harry Quelch, for example, appeared only in 1900. There was a similar delay in the publication of Engels's work. *The Condition of the Working Class in England* (the translator was Florence Wischnewetsky) was only published in New York in 1887 and in London in 1892, the same year in which Aveling's translation from Engels, *Socialism, Utopian and Scientific*, was published. Mikhail Bakunin's *God and the State* was published in Boston, in a translation by B. R. Tucker, in 1883 and reprinted by the Commonweal in London in 1893; H. M. Hyndman translated Pyotr Kropotkin's 'Aux jeunes gens' in 1889. Pierre-Joseph Proudhon, too, began to be commercially published late in the century, and an edition of his works, including *What is Property?*, was published in Massachusetts between 1876 and 1888.

One of Britain's main contributions to intellectual debate in the earlier nineteenth century was the development of a science of political economy, so there is not much important translated work in that area. Nonetheless, Jean-Baptiste Say, at least, ought to be mentioned. The *Traité d'économie politique* (1803), Say's best-known work, widely read for many years in Britain and America as well as in France, was translated in 1811 by C. R. Prinsep. Following on from Adam Smith, Say argued for a separation between politics and political economy and counterpoised the importance of a commercial economy to the agriculture-based economics of the French physiocrats. His sense of industry as fundamental and his invention of the (untranslatable) figure of the 'entrepreneur', as well as his commentary on England's economy, made him one of the central figures in early nineteenth-century thought. His radical ideas were what attracted his other translator, John Richter, a radical businessman. Richter was a leading reform politician of the late eighteenth and early nineteenth centuries and a member of the London Corresponding Society; he was imprisoned in the Tower of London with John Horne Tooke and (unsuccessfully) prosecuted for high treason in 1794. He was responsible for Say's *Catechism of Political Economy* (1816), *England and the English* (1816), a radical republican critique of England's post-war economy, and *Letters to Mr Malthus on Various Subjects of Political Economy* (1821).

LIST OF SOURCES

Translations

Austin, Sarah (1840). *The Ecclesiastical and Political History of the Popes of Rome during the Sixteenth and Seventeenth Centuries* [Ranke], 3 vols. London.
—— (1845–7). *History of the Reformation in Germany* [Ranke], 3 vols. London.
—— (1850). *On the Causes and Successes of the English Revolution of 1640–1688* [Guizot]. London.
Aveling, Edward (1892). *Socialism, Utopian and Scientific* [Engels]. London.
Beesly, Edward Spencer, et al. (1875–7). *System of Positive Polity* [Comte], 4 vols. London.
Bellingham, William (1850). *Cinq-Mars, or, A Conspiracy under Louis XIII* [Vigny]. London.
Clapp, Henry (1857). *The Social Destiny of Man, or, Theory of the Four Movements* [Fourier]. New York.
Cocks, Charles (1846). *The People* [Michelet]. London.
—— (1847). *History of the French Revolution* [Michelet]. London.
Congreve, Richard (1891). *The Religion of Humanity* [Comte]. London.
De Leon, Daniel (1898). *The Eighteenth Brumaire of Louis Bonaparte* [Marx]. New York.
Doherty, Hugh (1841). *Charles Fourier's Theory of Attractive Industry, and the Moral Harmony of the Passions* [Abel Transon]. London.
—— (1850). *The Passions of the Human Soul* [Fourier]. London.
Hare, Julius Charles, and Thirlwall, Connop (1828–32). *The History of Rome* [Niebuhr]. Cambridge.
Hazlitt, William (1846a). *The History of Civilization* [Guizot], 3 vols. London.
—— (1846b). *History of the English Revolution of 1640* [Guizot]. London.
—— (1847a). *History of the Roman Republic* [Michelet]. London.
—— (1847b). *Cinq-Mars, or, A Conspiracy under Louis XIII* [de Vigny]. London.
—— (1850). *Why was the English Revolution Successful?* [Guizot]. London.

Kelly, Walter K. (1842). *The History of the Popes* [Ranke]. London.
—— (1843). *The Ottoman and the Spanish Empires in the Sixteenth and Seventeenth Centuries* [Ranke]. London.
—— (1844–6). *History of France* [Michelet], 2 vols. (no more published). London.
Lloyd, Hannibal Evans (1842). *England in 1841* [Raumer], 2 vols. London.
—— and Austin, Sarah (1836). *England in 1835* [Raumer], 3 vols. London.
Martineau, Harriet (1853). *The Positive Philosophy of Auguste Comte, Freely Translated and Condensed*. London.
Moore, Samuel, and Aveling, Edward (1887). *Capital: A Critical Analysis of Capitalist Production* [Marx], 2 vols. London.
Prinsep, C. R. (1811). *A Treatise on Political Economy* [Say], 2 vols. London.
Reeve, Henry (1835–40). *Democracy in America* [Tocqueville], 2 vols. London.
—— (1840). *Washington* [Guizot]. London.
—— (1851). *American Institutions and their Influence* [Tocqueville]. London.
—— (1856). *State of Society in France before the Revolution of 1789* [Tocqueville]. London.
Richter, John (1816a). *Catechism of Political Economy* [Say]. London.
—— (1816b). *England, and the English People* [Say]. London.
—— (1821). *Letters to Mr Malthus on Several Subjects of Political Economy* [Say]. London.
Scoble, Andrew R. (1851a). *Monk, or, The Fall of the Republic and the Restoration of the Monarchy in England, in 1660* [Guizot]. London.
—— (1851b). *Monk's Contemporaries: Biographic Studies on the English Revolution* [Guizot]. London.
—— (1851c). *On the Causes of the Success of the English Revolution* [Guizot]. London.
—— (1852). *History of the Origin of Representative Government in Europe* [Guizot]. London.
—— (1854). *History of Oliver Cromwell and the English Commonwealth* [Guizot], 2 vols. London.
—— (1856). *History of Richard Cromwell and the Restoration of Charles II* [Guizot], 2 vols. London.
Smith, G. H. (1844–7). *History of France* [Michelet], 2 vols. London.
—— (1846). *The People* [Michelet]. London.

Other Sources
Burrow, John (1981). *A Liberal Descent: Victorian Historians and the English Past*. Cambridge.
Collini, Stefan (1991). *Public Moralists: Political Thought and Intellectual Life in Britain*. Oxford.
Hawthorn, Geoffrey (1976). *Enlightenment and Despair: A History of Sociology*. Cambridge.
Hazlitt, William (1991). *The Spirit of the Age*, ed. E. D. Mackerness. London.
Laughton, John Knox (1898). *Memoirs of the Life and Correspondence of Henry Reeve, C.B., D.C.L.*, 2 vols. London.
Lukács, Georg (1962). *The Historical Novel*, tr. Hannah and Stanley Mitchell. London.
Pankhurst, Richard K. P. (1952–3). 'Saint-Simonism in England.' *Twentieth Century* 152: 499–512 and 153: 47–58.
Robinson, Robert E. (1959). *William Hazlitt's Life of Napoleon Buonaparte: Its Sources and Characteristics*. Geneva.
Stedman Jones, Gareth, ed. (2002). *Karl Marx and Friedrich Engels: The Communist Manifesto*. London.

—— (2004). *An End to Poverty? A Historical Debate*. London.
Winch, Donald (1996). *Riches and Poverty: An Intellectual History of Political Economy in Britain 1750–1834*. Cambridge.
Worden, Blair (2000). 'The Victorians and Oliver Cromwell', pp. 112–35 in Stefan Collini, Richard Whatmore, and B. W. Young, eds., *History, Religion, and Culture: British Intellectual History 1750–1950*. Cambridge.

11.4 Exploring the World

Laura Dassow Walls

Introduction

In the nineteenth century, as the commercial and military empires of Europe and the United States expanded across the globe, works by explorers and naturalists, often read in translation, opened new worlds to enterprising nations and to individual readers. The most internationally famous of the era's explorers, Alexander von Humboldt, argued that the very progress of civilization demanded globalization—not just discovery and exploitation, but the free interchange of goods and knowledge across nations, continents, and oceans. In this process Humboldt assigned the key role to travel narratives. It had been, he recalled, a travel narrative translated from English to German, Georg Forster's *Voyage Round the World* (1777), which ignited his own desire as a youth to see new worlds beyond Europe. In this, Humboldt was the latest in a long tradition starting with Marco Polo's thirteenth-century travels and continuing with such works of the late eighteenth and early nineteenth centuries as Bougainville's *Voyage autour du monde*, Chateaubriand's *Voyages en Amérique* and *L'Itinéraire de Paris à Jérusalem*, and Lamartine's *Voyage en Orient*. Translators not only opened up the globe to all eyes but also, in an age of increasingly scientific specialization, helped turn the new discoveries of the scientific explorers—the geology of distant lands, the archaeology of lost ages, the astronomy of strange skies, the plants, animals, and peoples of exotic climates—into the talk of the street, the salon, and the Victorian parlour.

Costly voyages to distant lands became voyages of the mind in which any reader could participate, and translators often offered competing visions of an author's work, whether to suit varying national ideologies, changing aesthetic criteria, rising standards of scientific accuracy, or a growing mass market's hunger for cheap editions. Through their work they popularized the tradition which Volney helped to establish and within which both Goethe and Humboldt worked, in very different ways: that of the scientific traveller who seeks empirical truth, not to accumulate mere information but to rethink humanity's place in nature and in history. For Volney, travel led to a utopian vision of world revolution; for Goethe, to an inner revolution, the rebirth of the self; for Humboldt, to a synthesis of both, a conviction of humanity's ongoing progress through every individual's free exchange with fellow inhabitants of the Cosmos. The present discussion follows the fortunes of these three writers in Britain and America.

Volney's *Ruins*

This period began with revolution, in America and then in France, and Constantin-François Volney hoped to ignite the rest of Europe with his French Revolutionary spirit. Following a stint as a medical student in Paris, Volney travelled to the Middle East to investigate the cradle of civilization. In his first book, *Voyage en Égypte et en Syrie* (1787), he explored the complex interactions between human society and the physical environment, rejecting environmental determinism and concluding that civilizations fall through their own corruption; his book would help inspire the modernizing programme of Napoleon's invasion of Egypt. In *Les Ruines* (1791), completed while the French Revolution raged around him, Volney transformed his historical research into a visionary fable of civilization's rise, fall, and redemption. The narrator, meditating on the ruins of Palmyra (which, ironically, Volney never actually visited), sinks into profound melancholy at the waste and loss they represent. In his despair he is greeted by a Phantom in flowing robes who sweeps him into the heavens to show him the earth as a dappled globe. Before the narrator's eyes, primitive man gathers into societies and forms governments and laws; ancient states prosper, go to war, and collapse. But ruin is not inevitable. The Phantom shows all the nations and religions of the world gathering to argue out their differences, revealing the corruption of their rulers and false logic of their priests. In reaction, the common people rise up and declare they will be governed by the laws of nature alone, opening a dawn of hope for all humanity.

Ruins was translated immediately into English. Volney grumbled at its inaccuracies and speculated that the (anonymous) translator was too overawed by the government or clergy to render his ideas faithfully; nevertheless, according to E. P. Thompson, this translation of *Ruins* was the most influential text that circulated among the English Jacobins of the 1790s. It was available in cheap editions that 'remained in the libraries of many artisans in the nineteenth century', and the chapter in which the people declare to the priests that henceforth they will run their own affairs was frequently reprinted as a tract (Thompson 1966: 98–9). In 1797, while Volney was a refugee in the United States, his friend Thomas Jefferson translated the book's opening Invocation. His version would be often reprinted:

> O Ruins! to your school I will return! I will seek again the calm of your solitudes; and there, far from the afflicting spectacle of the passions, I will cherish in remembrance the love of man, employ myself on the means of effecting good for him, and build my own happiness on the promotion of his. (Barlow and Jefferson 1802: xii)

Ruins was altogether too radical for Volney's friend and fellow revolutionary Joseph Priestley, then living in Philadelphia, who, incensed by Volney's atheistic dismissal of religion, fired up a public controversy. In 1798, Volney was accused by President John Adams of spying for the French and forced to flee back to France, where he helped his friend Joel Barlow, a radicalized Connecticut wit then living abroad as an honorary French citizen, to complete a new, more accurate, and lyrical translation, which henceforward was regarded as standard. In its new form it made a deep impression on Shelley, who modelled on *Ruins* his first major poem, 'Queen Mab' (see Nablow 1989). His wife Mary Wollstonecraft Shelley had Frankenstein's monster commence his higher education by eavesdropping on a student being taught to read using Volney's *Ruins*. In mid-century, the American landscape painter Thomas Cole used Barlow's translation as a source for his epic series of paintings *The Course of Empire*, and it helped lead Ralph Waldo Emerson down the path of religious radicalism. Volney's *Ruins* continued to be popular throughout the century; at least eighteen editions had appeared in England by 1878 (often including Volney's 1793 sequel *The Law of Nature*), and Barlow's translation was reissued in New York in 1890.

Goethe's *Italian Journey*

In 1786, Johann Wolfgang von Goethe fulfilled a lifelong dream by stealing away from Germany to Italy. Once there, he, like Volney, meditated on ruins, but the questions he asked were very different: how could he become acquainted with himself through the objects he viewed? Whereas the ruins of Egypt had connected Volney with the course of empire, the ruins of Italy connected Goethe with the timeless universals of organic form. In his Romantic vision, mind or idea achieved fullness only through its phenomenal realization. Every object, whether artful or natural, embodied some thought, and true vision comprehended the particular object as a manifestation of universal thought. This organic vision unifies his travel narrative, *Italienische Reise*: aesthetically, Goethe distinguished between the organic unity of classic art and the fragmentary disunity of Romanticism; scientifically, he sought for the *Urpflanze* or 'Ur-plant', the essential idea of the plant visible in all its particular forms.

Italienische Reise had a complex publication history and was slow to be translated into English. The letters that form the bulk of the book were not published until 1816–17, and not until the final authorized edition of Goethe's complete works did they receive their modern title. (The last part, 'Second Sojourn in Rome', did not appear until 1829 and was not combined with the letters until much later in the century.) The work did not appear in English until 1849, when Henry G. Bohn issued the Revd A. J. W. Morrison's rather wooden translation of it as part of Goethe's autobiography; it was frequently reprinted thereafter. (Morrison, an Anglican clergyman, made sure to omit Goethe's favourable references to the Roman Catholic Church.) Curiously, for a relatively minor work the *Italian Journey* had an especially powerful impact on American literature and contributed to its mid-century romance with Italy. When Ralph Waldo Emerson found himself, late in 1832, alone, without a career, his health poor, and his faith shaken, he betook himself to Italy with a copy of Goethe's *Reise* in his pocket, which he read, in German, as his guidebook, translating passages into his journal and making them a major source of his thought. His friend Margaret Fuller celebrated Goethe as well, translating Eckermann's *Gespräche mit Goethe* and lamenting in an 1845 newspaper article that *Italienische Reise* had not yet been translated into English; she herself travelled to Italy shortly afterward, and plunged into the Italian Revolution of 1848. Like Fuller, Emerson's protégé Thoreau learned German so as to read Goethe in the original, and he used *Italienische Reise* as a model for his own works of travel. In England, by contrast, the book had little impact; in his influential biography of Goethe, George Henry Lewes voices deep disappointment in it as a literary work.

Humboldt's *Cosmos*

Alexander von Humboldt liked to call himself 'a man of 1789', recalling the glorious days of the French Revolution when, leaving his native Germany to visit Paris with his mentor Georg Forster, he helped build the Temple of Liberty. Years later, he would credit Forster with awakening in him the 'early and fixed desire to visit the land of the tropics' (Otté 1849–58: II, 20, 80). He too was fascinated by ruins, finding and documenting the vanishing relics of America's indigenous peoples; and he was a lifelong friend of Goethe, sharing his distinctive ability to unite empirical, observed particulars with their meaning in universal idea. Once Humboldt gained his freedom, he too headed south to warmth and sunshine—not to explore Europe's ancestral ruins, but to America, the 'new continent'. Against great odds he charmed the Spanish monarchy into giving him open access to the Spanish colonies, and for five years he and his companion, the botanist Aimé Bonpland, explored the coasts, deserts, jungles, mountains, and cities of South and Central America, returning home by way of the United States, where Humboldt made another lifelong friend in Thomas Jefferson.

Back in Paris, Humboldt found himself already a celebrity. His name became an international household word with the publication of *Essai politique sur le royaume de la Nouvelle-Espagne* (1808–11), a detailed portrait of Mexico's land, climate, peoples, and resources translated immediately into English by John Black as *Political Essay on the Kingdom of New Spain* (1810–11; see Rupke 1999). On its heels came Humboldt's popular narrative of his travels, published in French as *Relation historique* (1814–25) and translated into English as the *Personal Narrative* (1814–29) by his friend, the English radical poet and travel writer Helen Maria Williams, who had encouraged him to produce a book for the popular domain of the salon and lecture hall. (She hoped, as well, to recoup some of the expenses her publishing house had lost in printing Humboldt's 33-volume *Voyage en Amérique*.) Conceived on a mammoth scale, Humboldt's narrative covers barely the first two years of his five-year voyage, taking his readers to the Venezuelan coast, over the *llanos* and up the Orinoco into the deep jungles of the Amazon, then to Cuba and back to mainland South America, ending just as the travellers are on the verge of striking south to the Andes and their famed ascent of Chimborazo. (A concluding volume was apparently written but destroyed before publication; see Leask 2002: 284.)

Humboldt had been reluctant to write a personal narrative, and he worried that accounts of scientific voyages like his own lacked 'unity of composition' (Otté 1849–58: II, 29). The criticism was just, yet it understates what Humboldt accomplished. Far more than a narrative or catalogue, he offered a way of seeing: as Williams observed in her translator's preface, 'The appropriate character of his writings is the faculty he possesses of raising the mind to general ideas, without neglecting individual facts; and while he appears only to address himself to our reason, he has the secret of awakening the imagination, and of being understood by the heart' (Williams 1814–29: I, ix). The book throughout is imbued with Humboldt's relish for the richness of life in the tropics. He is never sick, seldom discouraged, always alive with joy, curiosity, and good humour. Indeed, his joy was infectious: young Charles Darwin, upon reading Humboldt's *Personal Narrative*, vowed he too would travel to South America and make some contribution to natural science. He carried Williams's translation with him on the *Beagle*, and when the time came to write his own travel narrative, he modelled it on Humboldt's. Humboldt repaid the compliment in *Cosmos*, praising Darwin as a worthy successor to his personal hero, Georg Forster.

The length and expense of Williams's translation made Humboldt's travel narrative relatively inaccessible until a second translation and abridgement by Thomasina Ross was issued in London in 1852. Ross's translation made Humboldt available to a new generation of British and American readers, including the young Henry David Thoreau, who adapted Humboldt's bold scientific approach and experimental style to his own ambition to live like a global traveller in his own local village of Concord, Massachusetts. Other abridgements also made Humboldt's travels and commentaries available to a wide audience. William MacGillivray's 1832 biography *The Travels and Researches of Alexander von Humboldt* brought Humboldt's mammoth text down to illustrated pocketbook size. Far more controversial was a second abridgement, J. S. Thrasher's *The Island of Cuba by Alexander von Humboldt* (1856), which used Humboldt to argue for the annexation of Cuba by American slave interests; Humboldt, furious, wrote a letter of protest that was widely reprinted in the United States.

Two other translations contributed to the surge of interest in Humboldt. *Ansichten der Natur* had already gone through two German editions, but only the third was translated into English, in two competing versions: *Aspects of Nature* (1848), by Elizabeth Juliana Sabine, and *Views of Nature* (1850), by Elise Otté and Henry G. Bohn. This series of nature essays was drawn from his American travels and blended poetry and science, relegating his typically verbose annotations to endnotes. Both translations circulated widely; Otté's and Bohn's became the standard edition, whereas Sabine's acquired a reputation as the more elegant and poetic of the two. The difference in titles points to a characteristic problem in translating Humboldt's German: the word 'Ansichten' implies a quality of intuitive visualization that helps to create the total picture; the English translations, 'aspects' or 'views', both suggest a reality separate from the viewer, losing the Humboldtian emphasis on the role of perception in composing, or even creating, the reality that is present to the mind.

Nearly simultaneously, the same translators issued two competing versions of Humboldt's last great work, *Kosmos*, published in German in five volumes from 1845 to 1862. (Augustin Prichard also issued a translation, but contemporaries regarded it as beneath notice.) Sabine translated the first two volumes (1846–8) under the scientific superintendence of her husband, the Humboldtian geophysicist Edward Sabine. At the time, her work was regarded as authoritative, and most British reviews of *Cosmos* were of this translation. Meanwhile the London publisher Bohn, eager to produce a cheap popular edition, engaged the highly respected scientific translator Elise Otté, who completed four of the five German volumes (1849–58). In her preface, Otté honoured her competitor's translation as 'singularly accurate and elegant', but distinguished her own as more scientifically accurate and completely uncensored, at a third the cost; Otté's translation became the standard. It was widely circulated, reissued in New York by Harper and Brothers (1850–9), and reprinted in 1997.

Cosmos became Humboldt's blockbuster, the global best-seller that crowned his career. The first volume detailed his unique approach to science and outlined the objective world from stars and planets to earth and its life forms, including man; his second volume took up the subjective realm, the history of the Cosmos as an *idea*. For Humboldt, nature becomes meaningful to us only through our representations, through art and poetry and science. This was the mark of modernity, the demand to know about distant lands and their inhabitants, and it was 'the common work of all civilized nations' to render by communication all parts of the earth accessible to each other. Thus, for this quintessential cosmopolitan, translation was the essence of the civilized. His final three volumes began the task of outlining all human knowledge of the universe; unsurprisingly, this task was too great even for Humboldt, and he died with his great survey unfinished. The final volume has never been translated into English.

The influence of Humboldt's *Cosmos* is difficult to calculate. Through his translators he had a powerful impact on individual writers and artists: Washington Irving, Emerson, Thoreau, Edgar Allan Poe, and Walt Whitman all made Humboldt's uniquely populist vision their own. The American artists Titian Ramsey Peale, Frederic Edwin Church, and George Catlin all followed Humboldt's footsteps to the tropics; British scientists such as Charles Lyell, William Whewell, and Charles Darwin extended Humboldt's ideas and changed the face of natural science; exploring expeditions modelled after Humboldt's mapped the Americas, Africa, Asia, and Australia; the pioneers of environmentalism, from Thoreau and Emerson to John Muir, John Burroughs, and George Perkins Marsh, extended Humboldt's insights into a call for environmental awareness and protection. Jules Verne planted a complete set of Humboldt's works on Captain Nemo's submarine the *Nautilus*; H. G. Wells exploded Darwin's Humboldtian vision of deep time, imagining the earth at the end of history and all humanity a ruin. Every age, Humboldt wrote, imagines itself to be at the furthest edge of knowledge, the end of science. He rejected such a view, arguing instead that all we have achieved is only a step to the attainment of higher things, to all that 'free humanity will attain in future ages by the progress of mental activity and general cultivation' (Otté 1849–58: II, 355). For Humboldt, there could be no limits to the Cosmos. Every step upward would reveal only a wider horizon.

LIST OF SOURCES

Translations

Anon. (1792). *The Ruins, or, A Survey of the Revolutions of Empires* [Volney]. London.

[Barlow, Joel, and Jefferson, Thomas] (1802). *A New Translation of Volney's Ruins, or, Meditations on the Revolution of Empires*, 2 vols. Paris.

Black, John (1810–11). *Political Essay on the Kingdom of New Spain* [Humboldt], 4 vols. London.

Morrison, Alexander James William (1848). *The Auto-biography of Goethe*, 2 vols. London (Bohn; the second volume contains *Travels in Italy*).

Otté, Elise C. (1849–58). *Cosmos: A Sketch of the Physical Description of the Universe* [Humboldt], 5 vols. London (printed in New York 1850–9).

—— and Bohn, Henry G. (1850). *Views of Nature* [Humboldt]. London.

Prichard, Augustin (1845–8). *Kosmos: A General Survey of Physical Phenomena of the Universe* [Humboldt], 2 vols. London.

Ross, Thomasina (1852). *Personal Narrative of Travels to the Equinoctial Regions of America, During the Years 1799–1804* [Humboldt], 3 vols. London.

Sabine, Elizabeth Juliana (1848). *Aspects of Nature*. [Humboldt]. London.

—— and Sabine, Edward (1846–8). *Cosmos: Sketch of the Physical Description of the Universe* [Humboldt], 2 vols. London.

Taylor, John (1824). *Selections from the Works of the Baron de Humboldt, Relating to the Climate, Inhabitants, Productions, and Mines of Mexico*. London.

Williams, Helen Maria (1814–29). *Personal Narrative of Travels to the Equinoctial Regions of the New Continent, during the Years 1799–1804* [Humboldt], 6 vols. London.

Other Sources

Botting, Douglas (1973). *Humboldt and the Cosmos*. New York.

Chinard, Gilbert (1923). *Volney et l'Amérique*. Baltimore, MD.

Dettelbach, Michael (1997). 'Introduction', pp. vii–xlvii in Alexander von Humboldt, *Cosmos*, tr. Elise C. Otté, vol. 2. Baltimore, MD.

Heffernan, Michael (1999). 'Historical Geographies of the Future: Three Perspectives from France, 1750–1825', pp. 125–64 in David N. Livingstone and Charles W. J. Withers, eds., *Geography and Enlightenment*. Chicago, IL.

Leask, Nigel (2002). *Curiosity and the Aesthetics of Travel Writing, 1770–1840*. Oxford.

Nablow, Ralph A. (1989). 'Shelley, "Ozymandias", and Volney's *Les Ruines.*' *N&Q* 36: 172–3.

Pratt, Mary Louise (1992). *Imperial Eyes: Travel Writing and Transculturation*. London.

Richardson, Robert D. (1984). 'Emerson's Italian Journey.' *Browning Institute Studies* 12: 121–31.

Rupke, Nicolaas (1999). 'A Geography of Enlightenment: The Critical Reception of Alexander von Humboldt's Work', pp. 319–39 in David N. Livingston and Charles W. J. Withers, eds., *Geography and Enlightenment*. Chicago, IL.

Thompson, E. P. (1966). *The Making of the English Working Class*. London.

12

The Translators: Biographical Sketches

The Translators: Biographical Sketches

The 108 biographical sketches that follow are intended primarily to complement the preceding chapters. They make no claim to cover the period comprehensively; only a small proportion of translators active in this period are included. Representativeness (of some sort) is only one of the criteria for inclusion; historical importance, literary merit, and the convenience of readers have also influenced the choice of subjects. The entries themselves concentrate on the activity of translating in the writers' lives. The further reading at the end of each entry is restricted to the standard works of biographical reference (the *Oxford Dictionary of National Biography*, the *Dictionary of American Biography*, and the *American National Biography*), the most important relevant biographies, and, where possible, critical works focused on translation. In the text, references to works are sometimes given in abbreviated form; the date normally refers to the year of first publication. Cross-references are included for a few figures who overlap with this period but are more fully treated in Vol. 3 or Vol. 5 of this *History*. The authors of the sketches can be identified by consulting the list of contributors at the beginning of this volume.

ANDERSON, Rasmus Bjørn (1846–1936), educator, author, editor, historian, insurance agent, diplomat, salesman, investor. He translated from English into Norwegian and from Norwegian, Swedish, Danish, and Old Norse into English. A controversial figure, Anderson was central to Norwegian cultural life in the United States. He attended Luther College and was expelled; he taught at Albion Academy and was dismissed. But from 1869 to 1882, he was professor at the University of Wisconsin, where he established the teaching of Norwegian and Old Norse. He was US Minister to Denmark, 1885–9. From 1898 to 1922, he edited the Norwegian-American newspaper *Amerika*.

Throughout his life, Anderson promoted Norwegian culture. He wrote books on Norse mythology, on the Norse discovery of America, on Norwegian immigration. His translations include versions of sagas and of the eddic poems, as well as a variety of non-literary works. In addition, Anderson was credited with translating several works by Bjørnstjerne Bjørnson, together with one by Georg Brandes, all of which were in fact translated by Anna Aubertine Woodward.

See further: Lloyd Hustvedt, *Rasmus Bjørn Anderson: Pioneer Scholar* (Northfield, MN, 1966). RB

ARCHER, William (1856–1924), the most influential drama critic of his day; translator from Norwegian, Danish, German; editor; playwright. Born in Perth, Scotland, he had strong family ties in Larvik, Norway, and was nearly fluent in Norwegian when he began studying at the University of Edinburgh in 1872.

The next summer he discovered Ibsen. He translated *The Pillars of Society* in 1878; though not published, it was staged in London in 1880 as *Quicksands*, the first production of an Ibsen play in English. Although Archer's Ibsen translations, culminating in *The Collected Works* (12 vols., 1906–12), were not, as is often thought, the first published in English, they dominated the field until the 1920s. Archer's translations also included plays by Gerhart Hauptmann (from the German) and Maurice Maeterlinck (from the French) as well as works by the Danish critic Georg Brandes and the Norwegian explorer Fritiof Nansen.

Archer's drama criticism greatly advanced the new drama of the day. His tireless support for a British National Theatre, beginning in 1873, resulted in the book *A National Theatre: Scheme and Estimates* (1904), written with Harley Granville-Barker. And he wrote over twenty original plays; one, *The Green Goddess*, became a silent film.

See further: *ODNB*; Peter Whitebrook, *William Archer: A Biography* (London, 1993).   RB

Arnold, Sir Edwin (1832–1904), journalist and poet. Born in Gravesend, near London, the son of a magistrate, Arnold excelled in school and went on a scholarship to University College, Oxford, where he won the Newdigate Prize in poetry. In 1856, he left England for India to become the Principal of a college at Poona and a Fellow at Bombay University. During his years in India he studied Sanskrit, Persian, Arabic, and Turkish. In 1861, having lost a child and with his wife continually unwell, he returned to England to work at the *Daily Telegraph* as both a writer and editor.

Arnold published translations of Bion, Homer, Hesiod, Sappho, and Theocritus in *Poets of Greece* (1869), and of Musaeus in *Hero and Leander* (1873). But his more widely known interest in eastern literature eventually emerged in his original work—*The Light of Asia* (1879) recounts the life of Buddha—and in his translations, which include the *Hitopadésa* (1861), Jayadeva's *The Indian Song of Songs* (1875), and *The Song Celestial* or *Bhagavad-Gîtâ* (1885), all from Sanskrit, and selections from the thirteenth-century Persian poet Saʻdī (1888 and 1899). The scholar Franklin Edgerton called his *Bhagavad-Gîtâ* 'a beautiful English rendering' and reprinted it in his edition for the Harvard Oriental Series. Arnold's travels in Japan later in his life inspired a number of shorter translations, many of which are found in *The Tenth Muse, and Other Poems* (1895).

See further: *ODNB*; Brooks Wright, *Interpreter of Buddhism to the West: Sir Edwin Arnold* (New York, 1957).   CD

Aston, William George (1841–1911), consular official, philologist, and translator from the Japanese; one of the most important early western scholars of Japan. Born in Londonderry, Aston completed his MA in modern languages and history at Queen's University, Belfast, where he was later awarded an honorary D.Litt. He arrived in Japan in 1864 as a student interpreter for the British Legation in Edo and was later appointed British consul at Nagasaki (1882) and then, provisionally, consul-general for Korea (1884). Plagued by ill health, he retired to Devon in 1889 at the age of 48.

Although he published a number of translations and studies of Japanese and Korean literature and language while in Asia, Aston is generally remembered for the works completed after his retirement. These include his translation—yet to be superseded—of the eighth-century state history *Nihongi: Chronicles of Japan* (1896), a difficult text written in a Japanized form of classical Chinese, and his ground-breaking *History of Japanese Literature* (1899); the latter work, which contains many translations, was the first, and for many years the only, book-length English-language survey of Japanese literature. Aston's final major work is his *Shinto (The Way of the Gods)* (1905), a text-based treatment of Shintō which has not stood the test of time as well as his literature-related works.

See further: *ODNB*; Peter Kornicki, 'William George Aston (1841–1911)', pp. 64–75 in Sir Hugh Cortazzi and Gordon Daniels, eds., *Britain and Japan 1859–1991: Themes and Personalities* (London, 1991). AC

AUSTIN (née Taylor), Sarah (1793–1867), translator, editor, and writer; born in Norwich and educated there by her mother. In 1820 she married the lawyer John Austin, with whom she resided in Britain, Germany, Malta, and France. Austin began translating in order to supplement her husband's income. She considered this occupation to be her calling and was regarded as one of the foremost translators of her time.

Among the French authors she translated were Guizot on the English Revolution and Victor Cousin on Prussian education, but she became best known for her translations from German, several of them going into two or more editions. They include Friedrich Carové's novel *The Story without an End* (1834), works by the historians Ranke and Niebuhr, travel writing (Pückler-Muskau), and studies of Goethe. Her compilation of sketches of German life entitled *Germany from 1760 to 1814* was read widely after its publication in 1854. Austin also edited her husband's work in jurisprudence and her daughter's *Letters from Egypt*. Lucie Duff Gordon, her only child, came to prominence as a travel writer, and she continued her mother's efforts in translating French and German literary and historical works.

See further: *ODNB*; Lotte and Joseph Hamburger, *Troubled Lives: John and Sarah Austin* (Toronto, 1985), and *Contemplating Adultery* (London, 1992).
SS

BELL, Clara Courtenay (1834–1927), prolific professional translator. The daughter of Ambrose Poynter, a distinguished architect and co-founder of the Royal Institute of British Architecture, and sister of the painter Edward Poynter, who became President of the Royal Academy, Clara Bell moved in artistic circles throughout her life; Burne-Jones (with whom she was connected by marriage) and George du Maurier (who thought her 'the cleverest woman of our acquaintance and the most exquisite amateur singer I ever heard') were particular friends. With her specialist knowledge she was much in demand to translate books on art, such as Chesneau's *Education of the Artist* (1886), or music (Spitta's *J. S. Bach*, with J. A. Fuller-Maitland, 1884), but most of her numerous translations were of fiction. In 1876 she translated the first of at least twenty German historical romances, principally by the Egyptologist Georg Ebers; she also translated from Dutch (e.g. Louis Couperus), Spanish (e.g. Pérez Galdós), Italian (e.g. A. G. Barrilio), and French (e.g. Pierre Loti, Guy de Maupassant, J. K. Huysmans). In all she translated at least fifty-nine books between 1876 and 1906.

Her reputation for reliability made her a natural choice when Ellen Marriage needed assistance with the complete new translation of Balzac's *Comédie humaine* published by Dent in 1895–8; she translated twelve of the forty volumes.

ML

Borrow, George Henry (1803–1881), writer, traveller, linguist. Born in Norfolk, the son of an army officer, he lived with his family in many parts of Britain and Ireland. After a spell in Grub Street, he travelled the world adventurously, loving the open road and the world of the Gypsies. As an agent for the Bible Society, he spent two years in Russia and several more in Spain and Portugal, settling in England again in 1840. His experiences, magnified and embellished, form the basis of the highly original prose works which brought him fame, *The Bible in Spain* (1843), *Lavengro* (1851), *The Romany Rye* (1857), and *Wild Wales* (1862).

He had a limited formal education but was a passionate and highly idiosyncratic amateur philologist; encouraged in his youth by William Taylor of Norwich, he translated from at least thirty languages, with a predilection for Danish and Welsh. Some translations are in prose, such as *The Sleeping Bard* (1860, from the Welsh allegory by Elis Wyn), but his energy was devoted above all to songs and ballads. He published *Romantic Ballads, Translated from the Danish* (1826) and *Targum, or, Metrical Translations from Thirty Languages and Dialects* (1835), but most of his numerous verse translations had little success and were published posthumously, if at all, notably in the *Works* edited by Clement Shorter (1923–4).

See further: *ODNB*; David Williams, *A World of his Own: The Double Life of George Borrow* (Oxford, 1982); and for a listing of his translations, Michael Collie and Angus Fraser, *George Borrow: A Bibliographical Study* (Winchester, 1984).

PF

Bowring, Sir John (1792–1872), businessman, politician, journalist, and compiler of anthologies of poetry from many languages. Born in Exeter, the son of a merchant, he began to learn languages as a young man, and travelled extensively on business throughout Europe. He was a committed radical, and the first editor of Bentham's *Westminster Review*, writing mainly on linguistic and literary topics. From 1835 to 1837 and again from 1841 to 1849 he was a Member of Parliament, and later held important official positions in China.

Bowring published on several subjects, including anthologies of poetry translated from Russian, Dutch, Spanish, Serbian, Polish, Hungarian, and Czech (see bibliography to § 6.8, above). He had a passion for lesser-known languages and cultures, claiming for instance to have introduced the Finnish *Kalevala* metre to Britain, but many, including the unreliable George Borrow (see 'The Old Radical' in *The Romany Rye*), cast doubt on his knowledge, and he certainly used unacknowledged sources. An ambitious man, he attracted hostility and criticism. Nevertheless, he saw the collection and translation of foreign poetry as a contribution to international understanding—his pioneering work is remarkable for this rather than for its literary distinction. His son Edgar (1826–1911) was an important translator of German poetry.

See further: *ODNB*; Joyce Youings, ed., *Sir John Bowring 1792–1872* (Plymouth, 1993). PF

BOYD, Henry (1748/9–1832), clergyman and poet, born in Co. Tyrone. Educated at Trinity College Dublin, Boyd translated partly from a desire to widen public knowledge of European literature. His verse translation of Dante's *Inferno* was published by subscription in 1785, with a specimen of Ariosto's *Furioso*—also in verse translation, never published in full. He dedicated it to Lord Frederick Hervey, then Bishop of Derry, whose passion for Italy almost certainly influenced Boyd's own.

Boyd worked for many years in Dublin as chaplain to Viscount Charleville before taking refuge in the country from the Irish Rebellion. Charleville shared his literary tastes, and Boyd dedicated his complete translation of the *Divine Comedy* (1802) to him. In 1805 he published *The Penance of Hugo*, an augmented translation of an anti-republican play by Vincenzo Monti, and a further verse translation, *Triumphs of Petrarch*, appeared in 1807, but he struggled without success to find a publisher for his version of the sixteenth-century Spanish epic *La Araucana* by Ercilla y Zúñiga. One or two of his own compositions were accused of vulgarity, but Boyd always carefully edited the translations: in his preface to Ariosto, he declares he has altered or omitted all licentious passages, trusting, too, that critics would not object to the 'suppression of a pleonasm'.

See further: *ODNB*. JY

BRIDGES, Robert Seymour (1844–1930), poet and translator of hymns, born at Walmer, Kent, and educated at Eton and Corpus Christi College, Oxford. After Oxford, he travelled (1867–8) and studied in Germany (1868–9), before becoming a medical student at St Bartholomew's Hospital. He graduated from there in 1874 and worked as a doctor until 1881, although he had already published *Poems* (1873), followed by *The Growth of Love* (1876) and two other volumes, *Poems by the Author of The Growth of Love* (second series, 1879, third series, 1880). In 1881 he had a life-threatening attack of pneumonia and gave up practising medicine. On recovery, he went to live at Yattendon, Berkshire, where he produced the *Yattendon Hymnal* (1895–9), in which he aimed to improve the standard of taste in Anglican worship. Alongside existing translations, the *Hymnal* contains his own rather free translations from Latin, Greek, and German, including such well-known hymns as 'The duteous day now closeth', 'O gladsome light, O grace', 'All my heart on God is founded', and 'Ah, Holy Jesu, how hast thou offended'. Bridges was made Poet Laureate in 1913 and continued to publish until *The Testament of Beauty* of 1929.

See further: *ODNB*; Catherine Phillips, *Robert Bridges: A Biography* (Oxford, 1992). JRW

BROOKS, Charles Timothy (1813–1883), clergyman and man of letters. Born and educated in Salem, MA, Brooks attended Harvard in 1828; on graduating in 1832, he spent three further years at the Harvard Divinity School. He was ordained as a Unitarian minister in 1837 and served as a pastor in Newport, RI, from then until 1871. Because of ill health, he spent many winters in Alabama and one year in India. In 1865–6, he spent nearly a year in Europe.

At Harvard, Brooks studied languages, especially German, with zeal. He wrote a good deal, including literary and theological essays, poems, and children's books. However, he is known primarily for his translations from German. The most important of these include Schiller's *Wilhelm Tell* (1838), *Songs and Ballads, Translated from Uhland, Körner, Bürger, and Other German Lyric Poets* (1842), the first part of Goethe's *Faust* (1856), and two novels by Jean Paul Richter (*Titan*, 1862 and *Hesperus*, 1865). Brooks's attachment to sentiment and gentility is evident in his choice of texts and his manner of translating.

See further: *ANB*; Camillo von Klenze, *Charles Timothy Brooks: Translator from the German and the Genteel Tradition* (1937); Joel Myerson, ed., *The Transcendentalists: A Review of Research and Criticism* (1984). KH

BROWNING, Elizabeth Barrett (1806–1861), poet, born in Durham into a family of wealthy landholders in the West Indies. Her parents encouraged her literary and poetical pursuits, including the study of languages. Although as a child she studied Greek with her brother's tutor, her learning was largely autodidactic. A lifetime of ill health contributed to her prodigious correspondence, and here her scholarly approach to the ancient languages is evident.

Time spent reading Greek with her classically inclined neighbour Hugh Stuart Boyd fuelled her initial interest in translation. At his suggestion, she undertook a translation of Aeschylus' *Prometheus Bound* (1833) that includes a preface where she considers the task of the translator. She would later refer to her first *Prometheus* as 'a sin of my youth' and criticize her objective, a literal rendering. During the 1840s, when her popularity as a poet was on the rise and she was corresponding with Robert Browning (they married in 1846), she translated *Prometheus Bound* again. This substantially reworked version first appeared in her *Poems* of 1850, which also includes her *Sonnets from the Portuguese*. Despite the title, these poems are not translations; they were inspired by her love for Browning.

In addition, her strong Christian faith prompted her to translate from the Greek Christian Fathers (1842). She continued to translate poetry until the end of her life, the majority of her other translations, mostly classical, being published posthumously. These include excerpts from the works of Apuleius, Bion, Euripides, Homer, Nonnus, Theocritus, Dante, and Heine.

See further: *ODNB*; M. Forster, *Elizabeth Barrett Browning: A Biography* (London, 1988). CD

BROWNING, Robert (1812–1889), poet, born in London. His father worked as a clerk in the Bank of England and amassed an extensive library that fostered Browning's literary and linguistic interests. He excelled in his studies, and since he was barred as a nonconformist from attending Oxford or Cambridge, he enrolled at London University for a year, studying Latin and Greek before beginning his career as poet.

Browning's first translations were of Euripides. In *Balaustion's Adventure, including a Transcript from Euripides* (1871), he works his own version of *Alcestis* into the poem. *Aristophanes' Apology, including a Transcript from Euripides, being the Last Adventure of Balaustion* (1875) contains a translation of *Heracles*. These translations occur within larger narrative poems whose plots both depend on and comment on the tragedies.

His most contentious contribution is his translation of Aeschylus' *Agamemnon* (1877). His declared intention in the preface was 'to be literal at every cost, save that of absolute violence to our language'. The strangeness of the ensuing English meant that the translation was not generally well received, not even by Carlyle to whom the effort was dedicated, and the gibe was that it was necessary to return to the Greek in order to understand the English.

See further: *ODNB*; William Irvine and Park Honan, *The Book, the Ring, and the Poet* (New York, 1974); Matthew Reynolds, 'Browning and Translationese', *Essays in Criticism* 53 (2003), 97–128. CD

BULWER LYTTON, Edward, *see* LYTTON, Edward Bulwer.

BULWER LYTTON, Robert, *see* LYTTON, Edward Bulwer.

BURTON, Sir Richard Francis (1821–1890) is best known as an explorer and author of accounts of explorations in Africa, India, Syria, and Arabia. In 1855–6 he published a controversial account of his journey to Mecca, suggesting he was the first non-Muslim to travel there in disguise. He was a brilliant linguist, claiming to know some forty languages. Much of his life was spent in isolated consular postings, since his erratic behaviour and obsession with sexology contributed to his insalubrious reputation. From 1880 he published mainly translations. *The Lusiads*, his version of Camões's Portuguese epic with which he felt great empathy, appeared that year. His wife Lady Isabel Burton, née Arundell (1831–96), is credited with making the first translation of a Brazilian work in English, Jose de Alencar's *Iraçéma, the Honey-Lips: A Legend of Brazil*, and in 1886 he and Isabel together translated another Brazilian work, Pereira da Silva's *Manuel de Moraes: A Chronicle of the Seventeenth Century.*

But his main translating interest lay in non-European languages. His pseudo-translation *The Kasîdah of Hâjî Abdû El-Yezdî*, a collection of his own poetry purporting to be the work of an imaginary Persian poet, was published in 1880; it is likely that he had hoped to rival the success of Edward FitzGerald's *Rubáiyát of Omar Khayyám*. In 1885–8 he published in ten volumes *The Book of the Thousand Nights and a Night: A Plain and Literal Translation of the Arabian Nights' Entertainments*, with extensive anthropological notes. His translations also include Latin, Persian, Sanskrit, and Arabic erotica, including the *Kama Sutra of Vatsayana*, jointly with F. F. Arbuthnot. These erotic works were privately printed, and after his death Isabel is said to have destroyed the manuscript of what he had hoped would be his major translation, *The Scented Garden*. His translation style is pedantic, and his penchant for archaisms and extensive footnotes meant that apart from the *Nights* none of his translations had much success.

See further: *ODNB*; Mary S. Lovell, *A Rage to Live: A Biography of Richard and Isabel Burton* (New York, 1998). SB

Busk (née Blair) **Mary Margaret** (1779–1863), reviewer, historian, poet. Daughter of a wealthy Birmingham manufacturer, she early gained knowledge of Latin and European languages, later strengthened through travel with her barrister husband William. However, William became destitute, and in her forties Busk started writing and translating for income, drawing on their 'wandering life'. She wrote on history and historical characters and published plays and poems. Her lengthier works, such as the *Manners and Customs of the Japanese in the Nineteenth Century* (1841), the first English work to concentrate on Japanese culture, or *Mediaeval Popes, Emperors, Kings and Crusaders* (1854–6), are combinations of exposition and translation.

Her place in the history of translation resides chiefly in her impressive contribution to periodicals. At first publishing under either her brother's name or the initials 'S.A.', she became a prominent reviewer and translator from the early 1820s. She reviewed in many journals and covered most European languages; in the *Foreign Quarterly* alone, she published almost forty articles, all distinguished by the unusually high percentage of translation. In a review-translation of Swedish literature (*Foreign Quarterly*, May 1834), she states the hope that her pages of direct translation will 'have afforded our readers ampler and better means of judging of the Swedish literary character, than they could have derived from the observations of any of the recent travellers to that country'.

See further: *ODNB*; Eileen Curran, 'Holding on by a Pen: The Story of a Lady/Reviewer', *Victorian Periodicals Review* 31 (1998), 9–30. JY

Byron, George Gordon, Lord (1788–1824), for a time Europe's most famous poet. He was brought up in Scotland until 1798, when he inherited his title, moved south, and attended Harrow School and Cambridge. He travelled widely in Europe and the Middle East, achieved fame with the first two cantos of *Childe Harold's Pilgrimage* (1812), and defended liberal causes in the House of Lords.

Ostracized for his scandalous private life, he left England for good in 1816, living mainly in Italy, where he was on close terms with Shelley. In 1824 he went to fight for Greek independence, but died of fever at Missolonghi.

Translation from Latin and Greek was part of his poetic apprenticeship; his first published collection was *Hours of Idleness: A Series of Poems Original and Translated* (1807). Thereafter he translated occasional short pieces, including epigrams by Martial, songs from Modern Greek, and ancient Armenian texts. Three major translations or imitations were a more integral part of his own poetry and polemics: the Juvenal-inspired *English Bards and Scottish Reviewers* (1809) was followed by *Hints from Horace* (1811), a Popean imitation of the *Ars Poetica*, and his lively version in *ottava rima* of Canto I of Pulci's comic epic *Morgante Maggiore* (1819) fed into his *Don Juan* and his advocacy of a non-Wordsworthian kind of Romanticism.

See further: *ODNB*; Leslie A. Marchand, *Byron: A Biography*, 3 vols. (New York, 1957); Peter Vassallo, *Byron: The Italian Literary Influence* (London, 1984).

PF

CALVERLEY, Charles Stuart (1831–1884), author of light verse and translator. Son of Henry Blayds, an Anglican clergyman, he was born in Martley, Worcestershire, spending his childhood near Bath. When he went in 1846 to Harrow School, he was already noted both for skill in versification in Greek, Latin, and English and for indolence and disrespectful ways. He lived up to his dual reputation at Balliol College, Oxford. Though awarded the Chancellor's Prize for Latin verse, he had to move to Christ's College, Cambridge, in 1852, the year he adopted the name Calverley. Though no model student, he continued winning prizes for verse composition, took a first-class degree in classics and gained a college fellowship. He married in 1863 and two years later qualified as a barrister. Ill health after a skating accident curtailed his career. An author of occasional poems and parodies, Calverley made translations of Theocritus, Homer, and Virgil, the Theocritus ranking among the most successful of the century. He also published Latin and Greek versions of English poems and wrote on verse translation, arguing that classical metres were not reproducible in English.

See further: *ODNB*; Richard B. Ince, *Calverley and Some Cambridge Wits of the Nineteenth Century* (London, 1929).

CS

CAMPBELL, John Francis, of Islay (1821?–1885), Gaelic scholar and folklorist. Educated at Eton and at Edinburgh University, he held a number of minor government posts, including secretary to the Lighthouse Commission and to the Coal Commission. He spent most of his spare time collecting, translating, and editing the oral traditions of the western Highlands, which he took down in Gaelic from native speakers. He also established a network of trained collectors across the region, setting new standards in the developing discipline of folklore. The results of his investigations were published in four volumes under the title *Popular Tales of the West Highlands* (1860–2) and form a crucial contribution to the field: Campbell's readable translations, which kept close to the syntax of the originals and preserved many dialect words, became key texts in the subsequent Gaelic revival, directly inspiring others such as Alexander Carmichael and, in Ireland, Douglas Hyde, to undertake similar work. Campbell was also an accomplished geologist and meteorologist: he invented the sunshine recorder, used in most British meteorological stations. He died at Cannes in February 1885.

See further: *ODNB*; Richard M. Dorson, *The British Folklorists: A History* (Chicago, IL, 1968), pp. 392–418.   M-AC

CARLYLE, Thomas (1795–1881). Born in Ecclefechan, Dumfriesshire, the son of a stonemason, he became a figure of prophetic stature in the English literature of his day. Intended originally for the ministry, he studied at Edinburgh University. He lived for a time with his wife Jane Welsh on a remote farm in Nithsdale, but from 1834 the couple lived in Chelsea, becoming a vital force in literary London. Jane's death in 1866 'shattered my whole existence'. Throughout his career, but especially early on, Carlyle wrote copiously for the periodical press, but he also produced a series of major critical and historical works, including a *History of the French Revolution* (1837), a life of Frederick the Great (1856–65), and the lectures *On Heroes, Hero-Worship and the Heroic in History* (1841).

His earliest translations, from French and German, were on scientific subjects, but he developed an intense interest in German literature, which greatly affected such of his own works as *Sartor Resartus* (1833–4). He adopted the mission of bringing German writers to the British reading public, both in numerous essays and in influential translations: Goethe's *Wilhelm Meister's Apprenticeship* (1824) and the four volumes of *German Romance* (1827), containing *Wilhelm Meister's Travels* and texts by Hoffmann, Tieck, and others.

See further: *ODNB*; Ian Campbell, *Thomas Carlyle* (London, 1974); Rosemary Ashton, *The German Idea* (Cambridge, 1980).   PF

CARY, Henry Francis (1772–1844). The son of an infantry officer, Cary was born at Gibraltar but brought up in England, spending his childhood in Staffordshire. Despite moving from school to school, he had a sound classical education and also learnt Italian. While a teenager, he published occasional verses and translations from Italian in the *Gentleman's Magazine*, attracting the attention of Anna Seward. After graduating from Christ Church, Oxford, he followed family tradition neglected by his father and took Anglican orders. In 1797 he started translating Dante; his version of the *Inferno* appeared in 1805–6. Moving from Kingsbury, Warwickshire, Cary settled in London in 1808. His translation of the *Commedia* was published in 1814 and reissued in a less cramped format in 1819. Among those who were impressed was Coleridge, who became a friend. To the *London Magazine* Cary contributed studies of early French poets with translations (reprinted as a book in 1846). In 1824 he published a version of Aristophanes' *Birds*; his *Pindar in English Verse* appeared in 1833. In 1826 he had become an

Assistant Keeper of Printed Books at the British Museum, but resigned when Anthony Panizzi was promoted over his head in 1837.

See further: *ODNB*; R. W. King, *The Translator of Dante: The Life, Work and Friendships of Henry Francis Cary* (London, 1925); Edoardo Crisafulli, *The Vision of Dante: Cary's Translation of 'The Divine Comedy'* (Market Harborough, 2003).

CS

CHAMBERLAIN, Basil Hall (1850–1935), scholar, philologist, and one of the most important early western scholars of Japan. Born in England, Chamberlain was brought up mainly in France and had mastered several European languages by the time he arrived in Japan in 1873 while travelling to improve his health. There he learnt Japanese—and studied Korean—and made several important early translations from the classical Japanese literary canon. These include the poetry and nō appearing in his *Classical Poetry of the Japanese* (1880), and the myth-history *Kojiki: Records of Ancient Matters* (1883), an extremely demanding eighth-century work. In addition to his translations, Chamberlain made a significant contribution to the field of linguistics in Japan. Appointed the first professor of Japanese and philology at the Imperial University in Tokyo in 1886, he influenced a generation of Japanese scholars. His works also include his clear and cogent 1888 grammar *A Handbook of Colloquial Japanese*, and *Things Japanese* (1890), a compendium of Japan-related information which was reprinted—and revised—no fewer than six times. After thirty-seven years of residence in Japan, Chamberlain retired to Geneva in 1911.

See further: *ODNB*; Richard Bowring, 'An Amused Guest in All: Basil Hall Chamberlain (1850–1935)', pp. 128–36 in Sir Hugh Cortazzi and Gordon Daniels, eds., *Britain and Japan 1859–1991: Themes and Personalities* (London, 1991).

AC

CLOUGH, Arthur Hugh (1819–1861), educator and poet, born in Liverpool, where his father was a largely unsuccessful cotton merchant. When he was a young child, his family emigrated to Charleston, South Carolina, but Clough returned at the age of 9 to attend Rugby while his parents remained in America. He then attended Balliol College, Oxford, and throughout his life worked as an educator: as Fellow and tutor at Oriel, as Principal of University Hall, London, and eventually, after time spent in Boston, MA, as an examiner in the Education Office.

In 1859 he published a revision of Dryden's five-volume edition of translations of Plutarch's *Lives*, a project which had engaged him intermittently for six years. As was his intention, he improved the translations with regard to their accuracy, concision, and readability. He considered the subject of translation and the particular problems of metre, syntax, and rhyme in several essays that incorporate his translations. 'Illustrations of Latin Lyrical Metres' (1847), for example, includes translations from Horace, Homer, Sappho, Sophocles, and Catullus, where Clough struggles to convey an 'adequate notion of the originals'. His review of

Poems and Ballads of Goethe (1859), translated by Aytoun and Martin, includes his general observations on 'that most difficult form of original composition—the translation of poetry into poetry' as well as his own translations of Goethe.

See further: *ODNB*; K. Chorley, *Arthur Hugh Clough: The Uncommitted Mind* (Oxford, 1962).   CD

COLERIDGE, Samuel Taylor (1772–1834), poet, critic. The son of a clergyman in Devon, he went at the age of 9 to Christ's Hospital, where he excelled in his classical studies. He attended Jesus College, Cambridge, but dropped out briefly during a period of depression, drinking, and (it was rumoured) opium use, a habit that would plague him for much of his life. In 1798 he travelled to Germany with Wordsworth. He studied German, attended the University of Göttingen, and read widely, in both literature and philosophy. His notebooks include numerous translations of excerpts from Lessing and many other writers, not all of which were published during his lifetime. Shortly after his return from Germany he translated two parts of Schiller's dramatic trilogy *Wallenstein: The Piccolomini* and *The Death of Wallenstein* (1800). In the prefaces he resolves to be literal whenever 'not prevented by absolute differences of idiom'.

His attraction to German writers persisted throughout his career. His striking translation of Mignon's song from Goethe's *Wilhelm Meister*, which was first published in 1829, is a testament to his skill as a translator. He also hoped to translate Goethe's *Faust*, but this plan fell through. In *Biographia Literaria* (1817) he borrows heavily from the works of Schelling, Maass, Jacobi, Kant, and others, including numerous translated passages without acknowledging his debt. In addition to German, his translations include two poems from the Hebrew of Hyman Hurwitz, a song from the Latin of Casimir Sarbiewski, and lines from Homer, Pindar, Virgil, and Dante.

See further: *ODNB*; Richard Holmes, *Coleridge: Early Visions* (London, 1989) and *Coleridge: Darker Reflections* (London, 1998); Rosemary Ashton, *The Life of Samuel Taylor Coleridge: A Critical Biography* (Oxford, 1996).   CD

CONINGTON, John (1825–1869), professor of Latin at Oxford, best known for his popular translation of Virgil (1866) into the ballad metre of Scott's 'Marmion'. Gifted with a prodigious verbal memory and educated at Thomas Arnold's Rugby, Conington was unenthused by the history and philosophy that dominated the study of classics at Oxford and by its narrowly philological approach to literary texts. Like Benjamin Jowett, he saw the Greek and Latin classics as living literature and translation as an essential means to their dissemination. In his earlier Oxford years he participated eagerly in the movement for reform, but in 1854, the year he took up the newly created chair of Latin, he underwent some kind of crisis that weakened his adherence to the liberal cause and left him estranged from Jowett, Mark Pattison, and others.

Though deeply attracted to the Greek tragedians, especially Aeschylus, it was Virgil with whom he became most closely associated, first with an edition that occupied him from 1852 for the rest of his life, then with the translation that grew out of it, an accurate but controversial translation in ballad metre. He also translated a great deal of Horace and finished off his friend Worsley's version of the *Iliad* in Spenserian measure.

See further: *ODNB*. AP

COWPER, William, *see* Volume 3.

CURTIN, Jeremiah (1838–1906), linguist and ethnographer. Born near Milwaukee, Wisconsin, he worked his way through college, learning languages from contact with local immigrant communities and graduating from Harvard in 1863. He then held various posts in St Petersburg, including that of assistant secretary at the US Legation. He travelled widely in Europe and Asia, collecting folklore and myth. Between 1883 and 1891 he worked for the Bureau of American Ethnology, then returned to world travel. Described in the *DAB* as 'one of the world's outstanding linguists', he is said to have known more than sixty languages.

As an ethnographer, he published several collections of myths and legends in his own very readable translations, notably *Myths and Folk-Lore of Ireland* (1890), *Myths and Folk-Tales of the Russians, Western Slavs and Magyars* (1890), and *Creation Myths of Primitive America* (1898). He also translated novels from Polish and Russian; in particular, though no longer read, his fairly accurate versions of many of the works of Henryk Sienkiewicz, including the much reprinted *Quo Vadis?* (1896) and the historical trilogy *With Fire and Sword* (1890), *The Deluge* (1891), and *Pan Michael* (1893) did much to establish the popularity of this writer.

See further: *DAB*; *Memoirs of Jeremiah Curtin*, ed. Joseph Schafer (Madison, WI, 1940). PF

DASENT, Sir George Webbe (1817–1896), journalist and translator of old northern texts. Son of a British colonial lawyer, Dasent was educated in London and Oxford, later taking up a diplomatic post in Stockholm in 1838. There he met George Stephens, learned old northern languages, and undertook his first major translations: Snorri Sturluson's prose *Edda* (1842) and *Brennu-Njáls saga* (published in 1861 as *The Story of Burnt Njal*). The success of *Burnt Njal* encouraged Dasent to translate *Gísla saga* (1866) and to write *The Vikings of the Baltic* (1875), a novelistic recreation of *Jómsvíkinga saga*. In robust essays on old northern literary and historical topics, he argued that all that was best in modern English institutions and values could be traced to Viking Age influences.

His most lasting contribution to old northern scholarship was to reactivate the floundering *Icelandic–English Dictionary* (1869–74), initiated by Richard Cleasby in the 1840s. Dasent persuaded the Icelandic philologist Guðbrandur Vigfússon to move to Oxford in 1864 where he completed the dictionary and saw it through the press. Though the relationship between the two philologists was often turbulent, they also produced a Rolls Series edition and translation (1887–94) of *Hákonar saga*, *Orkneyinga saga*, and other sagas relating to the British Isles.

See further: *ODNB*; Andrew Wawn, *The Vikings and the Victorians* (Cambridge, 2000). AW

DE QUINCEY, **Thomas Penson** (1785–1859), writer and journalist, born in Manchester. He showed early brilliance in Latin and Greek, learned German and Hebrew at Oxford, and later taught himself Danish (his translations from Danish versions of *Niels Klim* and Klopstock appeared in the *Foreign Quarterly Review*). He failed to take a degree from Oxford, but acquired there a taste for opium, famously described in *Confessions of an English Opium-Eater* (1821). The success of the *Confessions* ensured some financial stability, but De Quincey had a lifelong struggle with money and addiction. The needs of his five children were patchily met by the income from his vast literary output, often with help from well-placed friends.

Much of his work was for periodicals, and it is here that his translations are found. In the 1820s, he became known for his work from the German, and he has been seen as preceding Carlyle as a literary mediator between German and English: the *London Magazine* published lengthy translations from Buhle, Richter, Kant, Apel, and 'Dr. Schultz', and *Blackwood's* ran a 'Gallery of the German Prose Classics by the English Opium-Eater'. His approach to translation was usually to condense—only partially for editorial requirements—but sometimes to 'darn'. One of his longest commentaries on translation is found in the essay 'Protestantism'; see also his witty letters to Walter Scott and the German 'translator' of *Walladmor*, a pseudo-Waverley novel, 're'-translated and much darned by De Quincey.

See further: *ODNB*; Grevel Lindop, *The Opium-Eater: A Life of Thomas De Quincey* (London, 1981). JY

DICKINS, **Frederick Victor** (1838–1915), Japanologist, lawyer, and doctor, the son of a Manchester businessman. After becoming a naval surgeon, he ran the naval sick-quarters in Yokohama. Here he studied Japanese and in 1865 published one of the first English translations of Japanese literature: 'Translations of Japanese Odes, from the *H'yak nin is'shiu* (Stanzas from a Hundred Poets)'. Dickins returned that year to England, studied law, and married. In 1871 he left again for Japan with his wife, practised as a barrister, and edited the *Japanese Mail*. His translation of a 1748 Takeda Izumo puppet play was published as *Chiushingura, or, The Loyal League* (1875). In 1879, with health problems, he left for England with his family. Continuing his work on Japan, he contributed to the debate on Japanese transliteration, wrote and reviewed for periodicals, and published further translations: a complete revision of the *Chiusingura* in 1879; *The Old Bamboo-Hewer's Story* in 1887, with notes that included a romanized transcription, and *Primitive and Mediaeval Japanese Texts* (1906). Dickins was an important pioneer, not only as a translator of Japanese literature but also as a scholar convinced that Japan was worthy of western scholarship.

See further: *ODNB*. JY

DOLE, Nathan Haskell (1852–1935), translator, journalist, and miscellaneous writer. Best known as an early popularizer of Tolstoy in America, Dole was born in Chelsea, MA, the son of a Congregational minister of old colonial stock. After graduating from Harvard he taught in schools for four years, but from 1881 he was engaged in various literary activities: he was literary adviser to the publisher T. Y. Crowell and Co. from 1887 to 1901. He wrote novels, poems, and biographies and edited numerous volumes of poetry and prose, but his main activity was translation—from Italian, French, Spanish, German, and above all Russian. His own *Young Folk's History of Russia* (1881) and translation of Rambaud's *Popular History of Russia*, 3 vols. (1880–2) were followed by a translation of *Anna Karenina* (1886) which was a surprise success for T. Y. Crowell and Co. Thereafter Dole produced many Tolstoy translations in the 1880s (collected in *The Complete Works of Lyof N. Tolstoi*, 1899 and Tolstoy's *Dramatic Works*, 1923).

His knowledge of Russian was hardly profound; he admitted that to save time he occasionally referred to French translations of the text. However, he fulfilled a useful function. As the poet Harriet Monroe, a friend, said: 'He was not in the least fastidious in his writings,' but his work 'helped to build up the culture of his time and pass it on to the next generation'.

See further: *DAB*. ML

DOWSON, Ernest Christopher (1867–1900), poet. Born in Essex, the son of a dock-owner with strong literary inclinations, Dowson spent much of his early life in France and Italy, where his father's tuberculosis caused the family to live, and acquired an intimacy with contemporary French literature which was unusual for the period. A devotee of Pater while studying at Oxford, in London he aligned himself with such Decadents as Oscar Wilde, Arthur Symons, and Richard Le Gallienne, became an early member of the Rhymers' Club, and contributed poems to the *Yellow Book* and *Savoy*. However, economic necessity forced him to supplement his earnings by translating: poetry, including some by Verlaine and the previously expurgated parts of Voltaire's *La Pucelle*, and prose, including Zola's *La Terre* (1894) in an unexpurgated edition for the Lutetian Society; Couperus's *Majesty* (1894, with Teixeira de Mattos); Balzac's *La Fille aux yeux d'or* (1896); Laclos's *Les Liaisons dangereuses* (1898), the Goncourts' *Confidantes of a King* and *Beauty and the Beast* (both 1907). From about 1894 he led an increasingly dissolute life and was glad of any fees, however modest, but most of his identifiable translations also reflect his own literary passions and are of good quality.

See further: *ODNB*; Jad Adams, *Madder Music, Stronger Wine: The Life of Ernest Dowson, Poet and Decadent* (London, 2000). ML

EGERTON, Francis (1800–1857), politician, author, philanthropist. Born Leveson-Gower, on his father's death in 1833, Egerton assumed his uncle's surname and arms; he was later named first Earl of Ellesmere (1846). He was elected to Parliament in 1822, supporting liberal Tory policies; in the same year he married Harriet Greville, also an author and translator. He held several public posts, including Lord of the Treasury (1827) and Lord-Lieutenant of Ireland (1828–30), and was a committed philanthropist.

Egerton published some twenty-five books, of which about a third are adaptations or translations; the product of his enthusiasm for languages, travel, and literature, these achieved no lasting success. In 1823 (as Leveson-Gower), he published a verse translation of Part I of Goethe's *Faust*, with Schiller's *Song of the Bell*; this was followed in 1824 by a selection of translated poems, primarily from Schiller, accompanied by his own compositions. *Wallenstein's Camp*, a translation from Schiller's trilogy, appeared in 1830, again with his own poems. Egerton's approach to translation may be viewed in the preface to his blank verse version of Dumas's *Henri III et sa cour* (entitled *Catherine of Cleves* and published with his translation of Hugo's *Hernani* in 1832), where he says the changes and omissions of 'many incidents, speeches and entire scenes' were made to suit 'the taste of an English audience'.

See further: *ODNB*. JY

ELIOT, George (1819–1880), eminent novelist, born in Warwickshire, her real name being Mary Ann, later Marian, Evans. Having experienced at school a short-lived conversion to Evangelicalism, which continued to colour her later thinking, she started her career by translating controversial theological treatises by D. F. Strauss and L. Feuerbach from German. She also translated Spinoza's *Ethics* as well as parts of his *Tractatus Theologico-Politicus* from Latin and supported her partner, G. H. Lewes, in his work on the *Life of Goethe* (1855) by providing English versions of original German passages. Her wide-ranging linguistic competence also covered French, Italian, Spanish, Greek, and Hebrew. The translations, which Eliot carried out between 1843 and 1856, constituted a literary apprenticeship and allowed her to convey notions relating to her own spiritual development without having to expose herself as an independent author. At the same time, they influenced her fiction which appeared under her male pseudonym from 1857 onwards, whereas her translation of Feuerbach (*The Essence of Christianity*, 1854) was still published under her real name.

See further: *ODNB*; Rosemary Ashton, *The German Idea* (Cambridge, 1980), and *George Eliot: A Life* (London, 1996); Susanne Stark, 'Marian Evans, the Translator', pp. 119–40 in Susan Bassnett, ed., *Translating Literature* (Cambridge, 1997). SS

ELLIS, Henry Havelock (1859–1939), psychologist, essayist, critic, born in Croydon, son of a sea captain. He was educated privately, and at 16 he sailed with his father to Australia and South America, then lived in New South Wales for four years, where he taught, translated (including Heine's *Lieder*, some Goethe, and Renan's *Song of Songs*), and developed his twin interests in literature and science. He returned to England to study medicine but chose to write rather than practise, taking the name of Havelock. He joined several radical groups and was friendly with Arthur Symons, Eleanor Marx, and the writer Olive Schreiner, with whom he exchanged a lasting, passionate correspondence. At her suggestion, he translated *The Prose Writings of Heinrich Heine*. In 1891 he married the author Edith Lees, his amanuensis for the unexpurgated translation of Zola's *Germinal* (1894) which he did for the Lutetian Society. Their marriage, based on humanist vows, prompted Ellis's celebrated *Studies in the Psychology of Sex*, 7 vols. (1897–1928). During the *Studies* years, he travelled and wrote prolifically, including his *Sonnets with Folk Songs* translated from the Spanish (1925). Throughout his life he needed adoration; he would recite his life motto, Rabelais's 'Fay ce que voudras', to the women with whom he lived.

See further: *ODNB*; Havelock Ellis, *My Life* (London, 1940); Phyllis Grosskurth, *Havelock Ellis: A Biography* (New York, 1980). JY

EMERSON, **Ralph Waldo** (1803–1882). American essayist, poet, lecturer, and literary critic. He was born to an old Boston family, and his intellectual and literary talents were encouraged from a young age. He graduated from Harvard and later studied at Harvard Divinity School and was ordained as a Unitarian minister in 1829. A few years later, frustrated with the ministry and unable to subscribe to traditional Christian beliefs, he resigned his position. He subsequently made his living as a teacher, lecturer, and writer.

Perhaps the leading figure among the American Transcendentalists, a group of New England writers eclectically subscribing to philosophical idealism, Emerson found inspiration in the diverse sources that influenced the group: Plato and the Neo-Platonists, the Hindu religion, Swedenborg, German Romantic writers, Coleridge, and Carlyle. He also admired the essays of Plutarch, Montaigne, and Bacon and became an outstanding essayist. His translations, however, were mainly of poetry; they include Dante's *La vita nuova* (not published in his lifetime) and selections from other European authors, both ancient and modern. He published more than sixty translations of Persian poetry in his lifetime. Unable to read Persian, he translated at second hand, mostly through Joseph von Hammer's German translations. He was attracted in particular to Ḥāfiẓ's exuberant mysticism and to Saʻdī's sententiousness and moral rigour. His essay entitled 'Persian Poetry' was included in *Letters and Social Aims* (1876).

See further *DAB*; *ANB*; J. D. Yohannan, 'Emerson's Translations of Persian Poetry from German Sources', *American Literature* 15 (1943), 407–20; Robert D. Richardson, Jr., *Emerson: The Mind on Fire* (Berkeley, CA, 1995). PW

FERGUSON, **Sir Samuel** (1810–1886), poet and antiquary, born in Belfast and educated at Belfast Academical Institution and Trinity College Dublin. He studied at Lincoln's Inn, London, and was called to the Irish bar in 1838. He married Mary Guinness in 1848, and their Dublin home became a focus of intellectual and artistic activity. In the 1830s Ferguson was a contributor to *Blackwood's* and to the *Dublin University Magazine*, which published his influential critical essays on the translations from Irish in James Hardiman's *Irish Minstrelsy* (1831). His own lively translations of Irish poetry were a response to what he saw as the inadequacies of this collection. In his poetry he drew extensively on early Irish literature and mythology; his *Lays of the Western Gael* (1865) and *Congal* (1872), adaptations of old Irish legends, were much admired by a later generation of writers, especially W. B. Yeats. Ferguson was also devoted to the study of antiquities, and his major work, *Ogham Inscriptions in Ireland, Wales and Scotland*, came out posthumously in 1887. He was elected President of the Royal Irish Academy in 1882. In 1867 he was appointed Deputy Keeper of the public records of Ireland, where his thorough reorganization of the department won him a knighthood in 1878.

See further: *ODNB*; Peter Denman, *Samuel Ferguson: The Literary Achievement* (Savage, MD, 1990). M-AC

FITZGERALD, Edward (1809–1883), translator of the *Rubáiyát of Omar Khayyám*. He was born into the well-to-do Anglo-Irish family of Purcell; he later adopted the maternal name of FitzGerald. After a good classical education at Cambridge, he lived a life of cultivated leisure in Suffolk. He took pleasure in country life and in his late fifties engaged in a joint venture in boat ownership and herring-fishing. His friends included many artists, scholars, and writers (notably Tennyson, Carlyle, and Thackeray), and he left a very attractive correspondence.

FitzGerald had spent two years in France as a child; in addition to French, Latin, and Greek, he learnt Spanish, Persian, and some German. He wrote a small amount of poetry and some minor critical works, but his spasmodic creative energy went into translation. As well as the *Rubáiyát*, he translated *Six Dramas from Calderón* (1853), Jāmī's *Salámán and Absál* (1856), Aeschylus' *Agamemnon* (1865), a conflation of two tragedies of Sophocles (1880), and 'Aṭṭār's *Bird Parliament* (1889, posthumously). His translations made little stir with the exception of the *Rubáiyát*, a very free and personal reworking of poems purportedly by an eleventh-century Persian astronomer, which after a quiet appearance in 1859 went on to extraordinary success.

See further: *ODNB*; R. B. Martin, *With Friends Possessed: A Life of Edward FitzGerald* (New York, 1985). PF

FRERE, John Hookham (1769–1846). Son of the antiquary John Frere of Roydon Hall, Norfolk, and eldest brother of (Henry) Bartle Frere, he was educated at Eton and Cambridge. Envisaging a diplomatic career, he became a Member of Parliament in 1796 and in 1799 entered the Foreign Office and became Under-Secretary in succession to his friend Canning. He was entrusted with demanding diplomatic European missions throughout the first half of the Napoleonic period, but in 1809 he withdrew from public office, declining the ambassadorship to St Petersburg. Having married Elizabeth, Countess of Erroll, in 1812, he settled in Malta for the sake of her health and devoted himself to literature. He was friendly with most of the Romantic authors.

As well as composing occasional poetry, Frere made verse translations of plays by Aristophanes (*The Frogs, The Birds, The Acharnians,* and *The Knights*), which have continued to be admired for their fluent inventiveness, as well as excerpts from Homer, Euripides, and Catullus and versions of a number of psalms. His translations and imitations of passages from the comic epic *Morgante maggiore* of the Italian poet Luigi Pulici influenced Byron, and his version of the Spanish epic of *The Cid* was published as an appendix to Southey's translation of the chronicle. In his lifetime, his translations were privately printed.

See further: *ODNB*; *The Works of John Hookham Frere... with a Prefatory Memoir by his Nephews*, ed. W. E. and Sir Bartle Frere, 2 vols. (London, 1872); Gabrielle Festing, *John Hookham Frere and his Friends* (London, 1899). CS

FULLER, Sarah Margaret (1810–1850), scholar, author, and critic, born in Massachusetts, the daughter of a Puritan lawyer. She received a full education, including several languages; her intense work was to provoke lifelong health problems. She spent a period teaching and began to write and translate for periodicals, valuing translation for its contribution to international understanding. She was particularly interested in German literature: her version of Goethe's *Torquato Tasso*, done in 1833, was later published in her *Art, Literature and the Drama* (1860), and her other translations from German include Eckermann's *Conversations with Goethe* (1839) and *Günderode* (1842), a correspondence between Bettina Brentano and her friend Günderode.

Fuller was associated with the Transcendentalist group, and was the first editor of their journal *The Dial* (1840). In the 1840s she translated political articles from the German for the *New York Tribune* and in 1845 published *Woman in the Nineteenth Century*, a discussion of equal rights. A supporter of internationalist liberal causes, she visited Europe in 1846 as foreign correspondent and became involved in the Italian independence struggle. She married Count Ossoli, a follower of Mazzini, had a child by him, and composed a history of the Italian Revolution. Wishing it to be published in America, the family set sail for New York in 1850; their ship was wrecked in a storm, and Fuller, her family, and the manuscript were never found.

See further: *DAB*; *ANB*; Margaret Fuller, *Memoirs of Margaret Fuller Ossoli*, 3 vols. (Boston, 1852); Charles Capper, *Margaret Fuller: An American Romantic Life* (New York, 1992). JY

GARNETT, Constance, *see* Volume 5.

GILES, Herbert Allen (1845–1935), Chinese scholar, born in Oxford, son of the clergyman and translator John Allen Giles. After schooling at Charterhouse, in 1867 he joined the Chinese consular service as a student interpreter, then worked his way up to become consul at Tamshui in 1886 and Ningpo in 1891. He resigned in 1893 and returned to Britain to succeed Thomas Wade—with whom he had collaborated in creating a transliteration system for Chinese—as professor of Chinese at Cambridge. He held the chair until 1932.

Giles's vast literary output over more than fifty years helped to alter the perception of China as 'immoral and degraded' (as he noted in the preface to his 1875

Chinese Sketches). He is responsible for a wide range of translations from philosophy, poetry, and classical prose (including *Strange Stories from a Chinese Studio*, 2 vols., 1880). His *Gems of Chinese Literature* (1884) was the first anthology of Chinese prose in the English language; by 1925, interest in the culture had grown sufficiently for Giles to offer *Quips from a Chinese Jest-Book*. In 1922 he received the Gold Medal of the Royal Asiatic Society, for having 'humanized Chinese beyond all other living scholars'. Giles always held the general reader in mind when translating; he eliminated difficulties and rendered both verse and prose in a style and language familiar to the Victorian reader.

See further: *ODNB*. JY

GUEST, Lady Charlotte Elizabeth (1812–1895), born the daughter of the Earl of Lindsey. After a lonely, unhappy childhood from which she sought relief in reading and learning languages (including Arabic and Persian), she married in 1833 the leading ironmaster John Guest. Moving to Merthyr Tydfil, the site of the ironworks, she involved herself in the Welsh cultural revival, learnt the language, promoted educational reform, but also gave birth to ten children in thirteen years. After her husband's death in 1852, she ran the ironworks briefly, then married Charles Schreiber in 1855. Living with him in Roehampton, she engaged in philanthropy while amassing a collection of old china, fans, and playing cards.

Her translating activity was almost all confined to the years 1838–48. Working devotedly, and with important help from Welsh informants, she in 1849 produced her remarkable three-volume translation, with scholarly introductions and lavish illustrations, of the old legends and tales to which she gave the name *Mabinogion*.

See further: *ODNB*; Revel Guest and Angela V. John, *Lady Charlotte: A Biography of the Nineteenth Century* (London, 1989). PF

HAPGOOD, Isabel (1850–1928). Born in Boston, MA, she was educated at the Oread Collegiate Institute in Worcester and Miss Porter's School, Farmington, Connecticut, where she was taught French and Latin. After leaving in 1868, she learnt, largely on her own, many European languages, including Russian, Polish, and Old Church Slavonic, before embarking on a career as a literary translator. Her versions of French works—notably Hugo's *Les Misérables* (1887)—appeared in the same decade as translations from Spanish, Italian, Dutch, Polish, and above all Russian. In 1887 she visited Russia with her mother, perfecting her command of the language and meeting poets and writers, including Tolstoy, whose autobiographical trilogy she translated. She also translated prose by Gogol, Leskov, Gorky, and Bunin, but her greatest achievement was her sixteen volumes of Turgenev's novels and stories (1903–4). In 1902 she published *A Survey of Russian Literature*. Her *Service Book* for the Orthodox Church appeared in 1906, and nine years later she again ventured to Russia to collect material on Russian church music. For more than twenty years she was foreign correspondent, editorial writer, and reviewer for the New York *Evening Post* and the *Nation*.

See further: *DAB*. CS

HASTIE, William (1842–1903), Scottish scholar. Having read philosophy and theology at the universities of Edinburgh and Glasgow, Hastie became a licentiate of the Church of Scotland. He studied at universities in Germany, Holland, and Switzerland, spent time in France and Italy, and learnt the languages of all these countries, before going to Calcutta as Principal of the Church of Scotland College in 1878. Complaints about his conduct in office led to his dismissal; he returned to Scotland in 1883 and concentrated on literary work, but managed to succeed William Purdie Dickson (translator of Theodor Mommsen's *History of Rome*) as professor of divinity at Glasgow in 1895.

Hastie published theological works of his own both in India and in Britain, but the majority of his translations were done after his return to Scotland. Most were from German; he produced versions of major philosophical texts by Kant and Hegel and of several works on law, theology, and the history of religion by Schleiermacher and others. His translations also included work from Italian and French (a substantial history of German theology by Frédéric Lichtenberger) and religious poetry by Novalis and Friedrich Rückert, including a version of Rückert's translation of the Persian poet Rūmī, to which Hastie added a criticism of FitzGerald's *Rubáiyát of Omar Khayyám*.

See further: *ODNB*; Donald Macmillan, *The Life of Professor Hastie* (Paisley, 1926). SS

HAZLITT, William (1811–1893), editor and translator, born in London. When his father, the essayist, died in straitened circumstances in 1830, the younger Hazlitt, who had not been trained for any profession, fell back first on journalism, working for such papers as the *Morning Chronicle*, the *Daily News*, and *The Times*. But he was soon also editing Bogue's European Library, before instituting his own Romancist and Novelist's Library in 1839, of which he said that translations were 'a very important feature'. The many authors translated included Dumas, Hugo, and Paul de Kock as well as Goethe and Schiller—all available first in affordable twopenny numbers and then in book form. Hazlitt himself translated Hugo's *Notre-Dame de Paris* in 1833, a number of popular French historians, including Guizot, Thierry, and Michelet, and some German authors (Musäus, Ida Pfeiffer, Luther)—at least twenty-one titles before 1854. In that year he was at last appointed registrar in the London Bankruptcy Court—a 'post of a permanent character' such as he had been seeking since the age of 19, according to his son, **William Carew Hazlitt (1834–1919)**. The latter wrote or edited several major works on the Hazlitt family, including *Memoirs of William Hazlitt* (1867), *Four Generations of a Literary Family* (1897), and *The Hazlitts* (1911), as well as works on the Lambs and many bibliographical works, often on early English humorists. The only translation entirely by his hand was Legrand d'Aussy's *Norman Tales* in 1873, but he edited a revision (by his father) of Charles Cotton's classic translation of Montaigne (1877) and claimed (in *Four Generations*) to have helped with several of his hard-pressed father's translations: 'I am prouder of the bit of money which I then made for my parents than of any which I have since made for myself.'

See further: *ODNB* (for W. C. Hazlitt). ML

Hearn, Lafcadio (1850–1904), also known as Yakumo Koizumi from 1895, named after the Greek island Levkás, where he was born of Irish and Greek parentage. After a disrupted education in France and Dublin and a school accident that partially blinded him, at 19 Hearn travelled to the USA and worked as a journalist. In 1890 he moved definitively to Japan, where he lectured on literature at Tokyo Imperial University; he renounced his British citizenship following his marriage to a Japanese woman.

In his newspaper work, Hearn combined his interest in foreign literature with his taste for the 'whimsically grotesque and arabesque'; his translations of ghoulish selections from Gautier, Flaubert, and Loti appeared alongside gruesomely detailed reports of murders and hangings. He is probably best known, however, for his extensive writings on Japan, such as *A Japanese Miscellany* (1901), and *Kwaidan* (1904). He never spoke Japanese fluently; his Japanese translations are reinterpretations of stories recounted by his wife.

Hearn's other translations, largely posthumous, include Flaubert's *The Temptation of St. Anthony* (1910), Maupassant's *The Adventures of Walter Schnaffs, and Other Stories* (1931), and works by Daudet, France, Gautier, Loti, Maupassant, and Zola, he also translated from Creole and Spanish. His stated wider aim was for 'the English realization of a Latin style', which, along with his distaste for the 'bogus translations' of the time, must in part account for the heavily literal style of his translations.

See further: *DAB*; *ANB*; *ODNB*; Paul Murray, *A Fantastic Journey: The Life and Literature of Lafcadio Hearn* (Sandgate, Folkstone, 1993). JY

Hemans, Felicia (1793–1835), poet. Felicia Dorothea Browne was the daughter of a prosperous wine importer in Liverpool. While her father struggled to safeguard the family's wealth, her mother tutored her and encouraged her literary pursuits. *Poems* was published in 1808, and her future husband, Captain Alfred Hemans, was one of approximately 800 subscribers. They married in 1812, but in 1818, Captain Hemans left for Italy, ostensibly to restore his health, and never returned. She lived with her mother and five sons in Wales, and during these productive years, the commercial success of her poetry allowed her to support her family.

As a young woman Hemans studied several modern languages; these studies bore fruit in her *Translations from Camoens, and other Poets* (1818), consisting mainly of sonnets from Portuguese, Spanish, and Italian Renaissance poets, but also selections from German and French. Her decision to translate Camões stemmed from her comparison of Lord Strangford's translations (1803) with the originals and her subsequent distress at not finding 'any pretensions to fidelity'.

Her varied translations also include Mignon's song from Goethe's *Wilhelm Meister*, selections from Horace, and traditional songs from Welsh. *The Forest Sanctuary And Other Poems* (1825) included a poem by La Motte Fouqué and a song by Schiller. A small number of translations, including scenes from Goethe's *Iphigenie auf Tauris* and *Tasso* and from Alfieri's *Alceste*, appeared in periodicals during her lifetime.

See further: Henry F. Chorley, *Memorials of Mrs. Hemans*, 2 vols. (London, 1836); Harriet Browne Hughes, *The Works of Mrs. Hemans, with a Memoir by her Sister*, 7 vols. (Edinburgh, 1839); Peter W. Trinder, *Mrs. Hemans* (Cardiff, 1984).
CD

HILL, Isabel (1800–1842), writer and translator, born in Bristol. Like many jobbing translators of the early century, Hill started out with the ambition to be a writer, and in particular a dramatist and poet. A novel and a poem (*Constance* and *Zaphna*, both 1823) were well received but unremunerative, since their publisher failed. She further published two five-act tragedies (*Brian, the Probationer*, 1842, and *The Poet's Child*, 1820) and a novel (*Brother Tragedians*, 1834) and also prose and verse in a number of small periodicals, but none provided her with anything approaching a living. Out of necessity (and with some reluctance) she translated Madame de Staël's *Corinne* (1831), Chateaubriand's *Last of the Abencérages* (1835), and part of Manuel de Godoy's *Memoirs* (1836) for Richard Bentley. She also translated (anonymously) Chateaubriand's *Sketches of English Literature* (1836) for Henry Colburn and may have done other anonymous work. Her *Corinne*, though idiosyncratic, remained in print at least into the 1880s.

With her brother Benson Hill, she lived on the margins of the literary-theatrical world, writing mainly for keepsakes and annuals of the type published by Rudolf Ackermann or Frederic Shoberl; she eventually died (in debt) of consumption.

See further: *ODNB*; Benson Hill, 'Memoir of the Authoress', pp. 83–100 in Isabel Hill, *Brian, the Probationer* (London, 1842).
ML

HOLCROFT, Thomas, *see* Volume 3.

HOWES, Francis (1776–1844), clergyman. He was educated at Trinity College, Cambridge and like his father, he took holy orders, becoming a minor canon at Norwich Cathedral in 1815; later in life, he was rector at Alderford and Framingham Pigot.

Howes produced several volumes of translations: *Miscellaneous Poetical Translations* (1806), which in addition to translations from French, Greek, and Latin verse includes a Latin prize essay; *The Satires of A. Persius Flaccus* with notes (1809); *The Epodes and Secular Ode of Horace* (privately printed, 1841); and *The First Book of Horace's Satires* (privately printed, 1842). After his death in 1844, his son gathered his translations from Horace and published them in *The Epodes, Satires, and Epistles of Horace* (1845); all the translations were written in heroic couplets. In 1892 John Conington praised Howes's translations, noting sadly that they had been forgotten by the public. He called the version of Persius 'a work of decided ability', though it did not in his opinion reach the high level of his Horace: 'when it is good, which is not seldom, it is very good, unforced, idiomatic, and felicitous.'

See further: *ODNB*.
PW

HOWITT (née Botham), Mary (1799–1888). She was born in Gloucestershire, but grew up in Derbyshire. Like her husband William, she came of Quaker stock and early decided on a literary career. Both Howitts were prolific. Mary produced over sixty works (poems, children's books, novels, histories, etc.) as well as much journalism between the 1830s and 1870s. In 1847 she and William also edited *Howitt's Journal of Literary and Popular Progress*. In the 1820s, as their family expanded, both taught themselves German, with a view to supplementing their income by translating: Mary translated at least six German novels as well as several of Hans Christian Andersen's works from their German versions. She was most closely identified, however, with the Swedish novelist Fredrika Bremer, whom she 'discovered' in the early 1840s. Having taught herself Swedish (imperfectly, according to Bremer) she, together with William, translated virtually all Bremer's works, as well as novels by two other Swedes, Emilie Flygare-Carlén and M. A. Goldschmidt.

A strong advocate of women's independence, Mary saw translation as one means to that end: 'Girls must be made independent. I am bent on [my daughter] making £300 next year by translation,' she wrote to her sister in the 1840s. In later life she moved away from Quakerism—first to Unitarianism and in the 1880s, after she had settled in Italy, to Roman Catholicism.

See further: *ODNB*; Mary Howitt, *Autobiography* (London, 1889). ML

Hunt, James Henry Leigh (1784–1859), poet, critic, essayist. Although his father struggled to make a living as a preacher, Hunt received a solid education at Christ's Hospital. After graduation he worked as a legal clerk, theatre critic, and editor of various periodicals, including the *Examiner* from 1808 to 1821. A prolific writer, he published poetry, reviews, essays, plays, biographies, an autobiography, and a novel, *Sir Ralph Esher*. He had numerous literary acquaintances and introduced his readers to the leading poets of his time including Keats, Tennyson, and Browning. His friendship with Shelley lured him to Italy, but their plan, with Byron, to start a journal faltered after Shelley's death.

Hunt's first publication, *Juvenilia* (1801), included four translations from Anacreon and Horace. *Foliage, or, Poems Original and Translated* (1818) had translations from the Greek of Homer, Theocritus, Bion, and Moschus. Longer translations from Italian followed: Tasso's *Amyntas: A Tale of the Woods* (1820) and Redi's *Bacchus in Tuscany* (1825); *Stories from the Italian Poets* (1846) also included shorter translations. Many of Hunt's translations first appeared in periodicals. In *The Poetical Works of Leigh Hunt* (1832), they were followed by the originals, a decision he described as motivated by a 'willingness to shew the pains taken to do the originals justice'. His versatility and skill as a translator are in evidence in this collection, and his translations have been more consistently praised than his original poetry.

See further: *ODNB*; Leigh Hunt, *The Autobiography of Leigh Hunt: with Reminiscences of Friends and Contemporaries* (London, 1850); Ann Blainey, *Immortal Boy: A Portrait of Leigh Hunt* (New York, 1985). CD

Jebb, Sir Richard Claverhouse (1841–1905), Regius Professor of Greek at Cambridge, editor and translator of Sophocles. After a childhood spent in

Dublin, where his father was a solicitor, Jebb entered Trinity College, Cambridge, where in due course he became a Fellow, and to which he returned in 1889 after fourteen years in Glasgow. In 1891 he began a double life as a man of public affairs when he was elected Conservative Member of Parliament for the University of Cambridge, serving on many committees involved with education. He was active in founding the Society for the Promotion of Hellenic Studies, the British School of Archaeology at Athens, and the British Academy. He numbered among his friends many leading writers of the time, including Tennyson.

Jebb's translations into and out of Greek and Latin began in the 1860s and 1870s when he was a young Fellow at Trinity (they include a version of Browning's 'Abt Vogler' into Pindaric metres). He translated Theophrastus and Bacchylides, but it was his editions of Sophocles that brought enduring renown, first issued play by play from 1883 to 1896. These included a translation into English prose, justly admired both for its accuracy and its intrinsic literary qualities.

See further: *ODNB*; Caroline Jebb, *Life and Letters of Sir Richard Claverhouse Jebb* (Cambridge, 1907). AP

JOWETT, Benjamin (1817–1893), Regius Professor of Greek at Oxford, Master of Balliol College, and translator of Plato. Jowett's career was based in the Oxford which he entered as an undergraduate in 1836, which he helped to reform in the 1850s and to shake with his 'Interpretation of Scripture' in the controversial *Essays and Reviews* (1860), and over which, as Master of Balliol (from 1870) and then Vice-Chancellor, he wielded great influence. He was a leading figure in the liberalizing of Oxford's curriculum and constitution, and by virtue of the many pupils who passed through his hands to political, diplomatic, and administrative careers, he exerted considerable influence over the world outside the academy.

His active engagement with theology subsided after the furore of 1860, and he devoted himself to the philosopher about whom he had become enthusiastic in the 1840s. Through his teaching and writing, Jowett became indissolubly associated with the rise of Plato and Platonism, and their dissemination into English thought and culture in the later decades of the nineteenth century. The publication in 1871 of his translation of Plato in four volumes was a major event, and its revised and expanded editions (1875, 1892) established it as a contemporary masterpiece.

See further: *ODNB*; Geoffrey Faber, *Jowett: A Portrait with Background* (London, 1957). AP

LANE, Edward William (1801–1876), Arabic scholar. Born in Hereford, he attended grammar schools at Bath and Hereford and later chose engraving and eastern culture over Cambridge or the Church. He became known for his understanding of Arabic literature; living as a Muslim in Cairo, he devoted his life to explaining the culture and language to a largely ignorant West. His notes and drawings resulted in his first major work, *Manners and Customs of the Modern Egyptians* (1836).

Lane's 3-volume translation of *The Thousand and One Nights* (1839–41) corrected the representation established by earlier translations of Arabia as exotic dreamworld—although the publishers occasionally felt obliged to compromise ('it was thought that readers would more easily recognise their old friends Aladdin and Sindbad the Sailor, than 'Alá ed-Deen and Es-Sindibad of the Sea'). His *Selections from the Kur-an* (1843) similarly sought to expand and correct previous versions. His final work, *An Arabic–English Lexicon*, begun in 1842 and worked on for the rest of his life, offered an exhaustive thesaurus of the Arabic language.

See further: ODNB; Leila Ahmed, *Edward W. Lane: A Study of his Life and Works and of British Ideas of the Middle East in the Nineteenth Century* (London, 1978). JY

LANG, Andrew (1844–1912), man of letters. Born into a legal family in Selkirk, he attended the universities of St Andrews, Glasgow, and Oxford. In 1875, after seven years as a Fellow of Merton College, Oxford, he married and settled in London, quickly making his mark as an influential writer, an elegant stylist, an expert on folklore, and a devotee of the Middle Ages. He wrote innumerable essays and reviews for a variety of periodicals and published across a wide range of subjects and genres, from lyric verse to history and anthropology.

Translation was a relatively small but important part of his work. His *Ballads and Lyrics of Old France, and Other Poems* (1872) helped to establish in Britain medieval verse forms such as the *ballade*. Subsequently, he translated a good deal of Greek poetry, notably his versions in archaic prose of the *Odyssey* (with S. H. Butcher, 1879) and the *Iliad* (with Walter Leaf and Ernest Myers, 1883). His Homer was widely read, but his outstanding translation was probably the thirteenth-century French tale *Aucassin and Nicolete* (1887), where his mixture of medieval-sounding prose and pretty verse struck a chord with many readers. He went on to translate a companion piece, *The Miracles of Madame St. Catherine of Fierbois* (1889). His very popular series of *Fairy Books* contained many translations, generally by other hands.

See further: *ODNB*; Roger Lancelyn Green, *Andrew Lang: A Critical Biography*, (Leicester, 1946). PF

LAUN, Henri van, *see* VAN LAUN, Henri.

LEGGE, James (1815–1897), missionary and sinologist, born in Huntly, Aberdeenshire, the son of a drapery merchant. He developed a great facility in Greek and Latin at school, and in 1835 he graduated from King's College, Aberdeen. After teaching in a school, he decided to become a Congregational minister, studied Chinese, and became a member of the London Missionary Society. In 1839 he set out for the Anglo-Chinese College in Malacca, becoming Principal two years later. In 1843 he moved to Hong Kong to manage the Society's activities there. After retirement in 1873, he began a second career as an academic, becoming a Fellow of Corpus Christi College, Oxford, and in 1876 the university's first professor of Chinese language and literature.

Legge's publications were wide-ranging and voluminous. His annotated translations of both prose and poetry, published in the seven volumes of *Chinese Classics* (1861–72), remained in print throughout the twentieth century. Further translations of religious texts were published in Max Müller's Sacred Books of the East series. He was a committed and active advocate of the Christian faith, yet his encounter with Chinese culture, especially the Confucian tradition, led to his taking a comparative standpoint on the study of religion, which, in turn, enabled him to become a seminal figure in the development of sinology.

See further: *ODNB*; Norman J. Girardot, *The Victorian Translation of China: James Legge's Oriental Pilgrimage* (Berkeley, CA, 2002); Lauren F. Pfister, *Striving for the 'Whole Duty of Man': James Legge and the Scottish Protestant Encounter with China*, 2 vols. (Frankfurt am Main, 2004). RF

LELAND, Charles Godfrey (1825–1903), author, born in Philadelphia, PA, son of a wealthy merchant. While young, Leland started to study occult literature and languages, which absorbed him all his life. He graduated from Princeton in 1845, attended courses in Heidelberg, Munich, and Paris, and was admitted to the Philadelphia bar. Turning to journalism, he published translations from German in the *Knickerbocker Magazine*, and in 1857, the first of the 'Hans Breitmann' poems in 'Philadelphia German' appeared; immensely popular, they were collected into the *Hans Breitmann Ballads* (1871–95). Leland's most significant task of translation, the complete works of Heinrich Heine, was published in twelve volumes (1891–1905; first 8 vols. translated by Leland) and reissued many times. He constantly pursued his interest in folklore, and over twenty years he travelled (staying ten years in England where he met Carlyle and Borrow, who shared similar interests), studied languages, and published more than fifty works. At different times he stayed with and befriended the Tennessee Indians, the Gypsies in Europe, and the witches of Tuscany. He learnt Romany and published a metrical translation of *English Gipsy Songs* (1875), adding a glossary on Tennyson's advice. In 1879, he returned to Philadelphia, where he taught craft and successfully introduced industrial arts and craft into American schools.

See further: *DAB*; *ANB*; E. R. Pennell, *Charles Godfrey Leland* (Boston, 1906).

JY

LEVESON-GOWER, Francis, *see* **EGERTON, Francis.**

LEWIS, Matthew Gregory (1775–1818), novelist and playwright. Born in London, the son of a prominent family that derived its fortune from estates in Jamaica, he was educated at Westminster School and Christ Church, Oxford. He spent his vacations abroad, visiting Weimar in 1792 and perfecting his knowledge of languages with a view to a diplomatic career. While in his first post at The Hague, he wrote the Gothic novel *The Monk* (1795), after which he was known as 'Monk Lewis'. In 1796 he became a Member of Parliament, but took no interest in politics, resigning in 1802. In *Journal of a West Indian Proprietor* he records a visit to the

Caribbean in 1815; he went out again two years later, hoping to alleviate the lot of his slaves, but died of fever on the way back to Britain.

Translation is often hard to distinguish from original composition in Lewis's writings; *The Monk*, for instance, is full of borrowings from continental works. He reveals his acquaintance with contemporary German literature in such plays as *The Minister* (1797), after Schiller's *Kabale und Liebe*, and *Rolla* (1799), after Kotzebue, and in his free translations of two romances, Heinrich Zschokke's *The Bravo of Venice* (1805) and Christiane Naubert's *Feudal Tyrants* (1806). He also published some verse translations (e.g. of Goethe's 'Erlkönig'), as well as translating Juvenal's Satire 13 as *The Love of Gain* (1799).

See further: *ODNB*; D. L. Macdonald, *Monk Lewis: A Critical Biography* (Toronto, 2000). CS

Lockhart, John Gibson (1794–1854), writer, best known for his voluminous *Memoirs of the Life of Sir Walter Scott* (1837–8). He was born in Lanarkshire and attended the universities of Glasgow and Oxford. He was called to the Scottish bar but devoted himself to literature, becoming in 1817 a major contributor to the newly founded *Blackwood's Magazine* (where he attacked Keats and the 'Cockney poets') and from 1825 to 1853 the editor of the *Quarterly Review*. As well as his life of Scott (his father-in-law), he wrote a life of Burns (1828), four novels, and a witty sketch of Scottish literary life, *Peter's Letters to his Kinsfolk* (1819).

Lockhart worked hard as a journalist to stimulate interest in Spanish and particularly German literature—he had spent some months in Germany in 1817. In 1818 he published *Lectures on the History of Literature, Ancient and Modern*, a translation of Friedrich von Schlegel. As well as many reviews, the journals contain some of his verse translations (often anonymous), the most ambitious being his experimental hexameter versions of the first and last books of the *Iliad*, published in *Blackwood's* in 1846. He believed that critics should be 'merciful' to the thankless labours of the verse translator. His *Ancient Spanish Ballads, Historical and Romantic* (1823) enjoyed a lasting success.

See further: *ODNB*; Andrew Lang, *The Life and Letters of John Gibson Lockhart* (London, 1897); Gilbert Macbeth, *John Gibson Lockhart: A Critical Study* (Urbana, IL, 1935). PF

Longfellow, Henry Wadsworth (1807–1882), poet. Born in Portland, Maine, a prosperous lawyer's son, Longfellow attended nearby Bowdoin College. On graduating, he was offered a newly established professorship of modern languages at the college, provided he undertook preparatory study, at his own expense, in Europe. After three years in France, Italy, and Spain, he took up his duties. He was next appointed professor at Harvard, which again necessitated a spell in Europe, this time in Scandinavia, Germany, and Switzerland. His wife's death, in 1835, was the first domestic tragedy in an outwardly tranquil life; his second wife was burnt to death in 1861.

Both in his teaching at Harvard (until 1854) and in his literary work, Longfellow devoted his efforts to familiarizing American readers with older and contemporary European poetry and assimilating European influences in American literature. Echoing Goethe's *Hermann und Dorothea*, his *Evangeline* (1847) is a love story set in eighteenth-century America, and he was influenced by the Finnish *Kalevala* when he sought to recreate the ways of American Indians in *Hiawatha* (1855). Longfellow's activity as a translator is reflected in his ambitious *Poets and Poetry of Europe* (1845), a wide-ranging anthology of some 400 verse translations from ten languages, of which one tenth were his own work. The culmination of his translation work was his faithful rendering in blank verse of Dante's *Commedia* (1867), the first American translation of the entire poem.

See further: *DAB*; *ANB*; Newton Arvin, *Longfellow: His Life and Work* (Boston, 1963); Edward Wagenknecht, *Henry Wadsworth Longfellow: Portrait of an American Humanist* (New York, 1966). CS

LYTTON, Edward Bulwer (1803–1873), first Baron Lytton, novelist and politician. Born with the surname Bulwer, he changed it to Bulwer Lytton (unhyphenated) after his mother's death in 1843. He graduated from Cambridge in 1826 and married contrary to his mother's wishes; as a result he was for a time obliged to support himself by a prolific literary production, mostly novels but also poetry and plays. He entered Parliament in 1831 and was Secretary for the Colonies in 1858–9. In 1866 he became Baron Lytton.

In his two books of translations, *The Poems and Ballads of Schiller* (1844) and *The Odes and Epodes of Horace* (1869), both several times reprinted, Lytton showed a keen interest in metrical translation. While attempting to adhere to the metres of the original, he insisted that deviations were sometimes necessary, since metres have different associations in different literatures. He eschewed dactylic hexameter and elegiac couplets, replacing them with lines of blank verse. Faced with alcaics and sapphics, he developed several different models, ranging from direct imitations to verse which preserved only a bare suggestion of the original metre. His original poem *The Lost Tales of Miletus* (1866) was written in a metre that emerged from his long study of foreign prosody.

Lytton's son Robert Bulwer Lytton, first Earl of Lytton (1831–1891), diplomat and poet, published *Serbski Pesme, or, National Songs of Servia*, in 1861 ('No attempt has been made at accurate verbal translation from the original language', p. ix); many of these versions were reprinted in *Orval, or, The Fool of Time* (1869), a paraphrase of Zygmunt Krasinski's Polish verse drama *The Undivine Comedy*. The first appeared under his pseudonym Owen Meredith and the second under his own name.

See further: *ODNB*; Aurelia Brooks Harlan, *Owen Meredith: A Critical Biography of Robert, First Earl of Lytton* (1946); Leslie Mitchell, *Bulwer Lytton: The Rise and Fall of a Victorian Man of Letters* (2003). KH

MANGAN, James Clarence (1803–1849), poet, born in Dublin: his baptismal name was James, the 'Clarence' his own invention. His father, a grocer, went bankrupt, and James supported the family from the age of 15, working ten years as a copying clerk, first in a scrivener's office and then for an attorney. In 1833 he obtained a place with the Irish Ordnance Survey and began contributing poems and translations to the *Dublin Penny Journal* and the *Dublin University Magazine*; a committed nationalist, he later wrote for *The Nation* and the *United Irishman*.

Mangan was a flamboyant character, who wrote under a variety of masks and pseudonyms, translating, adapting, and occasionally inventing authors from German, Irish, Arabic, Turkish, and Persian literature. German apart, his knowledge of most of these languages is at best uncertain, but he did work with literal versions of Irish poems supplied by friends and colleagues. A distinctive style and a gift for bold imagery and unusual metres lift his work well above the run of mid-nineteenth-century translations into English. Most of his translations were scattered in newspapers and journals, but a *German Anthology* (1845) and *The Poets and Poetry of Munster* (1849) appeared during his lifetime. He died in 1849 at Meath Hospital, Dublin, of cholera.

See further: *ODNB*; Ellen Shannon-Mangan, *James Clarence Mangan: A Biography* (Blackrock, Ireland, 1996). M-AC

MARRIAGE, Ellen (1865–1946), professional translator from French. Born in Essex to a Quaker family, she attended the Mount School in York. Some time before 1895, Alfred Rayney Waller, who was working for the publisher J. M. Dent, suggested that the firm should issue a complete translation of Balzac's *Comédie humaine* ('a tremendous venture for a young house', according to Dent); he also proposed Ellen Marriage as translator, and she was found to be 'the ideal interpreter of Balzac, not only by the editor [George Saintsbury] but by other critics', as Dent observed in his *Memoirs*. In the end she needed assistance (Clara Bell and Rachel Scott) to complete the forty volumes, but she herself did twenty-seven (four of the 'bolder' titles under the pseudonym of 'James Waring'); several of them remained in print, in Britain or America or both, for over a century.

The *Comédie humaine* was issued from 1895 to 1898; in 1900 her translation of Prévost's *Frédérique* was published, in 1901 Murger's *Scènes de la vie de bohème*, and in 1902 Prévost's *Léa*, which virtually completed her oeuvre. In 1901 she had become a (non-tubercular) patient at a sanatorium, where she met her husband F. Edmund Garrett, the journalist and editor, who was gravely ill with tuberculosis. They married in 1903; four years later Garrett was dead. Ellen did no further published work apart from revising Garrett's translation of *Lyrics and Poems from Ibsen* (1912).

See further: J. M. Dent, *The Memoirs of J. M. Dent, 1849–1926* (London, 1928). ML

MARTIN, Sir Theodore (1816–1909), lawyer and writer. Born in Edinburgh, the son of a prosperous solicitor, Martin combined successful careers in law and literature. At Edinburgh University he added German to his classical acquisitions and collaborated with William Aytoun, a fellow student, on the comic pieces later published as *The Bon Gaultier Ballads* (1845). After practising as a solicitor in Edinburgh until 1846, he moved to London and worked as a parliamentary solicitor until 1907, preparing bills and piloting them through parliamentary committees. In 1851 he had married the dignified actress Helena Faucit. Their increasing reputations in Establishment circles led to Martin's being proposed as the author of the official biography of the Prince Consort (1875–9). He was knighted in 1880 and thereafter wrote a *Sketch of the Life of Princess Alice* (1885), the *Life of Lord Lyndhurst* (1883), and *Queen Victoria as I Knew Her* (1901).

In parallel Martin also pursued a prolific career as playwright, poet, and translator from several languages. He made adaptations of a number of foreign plays for Helena Faucit, translated plays from the Danish (Oehlenschläger) and the German (Schiller, Goethe); in particular he was responsible for frequently reprinted versions of the two parts of Goethe's *Faust* (1865, 1886). His translations of lyric poetry were equally numerous, even if they have not stood the test of time; they include separate volumes of the poems and ballads of Goethe and Heine, of poems by Catullus and Leopardi, of Books I–VI of Virgil's *Aeneid*, and a two-volume edition of the works of Horace (1881).

See further: *ODNB*; Carol Jones Carlisle, *Helen Faucit: Fire and Ice on the Victorian Stage* (London, 2000). ML

MARX-AVELING, Eleanor (1855–1898), the youngest of Karl Marx's three daughters, aspiring actress, author, lecturer, and editor. A committed socialist and authority on English socialism, she was deeply involved in the early labour movement and was considered the personification of the Marxian legacy. From 1884 she lived with Edward Aveling, fellow socialist, scientist, and atheist, but they never married. Aveling's shameless exploitation of her led to her final despair when she discovered he had married another woman while living with her. Apparently at her request, he seems to have obtained the prussic acid with which she committed suicide.

Translation from French, German, and Norwegian was a source of income for her, but the texts she translated were ones which spoke to her convictions. They include important political writings by figures such as Georgy Plekhanov, Eduard Bernstein, and Hippolyte Lissagaray. Her most famous literary translation is her sympathetic version of Flaubert's *Madame Bovary* (1886), which remained in print to the middle of the twentieth century. She also played a significant part in introducing Ibsen to the British public, learning Norwegian in order to translate *An Enemy of Society* (1888), *The Lady from the Sea* (1889), and *The Wild Duck* (1890).

See further: *ODNB*; Yvonne Kapp, *Eleanor Marx*, 2 vols. (1972–6). RB

MOORE, Thomas (1779–1852), poet, satirist, composer, and musician. A Catholic, Moore was able to enter Trinity College Dublin in 1795 due to a suspension of one of the rules of the Penal Code. While still a student Moore translated Anacreon into lush romantic verse that enjoyed a surprising success; he also did versions of Horace, Catullus, and poems from the Greek Anthology. At the same time, he became involved with members of the United Irish Society, including Robert Emmet, later hanged for his part in the aborted uprising of 1803. His discovery of

Edward Bunting's *General Collection of Ancient Irish Music* (1796) inspired the first volume of his *Irish Melodies* (1807). In all, ten volumes of these lyric poems had appeared by 1834, with music composed by Moore and Sir John Stevenson from traditional Gaelic airs. This romantic 'translation' of the Irish spirit, written by someone who knew no Irish, was extremely successful in Britain and Ireland, and the poems were translated into every European language; the work earned Moore some £500 annually for more than twenty-five years. He was subsequently paid a record £3,000 for his very popular Oriental poem *Lalla Rookh* (1817). A friend of Byron and Leigh Hunt, he lived in England for most of his life.

See further: *ODNB*; Brendan Clifford, *The Life and Poems of Thomas Moore* (Belfast, 1993).
M-AC

MORGANWG, Iolo, *see* WILLIAMS, Edward.

MORRIS, William (1834–1896), one of the most prolific writers and artists of his age. The son of a businessman, he was educated at Marlborough School and Exeter College, Oxford. Morris's achievements are legendary: from his early association with Dante Gabriel Rossetti and the Pre-Raphaelite circle, he went on to set up his own craft firm, founded the Kelmscott Press, designed textiles that continue to be international best-sellers, wrote a great deal of poetry, and in his latter years moved into his utopian socialist period when he wrote powerful visionary tracts such as *The Dream of John Ball* (1888).

As a translator, he was equally prolific. He published translations of Virgil's *Aeneid* (1875), Homer's *Odyssey* (1887), and (from a literal version) the Old English *Beowulf* (1895). He studied Old Norse and in collaboration with Eiríkr Magnússon set about translating the Icelandic sagas, publishing twenty-seven of them between 1869 and 1895. His own poetry and later prose show heavy Norse influence, as can be seen in *The Story of Sigurd the Volsung and the Fall of the Niblungs* (1876). He favoured archaic vocabulary and syntax, which proved difficult for contemporary readers; despite his passionate interest in the Viking world, his translations were not as successful as his designs.

See further: *ODNB*; David and Sheila Latham, *An Annotated Critical Bibliography of William Morris* (London, 1991); Fiona MacCarthy, *William Morris: A Life for our Time* (London, 1994).
SB

MÜLLER, Friedrich Max (1823–1900), philologist, born in Germany, the son of the lyric poet Wilhelm Müller. Upon his naturalization as a British citizen in 1855, he incorporated the name Max into his surname. Having studied at Leipzig, Berlin, and Paris, in 1845 he began work on his *magnum opus*, his edition of the Sanskrit text of the *Ṛg Veda* (6 vols., 1849–74). In 1846 he settled in Oxford, where he became a professor of modern languages and in 1868 professor of comparative philology. Much of his energy in the 1860s was devoted to the preparation of popular books and lectures, mostly in the fields of comparative religion and mythology. Max Müller became a leading figure of Victorian public life. His social success, together with the fact that he engaged in little original research in his later years, caused him to be criticized by more rigorous scholars. He was working on his autobiography at the time of his death.

From the mid-1870s his major occupation was his general editorship of the collection of translations entitled Sacred Books of the East, which is fully discussed in § 10.3, above. He himself did the translations for several volumes, including those devoted to the *Upaniṣads* and the *R̥g Veda*, though these are not among the most successful of the collection. In addition, he published in 1881 a stylish translation of Kant's *Critique of Pure Reason*.

See further: *ODNB*; F. Max Müller, *My Autobiography: A Fragment* (London, 1901); Nirad C. Chaudhuri, *Scholar Extraordinary: The Life of Professor the Rt. Hon. Friedrich Max Müller, P. C.* (London, 1974). RF

NEALE, John Mason (1818–1866), author and translator of hymns. Born in London, he was educated at several schools and Trinity College, Cambridge. He became a Fellow of Downing College, and one of the founders of the Cambridge Camden Society, which encouraged elaborate worship and ritual. Ill health and opposition to his high church views from bishops prevented him from becoming a parish priest, but in 1846 he was presented by the family of the Duke of Dorset to the wardenship of Sackville College, East Grinstead, a private charitable foundation for thirty poor and aged persons. He lived there for the remainder of his life; he decorated the chapel and altar (denounced by his bishop as 'spiritual haberdashery') and founded the nursing order of St Margaret's Sisterhood.

Neale was a voluminous writer on church history and doctrine and assisted in the revival of carols with *Carols for Christmas Tide* (1853), but apart from 'Good King Wenceslas' he is chiefly known for his translations of Latin and Greek hymns, which appeared in various collections, most notably *Mediaeval Hymns and Sequences* (1851), *The Hymnal Noted* (1852–4), and *Hymns of the Eastern Church* (1862). His contributions to the first edition of *Hymns Ancient and Modern* were more numerous than those of any other writer.

See further: *ODNB*; Leon Litvack, *J. M. Neale and the Quest for Sobornost* (Oxford, 1994). JRW

NEWMAN, Francis William (1805–1897). The son of a London banker, Newman grew up in a well-to-do and serious-minded family. Going to Oxford, he benefited from tuition and financial support from his elder brother, the future cardinal, from whom he was later estranged. He was elected Fellow of Balliol College, but resigned and left the university because of doubts about Anglicanism. After a spell of tutoring and participation in ill-conceived missionary ventures in the Middle East, he became a lecturer in classics and mathematics at Bristol College. Subsequently, he was appointed professor of classics first at Manchester New College, then, from 1840 to 1863, at University College London. Here he wrote on religious matters and provoked controversy by supporting liberal causes, from vegetarianism to social and political reform, in scores of pamphlets.

His *Odes of Horace Translated into Unrhymed Metres* (1853) was followed in 1856 by his *Iliad of Homer Faithfully Translated*, an avowedly foreignizing translation in which Homer is rendered in the ballad form that Newman deemed appropriate to oral poetry. After Matthew Arnold attacked his Homer in the first lectures he delivered as Professor of Poetry at Oxford, Newman fought back in *Homeric Translation in Theory and Practice* (1861); this polemic is a crucial document for nineteenth-century translation theories. Newman also translated Longfellow's *Hiawatha* into Latin in 1862 as a reader for his classics students.

See further: *ODNB*; Basil Willey, 'Francis W. Newman', pp. 11–52 in his *More Nineteenth-Century Studies: A Group of Honest Doubters* (London, 1956).

CS

NORTON, Charles Eliot (1827–1908), scholar and critic. On graduating from Harvard in 1846 he entered the business world, spending nearly two years abroad in India and then Europe, where he fell in love with the life and art of the Middle Ages. In 1856–7 he began the studies and translations of Dante that dominated his intellectual life and influenced those of many others. Through his friendships with Carlyle, Ruskin, Morris, and Arnold he acted as an important courier of ideas between Britain and America. In 1874 he returned to Harvard to teach the history of art.

Though he edited Donne's poems and *The Early Letters of Thomas Carlyle*, compiled a bibliography of Michelangelo, and wrote a biography of Kipling, his great contribution to learning was his work on Dante, whose poetry provided an antidote, he believed, to the modern world's widespread loss of religious faith. He translated *La vita nuova* in 1859 (revised in 1867) and the *Commedia* (in prose) in 1891–2 (revised in 1902). He was instrumental in founding the Dante Society and the Dante Collection at Harvard, and he took a leading role in starting the Loeb Classical Library.

See further: *DAB*; *ANB*; Kermit Vanderbilt, *Charles Eliot Norton: Apostle of Culture in a Democracry* (Cambridge, MA, 1959).

AP

NOTT, John (1751–1825), scholar and physician, born in Worcester, son of Samuel Nott, a friend of George III. Although he received medical training, there is uncertainty about his final degree. By inclination, he was a scholar and linguist, whose leaning to poetry turned quickly to translation. He travelled extensively, including two years in Pisa and three in China, when he learnt Persian (and later translated Ḥāfiẓ), before settling near Bristol. He provided the first book-length translations of Petrarch (1777), Propertius (1782), and Catullus (2 vols. in 1, 1795). His *Kisses* (1775, from the *Basia* of the neo-Latin poet Johannes Secundus) was reissued several times and then followed by another, quite different edition in 1824; as he put it in the preface to the 1779 edition, he saw it as his duty 'to revive a flame' for Love's 'Nuptual Torch'. Nott rewrote freely, providing the original for the reader who might and indeed should compare texts; most of his translations are accompanied by essays and copious notes, giving references and citations from other translations. His translations change radically among editions; in 1808 he published a volume entitled *Petrarch Translated*, which is quite unlike the anonymously published 1777 translation of Petrarch.

See further: *ODNB*; Lawrence Venuti, *The Translator's Invisibility* (London, 1995), pp. 84–95. JY

OXENFORD, John (1812–1877), prolific playwright, critic, and translator. Born in London, the son of a prosperous merchant, he was privately educated and became a solicitor in 1833. From an early age he showed a marked interest in literature and drama (German, Italian, French, and Spanish, as well as English). In 1846 he became *The Times*' drama critic and later contributed articles on literary, theatrical, and philosophical topics to the *Westminster Review* and other periodicals.

Oxenford was a pioneering popularizer of German literature; his translation of Lindner's article on Schopenhauer is said to have been among the first to create interest in the philosopher in England. His career as a translator of books began in 1844 with *Tales from the German* (with C. A. Feiling) and continued with Goethe's *Autobiography* (1848–9), the *Conversations of Goethe with Eckermann* (1850) and Delavigne's *Monastery of St Just* (1850), Callery and Ivan's *Insurrection in China* (1853), and Kuno Fischer's *Francis Bacon* (1857). He was also one of the editors of the 1857 edition of Flügel's German dictionary. However, his main interest was undoubtedly the theatre, for which he wrote at least fifty plays (often farces), many of which were, in the theatrical tradition, 'adaptations from the French'.

See further: *ODNB*. ML

PAYNE, John (1842–1916), poet and scholar born in London, the son of a businessman. He revealed an early love of poetic composition and translation, but family circumstances forced him to leave school at 13; eventually settling in a solicitor's office in London, he studied languages privately. By 20 he had made many translations, including Dante's entire poetical works. He became involved in literary groups and counted as friends Mallarmé, Banville, and Swinburne. He worked, as he lived, intensely and eccentrically.

Payne's many books of poems include *The Masque of Shadows and Other Poems* (1870). The plentiful translations, mostly published privately by the Villon Society, include *The Poems of François Villon* (1878), *The Quatrains of Omar Kheyyam of Nishapour* (1898), and the complete works of Ḥāfiẓ (3 vols., 1901). Payne largely endeavoured to retain the original form and metre, an approach which caused his Ḥāfiẓ to be called a grandiose failure. Other translations include the first complete English *Decameron* (3 vols., 1886), and a four-part anthology, *Flowers of France* (1906–13). His greatest translation achievement, however, is his complete version of *The Book of the Thousand Nights and One Night* (1882–4). His extraordinary literary output probably reflects not only a lifelong obsession with literature but also a need for privacy and, finally, reclusion.

See further: Thomas Wright, *The Life of John Payne* (London, 1919). JY

PLANCHÉ, James Robinson (1795–1880), playwright, antiquarian, and musician. During a career of some sixty years, Planché wrote more than 150 plays and libretti for the London stage, many of them adaptations of foreign works. His first notable adaptation (from an English work) was *The Vampire, or, The Bride of the Isle* (1820) at the Lyceum which introduced the 'vampire trap' to the British stage. He produced English versions of *The Magic Flute* and *William Tell*, and his libretto for Weber's *Oberon* at Covent Garden in 1826 contributed to the opera's phenomenal success. During the 1830s, he was one of the most adept of Eugène Scribe's numerous English adapters. It was his extravaganzas, however, that constituted the cornerstone of his reputation, especially the 'fairy' extravaganzas of the 1840s and 1850s, such as *The Island of Jewels* (1849). This genre essentially represents a naturalization of the French *féerie* by the incorporation of elements of English pantomime. Planché also adapted *The Birds* of Aristophanes (1846) and published translations of the fairy tales of Mme d'Aulnoy (1855). He was the author of an authoritative *History of British Costume* (1834).

See further: *ODNB*; J. R. Planché, *Recollections and Reflections* (1872); Kathy Fletcher, 'Aristophanes on the Victorian Stage: J. R. Planché's Adaptation of *The Birds*', *Theatre Studies* 26–7 (1978–81), 89–98.   TH

RALSTON, William Ralston (Shedden) (1828–1889), Russian scholar and translator. Son of a Calcutta merchant, William Shedden was born in London, educated privately, and graduated MA from Cambridge. He qualified for the bar, but, prompted by a family lawsuit, changed his surname and career, working for the next twenty-five years at the British Museum, where he acquired a good knowledge of Russian language and literature and developed an interest in folklore. A frequent traveller to Germany, Belgium, Switzerland, and above all, Russia, he forged a lasting friendship with Turgenev, and became a corresponding member of the Imperial Academy of Sciences of St Petersburg in 1886.

Ralston's translations include *Kriloff and his Fables* (1869), Turgenev's *Liza* (1869), *The Songs of the Russian People* (1872), *Russian Folk-Tales* (1873), and *Tibetan Tales* (1882, translated from Anton von Shiefner's German). His work was partially motivated by a fascination with the universal nature of folk tales and the problem of their classification (see his *Notes on Folk-Tales*, c.1878). Ralston describes his approach to translation by analogy: 'An untouched photograph is ... infinitely preferable to one which has been "worked upon" ' (*Russian Folk-Tales*, introduction). Against current taste, he rendered verse as prose. A frequent contributor to journals, and a generous and witty man, Ralston also composed introductions to translations of Portuguese and Indian folk stories.

See further: *ODNB*.   JY

READE, Charles (1814–1880), playwright, novelist, and social reformer. Born in Oxfordshire, the son of a country gentleman, he graduated from Oxford in 1835, became a Fellow of Magdalen College, and enrolled at Lincoln's Inn to study law, being called to the bar in 1843. Although he himself made much use of the texts of others, he later campaigned in favour of intellectual property rights; *The Eighth Commandment* (1860) records his dealings with pirates, collaborators, and legal opponents. He wrote several reforming novels, but is best known as the author of the historical novel *The Cloister and the Hearth* (1861).

He was a successful playwright, many of his plays being adaptations from the French. These include: *The Ladies' Battle, or, Un Duel en Amour* (1851, from a play by Scribe and Legouvé); *Angelo* (1851, from the play by Victor Hugo); *The Lost Husband* (1852, from a play by Anicet Bourgeois); *The Courier of Lyon, or, The Attack Upon the Mail* (1854, from a play by Moreau, Siraudin, and Delacour); and *Poverty and Pride* (1856, from a play by Brisebarre and Nus). *Jealousy* (1878, from Sardou) and *Drink* (1879, an adaptation of Zola's *L'Assommoir*) brought his theatrical career to a conclusion, the latter earning him considerable royalties.

See further: *ODNB*; W. Burns, *Charles Reade: A Study in Victorian Authorship* (New York, 1961).　　　　　　　　　　　　　　　　　　　　　　　　　　　　TH

REEVE, Henry (1813–1895), journalist and public servant, born in Norwich. His father was a doctor, who died when he was a child, and his mother the elder sister of the translator Sarah Austin. At 15 he left school in Norwich, perfected his French in Paris, and continued his education in Geneva, where he attended lectures on a wide variety of subjects, including law, and became friendly with the Polish poet Mickiewicz, whose *Farys* he translated. Returning to London in 1831, he met Carlyle, Godwin, and Thackeray; in 1832 he returned to Paris, travelled to Italy, and spent eight months in Munich, becoming fluent in German.

Once back in England, he began to translate for the monthly press, then to write articles on his own account, joining the staff of *The Times* in 1840. He continued to meet a wide circle of influential people, including Alexis de Tocqueville, whose close friend and confidant he became. In 1835 he published his translation of Tocqueville's *La Démocratie en Amérique*, which was much reprinted; subsequently he was to translate Tocqueville's *L'Ancien Régime* in the year of its French publication (1856) and Guizot's *Washington* (1841). In 1837 he had been appointed clerk of appeal to the judicial committee of the Privy Council, becoming its registrar in 1843. In 1855 he took over as editor of the *Edinburgh Review*, a position he held for the next forty years. His best-known work was his three-volume edition of the *Greville Memoirs* (1875–87).

See further: *ODNB*; J. K. Laughton, *Memoirs of the Life and Correspondence of Henry Reeve, C.B., D.C.L.* (London, 1898).　　　　　　　　　　　　　　　　　　IP

RODWELL, John Medows (1808–1900), clergyman and Oriental scholar. Born in Suffolk, he graduated from Cambridge (where Darwin was a contemporary and friend) and was ordained as deacon in Norwich in 1831. He was active in the Church for the next fifty years, largely in deprived areas of London; he became secretary of the Society for More Clergy in Populous Places and argued strongly against the disendowment and disestablishment of the Church. In 1843 he was given the rectorship of St Ethelburga's, Bishopsgate, which he held until his death.

As a young man Rodwell acquired a good knowledge of Hebrew and Arabic and translated several religious works, including the Book of Job (from the Hebrew, 1864), *Aethiopic Liturgies and Hymns* (1864), and liturgies from a thirteenth-century Coptic manuscript (1866). His largest work of translation is *The Koran* (1861), in which he endeavoured to arrange the *sūrahs* (sections) in chronological order, with notes and index. In the preface, speaking of his translation style, Rodwell cites the middle way of St Jerome, saying that he translated the poetic parts freely, but aimed at a more literal prose. In recognition of his work, his college, Gonville and Caius, elected him Honorary Fellow in 1886.

See further: *ODNB*. JY

ROSCOE, Thomas (1791–1871), translator, editor, and writer. Born at Toxteth Park near Liverpool, he was the son of William Roscoe, a Member of Parliament, a banker, and a distinguished writer. In 1816 William failed financially and Thomas perforce entered on a busy literary life, working first for local journals, then writing or editing a large number of individual works and series (e.g. The Novelist's Library, 17 vols., 1831–3; editions of Fielding, Swift, and others). He made many translations from Italian, including Cellini's *Memoirs* (1822) and Silvio Pellico's *My Imprisonments* (1833). He also translated from French (notably Sismondi's *Literature of the South of Europe*, 1823) and from German and Spanish. Particularly noteworthy are his three anthological collections: *The Italian Novelists* (4 vols., 1825); *The German Novelists* (4 vols., 1826); and *The Spanish Novelists* (3 vols., 1832). Several of these translations drew heavily (without acknowledgement) on earlier versions. At the same time he wrote several travel books.

The second half of Roscoe's adult life was far less prolific than the first and occupied chiefly by new editions of his father's works and his own. In 1839 he was awarded £50, as a needy writer, by the Royal Literary Fund. After his death the Fund's secretary refused a similar request from his even needier daughters, on the grounds that his marriage might have been irregular.

See further: *ODNB*. ML

ROSSETTI, Dante Gabriel (1828–1882), poet and painter, one of the founders of the Pre-Raphaelite Brotherhood. He was the second of four children, his father and maternal grandfather being Italian political refugees. He studied painting at the Royal Academy, and then as a result of his interest in medieval art forms he began to experiment with verse, writing poems that drew on English and Italian medieval models.

Among his greatest literary achievements was his translation of Italian medieval poets. *The Early Italian Poets* appeared in 1861, with a short preface outlining his theory of translation; in 1872 it was reissued in an expanded form as *Dante and his Circle*. The first part is devoted to poets writing before Dante, while the second part contains translations of Dante, including *La vita nuova*, along with poems by other writers in Dante's circle including Cavalcanti and Guinizelli. Rossetti saw the translator as the servant of the original; typically, he represented that relationship in medieval terms, portraying the humility of the translator born to serve the more powerful lordly original. Yet in his translation practice, he was not humble, often taking considerable liberties with the source texts in order to create aesthetically satisfying translations.

See further: *ODNB*; Russell Ash, *Dante Gabriel Rossetti* (London, 1995): Jan Marsh, *Dante Gabriel Rossetti: Painter and Poet* (London, 1999). SB

SCOBLE, **Sir Andrew Richard** (1831–1916), lawyer and politician. He was born in London in 1831, the second son of John Scoble, a Devon man who had been a member of the Provincial Parliament of Canada. He was educated at the City of London School, and was called to the bar at Lincoln's Inn in 1856. He was appointed QC in 1876, became Advocate-General and a member of the Legislative Council in Bombay in 1872. From 1886 to 1891 he was a member of the Council of the Governor-General of India, before becoming Conservative Member of Parliament for Hackney Central (1892–1900) and Treasurer of Lincoln's Inn. He was appointed to the judicial committee of the Privy Council in 1901.

His prodigious output of translations—twelve very substantial volumes, seven by Guizot (for six of these see the bibliography to § 11.2, above), in addition to Merimée's *Colomba, Charles IX*, and *Demetrius the Impostor*, Mignet's *History of Mary Queen of Scots*, and Lamartine's *Geneviève* in the space of five years—was achieved while he was reading for the bar. Despite the pressure he must have been under, they are remarkably effective. They were, perhaps understandably, the only translations he undertook.

See further: *Who Was Who, 1916–1928* (London, 1929). IP

SCOTT, **Sir Walter** (1771–1832), poet and novelist, the son of an Edinburgh lawyer. After an education at Edinburgh High School and Edinburgh University, he was called to the bar in 1792 and became Sheriff-Depute of Selkirkshire in 1799, but he devoted much of his time to writing. His literary fame began with his collection of popular ballads *Minstrelsy of the Scottish Border* (1802–3) and with such long poems as *Marmion* (1808) and *The Lady of the Lake* (1810); the proceeds from these enabled him to build the romantic residence of Abbotsford. Then he turned to fiction: *Waverley*, anonymously published in 1814, was the first in a long series of historical novels which had an incalculable influence throughout Europe. He also wrote many historical and critical works and left an interesting journal, first published in 1890. He was created a baronet in 1820.

Influenced by a lecture on German theatre by Henry Mackenzie, Scott and his friends began learning German in 1792. His translations of ballads by Bürger (including the famous 'Lenore') were anonymously published as *The Chase and William and Helen* (1796). He went on to translate various ballads and lyrics, as well as some modern German plays that remained unpublished except for a free and inaccurate version of Goethe's *Götz von Berlichingen* (1799) and *The House of Aspen*, a melodramatic adaptation of a play by Wächter, included many years later in his *Poetical Works*.

See further: *ODNB*; Edgar Johnson: *Sir Walter Scott: The Great Unknown*, 2 vols. (London, 1970).
PF

SHELLEY, Percy Bysshe (1792–1822), poet. Born in Sussex, the eldest son of a Member of Parliament, he studied at Eton and proceeded to University College, Oxford, in 1810. Precocious and talented, he found himself at odds with authority and was expelled in March 1811. A few months later, he eloped with Harriet Westbrook, but their relationship was unhappy. After the death of his wife in 1816, Shelley married Mary Godwin, with whom he lived until his death by drowning in the Bay of La Spezia in July 1822.

Shelley was perhaps the most versatile and accomplished verse translator of his time. He derived pleasure from working and reworking his translations, and while he shared his versions with friends, he published few of them in his lifetime. He studied the classics in school (supposedly one of his earliest translation exercises was of Pliny the elder), and he was intensely devoted to the literature of ancient Greece. His translations included Euripides' satyr play *Cyclops* and eloquent versions of seven of the *Homeric Hymns*; in 1816 he rendered the Aeschylean *Prometheus Bound* aloud to Byron. Shelley loved Plato passionately, translating the *Symposium* and *Phaedo* and passages from the *Ion*, *Republic*, *Crito*, and *Menexenus*. He also translated modern authors, though only in a fragmentary way: selections from Dante's *Divine Comedy* and scenes from Goethe's *Faust* and Calderón's *El mágico prodigioso*.

See further: *ODNB*; Richard Holmes, *Shelley: The Pursuit* (London, 1976); Timothy Webb, *The Violet in The Crucible: Shelley and Translation* (Oxford, 1976).
PW

SHOBERL, Frederic (1775–1853), translator, editor, and miscellaneous writer. Born in London of a German-speaking family and educated at the Moravian school in Yorkshire, Shoberl was a characteristic example of the literary all-rounder in the first half of the century. His translations from German and French followed the literary fashions, ranging from Klopstock (*Messiah*, 1817), Kotzebue (*The Patriot Father*, 1819), and Chateaubriand (*René*, 1813) earlier in his career to Hugo (*The Hunchback of Notre Dame*, 1833), Thiers (*History of the French Revolution*, 1838), and Vigny (*Lights and Shades of Military Life*, 1840) later on; he also translated travel books throughout the period, for instance the *Travels in the Caucasus* of Heinrich Julius von Klaproth (1814) and *Excursions in Normandy* by Jacob Venedey (1841).

Shoberl's own books include *A Natural History of Quadrupeds* (1834), *Prince Albert and the House of Saxony* (1840), and *The Persecutions of Popery* (1844), and he contributed volumes to *The Beauties of England and Wales* (1815) and other collections. In addition he exerted considerable influence as the editor of such popular periodicals and keepsakes as the *New Monthly Magazine* (published by Henry Colburn), Ackermann's *Repository of Arts*, and the *Forget-me-Not*, which carried translated verse and prose among other material.

See further: *ODNB*.
ML

SOUTHEY, Robert (1774–1843), poet, the son of a Bristol linen-draper. Expelled from Westminster School, he studied at Oxford and became an ardent supporter of the French Revolution, making unrealized plans to found a utopian colony in America with S. T. Coleridge. In 1803 he settled with Coleridge in Greta Hall near Keswick, where he lived with his family until his death. A man of strong views, he became more conservative in outlook and from 1809 wrote frequently for the Tory *Quarterly Review*. In 1813 he was appointed Poet Laureate and subsequently became embroiled in controversy with Byron.

As a writer, Southey was outstandingly productive, though few of his writings have stood the test of time. As well as many narrative poems, his work includes histories of Brazil and the Peninsular War and a life of Nelson. A youthful stay in the Iberian peninsula gave him a love for Portuguese and Spanish literature (of which his library contained a notable collection) and resulted in several translations. After translating an old Portuguese romance as *Amadis of Gaul* (1805) and reworking Anthony Munday's sixteenth-century version of *Palmerin of England* (1807), he produced his still impressive *Chronicle of the Cid* (1808), compiled from Spanish medieval sources. He also translated lyric poetry, much of it published anonymously in journals or included in his *Letters Written during a Short Residence in Spain and Portugal* (see the 3rd edn., 1808).

See further: *ODNB*; Mark Storey, *Robert Southey: A Life* (Oxford, 1997).

PF

STEPHENS, George (1813–1895), philologist and runologist. Born in Liverpool, the son of a methodist minister, he studied at University College London before moving to Stockholm, where his brother Joseph introduced him to Scandinavian languages and literature. He became professor of English language and literature at the University of Copenhagen in 1855, where he promoted his controversial pro-Scandinavian and anti-German philological and political agenda.

His publications include a verse translation (1839) both of Esaias Tegnér's *Frithiof's Saga* and of the medieval Icelandic saga on which the poem was based. This was the first English translation of a complete Icelandic saga ever published. In the saga verses and also in his translation of the Old English poem *The Phoenix* (1844), he sought to retain the alliteration of the original verse and favoured anglicized forms of old northern rather than Graeco-Roman and French vocabulary. In 1860 he edited and translated fragments of the hitherto unknown Old English poem *Waldere*. His most celebrated work was *The Old-Northern Runic Monuments of Scandinavia and England* (4 vols., 1866–1901). Though his philological preconceptions and misguided enthusiasms led him into error in all these projects, Stephens was widely and properly honoured for his pioneering contribution to old northern scholarship.

See further: *ODNB*.

AW

SWANWICK, Anna (1813–1899), writer, translator, and philanthropist, the daughter of a Liverpool merchant of liberal and Unitarian beliefs. She received a girl's education, but independent income allowed her to study Greek, German, Hebrew, and philosophy in Berlin and mathematics in London with F. W. Newman, translator of Homer. Her works included *Poets, the Interpreters of their Age* (1892) and *Evolution and the Religion of the Future* (1893). She championed social causes, particularly women's education; she was awarded an honorary LL D by Aberdeen University.

Swanwick translated German and Greek drama. Her first translation was *Selections from the Dramas of Goethe and Schiller* (1843); other works include *The Dramatic Works of Goethe* (1846) and the first verse translation of Part I of *Faust* (1850); Parts I and II appeared together in 1878). In 1865 she turned to Greek with *The Trilogy of Aeschylus*; in 1873 *The Complete Dramas of Aeschylus* appeared. Her approach to translation ran contrary to domesticating tendencies; she believed that a translation must 'approximate to the original . . . in form as well as in spirit' ('Translator's Preface', *Faust*, 1879). Her work won considerable praise, including a letter from Gladstone addressed to A. Swanwick, Esq.

See further: *ODNB*; Mary L. Bruce, *Anna Swanwick: A Memoir and Recollections* (London, 1903); Joan Bellamy, Anne Laurence, and Gill Perry, eds., *Women, Scholarship, and Criticism: Gender and Knowledge c.1790–1900* (Manchester, 2000).

JY

SWINBURNE, Algernon Charles (1837–1909), poet, dramatist, and critic. He was born into a wealthy and established family and thanks in large part to his mother, Lady Jane Henrietta, he acquired a knowledge of French and Italian at an early age. A voracious reader of classical, medieval, and modern literature, he was schooled privately and at Eton, and he later entered Balliol College, Oxford, where he impressed the Master, Benjamin Jowett, but left before graduating. He began to write poems and tragedies as a young man and became famous with *Poems and Ballads* (1866), a work which outraged moralizing critics but sold well. Both praised and reviled, he continued to publish poetry until his death in 1909.

Swinburne interwove allusions, translations, and imitations into his original works. For example, his 'Phaedra', published in the first *Poems and Ballads*, includes a translation of a six-line fragment from Aeschylus' *Niobe*, while 'Anactoria' contains several fragments of Sappho. Other poems, 'Hendecasyllabics' and 'Sapphics' for example, adapt into English the metres of Catullus and Sappho. The volume also includes a handful of other translations, as does the second series of *Poems and Ballads* (1878), which contains his fine translations from Villon. His version of a chorus from Aristophanes' *Birds*, published in *Studies in Song* (1880), has been especially praised.

See further; *ODNB*; Rikky Rooksby, *A. C. Swinburne: A Poet's Life* (Aldershot, 1997); Swinburne, *Poems and Ballads & Atalanta in Calydon*, ed. Kenneth Haynes (London, 2000).

PW

SYMONDS, John Addington (1840–1893), poet and critic. The son of a physician, he was educated at Harrow and Oxford. Suffering from chronic lung disease, which prompted a move to Davos in 1878 (and a friendship with Robert Louis Stevenson), Symonds earned his living through writing. Translator principally of Greek and Italian, he included many of his shorter verse translations (from Sappho, Poliziano, Boiardo, Pulci, and others) in his prose works: *An Introduction to the Study of Dante* (1872), *Renaissance in Italy* (7 vols., 1875–86), *Studies of the Greek Poets* (two series, 1873 and 1876), and *The Life of Michelangelo Buonarroti* (1893). His full-length translations include *The Sonnets of Michel Angelo Buonarroti and Tommaso Campanella* (1878); *Wine, Women and Song* (1884), a verse collection of medieval Latin students' songs which acquired great vogue; *The Life of Benvenuto Cellini* (1888); and *The Memoirs of Count Carlo Gozzi* (1890). In his translations Symonds adopts the archaic, flowery style of his own poetry; as he states in his introduction to Buonarroti's sonnets, 'the translator cannot wholly refrain from softening, simplifying, and prettifying Michel Angelo'.

Symonds married and fathered four daughters, but his memoirs reveal the significance of a repressed homosexuality: Phyllis Grosskurth finds that his works—including some translations—were prompted by a thwarted desire to 'speak out'. *A Problem in Greek Ethics* (1883), *A Problem in Modern Ethics* (1891), and his *Sexual Inversion*, written in collaboration with Havelock Ellis, indicate the centrality of these concerns.

See further: *ODNB*; *The Memoirs of John Addington Symonds*, ed. Phyllis Grosskurth (London, 1984); Phyllis Grosskurth, *John Addington Symonds: A Biography* (London, 1964). JY

SYMONS, Arthur, *see* Volume 5.

TAYLOR, Bayard (1825–1878), novelist, poet, and travel writer. Born and educated in rural Pennsylvania, Taylor became a printer's apprentice upon leaving high school in 1842. A few years later he reached an agreement with several newspapers that enabled him to tour Europe for two years (he spent six months in Frankfurt) in exchange for providing them with accounts of his travels. In 1848 he began his lifelong association with the *New York Tribune*. Further travels ensued: in the Near and Far East and in Europe, including St Petersburg (1862–3, as a member of an official US delegation). From 1857 he gradually retired to Pennsylvania and from 1870 to 1877 was a non-resident professor of German literature at Cornell.

Taylor enjoyed considerable fame in his later years but was subsequently forgotten. His reputation now rests on his translation of *Faust* (2 vols., 1870–1). In it he reproduced the lines, metres, and rhyme scheme of the original, while taking pains not to deviate from the literal meaning of the German. Some features of the German language were preserved: the frequent use of particles, inversions, capitals, delayed verbs, and nominalized adjectives recalls German. The translation has sometimes been criticized for these features, but it has generally received high praise and has often been reprinted. His other translations, mostly from German lyric poets, appeared in diverse writings and were collected posthumously by his daughter in *A Sheaf of Poems* (1911).

See further: *ANB*; *DAB*; Julianna Haskell, *Bayard Taylor's Translation of Goethe's Faust* (1908); John T. Krumpelmann, *Bayard Taylor and German Letters* (1959); Paul C. Wermuth, *Bayard Taylor* (1973). KH

TAYLOR, **Edgar** (1793–1839), lawyer. Born in Norfolk to a dissenting family, he attended a school in Suffolk, where he learned to read Greek and Latin. In 1809, he became an apprentice to his uncle, a solicitor. By the time he arrived in London in 1814, he had also learned Italian and Spanish, to which he later added French and German. In 1817 he founded a law firm with a partner and thereafter enjoyed a profitable legal career. In 1827 he became ill and by 1832 was unable to do much professional work. Throughout his adult life he was active in campaigns to secure the rights of dissenters.

German Popular Stories (2 vols., 1823–6), Taylor's translation of stories collected by the Grimm brothers, established itself as a classic and was reprinted several times in the course of the century. At this time he also was involved with the *Lays of the Minnesingers* (1825), which he wrote with his cousin Sarah Austin, who was responsible for almost all the translations of poetry, while Taylor was mainly concerned with the commentary. His translation of part of the *Roman de Rou* appeared in 1837 as *Master Wace, His Chronicle of the Norman Conquest*; he translated in prose in order to maintain fidelity to the narrative rather than to the poetry. Before his death, he was engaged in a revision of the King James version of the New Testament; this was completed by an unnamed editor who published it in 1840.

See further: *ODNB*; Lotte and Joseph Hamburger, *Troubled Lives: John and Sarah Austin* (1985); William E. Paul, *English Language Bible Translators* (2003). KH

TAYLOR, **Thomas** (1758–1835), mathematician and philosopher. The son of a nonconformist London stay-maker, Taylor overcame the ills of a sickly childhood and developed broad interests in mathematics, philosophy, and science. He learned the rudiments of Greek and Latin from his teachers but was primarily self-taught.

More than anyone else in his time, Taylor was responsible for introducing Plato and Neo-Platonic philosophy to the English-speaking public. His edition of Plato's dialogues, *The Works, viz. his Fifty-five Dialogues, and Twelve Epistles* (1804), includes revisions of nine translations by Floyer Sydenham (1710–87), whom Taylor knew and who inspired him to complete the project. Other published translations include works by Aristotle, Apuleius, Porphyry, and Proclus. Despite his enthusiasm, Taylor's translations were not well received: opponents criticized their obscurity, and Taylor's militant theological heterodoxy alienated many. Nevertheless, he found kindred spirits among the English Romantic poets, especially Blake, as well as the American Transcendentalists. They admired his unabashed Platonism and were greatly influenced by his translations, which indeed influenced everyone who could not read Plato in Greek or in Latin translation—at the time they were the only complete English rendering of Plato.

See further: *ODNB*; Kathleen Raine and George Mills Harper, *Thomas Taylor The Platonist: Selected Writings* (London, 1969). PW

TAYLOR, Tom (1817–1880), lawyer, playwright, and journalist. Son of a self-made Cumbrian who set up as a brewer, he was born in Bishop-Wearmouth, Sunderland. After two terms at Glasgow University, he read classics at Cambridge. In 1844 he went to London, teaching English at University College while reading law; he was called to the bar two years later. In 1850 he was appointed Assistant-Secretary at the Board of Health, a post he retained for twenty years. He had time, however, for much journalism, becoming editor of *Punch* in 1874; he was also one of the most popular playwrights of the mid-Victorian age.

He began with slight entertainments, but in his work for the Olympic Theatre he introduced the techniques of Eugène Scribe's French 'well-made plays' to English theatregoers, many of his plays being adaptations of French ones. One of his most successful plays, *Still Waters Run Deep* (1855), described as an 'original comedy', is largely based on Charles Bernard's *Le Gendre*, transposed to London, and the melodrama *The Ticket-of-Leave Man* (1863) is a reworking of *Léonard* by Édouard Brisebarre and Eugène Nus. Similarly for *The Fool's Revenge* (1858) he adapted Victor Hugo's *Le Roi s'amuse*. In 1864 he broke new ground in his free translation of Villemarqué's *Ballads and Songs of Brittany*.

See further: *ODNB*; Winton Tolles, *Tom Taylor and the Victorian Drama* (New York, 1940). CS

TAYLOR, William (1765–1836), translator, reviewer, and historian of German literature. He was born in Norwich, the son of a merchant. While on a long business trip to Detmold in 1781–2, he learned German and developed literary interests. In the early 1790s he gave up the family business and devoted himself to letters. He had by this time translated Goethe's *Iphigenie auf Tauris*, Lessing's *Nathan der Weise*, and Bürger's literary ballad 'Lenore'. These were privately printed or circulated in manuscript before being published; his version of 'Lenore' became particularly celebrated. He contributed regularly to the *Monthly Review* and became one of the most prolific reviewers of the 1790s; Hazlitt, in *The Spirit of the Age*, identified Taylor as the one who introduced 'philosophical criticism' into British letters at this time. After 1800 financial anxiety resulted in his writing more and less well. His *Historic Survey of German Poetry: Interspersed with Various Translations* (3 vols., 1828–30) gathered much of his previous writing on this topic, both criticism and translation, but Taylor's knowledge of German literature had not developed since the turn of century, and the book was harshly reviewed by Carlyle.

See further: *ODNB*; David Chandler, 'William Taylor's Pluralist Project: The Major Translations, 1789–91', *European Romantic Review* 11 (2000), 259–76.

KH

TEIXEIRA DE MATTOS SAN PAYO Y MENDES, Alexander Louis (1865–1921), man of letters and translator. Born in Amsterdam, where most of his aristocratic family remained, Teixeira was educated at the Jesuit Beaumont College in Windsor and made his career largely in England. In the 1890s he was associated with avant-garde work in both the theatre and literature. He was a familiar figure in Decadent circles, though he was felt by them to be something of an outsider, with his habits of punctuality and regular industry. The publisher Leonard Smithers recruited him to select and organize translators for the Lutetian Society (set up to publish *éditions de luxe* of works which might, at lower prices, have attracted prosecution) and in particular for an unexpurgated edition of Zola's novels (1894–5); Teixeira himself translated *Pot-Bouille*.

In 1900 he married the widow of Willie Wilde, Oscar's brother; in the new century he became particularly well known for his many translations of Maeterlinck, the Dutch novelist Louis Couperus, and the entomologist Jean-Henri Fabre, as well as miscellaneous work ranging from Chateaubriand's *Memoirs* (1902) to Gaston Leroux's *Phantom of the Opera* (1911), Georgette Leblanc's book on Helen Keller (1914), and G. H. Marius' *Dutch Painting in the 19th Century* (1908). During the First World War he put his language talents at the service of the Department for the Prevention and Extinction of Enemy Trading and became, according to Jepson, 'the friend of Prime Ministers'.

See further: Stephen McKenna, *Tex: A Chapter in the Life of Alexander Teixeira de Mattos* (New York, 1922); Edgar Jepson, *Memories of a Victorian* (London, 1933).

ML

THOMSON, James (1834–1882), Scottish-born poet and journalist, who published his early work as 'B.V.', the letters standing for two admired poets, Shelley ('Bysshe') and Novalis ('Vanolis'). Born in Port Glasgow, the son of a merchant seaman, he soon moved to London, where he attended the Royal Caledonian Asylum for the children of Scottish sailors and soldiers. He worked in Ireland and England as an army schoolmaster but was discharged in 1862; thereafter he made a precarious living as a journalist in London, writing in particular for Charles Bradlaugh's freethinking *National Reformer*. Many of his writings appeared here, the best known being the long poem *The City of Dreadful Night* (published in book form in 1880 with a dedication to the memory of 'the younger brother of Dante, Giacomo Leopardi, a spirit as lofty, a genius as intense, with a yet more tragic doom').

He translated only a few works, always out of sympathy or admiration: poetry and prose by Goethe, Heine, and Novalis, but above all a pioneering series of translations of prose texts by the lyrically pessimistic Leopardi. The first were published in the *National Reformer* in 1867–8, *Twelve Dialogues* came out posthumously in 1893, and *Essays, Dialogues and Thoughts* appeared in 1905, edited and considerably altered by Bertram Dobell. These translations continued to be read and praised for much of the twentieth century.

See further: *ODNB*; Tom Leonard, *Places of the Mind: The Life and Work of James Thomson ('B.V.')* (London, 1993).

PF

THOREAU, Henry David (1817–1862), essayist and naturalist. Born in Concord, Massachusetts, into a family that subsisted on their pencil-making business, he attended Harvard where he primarily studied languages, both classical and modern. In addition to writing, he worked variously as a schoolteacher and surveyor as well as helping with the family business. *Walden* (1854), his most famous book, is based on his experience of living a nearly solitary life of reading and observing nature for two years in his cabin at Walden Pond.

Through his friendship with Ralph Waldo Emerson, he became involved with the Transcendentalists; it was in their journal, *The Dial*, that he published his translations of Aeschylus' *Prometheus Bound*, Anacreon, and Pindar. This choice of works reflects his interest in ancient poetry and mythology. His style of translation, articulated in the headnote to *Prometheus Bound* (1843), 'in which fidelity to the text, and to the best text, is what is mainly attempted' signalled his belief in the superiority of the 'primitive' languages. This fidelity also anticipated the preference for literal translations favoured by his reviews in *The Dial*. In addition, he translated *The Transmigrations of the Seven Brahmans*, an excerpt from the *Mahābhārata* (via a French translation) and Aeschylus' *Seven Against Thebes*, but these translations were not published during his lifetime.

See further: *DAB*; *ANB*; Robert D. Richardson, Jr., *Henry Thoreau: A Life of the Mind* (Berkeley, CA, 1986). CD

THORPE, Benjamin (1781/2–1870), scholar of Old English and Scandinavian studies. Nothing is known of Thorpe's life until 1826 when, while in Copenhagen, he began studying with Rasmus Rask. His membership of the city's Icelandic Literary Society signalled the direction of his enthusiasms. He worked at a frenetic pace, editing and translating long-neglected or previously unknown Old English works, among them *Cædmon's Metrical Paraphrase of Parts of the Holy Scriptures in Anglo-Saxon* (1832), *Codex Exoniensis* (1842), *The Homilies of Ælfric* (1844–6), *The Anglo-Saxon Poems of Beowulf, the Scôp or Gleeman's Tale; and the Fight at Finnesburg* (1855), and *The Anglo-Saxon Chronicle* (1861). His description of his last translation, *The Edda of Sæmund the Learned* (1866), as 'faithful though homely . . . a stop-gap until made to give way to a worthier work' reflects an unduly modest view of his overall achievement.

Thorpe was an admirer of the philological scholarship emerging from Denmark and Germany. His *Northern Mythology* (1851–2) bears the distinctive methodological stamp of Jacob Grimm. Pedagogical texts such as his 1830 translation of Rask's *Angelsaksisk Sproglære* (1817) and his own *Analecta Anglo-Saxonica* (1834) signal his eagerness to revitalize Old English studies in early Victorian Britain.

See further: *ODNB*; Phillip Pulsiano, 'Benjamin Thorpe', pp. 75–92 in Vol. 2 of Helen Damico and Joseph B. Zavadil, eds., *Medieval Scholarship: Biographical Studies on the Formation of a Discipline* (New York, 1999). AW

TYTLER, Alexander Francis, Lord Woodhouselea, *see* Volume 3.

VAN LAUN, Henri (1820–1896), schoolmaster, one of the first examples of an academic translator working from French. He was born in the Netherlands and educated in France, settling in Britain in 1848. He taught in schools in the Isle of

Man, Cheltenham, and Edinburgh before moving to London, where for twenty years he was French examiner for the Civil Service Commission.

His *History of French Literature* (3 vols., 1876–7), partly inspired by Hippolyte Taine's *Histoire de la littérature anglaise*, which he had translated, was the first work of its kind in English. Spanning the centuries from the Middle Ages to 1848, it contains many sizeable translations, which together make up a kind of anthology for such fields as Romantic poetry. He also published a series of large-scale translations: the plays of Molière in prose (6 vols., 1875–6); the *Caractères* of La Bruyère (1885), and Le Sage's *Gil Blas* (3 vols., 1886). He describes his Molière as 'faithful and literal'; like his other translations, it is heavy and wooden, but scholarly, offering information about such matters as sources, production history, earlier translations, and adaptations.

See further: *ODNB*. PF

VIZETELLY, Henry Richard (1820–1894), publisher specializing in translations. Born in London to a family of printers, he began life as a wood engraver but soon moved into magazine publishing. From 1865 to 1872 he was the Paris correspondent of the *Illustrated News*, becoming increasingly familiar with the contemporary literary scene in France. In 1872 he started his own publishing house, issuing many translations (he himself had translated Topin's *Man in the Iron Mask* in 1870). These were mainly from French (e.g. Flaubert, Sand, Mérimée, authors whose translations were partly subsidized by the 'sensational' Gaboriau and Du Boisgobey) and Russian. His Mermaid Series of early English dramatists, unexpurgated, began in 1886; at the same time he was publishing many lightly expurgated translations of Zola's novels, which led to his prosecution and ruin (the case is described on p. 54, above).

After the firm's liquidation, his son Ernest Vizetelly (1853–1922) took over Zola's cause. Previously he had been a foreign correspondent and then an editor in the firm; now he turned to translation and writing, originating or revising English versions of twenty-three novels by Zola, who considered him a trusted friend. He also wrote some fifteen titles of his own, including *Émile Zola: Novelist and Reformer* (1904) and *With Zola in England* (1899), an account of his assistance when Zola was fleeing the fallout from the Dreyfus affair. Ernest's brother Edward Vizetelly (1847–1903) was also a translator; in the 1890s he was responsible for three novels and the *Stories for Ninon* of Zola, as well as Daudet's *Fromont Junior and Risler Senior* (1894).

See further: *ODNB*; Henry Vizetelly, *Glances Back Through Seventy Years* (London, 1893). ML

WARDROP, Sir John Oliver (1864–1948) and WARDROP, Marjory Scott (1869–1909), his sister, pioneers in the translation of Georgian literature, both ancient and modern. Marjory's interest in Georgia was aroused by her brother's *The Kingdom of Georgia* (1888), a travel book containing a chapter on the language and literature of the country, and at the age of 20 she resolved to devote herself to the study of Georgian language and culture, working at first from an alphabet and a Gospel. Thereafter she lived mainly abroad, speaking several European languages and dying in Bucharest. She first visited Georgia in 1894, returned there in 1896, and made many friends and literary acquaintances, including Prince Ilia Chavchavadze, one of whose narrative poems she translated as *The Hermit* (1895). Her other translations are a book of *Georgian Folk Tales* (1894) and her *magnum opus*, *The Man in the Panther's Skin*, a prose version of the great medieval epic-romance of Shota Rustaveli; this was left in manuscript at her death and was published in 1912 by the Royal Asiatic Society with an introduction by her brother.

Oliver, who outlived his sister by nearly forty years, had a long and varied diplomatic career after studying at Balliol College, Oxford, and serving in the army. In later years he became a senior figure in Georgian studies. His principal translation is a fine rendering of the chain of fables by the eighteenth-century writer Sulkhan-Saba Orbeliani under the title *The Book of Wisdom and Lies* (1894); he subsequently published *Visramiani: A Romance of Ancient Persian* (1914), translated from a Georgian text.

See further: *ODNB*; N. Wardrop, 'Oliver, Marjory and Georgia', *Bodleian Library Record* 14 (1994), 501–23.   PF

WEBSTER (née Davies), Augusta (1837–1894), poet, dramatist, novelist, essayist, and translator of the Aeschylean *Prometheus Bound* (1866) and Euripides' *Medea* (1868). Born in Dorset, daughter of a vice-admiral, she studied at the Cambridge School of Art and in Paris and Geneva, and taught herself Greek. In 1863 she married Thomas Webster, a Fellow of Trinity College, Cambridge, and subsequently a solicitor in London. She was active in the cause of extending women's educational opportunities and was twice elected to the London School Board.

Webster's liberal and feminist sympathies influenced her choice of the two Greek plays she translated; they further revealed themselves in the dramatic monologues in blank verse, showing the influence of Robert Browning and Felicia Hemans, gathered in *Dramatic Studies* (1866) and *Portraits* (1870). These explored the consciousness of female figures both ancient and modern in poems such as 'Circe' and 'Medea in Athens', and 'By the Looking-Glass' and 'A Castaway'. Her poetry was highly regarded by some while others found its realism—'A Castaway' addresses the issue of prostitution—hard to digest. She published a novel (pseudonymously), four plays, further poetry, and numerous essays and reviews, some of which, including two pieces on translation, are collected in *A Housewife's Opinions* (1879).

See further: *ODNB*; Janet Todd, ed., *Dictionary of British Women Writers* (London, 1989).   AP

WILLIAMS, Edward ('Iolo Morganwg') (1747–1826), poet and stonemason (and, at various times, farmer, bookseller, grocer, radical, Unitarian, opium-eater, and debtor) from Glamorgan, South Wales. A prime mover in the nineteenth-century Welsh cultural revival, Iolo is best known for his literary and historical forgeries, which include imitations of the fourteenth-century poet Dafydd ap Gwilym and the arcane Gorsedd ceremony, now part of the National Eisteddfod. Though not prolific in his publications, Iolo was a fervent mediator of Welsh culture, and his work reached a wide network of friends and supporters in literary and radical circles from the 1790s onwards. His influence is apparent in poems such as Robert Southey's *Madoc* (1804) and above all in the work of the lexicographer William Owen Pughe. Iolo's *Poems, Lyric and Pastoral* (1794) contains various translations, genuine and spurious, from Welsh poetic and bardic tradition; the translations in the posthumous *Iolo Manuscripts* (1848) added further pseudo-historical material to the mix. Iolo's vision of an unbroken druido-bardic tradition influenced notions of Welshness throughout the nineteenth century and became a model for subsequent cultural revivals in Brittany and Cornwall. An obsessive and paranoid character, he managed to alienate most of his friends during a long and difficult life dogged by ill health and financial hardship.

See further: *ODNB*; Prys Morgan, *Iolo Morganwg* (Cardiff, 1975). M-AC

WILLIAMS, Helen Maria (1761–1827), writer and translator, born in London, the daughter of an army officer. She received no formal education, but at 20 published her first verse story, 'Edwin and Eltruda', to some acclaim. From 1788 she lived almost entirely in Paris, sympathizing with the Girondists and chronicling the events of the Revolution in epistolary form. She knew Mme Roland well, and like her was imprisoned and vilified. In 1795 she completed a translation of *Paul et Virginie* by Bernardin de Saint-Pierre (also among her circle of friends), which was written 'amidst the horrors of Robespierre's tyranny' and became very popular. In the preface, she explains her omission of several pages of general observations on the grounds that although 'the gay and restless Frenchman listens attentively to long philosophical reflections... the serious Englishman requires... much bustle and stage effect'. Her other translations included Humboldt and Bonpland's massive *Personal Narrative of Travels to the... New Continent* (7 vols., 1814–29) and *The Leper of the City of Aoste* by Xavier de Maistre (1817). Both in London and Paris, she became renowned for her salons.

See further *ODNB*; Lionel D. Woodward, *Une Anglaise amie de la révolution française: Hélène-Maria Williams, et ses amis* (Paris, 1930). JY

WINKWORTH, Catherine (1827–1878), and **WINKWORTH, Susanna** (1820–1884), well known as translators of German texts. Both sisters were born in London and educated in Manchester, where the family moved in 1829. Among others they were taught by the Unitarian clergymen William Gaskell and James Martineau. The Winkworths moved in the Gaskells' social circle, and it was Mrs Gaskell who recommended Susanna to C. K. J. von Bunsen, the Prussian ambassador to London from 1842 to 1854, as a translator of a biography of B. G. Niebuhr. This project, for which Susanna did original research in Bonn, was published in 1852. Among her other translations were the anonymous *Theologia Germanica* (1854), the life and sermons of the German theologian Johannes Tauler (1857), Max Müller's

German Love (1858), and Bunsen's *Signs of the Times* (1856) and *God in History* (1868–70).

Bunsen also had a significant impact on the literary work of Catherine Winkworth who became known for her influential translations of German hymns from his collection. The first series of her *Lyra Germanica*, which went into over twenty editions, was published in 1855. Moreover, through her biographies Catherine made the lives of Amalia Sieveking (1863) and Pastor Fliedner (1867) known to English readers, and she was also the author of a history of German hymnody entitled *Christian Singers of Germany* (1869).

Both sisters visited and worked in Germany on several occasions. After a financial setback the Winkworth family moved to Clifton in 1862, where Catherine and Susanna became active in the promotion of education for women and in philanthropic work.

See further: *ODNB*; Margaret J. Shaen, *Memorials of Two Sisters: Susanna and Catherine Winkworth* (London, 1908); Peter Skrine, *Susanna and Catherine Winkworth* (Croydon, 1992). ss

WORDSWORTH, William (1770–1850), poet, born in Cockermouth, the son of a lawyer. He received a good classical education at Hawkshead Grammar School, studied at Cambridge, and spent a year in France at the height of the Revolution. After living in the West Country and visiting Germany with his friend Coleridge, he and his sister Dorothy settled in 1799 in their native Lake District, where they were to live for over fifty years; in 1802 William married Mary Hutchinson. A radical in his youth, he became more conservative with age. He published many volumes of poetry, becoming a classic in his own lifetime, and in 1843 he succeeded Southey as Poet Laureate.

Wordsworth's engagement with translation began at school and university. His early poems include versions of Anacreon, Catullus, Horace, and others; later he translated poems from modern languages, notably Italian. In 1802 he amused himself by modernizing passages from Chaucer's *Canterbury Tales* and *Troilus and Criseyde*, and in 1823 he embarked on a verse translation of Virgil's *Aeneid*, an attempt to produce a more faithful rendering than Dryden's. Friends and patrons reacted lukewarmly and he abandoned the project at Book III; the translation was not published in full until 1947.

See further: *ODNB*; Stephen Gill, *William Wordsworth: A Life* (Oxford, 1989); William Wordsworth, *Translations of Chaucer and Virgil*, ed. Bruce E. Graver (Ithaca, NY, 1998). PF

WORMELEY, Katharine Prescott (1830–1908), social pioneer, Civil War relief worker, and translator. Her parents were Virginians, but she was born in Ipswich and spent her formative years in England (with a three-year stay in 1839–42 in France and Switzerland). After her return to America she frequented the literary élite of New England. However, her translating career did not begin until the

1880s, after she had worked for the poor during the Civil War, organized supplies of clothing for soldiers, and later become the Superintendent of the Women's Department of the Lowell General Hospital in Rhode Island. After the war she founded the Newport Charity Organization and a Girls' Industrial School and also set up classes for poor women.

In her fifties she turned to translation, producing a very capable forty-volume version of Balzac's *Comédie humaine* (1885–93) single-handed—previously Balzac had been little known in America—followed in 1894–1904 by many works by Sand, Dumas, and Daudet and by a large number of French memoirs from the sixteenth, seventeenth, and eighteenth centuries (e.g. Brantôme, the duc de Saint-Simon, Élisabeth de France). Despite her prolific production, she is usually a reliable, and often a satisfying, translator.

See further: *DAB*; *ANB*.   ML

WRAXALL, Sir Frederic Charles Lascelles, third Baronet (1828–1865), soldier and man of letters, born in Boulogne, France. Educated at Shrewsbury School and Oxford, he spent most of his life abroad, dying in Vienna. He served in the Crimean War, but most of his life was devoted to writing. He succeeded to the baronetcy on the death of his uncle in 1863.

His publications show his interest in military matters and in modern European history, but also include many stories of crime and adventure. In the year of his death he published his *The Second Empire as Exhibited in French Literature*, a two-volume set of critical essays on current French writing. He is best known as the author of what was described as the authorized translation of Victor Hugo's *Les Misérables* (1862), in which he prided himself on his 'scrupulous fidelity'; although lacking in verve, this nearly complete and generally accurate translation was much reprinted. His translations also include two romances by Edmond About, two travel books by Henri-Alphonse Esquiros, seven adventure stories by Gustave Aimard, memoirs by the police chief Canler and the illusionist Robert-Houdin, and German works on war, travel, and adventure.

See further: *ODNB*.   PF

YORK POWELL, Frederick (1850–1904), lawyer, Icelandic scholar, and (from 1894) Regius Professor of Modern History at Oxford. He was educated at Rugby School and at Christ Church, Oxford. By 1870 he had translated *Hervarar saga* and *Gullfióris saga* (both now lost); his version of *Færeyinga saga* was published in 1896. He became a close colleague of Guðbrandur Vigfússon, after the Icelandic philologist arrived in Oxford to complete the *Icelandic–English Dictionary* (1869–74). The two men collaborated on *An Icelandic Prose Reader* (1879), *Corpus Poeticum Boreale* (1883), and *Origines Islandicae* (1905).

York Powell had a dualistic vision of life and letters. He dedicated his translation of *Færeyinga saga* to a professor and a fisherman; he embraced both roles himself, dressing in navy blue fisherman's clothing to associate himself with the Viking Age virtues he identified in deep-sea fishermen. He believed that medieval

Faeroese society had been nourished by the interaction of earthiness and saintliness dramatized in *Færeyinga saga*. York Powell admired the neutrality of medieval saga narrators and loathed modern Christian moralists. In the words of his biographer, York Powell 'loved heathendom, being himself a heathen' (Elton 1906: I, 29). He was a founding father of Ruskin College, Oxford.

See further: *ODNB*; Oliver Elton, *Frederick York Powell: A Life*, 2 vols. (Oxford, 1906). AW

Index

Note: References in bold figures denote major discussions, those in italics refer to the biographical sketches of Chapter 12.

References to foreign authors and their works, and to foreign literatures, are to English translations, unless otherwise indicated. The work of individual translators is indexed primarily under their own names rather than that of the source author.

Abbott, Thomas Kingsmill 482–3
About, Edmond 93
acculturation *see* domestication
accuracy 61, 74, 78–9
   in USA 24, 26, 28, 29
   see also fidelity; literal translation
Achilles Tatius 203
Adams, John (1704–1740) 28–9
Adams, John (1735–1826) 499
Adams, John Quincy 22
Adamson, John 265, 267, 268
adaptation 36, 41–2, 114–15
   based on literal translations 113, 114–15, 297, 350
   fiction 36, 41–2, 371–2, 380
   for musical performance 218, 225, 421, 422
   Sappho 61, 78, 160
   see also under children's literature; Morris, William; theatre, popular
Addison, Joseph 421, 421
Adlington, William 204
adventure novel 239–40, 371–3, 401
advertising 87, 390
Aeschylus 11, **178–80**
   Agamemnon 67, 75, 102, 119, **179–80**;
      Browning 52, 62, 67, 70, 79, 106, 179–80, 183–4
   poets inspired by 157, 178
   Potter's complete translation 158, 178
   [*Prometheus Bound*] 26, **178–9**; Barrett Browning 77–8, 111, 112–13, 178; Webster 66, 74, 77, 179
   Seven Against Thebes 26
Aesop, fables of 202–3, 399
African literature 99, 436, 437, 439
Aimard, Gustave (*pseud.* of Olivier Gloux) 93, 241, 374
Ainu folk tales 365
Aladdin, tale of 395
Alarcón, Pedro Antonio de 271
alcaics 15, 193–4, 194–5, 197
Aldana, Francisco de 264
Alexander, Cecil Frances 418
alexandrines 179, 235

Alfieri, Vittorio, Count 254
Alford, Henry 444
Alha 351
All the Year Round 41, 42
Allison, Alfred Richard 89, 204
alliteration 191, 192, 281–3
Alma Tadema, Laurence 237
Amazing Stories 378
American Folk-Lore, Journal of 438
Amiel, Henri-Frédéric 237
Anacreon 26, 99, 160
Ancient Classics for English Readers 118
Andersen, Hans Christian 138, 139, 394, **286–7**, **397–8**
   secondary translation 91, 92, 287
Anderson, Rasmus Bjørn 289, *507*
Angiolieri, Cecco 256
Anglo-Saxon literature 51–2, 114, 274, 278, 279–80, **281–3**
Anglo-Saxonisms in translation 51–2, 70, 114, 173, 174–5, 192, 281
anonymity 88, 125
   amateur translators 6, 38, 101–2
   norms 74–5, 86, 264–5, 394, 489
   in USA 20, 22
Anquetil du Perron, Abraham-Hyacinthe 458
anthologies 75, 182, 195, 226, 236, 237
   French, of German literature 212
   German theatrical 218
   in USA **27–9**, 264–5
anthropology 163, 180
Antier, Benjamin 386
Anti-Nicene Library, Clark's 448–9
Anugītā 463
Appleyard, E. 45
Apuleius 204
The Arabian Nights Entertainments see The Thousand and One Nights
Arabic literature 4, 7, 144, **323–31**
   cribs 324, 325
   in Sacred Books of the East 120, **466–7**
   see also *The Thousand and One Nights*
archaeology 23, 180

archaizing translation 63, **51–2**, 67–70
  Anglo-Saxonizing 51–2, 70, 114, 174–5, 192, 281
  Arnold-Newman debate 52, 56, **67–70**, 168–9, 173, 178–9, 432
  of Bible, American abandonment 456
  of Greek texts 70, 122, 162, 173–4, 205, 477; *see also* Browning, Robert (Aeschylus' *Agamemnon*) *and under* Homer
  of medieval and Renaissance texts 12, 13–14, 52, 70, 215, 231, 232, 233, 258, 262–3
  in physical presentation of translations 114
  The Thousand and One Nights 329
  see also biblical language, translations in
Archer, Charles 290
Archer, Frances 290
Archer, William 95, 290, *507–8*
Ardhamāgadhī 464, **466**
Ariosto, Ludovico 139, 248, **249–50**, 253
Aristophanes 55, **184–5**
  The Birds 11, 15, 181, 184, 185
Aristotle 473–5
Ariwara no Narihira 364–5
Armour, Margaret 215
Árnason, Jón 291
Arndt, Ernst Moritz 213
Arnim, Bettina von (*née* Brentano) 27
Arnold, Sir Edwin 161, 164, 236, 333–4, 348–9, *508*
Arnold, Matthew 14, **67–70**, 165, 213, 313
  on Celtic character 294, 301
  on classical authors 159, 164, 180, 190, 478, 479; *see also under* Homer
  on cultured society 46, 213
  'Sohrab and Rustum' 338
Arnold, Thomas 201
Arriaza, Juan Bautista de 265
Asbjørnsen, P. C. 398
asclepiads 193
Ash, Edward 212
Ashurst, Eliza 239
Asiatic Society of Japan 363, 364, 365, 367
Aston, William George 363–4, 365, *508–9*
Aśvaghoṣa; *Buddhacarita* 348, 464, 467
Athanasius, St 448
Atharva Veda 461
The Athenaeum 146, 309
Atkinson, James 337–8
'Aṭṭār 337
Auber, Daniel-François-Esprit 422
Aubertin, John James 267, 268, 269
Aucassin et Nicolette 231
Augustine of Hippo, St 139, 447, 448
Aulnoy, Marie-Catherine Le Jumel de Barneville, Comtesse d' 394–5, 396
Aurelius, Marcus 139, 479
Austen, Jane 105, 218, 373

Austin (*née* Taylor), Sarah 125, **126**, 127, 399, *509*
  and German 126, 214, 492
  and history 489, 491, 492
  on translation 126, 128, 492
Australia 377
authorship, attitudes to 20–1, 28, 64, 65
Aveling, Edward 130, 494
Avesta 458, 466
Avrillon, Jean-Baptiste Élie 446
Ayrton, William 422
azioni sacre 420, 425
Aztec literature 438

Babbitt, Irving 122
Baculard d'Arnaud, François-Thomas-Marie de 372
Bagehot, Walter 235–6
Bagnell, Gibbons 99
Baillot, A. 88
Bain, R. Nisbet 397
Bakunin, Mikhail 494
'Baldrs draumar' 275
Ball, William 425
ballad metre translations 119, 192, 295, 431–2
ballade 11, 232, 233
ballads and folk songs 4, 72, 106, 430, **434–6**, 439
  Celtic 4, 49, 51, 304
  Central and East European 309, 310–11, 435, 436
  Danish 287, 434, 436
  German 4, 106, 227, 434–5
  Homeric epic and 68, 158–9, 431–2
  literary 4, 227, 434–5
  and nationalism 310–11
  Spanish 4, 106, 139, 262, **263–4**, 434, 435–6
Ballard, Susan 366–7
Balzac, Honoré de 42, 63, 139, 142, **240–1**, 375
  Dent's *Comédie humaine* 86, 87, 89, 94, 510
  Dowson's translations 37, 106
  translation begins late 34, 39, 42, 44
  US editions 44, 241
Bāṇa Bhaṭṭa; *Harṣacarita* 348
Bancroft, George 21
Baptist Church, American 444
Barbauld, Anna 219
bardic tradition, Celtic 103, 301, 302
Barham, Francis Foster 478
Baring-Gould, Sabine 418
Barker, Theodore T. 426
Barlow, Joel 499–500
Barnard, Mordaunt 171
Barnes, William 446
Barnett, C. Z. 386
Barnum, Phineas Taylor 423
Barrow, William 93, 240
Barth, C. G. 400

Bartholomew, William 181, 424
Basford de Wilson, F. A. 475
Bashkirtseff, Marie 238
Basile, Giambattista 398
Baudelaire, Charles 11, 13, 235, **237**, 377
Bax, Ernest Belfort 483, 485
Beal, Samuel 467
Beardsley, Aubrey 185, 189
Bechstein, Ludwig 397
Beckford, William 36, 395–6
Beckwith-Lohmeyer, Charles 287
Beddoes, Thomas 212
Bedell, G. T. 400
Belgium 37, 237
Belgravia 41
Bell, Clara Courtenay 94, *509–10*
Bell, John 220
Bell & Daldy (*later* George Bell & Sons) 8, 53–4
Bellingham, William 490
Bellini, Vincenzo 423
Belot, Adolphe 378
Bengali literature 99, 351–2
Benjamin, Park 240
Bennett, Arnold 315
Bentley, Richard (publisher) 8, 41, 87, 88
Bentley, Richard (scholar) 172
Bentley's Miscellany 145, 235
Beowulf 51–2, 114, 274, **281–3**
Béranger, Pierre-Jean 235–6, 426–7
Bere, C. S. 414
Bergner, L. T. 254
Berlioz, Hector 426
Bernard, Charles 387
Bernard, John Henry 117, 482
Bernard of Morlaix, *or* Cluny 416
Bernardes, Diogo 263
Bernardin de Saint-Pierre, Jacques-Henri 138, 141, **238**
Berne Convention *see under* copyright
Berners, John Bourchier, second Baron 231
Berni, Francesco 252
Berquin, Arnaud 399
Bhagavad Gītā 341, 342, 343, 349, 351, 463
Bhagavata Purāṇa 347–8, 458
Bhavabhūti 346, 352
Bibelot 237
Bible **443–6, 451–7**
 American Standard Version 456
 Authorized (King James) Version 14–15, 105; revision 444, 451–7
 Clare's paraphrases 446
 commentaries on 138, 139, 443
 dialect versions 446
 literal or literary translation 445, 451–7
 New Testament 443, 444, 445, 451, 452; Revised Version 451, **452–4**
 Old Testament 140, 443, 444–5, 446; Revised Version 452, **454–6**
 Psalms 443, 445–6
 Revised Version 444, **451–7**
 US translations 444, 445, **456**
 Webster's revision 444, 456
biblical language, translations in
 FitzGerald's 79
 Homeric 162, 173–4
 Jowett's Plato 122, 477
 Legge's Chinese prayers 359
 Norton's Dante 122
 Palmer's Qur'ān 466–7
 Robinson's *Shāhnāma* 338
 Southey's *El Cid* 262–3
Biggs, Maude Ashhurst 312
Bingham, Caleb 373
Binyon, Laurence 364
biography 137, 138, 139, 148, 150, 151
 Chinese 357
Birch, Jonathan 215
Bishop, Henry Rowley 422
Bjørnson, Bjørnstjerne 139, 286, **289**
Black, John 248, 501
Black, Robert 491
The Black Cabinet 44
Blackie (publishers) 492–3
Blackie, John Stuart 118–19
Blackmore, R. D. 191
Blackwood's Edinburgh Magazine 3, 5, 87, **143–5**, 147, 214, 235
 reviews and essays 143, 146, 150, 313
Blake, William 216
Blanc, Louis 39, 88
blank verse translations
 Dante 29, 67, 250, 256
 French alexandrines 235
 German poetry 220, 223–4
 Homer 29, 170–1, 171–2, 174
 Lucretius 190
Blind, Mathilde 481, 487
Bloomfield, Maurice 461
Boas, Franz 438
Boccaccio, Giovanni 4, 54, 254, **258**
Boden, Lieut Colonel Joseph 347
Boehme, Jakob 216
Boer War 49, 138
Bogan, Zachary 173
Bogue, David 8, 56
Bohn, Henry G. **8–9**, 53–4, 140–1, 165
 Classical Library 42, 65, **165**
 literalism 61, 63, 65, 78, 165
 own translations 8, 236, 502–3
 Philosophical Library; Kant 482
 Standard Library **8–9**, 42, 65, 214
 standards of taste 53–4, 203–4
 and translators 75, 87
 widens readership 8–9, 42, 46

Boïeldieu, François-Adrien 422
Boileau, Daniel 89–90
Boldey, Ella 396
Bolland, W. E. 475
Bombay University 345
Bonaparte, Prince Lucien 446
Boner, Charles 397
Boniface, Joseph-Xavier (*pseud.*
　Xavier Saintine) 238
Bonpland, Aimé 501
booksellers 6, 377
Booth, Eleanor Worthington 493
Booth's Library 38–9
Boothby, Sir Brooke 202
Borg, Selma 289, 291
Borrow, George 301, 308, *510*
　and ballads 106, 287, 436
　and East European literature 310, 312, 313
Borthwick, Jane Laurie 414
Bosanquet, Bernard 483, 484
Boswell, Robert Bruce 234
Boucicault, Dion 77, 386, 388
Bougainville, Louis-Antoine de 38
Bourdillon. F. W. 231
Bourget, Paul 241
Bourne, Vincent 159
Bouvier, Alexis 378
bowdlerization *see* expurgation
Bowen, Sir Charles 191
Bowring, Edgar 93, 213, 225, **226–7**
Bowring, Sir John 37–8, **71–2**, 100, 102,
　308–10, *510–11*
　anthologies 71–2, 75
　and ballads 72, 264, 436
　metrical translation 72, 264
　Portuguese poetry 265, 268
　principles of translation 66, 71–2
　on Russian power 71, 311
Boy's Own Paper 379
Boyd, Erskine 377
Boyd, Henry 246–7, *511*
Boylan, R. D. 93, 217
Boyle, Eleanor Vere 399
Braddon, M. E. 37, 41, 45, 376, 389
Bradley, Katharine *see* Field, Michael
Brækstad, Hans Lien 290
Brahma Sūtra (*Vedānta Sūtra*) 461
Brāhmaṇas 459, **461**
Brazilian literature 100
Bremer, Fredrika 39, 92, 139, 286, **288–9**
Brentano, Bettina (Bettina von Arnim) 27
Brentano, Clemens 397
Breton literature 145, 294, 301, **304**
breviaries 414, 415
Bṛhadāraṇyaka-upaniṣad 349–50
Bridaine, Jacques 417–18
Bridges, Robert Seymour 204, 417, *511–12*
Bridgman, Elijah 357
Brinton, Daniel 438

Brisebarre, Edouard 387
Bristol 212, 213
British and Foreign Library 7
British Museum 92–3, 99, 101, 103
Brækstad, H. L. 398
Brontë, Charlotte 15, 37, 105, 234
Brontë, Emily 37, 105
Brooke, Charlotte 295
Brooks, Charles Timothy 21, 27, 28, 213, *512*
Brooks, Louise 402
Brotherhood Publishing Company 316
Brough, Robert B. 426–7
Broughton, Thomas Duer 351
Brown, David 453
Brown, Marie Adelaide 289, 291
Brown, T. E. 303
Brown, Thomas 64
Browne, Robert William 474
Browning, Elizabeth Barrett 77–8, **111–13**, 178,
　254, *512–13*
　translations: Apuleius 204; Dante 75, 112;
　　Greek Christian poets 159; Heine 112,
　　226; *Prometheus Bound* 77–8, 111,
　　112–13, 178; Theocritus 163–4;
　　Nonnus 159
Browning, Robert 173, 178, 183–4, 336, *513*
　Aeschylus' *Agamemnon* 52, 62, 67, 70, 79,
　　106, **179–80**, 183–4
　Aristophanes' Apology 183–4
　Balaustion's Adventure 183–4
　The Ring and the Book 76
Brun, Friederike 108, 221
Bryant, William Cullen 29, 171, 264, 435
Büchner, Georg 213, 218
Buckley, Theodore Alois 86, 163, 182, 475
Buddhism 344–5, 347, 348–9, 458, **463–6**
Bühler, Georg 462
Bulgarian literature 140, 312
Bulwer Lytton, Edward *see* Lytton, Edward
　Bulwer
Bunsen, C. K. J. von 126, 128, 412, 414
Buntline, Ned (*pseud.* of E. Z. C. Judson) 376
Bunyan, John 99
Bürger, Gottfried August 219, 434
Burges, George 75
Burke, Edmund 372
burlesque 185, 383, 423
Burnet, John 477
Burnham, I. G. 236
Burnouf, Eugène 458
Burns, James 394
Burns, Robert 28
Burton, (*née* Arundell), Lady Isabel 100,
　513, 514
Burton, Sir Richard Francis 53, 101, 189, 265,
　333, 349, *513–14*
　Camões 100, 101, 267–8, 269
　The Thousand and One Nights 53, 98, 326,
　　328–9; preface and notes 50–1, 328

Burton's Gentleman's Magazine 376–7
Busby, Thomas 478
Busch, Wilhelm 404
Bushby, Anna S. 287
Busk (*née* Blair), Mary Margaret *514*
Butcher, S. H. 173, 174, 475
Butler, Samuel 175–6
Byerley, J. Scott (*pseud.* John Scott Ripon) 253
Byrnes, Thomas F. 375
Byron, George Gordon, sixth Baron 14, 57, 343, 372, *514–15*
  Beppo 16, 248
  and classical literature 105, 155, 157, 160, 178
  Don Juan 157, 248
  and Goethe 221, 222
  and Italian literature 15, 16, 247, 248, 254
  translations and imitations 138, 435; Catullus 189; Dante 75, 246; Horace 76, 105, 155, 193, 197; in *Hours of Idleness* 76, 105, 189; Juvenal 196; Martial 196; Pulci 248; Spanish poetry 262, 264

Caesar, Julius 201
Caigniez, Louis 386
Caillé, René 38
Caird, Edward 122, 483
Calcutta 50, 325, 345, 348
Calcutta Review 351
Caldéron de la Barca, Pedro 269–70
  popularity 139, 262, 265
  translations 61, 102, 223, 264
Callaway, Henry 439
calligraphic editions, Morris's 114
Callimachus 159
Calverley, Charles Stuart 100, *515*
  translations 164, 171, 182, 191, 194–5
Calvert, George Henry 213
Calvin, John 139
Cambridge University 117, 118, 119, 120, 181, 360, 348
Cameron, Alexander 302
Camões, Luís de 98, 139, 262, 265, **267–9**
  lyric poetry 100, 101, 261, 263, 268
  Os Lusíadas 65, 100, 101, 262, **267–8**, **268–9**
Campbell, Alexander 303
Campbell, Jane Montgomery 414
Campbell, John Francis 100, 302, *515–16*
Campbell, Lewis 119, 181, 182
Campe, J. H. 400, 401
Canada 26, 483
canon of world literature 7, 8, 45–6
Capacelli, Albergati 254
Cardus, Neville 95
Carey and Lea 31
Carlyle, John Aitken 141
Carlyle, Joseph 324

Carlyle, Thomas 6, **109–11**, 430, *516*
  The French Revolution 111
  and German literature 110, 213, 215, 225; promotes in Britain 15, 16–17, 22, 109–11, 213, 215, 216–17
  Life of Schiller 74, 213
  principles of translation 62, 71, 79, 216, 217–18, 225
  Sartor Resartus 15, 110
  translations 71, **109–11**, 213, 411–12, 492; Goethe's *Wilhelm Meister* 78–9, 110, 111, 213, 216–17, 217–18, 225
Carmichael, Alexander 100, 302
Carolan 295, 296
Carové, F. W. 399
Carrington, Henry 234–5, 304, 447
Carroll, Lewis (*pseud.* of C. L. Dodgson) 111
carvals, Manx 303
Cary, Henry Francis 99, 184, 476, *516–17*
  Dante's *Divine Comedy* 4, 67, 99, 141–2, 250–1
  The Early French Poets 99, 231–2
Cassell 88, 141
Casti, Giambattista 252
Castlereagh, Robert Stewart, Viscount 36, 37
Caswall, Edward 415
Cattley, H. 312
Catullus, Gaius Valerius 75, **188–9**, 197
Cavalcanti, Guido 12–13
Cayley, C. B. 67
Celtic literature **294–307**
  folk and fairy tales 398, 437
  imitations and forgeries 299–300; *see also* Ossianic literature
  hymns 418
  politics of translation 51, 294–5, 304–5
  publication data 137, 139, 144, 149
  relationships with English 295, 298
  revivals 294, 301, 304, 305
  scholarship 119, 304–5
  see also bardic tradition; Breton, Cornish, Irish, Manx, Scottish *and* Welsh literature; *and under* ballads and folk songs
censorship 53–5
  in India 99, 351–2
  informal, by publishers, bookshops, and libraries 40–1, 53
  obscenity laws 53–4, 230, 242, 349
  politically-motivated 54, 99, 351–2
  private publication or performance avoids 53, 55, 88, 242, 327, 349
  see also expurgation; immorality
Central and Eastern Europe, literatures of 93, 117, **308–19**
  folklore 100, 310–11
  publication 136, 137, 138, 139–40, 149
  see also individual national literatures and under ballads and folk songs

Cervantes (Saavedra), Miguel de 267
  Don Quijote 139, 141, 262, **265–7**, 402
Challoner, Richard 444, 447
Chalmers, John 355–6
Chamberlain, Basil Hall 363, 364–5, 366, *517*
Chambers's Edinburgh Journal 375
Chamisso, Adalbert von 396
Champion, Joseph 337
chanson de geste 231
chapbooks 395
Chapman, George 69
Chapman, John 289
Chapman and Hall 45, 376
Chapponier, Alexandre 386
Chariton 203
Charlemont, James, late Earl of 247
Chartism 95, 236, 494
Chartres, J. S. 241
Chase, D. P. 474
Chateaubriand, François-René, Vicomte de 235, 238, 373
Chatelain, Mme de 397, 403
Chatrian, Alexandre 41, 240
Chaube, Pandit Ram Gharib 351
Chaucer, Geoffrey 105
Chavchavadze, Ilya 312
Chavette, Eugène 377
cheap editions 34, 35, **42–6**, 72–4, 486, 498, 499, 503
  translators 91, 93, 271, 489
  see also dime novels; penny press; series, publishing; shilling editions
Chenery, Thomas 325
Cherbuliez, Victor 241
Cherokee literature 437
Chertkov, Vladimir 316
Chiabrera, Gabriello 105, 252–3
Childe, C. O. 254
children's literature 15, 34, **394–407**
  adaptations 394, 395, 396; Aesop 203, 399; *Don Quijote* 266, 402; *Mabinogion* 403; *The Thousand and One Nights* 15, 395
  adventure stories 401
  Chinese 357
  contemporary life, stories of 402
  fairy tales 15, 436, 437, **394–8**
  folklore and folk tales 15, 366–7, 394, 398, 436, 437, 439
  fantasy 402–3
  French 231, 379, 394–5, 399, 401, 402
  German 15, 394, 395–7, 399–400, 401, 402–3, 403–4, 436
  history 401
  moral, religious, and didactic tales 398–400
  Norwegian 394, 398
  in periodicals 379
  picture books 394, 395, **403–4**
  publication data 137–8
  Robinsonades 400–1
  writers influenced by 203, 498
  see also Andersen, Hans Christian
Childs, M. Anna 402
China Review 358
Chinese literature 5, 7, 17, 50, **355–62**
  bibliography 356, 357–8, 360
  dialects 359
  periodicals 357–8
  promotion in Britain 99, 117, 360
  publication data 137, 140, 144
  Ruist ('Confucian') classics 355, 356, 357, 358–9, 467
  in Sacred Books of the East 120, 359, **467**
  transliteration systems 355–6
  see also Giles, Herbert Allen; Legge, James
Chinese Recorder 358
Chinese Repository 357, 357, 358
Chinese-English, US 30
Chorley, Henry F. 424
Chowkhambha Sanskrit Series Office 352
Christian texts *see under* sacred and religious texts
Christie, Ella R. 398
chronicles, medieval French 231
Chrysanthemum 366
Chulalankarana, King of Siam 464
Church, Frederic Edwin 503
Church Fathers 98, 139, 160, 443, **447–9**
Church of England 156, 411–19, 447–8
  see also Oxford Movement
Churchill, James 220
Churchill, John 310
Cicero, Marcus Tullius 202, **204–5**, 478
El Cid 106, 262–3, 432
Cinthio, Giovanni Battista Giraldi 254
civil service, British 117, 156, 489
Clairmont, Claire 222
Clare, John 446
Clarion 316
Clark, J. W. 266, 267
Clark, T. & T. 138, 448–9
classic translations reissued 9, 141, 449
classical 105, 138, 200, 205
  French 231, 233, 240
  Iberian 65, 139, 262, 265–6, 267
  Italian 139, 247
classical literature **153–207**
  cribs 63, 65, 86, 91, 112–13, 138, 164–5, 183, 201, 202, 233
  fidelity in translation 48, 63, 74, 112–13, 191
  and Indo-European philology 51
  methods applied to Sanskrit 350
  overview of translation 157–60
  publication data 136–7, 138–9, 149
  quantity in verse 66, 69–70
  readership 46, 118, 156, 165

status 24–5, 48, 155–7
see also individual authors and genres; Greek, ancient; Latin, classical; *and under* education; politics; women
Classicism, German 213, 226
Claudel, Paul 237
Claudius, Matthias 414
Clausewitz, Karl von 38
Clough, Arthur Hugh 15, 76–7, 175, 195, 200, 517–18
Cobbett, Susan 402
Cocks, Charles 87
Coe, Ernest Oswald 235, 236
Cogswell, Joseph G. 21, 22
Colburn, Henry 7–8, 378
Cole, J. W. 491
Cole, Thomas 500
Colebrook, H. T. 458
Coleridge, Samuel Taylor 15, **107–9**, **219–20**, 343, 430, *518*
  and Dante 246, 250
  and German literature 37, **107–9**, 110, 212, **219–21**
  'Hymn before Sun-Rise' 108
  influence of translation on writing 15, 220
  plagiarism 17, 109, 221
  poetic language 221
  on Pope's Homer 172
  on Seneca 478
  translations: Brun 108; Goethe 108, 221; Schelling 17, 109, 221; Schiller 75, 107, 108, 109, **219–21**
  on Virgil 159, 190, 191
Collins, W. Lucas 118
Collins, Wilkie 35, 37, 254, 372
Collodi, Carlo 394, 403
Collyer, Joseph 216
Collyer, Mary 215–16
colonial rule 27, **49–51**, 248, 267
  British in India 323, 332, 344, 462
  knowledge of languages 98, 99, 324, 325, 326, 332, 341, 351
  power relations 49–51, 340, 344, 350
  translation of local literature 439
Columba, St 418
commentary, learned 50–1, 179, 220, 346
  see also notes
Communist Manifesto 494
compensation, principle of 220–1
composition-translation boundary 64, 75–7, 264
Comte, Auguste 7, 127, 128, 493–4
'concealed' translation 36, 41–2
  see also adaptation
Confucius (Master Kŏng) and Confucian classics 355, 356, 357, 358–9, 360, 467
Congreve, Richard 494
Conington, John 118, **119–20**, 159, 188, 192, 193–4, *518–19*

Conrad, Joseph 14
Constant, Benjamin 238
Contemporary Review 7
contemporary translation 13
Conybeare, J. J. 279, 282
Cooney, Myron A. 241
Cooper, Edith *see* Field, Michael
Cooper, James Fenimore 21, 373
Cooper, Revd Mr (*pseud.* of Richard Johnson) 395
copy, definition of 65–7
copyright 20–1, 43, **55–6**, 147, 388–9, 391–2
  Anglo-French convention 56, 388
  Berne Convention for the Protection of Literary and Artistic Works 43, 56, 391–2
  British law 20, 21, **55–6**, 388; statute of 1710 55; Copyright Act (1814) 55; Dramatic Copyright Act (1833) 388; International Copyright Act (1838) 55; Literary Copyright Act (1842) 55, 56; International Copyright Act (1852) 388; International Copyright Act (1886) 391–2
  in France 56, 388
  in popular theatre 77, **388–9**, 391–2
  secondary rights 389
  US law 20–1, 43, 56, 391–2; International Copyright Act (1891) 21, 43, 56, 391–2
Cornhill Magazine 41, 147, 240, 364
Cornish literature 294, 301, **303–4**
Cornwall, Barry (*pseud.*) 258
Cory, William 159
Costello, Louisa Stuart 231, 232, 252, 304, 336
Cottin, Sophie (*née* Marie Ristaud) 238, 401
Cotton, Charles 233
Cotton, W. C. 404
Courtiras, Cisterne de, Vicomtesse de Poilloüe de Saint-Mars (Madame la Comtesse Dash) 39
Cousin de Grainville, Jean-Baptiste 378–9
Coutier, Louis 491
Coventry 213, 486
Cowell, Edward Byles 5–6, 102, 335, **348**, 461, 464
Cowley, Abraham 61
Cowper, William 69, 158, 161,170, 171, 175
Cox, Frances Elizabeth 412
Craddock, Thomas 493
Craig, Mary A. 258
Craigie, W. A. *and* J. K. 398
Craigie, Sir William 291
Crane, Lucy 396
Crane, Walter 396, 402
Crawford, John 433
Crawley, Richard 200
Crawley, Rowland 315

cribs
  Arabic 324
  classical languages 65, 86, 138, 165, 183, 201, 202, 233
  French 230
crime, mystery and detective fiction 17, 23, 43, 371, **375–8**
Crimean War 49, 138, 311
Crisis 492
criticism
  German 481, 482, 483, 485
  publication of translated 137, 138, 148, 150, 151
  of translation, in periodicals 143, **146–7**, 150–1
Croker, John Wilson 40, 239, 490
Crompton, A. 257
Crooke, William 351
Crosland, Mrs Newton 236
Crowell, T. Y. and Co. 87, 88–9
Croxall, Samuel 202–3
Cruikshank, George 396
Cruikshank, Percy 402
Cumberland, Richard 184
Cundall, Joseph 394
Curran, Henry Grattan 296
Currie, I. 217
Curtin, Jeremiah 100, 298, 311, 312, *519*
Curwen, Harry 235, 237
Cushing, Frank 438
Custine, Astolphe, Marquis de 38
Cuvelier de Tyre, Jean 386
Czech literature 49, 309, 312

Dafydd ap Gwilym 300, 301
Dahlmann, F. C. 490
Dakyns, H. G. 201
Dale, Thomas 181
Dallas, Robert Charles 490
D'Alton, John 296
Dalton, John 447
Dandin 346
Danish literature 144, 145, 279, **286–7**, 378
  hymns 411, 418
  oral 287, 434, 436
  secondary translation 91, 287
  see also Andersen, Hans Christian
D'Annunzio, Gabriele 13
Dante Alighieri 4, 15–16, 63, 76, 122, 141
  publication 139, 141–2, 142–3
  revaluing of 4, 15–16, 246, 256, 258
  metrical translations 66–7, 112, 256
  translators: Barrett Browning 112; Byron 66–7, 246; Cary 4, 67, 99, 141–2, **250–1**; Emerson 29; Longfellow 29, 141, 256; Norton 121, **122**, 256; Rossetti 12–13, 255, 256; Shelley 15–16, 106, 246; Wicksteed 141

WORKS
  Divina Commedia 29, 75, 121, **122**, **246–7**, **250–1**, 256; *Inferno* 76, 256; Cantos V and XXXIII 246–7; *Purgatorio* 246, 256
  minor poems 246
  La vita nuova 29, 122, 255
Daoism 467
da Ponte, Lorenzo 252
Darby, Howard Nelson 445
Darmesteter, James 466
Darwin, Charles 502, 503
Dasent, Sir George Webbe 277, 280–1, 398, *519–20*
Dash, Madame la Comtesse (*pseud.* of Cisterne de Courtiras, Vicomtesse de Poilloüe de Saint-Mars) 39
Daudet, Alphonse 86, 241
Davidson, John 13, 106
Davies, Edward 'Celtic' 301
Davies, J. Llewelyn 476
Davies, John Fletcher 67
Davis, Henry 476
Davis, John Francis 356–7
Davis, Matilda 396
Day, Angel 203
Dayman, John 67
Dean of Lismore, Book of the 302
de Benham-Yakobi, Julius 216
decadence 4, 37, 203, 214–15, 237, 258
  Italian 253, 258
Defoe, Daniel 400
Delacour, Alfred 388
Demmler, Franz 93
democracy 155, 473, 476, 477, 491–2
Demosthenes 202
demotic languages 30, 345, 350–3, 376
  see also dialects; oral literature
Dennery, Adolphe Philippe 386
Dent, J. M.
  Balzac's *Comédie humaine* 86, 87, 89
  Everyman's Library 9, 196, 215, 317
  Temple Classics 45
De Quincey, Thomas Penson 3, 15, 99n, 107, *520*
Derby, Edward Stanley, Earl of 171–2
Desbordes-Valmore, Marceline 235
detective fiction 17, 23, 43, 376–7, 377–8
de Vere, Aubrey 252
de Vere, Sir Stephen 194
devotional texts 98, 443, **446–7**
Dhammapada 458, 465
dharma, works on **461–2**, 463
The Dial 21, 25, 27, 28, 145–6, 237
dialects 28
  British 302, 398, 446
  Chinese 359
  US 30

diaries and memoirs, French 237–8
Dickens, Charles 15, 21, 41, 105
Dickins, Frederick Victor 99, 363, 364, 365–6, 520
dictionaries
  Chinese 355–6
  of demotic languages 30
  foreign-language 92, 94, 95
  Japanese 366
Diderot, Denis 234
difference between languages 25–6, 28, 64, 67, 71–4
  Celtic and English 295, 298, 301–2, 303
  English and ancient Greek 106, 180
  German and ancient Greek 222
dime novels 377
Dinis, Júlio (*pseud.* of Joaquim Gomes Coelho) 271
Dircks (*née* Goddard), Sara Hay 485
Disraeli, Benjamin 249
Ditson, Oliver 424
Dobson, Susannah 247
Dodgson, C. L. (*pseud.* Lewis Carroll) 111
Doherty, Hugh 493
Dole, Helen B. 402
Dole, Nathan Haskell 95, 316–17, *521*
domestication 48–9, **52–5**, 56–7, 63–4, 68, 71–4, 79–80
  of children's literature 394, 395, 396
Donaldson, James 449
Donizetti, Gaetano 423
Doré, Gustave 141, 238
Dostoevsky, Fyodor Mikhailovich 43, 313, 314, 317
Dowden, Edward 236
Downman, Hugh 275
Dowson, Ernest Christopher 13, 37, 88, 106, 241, 242, *521*
Doyle, Arthur Conan 377
drama
  Chinese 356, 357
  French 24, 55, 56, 63, 77, 100, 233, 234, 236, 388
  German 5, 86, **218–21**; *see also* Schiller, Johann Christoph Friedrich von
  Greek classical 46, 55, 62, 138–9, **158**, **178–87**; performance 119, 180, 181; *see also individual Greek dramatists*
  Italian 254, 258
  Japanese: 364–5, 366
  Norwegian *see* Ibsen, Henrik
  private performances 55, 119
  Spanish 267; *see also* Calderón de la Barca, Pedro
  publication data 136, 137, 138, 148, 150, 151
  theatre translation 55, 77, 218–21, 234, 236, 388
  see also theatre, popular

Drugulin, William 400
Drummond, William Hamilton 190, 296, 298, 478
Dryden, John 63, 64, 71, 194, 200
  Virgil 71, 105, 119, 138, 141, 190
du Boisgobey, Fortuné 43, 375, **377–8**
Dublin
  Abbey Theatre 258
  periodicals 145, 296, 297
  Trinity College 117, 118
Ducange, Victor-Henri-Joseph-Brahain 24
Ducray-Duminil, François-Guillaume 385
Duff, Robert ffrench 267–8, 269
Duffield, Alexander James 265
Dugdale, William 45, 376
Dulcken, Henry W. 240, 397, 404
Dumarsais, César Chesneau 164
Dumas, Alexandre ('Dumas *père*') 8, 39, 77, 100, 239, **240**, 241
  children's reading of 402, 403
  publication 8, 44, 45, 89, 93, 139, 141, 240
Dumas, Alexandre ('Dumas *fils*') 54–5
Dumoulin, James 333
Dunlap, William 24, 384
Dunn, Catherine Hannah 414
Duse, Eleonora 258
Dutch literature 95, 137, 140, 144, 145, 149, 378
Duyckinck, Evert Augustus 21, 23–4
Dvořák, Antonin 426
Dyde, Samuel Walters 483, 484

earlier translation embedded in new 89, 181
East India Company 4, 340, 341, 343, 462
  language training 325, 332, 345
eastern literatures 4–5, 7, **49–51**, **321–68**
  European reaction against 343–4
  knowledge of languages in west 323, 324, 325, 332, 341, 345–6, 347, 358
  publication data 136–7, 140, 142, 144, 149
  see also individual literatures and Sacred Books of the East; *The Thousand and One Nights*
Eastlake, Elizabeth 129
Eastwick, Edward 333
Eça de Queirós, José Maria 271
Echegaray y Eizaguirre, José 271
Eckenstein, L. 397
Eckermann, Johann Peter 27, 28, 214, 501
economy, political 493–5
Eddas 29, 275, 276–7, 280
Edgar, John 163
Edinburgh
  intellectual circles 180, 181, 211–12, 213, 219, 489–90
  publishing 138, 443, 448–9
  University 119

editor-translators 90–1
Edmonds, J. M. 205
education
  in classical languages 38, 156, 165, 193, 414;
    translation in 105, 109, 117
  in eastern languages 323, 324, 325, 332, 341,
    345–6, 347, 358
  élite, in languages 36–8, 39, 46, 98
  in French 36–7, 230, 234, 236
  in German 37–8, 107–8, 414, 490
  in Germany, of British and Americans 21, 30,
    37, 107–8, 219–20, 414, 490
  lists of recommended reading 7
  translation as means of language learning 87,
    94, 105, 109, 113, 117, 221–2
  in USA 21, 24–5, 30, 37, 122; *see also under*
    universities
  working class 7, 35, 45, 7, 120, 122
  see also cribs; universities *and under*
    individual national literatures and
    women
Edwardes, Charles 257
Egerton, Francis 38, 100, 225–6, 236,
    521–2
Egestorff, Georg Heinrich 216
Eggerling, Julius 461
Egypt 23, 94
Eichendorff, Joseph, Freiherr von 426
Eichhorn, J. G. 108
Eivind, R. 398
Eliot, George (*pseud.* of Mary Ann (Marian)
    Evans) 127, 128, 203, 522
  anonymous translations 127, 486
  and German literature 37–8; translates
    theology 127, 128, 214, 481, 486–7
  Greek allusions 157, 160, 205
  on translation 106, 127
élite, educated 35–6, 36–40, 46, 98, 156, 165
Ellicott, Charles 452, 453
Ellis, Henry Havelock 88, 93, 94, 242,
    522–3
Elson, Louis C. 426
Elton, Sir Charles 190, 195
Elton, Oliver 277
embedding of translations in original works 17,
    76–7, 106, 109
Emerson, Ralph Waldo 4, 25, 29, 165, 493, 523
  translates Persian poetry 23, 333
  and travel literature 500, 503
émigré translators 95, 89–90, 373–4
Emmet, Robert 295–6
Empire, British *see* colonial rule
Engels, Friedrich 27, 494
English, earlier forms of 11, 51–2, 105
  see also archaizing translation; biblical
    language; Old English
English Republic 236
Enlightenment 212, 286
environmentalism 503

epic
  Finnish *Kalevala* 432–4
  French medieval 231
  Indian folk- 351
  Old English 279–80
  O Uraguay 100
  oral 192, 351, 430, **431–4**; as national epic
    430, 431, 433
  Persian 333, **337–8**
  'primary' and 'secondary' 173, 192
  Sanskrit 341, **462–3**
  Spanish medieval 4, 106, 139, 262–3, 432
  see also Camões, Luís de; Homer
equivalence of effect 26, 65, 68–9, 218
Erasmus, Desiderius 139
Erckmann, Émile 41, 240
Ernest, George A. O. 377
eroticism 203, 373
  eastern 53, 101, 328, 333, 346, 349–50
  see also expurgation; homosexuality;
    immorality
Espronceda, José de 265
essays
  translated 137, 138, 148, 150, 151
  on translation 143, **146–7**, 150–1, 179
Estes and Lauriat 377
ethnography 28, 30, **437–9**
Euripides 178, 179, 181, **182–4**, 185
  Medea 179, 182, 183, 185
Eutropius 201
Evans, Mary Ann (Marian) *see* Eliot, George
Everett, Edward 21–2
Everyman's Library 9, 196, 215, 317
evolution, theories of 190, 459
Ewald, Johannes 287
Ewing, Alexander 403
expurgation 53, 89
  private editions or performances avoid 53, 55,
    88, 242, 327, 349
extracts, translation of 75, 108, 182
Eyrbyggja saga 277

fables 202–3, 233, 399
fabliaux 231
facsimiles 301
Fairfax, Edward 247
fairy tales 16–17, 291, **394–8**, 436, 437
  see also Andersen, Hans Christian
Family Chronicle 63
Family Herald 34, 44, 147
Family Weekly 73
Fanshawe, Sir Richard 267, 268
fantasy 111, **402–3**
Faucit, Helen 181
Fausböll, Victor 458, 465–6
Făxiăn 360
Featherstonhaugh, George William 478
Feiling, C. A. 397
Felton, C. C. 26

feminism 27, 78
Fénelon, François de Salignac de la Mothe- 99, 141, 234, 399
Fenian tradition 295, 302
Ferguson, Sir Samuel 296, 523–4
Ferretti, Jacopo 423
Ferry, Gabriel 374
Feuerbach, Ludwig 127, 128, 213, 481, **486–7**
Feuillet, Octave 41
Fichte, J. G. 481
fiction
    in classical languages **202–4**
    publication statistics 137–8, 148, 150, 151
    see also Gothic fiction; novel; popular fiction; short stories
fidelity **61–77**
    acculturation destroys 53
    Carlyle on 71, 217–18
    difference between languages and 24, 28, 53, 71–4
    and elegance 28, 65, 74
    and equivalence of effect 26, 68
    prestige of source language and 48
    in US translations 24, 26, 28, 29
    see also accuracy; literal translation; principles and norms of translation
Field, Frederick 453–4
Field, Michael (*pseud.* of Katharine Bradley and Edith Cooper) 61, 78, 161
Filicaia, Vincenzo 252
Findlater, Sarah Laurie 414
Finnish literature 49, **291**, 398, 432–4
Firdausī; *Shāhnāma* 337–8
Fischer, G. E. 399
Fischer, Kuno 128
Fitzball, Edward 386
FitzGerald, Edward 7, **101–2, 335–7**, 524
    freedom of translation 48, 61, 79–80, 179, 336
    and homoeroticism 335, 336
    on Persian poetry 48, 52, 102
    TRANSLATIONS
    Aeschylus' *Agamemnon* 102, 179, 180
    'Aṭṭār 337
    Calderón 61, 63, 102, 270
    Jāmī 335–6, 337
    Rubáiyát of Omar Khayyám 4, 5–6, 9, 48, 79–80, **101–2**, 141, **335–7**; publication 6, 101, 336; re-ordering of poems 75, 102, 336
    Sophocles 181
Fitzgerald, Francis 234
Flach, Pauline Bancroft 288
Flaubert, Gustave 41, 43, 130, 139, 241, 313
Flaxman, John 155
Fleay, F. 304
Fletcher, Alice C. 438
Fliedner, Theodore 126
Florenz, Karl 367
Florian, Jean-Pierre-Claris de 401

Florio, John 9, 233, 437
Flower, Robin 299
Flygare-Carlén, Emilie 288, 289
folklore and folk tales 30, 158, **436–7**
    Celtic 100, 295, 298–9, 302, 304
    children's versions 394, 398, 436, 437
    Indian 351, 398, 437
    Japanese 365
    Russian and East European 100, 310–11
    Scandinavian 291, 394, 398
    see also ballads and folk songs; fairy tales
Folk-Lore Society, London 365, 436, 437
Ford, J. 252
Foreign Quarterly Review 146, 147, 225, 309
foreignization **63–4**, 65, **71–4**, 79–80, 114
    and Homer 67–8, 70
Forestier, Auber (*pseud.* of Anna Aubertine Woodward) 289
forgeries 299–300
    see also Ossianic literature
Forster, E. M. 180
Forster, Georg 498, 501
Fortescue, Eleanor, Lady 414
Foscolo, Ugo 251, 252, 253, 254
Fouché, Joseph 39
Fouqué, Friedrich Heinrich Karl, Baron de la Motte 138, 213, 396
Four Books, Chinese 358–9
Fourier, Charles 493
Fournier, L. P. N. 388
fourteeners (iambic heptameters) 159, 184, 192
Fowle, J. 253
Fox, Henry Richard Vassal 196
France and French literature **230–45**
    argot 72–3
    British distrust of 109, 230
    British knowledge of language 36–7, 38, 39, 46, 230, 234, 236, 399, 402
    classic translations reissued 231, 233, 240
    copyright 56, 388
    cultural dominance 22, 230, 380, 391–2
    De Quincey's criticism 3
    devotional texts 446
    1848 uprising 27, 30
    medieval and Renaissance 231–3
    oriental studies 344, 352, 356, 357–8
    publication of translations: books 4, 8, 9, 136, 137, 138, 139, 149; penny press 44; periodicals 142, 144, 145, 146, 147, 150
    reviews in periodicals 146, 147, 150
    Revolution 38, 138, 385, 489, 490, 499, 501
    Revolutionary Wars 49
    translations into French: English literature 235, 238; Russian literature 314, 315, 316; secondary translation mediated through 26, 89, 91, 93, 218, 315, 316, 435
    women translators 125
    see also individual authors and genres and Napoleonic Wars

Francis of Assisi, St 447
Francklin, Thomas 158, 178, 181, 204, 234
François Villon Society 258, 327
Franklin, Benjamin 22, 30–1
Fraser's Magazine 6, **143–5**, 147
  reviews and articles 61, 110, 192, 310, 411
  translations 61, 235, 252, 431
free translation 61, 63, 75–6
  Dryden 63, 64, 71
  FitzGerald 48, 61, 79–80, 179, 336
  of Iberian poetry 261, 267, 268, 269
  of novel 41–2, 271
  Winkworth's judgment 413–14
  see also acculturation; adaptation; domestication; imitation; paraphrase
Freese, J. H. 202
Freiligrath, Ferdinand 28
Frere, John Hookham 16, 184, 445–6, *524–5*
  Spanish literature 262, 263, 264, 432, 435
Friedlænder, E. A. 289
Friðþjófs saga 277–8, **278–9**
Froissart, Jean 141, 231
Froude, James Anthony 217–18
Fry, Henrietta Joan 414
Fuller, Sarah Margaret **26–7**, 28, 214, 500–1, *525*
Fulton, Chandos 375
Furlong, Thomas 296, 297
Fuseli, Henry 155

Gaboriau, Émile 43, 46, 241, 375, **377–8**
Galdós, Benito Pérez 271
Galland, Antoine 53, 323, 325, 394
galliambics 189
Galsworthy, John 315
Galt, John 254
Gandhi, Mohandas Karamchand 349
Ganguly, Kisari Mohan 352
Garcilaso de la Vega 263
Garnett, Constance **14**, 88, 94, 95, 314, 315–16, 317
Garnett, Edward 95
Garnett, Richard 146, 257, 268
Garstin, Annie 87
Gāthās 466
Gautier, Théophile 11, 242
Gayot de Pitaval, François 372
Gellert, Christian Fürchtegott 212, 412
gender
  and academic authority 74, 77–8, 112–13, 486
  Gothic novel altered for female audience 372
  and knowledge of languages 37, 86–7, 94, 111, 125, **213–14**, 414
  men's concealment 288
  women's concealment 86, 216, 241, 242, 289, 378, 486, 494; *see also* Field, Michael
  women's trans-gendering 77–8
Genji, Tale of 140, 366
Genlis, Stéphanie-Felicité du Crest, Mme de 238, 399

genre, and norms of translation 64, 74–7
Gentleman's Magazine 9, 236
Gentz, Friedrich von 22
Georgia, Caucasus; literature of 312
Gerard; Chateaubriand's *Atala* 235, 238
Gerhardt, Paul 417
Germany and German literature **211–29**
  awareness of literature abroad 3, 5, 89, 213, 211, 218; in British provinces 5, 211–12, 213, 216, 219, 425, 489–90; Carlyle and 15, 16–17, 22, 109–11, 213, 215, 216–17; Coleridge and 107–9; Mme de Staël and 3, 22, 212–13; in universities 117, 213; in USA 21–2, 23–4, 27, 30, 118–19, 213–14, 225, 483, 500–1
  British knowledge of language 37–8, 107–8, 213, 414, 490
  emigrants in USA 27, 30–1, 373–4
  historical overview 211–14
  influence on British literature 3, 15, 111, 213, 225
  medieval 213, **214–15**, 216, 446–7
  musical theatre adaptations 218, 225
  oral 106, 311, 430, 434–5
  publication: books 8, 9, 136, 137, 138, 139, 149; periodicals 142, 144, 145, 150, 214; reviews in periodicals 146, 147, 150
  translations into German 43, 222, 343
  translators into English 89, 93, 106, 373; women 125, 126, 127, 128, 213–14, 414
  treatises on translation 23
  see also individual authors, and under individual genres and Coleridge, Samuel Taylor; education; Romanticism; secondary translation; United States of America; universities
Gernsback, Hugo 378
Gerstäcker, Friedrich 374, 401
Gessner, Salomon 212, 215–16
Gibbings's Standard British Classics 141
Gibbon, Charles 377
Gibbon, Edward 201
Gibson, James Young 267, 435–6
Gifford, Aimée G. 399
Gifford, William 196
gift books 27–8
Gilbert, Davies 303–4
Gilbert, Sir John 265, 265
Gilbert, W. S. 423
Giles, Herbert Allen 99, 117, 356, **360**, *525–6*
Gillies, John 473–4, 475
Gillies, R. P. 5, 16–17
Gilpin, William 445
Gisborne, Mary 221
Gísla saga 280
Gissing, George Robert 157, 256, 315
Gīta-Govinda of Jayadeva 349
Gladstone, William Ewart 100, 189, 194, 200, 253, 431

Gladwin, Francis 333
Glasier, J. Bruce 46
Glassbrenner, Adolf 403
Gloux, Olivier (*pseud.* Gustave Aimard) 93, 241, 374
Gododdin 300
Godwin, Parke 23–4
Godwin, William 400, 401
Goethe, Johann Wolfgang von 6, 48, 213, **216–18, 221–6**, 501
  ballads 227, 434
  and eastern literature 48, 325, 343
  Eckermann's *Conversations with Goethe* 27, 28, 214, 501
  immoral reputation 214, 217, 226
  publication data 139, 142
  Schiller's correspondence 213, 214
  secondary translation through French 212, 217
  translators: Birch 215; Blackie 119; Bowring 226, 227; Carlyle 78–9, 110, 111, 213, 225; Clairmont 222; Coleridge 108, 221; Godwin 23–4; Froude 217–18; Hayward 225–6; Lawrence 214, 217, 219; Scott 16, 219; Shelley **221–4**, 225; Soane 222–3; Swanwick 214; Taylor 15, 29, 225; US 213
  in USA 22, 213, 214, 500–1
  widening of readership 22, 46, 214
  WORKS
  'Die Braut von Korinth' 226
  Dichtung und Wahrheit 23–4, 214, 217, 222
  Faust 9, 10–11, 15, 29, 119, 214, 215, **221–6**
  Götz von Berlichingen 16, 214, 217, 219
  Iphigenie 212
  Italian Journey 498, **500–1**
  Lieder by 426
  'Das Märchen' 213
  'Roman Elegies' 226
  short poems 108, 226
  Torquaton Tasso 247
  'Der untreue Knabe' 219
  Die Wahlverwandtschaften 217–18
  Werther (*Die Leiden des jungen Werther*) 212, 217
  Wilhelm Meister 78–9, 108, 110, 111, 213, 225
Gogol, Nikolai Vasilievich 313, 314, 315
Goldoni, Carlo 254, 258
Goldschmidt, Meïr Aron 287
Gollancz, Hermann 444
Gollancz, Israel; Temple Classics 9, 141
Gomes Coelho, Joaquim (*pseud.* Julio Dinis) 271
Goncharov, Ivan Alexandrovich 14, 88
Goncourt, Edmond *and* Jules 242
Gooch, Walter 388–9
Good, John Mason 190, 478
Gordon, Lucie Duff 129, *509*
Gosse, Edmund 215, 253, 289

Gothic fiction 5, 17, 212, 225, 255, 275, **371–3**
Göttingen University 21, 107–8, 219–20
Goudie, Gilbert 277
grammars, foreign-language 92, 94
Grangé, Eugène 77, 386
Grant, Alexander 474
Graves, Robert 217, 301
Gray, John 13, 78, 237
Gray, Thomas 275, 299
Greek Anthology 75
Greek literature, ancient 4, **155–7, 157–9**
  anthropological approach 163
  drama 62, 138–9, **158, 178–87**; performance 119, 180, 181; *see also individual Greek dramatists*
  publication data: books 9, 136, 137, 138–9, 149; periodicals 142, 144, 145, 150
  reviews in periodicals 146, 150
  Swinburne and 9, 15, **11–12**
  taste for 155, 156–7, 201
  women translators 66, 74, 77–8, 111–12, 112–13, 178–9, 182–3
  see also individual genres and authors and classical literature
Greek literature, modern 311, 435
Greek literature, patristic 159, 411, 414, **416–17**, 445
  see also Bible; Church Fathers
Green, Anna Katherine 377, 378
Greene, G. A. 13
Gregory I, St (Gregory the Great) 448
Gregory, Augusta 298
Gresset, Jean-Baptiste-Louis 234
Grey, George 439
Gṛhya Sūtras 462
Griffiths, Arthur 377
Griffiths, Robert 337
Grimm, Albert Ludwig 397
Grimm, Jacob *and* Wilhelm 15, 394, **396**, 436
Grote, George 156, 476–7
Growse, F. S. 351
Guest, Lady Charlotte **102–3**, *526*
  Mabinogion 4, 13–14, 51, **103**, 300–1, 302, 403
Guicciardini, Francesco 253–4
Guinizelli, Guido 12–13
Guizot, François-Pierre-Guillaume 93, 126, 139, 140, 142, **490–1**
Gunning, Elizabeth 89
Gunnlaugs saga ormstungu 277
Gurney, Hudson 204
Guthrie, William 204
Gutzlaff, Charles 357, 358
Gyll, G. W. J. 267
Gypsies 436

Ḥāfiẓ 334–5
Hagedorn, Friedrich von 221
Haldane, Elizabeth Sanderson 483, 484, 485
Haldane, Richard Burdon 481, 483, 485

Halford, John 225
Halhed, Nathaniel Brassey 340, 342
Hall, Gertrude 237
Hall, William Henry 216
Hallard, J. H. 164
Hamilton, Anthony 54, 234, 395
Hamilton, James 165
Hannigan, D. F. 241
Hanstein, J. T. 396
Hapdé, Jean-Baptiste 386
Hapgood, Isabel 87, 95, **129**, 239–40, 315, 317, 526
Hardiman, James 296, 297
Hardingham, George G. 478
Hardman, Frederick 93
Hardy, Emma 93
Hardy, Thomas 157
Hare, Julius 117
al-Ḥarīrī 325
Harivaṃśa 26
Harper and Brothers 20, 503
Harrington, R. M. 493
Harris, Flora Best 366
Harris, James 302
Harris, Richard 269
Harris, William Torrey 483
Harrison, Frederic 7, 489, 494
Harry, James Spence 238
Hartmann von Aue 215
Harvard University 21, 22, 24–5, 121, 122
 Harvard Oriental Series 352
Harvey, Franklin 475
Harvey, G. J. 494
Harvey, Robert 218
Harvey and Darton 399
Haselfoot, F. K. H. 67
Hastie, William 117, 483, 484, 527
Hastings, Warren 342
Hatch, Walter M. 475
Hauff, Wilhelm 396–7
Hawkesworth, John 141
Hayes, B. J. 183
Hays, Matilda M. 239
Hayward, Abraham 225–6
Haywood, Francis 482
Hazlitt, William, the elder 489, 490
Hazlitt, William, the younger 85, 91, 233, 422, 527
 translations from French 93, 231, 239; history 489, 490, 491, 492
Hazlitt, William Carew 233, 527
Head, Sir Edmund 274
Head, Frances Anne 214, 216
Head, Sir George 204
Heaney, Seamus 305
Hearn, Lafcadio 242, 367, 528
Heart Sūtras 464
Heath, I. 287
Heberden, William, the younger 205

Hebrew literature 140
 see also Bible (Old Testament)
Hegel, Georg Wilhelm Friedrich 178, 213, 350, 477, 481, **483–4**
 translations 117, 483
Heimskringla 274, 280
Heine, Heinrich 29, 30, 112, 213, 214, **226–7**, 426
Heinemann, William 88, 95
 International Library 8, 140
Heliodorus 203
Helme, Elizabeth 401
Helvétius, Claude-Adrien 234
Hemans, Felicia 28, 212, 254, *528–9*
hendecasyllabics, Latin 15
Henderson, Ebenezer 290–1
Henley, W. E. 9, 140, 236
Henry, James 191–2
Hepburn, James 366
Heraclitus 477
Herbert, William 275, 276–7
Herder, Johann Gottfried von 26, 311, 430, 434, 481
Heredia, José Maria de 146
Herodotus 200, 201
heroic narrative 231, 262–3, 265, 267, 295
 see also epic; sagas
Heron, Robert 323
Hertz, Henrik 287
Hervarer saga 275
Hetzel, P.-J. (*pseud.* Pierre-Jules Stahl) 379, 401
Hewetson, William B. 401
Hewitt, James Edwin 268, 269
hexameters 15, 66, 67–70, 76–7, 119
 metrical translations 15, 66, 69–70, 170, 175, 216, 227
Hey, Wilhelm 404
Heywood, Abel 398
Heywood, Thomas 200
Hick, R. 400
Higginson, Thomas Wentworth 160
Higuchi Ichiyō 364
Hill, Aaron 234
Hill, Herbert 261
Hill, Isabel 87, 90, 238, *529*
Hindi literature 351–2
historical novel 16, 239–40
history and historical biography 36, **489–93**
 classical 157, **200–1**
 children's versions 401
 French 139, 230, 231, 490–2
 German 139, 213, 489, 492–3
 Italian 253–4
 Japanese 363
 publication: 8, 137, 138, 148, 150, 151
 translators 86, 93, 117, 489–93
Hitopadeśa 120, 341, 349
Hjaltalín, Jón 277
Hobbes, Thomas 200

Index

Hoblyn, Robert 191
Hodges, E. Richmond 65
Hodgson, Francis 196
Hoffmann, E. T. A. 5, 16–17, 110, 111, 213, 402–3
Hoffmann, Heinrich 403
Hofland, Barbara 401
Hogg, James 303
Hokkaidō, Japan 365
Holbach, Paul-Henri Thiry, Baron d' 234
Holberg, Ludvig 286
Holcroft, Fanny 254, 269
Holcroft, Thomas 218, 385, 389, 399
Hölderlin, Friedrich 222, 226
Holland *see* Dutch literature
Holland, Philemon 200
Holmes, Edward 422
Holt, Henry 314
Homer **158–9, 168**–77
   archaizing translations: Morris's *Odyssey* 70, 114, 171, 174–5; Newman's *Iliad* 52, 56, 67–70, 168–9, **173**, 178–9, 432
   Arnold and 157, 159, 170, 172, 431–2; dispute with Newman over archaism 52, 56, 67–70, 168–9, 173, 178–9, 432; hexameter translations 66, 69–70, 170, 175
   and ballad 68, 158–9, 431–2
   in biblical prose 173–4
   Joyce and 175
   Melville and 169
   metres of translations: ballad 431–2; blank verse 29, 170–2, 174; hexameter 15, 66, 69–70, 170, 175; Spenserian stanzas 174–5
   oral origin, theory of 158–9, 192, 431–2
   publication 142
   and statecraft 171–2
   Whitman and 169–70
   Wilson's essays on 143
   TRANSLATIONS
   complete: Cowper 69, 158, 169, 170, 175; Pope 105, 119, 138, 141, 158, 170, **172–3**
   Homeric hymns, Shelley 161–3
   Iliad: Blackie 119; Bryant 29; Calverley 171; Chapman 69; Conington 119, 159, 169; Derby 171–2; Lang, Leaf, and Myers 173–4; Meredith 171; Newman 52, 56, 67–70, 168–9, **173**, 178–9; Pallis 173; Tennyson 170–1; Worsley 119, 159
   Odyssey: Bryant 29; Butcher and Lang 173–4; Butler 175–6; Chapman 69, 168; Maginn 159, 431–2; Morris 70, 114, 171, 174–5; Worsley 169, 174–5
homosexuality 157, 333–5, 336
Hoole, John 139, 247, 248, 249, 252
Hooper, William 378
Hope, Ascott R. 403
Hopkins, Gerard M. 193, 445
Horace (Q. Horatius Flaccus) **193–5**
   imitations: Byron's *Hints from Horace* 76, 105, 155, 197; Tennyson 197
   publication 139, 142
   translators: Adams 28–9; Bulwer Lytton 15; Conington 119; Dryden 194; Housman 232; Howes 13, 99, 195; Newman 67–8; Smart 65
   WORKS
   Ars Poetica 119, 155, 197
   Epodes 15
   Odes 15, 28–9, 67–8, 146, 193–5, 232
   Satires and Epistles 13, 99, 195
Hosemann, Theodor 403
Housman, A. E. 121, 182, 193, 232
'How to Pass' series 117–18
Howard, Luke 444–5
Howell, Francis (*pseud.* of Isaac Taylor) 205
Howells, William Dean 314
Howes, Francis 13, 98–9, 195, 529
Howitt, Margaret 288
Howitt (*née* Botham), Mary 87, 92, 248, 288, 289, *529–30*
   children's literature 287, 397, 402, 404
Howitt, William 288, 402, *529–30*
Hugo, Victor 13, 235, **236**, **239–40**
   publication 95, 139, 141, 142
   theatrical adaptations 55, 236, 388
   translators 87, 93, 100, 129, 235, 236, 239–40
   WORKS
   Angelo 235, 388
   'La Captive' 426
   Hernani 100, 236
   Les Misérables 87, 93, 129, 239–40
   Notre-Dame de Paris 87, 93, 129, 239
   Ruy Blas 55
Humboldt, Alexander von 213, 498, **501–4**
Hume, Fergus 377
Hume, W. E. 99
Hungarian literature 49
   folk-tales 311, 436
   novels 140, 312
   poetry 72, 100, 309, 310
Hunt, Leigh 10, 159, 163–4, 246, 249, *530*
Hunt, Margaret 396
Huntington, Archer Milton 263
Huon de Bordeaux 231
Hutchison, William George 486
Huysmans, Joris-Karl 242
Hyde, Douglas 296, 298, 302
hymns **411–19**, 443
   Celtic 303, 418
   Danish 411, 418
   French 417–18
   German 126, 128, **411–14**, 417
   Greek 411, 414, **416–17**
   Hebrew 140
   Latin 411, **414–16**, 417
   metrical translation 412, 413–14, 416
   parallel texts 417
   Russian Orthodox 129
   Sanskrit 460–1

Hymns Ancient and Modern 411, 412, 417–18
Hyndman, H. M. 494

iambic lines
 four-beat 179
 heptameters (fourteeners) 159, 184, 192
 pentameters 216
Iberia **261–73**
 bias in British view of 262–3, 265, 267
 naturalism 261, 270–1
 Peninsular Wars 261–3
 see also Spanish literature; Portuguese literature
Ibsen, Henrik 55, 95, 130, 139, 286, **290**
Icelandic literature 290–1
 see also Old Norse and Icelandic literatures
illuminated manuscripts, Morris's 114
illustrated editions 45, 103, 203, 265, 301
 children's picture books 396, 402, **403–4**
 see also Beardsley, Aubrey; Boyle, Eleanor Vere; Cruickshank, George; Doré, Gustave; Gifford, Aimée G.; Retzsch, August Moritz
imitation
 blended with translation 63
 of classical literature 62, 157, 161, 188, 196, 197; *see also under* Byron; Horace; Wordsworth, William
 incorporated into original poems 188
 with literal translation and text 75, 303
 popular fiction 17, 73, 373, 380
 see also adaptation; free translation; paraphrase; *and under* Celtic literature
The Imitation of Christ (*attr.* Thomas à Kempis) 447
immorality, allegations of
 and anonymity of translators 74, 86
 Blue Books Report (1847) 301
 foreignness and 36, 40–1, 109
 prosecutions 43, **53–4**, 230, 242
'Imrū' al-Qays 325
Inca literature 438
Inchbald, Elizabeth 24, 105, 218
incorporation of translation
 into original works 11, 76–7, 106, 109
 previous translation into new 89, 181
 see also plagiarism
India and Indian literatures **340–54**
 censorship 99, 351–2
 classical canon 344–8
 colonial rule 323, 332, 340, 344, 345–6, 462; officers' linguistic knowledge 117, 324, 326, 332, 345, 351
 education system 345–6
 impact of translations in west 342–4
 Islamic culture 332, 340
 laws 340, **461–2**
 missionaries 347, 348, 351–2
 nationalism 353

native informants to translators 333, 349, 351
native translators 345, 352–3
Orientalist-Anglicist controversy 345
periodicals 351
Persian court culture 332, 340
popular translations 348–50
publishing 140, 352
translation between Indian languages 50
vernaculars 345, **350–3**
see also Buddhism; Hindi literature; Jainism; *and* Pali, Prakrit, Sanskrit, *and* Tamil literatures, *and under* folklore and folk tales
Indo-European philology 50, 51, 459
influence of translations 3, 4, **14–17**
 on children 203, 498
 and metrical experimentation 9, 11, 15
 and novel 16, 17, 314
 stanza forms 11, 15–16
 on translators' original writing 106–7, 111–13, 188, 197, 220
 translator's status and 74, 486
Ingemann, Bernhardt Severin 418
Innocent III, Pope 415
interlinear translations 164–5
International Working Men's Association 494
'Irāqī 334–5
Irenaeus 448
Irish literature 49, 51, 294, **295–9**, 302, 403
 translations in periodicals 144, 145
Irving, Henry 225
Irving, Washington 503
Islam 332, 466–7, 467–8
Íslendingasögor 274, 277–81
Isocrates 202
Italian literature **246–60**
 and cult of sensibility 246, 247
 expatriates in London 251, 254
 fairy tales 398
 opera 251–2, 254
 original works read in Britain 37, 38, 252
 poetry 15–16, 252–3; medieval and Renaissance 9, **12–13**, 70, 79, 106–7, **254–6**, 258
 provincial writing 258
 publication: books 8, 137, 139, 149; periodicals 142, 144, 145, 146, 150
 Risorgimento 27, 252–3, 253–4, 501
 see also individual authors and genres
Ives, G. B. 241

Jablonski, Leon 312
Jacobi, Hermann 466
Jacobs, Joseph 114, 398, 437
Jainism 344–5, 347, 466
James, Henry 241–2, 314–15
James, Joseph C.; Library of Foreign Romance 91–2
James, Thomas 203

Jameson, Anna 26
Jāmī 333, 335–6, 337
Jamieson, Robert 434
Japan Mail 366
Japanese literature 5, 99, 140, **363–8**, 467
  in classical Chinese 356
Jarvis, Charles 139, 141, 266–7, 402
Jātakamālā 348, 464
Jayadeva; *Gīta-Govinda* 349
Jean Paul *see* Richter, Johann Paul Friedrich
Jebb, Sir Richard Claverhouse 118, 119, 181, 202, 205, *530–1*
Jefferson, Thomas 499, 501
Jenkin, Fleeming 119, 180
Jenkins, John 302
Jephson, Robert 252
Jerrold, Maud 257
Jeyes, S. H. 475
Jikkinshō 367
John of the Cross, St 447
Johnes, Arthur James 300
Johnes, Thomas, of Hafod 141, 231
Johnson, R. U. 310
Johnson, Richard (*pseud.* Revd Mr Cooper) 395
Johnson, Samuel 158, 159
Johnston, Miss F. 399
Johnstone, James 218, 277
Jolly, Julius 462
Jones, Edmund O. 302
Jones, Henry Arthur 382, 391, 392
Jones, John (bardic name Tegid) 103
Jones, M. 402
Jones, Sir William 4, 50, 323–4, 337, 340, 342, 356
  Gīta-Govinda of Jayadeva 349
  Ḥāfiẓ lyric 334
  Indian laws 462
  Muʿallaqāt 4, 323–4, 324–5
  Śakuntalā of Kālidāsa 50, 341–2, 342–3, 349, 350
Jonson, Ben 63, 64
Journal asiatique 357–8
Journal des débats 375, 379
journals *see* periodicals
Jouy, Victor-Joseph-Étienne de 24
Jovellanos, Gaspar Melchor de 265
Jowett, Benjamin 118, 119, 200, 475, *531*
  Plato **121–2**, 477
Joyce, James 77, 175
Jubainville, Arbois de 298
Judson, Edward Zane Carroll (*pseud.* Ned Buntline) 376
Justin 201
Juvenal (Decimus Junius Juvenalis) 196

Kalevala 432–4
Kālidāsa
  Meghadūta 48, 346–7, 350
  Śakuntalā 50, 341–2, 342–3, 349, 350

Kāma Sūtra of Vātsyāyana 53, 349
Kama-Sastra Society 333, 349
Kamo no Mabuchi 365
Kāng Xī dictionary 355
Kant, Immanuel 110–11, 142, 481, **482–3**, 485
  Coleridge and 107–8, 221
  translators 117, 120–1, 481, 482–3, 485
Karadžić, Vuk 310–11
Keats, John 4, 246, 250, 258, 343
  and classical literature 156, 158, 204
Keble, John 412, 415, 416, 417, 447, 448
Kedney, John Steinfort 483
Keightley, Thomas 398
Keigwin, John 303–4
Kelly, George 266
Kelly, Michael 218
Kelly, Walter Keating 86, 203–4, 492
Kelmscott Press 114
Kemble, Adelaide 424
Kemble, John 274, 282
Kemp, John 485
Kempis, Thomas à (*attr.*); *The Imitation of Christ* 139, 447
Kennedy, Benjamin Hall 118, 179, 180, 181
Kennedy, Charles Rann 202
Kennedy, James 265
Kenney, Charles Lamb 421
Kenney, James 236
Kenrick, Francis 444
Kern, John Hendrik Caspar 463–4
Kettell, Samuel 28–9
Khayyām, ʿUmar (Omar); *Rubáiyát* 336
  see also under FitzGerald, Edward
Kielland, Alexander 130, 290
Kindersley, E. N. 350
Kingo, Thomas 418
Kingsley, Charles 111, 446–7
Kingston, W. H. G. 379
Kleist, Heinrich von 218
Klopstock, Friedrich Gottlieb 214, 216
Knittelvers 215
Knorring, Sophie von 87
Kŏng, Master *see* Confucius
Kochanowski, Jan 309
Kock, Paul de 39
Kojiki 365, 366
Kokinshū 364–5, 365–6, 367
Konjaku monogatari 367
Kormáks saga 277
Kotzebue, August Friedrich Ferdinand von 24, 54, 105, 139, **218**, **384**
Krasinski, Zygmunt 312
Krause, Alex L. 289
Kravchinsky, S. M. (Stepniak) 14, 94
Kroeker, Kate Freiligrath 397
Kropotkin, Pyotr 494
Krummacher, F. A. 399
Ku Hung-ming 360
Kwakiutl literature 438

L. E. L. (Letitia Landon) 28, 90
Labīd 324
La Bruyère, Jean de 233
Lach-Szyrma, Krystyn 314
Lachmann, Karl 431
Lacoste, Amand 386
Lacy, Michael Rophino 422–3
La Fayette, Marie-Madeleine Pioche de La Vergne, Comtesse de 233–4
Laffan, May 402
La Flesche, Francis 438
La Fontaine, Jean de 233
Lagerlöf, Selma 288
Laing, Samuel 280
Lamartine, Alphonse de 27, 29, 235, **236**, 490
Lamb, Charles 75, 159
Lamb, George 189, 196
Landon, Letitia (L. E. L.) 28, 90
Landor, Walter Savage 160, 164, 188–9
Lane, Edward William 53, **326–7**, 328, 329, *531–2*
Lang, Andrew 114, 532
  classical languages 163, 164, 173–4
  Fairy Books 398, 437
  and folklore 435, 437
  French literature 231, 236, 435
Langhorne, John *and* William 200
Langlois, S. A. 26
Lao tzu 360
Larken, Edmund R. 239
La Rochefoucauld, François, Duc de 233
Las Cases, Emmanuel Augustin Dieudonné, Comte de 38
Lassen, Christian 458
Latham, Robert Gordon 288
Latin literature, classical 157, 159, 188–9, 200, 201–2, 203–5
  Byron and 155
  education in 193
  publication: books 136, 137, 139, 149; periodicals 142, 144, 145, 150
  reviews in periodicals 146, 150
  see also individual genres and authors and classical literature
Latin literature, post-classical 139, **159–60**
  hymns 411, **414–16**, 417
Laun, Henri van *see* van Laun, Henri
La Villemarqué, Hersart de 304
Lawrence, D. H. 258
Lawrence, Rose (*née* D'Aguilar) 212, 214, 217, 219
laws
  British theatrical licensing 54, 383, 384
  Müller on religious authority of 459
  Qīng code 356
  Sanskrit texts 340, **461–2**
  see also censorship; copyright; Parliament (Acts)
Lawson, Edward 296

Laxdæla saga 277, 281
The Leader 127
Leaf, Walter 173–4
Le Braz, Anatole 304
Lecky, W. E. H. 203
Lee, Harriet 37, 371
Lee, Robert E. 479
Lee, Sophia 37, 371, 374
Leeds Library 39
Legge, James 140, 355, 357–8, **358–60**, 467, *532–3*
  promotes study of Chinese 99, 117, 458
Legouvé, Ernest 388, 389
Le Grand d'Aussy, Pierre Jean-Baptiste 231
Le Grice, C. V. 203
Leith, Mrs Disney 291
Leland, Charles Godfrey 30, 213, 213, 226, 436, *533*
Leland, Thomas 202
Le Mesurier, Thomas 252
Lemon, Mark 396
Lenape literature 438
Lentino, Jacopo da 255
León, Luis de 261
Leopardi, Giacomo 256–7
Le Prince de Beaumont, Mme 395
Léri, Jean de 437
Lermontov, Mikhail Yurievich 313, 317
Le Sage, Alain-René 234
Lessing, Gotthold Ephraim 212, 213, 214, 218
  Coleridge and 108, 109, 220
L'Estrange, Sir Roger 203
letters, Latin 204–5
Lettsom, William Nanson 215
Leveson-Gower, Francis *see* Egerton, Francis
Levy, Amy 183
Lewes, George Henry 253, 482, 501
Lewis, David 447
Lewis, George Cornewall 184
Lewis, John Delaware 205
Lewis, Matthew Gregory ('Monk') 36–7, 219, 434, 435, *533–4*
  Fairy Tales and Romances 395
  and German literature 212, 218, 221, 373
  The Monk 371, 373
lexicography *see* dictionaries
Lhéritier de Villandon, Marie-Jeanne 395
libraries
  circulating 35, **38–40**, 40–1, 45, 46, 53, 270
  personal 35, 37, 38, 39
  public 45, 92–3
  research 92–3
'Libraries' (publishing series) *see under* series
Library of Foreign Romance 91–2
libretti 86, 136, 218, 251–2, 254, 425
  dual-language printed 421, 423
Lie, Jonas 290
Lightfoot, Joseph Barber, Bishop of Durham 452

limited editions *see* private publication
linguistics, comparative 24, 50, 51
Linton, W. J. 236
Lippard, George 376
Lissagaray, Prosper-Olivier 130
lists of recommended reading 45
literacy rates 109–10, 420
literal translation 63–7
  adaptations based on 113, 114–15, 297, 350
  of Bible 445, **451–7**
  Bohn Libraries 61, 63, 65, 78, 165
  Celtic translations favour 304–5
  classical languages 63, 91, 112–13
  cribs for students 36, 117–18, 183; classical languages 65, 86, 138, 165, 183, 201, 202, 233; eastern languages 324, 325, 332
  Fraser's preference for 61
  freer version given with 75, 279–80, 303
  in penny press 93
  trend towards 63, 65, 91, 205, 268
Littledale, R. F. 418
Liverpool 173, 212, 213, 219, 489–90
Livy (Titus Livius) 201
Lloyd, Arthur 367
Lloyd, Charles 254
Lloyd, Hannibal Evans 489, 491
Llywarch the Aged 299
Locke, John 164, 165
Lockhart, John Gibson 10, 87, 214, *534*
  translations 5, 15, 175, 214, 310–11; Spanish literature 263, 264, (ballads) 4, 106, 263–4, 435
Loeb Classical Library 122, 182, 185, 448
London
  libraries 38–9, 92–3
  theatres 383–4, 386, 387, 388–9, 391, 422–3
  University 117, 180, 183, 213
London Journal 34, 44, 45, 145, 147, 240
  foreignizing translations 63, 73
London Magazine 3
London Pioneer 44
Long, George 200, 479
Long, James 99, 351–2
Longfellow, Henry Wadsworth 6, 22, 24–5, 29, 215, *534–5*
  The Poets and Poetry of Europe 29, 264–5
  The Song of Hiawatha 432, 433, 438
  translations 28, 287: Dante 29, 141, 256; Spanish poetry 264, 265, 435
Longinus 202
Longmans 103, 220
  Longman's Magazine 41
Longus 203
Lönnrot, Elias 432
Lope de Vega *see* Vega Carpio, Lope de
Lord, Henrietta Frances 290
Loti, Pierre 241
Lotus Sūtra 463

Louvet de Couvray, Jean-Baptiste 53
Lowell, James Russell 433–4
Lowrie, Walter 357
Lubbock, Sir John 7
Lucian 205
Lucretius Carus, Titus 157, **189–90**, 197, **477–8**
Lumsden, H. W. 282–3
The Lusitanian 269
Lutetian Society 88, 89, 106, 242
Luther, Martin 411–12, 414
Lyall, Sir Charles James 324, 379, 503
Lynch, Lawrence L. (*pseud.* of Emma Murdoch van Deventer) 378
lyric poetry 145, 226
  French **231–3**, 234–7
  Italian 12–13
  see also individual poets
Lytton, Edward Bulwer, first Baron 15, 37, 253, *535*
Lytton, Robert Bulwer, first Earl of (*pseud.* Owen Meredith) 310, *535*

Mabinogion 4, 13–14, 51, 103, 300–1, 302, 403
Macartney, George, first Earl 356
Macaulay, Thomas Babington, first Baron 252
  in India 50, 340, 345
  Lays of Ancient Rome 157, 431
McCarthy, Denis Florence 269–70
McCarthy, Justin Huntly 334
MacColl, Norman 270
MacDonald, George 111
Macdonell, Annie 395
McFarlane, Helen (*pseud.* Howard Morton) 494
MacGillivray, William 502
MacGregor, Duncan 418
Machiavelli, Niccolò 253, 254
Macintyre, Duncan Ban 303
Mackay, Robert (Rob Donn) 303
MacKenna, Stephen 447
Mackenzie, Henry 5, 211–12
MacLauchlan, Thomas 302
MacLush, John 404
Macpherson, James 51, 158, 294, 338, 430
Macquet, Auguste 388
Macready, William Charles 86
Madras University 345
Maeterlinck, Maurice 237
Maggione, Manfredo 421
Maginn, William 159, 431–2
Magnússon, Eiríkr 113, 277, 281, 291
Magyar literature *see* Hungarian literature
Mahābhārata 26, 341, 347–8, 351, 352, **462–3**
Mahaffy, John Pentland 482
Mahāparinibbāna Sutta 465
Maistre, Xavier de 238
Malan, César Henri Abraham 137–8
Maldonado, López 265

Malkin, B. H. 234
Mallarmé, Stéphane 237
Mallès de Beaulieu, Mme 401
Mallock, W. H. 190
Malot, Hector 402
Malthus, Daniel 217, 238
Man, Isle of 294, **303**
Mānava Dharmaśāstra (*Manu Smṛti*) 462
Manchester 213
Mangan, James Clarence 297, *535–6*
manifestos, political 494
Manning, Cardinal Henry Edward 447
Manrique, Jorge 264, 265
Mant, Richard 415, 416
Manu Smṛti (*Mānava Dharmaśāstra*) 462
manuscripts, collecting of 302, 325, 346
Manx literature 294, **303**
Man'yōshū 364, 365, 367
Manzoni, Alessandro 89, 253, 254
Maori literature 439
Marcus Aurelius 139, 479
Maretzek, Max 423
Marguerite de Navarre 231
Marie de France 231
Marino, Giambattista 253
Markham, Clements 438
Marmontel, Jean-François 234, 384
Marriage, Ellen 86, 87, 94, 95, 241, *536*
Marsh, Anne 231
Marsh, Herbert 108
Marsh, William Heath 196
Marshall, Beatrice 396
Martial (M. Valerius Martialis) 196
Martin, Emma 253
Martin, Sir Theodore 86, 100, 189, 194, 225, 226, 287, *536–7*
Martineau, Harriet 106, **127**, 212, 489, 493–4
Martineau, James 212
Martínez de la Rosa, Francisco 265
Marx, Karl 27, 203, 478, 494
Marx-Aveling, Eleanor 43, **129–30**, 241, 290, 489, *537*
Mary, Jules 378
Mason, A. J. 418
Massie, Richard 414
Matéaux, C. L. 402
Matthews, Washington 438
Maude, Aylmer 95, 316
Maude, Louise (*née* Shanks) 95, 316, 317
Maupassant, Guy de 241–2
Max Müller, Friedrich *see* Müller, Friedrich Max
Maxwell, J. & R. 43
May, Karl 374
Maya literature 438
Maybury, Augustus C. 117–18
Mazzini, Joseph 253
Medhurst, William H. 357

medieval literature and medievalism 4, 106, 113–14, 214, **254–6**
Celtic 102–3, 295, 296, 298–9, 301, 303–4, 403
see also under individual national literatures
Medwin, Thomas 246
Meiklejohn, John Miller Dow 93, 315, 482
Meilan, M. A. 399
Mélesville, Anne 386
Melmoth, William 204, 205
melodrama 24, 225, **384–7**
Melville, Herman 169
memoirs 38–9, 86, 237–8, 490
Mencius (Mengzi) 17
Mendel, S. 397
Mendelssohn, Felix 181, 424–5
Mendès, Catulle 236
Mendoza, Diego Hurtado de 263
Mengzi (Mencius) 17
Mercier, Sébastien 378–9
Meredith, George 171
Meredith, Owen *see* Lytton, Robert Bulwer
Mérimée, Prosper 93, 240
Merivale, John Herman 16
Merle d'Aubigny, J. H. 493
Merrill, Stuart 237
Metastasio, Pietro 105, **252**, 253
metempsychosis, translation as 64–5, 66
Methuen & Co 89
  Little Library 141
metre
  experimentation in 9, 11, 15, 191–2
  see also alcaics; asclepiads; ballad metre; fourteeners; hexameters; iambic lines; *Knittelvers*; metrical translation; octosyllabics; sapphics; stanza form; trochaic metres
metrical translation 15, 66, 69–70, 443
  hymns 412, 413–14, 416
  see also hexameters; stanza form
Mexico 501
Meyer, F. S. 399
Meyer, Kuno 298
Meyerbeer, Giacomo 423
Meysenbug, Malwida von 316
M'Farlan, James 445
Michaelis, J. D. 108
Michelangelo Buanarroti 105, 257
Michelet, C. L. 484
Michelet, Jules 490, 492
Michon, J. H. 88
Mickiewicz, Adam 49, 309, 311, **312**, 317
Mickle, William Julius 65, 262, 267, 268, 269
middle classes 35, **40–4**, 420
Middleton, Conyers 204
Mijatovich, E. L. 310
Mikszáth, Kálmán 312
Milindapañha 465

Mill, John Stuart 37–8, 475–6, 492
Mills, Lawrence Heyworth 466
Milner and Sowerby 395
Milton, John 216, 249, 250, 251, 290
  and Homer 174, 176
  Latin poetry 159–60
minstrel troupes, US 422, 423
miracle plays, English 11
mirror metaphor of translation 65, 66
missionaries 50, 347, 439
  translators 98, 99; of Chinese 117, 355, 356, 357–8, 360; of Indian languages 99, 341, 351–2
Mitchell, Thomas 184
Mitchell, Sir Thomas Livingstone 267, 268, 269
Mitford, A. B. 366
Mitra, Dinabandhu; *Nil-Darpana* 351–2
modernism 5, 9–10
modernization 196, 202–3
Moe, J. I. 398
Moghuls 332, 344
Mohl, Jules 338
Moir, George 65
Moleville, Bertrand de 490
Möllhausen, Balduin 374
Moltke, Helmuth, Count von 94
Moncrieff, William 386
Mongan, Roscoe 182
Monier-Williams, Sir Monier 347
monshees 333
Montaigne, Michel de 9, 233, 437
Montépin, Xavier de 77
Montesquieu, Charles de Secondat, Baron de 106, 234
Montgomery, James 75, 445
Monthly Magazine 434
Monthly Repository 475–6
Montolieu, Isabelle de 400
Moore, A. W. 303
Moore, Charles 195
Moore, George 43, 315
Moore, Paul Elmer 122
Moore, Samuel 494
Moore, Thomas 160, 188, 189, 295–6, 343, *537–8*
Moorish ballads 263, 264
Mór (or Maurus), Jókai 140, 312
moral tales for children 398–400
Moratín, Leandro de 265
More, Sir Thomas 139
Moreau, Eugène 388
Morell, John Reynell 493
Morfill, William Richard 117
Morganwg, Iolo *see* Williams, Edward
Morley, John 493
Morris, Sir Lewis 204
Morris, William 4, **113–15**, *538*
  archaism 70, 52, 114, 174–5, 192, 281, 283
  ADAPTATIONS 114–15
  Apuleius' *Cupid and Psyche* (*The Earthly Paradise*) 204
  Old French romances 114
  sagas: *Laxdaela saga* ('The Lovers of Gudrun') 281; *Völsunga saga* (*Sigurd the Volsung*) 114–15, 281
  TRANSLATIONS
  Beowulf 114, 283
  Homer, *Odyssey* 70, 114, 171, 174–5
  sagas 113–14, 277, 281
  Virgil, *Aeneid* 70, 114, 159, 192
Morrison, A. J. W. 500
Morrison, John Robert 357
Morrison, Robert 355
Morshead, E. D. A. 179
Morton, Howard (*pseud.* of Helen McFarlane) 494
Moses, Henry 222
Motoori Norinaga 365
Motteux, Peter Anthony (Pierre Le Motteux) 139, 141, 233, 266
Mozart, Wolfgang Amadeus 252, 422
Muʿallaqāt 4, 323–4, 324–5
Mudie's Circulating Library 35, 40–1, 53
Müller, Friedrich Max 120–1, 178, **347–8**, *538–9*
  cultural and religious views 120–1, 347–8, 459, 460
  and Sacred Books of the Buddhists 464
  and Sacred Books of the East 120, 347–8, **458–9**, 462, 467
  TRANSLATIONS
  Dhammapada 465
  Kant 120–1, 482
  Mahāyāna sutras 464
  Ṛg Veda 120, 121, 347, 460
  Sanskrit 120–1, 349–50, in Sacred Books of the East 460, 464, 465, 468
  Upaniṣads 120, 349–50, 460
Munch, Peter Andreas 289
Munday, Anthony 262
Munro, H. A. J. 90, 478
Munro, Robert 303
Murphy, Arthur 196
Murray, Gilbert 122
Murray, John 221, 492
Murray, Mary Alice 304, 394, 403
Musäus, J. K. A. 213, 395–6
Musgrave, George 67
Musgrave, Thomas Moore 267, 268, 269
music, texts for **409–29**
  amateur peformance 420, 424, 425–7
  popular musical theatre 218, 225
  see also hymns; opera; songs
Musset, Alfred de 235
Myers, Ernest 173–4
Myfyr, Owain (Owen Jones) 300

Nabokov, Vladimir 314
Nahuatl literature 438
Napoleon I, Emperor of France 251, 253, 384, 490
Napoleonic Wars 3, 4, 49, **261–3**, 267
Nash, D. W. 301
The Nation 298
National Vigilance Association 54, 242
nationalism and national literatures
  acculturation and 56–7
  archaism and 51–2
  and attitudes to foreign literature 36, 40–1, 214, 230, 248–9
  Central and Eastern European 57, 310–11
  foreign contact and national character 27
  Greek 311
  Indian 353
  Irish patriot movement 295–6, 297
  and music 427
  national languages: and collective consciousness 25–6; *see also* difference between languages
  oral literature and 310–11, 430, 431, 433, 439
  poets as 'specimens' of nationalities 71
  theories of national poetry 26, 430, 431, 433
  US 23–4
Native Americans 501
  literature 30, 100, **437–8**
native informants 92, 93, 94, 333, 351, 367
native translators 345, 352–3, 360, 366
naturalism, Iberian 261, **270–1**
Nauthusius, Marie 402
Navajo literature 438
Neale, John Mason 416–17, *539*
Nepos, Cornelius 201
Nerval, Gérard de 235, 435
Netherlands *see* Dutch literature
Neumark, Georg 413
New York 384, 425
New York Tribune 27
New Yorker Staatszeitung 27
Newcombe, William 444n
Newman, Francis William 67–8, *539–40*
  Homer's *Iliad*; archaism, and debate with Arnold 52, 56, 67–70, 168–9, **173**, 178–9, 432
  Horace's *Odes* 67–8
Newman, George; Penny Library of Famous Books 45–6
Newman, John Henry 98, 414, 416, 447, 448, 478
newspapers 34, 95, 298, 366, 489, 493, 494
  US 21, 27, 30–1
Newth, Samuel 453
Nibelungenlied 51–2, 213, 215
Nicholson, Reynold 335
Niebuhr, Carsten 117, 126, 128, 323
Nieritz, Gustav 401
Nietzsche, Friedrich Wilhelm 481

Nihon shoki 363, 365
Nineteenth-Century Short Title Catalogue (NSTC) 125, 135–6, 138, 149
Niẓāmī 337
Njáls saga 275, 277, **280–1**
Nodier, Charles 385
Noiré, Ludwig 482
Nonnus 159
norms *see* principles and norms
Norris, Edwin 304
Norse literature, early *see* Old Norse and Icelandic literatures
North, Christopher *see* Wilson, John
North, early literature of the **274–85**
  cultural politics 274, 278, 280, 283
  see also Old English literature; Old Norse and Icelandic literatures
North, Sir Thomas 9, 200
North American Review 21, 22, 23, 24, 146–7, 150–1, 309
North Indian Notes and Queries 351
Norton, Charles Eliot 121, **122**, 256, *540*
Norwegian literature **289–90**, 394, 398
  see also Ibsen, Henrik
Norwich 5, 212, 213, 425, 489–90
notes
  to Aeschylus 75, 179
  Bowring's, giving original text 66
  to eastern literature 326–7, 328, 348, 359
  Coleridge's, to Schiller 75, 220
  Guest's, to *Mabinogion* 301
  Hill's carping 90
Nott, John 188, 189–90, 247, 334, *540–1*
Novalis (*pseud.* of Friedrich von Hardenberg) 111, 213
novel
  Chinese 356, 357, 358, 360
  classical languages 203–4
  free translation 41–2, 271
  French 4, 8, 42–3, 43–4, 77, 233–4, **237–42**
  Iberian naturalist 261, **270–1**
  influence of translation on 16, 17, 314
  Italian 253, 254, 258
  Japanese 366
  multi-volume 40, 46
  in periodicals 34, 41–2, 44, 240, 377
  professional translators 86, 93, 271
  see also individual authors and adventure novel; Gothic fiction; historical novel; popular fiction; realism
Noyes, George 444
Nus, Eugène 387
Nutt, David 215, 233

O Uraguay 100
obscenity *see* censorship; immorality; pornography
O'Callaghan, M. 397
Oceanic literature 439

octosyllabics 119
O'Curry, Eugene 298
O'Daly, John 297
O'Donovan, John 298
Oehlenschläger, Adam Gottlob 286, **287**
O'Flanagan, Theophilus 298
O'Grady, Standish Hayes 298
O'Grady, Standish James 299, 403
Ogura Hyakunin isshu 365–6
O'Hagan, John 100, 231
O'Halloran, Sylvester 295
Ohnet, Georges 43, 241
Ojibwa literature 438
Okey, Thomas 141
Old English literature 51–2, 114, 274, 278, 279–80, **281–3**
Old Norse and Icelandic literatures 51, 139, 145, **113–15**, 274–85, 287
    cultural heritage 274, 278
    Stephens's translations 277–80
    see also *Eddas*; sagas
Oldenberg, Hermann 460, 462, 465
Omahan literature 438
Omar Khayyām *see* Khayyām, 'Umar
opera 372, **420–4**
    opera seria 251–2
    see also libretti; musical theatre
oral literature 311, **430–40**
    Sanskrit revealed literature 459–60
    transmission to written tradition 439
    see also ballads and folk songs; epic; folk lore and folk tales; *and under individual national literatures and* nationalism
oratorio 424–5
oratory *see* rhetoric and oratory
Orbeliani, Sulkhan-Saba 312
oriental literatures *see* eastern literatures
Oriental tale 323
Oriental Translation Fund 4, 140, 325
Orientalism 4, 323, **342–4**, 346, 350, 352
    and Indian laws and customs 345, 462
    Orientalist-Anglicist controversy 345
Ormsby, John 263, 265, 266–7
Orr, W. S., Simms and M'Intyre; Parlour Novelist collection 45
Orthodox church 129, 315
Osgood and McIlvaine 258
O'Shaughnessy, Arthur W. E. 231, 236
Ossianic literature 26, 139, 303
    controversy over 51, 294, 295, 299, 302, 430
    influence 51, 158, 294, 338, 430
Oswald, Eugene 494
Otley (publisher) 7
ottava rima 16, 161–2, 248–9, 267–8
Otté, Elise 502–3
Oulton, W. C. 216
Ovid (P. Ovidius Naso) 195
Owen, Daniel 302
Owen, Robert 492

Owen (Pughe), William 299, 300
Oxenford, John 89, 93, 269, 484, 485, *541*
Oxford Movement, Tractarianism 411, 414–17, 446, 447
    see also Newman, John Henry; Pusey, Edward Bouverie
Oxford University 180, 171, 347
    translators 117, 118, 119, 120, 121
    University Press **347–8**, 458; World's Classics 9, 240
Ozaki Kōyō 364

Pahlavi literature 120, **466**
Paley, F. A. 75
Palgrave, Francis Turner 160
Pali literature 120, 344–5, 348, 350, 458, **464–6**
Pall Mall Gazette 7
Pallis, Alexandros 173
Palmer, Edward Henry 291, 466–7
Palmer, Samuel 191
Pálsson, Ólafur 291
Pañcatantra 341
'Pandnāmeh' 333
Panin, Ivan 313
parallel texts 11, 108, 138, 183, 267
    Celtic 296, 298, 301, 303
    Chinese 359
    classical 65–6, 76, 161, 179, 181
    hymns 412, 417
    implied 66, 76
paraphrase 114–15, 160, 281, 446
Pardo Bazán, Emilia, Condesa de 271
Parliament
    acts: Obscene Publications (1857) 349; Theatres (1843) 54, 383, 384; *see also under* copyright
    and trial of Vizetelly 54, 242
Parnassians, French 236–7
parody 175, 310, 421–2, 423
Parry, Judge 402
Parzifal 215
Pascal, Blaise 233
Pater, Walter 204, 231
Patrick, St 418
Patrick, G. T. W. 477
patriotism *see* nationalism
Pattison, Mark 118
Pattison, Thomas 303
Paul, Adrien 401
Paull, Mrs H. B. 396
Payn, James 35
Payne, John 233, 258, 334, *541*
    Thousand and One Nights 53, 326, **327–8**, 329
Payne, John Howard 24
Payne, W. H. 493
Peabody, Elizabeth 26
Peachey, Caroline 397
Peacock, Thomas Love 159
Peale, Titian Ramsey 503

Peck, Harry Thurston 203
pederasty 333–5, 336
Peirce, George 45
Peninsular Wars 4, **261–3**, 267
penny press 35, **44–6**, 63, 73–4, 93, 147, 376
   see also *Family Herald*; *London Journal*
Perce, Elbert 289
Percival, James 252
Percy, Thomas 275, 430, 434
Pérez Galdós, Benito 271
performance translation 218–21, 234, 236
   Greek drama 119, 180, 181
   opera 420–1
   see also theatre, popular
periodicals 5, 34–5, **142–7**
   anonymity of contributors 74, 264–5
   Central and East European literature in 309–10
   cheap mass-circulation 34, 44, 147; see also *London Journal*
   in China 357–8
   decadent 145–6, 235, 237
   Dublin 145, 296, 297
   growth 34, 109–10
   in India 351
   in Japan 367
   pay for original or translated work 41–2
   poetry in 23, 226, 252, 264–5
   in Portugal 269
   quantitative survey 142–7
   reviews and essays on translation(s) 23, 143, **146–7**, 150–1
   serials in 22, 41, 44, 240, 377
   social stratification 35, 147
   translations by genre 150, 151
   in USA 21, 23, 27, **146–7**, 150–1, 214, 226; ethnic groups' 27, 30–1
   in Wales 300
   see also *individual titles* and newspapers; penny press; serialization
Perrault, Charles 395
Perry, Thomas Sergeant 233–4
Persian literature 4, 7, **332–9**
   FitzGerald on 48, 52, 102
   at Indian courts 332, 340
   pederasty 333–5, 336
   publication 140, 144
   secondary translation through German 4, 23, 333, 336
   Sufism 334–5
   university study of 325, 345–6
   see also Khayyām, 'Umar
Persius (A. Persius Flaccus) 99, 196
Peters, F. H. 475
Petőfi, Sándor 100, 309
Petrarch 143, 146, 246, **247**, 251, 252, **257**
Petronius Arbiter 165, 203–4
Peuchet, Jacques 386

Pfizmaier, August 366
Phaedrus 202, 399
The Phalanx 493
Philadelphia 24, 30–1
Phillipps, Sir Thomas 38
Phillips, Walter Alison 214–15
philology, comparative 50, 51, 459
philosophes, French 234
philosophy **473–88**
   Chinese 357, 360
   classical 122, 473–80
   French 230, 234
   German 107–8, 213, **481–8**; translation difficulties 482, 484
   publication statistics 137, 138, 148, 150, 151
   see also *individual authors*
Pilkington, J. G. 448
Pindar 26, 61, 222
Pinkerton, Percy E. 397
pioneer novels and westerns 371, **373–4**
Pitt, George Dibdin 386
Pixerécourt, Guilbert de 24, 385–6
plagiarism 17, 77, 89, 373
   Coleridge and 17, 109, 221
Planché, James Robinson 542
   children's literature 87–8, 394–5, 403
   popular theatre 383, 386, 387, 389–90
Plato 10, **121–2**, 142, 156, 162, **475–7**
Platts, John 333
Plekhanov, Georgy Valentinovich 130
Plesner, Augusta 289, 397
Pletsch, Oscar 404
Pliny the Younger 205
Plumptre, Anne 54, 90
Plutarch 9, 200, 201
Plymouth Brethren 445
Poe, Edgar Allan 23, 37, 111, 375, 376–7, 503
poetry
   arranged in narrrative sequence 75, 336
   principles and norms of translation 75–6, 77
   publication: books 137, 138, 148, 235; periodicals 145, 150, 151
   translations in collections of original 76
   see also *individual authors and types* and under *individual national literatures*
Polish literature 140, 309, 310, 311, **312**, 317
political economy 493–5
politics **48–58**, **493–5**
   archaism and national identity 51–2
   British attitudes to Continent 109, 230, 262, 384
   classical literature and 155, 156, 202–3, 477
   events, and interest in translations 138, 147; see also Napoleonic Wars
   feminist 27
   Iberian 262, 265

in India 99, 351–2, 352–3
Irish 49, 51, 295–6, 297, 298
Italian theoretical writings 253–4
melodrama and French Revolution 385
northern cultural 274, 278, 280, 283
politicians as translators 100, 171–2, 481, 489; *see also* Gladstone, William Ewart
translation used in support of 27, 49, 202–3, 265, 502
US 27, 274, 374, 502
see also censorship; Chartism; copyright; democracy; independence movements; nationalism and national literatures; power relations; radicalism; Republic of Letters; socialism
Pollard, Alfred 182
Pollock, T. B. 417–18
Polybius 200
Ponte, Lorenzo da 425
Poole, Edward Stanley 326
Poole, Stanley Lane 53
Pope, Alexander; Homer 119, 170, **172–3**
enduring popularity 105, 138, 141, 158
Pope, G. U. 351
popular culture **369–407**
French literature as major source 230
Orientalism 323
see also children's literature; popular fiction; theatre, popular
popular fiction 371–81
adaptation 36, 266, 371–2, 380
Chinese 358
'concealed' translation 36
foreignizing translation 63
French 43, 44, 230, 371–3, 375, 377–8, 378–9, 380
imitation 17, 73, 373, 380
Japanese tales 366–7
in mass-circulation periodicals 147
publication data 136, 147
pioneer novels and westerns 371, **373–4**
science fiction 371, **378–80**
see also crime, mystery and detective fiction; Gothic fiction
pornography 35, 53
Porson, Richard 173
Port Folio 22
Porter, John A. 432–3
Portuguese literature 261, 262, 263, 265, 270–1, 436
publication 9, 137, 139, 145, 146, 149
see also Camões, Luís de
postcolonial research 49, 50
Postl, Carl (*pseud.* Charles Sealsfield) 373–4
Potter, Robert 158, 178, 181, 182
Pound, Ezra 9–10, 364
Powell, Frederick York *see* York Powell, Frederick

Powell, George 291
power relations **48–9**, 50, 52, 53, 56–7
Celtic-English 294–5, 304–5
colonial 49–51, 340, 344, 350
French cultural dominance 22, 230, 380, 391–2
Prakrit literature 120, 344–5, 350, 464, **466**
Pre-Raphaelites 6, 214
Prescott, William Hickling 438
Presocratic philosophers 477
Press, Muriel 277
Prestage, Edgar 265
prestige of individual languages 24–5, 48, 51–2
previous translation embedded in new 89, 181
Prévost, Antione-François, abbé 371–2
Price, Thomas (*bardic name* Carnhuanawc) 103
Prichard, Augustin 503
Priestley, Joseph 499
primitivism 26, 158, 255, 430, 432, 433, 434
principles and norms of translation **59–82**
definitions 61–3; of copy 65–7
transformation of translator 77–80
Tytler on 62, **63–5**
variation with genre 64, 74–7
see also accuracy; adaptation; archaizing translation; difference between languages; domestication; equivalence of effect; fidelity; foreignization; free translation; imitation; literal translation; metrical translation; prose translation of verse; re-creation; taste; verse translations
Prinsep, C. R. 495
print runs 35, 43, 140, 141, 376
printing technology 35, 46, 141
Pritchard, T. J. Llewelyn 300
private publication or performance 101, 141, 185, 235, 241, 242, 334
evades censorship 53, 55, 88, 242, 327, 349
prompt books 390
Propertius, Sextus 195
prose
Arabic rhymed 327, 328–9
discursive 75–7, 139, 200–7, **471–504**; *see also individual types*
verse translated into 66, 75, 119, 165, 216, 220, 225
prose narrative
medieval Japanese; *Genji* 140, 366
see also novel; popular fiction; sagas
prosody *see* metre
prosimetrum; Saʿdī's *Gulistān* 333
protestantism 411, 414, 461
Proudhon, Pierre-Joseph 494
Prout, Father 252
provincial centres, British 212, 213, 384, 486, 489–90
see also Edinburgh; Liverpool; Norwich

Prudentius, Aurelius Clemens 415
Psalms 443, 445–6
pseudonyms, translators' 86
　women use male 86, 241, 242, 289, 378, 494;
　　see also Field, Michael
publishing 34–47, 133–51
　collected volumes 235
　de luxe editions 45, 141, 552
　in India 50, 352
　print runs 35, 43, 140, 141, 376
　quantitative survey 133–51; books 34,
　　135–42, 443; periodicals 34, 142–7
　technology 35, 46, 141
　translators' pay, conditions and recruitment
　　87–9, 98, 101, 125, 271
　in USA 27, 28
　see also anthologies; booksellers; censorship;
　　cheap editions; copyright; illustration;
　　limited editions; newspapers; penny
　　press; periodicals; private publication;
　　railway literature; readership; reprints;
　　serialization; series, publishing; shilling
　　editions
Pückler-Muskau, Hermann, Fürst von 128
Pulci, Luigi 16, 248
puppet theatre 365, 383
purāṇas 351, 463
Purleigh Brotherhood 316
Pusey, Edward Bouverie 98, 446, 447, 448, 449
Pushkin, Aleksandr Sergeevich 100, 310, 313–14

Quakers 444–5
quantity; stress substituted for 66, 69–70
Quaritch, Bernard 6
Quarterly Review 40, 239
Les Quatre fils Aymon 231
Quelch, Harry 494
Quental, Antero de 146, 265
Quevedo, Francisco de 261
Quillinan, Edward 267, 268, 269
Quintana, Manuel José 265
Quintilian (Marcus Fabius Quintilianus) 202
Qur'ān 466–7

Rabb, Kate 431
Rabelais, François 54, 141, 233
Rabillon, Léonce 231
Radcliffe, Ann 37, 212
radicalism 212, 286, 376, 489, 494, 495, 500
Ragnarr loðbrók ('Regnar lodbrog') 275–6
railway literature 8, 35, 42, 141, 239
Rainy, Charlotte Ada 216
Rājaśekhara 352
Raleigh, J. 397
Ralston, William Ralston (Shedden) 101, 315,
　542
Rāmānuja 461
Rāmāyaṇa 347–8, 351, **462–3**
Randolph, Thomas 159

Ranke, Leopold von 139, 213, 214, 490, **492–3**
Rawlinson, George 200
Ray, Catherine 290
Reade, Charles 388–9, 390, *542–3*
readership 34–47
　growth 7–9, 35, 109–10, 420
　social composition 7–9, 35–6, 45, 46, 118; see
　　also élite, educated; middle classes;
　　women (readers); working class
reading lists 7, 45
realism 43, **78–9**, 203–4, 374
　Russian 43, 314, 315
　Scandinavian 288, 290
re-creation, translation as 17, 348–9
Red Republican 494
Redhouse, James 335
Reeve, Clara 37, 371, 374
Reeve, Henry 489, 491–2, *543*
Reeve, Sophia 372
Reeves, Arthur 277
register, conveying of 329, 359
Rehatsek, Edward 333
Reid, Captain Mayne 374
reissues *see* reprints
relay translation *see* secondary translation
religion
　anticlericalism 253–4, 499
　bias in translations 461, 492–3
　German challenge to conventional 212, 213,
　　226
　in India 344–5, 347, 348
　Müller's theories of 459
　Volney's radicalism 499, 500
　Tasso and revival 248–9
　see also Buddhism; Church of England; Islam;
　　Jainism; Orthodox Church; sacred and
　　religious texts
Religious Tract Society 400
Renan, Ernest 129, 294, 481–2, **485–6**, 487
reprints 7–9, 20–1, 136, **140–2**, 315, 449
　see also classic translations reissued; series,
　　publishing
research by translators 92–3, 95, 103, 128
Retzsch, August Moritz 222–3
reviews and essays on translations 143, **146–7**,
　150–1
revival of translations *see* reprints
revolutions
　American 489, 490, 499
　French 38, 138, 385, 489, 490, 499, 501
　of 1848 27, 30, 49, 211, 498, 499, 501
reworking *see* adaptation
Reynolds, F. 218
Reynolds, G. W. M. 44, 236, 376
Reynolds' Miscellany 147
Ṛg Veda 120, 121, 346, 347, 458, 460
rhetoric and oratory, classical 201–2
Rhymers' Club 13
Rhys Davids, Thomas William 465, 466

Richardson, Mrs Charles 27
Richardson, G. F. 220
Richardson, J. 212
Richardson, John 482
Richter, Johann Paul Friedrich (*pseud.*
    Jean Paul) 3, 27, 71, 213, 214
Richter, John 495
Rimbaud, Arthur 237
Ripley, George 28
Ripon, John Scott (*pseud.* of J. S. Byerley) 253
Ristori, Adelaide 185
Roberts, Alexander 449
Roberts Brothers 44
Robertson, William John 235
Robins, E. P. 241
Robinson, Agnes Mary Francis 183
Robinson, Henry Crabb 5, 110, 161, 213
Robinson, Samuel 338
Robinsonades 400–1
Robson, Frederick 185
Robson, William 85, 93, 240, 491
Rodwell, John Medows 466–7, *543–4*
Rogers, Alexander 337, 338
Rogers, Benjamin Bickley 185
Rogers, Charles 303
Rogers, Henry 475
Rogers, W. H. 404
Roland, Song of 231
romance, translation as 78, 79
romances 16, 73–4, 114, 215, 231, 262
    modern 'researched' historical 94
Romancist and Novelist's Library 91
Romanian literature 312
Romanticism 4, 14, 214, 268, 391
    and classical literature 155–6, 189, 190–1
    and eastern literature 324–5, 342–3
    Finnish national 291
    German 3, 22, 111, 212–13, 396, 498, 500
    in US 21–2, 23–4, 25–7, 30, 213–14, 225
    see also individual authors
rondels 233
Root, Frederic W. 426
Roscoe, Thomas 91, *544*
    Iberian literature 263, 264, 265, 268
    Italian Novelists 75, 254
Roscommon, Wentworth Dillon,
    fourth Earl of 64
Rose, William Stewart 248, **249–50**
Rosetta Stone 23
Ross, James 333
Ross, John Lockhart 99
Ross, Thomasina 502
Rossetti, Dante Gabriel 6, **12–13**, 225, 255, 256, 336
    Hartmann von Aue 215
    Italian medieval lyric poetry 9, **12–13**, 52, 70, 79, 106–7, **254–6**
    Sappho 160
    Villon 4, 232, *544–5*

Rossini, Gioacchino Antonio 372, 421, 422, 423, 425
Roth, Edward 379
Rotherman, Joseph 445
Rousseau, Jean-Jacques 234, 399, 493
Routledge, George 43, 44, 45, 87–8
    Libraries: Every Boy's 379; Popular 141; Railway 8, 42
Roy, Ram Mohun 352
Royal Asiatic Society 4, 140, 325, 356, 358
Ruǎn Yuán 359
Rudolphi, J. J. 397
Rugeley-Powers, Susan 289
Rūmī 335
Runeberg, Johan Ludvig 291
Rush, Richard 36
Ruskin, John 15, 173, 255, 336, 396
    and Italian poetry 253, 258
Russell, William (*pseud.* 'Waters') 375
Russian literature 3, 34, 308, **312–17**
    folk and fairy tales 310, 398
    publication 9, 136, 137, 138, 140, 145, 149, 150
    realism 43, 314, 315
    secondary translation 91, 314, 315, 316
    translators 100, 129, 308, 309, 311
Rustaveli, Shota 312
Ryūtei Tanehiko 366

Sabine, Edward 503
Sabine, Elizabeth Juliana 502
Sacchetti, Franco 252, 256
sacred and religious texts **441–69**
    children's versions 399–400
    Christian 36, 98, 139, 303–4, **443–57**;
        German 139, 212, 213, **215–16**, 399–400;
        see also Bible; Church Fathers; hymns; oratorio
    eastern **458–69**; *see also* Sacred Books of the East
    publication 137, 138, 142, 148, 150, 151
Sacred Books of the Buddhists 464
Sacred Books of the East 140, **458–69**
    Arabic works 466–7
    Avestan and Pahlavi texts 466
    Chinese works 359, 467
    funding 4, 458
    and Islam 466–7, 467–8
    Müller and 120, **458–9**, 462, 467;
        translations in 460, 464, 465, 468
    Pali texts 464–6
    Prakrit (Ardhamāgadhī) texts 464, **466**
    Sanskrit texts 120, 347–8, 459–61, 462–3, 463–4, 468
    selection of material 347–8, 459, 460, 461, 462, 467–8
Sacy, Silvestre de 323
Saddharmapuṇḍarīka Sūtra 463
Sade, Donatien-Alphonse-François,
    Marquis de 11

Sa'dī 332, **333**, 334
Safford, Mary 94
sagas 4, 139, 145, 274, **277–9**, **280–1**
　archaism in translation 51–2, 277, 281
　Morris and 113–14, 114–15, 277, 281
　Vínland 277, 280
Saga Library 113
Said, Edward 344
St John, Percy Bolingbroke 374
Saint Paul's Magazine 41
Saint-Pierre, Jacques-Henri Bernardin de 138, 141, **238**
Saint-Simon, Claude-Henri de Rouvroy, Comte de 491, **492**, 493
Saintine, Xavier (*pseud*. of Joseph-Xavier Boniface) 238
Saintsbury, George 89, 94, 236
Śakuntalā see under Kālidāsa
Sala, George Augustus 196
Sallust (Gaius Sallustius Crispus) 200, 201
Salvo, Marchesa di 447
Salzmann, C. G. 399
Samber, Robert 395
Sampson Low 379
Sanatsujātīya 463
Sand, George 39, 88, 93, 95, 239, 388
Sanderson, J. Burdon 484
Śaṅkara 461
Sannazaro, Jacopo 252
Sanskrit literature 4, 7, 50, **120–1**, **340–50**, **459–64**
　canon 344–8
　epic 26, 341, **462–3**; see also *Mahābhārata*
　German translations 343
　hymns 460–1
　impact of early translations 342–4
　Müller and **120–1**, 349–50, 460, 464, 465, 468
　oral tradition 459–60
　publication data 9, 140, 144, 145
　in Sacred Books of the East 120, 347–8, 459–61, 462–3, 463–4, 468
　secondary translation through Persian 340
　university study 344, 347, 460–4 *passim*
　see also individual authors and works
Santillana, Iñigo López de Mendoza, Marqués de 263
sapphics 15, 161
Sappho 11, 15, 53, 61, 78, **160–1**
Śatapatha Brāhmaṇa 461
satire 196, 202–3
Satow, Sir Ernest Mason 363, 365
Saturday Night 377
satyr play; Euripides' *Cyclops* 184
Saunders, Thomas Bailey 481, 484–5
Savile, Sir Henry 200
The Savoy 237
Say, Jean-Baptiste 495
Sayers, Frank 275

Scandinavian literature, modern 4, **286–93**
　publication 137, 138, 139, 144, 149
　see also individual national literatures
Schaff, Philip 449
Schelling, Friedrich Wilhelm Joseph von 17, 109, 221, 343, 481
Schiller, Johann Christoph Friedrich von 8, 139
　Carlyle's *Life of Schiller* 213
　reputation in Britain 107, 212, 213
　translations 213, 214, 218–19, 226; Coleridge 75, 107, 108, 109, **219–21**
　WORKS
　correspondence with Goethe 213, 214
　'Götter Griechenlands' 226
　lyric poetry 108, 214, 226
　Die Piccolomini 75
　Die Räuber 212, 218–19
　Wallenstein trilogy 219–21
Schirmer, Walter 211
Schlegel, August Wilhelm von 71, 214, 221
Schlegel, Friedrich von 214, 343
Schleiermacher, Friedrich Daniel Ernst 213, 481
Schmid, Christoph von 399–400
Schoolcraft, Henry Rowe 437–8
Schopenhauer, Arthur 481, **484–5**
Schoppe, Amalie 402
Schreiner, Olive 88
Schubert, Franz 426
Schubring, Julius 424
Schuyler, Eugene 93, 316, 433
Schwartz, Marie Sophie 286, 288, **289**
science 137, 148, 411, 477
science fiction 17, 371, **378–80**
Scoble, Sir Andrew Richard 93, 491, 545
Scott, David Dundas 489
Scott, Jonathan 325
Scott, Sir Walter 21, 219, 245–50, 275, 490, 545–6
　and folk literature 106, 303, 311, 430, 434–5
　and German literature 5, 16–17, 106, 212, 219
　Rob Roy 250
　translations 16, 106, 219, 303, 311, 435
Scottish literature 28, 100, 294, **302–3**
　see also Ossianic literature
Scribe, Eugène 386–7, 388, 389
Sealsfield, Charles (*pseud*. of Carl Postl) 373–4
secondary translation 91–2
　with French as intermediary 91; Breton 304; Danish 287; eastern 325, 435; German 89, 217, 218, 394, 400–1, 403; modern Greek 435; Russian 91, 93, 95, 315, 316
　with German as intermediary 91; ancient Greek 26; Danish 91, 92, 287; Finnish 432–3; Japanese 367; Persian 4, 23, 333, 336; Serbian 311
　Old Norse through Latin 275
　Sanskrit through Persian 340
secularism 323, 411, 473, 475

self
  Romantic discovery 498, 500
  women translators' assertion or effacement 126–30
Seneca, Lucius Annaeus, the Younger 478
sensibility *or* sentiment, cult of 5, 246, 247
sentimental popular fiction, French 371–3
Sephton, John 277
Serbian literature 49, 309, 310–11, 435, 436
serialization 22, 37, 41, 44, 240, 377
series, publishing 7–9, 46, 140, 141
  present-day 9, 240
  see also Bohn, Henry; Collins, W. Lucas; Dent, J. M.; Gollancz, Israel; Heinemann, William; James, Joseph C.; Japanese Fairy Tale Series; Loeb Classical Library; Methuen & Co; Nutt, David; Orr, W. S., Simms and M'Intyre; railway literature; Routledge, George; Smith's Standard Library; Specimens of Foreign Standard Literature; Tudor Translations; Unwin, T. Fisher; Valpy; Ward, Lock, & Tyler; Warne; Works of the Greek and Roman Poets
Serrano, Mary Jane 271
Seward, Anna 275
Sewell, William 191
Shabistarī 335
Shadwell, Charles Lancelot 66–7
Shakespeare, William 120, 172, 220
Shand, A. Innes 375
Sharp, R. Farquharson 236
Sharpe, Samuel 444
Shaw, George Bernard 130
Shaw, Thomas Budge 313
Shelley, Mary 372, 378
Shelley, Mary Wollstonecraft 500
Shelley, Percy Bysshe 10–11, 224, 343, *546*
  influences on: Bible 162; classical 106, 156, 178, 202; Italian 76, 106, 247; Volney 500
  and 'the spirit of the age' 489
  and *terza rima* 15–16, 76
  on translation 63, 223
  translations: Calderón 223, 264, 269, 270; Dante 15–16, 75, 106, 246; Euripides 184; Goethe 10–11, **221–4**, 225; Homeric Hymns 10, 156, **161–3**; Plato, 10, 162, 476; Spanish poetry 262
  WORKS
  Adonais 156
  The Cenci 55
  A Defence of Poetry 63, 223
  'From the Arabic' 4
  Hellas 156
  Posthumous Poems 10
  Prometheus Unbound 156, 178, 343
  'Queen Mab' 500
  'The Triumph of Life' 15–16, 76, 106

Shelton, Thomas 266
Shepherd, Richard Herne 237
Sheridan, Richard Brinsley 218, 382, 384
Sherwood, Mary Neal (*pseud*. John Stirling) 242
shilling editions 141, 378
Shioi Ukō 364
Shoberl, Frederic 87, 90, 93, 216, 239, 399, *546*
short story 41, 147, 378
Shortall, Edward 439
Shuck, J. L. 357
Shuckburgh, Evelyn 200, 205
Shuō wén dictionary 355
Sibree, John 483–4
Sicily 258
Sienkiewicz, Henryk 100, 140, 312, 317
Sieveking, Amalia 126
Sigerson, George 298
signatures, translators' 74–5
Sigourney, Lydia 28
Simrock, Karl 215
Sims, George R. 376, 390–1
'Sir Marvellous Crackjoke' 402
Siraudin, Paul 388
Sismondi, Léonard Simonde de 74, 263
Skene, W. F. 302
Skírnismál 276–7
slang, jargon and cant 30, 72–3, 376
Slavonic literatures *see* Central and Eastern Europe
Sleath, Eleanor 373
Smart, Christopher 65, 202
Smart, Martin 234
Smirke, Mary 265, 266
Smirke, Robert 265
Smith's Standard Library 238
Smith, C. L. 247
Smith, Charlotte 37, 371–2
Smith, Elder and Co. 41
Smith, G. H. 93, 492
Smith, James *and* Horatio 194
Smith, James Elimalet 492, 493
Smith, James T. 235
Smith, Joseph 444
Smith, Julia 445
Smith, Rowland 203
Smith, Samuel 185
Smith, Samuel, MP 54
Smith, Sidney 165, 238
Smith, W. F. 233
Smith, W. H. 40, 53
Smithers, Leonard 185
Smithsonian Bureau of Ethnology 437, 438
Smollett, Tobias 138, 141, 234, 266
Soane, George 222–3
Soboleski, Paul 309
social and economic conditions 155, 211
  see also readership
social sciences 137, 148, 150, 151, 491–2

socio-political theory 489, **493–5**
socialism 129–30, 494
songs
  art 136, 420, 424, **425–7**
  medieval students' 160
  see also ballads and folk songs
Sonnenschein 494
sonnet 66, 257
Sophocles 46, 55, **180–2**
  Francklin's 158, 178, 181
Sotheby, Elizabeth (*or* Eliza) 258
Soulié, Frédéric 39, 73
Southey, Robert 212, 262–3, 300, 344, *547*
  Camões's lyric poetry 261, 268
  El Cid 4, 106, 262–3, 267, 432
  Spanish ballads 262, 263, 435
Souvestre, Émile 304
Spalding, H. 100, 313–14
Spanish literature 38, **263–5, 269–71**
  multiple languages and literatures 262, 264
  publication: books 8, 9, 137, 139, 149; periodicals 142, 144, 145, 150
  see also individual authors and genres
Specimens of Foreign Standard Literature 28
Speckter, Otto 404
Spedding, James 66
Speirs, Ebenezer Brown 484
Spenserian stanza 67, 159, 174–5, 248–9
Speyer, J. S. 464
Spohr, Louis 425
Spyri, Johanna 402
Śrībhāṣya 461
Staël, Anne-Louise-Germaine Necker, Mme de 3, 26, 71, 90, 214, 238
  promotes German literature 3, 22, 212–13
Stahl, Pierre-Jules (*pseud*. of P. J. Hetzel) 401
Stanley, Louise Dorothea 267
stanza form 15–16, **66–7**
  adherence to original *see* metrical translation
  five-line, for Japanese thirty-one-syllable poetry 365–6
  In Memoriam, for alcaics 194–5
  influence of translation on new writing 11, 15–16
  Spenserian 67, 159, 174–5, 248–9
  see also ottava rima; terza rima
Staunton, George 356
Steere, Edward 99, 439
Steingass, F. 325
Steinkopff, Ann 399
Steinthal, Heymann 431
Stendhal (*pseud*. of Henri Beyle) 139, 238
Stephens, George **277–80**, 288, *547*
Stephens, Thomas 301, 302
Stepniak (S. M. Kravchinsky) 14, 94
Sterling, Edward 421–2
Sterne, Laurence 3
Sterrett, J. Macbride 483
Stevenson, Robert Louis 37, 196, 377

Stewart, Aubrey 200, 478
Stewart, Dugald 219
Stirling, Edward 386
Stirling, James Hutchison 482, 483
Stirling, John (*pseud*. of Mary Neal Sherwood) 242
Stock, St George William Joseph 475
Stokes, Whitley 304
Stolberg, Friedrich Leopold 108, 221
Stowe, Harriet Beecher 43
Strand Magazine 41, 145, 147
Strangford, Percy Clinton Sydney Smythe, sixth Viscount 263, 265, 268
Strauss, David Friedrich 127, 213, 481, **485–6**, 487
Street, Stephen 445
stress substituted for quantity 66, 69–70
Strong, William 288
Strubberg, Friedrich Armand 374
Sturges, Jonathan 241–2
Sturluson, Snorri 274, 280
styles of translation **59–82**
  equivalence 65, 68–9, 218
  variety and competition 62–3
  see also accuracy; adaptation; archaizing translation; domestication; fidelity; foreignization; free translation; imitation; literal translation; metrical translation; prose translation of verse; re-creation; verse translations
sublime, the 160, 275, 372
Śūdraka 352
Sue, Eugène 39, 77, 79, 93, 240, **375–6**
  publication 34–5, 44, 45, 95, 139, 376
  slang 72–3, 376
Suematsu Kenchō 366
Suetonius Paulinus, Gaius 200, 201
Sufism 4, 334–5
Sukhāvatīvyūha Sūtras 464
Sully Prudhomme (*pseud*. of René-François-Armand Prudhomme) 236
Sunday School reward books 400
Suppression of Vice and the Encouragement of Religion and Virtue, Society for the 53
Sutta Nipāta 465–6
Sutta Piṭaka 464, 465
Swahili literature 99, 437, 439
Swan, Charles 89, 253
Swanwick, Anna 9, 178–9, *547–8*
  German translation 128–9, 212, 214, 225
Swedenborg, Emanuel, and Swedenborgianism 139, 443
Swedish literature 8, 39, 92, **288–9**, 291
  see also Bremer, Fredrika
Swinburne, Algernon Charles 10, 14, 254, 336, *548*
  imitation of Greek literature 62, 157, 161
  influence of translation on writings 9, 15, 234; on metres 9, 15, 161
  metrical translation 161, 185

and Sappho 11, 160, 161
translation incorporated into poems 11
TRANSLATIONS 11–12
  Greek poetry 9, 11–12, 15, 185
  medieval lyrics 4, 11; Villon 4, 11–12, 70, 106, **232**
  modern French poetry 4, 11, 230, 234
Sydenham, Floyer 475
symbolists, French 236–7
Symington, Andrew James 291
Symonds, John Addington 160, 161, 164, 257, 478, **548–9**
Symons, Arthur 13, 37, 106, 237, 241–2
Synge, John Millington 298

Tacitus, Cornelius 200, 201
Tadema, Laurence Alma 237
Tagore, Rabindranath 352
Takakusu, J. 464
Takasago 364, 366
Takeda Izumo 365
Taliesin 300
  'Tale of', in *Mabinogion* 301
Tamil literature 345, **350–1**
Tansillo, Luigi 146
Tasso, Torquato 139, **247–9**, 251
taste 64
  accommodation to readers' 77, 79, 89, 95
  Bohn's standards 53–4, 203–4
  for Greek culture 155, 156–7, 201
  rebellion against Victorian 258
Tauchnitz, Karl Christoph Traugott 8
Tauler, Johannes 447
Taylor, Bayard 15, 23, 29, 225, **549–50**
Taylor, E. Fairfax 159
Taylor, Edgar 90, 214, 394, 396, 436, *550*
Taylor, Edward 425
Taylor, Isaac (*pseud*. Francis Howell) 205
Taylor, John Edward 396, 398
Taylor, Thomas 204, 474, 475, *550–1*
Taylor, Tom 304, **386–7**, 390, *551*
Taylor, William, of Norwich 5, 212, 219, 434, *551*
Taylor, William Ernest 99, 439
Tchaikovsky, Pyotr Ilich 403
technology, printing 35, 46, 141
Tegnér, Esaias 277–8, 286, 288
Teixeira de Mattos San Payo y Mendes, Alexander Louis 89, 95, *551–2*
Telang, Kashinath Trimbak 463
Temple Bar 41
Le Temps 379
Tenant, William 16
Tennyson, Alfred, first Baron 7, 14, 194
  and classical literature 105, 157, 160, 163, 170–1, 191, 197; use of metres 15, 194
  'Locksley Hall' 4, 325
  'Ulysses' 76
Tennyson, Frederick 161
Teresa of Avila, St 447

terza rima 15–16, 66–7, 76, 112
  blank verse translations 29, 250, 256
Thackeray, William Makepeace 37, 236, 403
theatre, popular **382–93**
  adaptations for stage 139; French plays 24, 36, 56, 63, 77, 139, 382, **385–6**, **386–7**, 388, **389–91**; French novels 77, 385, 387, 388–9, 390; German plays 86, 139, 384; *see also* Kotzebue, August Friedrich Ferdinand von
  attribution 36, 77, 385–6, 390–1
  burlesque 185, 383, 423
  and censorship 54–5
  copyright **388–9**, 391–2
  imitations 386
  legitimate and illegitimate drama 383
  licensing laws 54, 383, 384
  melodrama 24, 225, **384–7**
  musical 218, 225
  repertoire 384–7
  in USA 24, 384, 386
The Theatrical Recorder 218
Theocritus 157, **163–4**
Theologica Germanica 216, 446–7
theology
  Essays and Reviews controversy 121
  German 107–8, 127, 128, 213, 443, 481, **485–7**
  Renan 481–2, **485–6**, 487
  see also Oxford Movement
Theophrastus 205
Thibaut, George 461
Thiers, Adolphe 44, 490, 491
Thiersch, Friedrich 26
Thilo, Marie von 317
Thirlwall, Connop 117
Thomas, F. W. 348
Thompson, Annie 447
Thompson, Benjamin 24, 86, 218, 384
Thompson, John 183
Thompson, W. H. 118
Thompson, William 493
Thoms, W. J. 396
Thomson, Alexander 201
Thomson, James 226, 256–7, *552*
Thomson, Ninian Hill 253
Thomson, William M. 485
Thorarensen, Bjarni 291
Thoreau, Henry David 17, **25–6**, 501, 502, 503, *552–3*
Thorkelín, Grímur 274, 277
Þorláksson, Jón 290–1
Thornley, George 203
Thorpe, Benjamin 276–7, 279, *553*
The Thousand and One Nights 50–1, 53, 98, 140, 394, **325–9**
  children's adaptations 15, 395
  popularity 49–50, 98, 142
Thrasher, J. S. 502
Thucydides **200**, 200, 201

Thurneysen, Rudolf 298
Ticknor, George 21, 22, 118–19
Tieck, Ludwig 110, 213
Tighe, Mary 204
Timberlake, Henry 437
Tipu Sultan 344
Tirukkural 351
Tocqueville, Alexis de 491–2
Tod, James 353
Tolstoy, Count Lev Nikolaevich 14, 88–9, 95, 140, 313, 315, **316–17**
Topelius, Zacharias 291, 398
Torrens, Henry 326
Tosa Diary 363, 366
T'oung Pao 358
Townsend, G. F. 202–3
toybooks 395, 402
Tozer, H. J. 493
Tractarianism *see* Oxford Movement
Transcendentalists, American **25–7**, 333
  see also individual authors
transfusion, translation as 64–5, 66
translators **83–132, 507–59**
  academics **117–24**, 188, 189–90, 193–4, 481, 460–4 *passim*
  amateurs and enthusiasts **98–104**, 189–90, 194–5, 200
  author assistance 92, 93
  biographical sketches *507–59*
  crediting of 74–5
  editors also working as 90–1
  émigrés 95, 89–90, 373–4
  of multiple languages and genres 86
  native, of eastern languages 345, 352–3, 360, 366; assistants to westerners 92, 93, 94, 333, 351, 367
  pay, conditions and recruitment 87–9, 98, 101, 125, 271
  professional **85–97**, 98, 102, 125–6, 271, 489
  specialization 86
  speed of working 88, 91, 92, 94, 271
  transformed by translating 77–80
  travel and residence abroad 98, 99–100
  see also anonymity; pseudonyms; research;
    and under cheap editions; missionaries;
    women; writers
Transon, Abel 493
travel 98, 99–100, 323, 325
  literature of 38, 50–1, 86, 93, 128–9, **498–504**
Tremenheere, J. H. A. 75
Tremenheere, S. G. 195
Trench, Richard Chenevix 270
trial reports, French 372
Tristan and Iseult 215
trochaic metres 193, 413, 433–4
Trollope, Anthony 46, 202
Trotz, Selma Ahlström 288
Tsubouchi Shōyō 364, 367
Tucker, B. R. 494

Tudor Translations 9, 140, 200, 233
Tulsi Das; *Ramacharitamanas* 351
Turgenev, Ivan Sergeevich 17, 91, 93, 311, **314–16**
  translators 14, 93, 101, 129, 314–15
Turner, C. E. 313, 315
Turner, Sharon 299
Twain, Mark (*pseud.* of S. L. Clemens) 30
Tyndale, William; New Testament 445, 452
Tyrrell, R. Y. 118
Tytler, Alexander 62, **63–5**, 212, 218–19, 247

Ukrainian literature 310
Ulster cycle 295
'Umar Khayyām *see under* Khayyām
unauthorized publication 20–1, 43–4, 374, 375, 377
  see also copyright
uncanny and supernatural, tales of 16–17
Unitarian Church 444
United States of America 3, **20–33**
  Civil War 169–70
  and Cuba 502
  Dante in 29, 122
  eastern literature in 23–4, 352
  immigrant populations 27, 211, 373–4, 424
  multilingualism 20, **30–1**
  northern cultural heritage 274, 277, 280
  novelists published in Europe 3, 40
  opera 420, 424
  reprints 20–1, 449
  Revolution 489, 490, 499
  socio-political theories 27, 493
  theories of translation 23, 25–6, 28, 29, 146–7, 150–1
  translations published in Britain 43–4, 88
  unauthorized publication 20–1, 43–4, 374, 375, 377
  see also individual translators, Native
    Americans; Transcendentalists,
    American *and under* Bible; copyright;
    dialects; education; fidelity; Germany;
    periodicals; politics; popular fiction;
    Romanticism; theatre, popular;
    universities; women (translators)
universities **117–19**
  German 21, 30, 37, 107–8, 118–19, 219–20
  Indian western-style 345–6
  Japanese 365
  new disciplines eastern languages 325, 344, 347, 348, 356, 360, 460–4 *passim*;
    German 117, 213; Old English 283; Old Icelandic 283
  Scottish 118–19, 181
  US 22, **24–5**, 118–19, 283, 356
  and women 94, 414
  see also individual universities
University Tutorial Series 183
Unwin, T. Fisher 398, 403
upaniṣads 120, 352, 459, **460**

upper class 35–6, **36–40**, 46, 156, 165
urban life 35, 73
Urquhart, Sir Thomas 141, 233
utopianism 498

Valdés, Armando Palacio 271
Valera, Don Juan 271
Valpy; Family Classical Library 165, 182
van Deventer, Emma Murdoch (*pseud.*
    Lawrence L. Lynch) 378
van Laun, Henri 94, 233, 234, *553–4*
Vātsyāyana; *Kāma Sūtra* 53, 349
Vaughn, David James 476
Vedānta Sūtra (or *Brahma Sūtra*) 461
Vedas 459, **460–1**
Vega Carpio, Lope de 261, 264, 265
Venantius Fortunatus 416
Verdi, Giuseppe 55, 424
Verga, Giuseppe 258
Verhaeren, Émile 146, 237
Verlaine, Paul 13, **237**
Verne, Jules 378, **379**, 402, 503
Verrall, Arthur Woollgar 120, 182
verse translations
  of prose texts 99, 234, 235, 238
  of poetry 66–7; *see also* metre; metrical
    translation; stanza form
Victoria, Queen of Great Britain 55
Vidocq, Eugène-François 375
Vidyākara; *Subhāṣitaratnakoṣa* 352
Víga-Glúms saga 274, 277
Vigfússon, Guðbrandur 274, 276–7, 283
Vigny, Alfred de 235, 240, 490
Villegas, Esteban Manuel de 263
Villon, François 4, 11–12, 70, 106, **232–3**
  François Villon Society 258, 327
Vinaya Piṭaka 464–5
Vínland sagas 277, 280
Virgil (P. Virgilius Maro) 139, 157,
    159, 190–2
  Dryden and 71, 105, 119, 138, 141, 190
  Tennyson's 'To Virgil' 191
  TRANSLATIONS
    Aeneid 190–1, 191–2; Conington 119, 159,
      192; Dryden 105, 141; Henry 191–2;
      Morris 70, 114, 159, 192; Wordsworth
      190–1, 105
    Eclogues 157, 191
    Georgics 191
Viṣṇu Purāṇa 346, 458
Vizetelly, Ernest 88, 95, 242
Vizetelly, Henry Richard 8, **42–3**, *554*
  and French fiction 46, 230, 241, 242, 378;
    Zola 42–3, **54**, 74, 95, 230, 242
  range of editions 35, 43, 378
  and Russian novels 313, 315, 317
  translators 46, 74, 88
  trials and ruin 43, **54**, 230, 242
Vizetelly, James 42

Vogüé, Melchior, Vicomte de 313, 317
Voïart, Élise 401
Volkmann-Leander, Richard von 397
Volney, Constantin-François 498, **499–500**
Völsunga saga 114–15, 281
Voltaire (François-Marie Arouet) 105, 234
Voss, Johann Heinrich 71, 175

Wace, Henry 449
Wade, Thomas 356, 357
Wagner, Richard 215
Waldere fragments 279–80
Walford, Edward 475
Walker, Alexander 238
Walker, Joseph Cooper 295
Wallace, J. 415
Wallace, William 117, 483, 485
Walpole, Horace 36, 371
Walsh, Edward 297–8
Walther von der Vogelweide 214–15
Walton, William 234
Ward, H. L. D. 397
Ward, Mrs Humphry 237
Ward, Lock & Co. 42, 43
Ward, Lock, & Tyler 397
  Erckmann-Chatrian Library 240
  Jules Verne Library 379
Ward and Langcake; translation of Boehme 216
Wardrop, Sir John Oliver 312, *554–5*
Wardrop, Marjory Scott 312, *554–5*
Warne's Chandos Classics 141
Warner, Arthur *and* Edmond 338
Warr, George 180
Waterfield, William 351
'Waters' (*pseud.* of William Russell) 375
Waters, W. G. 398
Watson, John 483
Watson, John Selby 202, 478
Watts, Henry Edward 265, 266–7
Watts, William 448
Way, Arthur S. 182
Way, Gregory Lewis 231
Weber, T. 286, 290
Webster (*née* Davies), Augusta 66, 74, 77, 179,
    182, *555*
Webster, Noah 444, 456
Webster, W. F. 461
Wedderburn, G. F. 373
Weedon, L. L. 396
The Weekly Freeman 298
Welldon, J. E. C. 475
Wells, H. G. 503
Welsh literature 51, 102–3, 294, **299–302**
  see also *Mabinogion*
Wesley, John 444, 447
West, Edward William 466
Westcott, Brooke Foss 453, 454
Westminster Review 146, 239, 309, 310
Westminster School 36

Weston, Jessie L. 215
Weston, Stephen 337
Wharton, Henry Thornton 161
Wheatley, L. A. 396
Wheeler, Anna 492, 493
Whewell, William 476, 503
Whibley, Charles 9
Whinfield, E. H. 335
Whishaw, Frederick J. 314, 317
White, John 439
Whitehead, Mrs A. E. 304
Whitman, Sarah Helen 26, 27
Whitman, Walt 4, 23, 28, 169–70, 503
Whittier, John Grenleaf 27
Wicksteed, Philip H. 141
Wieland, Christoph Martin 22, 212
Wiener, Leo 308, 316
Wiffen, J. H. 247–8, 248–9, 263, 264
Wilberforce-Clarke, H. 334, 337
Wilbour, Charles Edwin 239, 486
Wilde (née Elgee), Jane Francesca Agnes, Lady Wilde 268, 490
Wilde, Oscar 13, 37, 204
Wildermuth, Ottilie 402
Wilkins, Charles 50, 341, 342, 349, 463
Will, Peter 373
Williams, Dr John B. 377
Williams, Edward ('Iolo Morganwg') **299–300**, 301, *555–6*
Williams, Fred 377
Williams, Helen Maria 141, 238, 501–2, *556*
Williams, Henry Llewellyn 93, 240, 377
Williams, Howard 205
Williams, John 301
Williams, Robert 475
Williams, Samuel Wells 357
Williams, Taliesin 301
Williams, William 275
Willoughby, L. A. 218–19
Wilson, Horace Hayman 48, 346–7, 350, 458, 461
Wilson, John (*pseud.* Christopher North) 143
Winckelmann, Johann Joachim 155
Windisch, Ernst 298
Winkworth, Catherine 125, **126**, 128, **412–14**, 417, *556–7*
Winkworth, Susanna 125, **126**, 128, 216, 446–7, *556–7*
Winslow, Erving 237
Winternitz, Moriz 459
Wischnewetsky, Florence 494
Wiseman, Cardinal Nicholas 447
Wodhull, Michael 178, 182
Wolf, F. A. 431
Wolfram von Eschenbach 215
Wollstonecraft, Mary 399

women
  readers 271, 372, 378
  translators 86–7, 93, 102–3, **125–31**; academic authority 74, 77–8, 112–13, 486; of children's literature 394, 402; education 26, 37, 86–7, 94, 111, 125, 414; of Iberian languages 261, 271; of Scandinavian languages 288; on translation 106, 126, 127, 128, 130, 179, 492; US **26–7**, 27–8; *see also* gender *and under* Germany; Greek literature
  writers 254, 288–9, 129; translation as apprenticeship 26, 106, 127, 128; *see also* individual names
Wood, Annie 289
Wood, Robert 172
Woodward, Anna Aubertine (*pseud.* Auber Forestier) 289, *507*
Wordsworth, Dorothy 107
Wordsworth, William 15, 212, 261, 325, 391, *557*
  classical education 105, 155–6, 200
  and Coleridge 107, 221
  translations and imitations: Chaucer 105; classical 105, 155, 190–1, 193, 196, 197; Italian 105, 253
working class 7, 35, **44–6**, 95, 118, 120, 122, 157
Works of the Greek and Roman Poets 165
world literature **6–9**, 22, 27, 45–6
Worm, Ole 275
Wormeley, Katharine Prescott 95, 241, *557–8*
Worsley, Philip Stanhope 119, 159, 169, 174–5
Wrangham, Francis 247
Wraxall, Sir Frederic Charles Lascelles, third Baronet 93, 239, *558*
Wright, Elizur 233
writers as translators 93–4, **105–16**, 481
  motivation 105–6, 106–7, 111–13, 127, 128
  original writing affected 106–7, 111–13, 188, 197, 220
Wyatt, A. J. 114, 283
Wyatt v. Barnard (1814) 56
Wycliffe, John 445
Wylie, Alexander 356
Wyn, Elis 301
Wyndham, Charles 391
Wyss, Johann David 400–1

Xenophon of Athens 201
Xenophon of Ephesus 203

Yajñaparibhāṣa Sūtras 462
Yeats, William Butler 115, 296, 298
Yellow Book 145–6, 237
Yonge, Charles Duke 160–1, 204, 478

York Powell, Frederick 274, 276–7, 283, 558–9
Young, Sir George 181, 182
Young, Robert 445

Zarathustra 466
Zend 120
Zhū Xī 357, 358
Zhuāngzǐ 360

Zimmern, Helen 398
Zola, Émile 4, 43–4, 145, **242**, 388–9
  Lutetian Society edition 37, 88, 89, 106
  Vizetelly and 42–3, **54**, 74, 95
Zoroastrianism 458, **466**
Zschokke, Heinrich 373
Zulu literature 439
Zuni literature 438

PR131 .0944 v.4

The Oxford history of
literary translation in
English

NOV 17 2006